With Reverence for the Word

Contents

List of Contributors

STEPHEN D. BENIN is professor of Judaic studies, the University of Memphis. His publications include *The Footprints of God: Divine Accommodation in Jewish and Christian Thought* (Albany: State University of New York Press, 1993) and "Jewish Popular and Philosophical Religion." He has also edited a special volume of the *Journal of Jewish Thought and Philosophy* (8 [1999]).

HAGGAI BEN-SHAMMAI is professor of Arabic at the Hebrew University, Jerusalem, chair of the Ben-Zvi Institute for the Study of Jewish Communities in the East, and director of the Center for the Study of Judeo-Arabic. His recent publications include *The History of Jerusalem: The Early Islamic Period, 638–1099* (co-editor with J. Prawer; Jerusalem: Yad Izhak Ben-Zvi, and New York: New York University Press, 1996), "Kalam in Medieval Jewish Philosophy," in *History of Jewish Philosophy*, ed. D. H. Frank and O. Leaman (London: Routledge, 1997), 115–48 and "Jerusalem in Early Medieval Jewish Bible Exegesis," in *Jerusalem: Its Sanctity and Centrality to Judaism, Christianity and Islam*, ed. L. I. Levine (New York: Continuum, 1999), 447–64.

HERBERT BERG is professor of Islamic studies, University of North Carolina at Wilmington. His publications include *The Development of Exegesis in Early Islam: The Authenticity of Muslim Literature from the Formative Period* (London: Curzon, 2000).

GERHARD BÖWERING is professor of Islamic studies, Yale University. His recent publications include *The Mystical Vision of Existence in Classical Islam: The Qur'ānic Hermeneutics of the Ṣūfī Sahl al-Tustarī* (Berlin; New York: W. de Gruyter, 1980) and *The Minor Qur'an Commentary of Abu 'Abd ar-Rahman Muhammad b. al-Husayn as-Sulami* (Beirut: Dar al-Mashriq, 1995; 2nd edition, 1997).

JOHN F. BOYLE is professor of theology at the University of St. Thomas (Minnesota). He is co-editor with L. E. Boyle of the critical edition of Thomas Aquinas' recently discovered second commentary on Peter Lombard's *Liber sententiarum*. His recent publications include "The Twofold Division of St. Thomas's Christology in the Tertia Pars," *The Thomist* 60 (1995): 439–47, and "The Ordering of Trinitarian Teaching in Thomas Aquinas' Second Commentary on Lombard's Sentences," *Recherches de théologie ancienne et médiévale, Supplementa* 1 (1995): 125–36.

ALAN COOPER is professor of Bible, Jewish Theological Seminary and Union Theological Seminary. His publications include "The Sense of the Book of Job," *Prooftexts* 17 (1997): 227–44, and "The Meaning of Amos's Third Vision (Amos 7:7–9)," in *Tehillah le-Moshe* (Winona Lake, Ind: Eisenbrauns, 1997), 13–21.

ABIGAIL FIREY is assistant professor, Department of History and Honors Program, University of Kentucky. Her recent publications include "Carolingian Ecclesiology and Heresy: A Southern Gallic Juridical Tract against Adoptionism," *Sacris erudiri* 39 (2000): 253–318, and "Lawyers and Wisdom: The Use of the Bible in the Pseudo-Isidorian Forged Decretals" in *The Study of the Bible in the Carolingian Era*, ed. Celia Chazelle and Burton Van Name Edwards (Turnhout: Brepols, forthcoming).

DANIEL FRANK is assistant professor of Near Eastern studies at Ohio State University. His publications include "Karaite Exegesis," in *Hebrew Bible/Old Testament: The History of Its Interpretation*, vol. I/2, ed. Magne Saebø (Göttingen: Vandenhoeck & Ruprecht, 2001), and "The Shoshanim of Tenth-Century Jerusalem: Karaite Exegesis, Prayer, and Communal Identity," in *The Jews of Medieval Islam: Community, Society, and Identity*, ed. Daniel Frank (Leiden: E. J. Brill, 1995), 199–245.

JAMES R. GINTHER is senior lecturer in medieval theology at the University of Leeds. His recent publications include "Theological Education at the Oxford Studium in the Thirteenth Century: A Reassessment of Robert Grosseteste's Letter to the Oxford Theologians," *Franciscan Studies* 55 (1998): 83–104, and "A Scholastic Idea of the Church: Robert Grosseteste's Exposition of Psalm 86," *Archives d'histoire doctrinale et littéraire du moyen âge* 66 (1999): 49–72, and "Natural Philosophy and Theology at Oxford in the Early Thirteenth Century: An Edition and Study of Robert Grosseteste's Inception Sermon." *Medieval Sermon Studies* 44 (2000): 108–34. He is also the director of the Electronic Grosseteste Project: http://www.grosseteste.com/

JOSEPH W. GOERING is director of the Centre for the Study of Religion, University of Toronto, and professor of history. His publications include *William de Montibus: The Schools and Literature of Pastoral Care* (Toronto: Pontifical Institute of Mediaeval Studies, 1992) and *Robert Grosseteste: Templum Dei* (co-editor; Toronto: published for the Centre for Medieval Studies by the Pontifical Institute of Mediaeval Studies, 1984).

GERALD R. HAWTING is professor of the history of the Near and Middle East in the School of Oriental and African Studies, University of London. His publications include *Approaches to the Qur'ān* (co-editor; London, New York: Routledge, 1993), *The First Dynasty of Islam: The Umayyad Caliphate, A.D. 661–750* (London: Croom Helm, 1986), and *The Idea of Idolatry and the Emergence of Islam: From Polemic to History* (Cambridge: Cambridge University Press, 1999).

ÉDOUARD JEAUNEAU is professor emeritus of philosophy at the Pontifical Institute of Mediaeval Studies, Toronto. His publications include *L' âge d'or des écoles de Chartres* (Chartres: Editions Houvet, 1995) and a critical edition of the *Periphyseon* of John Scottus Eriugena (Turnhout: Brepols, 1996–).

ERIC LAWEE is professor in the Division of the Humanities, York University, Toronto. His recent publications include *Isaac Abarbanel's Stance Towards Tradition: Defense, Dissent, and Dialogue* (Albany: State University of New York Press, 2001), and "The Path to Felicity: Teachings and Tensions in *'Even shetiyyah* of Abraham ben Judah, Disciple of Hasdai Crescas," *Mediaeval Studies* 59 (1997): 183–223.

†HAVA LAZARUS-YAFEH was professor of Arabic and Islamic studies at the Hebrew University of Jerusalem. Her publications include *Intertwined Worlds: Medieval Islam and Bible Criticism* (Princeton, N.J.: Princeton University Press, 1992) and *Some Religious Aspects of Islam* (Leiden: E. J. Brill, 1981).

FRED LEEMHUIS is professor of Arabic and Islamic studies, University of Groningen. His publications include "The Koran and Its Exegesis: From Memorizing to Learning," *The D and H Stems in Koranic Arabic* (Leiden: E. J. Brill, 1977), and *The Arabic Text of the Apocalypse of Baruch* (Leiden: Brill, 1986).

MARTIN LOCKSHIN is associate professor of humanities and Hebrew and director of the Centre for Jewish Studies at York University. His most recent book is *Rashbam's Commentary on Leviticus and Numbers: An Annotated Translation* (Providence: Brown Judaic Studies, 2001), the third volume of a four-volume series.

JANE DAMMEN McAULIFFE is dean of Georgetown College, Washington, D.C., and professor of Islamic history and of Arabic. Her publications include *Qur'ānic Christians: An Analysis of Classical and Modern Exegesis* (Cambridge: Cambridge University Press, 1991), *'Abbāsid Authority Affirmed: The Early Years of al-Manṣūr* (Albany, N.Y.: State University of New York Press, 1995), and *The Encyclopaedia of the Qur'ān* (editor; Leiden: Brill, 2001–).

ALASTAIR J. MINNIS is professor of Medieval literature in the Department of English and Related Literature, University of York. His publications include *Medieval Theory of Authorship: Scholastic Literary Attitudes in the Later Middle Ages* (London: Scolar Press, 1984; 2nd., 1988) *Medieval Literary Theory and Criticism, c. 1100–c. 1375: The Commentary-Tradition* (co-editor; Oxford: Clarendon Press, 1988; 2nd., 1991, rpt. 2001), and *Magister amoris:* The Roman de la Rose *and Venacular Hermeneutics* (Oxford: Oxford University Press, 2001).

ANGELIKA NEUWIRTH is professor of Arabic and Islamic studies, University of Berlin, and a former director of Orient-Institut der DMG in Beirut, Lebanon. Her publications include *'Abd al-Latīf al-Bagdādī's Bearbeitung von Buch Lambda der aristotelischen Metaphysik* (Wiesbaden: Steiner, 1976) and *Studien zur Komposition der mekkanischen Suren* (Berlin: W. de Gruyter, 1981).

ANDREW RIPPIN is dean of humanities and professor of history, University of Victoria (British Columbia). His publications include *Muslims: Their Religious Beliefs and Practices*, 2nd ed. (London: Routledge, 2001), *Approaches to the History of Interpretation of the Qur'ān* (editor; Oxford: Oxford University Press, 1988), and *The Qur'ān: Formative Interpretation* (editor; Brookfield, Vt.: Ashgate, 1999).

MARC SAPERSTEIN is Charles E. Smith Professor of Jewish History and director of Jewish Studies at George Washington University. His publications include *Decoding the Rabbis: A Thirteenth-Century Commentary on the Aggadah* (Cambridge, Mass.: Harvard University Press, 1980), *Jewish Preaching 1200–1800* (New Haven: Yale University Press, 1989), and *"Your Voice Like a Ram's Horn": Themes and Texts in Traditional Jewish Preaching* (Cincinnati: Hebrew Union College Press, 1996).

MICHAEL A. SIGNER is Abrams Professor of Jewish Thought and Culture, University of Notre Dame. His publications include Andrew of St. Victor's *Expositionem in Ezechielem: A Critical Edition*, CCCM, 53E (Turnhout: Brepols, 1991), and "God's Love for Israel: Apologetic and Hermeneutical Strategies in Twelfth-Century Biblical Exegesis," in *Jews and Christians in Twelfth-Century Europe*, ed. Michael A. Signer and John H. Van Engen (Notre Dame, Ind: University of Notre Dame Press, 2001).

ROBERT SWEETMAN holds the H. Evan Runner Chair in the History of Philosophy at the Institute for Christian Studies, Toronto. His publications include "Thomas of Cantimpré, *Mulieres religiosae* and Purgatorial Piety: Hagiographical *Vitae* and the Beguine 'Voice,'" in *"In a Distinct Voice": Medieval Studies in Honor of Leonard Boyle, O.P.*, ed. Jacqueline Brown and William P. Stoneman (Notre Dame, Ind: University of Notre Dame Press, 1997), 606–28, and "Thomas of Cantimpré: Performative Reading and Pastoral Care," in *Performance and Transformation: New Approaches to Late Medieval Spirituality*, ed. Mary A. Suydam and Joanna E. Ziegler (New York: St. Martin's Press, 1999), 133–67.

†EDWARD SYNAN was professor emeritus in philosophy at the Pontifical Institute of Mediaeval Studies, Toronto. His publications include *The Popes and the Jews in the Middle Ages* (New York: Macmillan, 1965) and *The Works of Richard Campsall* (editor; Toronto: Pontifical Institute of Mediaeval Studies, 1968–82).

BARRY D. WALFISH is Judaica specialist at the University of Toronto Library and a member of the faculty of the Centre for the Study of Religion, University of Toronto. His publications include *Esther in Medieval Garb: Jewish Interpretation of the Book of Esther in the Middle Ages* (Albany, N.Y.: State University of New York Press, 1993) and *The Frank Talmage Memorial Volume*, 2 vols. (editor; Haifa: Haifa University Press, 1992–93).

STEFAN WILD is professor of Islamic studies at the University of Bonn. His recent publications include *The Qur'an as Text* (editor; Leiden: Brill, 1996), *Norm und Abweichung: Akten des 27. Deutschen Orientalistentages* (co-editor; Würzburg: Ergon, 2001), and *Studien aus Arabistik und Semitistik* (co-editor; Wiesbaden: Harrassowitz, 1980).

ELLIOT R. WOLFSON is the Abraham Lieberman Professor of Hebrew and Judaic studies, New York University. His recent publications include *Along the Path: Studies in Kabbalistic Myth, Symbolism, and Hermeneutics* (Albany, N.Y.: State University of New York Press, 1995), *Through a Speculum that Shines: Vision and Imagination in Medieval Jewish Mysticism* (Princeton, N.J.: Princeton University Press, 1994), and *Abraham Abulafia–Kabbalist and Prophet: Hermeneutics, Theosophy, and Theurgy* (Los Angeles: Cherub Press, 2000).

Abbreviations

BJRL	*Bulletin of the John Rylands Library, Manchester.*
BSOAS	*Bulletin of the School of Oriental and African Studies.*
BT	Babylonian Talmud.
CCCM	*Corpus Christianorum, Continuatio mediaevalis.* Turnhout: Brepols, 1966–.
CCSL	*Corpus Christianorum, Series latina.* Turnhout: Brepols, 1953–.
CSEL	*Corpus scriptorum ecclesiasticorum latinorum.* Vienna, 1866–.
EI, new ed.	*Encyclopaedia of Islam.* New ed. Leiden: E. J. Brill, 1960–.
EIr	*Encyclopaedia iranica.* Ed. Ehsan Yarshater. London; Boston: Routledge & Kegan Paul, 1985–.
GAL	Brockelmann, Carl. *Geschichte des arabischen Litteratur.* 2 vols. Weimar: Felber, 1898–1902.
GAL Supplementa.	*Geschichte des arabischen Litteratur. Supplementa.* 3 vols. Leiden: E. J. Brill, 1937–42.
GAS	Sezgin, Mehmed Fuat. *Geschichte des arabischen Schrifttums.* Vol. 1. Leiden: E. J. Brill, 1967.
GdQ	Nöldeke, Theodor. *Geschichte des Qorans.* Ed. Friedrich Schwally, G. Bergsträsser, and P. Pretzl. 3 vols. Leipzig: G. Olms, 1909–38.
HUCA	*Hebrew Union College Annual.*
JSAI	*Jerusalem Studies in Arabic and Islam.*
JQR	*Jewish Quarterly Review.*
MT	*Mishneh Torah*
OḤ	'Oraḥ ḥayyim
PG	*Patrologia graeca.* Ed. J. -P. Migne. 161 vols. Paris: Garnier, 1857–86.
PL	*Patrologia latina.* Ed. J. -P. Migne. 226 vols. Paris: Garnier, 1841–81.
SC	*Sources chrétiennes.* Paris: Cerf, 1941–.

PART I

MEDIEVAL JEWISH EXEGESIS OF THE BIBLE

1

An Introduction to Medieval Jewish Biblical Interpretation

BARRY D. WALFISH

The Hebrew Bible is the classic example of a sacred text frozen in time which must satisfy the religious needs of succeeding generations of believers. The need to make this text relevant to generations far removed from it both temporally and culturally has existed ever since its canonization. Early on in its history, Judaism developed the concept of an oral tradition which expanded upon and interpreted the text of sacred scripture. This oral tradition was in turn codified and recorded and attained authoritative status among the sacred works of Judaism. Subsequent generations were faced with the question of whether it was permissible to go beyond what the Sages had said and seek new ways to interpret and elucidate the text, even if doing so meant contradicting the words of the Sages. This is the issue that Stephen Benin explores in his wide-ranging study on the authority of each generation to interpret its sacred texts in a way that makes them meaningful and relevant. Benin shows that similar concerns were shared by medieval Jewish and Christian scholars on this issue, all of them concluding that the pursuit of the truth takes precedence over any consideration for the reputation and authority of the ancients.

The Jewish study of the Bible in the Middle Ages begins with the Geonim of Babylonia (9th–11th centuries),[1] who under the influence of the Islamic sages of the Qur'ān began to subject the biblical text to the same kind of critical and textual analysis as was being applied to the Qur'ān by their Muslim compatriots.[2] The best-known exegete of this period is Saadia Gaon, a polymath, who did pioneering scholarly work in many areas,[3] and who was followed in the exegetical field by others, such as Samuel ben Hofni and Aaron Sarjado. Saadia's exegetical method has been much studied, and many of his works were published from manuscripts found in the Cairo Genizah. Haggai Ben-Shammai, in his article on Saadia, analyzes one term from Saadia's lexicon to show the necessity of maintaining a balance between the concept of freedom of interpretation and authoritative tradition, an issue that must have been heatedly discussed in Islamic circles as well. We see that for Saadia, unlimited freedom of interpretation was unthinkable and exegetical freedom had to be limited by the dictates of tradition, a view that often led to interpretations far from what we would consider the plain sense.

The Karaite movement had its beginnings in Babylonia in the eighth century, when Anan ben David rejected the authority of the Rabbis and formed a rival school that derived law from scripture using similar hermeneutical rules, but which was often more severe in its interpretation of scripture. Anan's group, the Ananites, was probably absorbed into the Karaite movement in the ninth century and a slogan attributed to him, "Search well in scripture, and do not rely on my opinion," helped inspire an efflorescence in biblical scholarship which would reach its zenith in Jerusalem in the tenth century with the commentaries of Japheth ben Eli, Salmon ben Jeroham, Jeshua ben Judah, and others. There is much in Karaite exegesis that is tendentious and polemical, but there is also a lot of good sound exegesis based on solid grammatical and lexicographical foundations. In his paper, Daniel Frank examines the commentaries to the Song of Songs produced in the tenth century among the circle of the Mourners for Zion, an ascetic group of Karaites living in Jerusalem, who devoted themselves to mourning the destruction of the Temple and who constituted the spiritual and intellectual heart of the Jerusalem Karaite community.

In the late Geonic period the intellectual and spiritual center of medieval Jewry moved to Muslim Spain, and biblical scholarship was enhanced by the important grammatical work done by Judah Ḥayyuj (ca. 945–ca. 1000) and Jonah ibn Janaḥ (11th century), who raised the scientific study of Hebrew grammar to new heights. While they did not write commentaries themselves, there is much exegetical material in their grammatical treatises, *Sefer ha-Shorashim* (Book of roots) of Ḥayyūj, and *Kitāb al-Luma'* (*Sefer ha-Riqmah*; Book of variegated flower-beds) and *Kitāb al-Uṣūl* (*Sefer ha-Shorashim*; Book of roots) of Ibn Janaḥ, and exegetes who followed them were greatly influenced by their work. The commentaries of Abraham Ibn Ezra (1092–1167) mark the culmination of the Spanish-Arabic period of exegesis. Ibn Ezra was a transitional figure who carried the burden of the Spanish-Arabic tradition with him to Italy and later France and England and who conveyed much of the wisdom of this tradition to new audiences in these lands.[4] Another key figure in this tradition of *peshaṭ* (contextual) exegesis, which was based on the pillars of grammar, lexicography, and reason, foundations was David Kimḥi (ca. 1160–1235), whose father, Joseph, had moved from Spain to Provence at about 1150, in the wake of the Almohade persecutions. Kimḥi's commentaries and especially his grammatical works, *Sefer ha-Shorashim* (Book of roots) and *Sefer Mikhlol* (Comprehensive Hebrew grammar), as well as those of Ibn Ezra proved to be extremely popular and helpful to all those seeking to understand the basic meaning of the biblical text.[5] Both of these exegetes were philosophically trained—Ibn Ezra in Neoplatonism, Kimḥi in Maimonidean Aristotelianism—and both introduce many philosophical ideas into their commentaries, which popularized these views while also exposing their authors to criticism from more conservative anti-philosophical coreligionists.

In Northern France, at about the same time, another school of exegesis developed, with similar goals and slightly different results. Its inspiration was the eleventh-century scholar Solomon ben Isaac (Rashi, 1040–1105). Rashi wrote commentaries on almost the entire biblical corpus as well as an indispensable and arguably more important commentary on the Talmud. His Bible commentary, especially that on the Torah, became immensely popular, an inseparable companion of the text, almost like the *glossa ordinaria* on the Vulgate, to which it has been compared. In fact, the claim has been made that Rashi's commentary continues the trend of vernacular glosses on the biblical text that had begun in ancient times.[6] But Rashi was also faithful to the rabbinic tradition of interpretation and made judicious use of rabbinic commentary when it met his criteria for acceptability, carefully editing his sources and molding them to suit his exegetical goals. Rashi was a brilliant master of language, and his clarity, concision, and felicity of expression have helped assign his commentary to a lofty place in the canon of classic Jewish texts which are still studied widely today.

While Rashi did have some sense of the concept of *peshaṭ*, that is, explaining the biblical text in its context without resort to the meaning assigned to it by tradition, his conception was not fully developed.[7] It was his grandson, Samuel ben Meir (Rashbam) (ca. 1080/85–ca. 1174), who became the champion and most radical follower of the *peshat* method of exegesis, adhering to his method regardless of the consequences, and drawing a clear line between the meaning of the text in its context and the traditional interpretations of the Sages, who often took great liberties with the text for various reasons, whether polemical, didactic, or homiletical. While never questioning the authority of the Sages in matters of *halakhah*, the *peshaṭ* exegetes felt free to interpret the text contextually, even, on occasion, contradicting the interpretation assigned by tradition. The vast body of midrashic interpretation was for the most part ignored by these exegetes. Rashbam had a number of colleagues in his school of exegesis, most prominently Joseph Kara (b. ca.1060–1070), Joseph Bekhor Shor (12th century), and Eliezer of Beaugency (12th century), all of whom produced commentaries that were of considerable value and interest but did not enjoy much popularity in later generations. In fact, Rashbam's Torah commentary was preserved in a single manuscript, a hair's breadth from extinction, and was first published only in 1705. In recent years interest in these exegetes has grown, precisely because of their willingness to put aside the body of traditional commentary and study the text on its own terms. One of the intriguing aspects of the northern French school is their seeming modernity and interest in matters that concern modern literary scholars and biblical exegetes. In his essay, Martin Lockshin tests Rashbam's literary sense and concludes that one needs to be cautious in attributing modern concerns to medieval exegetes such as Rashbam.[8]

The interest in the biblical text shown by this school of northern French exegetes, has invited comparisons with similar trends in Christian scholarly circles at the time, notably the School of St. Victor in Paris, where the monk Andrew of St. Victor pursued the *hebraica veritas* with the same assiduousness as Rashbam and his colleagues pursued the *peshaṭ*. This similarity has led to suggestions of contacts and collaboration between the two schools, which, while possible and even likely, have to this date not been undeniably verified. The issue has been explored by Beryl Smalley in her classic pioneering work on the School of St. Victor, *The Study of the Bible in the Middle Ages*,[9] and more recently by Elazar Touitou[10] and especially Michael A. Signer,[11] who has done significant work on the Victorine school itself. In his essay in this volume, Signer examines Rashi's exegesis from the point of view of narrative theory and demonstrates quite convincingly that Rashi was concerned with the narrative flow of the text and that he shared this concern with exegetes of the School of St. Victor. He further speculates that this concern helped bring medieval readers closer to the biblical text from which many may have been alienated by the disjunctive readings of the Sages and the Fathers.

In the late Middle Ages (13th–15th centuries), exegesis followed along several new paths as scholars trained in philosophy and mysticism applied their knowledge to the biblical text. Those of a philosophical bent tended to interpret scripture through the prism of the philosophical school to which they adhered. Two important examples are Levi ben

Gershom (Ralbag; 1288–1344) and Joseph ibn Kaspi (1279–1340), both Aristotelian rationalists, who followed the teachings of Maimonides. Ralbag was probably the most significant and original Jewish thinker of the later medieval period. His philosophical exegesis has recently been the subject of a fine study by Robert Eisen,[12] and Kaspi's *Gevia' kesef* (Goblet of silver) was translated and analyzed by Basil Herring.[13] Ralbag was the first exegete to introduce sections in his commentaries devoted to moral lessons to be derived from the biblical text, quite possibly under Christian influence.[14]

In the late twelfth and thirteenth centuries in Ashkenaz, a circle of pietists developed, led by Judah ben Samuel, he-Ḥasid (d. 1217), and Eleazar ben Judah, of Worms. This circle produced a large body of commentary, some of it devoted to *peshaṭ* exegesis, but much more devoted to exegesis meant for initiates, using various esoteric techniques, which atomize the text, breaking it up into units as small as single letters and recombining them in various ways in order to decipher the esoteric meaning of the text. In his *Sefer ha-Ḥokhmah* (Book of Wisdom), Eleazar ben Judah recorded seventy-three (the *gemaṭria* or numerical value of *ḥokhmah*) exegetical techniques that could be used to elucidate the fifty gates of understanding the mysteries of sacred scripture. Some of these, such as *gemaṭria* (assigning numerical values to words and equating or comparing them with words or phrases of equal numerical value) or *noṭariqon* (seeking significance in the words formed by the beginning or ending letters of a series of words), are well known and already appear in rabbinic literature; others are far more complex and less well known. These rabbis believed that they were the bearers of a sacred esoteric tradition which was given to Moses at Sinai and which carried with it the true understanding of scripture.[15]

The kabbalists of the thirteenth century, who developed the theosophical-mystical system of the *sefirot*, read the Bible as a text that revealed the mysteries of the divine names. One of the most famous exegetes with kabbalistic orientation was Moses ben Naḥman (Ramban, Naḥmanides; 1194–1270). Ramban's commentary is of special importance because it operates on several levels. Ramban frequently engages with his two great predecessors, Rashi and Ibn Ezra, usually citing their comments and then giving his own opinion, thus setting the stage for "the emergence of the triumvirate which still casts its shadow over all Bible study," raising "exegetical problems and hermeneutical issues," which remained central to the history of exegesis.[16] His commentary is noted for its psychological insights and understanding of human nature. Naḥmanides was also a genuine kabbalist, who included in his commentary, which was intended for a popular audience, numerous allusions to hidden meanings of the Torah verses, thereby stimulating kabbalistic activity and lending an aura of legitimacy to the esoteric understanding of the Torah as propounded by kabbalistic theosophy.[17] Ramban was active in Gerona, Spain, in the second half of the thirteenth century; his generation preceded Moses de Leon and his circle, who compiled or composed the Zoharic corpus of mystical texts.

The Zohar is the primary kabbalistic text of the Middle Ages. Ascribed to Moses de Leon and his circle of the late thirteenth century, it is organized as a commentary on the Pentateuch as well as on the Five Scrolls.[18] It contains a wealth of mystical lore and stories about Rabbi Simeon ben Yoḥai, the putative author of the Zohar, and his students and contemporaries. Along with the Zohar ḥadash and other texts from the era, it is an inexhaustible source of theosophic mysticism.[19] In his essay, Elliot Wolfson makes an important contribution to the study of Zoharic hermeneutics with an analysis of the place of the Song of Songs in the mystical *Weltanschauung* of the authors of the Zohar. His conclusions concerning the centrality of this book in the mystic's worldview and the homoerotic spiritualizing tendencies expressed in this literature are certain to provoke discussion and debate.

While one can distinguish levels of interpretation in the commentaries of the German Pietists,[20] Naḥmanides,[21] and others such as Isaac Ibn Latif[22] and Abraham Abulafia,[23] it is in the last quarter of the thirteenth century, particularly in the Zohar and other writings of Moses de Leon, that one first encounters the use of the acronym *pardes* to refer to the four levels of interpretation of the biblical text, *peshaṭ*, *remez*, *derash* and *sod*, or historical, philosophical, homiletic, and mystical. The mystical is sometimes referred to as *derekh ha-'emet*, or the way of truth. This usage is restricted primarily to kabbalistic writings and did not achieve the almost universal application that the four senses achieved in medieval Christian exegesis. As Moshe Idel has pointed out, the first three methods of interpreting the text—the *peshaṭ*, philosophical, and homiletical—already existed and were widely applied by exegetes of various persuasions. By introducing a fourth level and presenting it as the culmination of the exegetical process, the most profound understanding of the biblical text attainable, the kabbalists were validating the work of their predecessors while also claiming pride of place for their own innovative approach to the text.[24]

Another important exegete from this period with a kabbalistic orientation was Baḥya ben Asher (13th century). His commentary, written around 1291 in Saragossa, was more formally organized along the lines of the commentaries of the medieval Christian exegetes, with several levels of interpretation, although few verses are interpreted on all four levels. Instead of *remez*, Baḥya uses the term *derekh ha-śekhel* (the way of the intellect) for philosophical allegory. Baḥya was not yet familiar with the term *pardes*, which appears only in the later parts of the Zohar, which had not yet been published. But, with the exception of Baḥya, there are few examples of exegetes who analyze a book using all four methods consistently as did the Christians.[25]

Typological exegesis is usually identified with Christian commentary, patristic and medieval, which often portrays the events of the New Testament, especially Jesus' life, as being prefigured in the Hebrew Bible. By and large, Jewish exegetes shied away from this type of exegesis, but there are examples of it, such as Rashi's commentary on the Song of Songs, the commentary of Ramban (Naḥmanides) on the Torah, and other works of the late Middle Ages and early modern period. My essay in this volume discusses an unusual commentary on the book of Ruth, by Isaac ben Joseph ha Kohen, which develops a rich typology of Jewish history based on the characters of the book. This commentary is unique in Jewish literature, and its existence raises further questions about the extent of the use of typology by Jewish exegetes.

In the fourteenth and fifteenth centuries, exegetes tended, by and large, to devote less effort to clarifying the *peshaṭ* in order to follow homiletic, philosophical, or mystical lines of interpretation. We also see an increasing tendency toward prolixity, which climaxes in the voluminous commentaries of Don Isaac Abarbanel (1437–1508), the greatest exegete of the fifteenth century.[26] Abarbanel's commentary is very rich and sophisticated, judiciously using midrashic material[27] and incorporating discussions of philosophical and theological issues. Especially important are his commentaries on Samuel and

Kings, in which he draws upon his experience in the royal courts to exegete the text and to elaborate his own political philosophy. The sermons on the Pentateuch (*'Aqeidat Yiṣḥaq*; The binding of Isaac) and the commentaries on the Five Scrolls of Isaac Arama (ca. 1420–94), Abarbanel's teacher, are exemplary models of homiletic exegesis, blending exegetical innovation with psychological and philosophical insight.

Two features of late medieval commentaries are the subjects of essays in this volume. Marc Saperstein explores the tendency among late medieval exegetes to raise a series of conceptual questions at the beginning of a biblical passage and then answer these questions in the course of the ensuing discussion. This technique is especially characteristic of the commentaries of Isaac Arama and Isaac Abarbanel. Saperstein tries to trace it back as far as possible, to its earliest Jewish antecedents, and also attempts to identify possible Christian sources for this practice. The consequences for the exegete of this practice and the pitfalls it may have presented him are also discussed.

Eric Lawee engages in a similar exercise with regard to the question of introductions to scriptural works, referred to in Latin as *accessus ad auctores*. Lawee, whose main focus is Abarbanel, also tries to trace back as far as possible the practice of writing introductions in medieval Jewish exegesis, and he endeavors to determine to what extent parallels can be drawn with Christian works. The results are mostly negative, except with regard to Joseph Ḥayyun, the famous fifteenth-century Portuguese rabbi, who wrote fully developed introductions to several biblical books, with a very modern ring to them. The question is an important one and Lawee's preliminary study offers a solid foundation for further research.

One of the important goals of research in medieval scriptural exegesis is to determine the role that sacred scripture played in the cultural life of the people of the period. The book of Proverbs, with its numerous moral and ethical admonitions and prescriptions, proved a rich source of ethical guidance for exegetes and other scholars. Alan Cooper in his essay examines the history of the exegesis of the verse "Educate the child according to his way" (Prov 22:6) and shows how different philosophies of education and attitudes toward children are expressed in the comments on this verse over the ages. This chapter demonstrates how the Bible mirrors changing cultural attitudes and provides authoritative sanction for them. In this way, the Bible has maintained its centrality and relevance in the life of the people for countless generations.

Medieval Jewish exegesis maintains an important position in the canon of Judaism to this very day. The commentaries of Rashi, Ibn Ezra, Ramban, and others are still studied assiduously in schools, yeshivot, seminaries, and by educated laity. Rashi's Torah commentary has been translated into English at least four times in the last century, the most recent translations appearing within the last decade.[28] Most of the major Torah commentaries are available in English editions aimed at a popular audience. Most have appeared since 1970.[29]

Since the sixteenth century[30] many editions of the Hebrew Bible have been published featuring the Hebrew text of the Bible and the Aramaic targum surrounded by several medieval commentaries. In the nineteenth century, publishers in Eastern Europe began calling such Bibles *Miqra'ot gedolot* (Great scriptures). This juxtaposition of exegetes of different generations and backgrounds allows them to interact with each other through the mediation of the reader[31] and such editions have remained very popular to this day. In recent years, modern editions of *Miqra'ot gedolot* have appeared in Israel, instilling new life into these venerable commentaries and making them more accessible. The *Torat ḥayyim* edition of the Pentateuch with commentaries published by Mossad Harav Kook is a popular edition based on earlier semicritical editions of commentaries published by this popular press, which is affiliated with the Religious Zionist movement. The *Keter*, a new edition published by Bar-Ilan University under the editorship of Menachem Cohen, has set a new standard for critical scholarship and textual accuracy. The biblical text is based on the most reliable manuscript in existence, the tenth-century Aleppo Codex, and the texts of the commentaries are all based on the best manuscripts available. This edition, which is intended for both educated laity and scholars, is one of the most significant publishing ventures in biblical scholarship in the last generation and attests to a continued interest in medieval commentary in the religious and academic sectors of the Jewish community.[32]

This continued interest in medieval commentary is similar to the situation in Islam, described by Jane McAuliffe in her introduction to Islamic exegesis, and contrasts with the situation in Christianity, where medieval commentaries are studied primarily by academics. One reason for this lack of interest among modern Christians is the fact that the Bible is studied by the laity only in translation, and the Latin, Hebrew, and Greek texts are the sole purview of academics (and the more scholarly clergy). In Judaism and Islam, however, the sacred texts of scripture are studied in their original Hebrew and Arabic along with the traditional commentaries. In Jewish law, for instance, every individual is obligated to read the weekly Torah reading twice in the original and once in the Aramaic translation of Onkelos as preparation for hearing the reading of the Torah in the synagogue on Saturday morning. According to some, one may fulfill the translation part of this obligation by reading Rashi's commentary.

Another reason for the continued popularity of the Jewish commentary tradition may be the fact that many of the commentaries try to understand the plain meaning of the text primarily on the basis of sound philology and lexicography. Commentaries that are philosophical or mystical in nature have much less popular appeal because they are less accessible. In medieval Christianity, the fourfold interpretation of scripture gave pride of place to the three nonhistorical senses, while the historical sense, except in the School of Saint Victor[33] and to some extent in the commentaries of Nicholas of Lyra, was given short shrift.[34] This tendency also contributes to the lack of appeal of medieval Christian exegesis to the modern Christian. In general, the impact of modern critical biblical scholarship on Christianity has been so profound that, until recently, there was little sympathy for the medieval approaches, which were so far removed from the literal meaning of the text.[35] In traditional Judaism, modern biblical scholarship has made limited inroads; this fact also helps account for the continued appeal of the medieval commentary tradition, which in general presents less of a challenge to traditional faith.[36] In Islam, the situation is similar, although the distance between traditional and critical scholarship is even greater, since critical scholarship is carried out chiefly by Western non-Muslim scholars and is often ignored by Muslims.[37]

The chapters in this volume advance the study of this important area of Jewish thought in several ways, some opening up new areas of research, others providing new insights into topics or exegetes already well researched. In reading these essays, I was struck by the unique position occupied by the chapters in the Jewish section. In the Middle Ages, the Jews served as mediators of culture, translating the major works of science and philosophy from Arabic and Greek into Latin via Hebrew. Jews as a minority had their feet in both cultures and were influenced by both. It would seem that in the modern academy as well, Jewish scholars tend to essay more comparative research, delving more deeply into Islam and Christianity than scholars of these religions do into Judaism. I am convinced that scholars of Islam and Christianity would benefit greatly from a greater familiarity with Jewish scholarship in areas of related interest. Bringing together a small group of scholars of the three Abrahamic religions in a symposium in which they heard each other speak and where they could interact both formally and informally was an important first step in the facilitation of such an exchange of ideas. If the juxtaposition of these studies on Jewish, Islamic, and Christian scriptural exegesis encourages cross-fertilization and exploration of topics of shared interest in this and other areas of medieval religious thought among a broader group of scholars, the publication of this volume will have served an important purpose.

Notes

1. The Geonic period actually begins near the end of the sixth century and ends with the death of Hai (Hayya) Gaon in 1038. On the problems of periodization see Robert Brody, *The Geonim of Babylonia and the Shaping of Medieval Jewish Culture* (New Haven, Conn.: Yale University Press, 1998), 3–18.

2. See S. W. Baron, "Restudy of the Bible," in *A Social and Religious History of the Jews*, 2d ed., vol. 6 (New York: Columbia University Press, 1958), 235–313, and, most recently, Brody, *The Geonim of Babylonia*, 300–315.

3. See Henry Malter, *Saadia Gaon: His Life and Works* (Philadelphia: The Jewish Publication Society of America, 1921), still the authoritative introduction to Saadia, and Saadia ben Joseph, *The Book of Theodicy*, trans. L. E. Goodman (New Haven, Conn.: Yale University Press, 1988), a translation of Saadia's commentary on Job, with an extensive introduction and notes. See also Moshe Zucker, ed., *Peirushei R. Se'adyah Ga'on li-Vereshit* (New York: Jewish Theological Seminary of America, 1984).

4. For a convenient introduction, see Nahum M. Sarna, "Abraham Ibn Ezra as an Exegete," in *Rabbi Abraham Ibn Ezra: Studies in the Writings of a Twelfth-Century Jewish Polymath*, ed. Isadore Twersky and Jay M. Harris (Cambridge: Harvard University, Center for Jewish Studies; distributed by Harvard University Press, 1993), 1–27. Much has been written about Ibn Ezra by Uriel Simon. See, for example, his *Four Approaches to the Book of Psalms*, trans. Lenn Evan Schramm (Albany, N.Y.: State University of New York Press, 1991), much of which deals with Ibn Ezra and his exegetical methodology.

5. The best study of Kimḥi is Frank Talmage, *David Kimhi: The Man and the Commentaries* (Cambridge, Mass.: Harvard University Press, 1975).

6. See Menahem Banitt, *Rashi: Interpreter of the Biblical Letter* (Tel-Aviv: Tel Aviv University, Chaim Rosenberg School of Jewish Studies, 1985).

7. See Sarah Kamin, *Rashi: peshuṭo shel Miqra u-midrasho shel Miqra* (Jerusalem: Magnes Press, 1985).

8. Very useful for the study of Rashbam is Martin Lockshin's translation of his Torah commentary. So far three volumes have appeared, on Genesis, Exodus, and Leviticus-Numbers. See bibliography of Lockshin's chapter in this volume.

9. 4th ed. (Oxford: Basil Blackwell, 1984).

10. E. Touitou, "Shiṭato ha-parshanit shel Rashbam 'al reqa' ha-meṣi'ut ha-hisṭorit shel zemanno" (The exegetical system of Rashbam against the historical background of his time), in *'Iyyunim be-sifrut Ḥazal, ba-Miqra uve-toledot Yisra'el muqdash le-Prof. 'Ezra Ṣiyyon Melammed*, ed.

Y. D. Gilat, Ch. Levine, Z. M. Rabinowitz (Ramat-Gan: Bar-Ilan University Press, 1982), 48–74.

11. See Michael A. Signer, "Peshat, Sensus Litteralis, and Sequential Narrative: Jewish Exegesis and the School of St. Victor in the Twelfth Century," in *The Frank Talmage Memorial Volume*, part I, ed. Barry Walfish (Haifa: Haifa University Press, 1993), 203–16.

12. *Gersonides on Providence, Covenant, and the Jewish People: A Study in Medieval Jewish Philosophy and Biblical Commentary* (Albany, N.Y.: SUNY Press, 1995).

13. *Joseph Ibn Kaspi's Gevia' kesef: A Study in Medieval Jewish Philosophic Bible Commentary* (New York: Ktav, 1982).

14. See Colette Sirat, "Biblical Commentaries and Christian Influence: The Case of Gersonides," in *Hebrew Scholarship and the Medieval World*, ed. Nicholas De Lange (Cambridge: Cambridge University Press, 2001), 221–23.

15. See Ivan G. Marcus, "Exegesis for the Few and for the Many: Judah he-Ḥasid's Biblical Commentaries," *Jerusalem Studies in Jewish Thought* 9 (1989):1*–24*.

16. See Isadore Twersky's "Introduction," to *Rabbi Moses Naḥmanides (Ramban): Explorations in His Religious and Literary Virtuosity* (Cambridge, Mass.: Harvard University, Center for Jewish Studies; distributed by Harvard University Press, 1983), 4.

17. See Elliot R. Wolfson, "By Way of Truth: Aspects of Naḥmanides' Kabbalistic Hermeneutic," *AJS Review* 14 (1989): 103–78, esp. 103–5.

18. Song of Songs, Ruth, Lamentations, Ecclesiastes, and Esther, the five biblical books read in the synagogue on the holidays of Passover, Shavuot, Ninth of Av, Sukkot, and Purim. These scrolls, because of their popularity and role in synagogue ritual, were often published together with the Pentateuch, and commentaries upon them proliferated.

19. On the hermeneutics of the Zohar, see Elliot R. Wolfson, "Beautiful Maiden Without Eyes: *Peshat* and *Sod* in Zoharic Hermeneutics," in *The Midrashic Imagination: Jewish Exegesis, Thought, and History*, ed. Michael Fishbane (Albany, N.Y.: State University of New York Press, 1993), 155–203.

20. They distinguished three levels of interpretation: *peshaṭ*, *derash*, and *sod*. See Marcus, "Exegesis for the Few," 11.

21. See Wolfson, "By Way of Truth," 122–25 and passim.

22. Ibn Latif in his *Sha'ar ha-shamayim* (Gate of Heaven), written before 1238, mentions four levels of interpretation. See Sara O. Heller Wilensky, "Isaac Ibn Latif: Philosopher or Kabbalist," in *Jewish Medieval and Renaissance Studies*, ed. Alexander Altmann (Cambridge, Mass.: Harvard University Press, 1965), 219. This must have been one of the earliest elaborations of a fourfold system.

23. Abulafia developed a sevenfold exegetical system in which his peculiar version of ecstatic kabbalah was credited with being the source of the deepest exegetical insights. See Moshe Idel, *Language, Torah and Hermeneutics in Abraham Abulafia* (Albany, N.Y.: SUNY Press, 1989), 82–124.

24. See Moshe Idel, "PaRDeS: Some Reflections on Kabbalistic Hermeneutics," in *Death, Ecstasy, and Other Wordly Journeys*, ed. John J. Collins, Michael Fishbane (Albany, N.Y.: State University of New York Press, 1995), 251–52. See the notes on p. 264 for other literature on this subject, esp. the articles by Bacher, Scholem, Sandler, and van der Heide.

25. In any case, as several scholars have pointed out, the four methods of the Christians do not correspond to those of the kabbalists, so the question of whether there was direct Christian influence in this development or whether this system was an internal Jewish development still has not been resolved. In the most recent review of the problem, Moshe Idel seems to favor the view that this was an internal Jewish development. See his "PaRDeS," 250–53.

26. Abarbanel has been the subject of several recent studies by Eric Lawee. See bibliography in Lawee's essay in this volume.

27. On his use of midrash and his exegesis in general, see especially, Eric Lawee, "The 'Ways of Midrash,' in the Biblical Commentaries of Isaac Abarbanel," *HUCA* 67 (1996):107–42.

28. Artscroll ed., trans. Y. I. Z. Herczeg, et al., 5 vols. (Brooklyn: Mesorah Publications, 1994–99), and trans. Shraga Silverstein (Jerusalem; Southfield, Mich.: Targum Press, 1997).

29. E.g., Charles B. Chavel's translation of Ramban (5 vols; New York: Shilo, 1971–76) and H. Norman Strickman and Arthur M. Silver's translation of Ibn Ezra on the Pentateuch (3 vols. to date; New York: Menorah, 1988–99).

30. 1st ed: Venice, 1517–18; 2d ed.: Venice 1524–25; 3d ed.: Venice, 1546–48.

31. See Edward L. Greenstein, "Medieval Bible Commentaries," in *Back to the Sources: Reading the Classic Jewish Texts*, ed. Barry W. Holtz (New York: Summit Books; Philadelphia: The Jewish Publication Society of America, 1984), 213–59.

32. So far seven volumes have appeared (1992–2000): Joshua–Judges, Samuel, Kings, Isaiah, Genesis (in 2 parts), and Ezekiel.

33. Primarily in the commentaries of Andrew, who was somewhat of a maverick, not at all representative of the school. Hugh and Richard were much more mainstream, valuing the nonhistorical senses more than the historical.

34. See chapters by Synan, Jeauneau, and Ginther in this volume.

35. This situation has changed somewhat in scholarly circles in the last ten or twenty years, where an increased interest in medieval exegesis has been manifested, but I suspect that very few of the fruits of this scholarship have been made available to the average lay Christian reader.

36. But the medieval commentaries are also studied by non-Orthodox scholars and rabbis for their intrinsic interest and the insights they can provide into the biblical text and for the moral and theological issues that they raise. No one has done more to raise the profile of medieval commentary tradition and show its relevance to the modern religious Jew than Nechama Leibowitz, biblical scholar and teacher extraordinaire, who for over fifty years successfully promoted the study of the Bible with its medieval commentaries among the Israeli public. Her teaching and her written works have had far-reaching influence, and her works continue to be studied widely today. Her series of studies on the weekly Torah portions have been translated into English and several other languages.

37. It would seem that in general Muslim society is more insulated from Western influence and would be closer to the situation of the Ḥaredim, or ultra-Orthodox Jews, who study Jewish texts in their yeshivot according to traditional norms without recourse to Western modes of thinking or scholarship. Many modern Orthodox Jews, however, participate fully in the academic tradition and, indeed, much of the critical historical scholarship on the Middle Ages in the field of biblical exegesis, philosophy, mysticism, and other areas is carried out by modern Orthodox scholars. I would suspect that as Muslim populations in Western countries grow and Muslims become more acculturated to Western society and study Islam in Western universities, this situation will change among Muslims as well.

2

The Search for Truth in Sacred Scripture

Jews, Christians, and the Authority to Interpret

STEPHEN D. BENIN

In the last part of the *Phaedrus*, Socrates, while discussing the interpretation of texts, notes an ambiguity:

> . . . anyone who leaves behind him a written manual and, likewise, anyone who takes it over from him, on the supposition that such writing will prove something reliable and permanent, must be exceedingly simple-minded . . . if he imagines that written words can do anything more than remind one who knows that which the writing is concerned with.[1]

How do texts remind us if we do not *already* know? How did medieval Jews and Christians, so temporally and culturally distant from the sacred text they endeavored to understand, ever know "that which the writing is concerned with"? As latecomers, were they perpetually banned from understanding a text from an earlier time and a different culture? The rabbinic Sages, in their attempt to explain the eternal validity of a time-bound text, simply, yet quite boldly, claimed that all their teachings stemmed, at least in principle, from Sinai and were accordingly part of revelation itself. As the Sages asserted: "Moses received the Torah at Sinai and transmitted it to Joshua, and Joshua to the Elders, and the Elders to the Prophets, and the Prophets to the men of the Great Assembly" (M. Avot 1.1).[2] A received chain of tradition linked the generations, and this unbroken chain of tradition guaranteed the chance for legitimate interpretation.[3]

The predicament confronting the interpreter was described by Socrates when, a bit further in the dialogue, he observed:

> You know, Phaedrus, that's the strange thing about writing, which makes it truly analogous to painting. The painter's products stand before us as though they were alive, but if you question them, they maintain a most majestic silence. It is the same with written words; they seem to talk to you as though they were intelligent, but if you ask them anything about what they say, from a desire to be instructed, they go on telling you just the same thing forever.[4]

The "majestic silence" of the text must somehow be made audible through the voice of the exegete. The Rabbis believed that their oral teachings could release the words of Torah for all subsequent generations.[5] "Revelation occurred once, written and inscribed;

but human learning . . . is perpetual, oral, and described. Nevertheless, it is precisely the many interpretive words of the Rabbis that attest to their ultimate distance from Sinai, and to the majestic silence which the written word maintains before and after all exegesis."[6] Readers of the Bible were engaged in a perpetual struggle with the written, inscribed revelation.

Both Jews and Christians developed interpretive traditions, and these very traditions presented an exegetical conundrum. After all, did Jewish scholars of later centuries have the same authority, indeed capacity, to interpret scripture as had the earlier Rabbis, and did successive Christian exegetes share the *auctoritas patrorum antiquorum*?[7] Did they have to agree with their forebears, or could they question and go beyond them? Might tradition stifle new approaches and avenues of interpretation? Medieval Jewish and Christian exegetes confronted this dilemma and found similar means and stratagems to address and surmount the problem of tradition. This study examines briefly the attempt of Jewish and Christian exegetes to explain in an innovative manner the eternal validity of a supposedly time-bound text while maintaining respect for received tradition, a position expressed in the medieval adage, "We are like dwarfs standing on the shoulders of giants."[8]

Before turning to the medieval developments on the theme of the eternal validity of the law, it is necessary to assess the rabbinic underpinnings of the matter, without which the medieval developments cannot be appreciated.

In searching rabbinic literature for historical examples of textual elucidation, Jewish scholars often turned to the talmudic story concerning the "oven of Akhnai," which elaborates on the exegesis of the Rabbis who came to decipher the Torah in ways that even Moses could not fathom. In this famous incident, Rabbis are portrayed discussing an issue of *halakhah*. Rabbi Eliezer brought forward almost every imaginable argument to support his view, but the assembled Rabbis rejected them. Finally, he said, "If the halakhah agrees with me, let this carob tree prove it!" The tree, we are told, moved one hundred cubits—or four hundred. The Rabbis retorted, "No proof may be brought from a carob tree!" He repeated his argument asking water to flow backwards to support him, which it did, and then he asked the walls of the academy to fall. We read that out of respect to Rabbi Eliezer they leaned, but out of deference to Rabbi Joshua, they did not fall. On each occasion the Rabbis responded that no proofs may be brought from unnatural occurrences. Finally a *bat qol*, a heavenly voice, cried, "Why do you dispute with Rabbi Eliezer, since in all matters the *halakhah* agrees with him?" Rabbi Joshua arose and said, "It is not in heaven!" (Deut 30:12). Rabbi Jeremiah said that the Torah had already been given at Sinai and we no longer pay attention to a *bat qol* because it is written in the Torah (Exod 23:2), "After the majority one must incline."

The tale continues that Rabbi Nathan met Elijah and asked, "What did the Holy One do then?" Elijah responded, "He laughed and declared, 'My children have defeated Me, my children have defeated Me!'"[9] This tale not only demonstrates in a vibrantly convincing manner the vigor of Jewish exegetical activities, but makes it abundantly clear that authority for interpretation had been transferred to humans, and that the miraculous and supernatural exercised no influence on legal decisions. Thus armed, the Rabbis were prepared boldly to go where none had seemingly gone before.

Yet the same story came to be used by medieval Christians as an example of insolent Jewish activity.[10] From the Jewish view, the Torah no longer being in heaven, it was the work of humanity to study it, to interpret it, and to ferret out all it contained. But the seeming rejection of divine aid in this process struck medieval Christians as scandalous. Rabbinic readers of the sacred text displayed an amazing synchronicity that leveled out entire epochs of history while at the same time opening up scripture as a vibrant florilegium of exempla.

Still, one ought always to recall Maimonides' admonition in *The Guide of the Perplexed* (1.2) that the Torah is not a book of history or poetry, but a book of laws.[11] And if the Torah and, *a fortiori*, its laws were bequeathed for all times, it cannot be read exclusively as an expression of one unique historical moment, that is, as a univocal text preserved in the amber of history. Rather, the Torah must be seen as part of an ongoing process or discussion between the divine and the human. And if it is a heritage—for Israel and for all humanity—then its normative message ought not to be spent in a single generation.[12]

Truth, for Maimonides, was paramount, and he declared quite plainly, "For only truth pleases Him, may He be exalted, and only that which is false angers Him" (*Guide* 2.48). And in his *Commentary on Ḥeleq*, Maimonides notes that one should believe truth for the sake of truth, and thus one "serves God out of love."[13] If this is so, then one may wonder if the writings of the Rabbis of the talmudic era on every subject have to be necessarily taken blindly with unswerving allegiance and without any questioning whatsoever. What about seeming changes or advances in science?

Such a question already arose with Abraham Ibn Ezra (1092–1167), a shrewd and keen scholar. In his biblical commentary, Ibn Ezra noted that Genesis is not a scientific and comprehensive account of creation *ex nihilo*, but rather of the creation of the sublunar realm through natural processes. He also questioned the seeming contradictions between astronomical observation and biblical statements concerning the relationship among planets in the supralunar realm:

> And should one inquire: do the astronomers (*ḥakhmei ha-sefirot*) not say that Jupiter and all the stars save Mercury and Venus are larger than the moon? How then could it be written [in scripture with regard to the sun and the moon] "the big ones"? The answer is that the meaning of "big" is not with respect to bodily size but with respect to light, and the moon's light, because of proximity to earth, is many times [stronger]. Thus it is written "luminary" [with regard to the moon].[14]

Simply put, it appears that the biblical account presents matters from the human perspective. If this is not abundantly clear from this comment, then it becomes manifestly obvious from Ibn Ezra's comment on Genesis 1:26.

> Know that all the works of creation came to be, for the sake of man, by God's command. [Scripture tells that] the earth and water produced plants and living creatures. After that, God said to the angels: "Let us make man"; that is, we, not the earth and water, will occupy ourselves with man's creation. We know that the Torah speaks the language of humans; for the speaker is human so also the hearer (*dibberah torah ki-leshon benei 'adam, ki ha-medabber 'adam gam ken ha-shome'a)*. Now a human cannot speak of things above or below him except by comparing them to man. Thus scripture uses expressions such as: "the mouth of the earth" (Num 16:30); "the hand of the Jordan" (Num 13:29); and "the head of the dust of the world" (Prov 8:26).[15]

Scripture thus speaks to humans on the human level, and in scientific matters such as astronomy the Torah speaks in a way that makes sense to humanity, even if it seems contradictory to "scientific fact."

The Torah may speak in human terms, but what of other sciences such as medicine and of seemingly magical practices being used in medicine? Maimonides, as a physician, reflected upon the use of magic in medicine as an example of Amorite usage (*mi-darkhei ha-'Emori*)[16] and voiced his opinion quite bluntly:

> You must not consider as a difficulty certain things that they [the Sages] have permitted, for example, the nail of one who is crucified and a fox's tooth (BT Shabbat 67a). For in those times these things were considered to derive from experience and accordingly pertained to medicine and entered into the same class [as other folk remedies]. . . . For it is allowed to use all remedies similar to these that experience has shown to be valid even if reasoning does not require them.[17]

Knowledge may advance and increase, and since the Rabbis of the talmudic period lived at a time when medicine was not as advanced as it was in his own day, one need not follow their medical advice. In a similar vein to Ibn Ezra, Maimonides argued:

> Do not ask me to show that everything they [the Sages] have said concerning astronomical matters conforms to the way things really are. For at that time mathematics were imperfect. They did not speak about this as transmitters of the dicta of prophets, but rather because in those times they were men of knowledge in those fields or because they had heard these dicta from the men of knowledge who lived in those times.[18]

The Rabbis did have authority, but not in every sphere of knowledge. It is clear that Maimonides did not accept every statement in rabbinic literature absolutely, but differentiated among their areas of expertise. In a discussion of rabbinic statements on how best to praise God, Maimonides, in an apparent swipe at the need to accept all rabbinic utterances, quips, "You also know their famous dictum—would that all dicta were like it. . . ."[19] The Rabbis had knowledge and authority but it was not catholic in nature or scope. Indeed, it was Maimonides' son, Abraham, who gave eloquent voice to this opinion:

> We are not obligated, in spite of the greatness of the wisdom of the talmudic Sages and the perfection of their understanding in Torah . . . to accept all that they say in matters of medicine or science or astronomy, and believe their statements as we believe them when they interpret the Torah. For the latter is the quintessence of their wisdom, and it is for them to rule on these matters to others, as it is said in the verse: "According to the Torah which they will teach you" (Deut 17:11).[20]

The authority and wisdom of the Sages were evidently circumscribed. Challenging the opinions of an authority in cases where his opinion is based on judgment does not necessarily entail a challenge to his authority. Indeed, Maimonides disagrees completely with the misguided opinions of the Sages who claimed that the motions of the celestial spheres produced mighty and fearful sounds, as he writes:

> Aristotle, however, does not accept this and makes it clear that the heavenly bodies produce no sound. You will find this statement in his book "On the Heaven"; from the passage there you will understand this. You should not find it blameworthy that the opinion of Aristotle disagrees with that of the Sages, may their memory be blessed, as to this point. For this opinion, I mean to say the one according to which the heavenly bodies produce sounds, is consequent upon the belief in a fixed sphere and in stars that return. You know, on the other hand, that in these astronomical matters they preferred the opin-

> ion of the Sages of the nations of the world to their own. For they say explicitly: The Sages of the nations of the world have vanquished. And this is correct. For everyone who argues in speculative matters does this according to the conclusions to which he was led by his speculation. Hence the conclusion whose demonstration is correct is believed.[21]

For Maimonides, the Sages of Israel recognized the wisdom of non-Jewish Sages in certain areas, and various traditional Jewish opinions, including exegetical ones, were not necessarily divorced from the particular context in which they were formulated.

One emergent exegetical trend seems to have been the attempt to rise above external factors in the interpretation of the law. On numerous occasions, the midrash notes that the law was given to an individual *lefi koḥo* or to groups *lefi koḥan*, that is, it was individually adapted, not given as a seeming generic dispensation in the language of all generations. Even Moses, according to Exodus Rabbah, received revelation uniquely. As the midrash states: "Moses spoke and the Lord answered him—in a voice Moses could bear."[22] Hence, the Jewish exegetical tradition could invoke intermittently the maxim *dibberah torah ki-leshon benei 'adam / scriptura humane loquitur* to explain how the Torah was given in a manner comprehensible to humanity, and midrashic texts could make claims for revelation adapted to individual or communal abilities.

Jewish exegetes also wondered why the language of the Torah appeared to be so repetitive and redundant. Maimonides addressed this in the *Guide*: "There are also things which belong to the mysteries of the Torah which have caused many people to stumble" (3.50), and he provided explanations and reasons for each apparent redundancy as well as a rationale for the commandments (*Guide* 3.25–50).

Other exegetes followed in his wake. Joseph ibn Kaspi (1279–1349), for example, in his *Gevia' kesef*, argued that the redundancies and lengthy explanations in the Torah were needed for the mass of humanity to comprehend its teachings. He additionally noted that "[Moses] repeated several things for the benefit of us who read the Torah today. Thus he said 'a copy of this law' [Deut 17:18—literally a "second Torah"], intending us to read some things in the book of Exodus in the wintertime, and to repeat them when we read the book of Deuteronomy in the summer."[23] For ibn Kaspi the prophets spoke in the same redundant manner, having learned the technique from the Torah. Citing Ezekiel 21:32, "a ruin, a ruin, a ruin, will I make it," and other cases of repetition and duplication, ibn Kaspi claims such language establishes something overpowering. "This purpose was pointed out by Him who gave the Torah most notably in the case of Joseph, who told Pharaoh, 'For that the dream was doubled unto Pharaoh twice, it is because the thing is established by God' (Gen 41:32). Other instances should be compared to this statement."[24] Therefore, scriptural style was, in this view, accommodated to human necessity.

Maimonides, in his historical-anthropological explanation for the "bloody sacrifices" of old, asserts unequivocally that the Torah took into account the passing and imperfect cultural situations of humanity at the time of the revelation at Sinai (*Guide* 3.32), for to have done otherwise would have been impossible, considering that the Torah, at least at its literal level—the *peshaṭ*—was formulated for humans bounded by the here and now. In some cases this relates merely to origins, and not to the eternal validity of what is commanded (MT, *Me'ilah* 8.8). As many commentators have suggested, even if we do not know why we should obey the law—anyone who understands *lefi kokho* may not understand enough about the divine teaching—that is no license for its abrogation. Yet in other cases, for example when trial by water was stopped (M. Sotah 9.9), changed circumstances involved a change in the way the *halakhah* was practiced but did not lead to its eradication.[25]

What we have then in Maimonides are cases that attempt to locate biblical law and history within changed and changing historical circumstances. In his approach and those of others may be seen the hermeneutical attempt to preserve and explain how a Torah given but once at a unique historical moment in our contingent world could speak eternally. Lest we think this was simply a medieval problem, what some have called gradualism or accommodation, scholars through the centuries continually addressed it. Even the adage *ḥadash 'asur min ha-Torah* was seemingly balanced by various *'aggadot* explaining the paradox of how God learned Torah from his creatures. The phrase was invoked by many, including Rabbi Ḥayyim of Volozhin, and the comment "Whatever a veteran student of the Law is destined to innovate *has already been said* to Moses at Sinai" begged for exegesis.[26]

Consider, for example, Rabbi Abraham Isaac Kook's discussion of biblical slavery. Rav Kook did not propose a willy-nilly evolving Torah, but rather one that was directed toward a predefined goal, and a vital element in his thought is that the providential coordination of appropriate historical factors is God's way of relating to a gradual progression of humanity's spiritual development. Yet, while Israel might have been morally able to renounce slavery, the Lord, by giving laws to make it as just as possible, allowed Israel gradually to be weaned from it and to progress to ever higher levels of morality.[27] In numerous Jewish sources, history was construed as an educational process guiding humanity toward some predefined goal.[28]

This idea also connoted some progressive quality to the historical process, and, in fact, one might argue that the Jewish tradition recognized that the text of the Torah itself might have been emended or adjusted at different times. There is a fascinating story related in the Talmud concerning the canonicity of the text of the Torah:

> Mar Zutra, or as some say, Mar 'Ukba, said: "Originally the Torah was given to Israel in Hebrew characters and in the sacred [Hebrew] language; later, in the time of Ezra, the Torah was given in *'Ashurit* (Assyrian) script and Aramaic language. [Ultimately], they selected for Israel the *'Ashurit* script and Hebrew language." It has been taught: R. Yose said: "Had Moses not preceded him, Ezra would have been worthy of receiving the Torah for Israel." Of Moses it is written, "And Moses went up to God" (Exod 19:3), and of Ezra it is written, "He, Ezra, went up from Babylon" (Ezra 7:6). As the going up of the former refers to the [receiving of the] Law, so does the going up of the latter. . . . And even though the Torah was not given through him [Ezra], its writing was changed through him. . . . It has been taught: Rabbi said: "The Torah was originally given to Israel in this [*'Ashurit*] writing. When they [Israel] sinned, it was changed into *ro'eṣ*.[29] But when they repented, [Assyrian characters] were reintroduced. . . . R. Simeon b. Eleazar said on the authority of R. Eliezer ben Perata, who spoke on the authority of R. Eleazar of Modi'im: "This writing [of the Law] was never changed. . . ."[30]

In this rabbinic presentation of revelation relating to the form of the canonical Pentateuch, Ezra played a not insignificant role. If in fact this is an example of a retrojection, it may, in fact, have reflected some historical memory, since the Samaritans also have a tradition recalling Ezra's role in the consolidation of the scriptures.[31] What also emerges clearly is that by the time of the last attribution, the notion that Ezra might have had anything to do with the consolidation of Scripture, in such crucial issues as orthography and language, was rather unpalatable. Such an assertion, at any time, threatens the sanctity of the written word.

And yet Judaism maintained that in ten specific places the very words of the text of the Torah presented such exegetical enigmas that they are marked with dots above them to indicate that they are not to be taken according to their plain meaning. Tradition attributes these markings (*'eśer nequdot / puncta extraordinaria*) to Ezra. In a midrashic analysis of these scriptural anomalies, the discussion concludes with this remarkable observation:

> Some give another reason why the dots are inserted. Ezra reasoned thus: If Elijah [some read "Moses"] comes and asks, "Why have you written these words? [i.e., why did you include these questionable selections?], I shall answer, "That is why I have dotted these passages." And if he says to me, "You have done well in having written them," I shall erase the dots above them.[32]

What is truly daring in this midrash is that it not only attributes the introduction of these marks to Ezra, but amazingly ascribes to Ezra the discretion to write—or not to write—these sentences in scripture. Not surprisingly, from the Middle Ages to the twentieth century, this text was seen as more than merely problematic. Azariah de Rossi (1513–78) denounced this passage as the work of a deviant student who entered this comment into the text without his teacher's knowledge, and in the twentieth century R. Moshe Feinstein decried it as unadulterated heresy and urged its excision from the text.[33]

Yet there were other voices that saw this and other parallel passages as much less dangerous. Scholars such as Ibn Ezra, Rabbi Judah the Pious, and more contemporaneously Rabbi Y. F. Lisser[34] believed that Ezra had some hand in the scribal correction of the text. Indeed, Ibn Ezra and Judah the Pious argued that some words and phrases had been added to the canonical text after the time of Moses.[35] David Kimhi expressed his view quite clearly:

> These differences in reading apparently developed because, during the first exile, the texts were lost, the scholars were dispersed, and the biblical experts died. Thus the members of the Great Assembly . . . found differences in the texts and followed the reading of the majority as far as possible. When they could not come to a decision, however . . . they wrote one in the margin and one in the text.[36]

The late medieval scholar Rabbi Moses Alashkar (1466–1542) wrote in a responsum: "It makes no difference whether the Torah was given via Moses or via Ezra as to whether Sages can expound upon it."[37] And Isaac Abarbanel (1437–1508) opined in his commentary on Jeremiah:

> How can I believe in my soul and bring forth on my lips that Ezra the Scribe found the book of the law of God and the books of His prophets and all others who spoke through the Holy Spirit to be questionable due to omission and confusion? . . . Behold, this is what has comforted us in our affliction: that God's Torah is with us in our exile. And if we think that the Torah has been subject to omission and confusion . . . then nothing firm will remain upon which we can rely.[38]

The attitudes of various Jewish scholars toward the history of the Torah's text and its interpretations were neither uniform nor univocal. These scholars addressed the issue of the eternal validity of the text by focusing on the familiarity of the Sages with scientific and medical knowledge, that is, areas of general education, and on the question of the nature of the text of the Torah itself and possible emendations to it. What emerges is the acceptance of the text's eternal veracity. The seeming shortcomings of the Sages in scientific and medical matters in no way impinged upon or negated the validity of their exegetical enterprise. And at the textual level, the unique authorship of the Torah by Moses was accepted.

Jewish Tradition and Progress

When it came time to interpret the sacred page, medieval Jews, as well as Christians, were in some ways compelled to work within confines established by their respective faiths, and they deferred ostensibly to long-established norms. Yet in several cases, we can discern the desire of some exegetes to stake out their original claims and give voice to their own fresh insights. Rabbi Levi ben Gershom (Ralbag/Gersonides) (1288–1344) took up one of the issues raised above: how did humanity seemingly achieve so much scientific knowledge in the relatively short time between creation and his own day? In his Genesis commentary, which was completed 5,090 years after creation, according to the traditional Jewish calculation, he answered that the early human forebears were extraordinarily long-lived and that longevity permitted individuals to accrue much more scientific knowledge than we may acquire now in our abbreviated lifetimes. Thus the sciences received, as it were, a jump start and developed quite rapidly.[39] So much for science, but what about exegesis?

In his commentary to Song of Songs 7:14, Gersonides writes:

> The meaning of her statement, "new and old, which I have laid up for you, O my beloved," is that what has been apprehended anew from these things through the senses, with what was apprehended of old, was all stored for him in the faculty of memory by her, so that the appropriate sensual repetition of this could be accomplished.[40] This is accomplished either through the senses or through what she apprehends from another, and this indeed is added to her, as is well known.[41] This is so because there [exist] here many things which cannot in any fashion be fully apprehended by any individual [alone], as is the case with the species of animals and what is similar to them, as Aristotle has mentioned in *On Animals*.[42] Thus, the correct way to proceed is to gather what has been apprehended concerning these matters by those among the ancients who are trustworthy and in this way to bring to completion what is needed from the senses.[43]

Thus we ought to rely upon those "ancients who are trustworthy." Gersonides was quite respectful of the work of his predecessors, straying from their path reluctantly, yet prepared to go his own way when necessary.[44] He does give instructions on how one ought to disagree with the ancients:

> But when deciding to dissent from the teachings of the ancients, one should do so with extreme care and scrutiny, deviating from their teachings as little as possible. This is appropriate because the ancients were lovers of truth and endeavored to approach it as closely as possible even when their principles prevented them from reaching it entirely. . . .[45]

And yet Gersonides was conspicuous for having relied so infrequently on the works of the ancients.[46] As he observes at the start of his discussion of astronomy in *Wars of the*

Lord 5.1.1: "None of the ancients whose works have reached us tried to investigate the science of astronomy in its perfection, and thus some gaps remain in it. For this reason we decided to investigate it here."[47] This independent attitude marks not only his philosophical and astronomical works, but his exegetical works as well. He makes the point abundantly clear in the Introduction to *Wars of the Lord*: ". . . our predecessors have not treated most of these questions philosophically, and what they do say philosophically about them is false, as will be demonstrated in our book."[48] His exegeses of the Song of Songs and Job voice similar attitudes. In the introduction to his commentary on Job, he states:

> We have not found among any of our predecessors whose commentaries have reached us an explanation of the meaning of the text. Rather, their purpose was merely to explain the words. Thus, they did not come near the real meaning [of the text] by [giving us] this kind of commentary. For it is necessary for an exegete to conduct his explanation of words and phrases according to the meaning of the content of the whole book, [especially] when the words are ambiguous, as they are in this book. If the exegete does not first pay attention to the understanding of the general meaning of the contents, he will not understand the words, except by accident. . . . Thus, the commentaries which we were accustomed to from our youth have prevented us from understanding this book for some time until we [finally] opened the eyes of our intellect and examined the contents of this book; on this basis we then explained the words therein. . . . We found no one who sought to investigate the various views of Job's friends who disputed with him except the little that the *Rav Ha-Moreh* [Maimonides] wrote on this in his celebrated book *The Guide of the Perplexed*. It was his remarks that stirred us to investigate these views in detail. . . .[49]

A similar critique of earlier commentators, even if based on different reasons, is articulated in the introduction to the Song of Songs:

> Said Levi ben Gershom: We have seen fit to comment on this scroll, the Scroll of Song of Songs, as we understand it, for we have not found any other commentary on it which could be construed as a correct explanation of the words of this scroll. Rather, we have seen that all the commentaries which our predecessors have made upon it and which have reached us adopt the midrashic approach, including interpretations which are the opposite of what was intended by the author of the Song of Songs.[50]

Hence the ancients either employed the wrong method in their exegesis of specific biblical books by ignoring the content and context and concentrating on isolated words, or they made excessive use of midrashic interpretive techniques, thereby misconstruing the true intentions of the author.[51] The midrashic approach was shunned by R. Levi since it tended to lead readers to wrong conclusions about the meaning of a text, and for him, when the Sages resorted to midrash, he could proffer another interpretation. In discussing Exodus 20:5, which identifies God as "a jealous God," who visits the guilt of the fathers upon the third and fourth generation of children, Ralbag demonstrates his own hermeneutical approach. In seeking to explain the exile suffered by the Jews since the first century C.E. he writes:

> For example, when our fathers rebelled they incurred the punishment of exile and the nations dispossessed their land. Now their progeny too suffered exile [simply] because they were born while their parents were in exile, so they could not avoid this evil unless they would have been exempted from it by virtue of the heavenly constellations or by

> virtue of their own perfection such that God Himself would miraculously take them out of exile. . . .[52]

Ralbag continues that this is no injustice since the punishment the children suffer is accidental, and this sort of evil, stemming from heavenly constellations, is terribly rare, while the benefits God causes in this manner are many. The type of evil caused by heavenly constellations may disappear before its appointed time because of individual divine providence. This type of evil cannot endure for a very long time along with individual divine providence and general providence, but the good that emanates from God may endure for a thousand generations. In this view, Israel's sufferings are more than compensated by divine benefits, and in this way Ralbag agrees with the rabbinic axiom that "no evil descends from above."

> Our Rabbis, however, have solved this problem in a different way. They have maintained that God visits the sins of the fathers upon the children when the latter continue the deeds of their fathers. This is no doubt true. . . . For the evil that emanates from God's exhortation is according to the rebellion [committed by those who have been exhorted], i.e., for someone who is slightly enmeshed in rebelliousness a slight exhortation suffices, whereas someone who is deeply involved in it such that it has become a strong habit requires a greater reproof. Accordingly, when someone sins by himself, a slighter reproof is sufficient, one weaker than what will be needed if his father had committed this vice and he persisted in it. . . . Our interpretation of this passage [however] is more consonant with the literal meaning of the text.[53]

Ralbag distinguishes his method, closer to the literal truth, from the rabbinic approach, which is much more homiletical. He remains considerate of rabbinic tradition while advancing his views. In subsequent centuries, Isaac Abarbanel was to break new ground in the entire area of biblical hermeneutics and the stance toward tradition.[54] He freely wonders about the authorship of the biblical text, the sources used, the differences among books that were written through mantic arts (*nevu'ah*) and those composed through the holy spirit (*ru'aḥ ha-qodesh*), and so on. As had many other exegetes, Abarbanel felt free to question the Rabbis on their use of midrash.[55] As Abarbanel states emphatically:

> Thus, it is clear to you that there are dicta in the Babylonian and Jerusalem Talmuds that one is not obligated to believe. . . . how much more in this case [with such other rabbinic compendia as] Sifra, Sifrei, Tosefta, Tanḥuma, Mekhilta, the various Rabbot . . . and the rest of the compilations and anthologies; for [the name of] those who created them are not preserved and we are unsure whether their final shapers (*me'abbedeihem*) were trustworthy or what exactly was their character.[56]

Much as earlier scholars claimed the Rabbis were not omniscient in all things, Abarbanel voices the same opinion. He refers to Aristotle's assertion that one should thank earlier scholars who initiate investigations even if they do not get the correct answers, since without their attempts later scholars could not complete the work.[57] This justification for new investigations is taken up in his discussion of the relationship between Samuel and Chronicles:

> . . . These are the plethora of doubts that beset this great question, and in seeking an answer and their resolution, I am bereft, with nobody working with me on them. For

> concerning this topic, I have found nothing, great or small, good or bad, from our Sages—not the early ones, the talmudic masters, nor the later writers and commentators. Not even one alluded to the difficulty at all and not one among them suggested a path toward its resolution.[58]

In the general introduction to his commentary on the Former Prophets, after discussing historical questions about the authorship of various biblical books, Abarbanel writes:

> Do not be amazed that I have deviated from the opinion of our Sages in this matter, since even in the *gemara*, they did not agree on these matters. They disagreed there as to whether Moses wrote the book of Job (BT Bava Batra 15a-b) and whether Joshua wrote [the last] eight verses of the Torah (Bava Batra 15a). Given that our Sages themselves exhibited doubts in a part of the dictum [concerning biblical authorship], it is not inadmissible for me also to choose a more plausible and satisfying approach as regards a part in accordance with the nature of the verses and their straightforward purport.[59]

Since the Sages themselves arrived at no unanimous and valid conclusions, it was not "inadmissible" for a scholar to search for a better and more complete answer. Abarbanel advocated respect for tradition with an acceptance of progress. In concluding his introduction to the Former Prophets, he acknowledges: "As for what I have understood of this, let the wise person pay heed and increase instruction."[60]

As Maimonides observed: "The great sickness of the 'grievous evil' (Eccl 5:12) consists in this: all the things that man finds written in books, he presumes to think as true—and all the more so if the books are old."[61] Thus received tradition, even that of "trustworthy ancients," which might have constrained attempts at expounding novel ideas and views, was respectfully challenged, and the call for future study is combined with respect for earlier scholars, who started the as yet incomplete work.

The Broad Field of Sacred Scripture

The issues raised by Gersonides and other Jewish exegetes regarding the ancients not surprisingly find expression in Christian exegesis as well. Indeed, it was the twelfth-century exegete Richard of Saint Victor who voiced his frustration with those who were unwilling to countenance novel approaches to scriptural interpretation, and Richard could well have said he was writing, as did Gersonides much after him, "to explain this book, because among earlier commentators we have not found one who stated the real meaning and content of the book."[62]

Richard, in his prologue to the vision of Ezekiel, a text much beloved and commented upon by the Fathers, especially Gregory the Great, whose interpretation merited pride of place among Christian authors, nevertheless offered his own interpretation while remaining respectful to Gregory.

> Many take much more pleasure in holy Scripture when they can perceive some suitable literal meaning. The building of the spiritual interpretation is more firmly established, so they think, when aptly grounded in the solid historical sense. Who can lay or firmly establish a solid foundation in a formless void? The mystical senses are extracted and formed from fitting comparisons of the things contained in the letter. How then, they ask, can the letter lead us to a spiritual meaning in those places where it contradicts itself,

or is merely ridiculous? Persons of this kind are often scandalized rather than edified when they come to such passages of Scripture.

The ancient Fathers, on the contrary, were glad to find passages which according to the letter could not stand. These "absurdities" of the letter enabled them to force certain persons, who accepted holy Scripture but mocked at allegorical interpretations, to resort to a spiritual meaning, since they dared not deny that the Holy Spirit had written nothing irrelevant, however foolish the letter might sound. This is the reason, in my opinion, why the ancient Fathers passed over in silence the literal exposition in certain more difficult passages, or treated it rather carelessly, when by perseverance they could doubtless have found a much more satisfying explanation than any of the moderns.

But here I must say that certain people, as though from reverence for the Fathers, will not attempt to fill their omissions, lest they should seem to presume. Having this excuse for laziness, they idle at leisure; they mock, they deride, ridicule other people's efforts to seek and find truth. . . . For our part, however, let us take with all greediness what the Fathers have discussed; let us investigate eagerly what they have left untouched; let us offer with all generosity the fruits of our research, that we may fulfill that which is written: "Many shall pass over, and knowledge shall be manifold" (Dan 12:4).

Lo! Blessed Gregory expounds the wonderful vision of celestial creatures, seen by the prophet Ezechiel, according to the mystical sense. But what it means literally he does not say. Of the second vision he says that it cannot mean anything according to the letter. This is true, but only according to the way he takes it here. If we decide to consider the same passage in a different way, perhaps we may be able to extract some suitable literal meaning. . . .[63]

For Richard, times have changed and the perception of different types of exegesis has also changed. In commenting on the prophet's second vision, Richard enunciates with great clarity his approach, as well as excusing himself for his words.

I know that the Fathers passed carelessly over certain passages of Scripture, which they could easily have grasped. They wanted to find, and rejoiced in, passages which according to the letter could not stand; their intention was at least by these means to persuade men that allegory ought to be accepted, which very few were willing to admit in those days. Let no one take scandal if I say something other, or otherwise than he finds in his glosses. Let no one scorn me for desiring to glean. Let it not surprise him that something has escaped the Fathers, or rather that they, who received the divine commandment and the divine boon to fill so many volumes with corn from the harvest of Scripture, have left something intentionally to the poor.

Do you wish to honour and defend the authority of the Fathers? We cannot honour the lovers of truth more truly than by seeking, finding, teaching, defending and loving the truth. Do not ask whether what I say is new, but whether it is true.[64]

As certain Jewish scholars could question use of midrash and other aggadic exegesis, Richard raised questions about different types of interpretation and what they might convey. The Fathers' work sought to encourage later generations to build upon their foundations, and for Richard, truth, not novelty, was the indispensable and fundamental quality of interpretation. He felt restricted, no doubt, by those who would not even acknowledge the possibility that something new might be proffered in explication of the holy word and who were so narrow in outlook that they could not even conceive of any creative insight into the sacred text. Elsewhere, Richard noted about his fresh insights into scripture: "I have said all these things on account of those who accept nothing which had not been accepted by the fathers."[65]

Given the reforms in scriptural studies emanating from Saint Victor, it fell to Andrew of Saint Victor, the "new Jerome,"[66] to elucidate most eloquently a defense of Victorine "naturalistic"[67] exegesis against its enemies:

> If Jerome had judged it idle, rash or presumptuous to expend enthusiasm and work for the sake of investigating the truth of the scriptures after the Fathers had taken such great care to elaborate upon them, then never would that wise, industrious, and good man, who kept in mind that it is written, "Make good use of your time," have worked so hard on this task or have spent his whole life at it. For he surely knew, that learned man knew—he knew, I say, and he knew best—how obscure truth is, how deep it lies buried, how far from mortal sight it has plunged into the depths, how it will admit only a very few, by how much work it is reached, how practically no one over succeeds, how it is dug out with difficulty and then only bit by bit. . . . Careful search can find it, but only in such a way that careful search can find still more. No one can bring out all of it but ferrets it out in bits and pieces and, when all is said and done, in vain. While fathers and forebears discovered it, more remained for sons and descendants to find. While it is sought, more always remains to be sought. While it is always being found, more always remains to be found (*Sic semper invenitur, ut semper supersit quod inveniatur*). Therefore, just because our forebears gave themselves over to the search for truth through studying and expounding sacred scripture, there is nothing dishonorable or presumptuous or wrong or idle or superfluous about us lesser men devoting ourselves to that same search.[68]

That the Church Fathers were lovers and seekers of truth does not preclude contemporary, lesser mortals from attempting to build on their substantial accomplishment. Truth endures always to be sought. The more truth is found, the more remains to be discovered. The issue Andrew confronted is the same that Rupert of Deutz would address, namely, how to honor the Fathers yet articulate a different opinion.

Just as there might be diversity within Christian unity, so might there be between old and new religious orders. A superb exegete such as Rupert of Deutz, who retained a fundamental belief in the validity of the historical periodization of four kingdoms and ages, nevertheless assaulted the very notion of any change or evolution in religious institutions.[69] Rupert attacked novel religious orders and, perhaps more important, the possible changes they heralded, and he complained about the comparison between the historical succession of the four kingdoms and the monastic orders.[70] Yet, despite such conservative attitudes, Rupert claimed unequivocally that he nonetheless had the right and liberty to discover new truths in scripture. He did not discard or demean the work of the Fathers. On the contrary, one could accept certain views while at the same time not accepting everything they said. In much the same way as some contemporary rabbis came to accept the limitations in the scope of the Sages' knowledge, Rupert and others came to view the Fathers. In the dedicatory letter to his commentary on the Gospel of John, a text on which Augustine was the authority, Rupert raised the possibility of adding to and complementing patristic exegesis.

> Since that voice of Christian law and spokesman for the catholic faith, Father Augustine, held forth on the Gospel of John in elegant discourses, they foolishly think it reprehensible or derogatory toward him that I have presumed to rework the same Gospel, nothing

> less than the word of God, after such a learned man; and they are angered because, as they think, I have dared out of pride (. . . *per superbiae spiritum ausus sim*) to usurp as an upstart (. . . *quasi novi homini*), a task for which only the noble ancients were fit.[71]

To make matters worse, some apparently denounced Rupert for having forsaken one of Augustine's opinions. No doubt feeling the sting of such accusations, Rupert defended himself and for that matter Augustine: "Necessity compels me to say that the writings of St. Augustine are not part of the canon and are not to be trusted in all matters as are the canonical books (*non esse in canone scripta beati Augustini, non esse illi[s] per omnia confidendum sicut libris canonicis*). And they have begun to malign me as a heretic for saying that St. Augustine was not canonical."[72]

Questioning any Father, let alone Augustine, paved the way for the critical examination of the entire patristic corpus, and this in turn legitimated new approaches to sacred writ which could no longer be denounced, in the words of 1 Timothy 6:20, "as profane innovations." Indeed, as Rupert declared:

> But someone will say: "What those far better and more holy and nevertheless more learned men discovered and wrote is already quite enough. It is wrong, it is rash to add anything to what was said by the renowned and catholic Fathers, and thus to wear readers out by swelling the multitude of commentaries."
>
> To which I reply: "The broad field of the sacred scriptures surely belongs to all the confessors of Christ, and the freedom to cultivate them cannot by right be denied to anyone, provided that, the faith remaining unscathed, he say or write what he knows. For indeed who may be properly indignant when, after the Fathers before them dug one or two holes, their sons and heirs dig more yet by their own labor in their common patrimony."[73]

Rupert had to rebut criticism similar to that leveled at Andrew of Saint Victor. Both claimed the right to find truth without being accused of contempt or impertinence toward the Fathers. Both were respectful, yet each felt free to go his own way.

What emerges plainly from this brief survey is that Jewish and Christian exegetes accepted the words of their forebears, yet felt free to depart from them, while at the same time aspiring to amplify and transcend them. As we have seen, Gersonides, Abarbanel, Richard of Saint Victor, and Rupert of Deutz not only sought innovative and timely approaches to scripture, but endeavored to accommodate their own interpretations to their exegetical legacy, thereby contributing to increased understanding and appreciation of the biblical text. It would be only a matter of time before their novelties became part of the tradition itself. Both Jews and Christians believed they had inherited an eternally valid text which could reveal the truth to those who sought it diligently. However, the search for truth is never-ending, and so scholars of each generation felt the need to take up the quest for themselves.

Notes

1. Plato, *Collected Dialogues*, 521.
2. For further elaboration see Herr, "Ha-reṣef."
3. See Urbach, *The Sages*, chapter 12, and Fishbane, *The Garments of Torah*, 112–20. Islam also came to recognize the authority and value of *isnad*, a received chain of tradition.
4. Plato, *Collected Dialogues*, 521.

5. See for example, Midrash Tanḥuma, Noaḥ, 3. See also: Rawidowicz, "On Interpretation."

6. Fishbane, *Garments of Torah*, 113. Also of value is Simon, "The Religious Significance of the *Peshat*."

7. On the decline of generations, see for example BT 'Eruvin 53a: "The hearts [i.e., minds] of the *rishonim* (early authorities) are like the doors of the *'ulam* [a chamber of the Temple in which the door was 20 cubits wide] and that of the *'aḥaronim* (later authorities) like the door of the *hekhal* [a smaller chamber of the Temple in which the door was 10 cubits wide] but ours are like the eye of a fine needle." For medieval uses of this idiom see Zlotnick, "Commentary of Rabbi Abraham Azulai," 162–68, and Lawee, "Isaac Abarbanel's 'Stance Toward Tradition,'" 165–98, esp. 175–79.

8. The remark is attributed to Bernard of Chartres by John of Salisbury in *The Metalogicon*, 167. The phrase made its way into Hebrew texts as well. See Zlotnick, "Commentary," 162–68; Azulai raises the question of how later halakhists—*'aḥaronim*—could argue with earlier ones—*rishonim*. See also Leiman, "From the Pages of Tradition," 93–94 n. 10; Guyer, "The Dwarf," 398–402; and Merton, *On the Shoulders*, 268.

9. On this episode see BT Bava Meṣia' 59b. For partial discussion of similar issues see Benin, *The Footprints of God*, and Benin, "Jews and Christian History."

10. The very expression "it is not in heaven" supports the notion that the Torah is now given to humanity and humans must make sense of it. See the discussion of the Christian understanding of the talmudic story in Saperstein, *Decoding the Rabbis*, 4–6. See also Grabois, "The *Hebraica Veritas*"; Berger, "Mission to the Jews"; Berger, "Gilbert Crispin"; Smalley, *The Study of the Bible*; and Touitou, "Shiṭato he-parshanit."

11. See *The Guide of the Perplexed*, trans. Pines, 24.

12. On this entire issue, see Benin, *Footprints of God*, passim; Twersky, *Introduction to the Code of Maimonides*, passim; Twersky, "Some Non-Halakhic Aspects of the *Mishneh Torah*"; Twersky, "Religion and Law"; and Funkenstein, *Perceptions of Jewish History*.

13. I use the translation in Twersky, ed., *A Maimonides Reader*, 406. For a discussion of the seeming paradox of increased knowledge and the idea of the "decline of the generations" see Kellner, *Maimonides on the "Decline of the Generations."*

14. *Peirushei ha-Torah le-rabbeinu 'Avraham 'Ibn 'Ezra*, ad Gen 1:16, ed. Weiser 1:17.

15. Ibid., ad Gen 1:26, ed. Weiser, 1: 18–19.

16. Part of the discussion in *Guide* 3.37, trans. Pines, 542–44.

17. Ibid., 544.

18. *Guide* 3.14, trans. Pines, 459.

19. *Guide* 1.59, trans. Pines, 140, discussing BT Berakhot 33b.

20. Cited in Ross, "Can the Demand for Change Be Legitimated," 481. The text appears in *Ma'amar 'al 'odot derashot Ḥazal [s.v. da' ki 'attah ḥayyav]* in editions of the '*Ein Ya'aqov*, at the beginning and in Maimonides, *Qoveṣ teshuvot ha-Rambam we-'iggerotaw*, 41a. See also Y. Levi, "The Sciences as the 'Maid Servants of the Torah.'"

21. *Guide* 2.8, trans. Pines, 267. The talmudic source is BT Pesaḥim 94b on the fixity of the spheres vs. the fixity of the constellations in which the rabbis conceded to gentile scholars that the constellations were fixed and the spheres rotated. Cf. *Guide* 3.14.

22. See Benin, *Footprints of God*, 127–38, for some midrashic uses, and see, for example, Genesis Rabbah 55.8, which comments on both Abraham and God acting "*lefi koḥo*." For Moses see inter alia, Exodus Rabbah 5.9, as well as Tanḥuma (Buber) Shemot 22. For use of the maxim "the Torah speaks the language of humans" see BT Berakhot 31b, inter alia, Funkenstein, *Perceptions of Jewish History*, 88–94, and Jacobs, *A Tree of Life*, 249–52.

23. Herring, *Joseph Ibn Kaspi's* Gevia' kesef, 258–59 (Chap. 19).

24. Ibid., 259.

25. The argument is expressed clearly by Ross, "Demand for Change," 481. In his explana-

tion for animal sacrifices, Maimonides argues that the Torah took into consideration the passing and less than perfect cultural situations of humanity (*Guide* 3.32), since to have done otherwise would have been an impossibility considering that the Torah was formulated on the literal level (*peshaṭ*) for humans limited by the present world. In some cases this may relate to origins, not the eternal validity of the Law, but in some cases changed circumstances involve a change in practice.

26. See BT Ḥaggigah, Chap. 1, passim, Menaḥot 29b. I quote the translation in Ross, "Demand for Change," 482. The text cited is in *Nefesh ha-ḥayim*, Sha'ar 4, chapter 6. Re: *ḥadash 'asur min ha-Torah*, whose polemical use by Rabbi Moses Sofer (Ḥatam Sofer) (1762–1839) against the Reform movement is well known, see Jacobs, *A Tree of Life*, 249–56.

27. See the discussion in Ross, "Demand for Change," 483–85.

28. Ibid., 483–86.

29. Other versions: *ra'aṣ*, or *da'aṣ*, one of the names for the primitive Hebrew script.

30. BT Sanhedrin 21b. Cf. the story in BT Menaḥot 29b, where God is depicted as busying himself with the "crowns" in the letters of scripture. The story in Sanhedrin seems much richer and nuanced in dealing with fundamental issues of the canonicity of text.

31. Halivni, *Revelation Restored*, 16–17. In what follows I agree with the arguments as set forth on 17–22.

32. Deuteronomy Rabbah 3.13.

33. For de Rossi see Azariah de' Rossi, *The Light of the Eyes*, trans. Joanna Weinberg, chap. 19, 328, and Moshe Feinstein, *'Iggerot Mosheh, Yoreh De'ah*, vol. 3, numbers, 114–15, both cited by Halivni in *Revelation Restored*, 93, notes 7 and 8. Halivni, n. 7, incorrectly cites *The Light of the Eyes*, chap. 9. R. Feinstein calls the selection "spurious and heretical."

34. See Halivni, *Revelation Restored*, 17.

35. See the discussion in Halivni, *Revelation Restored*, 16–22, 93–94 n. 11 (for sources and references to Ibn Ezra and Judah the Pious), and Halivni, *Peshat and Derash*, 141–44.

36. *Commentary on Chronicles* cited in Talmage, *David Kimhi*, 93. For Abarbanel's differing view, see Lawee, "On the Threshold of the Renaissance," 283–319, esp. 304–5.

37. Responsum 74, cited in Halivni, *Revelation Restored*, 18.

38. *Peirush 'al Nevi'im rishonim*, 299. I use the translation in Lawee, "On the Threshold of the Renaissance," 305.

39. See Levi ben Gershom, *Peirush 'al ha-Torah 'al derekh ha-bei'ur*, Venice ed., 16d; Israel ed., 68.

40. Kellner, "Gersonides on *Imitatio Dei*," 290, n. 41, "i.e., that the memory must store the impressions of previous sense experience if their repetition will be of any use to us."

41. Ibid., 290, n. 42, "Or, 'because it has become well-known,' i.e., the scientific accomplishments of others have become well-known and available to researchers."

42. As Kellner notes, ibid., n. 43, *On Animals* is actually *Parts of Animals*, bk. 1. Gersonides is here following the medieval Muslim bibliographic tradition.

43. I use the translation of M. Kellner in Levi ben Gershom, *Commentary on Song of Songs*, 68. Cf. Kellner, "Gersonides," 290.

44. See Kellner, "Gersonides," 275–96. Cf. Levi ben Gershom (Gersonides), *The Wars of the Lord*, trans. Feldman, 2:230–38. For an overview of Gersonides, see Dahan, ed., *Gersonide et son temps*.

45. *Wars of the Lord* 5.1.46; cited in Goldstein, "A New Set of Fourteenth-Century Planetary Observations," 385.

46. See the numerous studies of Bernard Goldstein cited in Kellner, "Bibliographia Gersonideana," 367–414, esp. 398–402.

47. I use the translation in Goldstein, *The Astronomy of Levi ben Gerson*, 22.

48. Levi ben Gershom, *The Wars of the Lord*, trans. Feldman, 1:93.

49. Ibid., 2:232.

50. I use the translation of Kellner in Levi ben Gershom, *Commentary*, 3.

51. On Ralbag and midrash, see Harvey, "Quelques reflexions," 109–16. On the issue of midrash in exegesis, see Smalley, *The Study of the Bible*, 149–56.

52. Levi ben Gershom, *Peirush 'al ha-Torah*, 76a. I use Feldman's translation, in *Wars of the Lord* 2:236–37.

53. Levi ben Gershom, *Peirush 'al ha-Torah*, 76a–b; trans. Feldman, in *Wars of the Lord* 2:237.

54. For Abarbanel, see Lawee, "Isaac Abarbanel's 'Stance'"; idem, "On the Threshold"; idem, "Don Isaac Abarbanel."

55. See Saperstein, *Decoding the Rabbis*, 8–12.

56. *Yeshu'ot meshiḥo*, fol. 17r cited in Lawee, "On the Threshold," 312. For subsequent disagreement with some of Abarbanel's views see Samuel Laniado (turn of seventeenth century), Meir Loeb ben Yeḥiel Michael Malbim, and Zadok ha-Kohen Rabinowicz of Lublin (nineteenth century).

57. *Perush 'al Nevi'im rishonim*, 13 cited in Lawee, "Don Isaac Abarbanel," 71, n. 12.

58. *Perush 'al Nevi'im rishonim*, 13 cited in Lawee, "Don Isaac Abarbanel," 71–2, n. 12.

59. Cited in Lawee, "Don Isaac Abarbanel," 70.

60. Cited in Lawee, "Don Isaac Abarbanel," 66. As Lawee points out, 72, n.14, Abarbanel uses this verse from Proverbs as a call for renewed and ongoing creativity by future students. One might also cite Abarbanel's comments concerning BT Ḥullin 7a: "My fathers have left me room whereby I might distinguish (*le-hitgadder*) myself." He would use this dictum to justify writing books without thinking everything had already been said by earlier authorities. For various applications of this dictum see Lawee, "Don Isaac Abarbanel," 176–77, n. 47.

61. See Maimonides, *Letter on Astrology*, 229.

62. See above, n. 39.

63. Richard of Saint Victor, *Prologus in visionem Ezechielis*, in *PL* 196. 527. I use the translation in Smalley, *The Study of the Bible*, 108–9.

64. Richard of Saint Victor, *Prologus in visionem Ezechielis*, in *PL* 196. 562. I use the translation in Smalley, *The Study of the Bible*, 109.

65. Richard of Saint Victor, *Expositio tabernaculi foederis*, in *PL* 196. 211.

66. See Smalley, *The Study of the Bible*, 112–95; Chenu, *Nature, Man and Society*, 168, and Schneider, *Geschichte*.

67. For the term, see Chenu, *Nature, Man and Society*, 17.

68. I use the translation in Chenu, *Nature, Man and Society*, 313; the text is reproduced there, 313–14, n. 7. The text is in Smalley, *The Study of the Bible*, 378–79. She transcribed Andrew's prologue *In Isaiam* from Paris MS Mazarine 175, fol. 40.

69. On Rupert see Van Engen, *Rupert of Deutz*.

70. Cited in Chenu, *Nature, Man and Society*, 215.

71. *Prologus in evangelium Joannis*, in *PL* 169. 202.

72. *Super quaedam capitula regulae divi Benedicti abbatis* 1, in *PL* 170. 496.

73. The text is in *Prologus in Apocalypsim*, in *PL* 169. 826.

Bibliography

Abarbanel, Isaac. *Perush 'al Nevi'im rishonim*. Jerusalem, 1979.

——. *Yeshu'ot meshiḥo*. Konigsberg, 1861.

Azariah de' Rossi. *The Light of the Eyes*. Trans. Joanna Weinberg. Yale Judaica Series, 31. New Haven: Yale University Press, 2001.

Benin, Stephen D. *The Footprints of God: Divine Accommodation in Jewish and Christian Thought*. Albany: SUNY Press, 1993.

——. "Jews and Christian History: Hugh of St. Victor, Anselm of Havelberg and William of Auvergne." In *From Witness to Witchcraft: Jews and Judaism in Medieval Christian Thought*. Ed. Jeremy Cohen, 203–219. Wolfenbütteler Mittelalter-Studien, 11. Wiesbaden: Harrassowitz, 1997.

Berger, David. "Gilbert Crispin, Alan of Lille, and Jacob ben Reuben: A Study in the Transmission of Medieval Polemic." *Speculum* 49 (1974): 34–47.

——. "Mission to the Jews and Jewish-Christian Contacts in the Polemical Literature of the High Middle Ages." *The American Historical Review* 91 (1986): 576–79.

Chenu, M. D. *Nature, Man and Society in the Twelfth Century: Essays on New Theological Perspectives in the Latin West*. Ed. and trans. Jerome Taylor and Lester K. Little. Chicago: The University of Chicago Press, 1968.

Dahan, Gilbert, ed. *Gersonide et son temps: science et philosophie médiévales*. Louvain: Peeters, 1991.

Fishbane, Michael. *The Garments of Torah: Essays in Biblical Hermeneutics*. Bloomington: Indiana University Press, 1989.

Funkenstein, Amos. *Perceptions of Jewish History*. Berkeley and Los Angeles: University of California Press, 1993.

Goldstein, Bernard R. *The Astronomy of Levi ben Gerson (1288–1344): A Critical Edition of Chapters 1–20 with Translation and Commentary*. New York: Springer-Verlag, 1985.

——. "A New Set of Fourteenth-Century Planetary Observations." *Proceedings of the American Philosophical Society* 132 (1988): 371–99.

Grabois, Aryeh. "The *Hebraica Veritas* and Jewish-Christian Intellectual Relations in the Twelfth Century." *Speculum* 50 (1975): 613–34.

Guyer, F. E. "The Dwarf on the Giant's Shoulders." *Modern Language Notes* 45 (1930): 398–402.

Halivni, David Weiss. *Peshat and Derash: Plain and Applied Meaning in Rabbinic Exegesis*. New York: Oxford University Press, 1991.

——. *Revelation Restored: Divine Writ and Critical Responses*. Boulder, Colo.: Westview Press, 1997.

Harvey, Ze'ev. "Quelques reflexions sur l'attitude de Gersonide vis-à-vis du *Midrash*." In *Gersonide et son temps*. Ed. Gilbert Dahan, 109–16. Louvain: Peeters, 1991.

Herr, M. D. "Ha-reṣef shebe-shalshelet mesiratah shel ha-Torah: le-verur ha-hisṭoryografyah ha-miqra'it be-hagutam shel Ḥazal" (Continuum in the chain of transmission of the Torah). *Ẓion* 44 (1979): 43–56.

Herring, Basil. *Joseph Ibn Kaspi's* Gevia' kesef: *A Study in Medieval Jewish Philosophic Bible Commentary*. New York: Ktav, 1982.

Ibn Ezra, Abraham. *Peirushei ha-Torah le-rabbeinu 'Avraham 'Ibn Ezra'*. Ed. A. Weiser. 3 vols. Jerusalem: Mossad Harav Kook, 1976.

Jacobs, Louis. *A Tree of Life: Diversity, Flexibility and Creativity in Jewish Law*. New York: Oxford University Press, 1984.

John of Salisbury. *The Metalogicon*. Trans D. D. McGrath. Berkeley and Los Angeles: University of California Press, 1962.

Kellner, Menachem. "Bibliographia Gersonideana: An Annotated List of Writings by and about R. Levi ben Gershom." In *Studies on Gersonides: A Fourteenth Century Philosopher-Scientist*. Ed. Gad Freudenthal, 367–414. Leiden: E. J. Brill, 1992.

——. "Gersonides on *Imitatio Dei* and the Dissemination of Scientific Knowledge." *JQR* n.s. 85 (1995): 275–96.

——. *Maimonides on the "Decline of the Generations" and the Nature of Rabbinic Authority*. Albany: SUNY Press, 1996.

Lawee, Eric. "Don Isaac Abarbanel: Who Wrote the Books of the Bible." *Tradition* 30 (1996): 65–73.

——. "Isaac Abarbanel's 'Stance Toward Tradition': The Case of '*Ateret zeqenim*." *AJS Review* 22 (1997): 165–98.

——. "On the Threshold of the Renaissance: New Methods and Sensibilities in the Biblical Commentaries of Isaac Abarbanel." *Viator* 26 (1995): 283–319.

Leiman, S. Z. "From the Pages of Tradition, Dwarfs on the Shoulders of Giants." *Tradition* 27:3 (Spring 1993): 90–94.

Levi ben Gershom. *Commentary on Song of Songs*. Trans. Menachem Kellner. New Haven, Conn.: Yale University Press, 1998.

——. *Peirush 'al ha-Torah 'al derekh ha-bei'ur*. Venice, 1547; reprint, [Israel: n.p., n.d.].

——. *The Wars of the Lord*. Trans. Seymour Feldman. 3 vols. Philadelphia: Jewish Publication Society, 1984–99.

Levi, Yehudah. "The Sciences as the 'Maid Servants of the Torah' in Maimonides' Writings." In *Moses Maimonides: Physician, Scientist, Philosopher*. Ed. Fred Rosner and Samuel Kottek, 97–104. Northvale, N.J.: Jason Aronson, 1993.

Maimonides, Moses. *The Guide of the Perplexed*. Trans. Shlomo Pines. Chicago: University of Chicago Press, 1963.

——. *Letter on Astrology*. Trans. Ralph Lerner. In *Medieval Political Philosophy*. Ed. Ralph Lerner and Muhsin Mahdi, 227–36. New York: Free Press, 1972.

Mishneh Torah. Standard editions.

Merton, R. K. *On the Shoulders of Giants: A Shandean Postscript*. New York: Free Press, 1965.

Plato. *The Collected Dialogues*. Ed. E. Hamilton and H. Cairns. Trans. R. Hackforth. Princeton, N.J.: Princeton University Press, 1987.

Rawidowicz, S. "On Interpretation." *Proceedings of the American Academy of Jewish Research* 26 (1957): 83–126.

Richard of Saint Victor. *Expositio tabernaculi foederis 1*. *PL* 196.211–55.

——. *Prologus in visionem Ezechielis*. PL 196.527–600.

Ross, Tamar. "Can the Demand for Change in the Status of Women Be Halachically Legitimated?" *Judaism* 42 (1993): 478–91.

Rupert of Deutz. *Prologus in Apocalypsim*. *PL* 169. 825–1214.

——. *Prologus in evangelium Joannis*. *PL* 169. 202–6.

——. *Super quaedam capitula regulae divi Benedicti abbatis*. *PL* 170. 477–536.

Saperstein, Marc. *Decoding the Rabbis: A Thirteenth-Century Commentary on the Aggadah*. Cambridge, Mass.: Harvard University Press. 1980.

Schneider, W. A. *Geschichte und Geschichtsphilosophie bei Hugo von St. Victor: Ein Beitrag zur Geistesgeschichte des 12. Jahrhunderts*. Münster: Verlag der Universitäts-Buchhandlung F. Coppenrath, 1933.

Simon, Uriel. "The Religious Significance of the *Peshat*." *Tradition* 23 (1988): 41–63.

Smalley, Beryl. *The Study of the Bible in the Middle Ages*. 1st pbk ed. Notre Dame, Ind.: University of Notre Dame Press, 1964.

Talmage, Frank E. *David Kimhi: The Man and the Commentaries*. Cambridge, Mass.: Harvard University Press, 1975.

Touitou, Elazar. "Shiṭato ha-parshanit shel ha-Rashbam 'al reqa' ha-meṣi'ut ha-hisṭorit shel zemanno" (Rashbam's exegetical method against the background of the historical reality of his time). In *'Iyyunim be-sifrut Ḥazal ba-Miqra u-ve-toledot Yisra'el: muqdash li-Prof. 'Ezra Ṣiyyon Melammed (Studies in Rabbinic Literature, Bible,* and *Jewish History*). Ed. Y. D. Gilat et al., 48–74. Ramat Gan: Bar-Ilan University Press, 1982.

Twersky, Isadore. *Introduction to the Code of Maimonides* (*Mishneh Torah*). New Haven, Conn.: Yale University Press, 1980.

——, ed. *A Maimonides Reader*. New York: Behrman House, 1972.

——. "Religion and Law." In *Religion in a Religious Age*. Ed. S. D. Goitein, 69–82. Cambridge, Mass.: Association for Jewish Studies, 1974.

——. "Some Non-Halakhic Aspects of the *Mishneh Torah*." In *Jewish Medieval and Renaissance Studies*. Ed. Alexander Altmann, 95–118. Cambridge, Mass.: Harvard University Press, 1967.

Urbach, E. E. *The Sages*. Trans. Israel Abrahams. 2d enl. ed. Cambridge, Mass.: Harvard University Press, 1987, c1979.

Van Engen, J. H. *Rupert of Deutz*. Berkeley and Los Angeles: University of California Press, 1983.

Zlotnick, Dov. "The Commentary of Rabbi Abraham Azulai to the Mishnah." *Proceedings of the American Academy for Jewish Research* 40 (1972): 147–68.

3

The Tension between Literal Interpretation and Exegetical Freedom

Comparative Observations on Saadia's Method

HAGGAI BEN-SHAMMAI

I do not intend to discuss here, in general or in detail, Saadia's exegetical activity nor to survey his exegetical works.[1] The exact number of biblical books which Saadia translated into Judeo-Arabic and interpreted in the same language is still debated among modern scholars. Suffice it to say here that Saadia had other priorities, and even if he had intended to write commentaries on the entire canon of the Hebrew Bible, he would not have managed to complete such a task. It may further be said in general that it is certain that Saadia wrote extensive commentaries on Genesis (the first half only?), Exodus, Leviticus, Deuteronomy 32, Isaiah, Psalms, Proverbs, Job, Daniel, The Song of Songs, Esther, and possibly the blessings of Jacob and Moses (Gen 49 and Deut 33). Most of these works have survived, some of them only in a fragmentary form. Most of the nonpentateuchal texts have been published, in critical or semicritical editions, mostly with translations into modern Hebrew. To date only his commentary on Job has been translated into English.[2]

Neither do I intend to discuss the entire exegetical terminology of Saadia. I will limit myself to the main terms relevant to the title of this chapter.

The term "literal" may be understood in different ways. It is used in the title as a convenient convention, and the terms and concepts relevant to Saadia in relation to that convention will be discussed.

Jewish Biblical Exegesis in Saadia's Time

Exegetical activity is an important hallmark of what is usually known as the Geonic period, that is, the ninth to the eleventh centuries, within the geographical boundaries of Islamic, mainly Arabic-speaking, countries.[3] This activity developed from the notion that the Hebrew Bible, or the biblical text, as holy scripture, deserves or needs to be studied in its own right. This was a very important innovation of the Geonic period. During that period the Bible had already occupied a focal position in religious thinking and attitudes.[4] It may well be that this trend could be seen as a result of external factors, such as the Christian interest in the Bible, but this does not make much difference. Saadia is well aware of the importance of scripture for Christians. He knows very well, as is attested in his writings, that scripture is the major source of inspiration and prooftexts for a number of central Christian doctrines, as well as for other religious movements.[5]

Saadia was not the first to interpret the Bible in general, or the Pentateuch in particular, in Judeo-Arabic. It seems that what we have in Saadia's work is almost the culmination of a process: periphrastic Judeo-Arabic translations, or, more simply put, Judeo-Arabic paraphrases, were developing since the early days of the Arab conquests, first orally and then in writing. There is now positive evidence for the existence of written Judeo-Arabic translations not later than the middle of the ninth century (they were written on papyrus), which Saadia could have used, and probably did, for his translations.[6] These paraphrases may have been modeled on similar Aramaic works in incorporating varying amounts of rabbinic materials in Arabic paraphrase.

This process, whereby Arabic interpretive translations take the place of old Aramaic traditional translation, is witnessed in an interesting responsum by Naṭronai Gaon, who was active in the middle of the ninth century, about a century before Saadia. Asked whether or not it is permitted to abandon the recital of the Aramaic translation in favor of the Arabic one, the Gaon (head of the *yeshivah*, the highest institution devoted to the study of rabbinic tradition, and the one responsible for making legal decisions) rendered the following decision:

> Those who do not translate, saying: "we do not have to recite the translation of the rabbis, we should rather translate in our language, the one used by the public," those people do not fulfill their obligation.

Further on he proves that the accepted Aramaic translation is based on the decisions of "our rabbis" and therefore it is obligatory to incorporate it into the liturgy of the synagogue. Whoever does not fulfill this obligation is liable to excommunication.[7] This means that quite early the Babylonian institutions sought to apply the severest sanctions available in order to maintain the status of the Aramaic translation against "the translation in the language used by the public," which in the Babylonian context is obviously Arabic. The Gaon concludes:

> If in some place the public wants [the Hebrew Scripture] to be interpreted to them, a person other than the one who recites the Aramaic translation may stand up and interpret for them in their language.

Again, the mention of the alternative language seems to be a rather clear reference to Arabic. To this evidence one may add that Saadia, in his own commentaries, refers often to previous interpreters. All these precedents could already have been known to Saadia during his early years in his hometown in the province of Fayyūm (Upper Egypt), around the year 900. Most of these early Arabic works, like most Aramaic translations and paraphrases, are of unknown authorship.[8] There are some Hebrew commentaries that are ascribed to ninth-century Karaites, which certainly contain early elements, such as the fragments ascribed to Benjamin al-Nahāwandi (early ninth century?) and Daniel al-Qūmisī (active in Iran and Jerusalem around 900 C.E.).[9]

Saadia's Exposition of His Exegetical Principles

Saadia's exposition of his exegetical principles is quoted here from "On Resurrection," the seventh treatise of his theological *summa*, entitled *Kitāb al-amānāt wa-l-i'tiqādāt* (The

Book of Beliefs and Convictions). It has become a *locus classicus* in modern scholarly discussions of Saadia's exegesis. Similar expositions, or brief references, are found also in other works of Saadia, such as his introduction to the Pentateuch,[10] as well as in his introductions to the other books of the Bible.[11] The exposition found in *Amānāt* seems to be the latest one but is not much different from the earlier ones, which may mean that Saadia's view on biblical exegesis remained consistent throughout his literary career. Saadia says:[12]

> I declare in the first place that one of the things of which we can be certain is that every statement found in the scriptures must be taken in its external sense.[13] Only for one of four reasons is it not permitted to take a statement in its external sense. These four reasons are the following:
>
> (1) If sense perception rejects the external sense of the passage, as in the statement, "The man named his wife Eve, because she was the mother of all the living" (Gen 3:20), seeing that we witness the fact that ox and lion are not the children of woman, so that is it necessary for us to accept the premise that the statement refers only to humans.
>
> (2) If reason repudiates it,[14] as in the statement "For the Lord your God is a consuming fire, an impassioned God" (Deut 4:24), [seeing] that fire is created, is in need of fuel and extinguishable; it is therefore not permitted, from the point of view of reason, to assume that God should be like it; it therefore follows that we must understand the statement in an elliptical sense, namely, that God's *punishment* is like a consuming fire, in the same way it says, "Indeed, by the fire of My passion, all the earth shall be consumed" (Zeph 3:8).
>
> (3) If there exists some clear text which renders the external meaning of a passage impossible; it then follows that this clear text should be used to interpret the text which is not clear, as in the statement "Do not try the Lord your God, as you did at Massah" (Deut 6:16); and it states further "And thus put Me to the test—said the Lord of Hosts. I will surely open the floodgates of the sky" (Mal 3:10). Both statements agree in this respect, that one should not try our Lord as to whether or not He is able to do a certain thing, after the manner of those of whom it is said "To test God was in their mind, when they demanded food for themselves; they spoke against God, saying, 'Can God spread a feast in the wilderness?'" (Ps 78:18–19). Of these it is said "As you did at Massah." But man may test his standing before God[15] to see whether or not He values man enough to produce a sign and miracle for him, in the same way as Gideon asked "Let me make just one more test with the fleece" (Judg 6:39), or as Hezekiah asked (2 Kgs 20:8), and others besides them; this is permissible.
>
> (4) If to the statement of scripture is attached some tradition which modifies it, we must interpret the passage in conformity with the reliable tradition, as in the case of the tradition that flogging consists of thirty-nine lashes, although it is written "He may be given [up to] forty lashes" (Deut 25:3).[16] We take this to be a figure of speech; the flogging consists of thirty-nine lashes, and the text of scripture mentions a round[17] figure, in the same way as it says "Corresponding to the number of days—forty days—that you scouted the land, a year for each day" (Num 14:34), although in fact it was only thirty-nine [years] because the first year was not included in this punishment.
>
> There are only these four reasons which necessitate the interpretation of the external meaning of the scriptural passages in an allegorical sense; there exists no fifth reason which would justify an allegorical interpretation.

With regard to this exposition the following remarks may be made:

1. Saadia is not the only one to discuss exegetical principles in the context of resurrection. It seems that in this particular context the problem of exegesis was especially disturbing for religious philosophers, or put otherwise: such thinkers were especially

concerned about the interpretation of scriptural references to resurrection that seemed to contradict rational reasoning or to be at variance with scientific truth.

2. There is the problem of the "correct" text of the seventh treatise of the *Amānāt*. The original Arabic text of the entire work has been preserved in two manuscripts (in Oxford[18] and in St. Petersburg[19]) which are almost complete[20] and which differ from each other on many points. The differences in the seventh treatise are especially meaningful.[21] However, the question of the relationship between the literal and the truly correct meaning of scripture is discussed in a similar manner in both versions.[22] Yet there is an interesting difference between the two versions, one that may appear to be only of an editorial nature but that seems to bear on the contents of the argument. In the Oxford MS the discussion is placed at the beginning of the treatise, immediately after the opening string of prooftexts, where it thus relates to the meaning of the prooftexts and is meant to be "neutral" with regard to the possibility that any factor (scripture, tradition, or reason) has an overriding authority. In the St. Petersburg ("Firkovich") MS it is placed in the context of the discussion as to whether any factor has absolute authority in determining the correct interpretation of the verses.[23]

In Saadia's exposition just quoted, the exegete moves between two different (but not opposed!) foci: *ẓāhir* and *ta'wīl*. *Ẓāhir* has been understood by many scholars as "plain"or "literal"meaning. So, for instance, Erwin Rosenthal, in an important study published many years ago,[24] states right at the beginning: "He [= Saadia] wanted to establish the plain meaning of scripture. He became thus the founder of Hebrew philology among the Jews." The difficulty of this statement is that, without defining plain meaning, the author makes the immediate connection, perhaps even equation, between this undefined "plain meaning" and a philological approach to scriptural interpretation.[25] Nevertheless, Rosenthal states shortly afterwards: "If the literal meaning would be incompatible with reason, Saadia would bring out the inner meaning of a word or passage." This statement seems to assign to reason a crucial role in deciding on the correct interpretation of scripture. It further may have encapsulated in a very concise way the meaning of *ta'wīl* as distinguished from *ẓāhir*.

It seems relevant to mention here that *ẓāhir* is well documented in Islamic exegetical discussions. A very close parallel to Saadia's "canon"[26] is found in the writings of the Spanish author *Ibn Ḥazm* (d. 1064), who is famous, among other things, for his affiliation with the trend known as *Ẓāhiriyya*.[27] *Ibn Ḥazm* taught:

> It is one's duty to interpret God's word literally (*'alā ẓāhirihī*).[28] This may be abandoned only when another written word of God, or the consensus [of the Companions of the Prophet], or a compelling fact[29] based on logical conclusion supplies conclusive evidence that a particular word of God should not be understood literally.[30]

This parallel does not mean, of course, that Saadia may be classified as a *Ẓāhirī*. It means only that a similar set of rules, with similar nomenclature, may have served exegetes of diversified approaches. A similar view of the obligation to adhere as closely as possible to the *ẓāhir* is quoted from the famous Mu'tazili teacher Abū 'Alī al-Jubbā'ī, an older contemporary of Saadia.[31] His motive for abandoning the *ẓāhir* is often, though not exclusively, theological, in verses in which the external, accepted meaning of the words does not pose any lexical or linguistic difficulty.

L. Goodman translated *ẓāhir* by "plain,"[32] as did Altmann before him. This as well as my own "external" may allude to the possibility of an alternative, hidden, meaning. And yet, all these renderings lack a more precise definition. Such may be gained from Saadia's use of a parallel (or, shall we say, synonymous) term, namely, *mashhūr* (i.e., commonly known, famous). A relevant occurrence of the term is found in a passage following the one quoted earlier, in which Saadia states:

> The correct view is that a verse should not be diverted from its apparent and common [meaning], except for one of the four convincing reasons which I have described. Anything that one of those four is not relevant to should be [understood] as heard.[33]

It should be noted that in this statement Saadia introduces another term, *masmū'*,[34] "heard, audible." It indicates something attained through sense perception, that is, audition, like *ẓāhir*, which indicates something attained through the sense of sight. The important point in this statement is the equation Saadia makes between the concepts *ẓāhir* and *masmū'* on the one hand, and *mashhūr* on the other hand.[35] It seems perfectly correct to understand the first pair of concepts as "apparent" and the latter as "commonly accepted sense."[36] The last definition especially points to something measurable. Given that we are not dealing here with the vocabulary of a spoken language, but with a specified corpus of written texts, the "common acceptability" of words may be, and has to be, measured by its distribution and documentation in the entire text of scripture. The principle underlying this requirement is that scripture was given to specific persons who share a common language. Scripture is a message which has to be perfectly understood by these persons. In other words: the language of the message has to be compatible with the language used by its recipients, who are its native or natural speakers, termed by Saadia as *ahl al-lugha*. The meaning of the latter term is proven, for instance, in his introduction to Isaiah, where Saadia lays down the rule for the interpretation (*'ibāra*, meaning mainly translation, perhaps with very minimal exegetical additions) of the original text of scripture (or of any given text, for that matter) in another language: "Declension and etymologies should not deviate from what is accepted among speakers of both languages concerned."[37] The term *ahl al-lugha* is used with the same meaning by other authors in the Geonic period as well. Samuel ben Ḥofni (Baghdad, d. 1013) uses the Arabic term as an equivalent to the Hebrew rabbinic term *leshon benei 'adam* (the language of ordinary humans).[38]

It should be noted that for Saadia the notion of *mashhūr* includes one more element in addition to the lexical, morphological, and syntactic aspects of the commonly accepted meaning. In his Introduction to the Pentateuch, Saadia discusses various kinds of deviations from the commonly accepted, or external meaning of verses. The textual condition of lists and classifications in this part of the Introduction is rather deficient, but several paragraphs are still intact and make perfect sense. There[39] Saadia lays down the important rule that one device employed by scripture in clarifying obscurities is the joining together[40] of words.[41] Saadia is probably referring to the division of verses into sentences, clauses, and phrases by means of the masoretic accents.[42] Accordingly, the *mashhūr* of a verse is its division in this way. Words attached to each other should be understood according to the *mashhūr*, which means that such clauses or phrases made up of words attached to each other (*ḍummat*) cannot be divided (*yufarraq*), just as words set apart by the accents should not be interpreted as attached to each other (*yu'allaf*). However, if it is necessary, in order to clarify the meaning of a verse, to break apart phrases or to join together words divided by the accents, doing so is permissible. This exegetical process is called here *takhrīj* (discussed in a later section). Examples cited are Genesis 3:22 and Exodus 25:34.[43] Saadia also promises his readers that he will discuss the topic in detail in his interpretation of Isaiah 6:2. The words in question there are *mi-ma'al lo*, describing the seraphim that Isaiah sees in his vision. These two words are joined by the accents and thus can (or should?) convey the meaning "Above Him (stood the seraphim)."[44] Unfortunately, Saadia's discussion has not come down to us, but we have at least his translation of the verse in question. There the word *lo* is detached from *mi-ma'al*, against the explicit division of the verse by the accents, and is interpreted in a possessive sense: He possesses angels who stand in exaltedness (or sublimity).[45]

About *ẓāhir* in Qur'ānic Exegesis

Ẓāhir is a quite common term in qur'ānic exegesis. An instructive example of its use and meaning is found in Ṭabarī's comment on Qur'ān 8:73: *wa-tawjīh ma'nā kalām allāh ilā 'l-aẓhar wa-'l-ašhar awlā min tawjīhihi ilā khilāf ḏālik* (To direct the interpretation of God's word to its most apparent and common meaning is more appropriate than to direct it toward the opposite meaning).[46] The equivalence of apparent and common, widely known, is evident in this quotation, as it is also in Ṭabarī's comment on Qur'ān 17:71: *wa-tawjīh ma'ānī kalām allāh ilā 'l-ašhar awlā mā lam tathbut ḥujja bi-khilāfihī* (To direct the interpretation of God's word to its commonest meaning is more appropriate as long as no proof has been established to the contrary).[47] The juxtaposition of *ẓāhir—ta'wīl* is aptly exemplified in a statement made by Ṭabarī in the name of earlier authorities with respect to the character of the verse Qur'ān 2:221: *innama hiya āyat*[un] *'āmm*[un] *ẓāhiruha khāṣṣ*[un] *ta'wīluha* (This is precisely a verse whose external meaning is general [or generalized], but its inner meaning [or true] interpretation is particular).[48]

It is interesting to see that when Ṭabarī states his own position regarding this verse, he repeats the statement with a slight change: instead of *ta'wīluha* he has *bāṭinuha*.[49] The usual term for inner, hidden (esoteric?) meaning comes up here. This is not to say that for Ṭabarī these two terms are identical or synonymous and can interchange freely. On the contrary, this is an exception to Ṭabarī's usual usage of *ta'wīl* to indicate precisely the correct interpretation and nothing beyond it. I would even suggest that Ṭabarī does not intend *bāṭin* here to carry more than the usual meaning of *ta'wīl*. He merely wants to indicate that the external meaning of this verse is misleading and cannot stand on its own without further clarification. The correct meaning has to be uncovered through exegetical methodology that in such cases calls in another verse(s), which in this case is Sura 5:5.[50]

Between Text and Context

Let us now turn back to Saadia's exposition of his rules. It is quite evident in this discussion that in all cases that are quoted as examples for the need, or rather the obligation (or requirement), to deviate from the "apparent" or "commonly accepted" meaning of words, there is not one case of any apparent or inherent literal, lexicographic, or syntactic difficulty. All the verses quoted are clear, precise, straightforward statements. All the difficulties presented by Saadia stem from premises that are drawn into the discussion from outside and belong to the areas of religious or legal philosophy. Consequently, we are dealing not with hermeneutical principles but rather with the parameters or commitments of the exegete. In spite of Saadia's repeated strong statements of commitment to the *ẓāhir*, it seems that there is no one objective, absolute *ẓāhir*. The acceptable *ẓāhir* is in every particular case dependent on the exegete's judgment. As we shall see, such a concept of *ẓāhir* can lead to surprising results. In addition, the *ẓāhir* defines mainly the words and the context, but this does not necessarily lead to what may be considered "plain" meaning (*peshaṭ*) as perceived, for example, by later Spanish commentators. I have shown elsewhere that, beyond the commonly accepted meaning, context (*nasq*, *siyāq*) plays a decisive role in determining the "apparent" meaning of a scriptural text.[51] Furthermore, the *ẓāhir* of a given verse may change when it is interpreted outside the context of a verse by verse commentary, such as in the course of a theological discussion.[52]

The connection between *ẓāhir* and context is also found in qur'ānic exegesis. So, for example, in Ṭabarī's comment on Qur'ān 22:73:

> *wa-innama qultu hādha 'l-qawl awlā bi-ta'wīl dhālika li-anna dhālika fī siyāq al-khabar 'an al-āliha wa-'l-dhubāb, fa-an yakūna dhālika khabar*[an] *'ammā huwa bihī muttaṣil ashbah min an yakūna khabar*[an] *'ammā huwa munqaṭi'* (I say that this suggestion is more appropriate as an interpretation of this verse, because it is in the course of the statement about the gods and flies; its being a statement about that to which it is attached [= its context] is more plausible than its being a statement about that from which it is detached).[53]

An explicit reference to *siyāq* is found in Ṭabarī's comment on Qur'ān 16:69:

> *wa-hādha 'l-qawl a'nī qawl qatāda awlā bi-ta'wīl al-āya li-anna qawlahū "fīhi" fī siyāq al-khabar 'an al-'asal, fa-an takūn al-hā' min dhikr al-'asal, idh kānat fī siyāq al-khabar 'anhū, awlā min ghayrihī* (This interpretation, i.e., Qatāda's, is the most appropriate to explain this verse, because he considers the word "*fīhi*" [= in it] in the context of the statement about the honey. Consequently, [Qatāda's] interpretation that the pronoun of the third person masculine singular indicates the honey, being in the context of the statement about honey, is more correct than other [interpretations]).[54]

A similar argument is found in Ṭabarī's comment on Qur'ān 16:83 (though without explicit mention of the term *siyāq*):

> *wa-dhālika anna hādhihi al-āya bayna āyatayn kiltāhumā khabar 'an rasūl allāh wa-'amma bu'itha bihī fa-awlā mā baynahumā an yakūn fī ma'nā mā qablahū wa-mā ba'dahū idh lam yakun mā yadullu 'alā 'inṣirāfihī 'ammā qablahū wa-'ammā ba'dahū* (This verse is between two verses, both of which are an informative statement about the Messenger of God and the message with which he was sent. It is most appropriate that a verse which is between these two have the meaning of that which is before and after it, since there is no indication that it deviates from that which is before and after it).[55]

Ẓāhir, ta'wīl, majāz

As I have already indicated, it is evident that *ẓāhir* and *ta'wīl* are two different concepts, constituting two alternative but mutually exclusive methods of interpretation.

When the first method is not acceptable or admissible, the exegete has to resort to the second.

Interestingly, in his comment on Isaiah 1:2, Saadia quotes six interpretations of Deuteronomy 32:1 ("Give ear, O heavens, let me speak; Let the earth hear the words I utter!").[56] Five of them he classifies as *ta'wīl*; in these, heaven and earth are interpreted "literally," and various methods are used to circumvent "literal" interpretation, such as by annexing "dwellers" to heaven and earth (as in the current version of Saadia's translation: "dwellers in heaven and dwellers on earth"). The sixth interpretation Saadia classifies as *takhrīj*, or more precisely, the *takhrīj* is applied to the interpretation of heaven and earth, which are accordingly understood in their concrete meaning, while their testimony is interpreted by *ta'wīl*: they testify by bringing happiness (*sa'āda*) or misery (*shaqā*) upon humans.[57]

The device by which *ta'wīl* can be attained is *majāz*. This term has been rendered by several scholars as "figurative speech,"[58] "metaphor," and similar terms taken mainly from the field of poetics or rhetoric. The meaning of *majāz* has been in recent years a matter of some controversy in the field of qur'ānic exegesis and has also been the topic of some thorough studies related to the literary and hermeneutical theories of early Arab critics.[59] In the later stages of medieval Judeo-Arabic biblical exegesis, *majāz* may indicate figurative or metaphoric speech, and it may have been used in this sense with respect to certain biblical statements. However, in Saadia's usage it has a much less defined, technical meaning, and it seems to have been broadly used to indicate paraphrases through less common meanings and usages for given words or particles.

In his translation of Saadia's exposition here under discussion, Altmann renders *majāz* as "figure of speech" (p. 158), but I doubt very much that this was Saadia's intention. I would suggest that what he means here is that the *majāz* of forty lashes is thirty-nine, which may mean that the deviation from the "commonly accepted sense" in this case is that the punishment is indeed thirty-nine, and Scripture "completed" it, "rounded it off" as it were, (by way of addition) to forty.[60]

Majāz (sometimes termed by a formula: *majāz min al-lugha*) is once defined by Saadia quantitatively, as opposed to *mashhūr*: while *mashhūr* is much used (*kathīr al-isti'māl*), *majāz* is scarcely used (*qalīl al-isti'māl*).[61] *Majāz* is a deviation from the commonly accepted meaning or usage (in the case of particles, prepositions, etc.) that can be supported and documented by scriptural prooftexts.[62] These show the limits of the commonly accepted usage (*musta'mal*) on the one hand, and of the possible expansion of that usage (*ittisa' al-lugha*[63]) on the other. Such prooftexts confer on the deviation an admissible status. The deviations can be relevant to any particle of speech. Saadia's notion of *majāz* is probably quite close to that of Abū 'Ubayda,[64] although Saadia is totally committed to a corpus of sacred texts (including rabbinic sources).

Parameters of Deviation from the *ẓāhir*

How is the exegete supposed to know or to decide that a given *ẓāhir* is not admissible? The answer to this question is contained in the rules laid down in the text under discussion. There are two criteria, two tools by which the exegete makes his decisions on this point: reason and tradition.[65] Elsewhere[66] Saadia described reason as preceding (*muqaddam*) scripture, and tradition as following it (*m'uakhkhar ba'dahū*). Without these two foundations (*aṣlān*) scripture cannot constitute a valid claim laid down by God to His servants. Reason operates by means of sense perception (*ḥiss*), immediate knowledge (*'aql*), and scientific data. Tradition consists of knowledge transmitted from the prophets to the Sages (*āthār al-anbiyā'*) and sanctified by the authority of the latter. If a *ẓāhir* does not agree with reason or tradition, exegesis is called in to resolve the apparent contradiction between two expressions of one and the same truth.

The importance of reason and tradition in deciding correct interpretation is elucidated at the beginning of Saadia's exposition of his exegetical approach in his Introduction to the Pentateuch, which is actually an introduction to all of scripture.[67] The Pentateuch was revealed in a human language. Every human language, by definition, includes unequivocal (*muḥkam*) and equivocal (*mutashābih*) components. The interpreter (*mu'abbir*) of the Torah is required to relate to abstract primary knowledge (*al-ma'lūmāt*) and to transmitted knowledge, that is, tradition (*al-manqūlāt*), as unequivocal (*muḥkam*) statements; and to everything, that is, every scriptural statement that does not agree with these two types of knowledge as equivocal (*mutashābih*) statements. The preference for reason and tradition over scripture is thus quite clear. But how much weight to give this preference is left to the exegete's discretion.

On the authority of reason in questions of faith Saadia says quite clearly at an early stage of his discussion of the Divine Attributes:

> I say as a rule: Whenever an expression is found in either the words in Scripture or in the speech of anyone of us monotheists, pertaining to the description of our Creator or to His action, which stands in contradiction to the requirement of sound reason, it [= this expression] no doubt has a meaning that deviates from the one that is customary in the common use of language;[68] the diligent students will find it if they seek it.[69]

The decision as to whether such contradictions that call for a special treatment by way of *ta'wīl* are discerned is thus dependent on the exegete, or rather on the premises, presuppositions, or convictions to which he is committed. The exegete applies his judgment to the best of his ability. It seems that this situation leaves the exegete plenty of room for maneuvering and creativity. And yet Saadia insists that as a rule, the *ẓāhir* should prevail whenever possible. So where are the limits to the exegete's freedom? The answer seems to be found in a further statement at the conclusion of the long discussion of the relationship between the apparent and "true" meaning of scripture.[70] The thrust of the conclusion, in itself a rather lengthy argument supported by several scriptural citations of a legal, doctrinal, or historical nature, is that absolute exegetical freedom is bound to result in absolute exegetical "anarchy," which will destroy the meaning of scripture as the foundation of faith and law. Since the main purpose of scripture is precisely to be the ultimate authority on all questions of faith and law confronting the community, such exegetical freedom is self-destructive. Therefore, the exegete has to justify any deviations from the *ẓāhir* = *mashhūr* (apparent, common) meaning by one of the four valid reasons (*ḥujja*) discussed earlier. Otherwise the verse has to retain its "literal" (*masmū'*) sense.[71] The polemical tone of the argument is probably aimed at an extreme allegoristic tendency (an actual, not hypothetical one). Although not stated explicitly, it is obvious from this presentation that the responsibility lies ultimately with the exegete. It is for him to judge whether or not one of the four deviations from the *ẓāhir* (or the *mashhūr*) has to be applied.

Among important contemporaries of Saadia whose views are relevant to this discussion one may mention also some Karaites, notably al-Qirqisānī. The only difference, and this is a highly significant one, is that in al-Qirqisānī's method tradition does not count; it assigns to reason an even higher authority, and to the exegete more freedom, in deciding between *ẓāhir* and *ta'wīl*.[72] Like Saadia, al-Qirqisānī also shows concern about the danger of exegetical "anarchy" and therefore emphasizes the importance of adhering to the *ẓāhir* as much as possible.

In the method of Saadia and his Rabbanite associates, as is reflected in the text under discussion, tradition might be thought to occupy an important position mainly with regard to the legal pronouncements in the Bible. But in fact this is not exactly so, and rabbinic traditions and homilies are applied or brought into play in a much wider range of contexts. I can quote here a somewhat trivial example which may illustrate the extent of this method's power. When Saadia says that the Land of Uz, the country of Job, was called so after a man who was Abraham's nephew, he adds that he accepts this ascription for a number of reasons, the first of which is that many of the ancients (*salaf*) have reported it (*anna kathīr*[an] *min al-aslāf yarwūna dhālik*).[73] Indeed Saadia's commentaries on narrative or other nonlegal sections of the Bible abound with rabbinic-midrashic materials. Sometimes these have nothing to do with what may be called the "plain meaning" or a "philological approach." The inclusion of such materials in his commentaries seems to reflect clearly his intention to integrate the rabbinic tradition into the Arabic readings of Jewish intellectuals.[74]

Recognizing that such are the limits of the exegete's freedom, one is not surprised to find, for instance, that David's words in his song, 2 Samuel 22:2–3, are interpreted by Saadia as an expression of ten articles of faith. In the course of this exercise Saadia does not even feel a need to apologize or to explain this deviation from the "commonly accepted sense" of the words. The reader is led to believe that this is the *ẓāhir* of these verses.[75]

Exoteric and Esoteric Interpretation

Finally I would like to mention that Saadia knows the notion of *bāṭin*, a concept often perceived as the opposite of *ẓāhir*, as constituting the hidden, esoteric, or mystical meaning of scripture.[76] Many of the instances in which Saadia makes use of this notion are found in his commentary on Proverbs. It seems that this book calls for such interpretations, since the "external" meaning of the words often conveys little more than popular wisdom, while a prophetic message is expected to convey more than that.[77] Yet the *bāṭin* in this commentary by Saadia, which is often taken from rabbinic-midrashic sources, seems to serve mainly an educational or edificatory purpose, by means of some lesson that lies beyond, in addition to the apparent, true meaning of the verses.[78] I wish to add a few notes on this matter.

First, the use of *bāṭin* is not exclusively limited to the commentary on Proverbs. Saadia's commentary on Isaiah contains a three-layered interpretation similar to that found in several interpretations of verses in Proverbs.[79] The first layer is the *ẓāhir*, which regarding this particular verse is interpreted as a simile (*mathal*) alluding to God's power in assisting and redeeming His servants from their hardships. The second layer is the *bāṭin*, according to which the elements mentioned in the verse are the nations and kingdoms (*al-duwal wa-'l-mamālik*) from whose oppression God had delivered Israel in the past and will redeem her in the future. The last layer is not defined by a technical term. It seems to be the most esoteric, as it gives the whole passage a philosophical meaning.[80] The distinction in this prophecy is not only between oppressors and oppressed, but among three groups of beings: animals, humans, and Israelites. The prophecy is intended to show the hierarchy (*tafāḍīl*) of these three groups. The first two interpretations are defined as *takhrīj*, though not the third one. It seems that this word is, in accordance with its concrete sense (to bring/take out), a general term for exegesis in its (Greek) basic literal meaning: bringing out/bringing to light/extracting an interpretation.[81] *Takhrīj* may thus serve as a less specific term, covering different modes or shades of interpretation. *Takhrīj* seems to be well attested in Arabic lexicography.[82] It is found occasionally in Saadia's commentaries[83] as well as in some Judeo-Arabic works by his contemporaries.[84] What is more important in these examples is the legitimacy that Saadia gives to a multilayered reading of scripture. The application of this mode of reading is again at the absolute discretion of the exegete.

Conclusion

Saadia is well aware of the far-reaching consequences that may result from deviating from the commonly accepted meaning of scripture. He warns against excessive resort to *ta'wīl*. He has in mind both the theological and legal aspects of the danger of such an exegetical approach. But according to the rules laid down by Saadia himself we are led to the dialectical situation in which the application of exegetical freedom or restraint is at the discretion of the commentator. The exegete knows that initially he should be committed to the *ẓāhir*, but that there are other modes (*wujūh*) of *takhrīj* (which is the term that comprises all exegetical modes) that are not mutually exclusive of *ẓāhir*. It is for the exegete to decide where only one mode can be tolerated and where two (or even three) may be accepted simultaneously. Such decisions are an essential part of the exegete's freedom, or shall we say: in Saadia's view, responsibility and freedom on the exegete's part are not mutually exclusive but rather complement each other. The exegete constantly moves between the two parameters of reason and tradition and is required to make sure that his interpretation agrees with both. Tradition seems to be a given, closed corpus but is in itself subject to interpretation. But with regard to reason, the exegete's job is even more delicate. How is he supposed to know exactly what are the reasonable criteria for judging his interpretation? Saadia probably saw in his collected works an adequate summation of scientific religious philosophy. But to be quite certain that the future exegete is adequately equipped with the basic data of philosophy and science, he included at the end of his extensive Introduction to the Pentateuch[85] a rather detailed exposition of his views on major theological principles.[86] This exposition should serve as an appropriate indicator of the right path for those who wish to avoid accepting interpretations that do not agree with empirical and abstract knowledge. Furthermore, the style of the Introduction to the Pentateuch, as well as other introductions (to Isaiah or Job) and expositions, is supposed to make them look like guides for whoever wishes to engage in exegesis. However, these statements were probably meant mainly to serve as explanations of Saadia's method in his interpretation of the entire Bible, a task that he would have liked to complete but was unable to, because of circumstances beyond his control.

Notes

1. To date the most comprehensive work on Saadia remains Malter, *Saadiah Gaon*; bibliographical supplements covering the years 1920-42 were published by Freimann, "Saadia Bibliography," 327-40 and Werfel, "Milu'im la-bibliyografyah," 644-57.

2. *The Book of Theodicy*, ed. and trans. Goodman.

3. See now Sklare, *Samuel ben Ḥofni Gaon*, 44; Brody, *The Geonim of Babylonia*, esp. 300-15.

4. See my survey, Ben Shammai, "Return to the Scriptures," 315-35.

5. See now Lasker, "Saadya Gaon on Christianity and Islam," 165-77. Jews who believed in the transmigration of souls also found it necessary to find biblical prooftexts for their belief; see my remarks, Ben-Shammai, "Gilgul neshamot," 117-36.

6. Blau, "On a Fragment of the Oldest Judaeo-Arabic Bible Translation Extant," 31-39.

7. Quoted in *Seder Rav 'Amram Ga'on*, 76-77; now published in *Teshuvot Rav Naṭronai bar Hilai Ga'on*, 1: 152-54 (no. 45) (with references to all relevant talmudic and geonic sources); see also p. 93 concerning the punitive excommunication which the Gaon threatens to apply to those who disobey his decision.

8. But unlike some Christian Syriac commentaries. About Christian (mainly Syriac) exegetical works of *Questions and Answers* see Molenberg, "An Eighth-Century Manual, 45-55.

9. See my remarks, Ben-Shammai, "Fragments of Daniel" 259-81.

10. The latest edition of this text is *Peirushei Rav Se'adyah Ga'on li-vereshit*, ed. M. Zucker, 18. 1-28.

11. For instance, his introduction to Job; see Saadia, *Book of Theodicy*, trans. Goodman, 131, where the reasons for deviating from the external sense of the scriptural text are condensed into two: reason and transmitted knowledge. The first represents both sense perception and theoretical (or abstract) knowledge, while the second represents both the Bible and rabbinic tradition. The differences in terminology between this text and others will be mentioned later.

12. The following translation is mostly quoted from Saadia, *The Book of Doctrines and Beliefs*, ed. and trans. Altmann, 157-58, except for some modifications in the translation of the Arabic and the adjustment of biblical quotations to the new translation of the Jewish Publication Society *Tanakh*. Another translation is by Rosenblatt, *The Book of Beliefs and Opinions*, 265-67. Yet another (partial) one is in Saadia, *Book of Theodicy*, trans. Goodman, 148, n. 68. The Arabic original text is found in Saadia, *Kitāb al-mukhtār fī 'l-amānāt wa-'l-i'tiqādāt*, ed. and trans. Qāfiḥ, 219-20.

13. Here and throughout I use "external" for *ẓāhir*. This is the closest I can get to a precise, factual, and concrete rendering. Others use "plain sense."

14. That is, the external sense of the passage.

15. "But man . . . so as"; Altmann's rendering reads: "But man may try the power of his Lord as to whether or not He is able." My translation is according to Qāfiḥ's emendation on p. 220:3, which is confirmed by the different wording, with similar meaning, in the parallel recension (mentioned below)—see Bacher, "Ma'amar teḥiyyat he-metim," 102—and is consistent with the argument that one may not try God under any circumstances; one may, however, put to the test one's own standing vis-à-vis God.

16. In his Introduction to the Pentateuch mentioned above, Saadia quotes another biblical example for this category, namely Exod. 23:19 (= 34:26; Deut. 14:21): "You shall not boil a kid in its mother's milk," which rabbinic tradition extended to any mixture of meat with milk.

17. Arabic *jabara*; Altmann's translation seems very adequate; without further elaboration I wish to add here that in several places throughout his exegetical works Saadia uses this term to indicate round numbers, or to point out the scriptural use of large or typological numbers to convey the notion of multiplicity.

18. Oxford, Bodleian Library, MS Pococke 148 (Neubauer-Cowley, no. 1222). The MS was written in 1470 by Mūsā b. ʿAbd al-Muḥsin. Both editors of the Judeo-Arabic text, S. Landauer and Y. Qāfiḥ, preferred this MS as the basis for their editions.

19. St. Petersburg, Russian National Library, MS Evr.-Arab I (formerly Firk. II), no. 127. Not dated. For many years it was known as the "Leningrad Recension."

20. In addition, there are numerous fragments, preserved in various libraries; so far over fifty have been identified.

21. I do not intend to discuss here the complex question of the relationship between the two recensions of *Kitāb al-Amānāt* in general, and of the seventh treatise in particular. I have already dealt with this question in Ben-Shammai, "Textual Problems in Saadya's *Kitāb al-Amānāt*." The only publication of the "St. Petersburg recension" of the seventh treatise is Bacher, "Die zweite Version 219–26, and Hebrew section, 98–122 (n. 15 earlier). Bacher suggested there, very convincingly, that Saadia himself integrated this version into his great opus at a late stage, replacing the original one.

22. The verses discussed as examples for the four reasons for deviation from the apparent meaning are identical in both discussions.

23. Note that Altmann, in Saadia, *Book of Doctrines, and Beliefs* 158, n. 4, argues that "the Leningrad Recension contains the same exegetical canon, but in a slightly less elaborate form than presented here," and refers to Bacher, "Die zweite Version," 102–3. I admit that the wording of the Leningrad Recension is different. I am not sure that it is less elaborate.

24. Rosenthal, "Saadya Gaon," 1–11. The article is actually based on Saadia's commentary on Proverbs. The following quotations are found on p. 1.

25. On the difficulty of defining what plain meaning is, and the tendency of modern scholars to impose or project their concepts on rabbinic approaches and methods, see the instructive and erudite analysis by Loewe, "The 'Plain Meaning' of Scripture," 140–85.

26. So Altmann; see note 27.

27. Altmann, in Saadia, *Book of Doctrines and Beliefs*, 158, n. 4, had first drawn attention to Ibn Ḥazm in this context, and referred to Goldziher, *Die Ẓâhiriten*, 122–23, 142–45; Goldziher's work is now available in English translation by Behn, *The Ẓāhirīs*, 115–17.

28. This is Behn's translation; Goldziher's original German text has *wörtlich*.

29. So Behn; another, perhaps preferable translation: sensible perception (which is perceived necessarily, by definition); in the original: *ḍarūrat ḥiss*; elsewhere Ibn Ḥazm mentions in a similar context (quoted n. 3 there) *ḍarūrat ʿaql*, which is not "logical necessity" (Behn), but rather "immediate/primary knowledge," parallel to Saadia's second reason.

30. Behn, 115.

31. Gimaret, *Une lecture muʿtazilite du Coran*, 63.

32. Saadia, *Book of Theodicy*, 148, n. 68; Goodman, "Saadiah Gaon's Interpretive Technique," 50. It seems, however, that Alfasi uses the term in a different sense, at least when applied to single words, as has been demonstrated by Maman, "Hashwa'at oṣar ha-millim," 126–27 (with reference to an earlier publication by D. Tene). In such cases the "audibility" refers to interpretation based on etymological identity of Hebrew and Arabic roots. According to Maman, Alfasi uses the term in another sense when applied to phrases. This sense as presented by Maman is apparently identical with Saadia's usage of the term.

33. Saadia, *Amānāt*, 224, l. 27–30 (English trans.: Rosenblatt, 273): *wa-lākin al-qawl al-ṣaḥlīḥ huwa allā yunqal fasūq ʿan ẓāhirihī wa-mashhūrihī illā bi-ḥujja min al-arbaʿ allatī waṣaftu fa-mā lam takun fīhi ḥujja minhā fa-huwa ʿalā masmūʿihī.* One should not rule out the possibility

that the use of *masmūʿ* here is influenced by derivatives of the Hebrew root *SHMʿ*, which are found in rabbinic sources in hermeneutic contexts (*mishmaʿ/mashmaʿ*, *shomeaʿ*); see Loewe, "The 'Plain Meaning,'" 169–70, 184. If this interpretation is accepted, it would mean that Saadia coined a new technical term by inventing a new meaning for an existent Arabic word, a meaning that he found in an etymologically and morphologically similar word in Hebrew. On a parallel case of such lexicographic invention by Saadia see my suggestion in Ben-Shammai, "ʿAseret ʿiqqerei ha-'emunah," 22–26. The word in question there is Arabic *amāna* in the sense of belief, article of faith; in this sense it is unattested elsewhere. Rosenblatt's translation is somewhat inconsistent with his translation elsewhere in the book; the words *ẓāhirihī wa-mashhūrihī* are rendered here "the obvious and generally recognized meaning."

34. The term is well attested in a famous Judeo-Arabic dictionary of biblical Hebrew written shortly after Saadia by David b. Abraham Alfasi, active probably in Jerusalem in the tenth century. For his use of *masmūʿ* see numerous references in the index to his dictionary *Jāmiʿ al-alfāẓ*, ed. S. L. Skoss, 2: cxxii.

35. Such equation is found in a number of pronouncements made by Saadia on the subject. The accepted usage of biblical Hebrew by its original users is also referred to by Saadia in his introduction to Job, where he lists the three principles according to which the interpreters (*al-muʿabbirūn*, a clear allusion to translators-commentators) interpret the books of the Bible (translation by Goodman, in Saadia, *The Book of Theodicy*, 131): (1) what is rooted in the proof of reason [i.e., implanted there by God; see Saadia, *al-Mukhtār fi 'l-amānāt*, 118]; (2) the linguistic usage of the people among whom the book [should probably be: Book] was written; (3) the links [or: circumstances; Arabic *al-asbāb*; Goodman: tropes] attested by the traditions of their ancestors [*al-qudamā'*, often used by Saadia to indicate the Rabbis] as going back to the prophets of God. This is Saadia's usual term for the rabbinic tradition, which he ascribes to the prophets; see my remarks in Ben-Shammai, "Haqdamat R. Seʿadyah," 398, n. 41. Goodman's note 67 on pp. 147–48 misses this point.

36. So Saadia, *Book of Theodicy*, 131; Goodman, "Interpretive Technique," 49.

37. *al-taṣrīf wa-'l-ishtiqāq yajib an yakūn lā yatajāwaz iṣṭilāḥ ahl tānīka[!] al-lughatayn*; the text may be found in Ben-Shammai, "Haqdamat R. Seʿadyah," 399.165 (Heb.) = Saadia, *Tafsīr Yeshaʿyah le-Rav Seʿadyah*, 250.1–2.

38. Samuel b. Ḥofni, *Peirush ha-Torah*, ed. Greenbaum, 465.27–30, and also 479.2–4. On the significance of the rabbinic term in the history of Jewish law see Urbach, *The Halakhah*, 104. The term *ahl al-lugha* is attested also in Islamic sources of a similar nature; see Gimaret, "Les *Uṣūl al-ḫamsa* du Qāḍī ʿAbd al-Ǧabbār," 92.

39. Saadia, *Peirushei Vereshit*, ed. Zucker, 19.17–25.

40. Or attaching to each other.

41. *wa-'l-qism al-rābiʿ min al-mūḍiḥāt al-ghawāmiḍ hiya al-ḍammāt*. So far I have not come across the term *ḍammāt* anywhere else.

42. The accents are probably indicated here by the Arabic term *al-qirā'a*, i.e., recital.

43. A detailed discussion of these examples in association with this particular case of exegesis is beyond the scope of the present observations.

44. Such a translation is actually found in *The Holy Scripture According to the Masoretic Text*. The King James Version has the seraphim standing "above it," i.e., above the Throne. *Tanakh* has them standing "in attendance on Him" (compare Gen 18:8).

45. *lahū malā'ika wuqūf fi-'l-ʿuluww*.

46. Ṭabarī, *Tafsīr*, 10:56.

47. Ṭabarī, *Tafsīr*, 15:127.

48. Ṭabarī, *Tafsīr*, 2:376.

49. Ṭabarī, *Tafsīr*, 2:377.

50. Ṭabarī takes this opportunity to state his position concerning the possibility that the

latter verse supersedes (*nāsikh*) the former. True to his principles, Ṭabarī rejects this possibility in favor of an interpretation that reconciles the two verses, as indicated; the details of this interesting matter are beyond the scope of this study.

51. See Ben-Shammai, "Haqdamat R. Se'adyah." See also the important study about the rabbinic notion *peshuṭo shel miqra* in Kamin, *Rashi*, esp. 23–56.

52. See my analysis in Ben Shammai, "Midrash prognosṭi be-khitvei Rasag", 1–19.

53. Ṭabarī, *Tafsīr*, 17:203.

54. Ṭabarī, *Tafsīr*, 14:141. According to alternative interpretations quoted by Ṭabarī the pronoun can refer to the Qur'ān.

55. Ṭabarī, *Tafsīr*, 14:158.

56. The text is found in Saadia, *Tafsīr Yesha'yah le Rav Se'adyah*, ed. Ratzaby, 158–59 (Hebrew translation on 254–55). The six interpretations are quoted in full by Samuel b. Ḥofni in his commentary on Deuteronomy 32:1, London, British Library MS Or. 8658, fol. 39r-v. I discussed both texts in Ben-Shammai, "Meṣi'ah 'aḥat she-hi shetayim," 329–30.

57. *Takhrīj* might thus be another equivalent of *ẓāhir*, but see further below.

58. See recently, e.g., Saadia, *Book of Theodicy*, 131; Polliack, *The Karaite Tradition of Arabic Bible Translation*, 85.

59. Wansbrough, "*Majāz al-qur'ān*, 247–66; idem, *Quranic Studies*, 219–38; Almagor, "The Early Meaning of *Majāz*," 307–26; Heinrichs, "On the Genesis of the *Ḥaqīqa-Majāz* Dichotomy," 111–40.

60. See earlier, n. 17.

61. Saadia, *Peirushei Vereshit*, 18.2–3 from bottom.

62. It is obvious that since *ẓahīr* is quantitatively established, there is no need to support it by proof texts.

63. On this term in medieval Judeo-Arabic exegesis, see the remarks of Vajda, *Deux commentaires karaïtes sur l'Ecclésiaste*, 189, n. 4.

64. See n. 59, earlier.

65. Cf. Saadia, *Book of Theodicy*, 148, n. 68.

66. Saadia, *Peirushei Vereshit*, 5.8–10.

67. The original Arabic term: *kayfiyyat tafsīr al-tawrāh*. Saadia, *Peirushei Vereshit*, 17, 1.22–28.

68. *lahū majāz min al-lugha* (about this phrase, see the preceding section here); Rosenblatt, as in other places, connects this phrase with "figurative sense."

69. *Amānāt*, ed. Qāfiḥ, 87 (English trans.: Rosenblatt, 100; the translation here is somewhat different).

70. Ed. Qāfiḥ, 224 (end of chapter 2) (English trans.: Rosenblatt, 272 [chapter IV; the translator changed the division into chapters of this treatise]). In the St. Peterburg version (see n. 20), because of its different arrangement and line of argumentation, this statement is found at a later stage of the discussion; for the edition of the original text, see Bacher, "Ma'amar," 106–8 (English trans.: Rosenblatt, 423–26). The examples quoted in both discussions are only partly identical.

71. See earlier, n. 33.

72. al-Qirqisānī expounds his views on this point in his Introduction to the Pentateuch, first published by Hirschfeld, *Qirqisānī Studies*, 43–44 (2nd hermeneutic principle); English translation in Nemoy, *Karaite Anthology*, 60–61.

73. See the translation of Goodman in Saadia, *Book of Theodicy*, 151, where the source is given as BT Bava Batra, 15a.

74. On this see Ben-Shammai, "Ha-sifrut ha-midrashit-rabbanit be-feirushei Rasag."

75. For a Hebrew translation and discussion of this interpretation see Ben-Shammai "'Aseret 'iqqerei ha-'emunah." Saadia's interpretation is in the main a philosophical exposition. It is

introduced by a bold prognostic homily which also incorporates midrashic materials; see the reference earlier in n. 52.

76. See earlier on the usage of this term by Ṭabarī, and compare Wansbrough, *Quranic Studies*, 151–53.

77. As proverbs, or parables (Heb. *meshalim*, Arabic *amthāl*), it would not be surprising to find that already in the Bible, and even more so in rabbinic literature, they are perceived as bearing a lower status or degree of divine message, but this is certainly a matter for another study.

78. This matter was first discussed by Rosenthal, "Saadya Gaon: An Appreciation;" I have discussed it quite extensively in Ben-Shammai, "Ha-Sifrut ha-midrashit-rabbanit."

79. In the comments on Isa 43:2–8: Saadia, *Tafsīr Yesha'yah*, ed. Ratzaby, 211 (Heb. translation, 320).

80. For a similar feature in Saadia on Proverbs see the references in n. 78.

81. Interestingly, the first definition of this verbal form in Lane, *Arabic-English Lexicon* is, "He resolved, explained, or rendered, a saying." In modern dictionaries, such as Wehr's, this meaning comes last. It may be added that in Saadia's commentaries and in commentaries by other authors one may find also occurrences of verbs from this root in the fifth form, meaning "to be interpreted"; see for instance the reference in Ben-Shammai, "Ha-sifrut ha-midrashit-rabbanit be-feirushei Rasag," 62.

82. See n. 81.

83. Apart from the instances already quoted, see, for example, Saadia, *Peirushei Vereshit*, 19.21 (referring to deviation from the accepted division of a verse by the accents, see n. 42 earlier).

84. See, for example, Alfasi, *Jāmi'*, 1:168.38.

85. To be sure, it seems that this introduction is one of Saadia's early works.

86. Saadia, *Peirushei Vereshit*, 21–23 (the text printed there constitutes only fragments of the full discussion).

Bibliography

Alfasi, David b. Abraham. *Kitāb Jāmi' al-alfāẓ*. Ed. S. L. Skoss. 2 vols. New Haven, Conn.: Yale University Press, 1936–45.

Almagor, E. "The Early Meaning of *Majāz* and the Nature of Abu 'Ubayda's Exegesis." In *Studia Orientalia memoriae D. H. Baneth dedicata*. Ed. J. Blau et al., 307–26. Jerusalem: Magnes Press, 1979.

Bacher, W. "Die zweite Version von Saadja's Abschnitt über die Wiederbelebung der Toten." In *Festschrift Moritz Steinschneider*, 219–26. Leipzig, 1896. Reprint, Jerusalem: Makor, 1969.

——. "Ma'amar teḥiyyat ha-metim le-rav Se'adyah Ga'on" (The treatise on resurrection of Rabbi Saadia Gaon). In *Tehillah le-Mosheh* (*Festschrift Moritz Steinschneider* [Hebrew section]). 98–112. Leipzig, 1896. Reprint, Jerusalem: Makor, 1969.

Ben-Shammai, H. "'Aseret 'iqqerei ha-'emunah shel Rav Se'adyah Ga'on" (Saadia Gaon's ten articles of faith). *Da'at* 37 (1996): 11–26.

——. "Fragments of Daniel al-Qūmisī's Commentary on the Book of Daniel as a Historical Source." *Henoch* 13 (1991): 259–81.

——. "Gilgul neshamot be-hagut ha-yehudit ba-mizraḥ ba-me'ah ha-'asirit" (Transmigration of souls in tenth-century Jewish thought in the Orient). *Sefunot* 20 (1991): 117–36.

——. "Haqdamat R. Se'adyah Ga'on li-Ysha'yah—mavo le-sifrei ha-Nevi'im" (Saadia's introduction to Isaiah as an introduction to the books of the Prophets). *Tarbiz* 60 (1991): 371–404.

——. "Ha-sifrut ha-midrashit-rabbanit be-feirushei Rasag: hemshekh we-ḥiddush" (The rabbinic literature in Saadia's exegesis: between tradition and innovation). In *Masoret we-shinnui ba-*

tarbut ha- 'arvit-ha-yehudit shel yemei ha-beinayim = Heritage and Innovation in Medieval Judaeo-Arabic Culture (Proceedings of the sixth conference of the Society for Judaeo-Arabic Studies). Ed. J. Blau and D. Doron, 33–69. Ramat-Gan: Bar-Ilan University Press, 2000.

——. "Meṣi'ah 'aḥat she-hi shetayim" (New findings in a forgotten manuscript: Samuel b. Ḥofni's commentary on Ha'azinu and Saadia's "Commentary on the Ten Songs"). *Qiryat sefer* 61 (1986–87): 313–32.

——. "Midrash prognosṭi be-khitvei Rasag" (Prognostic *Midrash* in the Works of Se'adya Gaon as Exemplified in his Introduction to the Commentary on the Song of David [2Sam. 22]), in *Me'ah She'arim: Studies in Medieval Jewish Spiritual Life in Memory of Isadore Twersky*. Ed. E. Fleischer et al., 1–19. Jerusalem: Magnes Press 2001.

——. "Return to the Scriptures in Ancient and Medieval Jewish Sectarianism and in Early Islam." In *Les retours aux Écritures: fondamentalismes présents et passés*. Ed. E. Patlagean and A. Le Boulluec, 315–35. Bibliothèque de l'Ecole des Hautes Études, Section des sciences religieuses, vol. 99. Louvain: Peeters, 1993.

——. "Textual Problems in Saadya's *Kitāb al-Amānāt*." In *Proceedings of the Seventh Conference of the Society for Judaeo-Arabic Studies* (1995). Ed. P. Fenton (forthcoming).

Blau, J. "On a Fragment of the Oldest Judaeo-Arabic Bible Translation Extant." In *Genizah Research after Ninety-Nine Years, the Case of Judaeo-Arabic: Papers Read at the Third Congress of the Society for Judaeo-Arabic Studies*. Ed. J. Blau and S. C. Reif, 31–39. University of Cambridge Oriental Studies, no. 47. Cambridge: Cambridge University Press, 1992.

Brody, R. *The Geonim of Babylonia and the Shaping of Medieval Jewish Culture*. New Haven, Conn.: Yale University Press, 1998.

Freimann, A. "Saadia Bibliography." In *Saadia Anniversary Volume*. Ed. B. Cohen, 327-40. New York: American Academy for Jewish Research, 1943.

Gimaret, D. *Une lecture mu'tazilite du Coran*. Louvain: Peeters, 1994.

——. "Les *Uṣūl al-ḫamsa* du Qāḍī 'Abd al-Ğabbār et leurs commentaires." *Annales islamologiques* 15 (1979): 47–96.

Goldziher, I. *Die Ẓāhiriten*. Leipzig: Otto Schulze, 1884.

——. *The Ẓāhirīs: Their Doctrine and Their History*. Trans. W. Behn. Leiden: E. J. Brill, 1971.

Goodman, L. E. "Saadiah Gaon's Interpretive Technique in Translating the Book of Job." In *Translation of Scripture: Proceedings of a Conference at the Annenberg Research Institute, May 15–16, 1989*, 47–76. Philadelphia: Annenberg Research Institute, 1990.

Heinrichs, W. "On the Genesis of the *Ḥaqaīqa-Majāz* Dichotomy." *Studia islamica* 59 (1984): 111–40.

Hirschfeld, H. *Qirqisānī Studies*. Jews' College Publications, no. 6. London: Hall, 1918.

Holy Scripture According to the Masoretic Text. Philadelphia: Jewish Publication Society of America, 1917.

Kamin, S. *Rashi: peshuṭo shel miqra u-midrasho shel miqra* (Rashi's exegetical categorization in respect to the distinction between *peshat* and *derash*). Jerusalem: Magnes Press, 1986.

Lane, E. W. *Arabic-English Lexicon*. 1 vol. in 8 pts. 1863–93. Reprint, Cambridge, 1984.

Lasker, Daniel J. "Saadya Gaon on Christianity and Islam." In *The Jews of Medieval Islam*. Ed. Daniel Frank, 165–77. Leiden: E. J. Brill, 1995.

Loewe, R. "The 'Plain Meaning' of Scripture in Early Jewish Exegesis." *Papers of the Institute of Jewish Studies London* 1 (1964): 140–85.

Malter, H. *Saadia Gaon: His Life and Works*. Philadelphia: Jewish Publication Society, 1921. Reprint, New York: Hermon Press, 1969.

Maman, Aharon, "Hashwa'at 'oṣar ha-millim, shel ha- 'ivrit la- 'arvit we-la-arammit le min Rasāg we-'ad Ibn Barun" (The comparison of the Hebrew lexicon with Arabic and Aramaic in the linguistic literature of the Jews from Rav Saadia Gaon [10th cent.] to Ibn Barun [12th cent.]). Ph.D. thesis, Hebrew University, Jerusalem, 1984.

Molenberg, C. "An Eighth-Century Manual: Iso' bar Nun's Questions and Answers on the Whole Text of Scripture as a Representative of a Genre." In *IV Symposium Syriacum*. Orientalia christiana analecta, no. 229. Rome: Pontificium Institutum Orientale, 1987.

Naṭronai bar Hilai, Gaon. *Teshuvot Rav Naṭronai bar Hilai Ga'on*. 2 vols. Ed. R. Brody. Jerusalem: Mekhon Ofek, 1994.

Nemoy, Leon, ed. *Karaite Anthology*. Yale Judaica Series, no. 7. New Haven, Conn.: Yale University Press, 1952.

Polliack, M. *The Karaite Tradition of Arabic Bible Translation*. Leiden: E. J. Brill, 1997.

Rosenthal, E. I. J. "Saadya Gaon: An Appreciation of His Biblical Exegesis." *BJRL* 27 (1942): 1–11.

Saadia ben Joseph. *The Book of Beliefs and Opinions*. Trans. S. Rosenblatt. Yale Judaica Series, no. 1. New Haven, Conn.: Yale University Press, 1948.

——. *The Book of Doctrines and Beliefs*. Ed. and trans. A. Altmann. Oxford: East and West Library, 1946.

——. *The Book of Theodicy: Translation and Commentary on the Book of Job*. Ed. and trans. L. E. Goodman. Yale Judaica Series, no. 25. New Haven, Conn.: Yale University Press, 1988.

——. *Kitāb al-mukhtār fī 'l-amānāt wal-i'tiqādāt = Sefer ha-Nivḥar be-'emunot uve-de'ot*. Ed. and trans. by Y. Qāfiḥ. Jerusalem, 1970.

——. *Peirushei Rav Se'adyah Ga'on li-Vereshit*. Ed. M. Zucker. New York: The Jewish Theological Seminary of America, 1984.

——. *Tafsīr Yesha'yah le-Rav Se'adyah* (Saadia's translation and commentary on Isaiah). Ed. Y. Ratzaby. Kiryat Ono, 1993.

Samuel b. Ḥofni. *Peirush ha-Torah le-Rav Shemu'el ben Ḥofni*. Ed. A. Greenbaum. Jerusalem: Mossad Harav Kook, 1978.

Seder Rav 'Amram Ga'on. Ed. E. D. Goldschmidt. Jerusalem: Mossad Harav Kook, 1971.

Sklare, D. E. *Samuel ben Ḥofni Gaon and His Cultural World*. Leiden: E. J. Brill, 1996.

Tanakh: A New Translation of the Holy Scriptures According to the Traditional Hebrew Text. Philadelphia: Jewish Publication Society, 1985.

al-Ṭabarī, Abū Ja'far Muḥammad b. Jarīr. *Jāmi' al-bayān fī tafsīr āy al-Qur'ān*. 30 vols. Cairo, 1954–68.

Urbach, E. E. *The Halakhah: Its Sources and Development*. Trans. R. Posner. Ramat Gan: Massada, 1986.

Vajda, G. *Deux commentaires karaïtes sur l'Ecclésiaste*. Leiden: E. J. Brill, 1971.

Wansbrough, J. "*Majāz al-qur'ān*: Periphrastic Exegesis." *BSOAS* 33 (1970): 247–66.

——. *Quranic Studies: Sources and Methods in Scriptural Interpretation*. Oxford: Oxford University Press, 1977.

Werfel, I. "Milu'im la-bibliyografyah." In *Rav Se'adyah Ga'on: Qoveṣ torani mada'i*. Ed. Yehuda Leib Fishman, 644–57. Jerusalem, 1943.

4

Karaite Commentaries on the Song of Songs from Tenth-Century Jerusalem

DANIEL FRANK

For Jews and Christians alike the Song of Songs (*Shir ha-shirim*) posed a special problem.[1] If its Solomonic authorship assured its scriptural standing, its frank eroticism demanded allegorization. In its depiction of love lost and regained, Jews discovered a parable for the historical relationship between God and Israel, one that sat well with such other biblical passages as Hosea 1–2, Isaiah 54:4–7, Jeremiah 2:2, and Ezekiel 16.[2] But the allegory still required interpretation. Determining the significance of its elaborate symbolism and fashioning a coherent reading of the work as a whole would engage many a Jewish exegete in the Middle Ages—and this even before the philosophers and kabbalists began to read *Shir ha-shirim* in new ways during the twelfth and thirteen centuries![3] It is not surprising, then, that Jews have probably composed more commentaries on the Song than on any other biblical book.[4]

The earliest Jewish interpretations of the Song were not, of course, proper commentaries but *midrashim* and *targumim*, the standard genres of rabbinic exegesis for over a thousand years.[5] It was only in the ninth century that Jews in the Islamic East began to write systematic compositions according to the classical models cultivated by their Muslim and Christian neighbors. The first Jew to write formal Bible commentaries was probably Dāwūd b. Marwān al-Muqammaṣ, an Iraqi scholar who converted to Christianity for a period before reverting to Judaism. During his lengthy Christian phase al-Muqammaṣ encountered genres that were not part of the traditional Jewish literary repertoire. When he rejoined his ancestral faith, he determined to compose new, Jewish works in Arabic on the patterns of the Christian and Islamic books he had studied. His *Twenty Chapters* is probably the first medieval Jewish speculative treatise.[6] His commentaries on Genesis and Ecclesiastes have not survived, but they were apparently translations and adaptations of Christian works.[7] During the first half of the tenth century, the genre was developed in Iraq by two other authors. Saadia Gaon, "First of Scholars in Every Discipline," was the real pioneer. His Bible commentaries feature comprehensive introductory essays, elegant Arabic translations of the scriptural text, and extensive discussions of speculative, philological, and polemical points.[8] His contemporary, the Karaite Ya'qūb al-Qirqisānī, wrote similar works from a sectarian perspective.[9] Although the commentaries of both these scholars were informed by traditional rabbinic learning, the works themselves breathe the rationalistic spirit of the current Islamic humanism.[10]

How then did these first Jewish exegetes approach the Song of Songs and how did they interpret its symbolism? The answer to these questions, alas, remains elusive. While Saadia wrote a commentary on *Shir ha-shirim*, it has not survived in its original form; the text ascribed to him is clearly an extensive reworking of later vintage.[11] But two Jewish commentaries on the Song do survive from tenth-century Jerusalem. Written in Judeo-Arabic by the Karaites Salmon b. Jeroham and Japheth b. Eli, both include substantial introductory observations on the nature of biblical song and incorporate full Arabic translations and verse-by-verse exegesis.[12] As would be expected, they differ markedly in form from the most popular Rabbanite treatments of the Song, Targum Shir ha-shirim and Shir ha-shirim Rabbah, which may be classified respectively as narrative and exegetical midrashim but not as true commentaries. Where the Targum speaks anonymously and Shir ha-shirim Rabbah cites multiple authorities, both Salmon and Japheth project clear authorial voices. Where the Midrash records diverse interpretations for each verse, the Karaites strive for a single, *correct* meaning. Though not infrequently they set down more than one explanation, they usually indicate which comment they favor—all the while looking forward to the advent of the Messiah who will solve every exegetical problem and eliminate interpretive dissension.[13] Salmon's comment on Song 3:8, makes his position as exegete clear:

> Now you must know, my brother, that the meanings of the Song of Songs are most obscure; not every one will venture upon its interpretation. For my part, I too acknowledge the deficiency of my own knowledge. I shall proffer only the most plausible explanations that I have found among the words of the Sages as well as those interpretations which I know might [feasibly] be suggested. And if what I have set down contains errors, may God in his great mercy forgive me, since in all that I write it is my sole intention to benefit Israel and to promote their love for the knowledge of scripture. For I see that they neglect it—some [occupy themselves] with Talmud, and some with the "external books," and some with [their] livelihoods.[14] I have therefore composed these books [i.e., his commentaries] in similar fashion in order to stimulate them to [study] God's scripture, for I know that repentance begins with the study of the Bible, speculation on its meaning, and performance of what is prescribed therein. And when Israel follows this path they will deserve to behold the salvation.[15]

Salmon's and Japheth's commentaries both reflect the particular outlook and needs of the sectarian community for which they were written.[16] The Mourners for Zion, or "Shoshanim," were an ascetic, messianic group of Karaites who settled in Jerusalem during the tenth century. They believed that they were living at the End of Days and hoped to hasten the final redemption through a strict regime of prayer, formalized lamentation, and Bible study. Referring scriptural prophecies to their own time, they also found eschatological significance in the Psalter and Song of Songs.[17] Examination and comparison of these two texts reveal much about the shared ideology of their readership and the interpretive strategies and techniques of their authors.

Until a few years ago, Salmon's commentary on the Song was thought to have been lost. Toward the end of the nineteenth century, Poznanski had succeeded in identifying eight folios of the work in a scarcely legible British Museum manuscript.[18] But it was only recently, when the great collections in St. Petersburg again became accessible, that the work was rediscovered. The 165 folios of Russian National Library MS Evr.-Arab. I.1406 contain virtually the entire commentary. While the title page, beginning, and end of the manuscript are missing, several other extensive fragments confirm the work's authorship and supply lacunae.[19] Composed in 956 C.E., it was one of several long commentaries that Salmon seems to have produced within a short period, perhaps no more than five years.[20] The speed at which he worked owed as much to his methods as to his diligence: he strove to record interpretations already current among the Mourners, and he freely transposed material from one work to another. By the time he had begun his exegetical project, the Jerusalem community was over half a century old.[21] It had evolved practices of its own as well as a method of translating and interpreting the Bible.[22] Since the Psalter and the book of Lamentations furnished the Mourners with their basic liturgy, Salmon's commentaries on these books were necessarily compilatory affairs. Indeed, it has been argued that Salmon's Commentary on Lamentations is no more and no less than the community's liturgy of mourning, featuring a biblical verse-cum-refrain at the end of each comment and incorporating many simple hymns.[23] On the other hand, the homilies and excursuses that Salmon embedded in his commentaries were his own; he tended to reproduce them in more than one place.[24]

One of the most interesting features of Salmon's commentaries are his programmatic introductions or *ṣudūr*. By his time, this subgenre was already well established in the Near East among Muslims, Christians, and Jews, serving to address questions of authorship, generic classification, function, and content.[25] Salmon's Introduction to Song of Songs is a substantial disquisition on the nature of divine communications, the function of metaphor in biblical prophecies, and the symbolism of *Shir ha-shirim*.[26] He commences with a standard invocation to the Creator, praising God for having communicated to his creatures via prophets. He then observes that God revealed his scripture in different modes in order to accommodate the different capacities of human souls. The biblical narratives, commandments and prohibitions, and divine promises and threats were all communicated plainly. But there are also esoteric communications that require interpretation. Some are revelations that can be understood only by means of the interpretations God himself furnishes through his prophets; an example of this is the Song of the Vineyard in Isaiah 5. Others, such as the Song of Songs, "require *scholars* to set forth their meanings, to explicate their purposes with subtlety, and to strive to reveal their benefits so that some reward may be obtained thereby."[27]

Qualified exegetes, then, both occupy privileged positions and bear the heavy responsibility of making esoteric discourse meaningful to their community. The Song, continues Salmon, "is a precious, sublime text. Were this not so, it would not have been included by the prophets among the twenty-four books of scripture. Nor would Solomon have set it down in the first place as part of Israel's literary heritage unless it were [a work of] wisdom, beneficial to both the elite and the masses."[28] The work's genre, authorship, and stature are all indicated in the first verse, "The Song of Songs that is Solomon's" (1:1). Now in scripture, says Salmon, the word *shir* denotes a song to God (*nashīd li-llāhi*), of which there are some half dozen different types. There are songs of praise, such as Exodus 15, which describe God's might and his destruction of those who vaunted their own power, before petitioning him to extend his favor to Israel. There are songs of testimony, such as Deuteronomy 32, and songs of thanksgiving, such as Judges 5.

In one crucial respect, Salmon's classification of biblical song aligns with the rabbinic enumerations found, for example, in the Targum and elaborated by Saadia Gaon in his commentary on Exodus 15: in none of these Jewish sources are aesthetic canons applied to biblical texts.[29] This absence is striking in light of Islamic claims concerning the Qur'ān's inimitable literary perfection—a clear mark of its superiority.[30] For Jewish authors, however, a song's value lies in its substance, not its form. What makes a biblical passage a "song" is its designation as such rather than any formal criteria with which it may or may not comply.[31]

According to Salmon, the Song of Songs contains three essential elements: a petition that God elucidate his Law (1:2); an expression of remorse at Israel's sin, and grief over its punishment (1:3); and finally, a declaration of Israel's longing for messianic salvation (5:8 and 8:1). These are all expressed by means of an extended parable in which Israel is depicted as a woman whose husband has favored her with food, clothing, and conjugal rights. Salmon stresses the allegorical nature of the work:

> Now you must know that this entire book is a parable (*kulluhu 'alā sabīl al-mathal*), as I have explained to you above. Reason only permits God to be called "father" inasmuch as he is the Governor and Creator. . . . All scriptural anthropomorphisms refer to God's actions, since reason decrees that the Creator has no (real) attributes (*laysa lahu ṣifah*). . . . But all of these attributes are [employed] only as a means of making [matters] more accessible to our intellects, as the Sages have expressed it, "Scripture speaks in human language."[32]

Having made his point, Salmon offers the following simple key to the Song:

> From the beginning of the book to 7:10 every expression denoting a man refers to the Creator; from 7:10 to the end of the book, such expressions refer to the Messiah son of David. Wherever the feminine is employed, the congregation of Israel is intended.[33]

Support for this reading of Song of Songs can be found in the Song of the Vine (Isaiah 5), which Salmon explicates before commencing his commentary proper.[34]

As was mentioned previously, the commentary includes a full Arabic translation. For the most part, it is a highly literal rendering with each Hebrew word represented by an Arabic equivalent.[35] Occasionally, the word *mithl* ("like," "as") is inserted to signal a metaphor: "I am *like* the narcissus of the plain, *like* the lily of the fields."[36] And where blasphemies might result, exegetical interpolations do creep in; "Draw me, we will run after your *worship* (*ṭā'atika*)," reads 1:4 in Salmon's Arabic.[37] But on the whole, the translation furnishes the Song's *peshaṭ* or *ẓāhir*, its exoteric meaning. The commentary, on the other hand, immediately decodes the parable, identifying speakers, glossing difficult words, and explaining the connection between verses.[38] Verse 1:13, for example—"My beloved to me is like a bag of myrrh, that lies between my breasts"—represents the words of *Keneset Yisra'el*.[39] Having described the cessation of the sacrifices and the lamentation of the priests, the speaker now recalls the time when God's glory dwelt between the cherubim in the Holy of Holies, the monarchy was at its zenith, and the nation enjoyed general prosperity.[40] But when the divine glory departed, the Temple was destroyed and the divine service suspended. Now this is a fair paraphrase of Salmon's comment—up to the point, that is, where he changes both style and language and launches into a terse, Hebrew dirge:

> *'ein melekh we-'ein sar, we-'ein mesharetei 'adonai*
> *'ein nevi'im we-'ein morim*
> *'ein ḥakhamim we-'ein yode'ei da'at*

'ein shofeṭim we-'ein shoṭerim
'ein kevod 'adonai we-'ein keruvim
'ein 'aron we-'ein badaw
'ein heikhal we-'ein devir
'ein 'ulam we-'ein ḥaṣer . . .

No king, no prince, no ministers to the Lord.
No prophets, no teachers
No sages, no scholars,
No judges, no officers,
No divine glory, no cherubs,
No ark, no coverings,
No sanctuary, no sanctum,
No hall, no court . . . [41]

This lament, in fact, reappears in a more embellished form in Salmon's Commentary on Lamentations 3:4 and formed part of the Karaites' liturgy of mourning for Zion.[42] From the unself-conscious way in which Salmon integrates the hymn into both commentaries, it is clear that he saw nothing wrong in mixing genres, or rather, that his notion of commentary was flexible.

By contrast, Japheth ben Eli's commentary adheres to strict organizational principles.[43] Active during the last third of the tenth century, Japheth was the first Jew to produce commentaries on the entire Bible. Although they are lengthy, detailed affairs, his works are carefully structured and fluently written, tending toward a scholastic rather than homiletic style. By the time he set about writing his commentary on the Song, he had developed a standard exegetical method and model.[44] For the Jerusalem Karaites of the late tenth century the consistency, orderliness, and precision of Japheth's compositions must have been a blessing. At last there were Bible commentaries that fully served the community's needs.

Japheth's Introduction to the Song, which centers on its first verse, exemplifies his systematic approach. A methodical survey of the Solomonic corpus—its generic classification, and the modes in which it was revealed—leads directly into a discussion of *Shir ha-shirim*, and a tripartite classification of song that resembles Salmon's: the wholly exoteric, the parable containing its own interpretive key (the Song of the Vine again!), and the wholly esoteric. *Shir ha-shirim* belongs to the latter category. "From beginning to end," says Japheth, "not a word of it is to be taken exoterically. It is, rather, condensed speech, rich in meaning which may be understood only through [recourse to] the prophetic books."[45] It was written as a parable in response to the prophecies of Ezekiel in which the relationship between a man and a woman is depicted negatively and Israel's abandonment of and by God deplored.[46] In the Song of Songs, Israel's return to God is celebrated through the female–male relationship. *Shir ha-shirim* takes its name from the thirty songs it comprises, which, says Japheth, correspond to the thirty Psalms that bear the word *shir* in their superscriptions. One of the tasks Japheth sets himself, consequently, is the identification of these poetic units.[47] The import of the work's Solomonic authorship prompts comment as well: the song is emphatically *not* autobiographical but *prophetic*. Solomon recited it with reference to the community of Israel and their leaders—"the Perfect of Way" and "the Mighty Ones of Israel"—and the Messiah.[48] The reason God revealed this song to Solomon alone among the prophets is that his reign was the most glorious in Jewish history, only to be surpassed by the messianic period, concerning which it prophesies. The object of the commentary is to relate the Song's metaphors to the players and events of the End of Days.

Broadly speaking, Salmon and Japheth offer similar readings of the Song. The allegory which they elucidate describes the relationship between God and the Jewish people—from the distinctive standpoint of Mourners for Zion. Three features characterize this interpretation: (1) an emphasis on the End which is identified with the present; (2) the isolation and explication of emblematic appellations; (3) a vigorous sectarian stance against Islam and rabbinic Judaism.

While the Karaite approach to the Song is rooted in the rabbinic tradition, the salvation history it proffers differs markedly from those given in Targum Shir ha-shirim, Midrash Shir ha-shirim, and Shir ha-shirim Rabbah. The Targum, for example, presents a coherent, chronological sequence from the Exodus and revelation at Sinai to the conquest of Canaan, the construction and destruction of the First Temple, the campaigns of the Maccabees, and the functioning of the Sanhedrin; only in chapters 7 and 8 are references to the eschaton discerned.[49] In contrast, the Karaites regard most of the Song as an apocalyptic prophecy relating to their own time—a prophecy that, to be sure, represents earlier episodes in Jewish history, but only as necessary background to the messianic present.

In reading the Song comprehensively, Japheth elucidates its various strands of discourse, its underlying structure, and the relations between each of its sections.[50] By inserting programmatic statements at key points, he shows his readers how to make sense of this abstruse work:

> This song contains four types [of discourse]: (1) the address of the Congregation of Maskilim[51] to the Lord, describing his deeds and beneficence to their ancestors and them, and beseeching him to fulfill his promises; (2) the plaint of the Daughters of Jerusalem concerning their condition, their rehearsal of God's deeds as a stimulus to serve him, and their request that he fulfill his promises; (3) the words of the people to each other concerning their affairs, e.g., the passage, "We have a little sister" (8:8); and (4) the Creator's response to the Maskilim concerning their petition and desire as well as an account of their excellence and beauty when they serve him, and their ranks, as we will explain in every section.[52]

Or, there is this comment on 6:11:

> Here ends one section and begins another in which is described how Israel's affairs run their course at the end of the Fourth Kingdom. For the Song of Songs contains three sections, each of which commences with the beginning of a time [period] and concludes with the Salvation. The first section is "Upon my bed at night" (3:1); it commences with the destruction of the Second Temple, as we have explained. The second section, "I slept" (5:2), begins with the kingdom of the Chaldees, as we have explained. This, the third section, refers to the end of the era of the Fourth Kingdom, as we will explain.[53]

Thorough in the extreme, Japheth takes pains to explicate every element of the Song's rich symbolism, frequently suggesting alternative interpretations which he rates as more or less plausible.[54] The comment on 2:6 gives a good idea of his penchant for order:

> "His left hand beneath my head and his right hand embracing me." They said "For I am sick with love" and then stated, "His left hand etc." Thus, they proclaimed that they long

for the embrace of his left and right hands. The plain sense (*al-ẓāhir*) of this statement derives from [Solomon's] having composed the book as a song concerning a man and his wife; they join beneath a single cover, he embracing her with his right and left hands. The allegorical interpretation (*ta'wīl*) yields several meanings. One [explanation] is that he protects them along both borders of their land, i.e., the north and south. . . . Another, plausible one is that he has mentioned the two Exiles [in this verse]: the first was when the kings of Assyria and Babylonia exiled [Israel] to the North; the second was the exile to the South by Edom [i.e., Rome]. By this verse they mean: "We are longing and yearning for him to reunite Israel who had been exiled in [the days of] the First and Second Temples." For this reason, they mentioned his left before his right. There are still other interpretations of this by [our] Sages; therefore, I have been brief.[55]

First Japheth renders the verse quite literally: five words of Arabic, corresponding precisely in sequence, form, and meaning to the five of the Hebrew original. The comment proper begins with a brief statement relating the verse to 2:5, thereby identifying the speaker with the Karaite leadership. Next he explains the verse's plain meaning in the context of the Song's guiding metaphor. These preliminaries completed, he embarks on the allegory proper, presenting three possible interpretations (only the first and last are given here). All three involve the linguistic connection between left and right and north and south respectively, the directions to which Israel was exiled and from which God will "embrace" or gather in Israel.[56] Japheth makes it clear that he does not know the precise significance of the metaphor; he is proposing only those interpretations that he deems soundest.

Naturally, there are verses whose Rabbanite and Karaite exegeses comfortably coincide—or nearly so. In Song 1:9 ("I have compared you my love to a mare of Pharaoh's chariots") Targum, Midrash, and Karaites all find an allusion to God's destruction of Pharaoh's forces (Exod 14:23–28). The interpretations differ, however, both in details and in significance. The Targum makes the verse a peg on which to hang an embellished paraphrase of Exodus 14; verses 10–14 will serve almost as nicely for the summary of Israel's journey to Mount Sinai, Moses' ascent and descent, the sin of the Golden Calf, and the building of the desert tabernacle.[57] Midrash Shir ha-shirim, for its part, contributes an *aggadah*: when the Egyptians pursued Israel, God made himself manifest to them by means of a cherub that took the form of a mare; the stallions drawing Pharaoh's chariots promptly plunged in after the phantom, and the Egyptian troops were destroyed.[58] Interestingly, Salmon and Japheth both mention the *aggadah* of the mare-siren, the former ascribing it to the Rabbanites, the latter to "one of the scholars." Salmon's concluding "God knows [if this is true]" sounds dismissive.[59] The real purpose of the verse is to draw a comparison; just as God preserved Israel from destruction at the Red Sea, so will he save them at the End of Days:

If you serve me [says God], I shall make My salvation manifest to you, just as I made it manifest to your ancestors. And I shall destroy your enemies, just as I destroyed Pharaoh and his people. . . . Just as I fought the Egyptians on your behalf, so shall I fight on your behalf in the future. . . . Just as I annihilated all of the Egyptians in the past, as it is written "For when the horses of Pharaoh with his chariots and his horsemen went into the sea, etc." (Exod 15:19), so will all the enemy horses be annihilated in the future, as it states: "On that day, says the Lord, I will strike every horse with panic, and its rider with madness" (Zech 12:4).[60]

For Japheth the rabbinic legend remains a possibility[61]—but only because it can enhance his eschatological scheme: "One of the scholars said that God made a mare appear in the sea and when Pharaoh's stallions beheld her, they sought her and this was the reason for their destruction. Now [Solomon] compared the Remnant of Israel (*she'erit Yisra'el*) to [this mare], for they will attract the nations who will then be destroyed."[62] The "Remnant of Israel"—that is, the Mourners for Zion—are, of course, the heroes of this apocalypse, at once lightning rods for gentile wrath and instruments of divine deliverance. For the Karaites the Song of Songs, then, is no less than a prophetic drama that gives their community the leading role in the final act of Israel's history.

"The Remnant of Israel," "Those Who Turn from Transgression," "The Perfect of Way," "The Mourners for Zion"—each biblical phrase that these Karaites applied to themselves evoked a different aspect of the group's identity.[63] Emblematic appellations, a prominent feature of the Jerusalem sectarians' writings, also facilitated prognostic interpretations and helped forge exegetical connections between biblical texts. One of their favorite names for themselves was the "Shoshanim" or "Lilies," an epithet deriving directly from the Song.

In his comment on 2:1, Japheth explains that the words *ḥavaṣelet* ("narcissus") and *shoshanah* ("lily") are metaphors for the "Maskilim of the Exile," that is, the Karaite leadership. Like the narcissus that flowers in midwinter and soon withers, the first "Maskilim" appeared in the midst of the Exile, then passed away. Latterly, however, a new generation of "Maskilim" has emerged. They are styled "Shoshanim," for like lilies they have come forth in the spring—the spring of Israel's Salvation.[64] They have turned the people toward God's Law and are called "those who promote righteousness" (*maṣdiqim*), since they teach the people and call them to repentance. It is on their account that God will return to Israel; this is the meaning of "I am my beloved's and my beloved is mine, who tends the *shoshanim*" (Song 6:3).[65] This exposition led Japheth to refer certain Psalms bearing the word *shoshanim* in their superscriptions directly to the Mourners for Zion.[66]

Epithets of this kind also figure prominently in polemical contexts. Medieval Jews—Rabbanites and Karaites alike—identified Edom with Christianity, Ishmael with Islam.[67] The Mourners' prognostic readings of biblical prophecies regularly use these nicknames when referring to the great kingdoms whose military conflicts would mark the End of Days. Upon encountering a verse containing one of these appellations, they are quick to comment. Thus, Salmon finds an allusion in "the tents of Kedar"[68] (Song 1:5) to "the kingdom of Hagar's son"—that is, Islam—which he identifies with the Fourth Kingdom.[69] Since both Salmon and Japheth present triumphalist interpretations of the Song, focusing on the imminent salvation of Israel and the defeat of her enemies, their commentaries contain numerous references to the Fourth Kingdom and its destruction.[70]

The polemical edge these compositions show can already be observed in ancient Jewish and Christian readings of the Song. The Rabbis and Fathers advanced competing allegories: for Jews the work described God's love for Israel; for Christians, his love for the Church. Modern scholars have argued convincingly that rabbinic and patristic exegeses of the Song betray mutual awareness, each side countering the other's claims.[71] But though the Karaite exegetes could comfortably adopt the rabbinic allegory in its broad outlines, they found certain elements to be unacceptable. By way of response, the Mourners' commentaries feature sharp anti-Rabbanite polemics; these sectarians were at least as troubled by the enemy from within as from without.

For Rabbanites, Song 7:3–5 signaled the triumph of talmudic Judaism: a restored Sanhedrin that would teach and administer Law; an *'av beit din* with the same power to coerce, convict, and punish that King Solomon possessed; and scribes who would determine the calendar for all Jewry.[72] For Japheth, however, Song 7:3 described a *biblical* utopia, a realization of Ezekiel 48, which details the allotment of the Land of Israel and accords prime portions to the priests and the *nasi*.[73] Now in his time, the Karaite leadership was vested not only in those "Maskilim" who studied, taught, and proselytized, but also in a hereditary line of *nesi'im* or princes who claimed Davidic descent—rivals, in other words, to the Babylonian exilarchs.[74] Responding directly to the rabbinic scheme, this interpretation reaffirms the preeminence of biblical institutions and associates the Karaite community's leaders directly with them.

The polemic is often explicit as well. A prime example may be found in Japheth's comment on Song 5:7, "The watchmen found me, as they went about in the city; they beat me, they wounded me, they took away my mantle, those watchmen of the walls":

> "The watchmen" refer to the judges (*dayyanim*) and rabbinic scholars (*benei beirav al-ḥaverim*) who went about in the lands collecting the pledges.[75] They exercise the power to permit, to prohibit, and to scrutinize the people's affairs. When reports of these seekers [i.e., the Karaites][76] reached them, the [Rabbanite scholars] questioned them concerning the different manner in which they kept their festivals and observances. Then the [Karaites] said: "Have *you* seen him whom my soul loves?" (Song 3:3), meaning: "You lack knowledge of the commandments that God has included in his Law—may he magnify and glorify it—that which he has forbidden and that which he has permitted. How then should we not investigate it and uphold it?" When the [Rabbanites] heard their words, they knew that the [Karaites] were leaving their jurisdiction.[77] They promptly struck them so that they should not defy them and alienate the people from them [i.e., the Rabbanites]. It is well known that wherever the Karaites have appeared in the lands of the Exile, these things have befallen them. Therefore, the verse states: "They beat me, they wounded me". . . . Now these "watchmen of the walls" are the Exilarchs and Heads of the Academies who ensure that the people observe their customs and invented traditions; they do not permit anyone to abandon them. . . ."[78]

Rabbinic exegesis refers this verse to a later *biblical* period, interpreting "the watchmen" as the Chaldeans or the governor Tatenai (Ezra 5)—in any event, an allusion to past injuries suffered by the Jews at the hands of gentiles.[79] But for Japheth the verse depicted a sharper pain, the deep wounds inflicted by the Rabbanite hierarchy of his day on the Karaite seekers, and on the Jewish people at large.

"The flowers appear on the earth, the time for *pruning* has come, and the voice of the turtledove is heard in our land" (2:12). In this verse, Japheth sees a clear reference to the emergence of the "Maskilim" or "Shoshanim," "the great teachers who are scattered in the diaspora." "With their advent," he declares, "has come the time for pruning away[80] the evildoers who have held power over Israel throughout the period of the Exile . . . for Israel's worship [of God] will not become sound until after the destruction of her evildoers (*rish'ei Yisra'el*) who harm the righteous." The true "watchmen on the walls," after all, are the "Maskilim" whose prayers, and pious, ascetic ways hasten the people's salvation. "'The voice of the turtledove,'" Japheth continues,

> alludes to "the Oaks of Righteousness," "the Mourners for Zion" (Isa 61:3) who come from the Exile to the Land of Israel, devoting themselves to knowledge, perpetually "seeking him by prayer and supplications" (Dan 9:3), never desisting from this until they have beheld the Salvation. Concerning them the prophet Isaiah pronounced: "Upon your walls, O Jerusalem, I have set watchmen; all the day and all the night they shall never be silent. You who put the Lord in remembrance, take no rest, and give him no rest until he establishes Jerusalem and makes it a praise in the earth" (Isa 62:6–7).[81]

Japheth's wrathful, vindictive tone reflects the virulent nature of the Karaite–Rabbanite debate in his time. The controversy raged around the question of exegetical authority, viz., who was authorized to interpret scripture. For the most part, battle was joined over a series of halakhic issues relating to the calendar, the observance of festivals, dietary regulations, and other ceremonial laws; it is differences of praxis that distinguish rabbinic and sectarian Judaism. As we have seen, however, certain nonlegal portions of scripture were also susceptible to partisan readings. While it is not a halakhic source, the Song of Songs is especially cherished as an affirmation of God's love for Israel. The Rabbis' interpretation of the Song elaborated God's historical relationship with his people, giving pride of place to rabbinic authority and institutions. Karaite exegetes adopted this approach, modifying it according to their own outlook and needs. At the same time, in their particular treatment of the text, its every word and nuance, they demonstrated a true reverence for the word. While their distinctive reading of the Song was virtually ignored by mainstream Rabbanite exegetes, their fidelity to scripture in general set new exegetical standards. Karaite scripturalism posed challenges that would inspire Rabbanite interpretations in the centuries to come.

Notes

1. I should like to thank Dr. Adena Tanenbaum and Mr. Samuel Rascoff, who read portions of Salmon's commentary with me in Oxford and made many valuable suggestions. I am also most grateful to Professor Michael Schwarz of Jerusalem for his helpful comments and corrections to the Hebrew version of this essay, "'We-qol ha-tor nishma' be-'arṣenu': peirushei ha-Qara'im Śalmon ben Yeroḥam we-Yefet ben 'Eli le-Shir ha-shirim," which contains the Judeo-Arabic texts. And I should like to thank the Ingeborg Rennert Center for Jerusalem Studies, Bar-Ilan University, and its director, Professor Joshua Schwartz, for permission to publish this English version.

2. See Cohen, "The Song of Songs and the Jewish Religious Mentality."

3. On philosophic exegesis of the Song by medieval Jews see: Halkin, "Ibn 'Aknīn's Commentary"; Rosenberg, "Ha-parshanut ha-filosofit"; and Kellner's trans. of Levi ben Gershom, *Commentary on Song of Songs*, esp. xv–xxxi. For the kabbalistic tradition see Vajda, *Le Commentaire d'Ezra de Gérone*, and Elliot Wolfson's contribution to this volume.

4. On exegesis of the Song by medieval Jews see: Salfeld, *Das Hohelied Salomo's*; Ginsburg, *The Song of Songs*, 34–58; and Walfish, "Bibliyografyah mu'eret." For medieval Christian interpretations, see Astell, *The Song of Songs in the Middle Ages*, and Matter, *The Voice of My Beloved*.

5. On traditional rabbinic exegesis of Song of Songs, see Loewe, "Apologetic Motifs"; Alexander, "Tradition and Originality"; and Boyarin, "Shenei mevo'ot." See also Strack and Stemberger, *Introduction*, 343–44, 347–48.

6. Stroumsa, *Al-Muqammiṣ's Twenty Chapters*.

7. Ibid., 20, and nn. 4–5. A small fragment of Muqammaṣ's Genesis Commentary (*Kitāb al-Khalīqa*) has been discovered. Stroumsa has demonstrated the work's dependence upon Christian exegetical texts; see "The Impact of Syriac Tradition."

8. For general characterizations of the Gaon's exegetical endeavor see Rosenthal, "Saadya Gaon," and Ben-Shammai, "Yeṣirato ha-parshanit," as well as Professor Ben-Shammai's contribution to this volume. On the significance of the phrase *rosh ha-meddaberim be-khol maqom* ("first of scholars in every discipline"), see Ben-Shammai, "Midrash prognosti," 1–2.

9. Nemoy, *Karaite Anthology*, 42–45, 53–68; Chiesa, "Dai 'Principi dell'esegesi biblica' di Qirqisani"; Vajda, "Du prologue de Qirqisānī"; and Chiesa and Lockwood, "Al-Qirqisani's Newly Found Commentary."

10. On Islamic humanism see Kraemer, *Humanism in the Renaissance of Islam*. On the development of new Jewish literary genres during the tenth century and a possible explanation for the phenomenon, see Drory, *Reshit ha-magga'im*, and idem, "'Al tafqidah."

11. For the text, see *Ḥamesh megillot*, ed. Qafiḥ, 17–129. Cf. Walfish, "Bibliyografyah mu'eret," 522, no. A.1.b.1. An authentic Saadianic composition, the unpublished "Commentary on the Ten Songs" does, however, contain a short homily on *Shir ha-shirim*; see n. 29 here.

12. On Karaite exegesis of the Song, see Salfeld, *Das Hohelied*, 126–34, secs. 39–40. The ninth-century Karaite Benjamin al-Nahāwandī composed a commentary, now lost; see the comment of Japheth b. Eli on Isaiah 53:12 in Neubauer and Driver, *The Fifty-Third Chapter of Isaiah*, 1:32 and 2:31. Among the Mourners for Zion, the lexicographer and exegete David b. Abraham Alfasi also composed a commentary on the Song; see Alfasi, *Kitāb Jāmi' al-alfāẓ*, 1:158, lines 67–68. Fragments of Judeo-Arabic commentaries on the Song apparently emanating from the Jerusalem Karaite group are extant in London and St. Petersburg.

13. Daniel al-Qūmisī (late 9th century) comments on Psalm 74:6: "Every word in the Bible has but one [true] interpretation, not two. But since people do not know [scripture's true] meanings, they will [continue to] interpret it in various ways until the advent of the Teacher of Righteousness"; see Marmorstein, "Fragments du commentaire," 196. On this and similar passages see Ben-Shammai, "Ha-parshan ha-qara'i," 52.

14. Cf. his comment on Song 1:6, St. Petersburg, Russian National Library, MS I.1406, fol. 36a: "Some occupied themselves with the Talmud of the Rabbis, others with the ways of the philosophers, and others with heretical [lit., 'external'] books."

15. *Com. Song* 3:8. St. Petersburg, Russian National Library, MS I.3959, fol. 5a. In the Introduction to his Commentary on Psalms he states that the errors of his predecessors motivated him to write the work; see Shunary, "Salmon ben Yeruham's Commentary on the Book of Psalms," 163, lines 2–4, and Alobaidi, *Le Commentaire des Psaumes par Salmon ben Yeruham*, 176–77 (Arabic), 287–88 (French). In his Introduction to Lamentations, Salmon expresses his reliance upon earlier authorities; see London, British Library, MS Or. 2525, fol. 12b.

16. For an overview of Karaite biblical interpretation with full bibliography, see Frank, "Karaite Exegesis."

17. On this group and their ideology see Frank, "The *Shoshanim*"; Ben-Shammai, "The Karaites"; Gil, *A History of Palestine*, 784–820; and Erder, "The Negation of the Exile"; and Walfish, "The Mourners of Zion."

18. Poznanski, "Karaite Miscellanies," 688, n.4, referring to British Library, MS Or. 2520 (Cat. 328/XII). See Salfeld, *Das Hohelied*, 127–28, and Walfish, "Bibliyografyah mu'eret," 521, no. A.1.a.2.

19. The manuscripts of Salmon's *Commentary on Song of Songs* [= Salmon, *Com. Song*] consulted for this study are (1) St. Petersburg, Russian National Library [= RNL], MS Evr.-Arab. I.1406; (2) RNL, MS Evr.-Arab. I.4252; (3) RNL, MS Evr.-Arab. I.3958; and (4) RNL, MS Evr.-Arab. I.3959.

20. See RNL, MS Evr.-Arab. I.1406, fol. 84b, on 2:12. In the course of a long excursus on messianic calculation, he gives the date of the work's composition as 888 after the destruction of the Second Temple and 345 A.H., both of which correspond to 956 C.E. The precise correspondence of the two dates rules out the possibility of scribal error. Other works completed between

953 and 957 include his *Commentary on Psalms* and *Commentary on Lamentations*. He also wrote a *Commentary on Ecclesiastes* (extant) and commentaries on Daniel, Isaiah, Proverbs, Job, and the Pentateuch that have not survived. On the dating of Salmon's commentaries see Poznanski, "Karaite Miscellanies," 688 and nn. 2–4, and Riese, "The Arabic Commentary of Solomon Ben Yeruham the Karaite on Ecclesiastes," xxxi–xxxiii; cf. Fuerst, *Geschichte des Karäerthums*, 3:87–90, which should be corrected accordingly. On the dating of *Com. Lam.* see Margoliouth, *Cat.* 1:192–93 on British Library, MSS Or. 2516 (Cat. 252) and Or. 2515 (Cat. 253).

21. For his account of Karaite history and the origins of the Shoshanim, see his comment on Psalm 69:1, in Marwick, *The Commentary of Salmon Ben Yeruham on Psalms*, 98. On this passage, see Gil, *A History of Palestine*, 618–19, and Ben-Shammai, "The Karaites," 201.

22. On these translations, see Polliack, *The Karaite Tradition*.

23. See Ben-Shammai, "Ha-yeṣirah ha-payyeṭanit."

24. For three examples of this practice see (1) the messianic calculation in *Com. Pss.* 102:14 found also in *Com. Song.* 2:12 [RNL, MS Evr.-Arab. I.1406, fols. 73a-85b], noted by Poznanski, "Miscellen über Saadja," 405, n. 1; (2) the comparison of Job's sufferings with those of Israel found in the Introduction to *Com. Lam.* and *Com. Song* 1:5 [RNL, MS Evr.-Arab. I.1406, fols. 30b-33a]; and (3) the exegesis of Psalm 42:6–7 found in *Com. Pss.* ad loc. and in *Com. Lam.* 3:20, noted by Ben-Shammai, "Ha-yeṣirah ha-payyeṭanit," 195. See also Marwick, "Studies in Salmon," 317, listing extended passages from Prophets discussed in *Com. Lam.*

25. Basing themselves upon classical models, Christian authors in the East developed the form; see Riad, *Studies in the Syriac Preface*. On the introduction as an Arabic genre, see Freimark, "Das Vorwort als literarische Form," and idem, "Mukaddima." On the academic prologue to scriptural commentary as a literary form in the Latin West, see Minnis, *Medieval Theory of Authorship*, ch. 2, esp. 42–58, on prologues to the Psalter and Song of Songs. On the function of the introduction (*haqdamah*) in medieval Jewish Bible commentaries, see Eric Lawee's contribution to this volume.

26. Salmon's Introduction is preserved in St. Petersburg, RNL, MS Evr.-Arab. I.1406, fols. 1a-4b, 7a-12b; the text between fols. 4b and 7a can be supplied from RNL, MS Evr.-Arab. I.4252, fol. 36. The beginning of the Introduction is missing; see RNL, MS Evr.-Arab. I.3958, fol. 19 for text preceding RNL, MS Evr.-Arab. I.1406, 1a.

27. RNL, MS Evr.-Arab. I.1406, fol. 1a.

28. RNL, MS Evr.-Arab. I.1406, fol. 1b. (slightly paraphrased and abridged translation).

29. On the rabbinic enumeration of ten biblical songs see Epstein, *Mi-qadmoniyot ha-Yehudim*, 2:251–54, and Goldin, *The Song at the Sea*, 68–76. Saadia composed a work that explicates these songs, *fasr wa-yosha'*; see Ben-Shammai, "Meṣi'ah 'aḥat she-hi shettayim," 313–32, esp. 323, on the homily on *Shir ha-shirim*, idem, "'Aseret 'iqqarei ha-'emunah," and idem, "Midrash prognosṭi." It should be noted that Salmon does *not* enumerate ten songs (as the rabbinic sources would have it), nor does he record songs enumerated by the Sages but lacking clear scriptural authority, e.g., the Song of Abraham mentioned by Saadia. His classification, therefore, may be seen as a *response* to the rabbinic lists.

30. For the Muslim argument concerning the inimitability (Ar. *i'jāz*) of the Qur'ān, see Abdul Aleem, "I'jāzu-l-Qur'ān," and von Grünebaum, *A Tenth-Century Document*.

31. Philo and the Church Fathers had already discussed the problem of the Bible's literary merit; see Kamesar, "Philo and the Literary Quality of the Bible." Abraham Ibn Ezra (12th century) would also ignore the Song of Songs' form while praising its content; see Simon, *Four Approaches*, 270, n. 62. During the twelfth to seventeenth centuries, certain Jewish scholars in Spain, Provence, and Italy would investigate the art of biblical poetry, seeking to establish its relationship to Arabic or classical norms. For a convenient overview see Berlin, *Biblical Poetry*, ch. 4, esp. 35–44, on rhyme and meter.

32. RNL, MS Evr.-Arab. I.1406, fol. 5a-b. Note that Salmon readily uses the rabbinic dictum "scripture speaks in human language" (BT Ber. 31b), which had become an exegetical commonplace.

33. RNL, MS Evr.-Arab. I.1406, fol. 7b.

34. RNL, MS Evr.-Arab. I.1406, fol. 8a-11b.

35. On Japheth's approach to translation, see Polliack, *The Karaite Tradition*, ch. 3, esp. 40.

36. RNL, MS Evr.-Arab. I.1406, Song 2:1, fol. 54b: *anā mithl narjisat al-sahl mithl sūsanat al-murūj*.

37. RNL, MS Evr.-Arab. I.1406, fol. 28ab. On the avoidance of anthropomorphisms through this type of addition, see Polliack, *The Karaite Tradition*, 230–32.

38. See, e.g., the identifications offered for the following verses: 1:2 (Israel to God); 1:3 (Israel to God);1:4 (Israel to God); 1:5 (Israel to Israel); 1:6 (Israel to Israel); 1:7 (Israel to God); 1:8 (God to Israel); 1:9 (God to Israel); 1:10 (God to Israel); 1:11 (God to Israel); 1:12 (Israel); 1:13 (Israel); 1:14 (Israel); 1:15 (God to Israel); 1:16 (Israel to God); 1:17 (Israel to God); 2:1 (Israel); 2:2 (God to Israel).

39. RNL, MS Evr.-Arab. I.1406, fol. 45a.

40. Midrashic sources also interpret the breasts in Song 1:13 as an allusion to the cherubim of Numbers 7:89; see Kasher, *Torah Shelemah*, 37:201, n. 351.

41. RNL, MS Evr.-Arab. I.1406, fol. 45b.

42. See Ben-Shammai, "Ha-yeṣirah ha-payyeṭanit," 214–15; as he observes (216), simple *piyyuṭim* of this kind may well have been modeled on ancient rabbinic litanies. Adena Tanenbaum has drawn my attention to a similar *piyyuṭ*—albeit an acrostic—from the *'avodah* of Yom Kippur which beguns: *u-me-rov 'awoneinu 'ein lanu/ lo 'ishshim we-lo 'asham/ lo vaddim we-lo velulah/ lo goral we-lo gaḥalei 'esh*. . . . On this hymn see *Maḥzor le-Yom Kippur*, 397; Davidson, *Thesaurus*, 1:143, no. 3050; and Beit-Arié, "Palimpsest," who dates the piece to the eighth century.

43. Bargès, *Rabbi Yapheth in Canticum Canticorum Commentarium*, with Latin translation [= Japheth, *Com. Song*].

44. On the probable sequence in which Japheth composed his commentaries, see Marwick, "The Order of the Books." On Japheth's exegetical approach see Birnbaum, *The Commentary of Yefet on Hosea*, "Introduction." See also Simon, *Four Approaches*, 72.

45. Japheth, *Com. Song*, p. 4: *min awwalihi ilā ākhirihi laysa fihi shay'in 'alā ẓāhirihi bal huwa kalām mukhtaṣar ghazīr al-ma'ānī wa-laysa yuqaf 'alā ma'nāhu illā min kutub al-anbiyā'*.

46. From Japheth's standpoint, it was, of course, perfectly natural for Solomon to respond prophetically to Ezekiel—who lived long after his time—just as it was entirely logical for them both to prophesy concerning the late tenth century C.E.!

47. Japheth does not, in fact, enumerate thirty "songs," although he does indicate where sections begin and end. Following these indications, Bargès identifies twenty-two such units in his "Praefatio," xix–xxii.

48. On the epithet "the Perfect of Way" or "Those Whose Way Is Blameless" (*temimei derekh*; Ps 119:1), see Wieder, "The Qumran Sectaries," 97–113, 289–91. For the "Mighty Ones," (or 'Terebinths') of Israel" (*'eilei Yisra'el*) see ibid., p. 292 and n. 148.

49. See Ginsburg, *The Song of Songs*, 38–34; Alexander, "Tradition and Originality," 332–34. Rashi (11th century) follows the Targum in developing a unified, coherent reading; see Marcus, "The Song of Songs in German Hasidism," 182–83, and Kamin, *Rashi*, 77–86, 247–62.

50. Cf. Japheth's explanations for the sequence of the Psalms; see: Simon, *Four Approaches*, 86; Frank, "The *Shoshanim*," 215, 220.

51. These are the leaders of the community of Mourners, the preachers and teachers of Karaism; see Frank, "The *Shoshanim*," 201 and n. 9 and further below.

52. Japheth, *Com. Song* 1:2, p. 5.

53. Japheth, *Com. Song* 6:11, pp. 90–91.

54. See, e.g., *Com. Song* 7:3, pp. 95–98, where Japheth offers three alternate interpretations. At the end of the first, he states: "This is a plausible approach (*maslik qarīb*) to this verse; but there is, in my view, another, even more plausible approach offering a superior interpretation. . . ." Cf. Birnbaum, *The Commentary of Yefet on Hosea*, viii–x.

55. Japheth, *Com. Song* 2:6, p. 27.

56. In both Hebrew and Arabic the root s/sh.m.l may signify either "left" or "north," while y.m.n. may designate "right" or "south," a consequence of orientation toward the rising sun.

57. See Sperber, *The Bible in Aramaic*, 4A: 128–29; *The Targum to "The Song of Songs,"* trans. Gollancz, 22–27.

58. See *Midrash Shir ha-shirim*, ed. Wertheimer, 34–35 and n. 150, for parallels. On this text, see Strack and Stemberger, *Introduction*, 347.

59. Salmon, *Com. Song*, RNL, MS Evr.-Arab. I.1406, fol. 42ab.

60. Salmon, *Com. Song*, RNL, MS Evr.-Arab. I.1406, fols. 40b–41b. Cf. Judah Goldin's observation, in a related context, that "every age is thus itself and also may be paradigmatic of another, for, according to the Rabbis, the biblical vocabulary addressed past generations, but present and future ones no less, each according to its requirements. . . ."; see Goldin, "Of Midrash and the Messianic Theme," 360. Significantly, Saadia emphasized this prognostic element in his *Commentary on the Ten Songs*; see earlier, n. 29, and especially Ben-Shammai, "Midrash prognosṭi."

61. For Japheth's critical attitude to certain *'aggadot* on biblical narratives, see Vajda, "Quelques aggadōt."

62. Japheth, *Com. Song* 1:9, pp. 14–15.

63. On the first three appellations, see Wieder, "The Qumran Sectaries"; on the last, see Gil, *A History of Palestine*, 619–21.

64. Japheth, *Com. Song*, 22. Cf. Japheth b. Eli, Comment on Psalm 45:1, cited in *Com. Song*, 185–86 (Latin) and Frank, "The *Shoshanim*," 201.

65. Japheth, *Com. Song* 6:3, p. 85. Cf. Wieder, *The Judean Scrolls*, 106–7. See also Japheth's comment on 2:16, p. 37, in which he explains that *ha-ro'eh ba-shoshanim* means "who tends us, who are called Shoshanim."

66. Specifically, Psalms 45, 69, and 80, also Psalm 23; see Japheth, *Com. Song* 4:5, p. 55, and 2:16, p. 37. See also Frank, "The *Shoshanim*," 223–24.

67. On appellations for Christianity and Christendom, see Cohen, "Esau as Symbol." On epithets for Islam, see Ben-Shammai, "The Attitude," 8–23.

68. Kedar, Ishmael's second son (Gen 25:13) also became a standard appellation for Islam.

69. RNL, MS Evr.-Arab. I.1406, fol. 34b. Cf. Japheth, *Com. Song*, 10; on this verse see Erder, "Yaḥaso shel Yefet la-'Islam," 35. Japheth's commentary contains other polemical references to Islam; see, e.g. *Com. Song* 2:15, p. 36, col. b, lines 7–12, where he states that the "little foxes" are the propagandists (*du'āh*) who missionize among the (Jewish) people, setting snares and ruining many of them. These *du'āh* were most likely Fatimid missionaries; see Stern, "Fatimid Propaganda." Cf. Erder, ibid., 38 and n. 53, who identifies them with the Carmathians.

70. For Japheth's position concerning the Four Kingdoms, see Frank, "The *Shoshanim*," 215–16, n. 69.

71. Polemical interpretations of the Song date back to antiquity; see Loewe, "Apologetic Motifs"; Urbach, "Homiletical Interpretations"; Kimelman, "Rabbi Yochanan and Origen"; and Hirshman, *Rivalry of Genius*, 83–94. For the medieval period, see Kamin, "Peirush Rashi 'al shir ha-shirim."

72. See Sperber, *The Bible in Aramaic*, 4A: 138 on Song 7:3–5 = *The Targum to "The Song of Songs,"* trans. Gollancz, 74–76. Cf. the fragment of a geonic commentary on Song of Songs

cited in Mann, *Texts and Studies*, 1:322, n. 47a, which interprets Song 8:14 as a reference to the two Babylonian academies.

73. Japheth, *Com. Song* 7:3, 95–98.

74. On the Karaite Nesi'im, see Gil, *A History of Palestine*, 790–94.

75. "Collecting pledges (*al-fasā'iq*)": these are the *pesiqot*; see Mann, *Texts* 2: 89, n. 112. On this institution, see Goitein, *A Mediterranean Society* 2: 106–9.

76. That "the seekers" are the Karaites can be seen from Japheth, *Com. Song* 3:2, p. 42.

77. Lit., "what they had enjoined, prohibited, and legislated."

78. Japheth, *Com. Song* 5:7, pp. 73–74. This passage was published by Mann, *Texts* 2:89–90 from a manuscript in St. Petersburg; see also Wieder, "The Dead Sea Scrolls Type of Biblical Exegesis," 98, n. 86.

79. See Sperber, *The Bible in Aramaic*, 4A: 135 = *The Targum to "The Song of Songs,"* trans. Gollancz, 60–61; *Midrash Rabbah Shir ha-shirim*, ed. Dunsky, 130.

80. Connecting Heb. *zamir* with the verb *zamar*; see Lev 25:4 and esp. Isaiah 5:6.

81. Japheth, *Com. Song* 2:12, pp. 31–32.

Bibliography

Abdul Aleem. "I'jāzu-l-Qur'ān." *Islamic Culture* 7 (1933): 64–82, 215–33.

Alexander, P. S. "Tradition and Originality in the Targum of the Song of Songs." In *The Aramaic Bible: Targums in their Historical Context*. Ed. D. R. G. Beattie and M. J. McNamara, 318–39. Sheffield: Sheffield Academic Press, 1994.

Alfasi, David ben Abraham. *The Hebrew-Arabic Dictionary of the Bible Known as Kitāb Jāmi' al-alfāz (Agron) of David ben Abraham al-Fāsī the Karaite*. Ed. Solomon L. Skoss. 2 vols. New Haven, Conn.: Yale University Press, 1936–45.

Alobaidi, Joseph. *Le Commentaire des Psaumes par le Qaraïte Salmon ben Yeruham*. Bern: Peter Lang, 1996.

Astell, Ann W. *The Song of Songs in the Middle Ages*. Ithaca: Cornell University Press, 1990.

Bargès, J. J. L. *Rabbi Yapheth Abou Aly in Canticum Canticorum Commentarium Arabicum*. Paris, 1884.

Beit-Arié, Malachi. "Palimpsesṭ Minkhen." *Qiryat sefer* 43 (1968): 411–28.

Ben-Shammai, Haggai. "'Aśeret 'iqqerei ha-'emunah shel Rav Se'adyah Ga'on" (Saadia Gaon's ten articles of faith). *Da'at* 37 (1996): 11–26.

——. "The Attitude of Some Early Karaites Toward Islam." In *Studies in Medieval Jewish History and Literature*. Vol. 2. Ed. I. Twersky, 3–40. Cambridge, Mass.: Harvard University Press, 1984.

——. "The Karaites." In *The History of Jerusalem: The Early Muslim Period, 638–1099*. Ed. J. Prawer and H. Ben-Shammai, 201–24. Jerusalem and New York: Yad Izhak Ben-Zvi and New York University Press, 1996.

——. "Meṣi'ah aḥat she-hi shettayim: peirush Ha'azinu le-rav Shemu'el ben Ḥofni u-feirush Wa-yosha' le-Rav Se'adyah Ga'on bi-khtav yad nishkaḥ" (New findings in a forgotten manuscript: Samuel b. Hofni's Commentary on *Ha'azinu* and Saadia's 'Commentary on the Ten Songs'). *Qiryat sefer* 61 (1986–87): 313–32.

——. "Ha-parshan ha-qara'i u-sevivato ha-rabbanit" (The Karaite exegetes and their rabbinic environment). In *Proceedings of the Ninth World Congress of Jewish Studies: Panel Sessions: Bible Studies and the Ancient Near East*, 43–58. Jerusalem: Magnes Press, 1988.

——. "Ha-yeṣirah ha-payyeṭanit we-sidrei ha-qinot shel 'Avelei Ṣiyyon ha-Qara'im: ha-misgeret we-ha-tekhanim" (Poetic works and lamentations of Karaite 'Mourners of Zion'—structure and contents). In *Keneset Ezra: Literature and Life in the Synagogue; Studies Presented to Ezra Fleischer*. Ed. S. Elizur et al., 191–234. Jerusalem: Ben-Zvi Institute, 1994.

——. "Midrash prognosṭi be-khitvei Rasag: petiḥat peirusho le-shirat David (Shemu'el Beit 22) ke-dugmah meyyaṣeget" (Prognostic *Midrash* in the Works of Se'adya Gaon as Exemplified in his Introduction to the Commentary on the Song of David [2Sam. 22]). In *Me'ah She'arim: Studies in Medieval Jewish Spiritual Life in Memory of Isadore Twersky*. Ed. E. Fleischer et al., 1–19. Jerusalem: Magnes Press, 2001.

——. "Yeṣirato ha-parshanit we-ha-hagutit shel Rasag: mif'alo shel manhig" (The exegetical and philosophical writing of Saadya Gaon: a leader's endeavor). *Pe'amim* 54 (1993): 63–81.

Berlin, Adele. *Biblical Poetry through Medieval Jewish Eyes*. Bloomington: University of Indiana Press, 1991.

Birnbaum, Philip. *The Arabic Commentary of Yefet Ben 'Ali the Karaite on the Book of Hosea*. Philadelphia: Dropsie College, 1942.

Boyarin, Daniel. "Shenei mevo'ot le-Midrash Shir ha-shirim" (Two introductions to the Midrash on the Song of Songs). *Tarbiẓ* 56 (1987): 479–501.

Chiesa, Bruno. "Dai 'Principi dell'esegesi biblica' di Qirqisani." *JQR* n.s. 73 (1982–83): 124–37.

Chiesa, Bruno, and W. Lockwood. "Al-Qirqisani's Newly Found Commentary on the Pentateuch: The Commentary on Gen. 12." *Henoch* 14 (1992): 153–80.

Cohen, Gerson D. "Esau as Symbol in Early Medieval Thought." In *Studies in the Variety of Rabbinic Cultures*, 243–69. Philadelphia: Jewish Publication Society, 1991.

——. "The Song of Songs and the Jewish Religious Mentality." In *Studies in the Variety of Rabbinic Cultures*, 3–17. Philadelphia: The Jewish Publication Society, 1991.

Davidson, Israel. *Thesaurus of Mediaeval Hebrew Poetry*. 4 vols. New York: Jewish Theological Seminary of America, 1924.

Drory, Rina."'Al tafqidah shel ha-sifrut ha-qara'it be-toledot ha-sifrut ha-yehudit ba-me'ah ha-'asirit" (The role of Karaite literature in the history of tenth-century Jewish literature). *Dappim le-meḥqar be-sifrut* 9 (1994): 101–10.

——. *Reshit ha-magga'im shel ha-sifrut ha-yehudit 'im ha-sifrut ha-'arvit ba-me'ah ha-'asirit* (The emergence of Hebrew-Arabic literary contacts at the beginning of the tenth century). Tel-Aviv: Hakibbutz Hameuchad, 1988.

Epstein, Abraham. *Mi-qadmoniyot ha-Yehudim*. 2 vols. Jerusalem: Mossad Harav Kook, 1967.

Erder, Yoram. "The Negation of the Exile in the Messianic Doctrine of the Karaite Mourners of Zion." *HUCA* 68 (1997): 109–40.

——. "Yaḥaso shel ha-qara'i Yefet ben 'Eli la-'Islam le-'or peirusho le-mizmorei tehillim 14, 53" (The attitude of the Karaite, Yefet ben Eli, to Islam in light of his interpretation of Psalms 14 and 53). *Michael* 14 (1997): 29–49.

Frank, Daniel. "Karaite Exegesis." In *Hebrew Bible/Old Testament: The History of Its Interpretation*, Vol. I/2. Ed. Magne Saebø, 110–128. Göttingen: Vandenhoeck & Ruprecht, 2000.

——. "The *Shoshanim* of Tenth-Century Jerusalem: Karaite Exegesis, Prayer, and Communal Identity." In *The Jews of Medieval Islam: Community, Society, and Identity*. Ed. D. Frank, 199–245. Leiden: E. J. Brill, 1995.

——. "The Study of Medieval Karaism, 1989–1999." In *Hebrew Scholarship and the Medieval World*. Ed. Nicholas De Lange, 3–22. Cambridge: Cambridge University Press, 2001.

——. "*We-qol ha-tor nishma' be-'arṣenu.*" *Peirushei ha-Qara'im Śalmon ben Yeroḥam we-Yefet ben 'Eli le-Shir ha-shirim* ("The voice of the turtledove is heard in our land": The commentaries of the Karaites Salmon ben Jeroham and Japheth ben Eli on the Song of Songs). International Rennert Guest Lecture Series, no. 7. Ramat-Gan: Bar-Ilan University, 2001.

Freimark, Peter. "Das Vorwort als literarische Form in der arabischen Literatur." Ph.D. diss., University of Münster, 1967.

——. "Mukaddima." *EI*, new ed. 7: 495–96.

Fuerst, J. *Geschichte des Karäerthums*. 3 vols. Leipzig, 1862–69.

Gil, Moshe. A *History of Palestine, 634–1099*. Cambridge: Cambridge University Press, 1992.
Ginsburg, Christian David. *The Song of Songs*. London, 1857; reprint, New York: KTAV, 1970.
Goitein, S. D. *A Mediterranean Society*. Vol. 2. Berkeley and Los Angeles: University of California Press, 1971.
Goldin, Judah. "Of Midrash and the Messianic Theme." In *Studies in Midrash and Related Literature*, 359–79. Philadelphia: Jewish Publication Society, 1988.
——. *The Song at the Sea*. Philadelphia: Jewish Publication Society, 1990.
Grünebaum, G. E. von. *A Tenth-Century Document of Arabic Literary Theory and Criticism*. Chicago: University of Chicago Press, 1950.
Halkin, A. S. "Ibn 'Aknīn's Commentary on the Song of Songs." In *Alexander Marx Jubilee Volume*, 389–424. Philadelphia: Jewish Publication Society of America, 1950.
Ḥamesh megillot . . . 'im peirushim 'attiqim. Ed. Joseph Qafiḥ. Jerusalem: Ha-Agudah le-Haṣalat Ginzei Teiman, 1962.
Hirshman, Marc. *Rivalry of Genius: Jewish and Christian Biblical Interpretation in Late Antiquity*. Albany: State University of New York Press, 1996.
Japheth, *Com. Song*. See Bargès.
Kamesar, Adam. "Philo and the Literary Quality of the Bible: A Theoretical Aspect of the Problem." *Journal of Jewish Studies* 46 (1995): 55–68.
Kamin, Sarah. "Peirush Rashi 'al Shir ha-shirim we-ha-wiqquaḥ ha-yehudi noṣri" (Rashi's commentary on the Song of Songs and Jewish-Christian polemic). In *Bein Yehudim le-Noṣrim* (Jews and Christians interpret the Bible), 31–61. Jerusalem: Magnes Press, 1991.
——. *Rashi: peshuṭo shel Miqra' u-midrasho shel Miqra'* (Rashi's exegetical categorization). Jerusalem: Magnes Press, 1986.
Kasher, Menaḥem M. *Torah Shelemah*. 45 vols. in 12. Jerusalem: Beth Torah Shelemah, 1992.
Kimelman, Reuven. "Rabbi Yochanan and Origen on the Song of Songs." *Harvard Theological Review* 73 (1980): 567–95.
Kraemer, Joel L. *Humanism in the Renaissance of Islam*. Leiden: E. J. Brill, 1986.
Levi ben Gershom (Gersonides). *Commentary on Song of Songs*. Trans. Menachem Kellner. New Haven, Conn.: Yale University Press, 1998.
Loewe, Raphael. "Apologetic Motifs in the Targum to the Song of Songs." In *Biblical Motifs: Origins and Transformations*. Ed. A. Altmann, 159–96. Cambridge, Mass.: Harvard University Press, 1966.
Maḥzor le-Yom Kippur. Ed. Daniel Goldschmidt. Jerusalem: Koren, 1993.
Mann, Jacob. *Texts and Studies in Jewish History and Literaure*. 2 vols. Cincinnati/Philadelphia: Hebrew Union College Press and the Jewish Publication Society of America, 1931–35.
Marcus, Ivan. "The Song of Songs in German Hasidism and the School of Rashi: A Preliminary Comparison." In *The Frank Talmage Memorial Volume*. Vol. 1. Ed. Barry Walfish, 181–89. Haifa: Haifa University Press, 1993.
Margoliouth, George. *Catalogue of the Hebrew and Samaritan Manuscripts in the British Museum*. Part I. London, 1899.
Marmorstein, A. "Fragments du commentaire de Daniel al-Kumisi sur les Psaumes." *Journal asiatique*, 2d ser., 7 (1916): 177–237.
Marwick, Lawrence. *The Arabic Commentary of Salmon Ben Yeruham on the Book of Psalms, Chapters 42–72*. Philadelphia: Dropsie College, 1956.
——. "The Order of the Books in Yefet's Bible Codex." *JQR* n.s. 33 (1942–43): 445–60.
——. "Studies in Salmon ben Yeruham." *JQR* n.s. 34 (1943–44): 313–20, 475–80.
Matter, E. A. *The Voice of My Beloved: The Song of Songs in Western Medieval Christianity*. Philadelphia: University of Pennsylvania Press, 1990.
Midrash Rabbah Shir ha-Shirim. Ed. Shimson Dunsky. Jerusalem/Tel Aviv: Devir, 1980.
Midrash Shir ha-shirim. Ed. Joseph Chaim Wertheimer. Ktav Yad Vasefer Institute, 1981.

Minnis, A. J. *Medieval Theory of Authorship*, 2d ed. Aldershot: Wildwood House, 1988.

Nemoy, Leon. *Karaite Anthology*. New Haven, Conn.: Yale University Press, 1952.

Neubauer, A., and S. R. Driver. *The Fifty-Third Chapter of Isaiah According to the Jewish Interpreters*. 2 vols. Oxford and London, 1876–77.

Polliack, Meira. *The Karaite Tradition of Arabic Bible Translation: A Linguistic and Exegetical Study of Karaite Translations of the Pentateuch from the Tenth to the Eleventh Centuries*. Leiden: E. J. Brill, 1997.

Poznanski, S. "Karaite Miscellanies." *JQR* o.s. 8 (1896): 681–704.

——. "Miscellen über Saadja, III: Die Berechnung des Erlösungsjahres bei Saadja." *Monatsschrift für die Geschichte und Wissenschaft des Judentums* 44 (1900): 519–29.

Riad, Eva. *Studies in the Syriac Preface*. Uppsala: Uppsala University, 1988.

Riese, Moshe. "The Arabic Commentary of Solomon Ben Yeruham the Karaite on Ecclesiastes." Ph.D. diss., Yeshiva University, New York, 1973.

Rosenberg, Shalom. "Ha-parshanut ha-filosofit le-Shir ha-shirim: he'arot mavo'" (Philosophical hermeneutics on the Song of Songs, introductory remarks). *Tarbiẓ* 59 (1990): 133–51.

Rosenthal, E. I. J. "Saadya Gaon: An Appreciation of His Biblical Exegesis." *BJRL* 27 (1942): 168–78. Reprint: *Studia Semitica, Volume I: Jewish Themes*, 86–96. Cambridge: Cambridge University Press, 1971.

Salfeld, S. *Das Hohelied Salomo's bei den jüdischen Erklärern des Mittelalters*. Berlin, 1879.

Salmon, *Com Song* = Salmon b. Jeroham, *Commentary on Song Of Songs*. References to St. Petersburg, Russian National Library [=RNL], MSS Evr.-Arab. I.1406, Evr.-Arab. I.4252, Evr.-Arab. I.3958, and Evr.-Arab. I.3959.

Shunary, Jonathan. "Salmon ben Yeruham's Commentary on the Book of Psalms." *JQR* n.s. 73 (1982–83): 155–75.

Simon, Uriel. *Four Approaches to the Book of Psalms*. Trans. Lenn J. Schramm. Albany: State University of New York Press, 1991.

Sperber, Alexander. *The Bible in Aramaic, Vol. IVA: The Hagiographa*. Leiden: E. J. Brill, 1968.

Stern, S. M. "Fāṭimid Propaganda Among Jews According to the Testimony of Yefet b. 'Alī the Karaite." In *Studies in Early Ismā'īlism*, 84–95. Jerusalem: Magnes Press, 1983.

Strack, H. L., and G. Stemberger, *Introduction to the Talmud and Midrash*. Edinburgh: T&T Clark, 1991.

Stroumsa, Sarah. *Dāwūd Ibn Marwān al-Muqammiṣ's Twenty Chapters ('Ishrūn Maqāla)*. Leiden: E. J. Brill, 1989.

——. "The Impact of Syriac Tradition on Early Judaeo-Arabic Bible Exegesis." *ARAM* 3 (1991): 83–96.

The Targum to "The Song of Songs." Trans. H. Gollancz. London, 1908.

Urbach, E. E. "The Homiletical Interpretations of the Sages and the Expositions of Origen on Canticles, and the Jewish-Christian Disputation," *Scripta hierosolymitana* 22 (1971): 247–75.

Vajda, Georges. *Le commentaire d'Ezra de Gérone sur le Cantique des Cantiques*. Paris: Aubier-Montaigne, 1969.

——. "Du prologue de Qirqisānī à son commentaire sur la Genèse." In *In Memoriam Paul Kahle*. Ed. M. Black and G. Fohrer, 222–31. Berlin: Alfred Töpelmann, 1968.

——. "Quelques aggadōt critiquées par Yefet ben 'Eli." In *Studies in Judaica, Karaitica, and Islamica Presented to Leon Nemoy*. Ed. S. R. Brunswick et al., 155–62. Ramat-Gan: Bar-Ilan University Press, 1982.

Walfish, Barry Dov. "Bibliyografyah mu'eret shel ha-parshanut ha-yehudit 'al Shir ha-shirim mi-yemei ha-beinayim" (An annotated bibliography of medieval Jewish commentaries on the Song of Songs). In *Ha-Miqra' bi-re'i mefareshaw* (The Bible in the light of its interpreters: Sarah Kamin memorial volume). Ed. Sara Japhet, 518–71. Jerusalem: Magnes Press, 1994.

——. "The Mourners of Zion (*'Avelei Ṣiyyon*): A Karaite *'Aliyah* Movement of the Early Arab Period." In *Eretz Israel, Israel and the Jewish Diaspora: Mutual Relations*. Ed. Menachem Mor, 42–52. Lanham, Md.: University Press of America, 1991.

Wieder, Naphtali. "The Dead Sea Scrolls Type of Biblical Exegesis among the Karaites." In *Between East and West: Essays dedicated to the Memory of Bela Horovitz*. Ed. Alexander Altmann, 75–106. London: East and West, 1958.

——. *The Judean Scrolls and Karaism*. London: East and West Library, 1962.

——. "The Qumran Sectaries and the Karaites." *JQR*. n.s. 47 (1956–57): 97–113, 269–92.

5

Restoring the Narrative

Jewish and Christian Exegesis in the Twelfth Century

MICHAEL A. SIGNER

In the past decades the concept of narrative has emerged as a significant theoretical framework across the spectrum of scholarly disciplines. Postmodern thinkers have defined the novelty of their approach by rejecting the notion of unifying "master narratives." Other philosophers and not a few literary critics have argued the opposite position. They claim that it is precisely the loss of a unifying narrative that allows for the cultural anomie and the decline of culture in our era. Whatever side of this intellectual battle students of the medieval world may take, it is clear that narrative—the construction of story—is central to defining the self and, by extension, one's community. The desire to become part of a human community impels the individual to engage in argument over narrative.

The theme of this volume, "With Reverence for the Word," places the analysis of twelfth-century Jewish and Christian biblical exegetes squarely within the argument over the construction of narrative or story. The Hebrew Bible, with its amalgam of narrative and nonnarrative genres, has its parallel in the Christian scriptures, whose Gospels are constructed of mixed genres and whose Epistles, with their arguments and exhortations, have, over the centuries, taxed the patience of many an exegete and preacher. In addition, both Jewish and Christian communities engaged in the continuing construction of literatures that have been considered normative or definitive for the lives of their followers.

What relationship does narrative have to the development of biblical commentary? How can the musings of modern literary theorists about the nature of narrative help students of medieval biblical commentary? We can begin with the argument that narrative demarcates, encloses, and establishes limits.[1] Therefore, when the medieval author sets his mind to writing a commentary, his selection of the lemma from the Bible demarcates and divides the text of scripture. Simultaneously, the phrases of the commentary itself break up the biblical text and establish a conjunction between verses, chapters, and even books of the Bible that come together through the imagination of the exegete. Through this conjunction of lemmata, the medieval commentator on scripture restructures the biblical text and introduces the possibility for a new narrative reading.

Jewish and Christian exegetes in the twelfth century inherited a wide range of possible readings for their respective communities. For Jews, midrash and talmudic *'aggadah* offer a dazzling array of imaginative readings of the biblical text. However, many of the classical rabbinic texts make no attempt to provide a link between successive verses in the biblical text itself. In the same way, patristic writings offer little guidance to the student who wishes to track the verses of scripture in their sequential order. Jewish and Christian exegetical literatures manifest consciousness of the distinction between "plain meaning" (*peshaṭ* or *sensus litteralis*) and derived or figurative meaning (*derash* or *sensus spiritualis*). However, there are very few twelfth-century commentaries on scripture, either Christian or Jewish, that present a sustained theoretical framework that helps the reader to distinguish between them. This lack of clear distinction poses a serious problem for the reader who wishes to enter the world of scripture. How was it possible to understand the biblical text through the framework of the exegetical tradition? This dilemma is described by Hans Frei: "When the pattern of meaning is no longer firmly ingredient in the story and the occurrence character of the text, but becomes a quasi-independent interpretive stance, literal and figurative reading draw apart, the latter gradually looking like a forced arbitrary imposition of unity on a group of very diverse texts."[2] Frei's description of the separation of literal and figurative readings applies to the cultural environment of the twelfth century, in which Jews read the midrashim of the Sages and Christians the lengthy disquisitions of an Augustine or Jerome and discovered that these works put them at a greater distance from the biblical text. Abelard describes this dilemma of the arbitrary imposition of the Fathers on the biblical text when he heard the lectures of Master Anselm at Laon.[3] Similarly, material from midrash or Talmud did not provide immediate access to the biblical readings in the synagogue. Abraham Ibn Ezra expressed his dissatisfaction with the biblical commentaries written in Christian lands that presented little more than midrash with no attention to the linguistic component of Scripture.[4]

Literary theory would suggest another paradigm for describing the difficulty facing Jewish and Christian biblical commentators in the twelfth century. With Northrop Frye we might describe the scriptural exegesis of the Sages and Church Fathers as "metaphoric reading," in which each word in the Bible provides an occasion to enter the entire thought world of the Sages or the Fathers. By contrast, Rashi and the Victorines offered what Frye calls a "metonymic" reading that provides links between each word of the biblical sentence in proper order.[5]

To illustrate the difference between these two readings, let us presume that the letters "A," "B," "C," and "D" each represent a single word in a verse. The "paradigmatic" reading would focus on only one of the letters—"A," for example—without considering how "A" relates to the sequence of "B–D." The "metonymic" reading, by contrast, would relate the word "A" directly to those letters that follow it. By shifting the emphasis from "metaphoric" to "metonymic" reading, the author of an exposition of a biblical verse facilitates the understanding of the sequence of words, sentences, chapters, or even entire biblical books.

The innovation of Rashi and the Victorines, I would argue, is the use of the narrative framework of Scripture as the basis of their commentaries in order to avoid the fragmentation or diffusion of the biblical text that they found in the literary forms of biblical commentary in their respective traditions. Their commentaries reveal a unity of theme or content where the biblical verse may seem disjointed. In order to realize this narrative unity, their commentaries develop exegetical techniques whereby biblical lemmata become embedded in the commentary. This process of embedding the biblical verse into the commentary itself provides the opportunity to "fill in the gaps" for the reader. In this manner Rashi would differ from the earlier midrashim, where the paradigmatic reading dominated. The Victorines differed from patristic commentary where the sequence of the verse was subordinated to a meditation on a single word or phrase. In their move to metonymic reading neither Rashi nor the Victorines strip the scriptural verse of its figurative or midrashic meanings. Twelfth-century exegetes strove to balance the traditional metaphoric readings with an emphasis on the sequence of words or chapters in the biblical text.

Let us begin with Rashi's exegetical works that reveal his efforts to restructure the biblical texts. In his commentaries we read the words of the Sages, but in an abbreviated or restructured form. Rashi's own voice interrupts the continuity of scripture with rabbinic literature when he states, "There are rabbinic homilies (*midreshei 'aggadah*) but I say. . . ."[6] The reader of Rashi's commentary might experience what Paul Ricoeur has called the "double eclipse," both from the text of scripture and from the explanations of the Sages which are removed from their context in the Talmud or midrash.[7] However, the eclipse does not occur, and the reader is drawn closer to the biblical text both through the Sages and through Rashi. It is this fusion rather than fission between text and tradition that occurs in Rashi's commentaries that constitutes their great achievement. The correlation and harmonization of biblical narrative with rabbinic tradition is what makes the appellation of "narrator" a significant description for the overall intellectual accomplishment of Rashi's commentaries.[8]

To understand the narrative process of exegesis in Rashi's commentary, we begin with his attention to the smallest linguistic units. Considerable attention has been focused on Rashi as a philologist and lexicographer of the Hebrew Bible.[9] Menahem Banitt has expanded our appreciation of Rashi's ability to link the words of the Bible with the world of his reader by translating biblical words into the vernacular.[10] Rashi's *le'azim* reveal the profound link between the study of the Bible in the eleventh-century classroom and the world of inherited exegetical rabbinic literature. This fusion of the vernacular with the Hebrew text drew the reader into the world of his inherited tradition.

Rashi also uses single words in scripture as semantic markers that propose conjunctive or disjunctive readings of biblical passages. In his comment on Psalm 2:2 Rashi raises the question, "What is the counsel they take?" This question moves the reader of the comment on toward the following verse as a response. The reader is drawn from Rashi's question forward into the text of scripture that Rashi frames as the words of the Philistine princes. A similar marker appears in Psalm 2:5, where the undetermined speaker is introduced in the biblical lemma, "Then he will speak to them." Once again, Rashi raises the question, "What is the word?" The answer is the next phrase in the Psalm itself,: "But I have installed my king." By this combination of question and response, Rashi establishes that the first six verses of the Psalm are to be understood in the following context, "Why did you assemble seeing that I have appointed for me this one [King David] to anoint and to be King over my holy Mount Zion?"[11] Further investigation of the narrative power of fusing questions with biblical lemmata will, I think, demonstrate the ability of Rashi to fuse biblical text, rabbinic tradition, and original exegesis.

In Rashi's commentaries a single word in the biblical text may be "translated" into a synonymous Hebrew term. The reason for the "translation" may be suggested by the lexical context of the Bible. However, as Abraham Grossman and M. Zohori have demonstrated, Rashi utilized the writings of the rabbinic Sages and adapted them for his own didactic purposes.[12] We shall select one example, Genesis 15:1, where the narrative of Abram's vision of God follows his conquest of the warring Canaanite tribes. God assures Abram with the words, "Do not fear (*'al tira*) Abram, I am a shield for you; your reward will be very great." Rashi comments on this verse:

> *After these things*. Every place that [scripture] uses the word *'aḥar* it joins the narratives (*samukh*). Every place that [scripture] uses the word *'aḥarei* it means that the texts should be separated (*muflag*) (Gen. Rab. 44:5). After the miracle was performed for him that he killed the kings [of Canaan], he was worried (*hayah do'eg*) and said, "Perhaps I have received the reward for all my righteous deeds." Therefore, God spoke to him and said, "Do not fear."[13]

The comment provides an amplification of the biblical verse. God urges Abram not to fear (from the root *y-r-'*). Rashi uses the word *do'eg*, "worry," to describe Abram's inner emotions that guide the divine response. Abram worries and God responds with the message that he is not to fear. He seems to have changed the language in Genesis Rabbah 44:4 where Abram's state of mind is translated by *mitpaḥed*, a much more literal translation of the Hebrew *y-r-'*. Rashi's use of *d-'-g* transfers the emotion of "fear" expressed in Genesis Rabbah to the dimension of "worry" and helps the reader gain a better understanding of the narrative, which begins with Abram's journey in Genesis 12 and is followed by encounters with the King of Egypt (Gen 12:10–29) and with the Canaanite kings (Gen 14). From the reading of Rashi's comment, the reader can discern the reciprocity between Abram's worry and God's reassurance. Abram does not need to worry, because he has nothing to fear. The seeming disjunction of Genesis 14, where Abram joins battle with the kings of Canaan, is now brought into harmony with earlier portions of the narrative and provides the setting for the affirmations of the divine promise in Genesis 15.

This close reading of Rashi on Genesis 15:1 demonstrates what we have earlier called "metonymic reading." The commentary first sets the narrative framework, which is then expanded in the following segments of the verse or verses. The dialogues between the biblical protagonist, Abram, and God are derived from the rewriting of earlier rabbinic sources. In Rashi's commentary the biblical dialogue and the rabbinic tradition appear as a seamless web. Rashi refocuses the reader on the episode immediately prior to the divine call to Abram as the stimulus for the vision. The effect of the commentary is to move the reader through the biblical passage with a more profound consciousness of how the individual episode contributes to the narrative.

A significant dimension of narrative perspective is provided by the prefaces that Rashi writes for biblical books. In Rashi one does not find the formal prologues that characterize the biblical exegetes who wrote under the influence of Islamic culture, such as Saadia Gaon or Abraham Ibn Ezra.[14] However, at the beginnings of biblical books, Rashi often indicates something about the author and the central themes that will be presented. In the prophetic books or the Hagiographa, the introductory statements can be clearly recognized. In his first comments on the book of Isaiah, Rashi recasts a number of midrashim into a coherent narrative. We learn of the prophet's ancestry and the geographic scope of his audience, which extended to both the northern and southern kingdoms. However, Rashi demonstrates that the initial vision provided only part of the prophet's audience, since there are also visions later in the book concerning other nations, such as Babylonia and Moab. The entire book as a cohesive narrative is Rashi's concern and not just the superscript of the first chapter, describing the prophet. The introductory comments also focus on the problem of whether or not the first book is the beginning of Isaiah's mission to Israel. Rashi argues that the vision in the Temple (ch. 6) is the first of Isaiah's prophecies.[15] The reader of Rashi's introductory remarks receives all the information that one could have gathered from the classical genre *accessus ad auctores*: who the prophet was, when he delivered his message, and the literary order of the prophecies set forth in the book. A. J. Minnis provides an account of the utilization of prologues that contain similar information in Christian biblical commentaries of the late eleventh and early twelfth centuries, and their use by the Victorines Hugo and Andrew will be discussed later.[16]

The most outstanding example in Rashi's exegesis of a prologue providing a narrative framework for an entire biblical book is in the commentary on Song of Songs. In this text he provides one of the most extensive theoretical statements about the coherence of the poetry in that book. He begins the prologue with a deliberate imitation of the *proem* or opening statement which is utilized in the homiletical midrashim, citing Psalm 62:12, "God has spoken one thing, Two things I have heard." Rashi applies this verse to the process of interpreting Scripture: "A scriptural verse may have many meanings, but the final result is that no scriptural verse goes beyond its context (*mashma'o*)."[17] The link between the Psalm verse and its application builds a framework for the act of interpretation. Divine revelation is a unified whole, but human beings "hear" (from the root *sh-m-'*) it as multivoiced. Rashi grants that any verse in scripture may have many meanings, but the act of interpretation requires that the context (*mashma'*—the way the verse is heard) set the boundary for understanding. This statement about *mashma'* indicates the metonymic dimension of Rashi's commentary. It is the "broad context" or horizontal relationship between the words and verses that follow the verse in question that sets the horizons for the interpretive activity.[18] Rashi then locates the Song within the category of prophecy and shows how it should be interpreted: "Even though the prophets spoke in types [or figures] (*dugma*), one must explain these types according to the order and characteristics of the verse, just as the scriptural verses follow one after the other." The use of the term *dugma* for type or figure is a locution unique to Rashi. After tracing the history of this word in rabbinic literature, Sarah Kamin determined that Rashi uses it to indicate a typological interpretation where the biblical text provides the paradigm for the interpretation of God's interaction with Israel throughout its history from Abraham through the end of days.[19] Prophetic statements, however, are restricted by the same general rule that Rashi made for scriptural verses. If the verse cannot transgress its context, the prophetic word should also be understood within a framework. This structure is built on the pattern of the verses in scripture that follow one another in order. The correct way to understand the historical orientation of the types in Song of Songs is in their proper sequential order.

The introduction then reviews the history of interpretation of the Song. Rashi asserts his auctorial voice:

> I have seen a number of aggadic midrashim on this book. Some of them explain the entire book in one continuous midrash. There are other midrashic comments on individual verses that are scattered [throughout the many books of midrash]. These comments do not fit in with the language of scripture and the order of its verses. I have therefore determined to grasp the *context* (*mashma'*) of the scriptural verses and to clarify them in their proper order. As for the midrashic interpretations, our Sages have set each one in its proper place.

In this passage we discern Rashi's assessment of the lack of coherence in the rabbinic exegesis. There are some commentaries, such as Songs of Songs Rabbah, that set the entire biblical book into a single collection (*midrash 'eḥad*). By contrast, one can discover midrashic interpretations of individual verses that are scattered throughout the books of *'aggadah*. Neither form of midrash takes its point of departure from the language of the Bible (*leshon ha-Miqra*) or the order of the verses (*seder ha-miqra'ot*). The task that Rashi sets for himself is to produce a commentary that is grounded in the context of biblical language. It is the context of the verses (*mashma' ha-miqra'ot*) that will be the determining factor in utilizing rabbinic midrash. Rashi does not intend to strip the Bible of rabbinic midrash and reduce his exegesis of the Song to lexicographical and etymological notes. His objective is to establish a foundation for rabbinic thought by providing a narrative context that is grounded in Scripture itself.

In the closing portion of his introduction, Rashi reveals the narrative that will control his selection of rabbinic material. He returns to the idea of auctorial intention: "I claim that Solomon understood by means of the Holy Spirit that the Israelites were destined to endure one exile after another—one destruction after another." In other words, Solomon's purpose in composing the Song of Songs was to prophesy about Israel's destiny. It would be a cycle of exile and destruction. This cycle diverges from a history of the Jewish people that leads from the destruction of the Temple and subsequent exile toward a final redemption with a triumphal return to the land. This pessimistic narrative has a pedagogic purpose. "They [Israel] will mourn in their current exile over their earlier position of honor and remember that they were God's first love—a treasured possession of the King of the Universe. . . . They would remember God's steadfast love and their transgressions and also the rewards that God promised them in the end of days." In this cycle of historical exiles, Rashi emphasizes that his comments refer to "this exile," their current status among the Christian nations. Let us note that Rashi conjoins Israel's mourning with a quotation from Hosea 2:9: "I will return to my first husband for then I fared better than now." However, Rashi does not use the image of the bride seeking her husband, but rather that of "living widow (*'almenut ḥayut*)" (2 Sam 20:3). This hapax legomenon in Scripture provides a more radical image that would force the reader of the commentary to reflect upon the status of those concubines whom David had left to care for his palace in Jerusalem during his absence. After his return, he restored them to his table but never enjoyed conjugal life with them again. In this status of living widowhood, Israel would cling to her beloved and remember her youthful love for him. This mournful longing evokes a response from her beloved, who "takes pity upon her sorrow." For God, the beloved is "still bound to her in a powerful love" and there is no divorce, "because she remains his wife and he remains her husband."

We can observe in Rashi's introduction to the Song of Songs a powerful restoration of a unifying narrative. The rabbinic traditions on the book provided a rich assembly of images, but their patterns of organization were too fragmented. It is the order of the biblical verses and chapters that sets the structure for organizing the rabbinic exegetical works. There is a strong apologetic motif in Rashi's introduction to Song of Songs. God's love for Israel is eternal. He has not "divorced" Israel. They remain his beloved people.[20]

The restoration of the narrative may also be discerned in the opening lines of Rashi's commentary on Genesis.[21] Rashi raises the question based on a rabbinic midrash, Tanḥuma, of why the Pentateuch commences with an account of the creation of the world rather than with the divine commandment for Israel to celebrate the Passover (Exod 12:2). His response is based on scriptural authority: "God tells the might of his deeds to His people to give them an inheritance of the nations" (Ps 111:6). The commentary then imagines a dialogue between Israel and the gentile nations. The nations suggest that Israel robbed the land of Israel from the seven Canaanite nations. Israel is then to respond, "All of the earth is the Lord's. He gives it to whomever is upright in His eyes. By his will He gave it to them, and by his will He took it from them and gave it to us."[22]

Here one can discern that Rashi wanted to fuse two literary structures: the narratives of Genesis with the legal structures of commandments in Exodus and other books of the Pentateuch. These two structures, seemingly distinct, merge into relationship with the introduction of the covenant between God, the people Israel, and the Land of Israel. Law and narrative are not in opposition to one another but part of a seamless web that drew Israel toward an unbreakable bond with God. This fusion of narrative and law resonates again in Rashi's comment at the conclusion of the first creation narrative (Gen 1:31):

> *The sixth day*. God added *he* [i.e., the letter, which has a numerical value of five] to the word 'sixth' at the end of creation because He made it a condition with Israel that they would take upon themselves the *five* books of Moses. Another interpretation: *The sixth day*. All of them [the works of creation] were suspended and waiting until the sixth day which was the sixth day of [the Hebrew month] Sivan—[a day] prepared for the giving of the law.[23]

This comment provides a concluding framework to the question raised in the preface. The reader comes to understand that what began as a narrative to inspire awe and gratitude among the people of Israel concludes with a foreshadowing of the revelation of the decalogue where Israel would be asked to observe the laws in "the five books of Moses." The narrative of creation is joined to the responsibilities of the commandments. Rashi tightens the complex meditations on the cosmology in the midrash collections such as Genesis Rabbah and Tanḥuma into a commentary that incorporates their most significant ideas directly into the lemmata of the biblical text.

We have been able to observe how Rashi's commentaries succeed in bringing about a fusion of the diverse texts of the rabbinic tradition with the biblical text. This fusion is established by his attention to the metonymic "one verse after another" structure of scripture. From our close reading of his introduction to the commentary on the Song of Songs and the opening lines of his commentary on Genesis, we have discerned that his purpose in drawing all of these diverse elements together was to demonstrate how they reveal God's continuing covenant with Israel. In her "current exile" Israel was to meditate on her fall from the glories of the biblical past and to concentrate on the rewards that God would provide in the world to come.

This effort by Rashi to restore the broad context of the biblical narrative has a strong resonance in the biblical commentaries written by Hugh and Andrew of Saint Victor. By "resonance" I refer to a similarity in approach to the biblical text and tradition rather than influence or interaction between Rashi and the Victorine scholars.[24] For the purpose of this essay, I would prefer to focus on the way that Hugh and Andrew attempt to provide a framework for the reading of scripture that balances the order of the biblical text with an appropriation of the patristic tradition.

Hugh of Saint Victor provided his students with guidelines for reading scripture in three of his works. The most extensive treatment is the *Didascalicon*, an attempt to recast Augustine's *De doctrina christiana*.[25] A more focused discussion may be found in *De scripturis et scriptoribus sacris*, which served as the "introduction" to his *Notulae* on the Pentateuch.[26] His extended discussion of a theological reading of scripture, *De sacramentis christianae fidei*, also begins with a set of directions for how the Bible should be read.[27]

Hugh's overarching concern with scriptural hermeneutics was to underline the importance of careful reading of scripture as the basis for theological reflection and meditation. This care is necessary because sacred reading entails the development of both the intellect and morals. Hugh warned against methods of study that urged the student to rush past the close reading of the biblical text in order to engage in allegory.

> Do not despise these lesser things. They who despise the lesser things gradually fail. If you scorn to learn your alphabet you will never even make your name as a grammarian. I know that there are some who want to philosophize immediately and say that fairy tales should be left to the false apostles. Their learning is asinine. Do not imitate such men.[28]

At the basis of all scriptural study is the literal or historical sense. For Hugh this reading implies an understanding of both language and narrative. As he put it, "We call by the name 'history' not only the recounting of actual deeds but also the first meaning of any narrative which uses words according to their proper nature."[29] By reading history, the student would acquire the "means through which to admire God's deeds." When approaching the reading of scripture, Hugh prescribes the proper order for reading historically. From the Old Testament one should read Genesis, Exodus, Joshua, Judges, Kings, and Chronicles; and in the New Testament the first four Gospels and then the Acts of the Apostles. Then, he might proceed to allegory, through which he could believe God's mysteries, and finally to morality, which would allow him to imitate God's perfection.[30] Allegory was to be constructed on the firm foundation of the letter, with the reader building it with great care. He was not to follow the letter slavishly but was to read carefully the beginning of Genesis, the last three books of Moses (Leviticus, Numbers, Deuteronomy) on the mysteries of the Law, Isaiah, the beginning and end of Ezekiel, Job, the Psalter, Song of Songs, Matthew and John, the Pauline Epistles, and the Apocalypse. Hugh emphasized the reading of the Pauline Epistles because they contain the perfection of the two testaments. The concordance of the two testaments in both their historical and allegorical readings is at the heart of Hugh's great theological work *De sacramentis*. Ultimately, the task of the Christian theologian is to utilize all the tools of learning to discern the narrative of divine redemption which is emplotted in scripture. This redemptive narration begins with the "work of creation" and continues through the end of time in what Hugh calls the "work of restoration."[31]

We can observe a far more explicit description of the theoretical basis for the relationship between narration and the literal sense in Hugh of Saint Victor than in Rashi. However, when we investigate his *Notulae* on the Pentateuch, the concern for coherent narrative that is grounded in history becomes clear. At the beginning of his notes on Genesis, Hugh argues that "Moses was an historical writer (*historiographus*) who composed a narrative from the beginning of the world until the death of Jacob. Through prophecy Moses was able to narrate what happened before the creation of humanity in the same manner as he predicts the matters after the death of Jacob which are introduced here." The juxtaposition of the historical genre with its realization in narrative is, therefore, central for understanding Hugh's exegetical enterprise. This alliance of lexical truth with narrative is emphasized in another passage in the same work: "Two things should be noted: the truth of things done and the forms of the words. Through the truth of the words we know the truth of things and through the truth of things we know more easily the truth of words. This is because we are moved forward through the historical narration to higher things."[32]

Andrew of Saint Victor was narrower in his intellectual efforts than his teacher.[33] Eschewing broad statements of method, he focused exclusively on the literal sense of the Hebrew Bible. However, his efforts to discover the literal sense did not mean that his exegetical writings were dry linguistic notes. Andrew described his exegetical endeavors as something of an adventure, and he often used colorful images to describe the project. We can discern this spirit from the preface to his commentary on Ezekiel: "With God as leader, who makes ways in the sea, paths in the stormy water, we take our way unfearing, through unknown, pathless places, no end in sight."[34]

He introduced the commentary on the Pentateuch with a keen sense of narrative. He asserts that Moses knew that a people enslaved would have difficulty keeping the commandments. Therefore, before he gave "hard and heavy precepts of the law to an untutored people lax from soft living and the many pleasures of Egypt," Moses related God's manifold blessings to them and their ancestors. He promised that more good things shall be given to them. The purpose of these narratives is "to educate his hearers to a more careful observance of the law he gives them by counting the great riches of heavenly favor." We should note here the progressive nature of the narrative. Both law and narrative are fused into the covenanted drama of divine grace.[35]

Andrew, though devoted to the literal sense, does not neglect the Christian hermeneutical framework of the Pentateuch. He does not attribute the omission of explicit reference of the Trinity to the blindness of the Jews. He ascribes it to the pedagogic reality facing Moses: "Lest he occasion backsliding to an untutored people prone to the worship of many gods which they had learned in the land of Egypt, he does not mention the Trinity." However, Moses does suggest the operations of the Trinity by the narratives of creation: "power in creating things from nothing; wisdom in disposing and guiding them; goodness in sustaining and cherishing them."

At the conclusion of his introduction he raises the issue of how and when the creation narrative was composed.

> How could Moses so long after creation have known about it? The grace of the Holy Spirit, which could reveal to him the future, surely could have revealed things past, for nothing is as apt as our knowledge of what is past. It is not absurd to believe that the

> Holy Fathers of old, Adam and his descendants, could commit the creation to memory by frequent recital or even in writing, for this especially causes us to praise God and love him. So might it have come to the knowledge of Moses who sought it by careful research.

Andrew's emphases on story, commandments, and praise of God are reminiscent of Rashi's introductory statements on the book of Genesis. In both Rashi and Andrew of Saint Victor, modern readers can discern the concerns of medieval readers. For the Jewish people in the late eleventh century, their lowly status and the growing strength of the Christian Church were the source of some anxiety about the possibilities of future redemption. Christians were experiencing confusion about the future directions of their sense of religious community and the fragmentation of theological knowledge. The resolution for each community, as this chapter suggests, may have rested in the shift from a metaphoric to a metonymic reading of scripture. To domesticate a narrative by limiting the potential expansions of its meanings provides a center from which members may diverge, but still define themselves. The lives of Jews and Christians in northern France diverged in their rites, rituals, and theology, but not in their goal—the discovery of a narrative that fused biblical text and ancient traditions for members of their communities.

Notes

1. Brooks, *Reading for the Plot*, 4.
2. Frei, *The Eclipse of Biblical Narrative*, 35.
3. Abelard, *Historia Calamitatum*, ed. Monfrin, 68–70, and idem, *The Story of Abelard's Adversities*, trans. Muckle, 21–24.
4. Ibn Ezra, "Introduction" in *Peirushei ha-Torah*, ed. Weiser, 1:7.
5. Frye, *The Great Code*, 5–27.
6. For example, *Peirush 'al ha-Torah* ad Gen 3:8, Exod 23:2.
7. Ricoeur, "What Is a Text?" 145–64.
8. Cf. Signer, "Rashi as Narrator."
9. Pereira-Mendoza, *Rashi as Philologist*; Englander, "Rashi's View of the Weak 'ayin-ayin and peh-nun Roots"; idem, "Grammatical Elements and Terminology in Rashi's Biblical Commentaries"; idem, "Grammatical Elements and Terminology in Rashi."
10. Banitt, *Rashi*.
11. See Signer, "King Messiah"; Gruber, *Rashi's Commentary on Psalms 1–89*, 52–57.
12. Grossman, *Ḥakhmei Tsarefat ha-rishonim*, 193–200. Zohori, *Midreshei halakhah*, 1–16.
13. Rashi, *Perush 'al ha-Torah* Gen 15:1, and *Ḥamishah ḥumshe Torah . . . Rashi ha-shalem*, 1:148–49.
14. Cf. Goodman, in Saadia, *The Book of Theodicy*, 56; he attributes the use of introductions by Saadia to the "Greco-Arabic *Isagoge* literature of which Porphyry's thematic introduction to the *Organon* of Aristotle was a model." Further discussions of the introduction to biblical books in the Islamic environment may be found in Simon, *Four Approaches*.
15. Cf. Rashi, "Commentary on Isaiah," in *Miqra'ot gedolot Ha-Keter: Yesha'yahu*, 2–3, for the relevant texts. I hope to provide an analysis of Rashi's commentaries on the prophetic writings in my forthcoming monograph on Rashi and the School of Saint Victor.
16. Minnis and Scott, eds., *Medieval Literary Theory and Criticism*, 1–11.
17. The text here is cited from the edition by Rosenthal, "Perush Rashi 'al Shir ha-Shirim," and compared to the transcription of MS L778 in the Jewish Theological Seminary of America by Kamin and Saltman in *Secundum Salomonem*, 81–99.
18. Halivini, *Peshat and Derash*, 79–80, and 159, n. 59, provides a discussion of the terms *peshaṭ* and *derash*. Lifschuetz, *Rashi*, 9–196, describes Rashi's use of the term *mashma'* to indi-

cate broad context. For a discussion of Rashi's introduction to the commentary on Song of Songs, cf. Kamin, *Rashi*, 77–86, 247–62.

19. Kamin, "Dugma."

20. Cf. Kamin, *Rashi*, 247–50 and her subsequent discussion of the meaning of exile on 251–60. Kamin also analyzes the Christian intellectual background to Rashi's commentary in her article "Peirush Rashi 'al Shir ha-Shirim." For another perspective on Rashi's commentary on Song of Songs, cf. Marcus, "The Song of Songs in German Hasidism."

21. I have treated this subject at greater length in my article "God's Love for Israel: Apologetic and Hermeneutical Strategies in Twelfth-Century Biblical Exegesis."

22. Rashi, "Commentary on Genesis," in *Miqra'ot Gedolot Ha-Keter: Bereshit*, 1:2. The translation is my own.

23. Rashi on Genesis 1:31, ibid., 30, "Commentary on Genesis," 1:31, 30. See also *Ḥamishah ḥumshei Torah . . . Rashi ha-shalem*, 1:20–21.

24. Smalley has discussed these mutual interactions in *The Study of the Bible*, 83–195. Awerbuch, *Christlich-jüdische Begegnung*, 215–30, provides a more extended discussion of parallels between Hugh and Rashi. For an investigation of Hugh's theological perspective on Jews and Judaism with some attention to his biblical commentaries, cf. Moore, *Jews and Christians*, 77–112.

25. Hugh of Saint Victor, *Didascalicon*, ed. Buttimer; *The Didascalicon of Hugh of St. Victor*, trans. Taylor.

26. *De scripturis et scriptoribus sacris praenotatiunculae*, in PL 175. 9–28D. Cf. Zinn, "The Influence of Augustine's *De doctrina christiana*."

27. *De sacramentis christianae fidei*, in PL 176.183–86; *Hugh of St. Victor on the Sacraments of the Christian Faith*, trans. Deferrari, 1–7.

28. *Didascalicon* 4. 3, trans. Taylor, 104–5; Smalley, *Study of the Bible*, 87.

29. *Didascalicon* 6. 3, trans. Taylor, 137; Zinn, "*Historia fundamentum est*."

30. *Didascalicon* 4. 3, trans. Taylor, 138.

31. Moore, *Jews and Christians*, 113–34; Sicard, *Huges de Saint-Victor et son école*.

32. Hugh of Saint Victor, *Adnotationes eluciditoriae in Pentateuchon*, in PL 175. 12–13.

33. The life and literary works of Andrew were first investigated by Smalley, *The Study of the Bible*, 112–85, and most recently by Berndt, *André de Saint-Victor (1175)*.

34. Andrew of Saint Victor, *Expositionem in Ezechielem*, ed. Signer, 1, trans. Smalley, *Study of the Bible*, 125.

35. Andrew of Saint Victor, *Expositio in Heptateuchum*, ed. Lohr and Berndt. All subsequent references in the paragraph will be found in this text; trans. Smalley, *Study of the Bible*, 131.

Bibliography

Abelard, Peter. *Historia Calamitatum*. Ed. J. Monfrin. Paris: J. Vrin, 1967.

——. *The Story of Abelard's Adversities*. Trans. J. T. Muckle. Toronto: Pontifical Institute of Mediaeval Studies, 1964.

Andrew of Saint Victor. *Expositionem in Ezechielem*. Ed. Michael Alan Signer. CCCM, 53e. Turnhout: Brepols, 1991.

——. *Expositio in Heptateuchum*. Ed. C. Lohr and R. Berndt. CCCM, 53. Turnhout: Brepols, 1986.

Awerbuch, Marianne. *Christlich-jüdische Begegnung im Zeitalter der Frühscholastik*. Munich: Chr. Kaiser Verlag, 1980.

Banitt, Menahem. *Rashi: Interpreter of the Biblical Letter*. Tel Aviv: University of Tel Aviv, 1985.

Berndt, Rainer. *André de Saint-Victor (1175): exégète et théologien*. Turnout: Brepols, 1991.

Brooks, Peter. *Reading for the Plot: Design and Intention in Narrative*. New York: Alfred A. Knopf, 1984.

Englander, Henry. "Grammatical Elements and Terminology in Rashi." *HUCA* 14 (1939): 387–429.

——. "Grammatical Elements and Terminology in Rashi's Biblical Commentaries." *HUCA* 11 (1936): 367–89; 12–13 (1937–38): 505–21.

——. "Rashi's View of the Weak 'ayin-ayin and peh-nun Roots." *HUCA* 7 (1930): 399–437.

Frei, Hans. *The Eclipse of Biblical Narrative: A Study in Eighteenth-and Nineteenth-Century Hermeneutics.* New Haven, Conn.: Yale University Press, 1985.

Frye, Northrop. *The Great Code.* New York: Harcourt, Brace, Jovanovich, 1982.

Grossman, Abraham. *Ḥakhmei Ṣarefat ha-rishonim.* Jerusalem: Magnes Press, 1995.

Gruber, Mayer I. *Rashi's Commentary on Psalms 1–89 (Books I–III) with English Translation, Introduction and Notes.* Atlanta, Ga: Scholars Press, 1998.

Halivini, David Weiss. *Peshat and Derash: Plain and Applied Meaning in Rabbinic Exegesis.* New York and Oxford: Oxford University Press, 1991.

Ḥamishah ḥumshei Torah: Ari'el . . . Rashi ha-shalem. 5 vols. to date. Jerusalem: Ari'el, 1986– .

Hugh of Saint Victor. *Adnotationes elucidatoriae in Pentateuchon.* PL 175. 29–86.

——. *De sacramentis christianae fidei.* PL 176. 183–618.

——. *De scripturis et scriptoribus sacris praenotatiunculae.* PL 175. 9–28D.

——. *The Didascalicon of Hugh of St. Victor: A Medieval Guide to the Arts.* Trans. Jerome Taylor. New York: Columbia University Press, 1961.

——. *Hugh of St. Victor on the Sacraments of the Christian Faith.* Trans. Roy J. Deferrari. Cambridge, Mass.: Medieval Academy of America, 1951.

——. *Hugonis de Sancto Victore, Didascalicon: de studio legendi. A Critical Text.* Ed. Charles Henry Buttimer. Washington, D.C.: Catholic University Press, 1939.

Ibn Ezra, Abraham. *Peirushei ha-Torah.* Ed. A. Weiser. 3 vols. Jerusalem: Mossad Harav Kook, 1976.

Kamin, Sarah. *Bein Yehudim le-Noṣerim be-farshanut ha-Miqra* (Jews and Christians interpret the Bible). Jerusalem: Magnes Press, 1991.

——. "Dugma be-feirush Rashi le-Shir ha-Shirim" (Dugma in Rashi's commentary on Song of Songs). *Tarbiẓ* 52 (1982–83): 41–58. Reprint in Kamin, *Bein Yehudim le-Noṣerim,* 13–30.

——. "Peirush Rashi 'al Shir ha-Shirim weha-wiqquaḥ ha-Yehudi Noṣeri" (Rashi's commentary on the Song of Songs and Jewish-Christian polemic). *Shenaton le-Miqra ule-ḥeqer ha-Mizraḥ ha-qadum* 7–8 (1982–83–1983–84): 218–48. Reprint in Kamin, *Bein Yehudim le-Noṣerim,* 31–61

——. *Rashi: peshuto shel Miqra u-midrasho shel Miqra* (Rashi's exegetical categorization in respect to the distinction between *peshat* and *derash*). Jerusalem: Magnes Press, 1986.

Kamin, Sarah, and Avrom Saltman, eds. *Secundum Salomonem: A 13th Century Latin Commentary on the Song of Songs.* Ramat-Gan: Bar-Ilan University Press, 1989.

Lifschuetz, E. M. *Rashi–Rabbi Shelomoh Yiṣḥaqi.* Warsaw, 1912. Reprint in *Ketavim.* Vol. 1. Jerusalem: Mossad Harav Kook, 1947.

Marcus, Ivan G. "The Song of Songs in German Hasidism and the School of Rashi: A Preliminary Comparison." In *The Frank Talmage Memorial Volume.* Vol. 1. Ed. Barry Walfish, 181–89. Haifa: Haifa University Press, 1993.

Miqra'ot gedolot Ha-Keter: Bereshit, Vol. 1. Ed. Menachem Cohen. Ramat-Gan: Bar Ilan University, 1997.

Miqra'ot gedolot Ha-Keter: Yesha'yahu. Ed. Menachem Cohen. Ramat-Gan: Bar Ilan University, 1996.

Minnis, A. J., and A. B. Scott, eds. *Medieval Literary Theory and Criticism c.1100–1375: The Commentary Tradition.* Oxford: Clarendon Press, 1988.

Moore, Rebecca. *Jews and Christians in the Life and Thought of Hugh of St. Victor.* Atlanta, Ga.: Scholars Press, 1998.

Pereira-Mendoza, Joseph. *Rashi as Philologist.* Manchester: Manchester University Press, 1940.

Ricoeur, Paul. "What Is a Text? Explanation and Understanding." In *Hermeneutics and the Human Sciences*. Ed. and trans. John B. Thompson, 145–64. Cambridge: Cambridge University Press, 1981.

Rosenthal, Judah. "Perush Rashi 'al Shir ha-Shirim" (Rashi's commentary on the Song of Songs). In *Sefer yovel li-khvod Shemu'el Qalman Mirsqi* (Samuel K. Mirsky Jubilee volume). Ed. S. Bernstein and G. A. Churgin, 130–88. New York, 1958.

Saadia ben Joseph. *The Book of Theodicy: Translation and Commentary on the Book of Job*. Trans. L. E. Goodman. New Haven, Conn.: Yale University Press, 1988.

Sicard, Patrice. *Huges de Saint-Victor et son école*. Turnhout: Brepols, 1991.

Signer, Michael A. "God's Love for Israel: Apologetic and Hermeneutical Strategies in Twelfth-Century Biblical Exegesis." In *Jews and Christians in Twelfth-Century Europe*. Ed. Michael A. Signer and John H. Van Engen, 124–37. Notre Dame, Ind.: University of Notre Dame Press, 2001.

——. "King Messiah: Rashi's Exegesis of Psalms 2." *Prooftexts* 3 (1983): 273–84.

——. "Rashi as Narrator." In *Rashi et la culture juive en France du nord au Moyen Âge*. Ed. Gilbert Dahan, Gérard Nahon, and Elie Nicolas, 102–10. Paris-Louvain: E. Peeters, 1997.

Simon, Uriel. *Four Approaches to the Book of Psalms*. Trans. Lenn J. Schramm. Albany: State University of New York Press, 1991.

Smalley, Beryl. *The Study of the Bible in the Middle Ages*. 3d ed. Oxford: Basil Blackwell, 1984.

Zinn, Jr., Grover A. "*Historia fundamentum est*: The Role of History in the Contemplative Life According to Hugh of St. Victor." In *Contemporary Reflections on the Medieval Christian Tradition. Essays in Honor of Ray C. Petry*. Ed. George H. Shriver, 135–58. Durham, N.C.: Duke University Press, 1974.

——. "The Influence of Augustine's *De doctrina christiana* upon the Writings of Hugo of St. Victor." In *Reading and Wisdom: The "De doctrina christiana" of Augustine in the Middle Ages*. Ed. Edward. D. English, 60–88. Notre Dame, Ind.: University of Notre Dame Press, 1995.

Zohori, M. *Midreshei halakhah we-'aggadah be-feirushaw shel Rashi*. Jerusalem: Dani Sefarim, Kanah, 1993.

6

Rashbam as a "Literary" Exegete

MARTIN LOCKSHIN

Rabbi Samuel ben Meir (Rashbam), who lived in northern France in the twelfth century, was a consistent and perhaps radical exponent of *peshaṭ* exegesis. He insisted on reading the biblical text in its "plain" sense and in its context, and he eschewed midrashic readings that are not textually anchored. But was he therefore aware of and sensitive to literary issues within the text? Is the *pashṭan*, the exegete dedicated to the "plain" meaning, always the most careful reader of the biblical text? Logically one would think so. However, the history of medieval Jewish exegesis shows that that was not always the case. Many examples show that some *peshaṭ* exegesis from this period purposely and self-consciously avoids "close reading" of the biblical text.

Rashbam's Sephardic younger contemporary, Abraham Ibn Ezra, argued passionately against "close reading" of texts. In a long tirade in his introduction to the Decalogue[1] and in other passages, Ibn Ezra argues that word choice in the Bible is not always of significance, that authors will choose to express themselves differently on different occasions for no particular reason. Ibn Ezra contrasts God's words to Cain (Gen 4:11), "You are cursed from the soil . . . if you till the soil it shall no longer yield its strength to you," with Cain's "rephrasing" of the same speech (4:14): "You have banished me this day from the soil." Ibn Ezra asks, "Who would be so mindless as to think that the meaning changes (*ha-ṭaʿam ʿeinenu shaweh*) because different words are used?" In all likelihood, many modern readers of the Bible would disagree with Ibn Ezra. They would say that the meaning *was* different, that a petulant and self-righteous Cain had changed the words in order to exaggerate the punishment that God had imposed on him.

Ibn Ezra suggests further that when a biblical story is written twice—for example, once in the words of the narrator and then retold in the words of one of the characters, as in Pharaoh's dream in Genesis 41—one ought to ignore the differences between the versions. Such an approach was later adopted by a number of other well-known *pashṭanim*, such as David Kimḥi, Joseph ibn Kaspi, and Joseph Kara.[2]

Modern readers, on the other hand, often do pay attention to the differences that occur in the retelling of a story. I often heard my teacher, the late Nehama Leibowitz—who was a gifted practitioner of close reading and who had the greatest respect for medieval Jewish commentators—speak disparagingly about the type of classical exegesis that failed to see significance in variations between versions of a repeated biblical story. We might expect that only those exegetes who do see significance in such variations are the ones who deserve to be called *pashṭanim*. In practice, however, many of the commentators whom history has labeled *pashṭanim* are the ones who ignore such variations.

Ibn Ezra's approach to the literary nature of biblical texts is difficult to understand. Uriel Simon once described Ibn Ezra's biblical commentaries as "lacking the literary-esthetic approach to the text that one might have anticipated from a great poet like him."[3] More investigation of Ibn Ezra's position is called for, but I would suggest that his approach may reflect an ambivalence about poetry and literary pursuits that was common in Sephardic intellectual circles. It is possible that Ibn Ezra, though a talented and accomplished poet, believed, as many philosophers did,[4] that poetic pursuits fall far below the level of philosophy, and that he therefore should hesitate to apply poetic analysis to the holy text of the Bible.

Ibn Ezra's position is presented here simply as a foil to that of his Ashkenazic contemporary, Rashbam. Rashbam was neither a poet nor a philosopher. Like most twelfth-century Jews who lived in Christendom, he had no reason to want to take part in the *adab*, the general culture, as a Sephardic Jew like Ibn Ezra did. As David Berger has recently argued, both Ashkenazic and Sephardic Jews in the high Middle Ages were involved in some form of "competitive imitation"[5] of their non-Jewish neighbors. Sephardic Jews competed with the Muslims in the fields of poetry and philosophy; Ashkenazic Jews competed with their Christian neighbors in the realms of piety and religious devotion.[6] Ibn Ezra's approach to literature is almost certainly a function of the spirit of the Muslim society from which he came. But it is hard to imagine that Rashbam, who presumably read no Latin,[7] developed a particular literary approach as a result of his contact with contemporaneous Christian writings.[8]

Despite all the differences in their backgrounds and worldviews, Rashbam and Ibn Ezra developed very similar exegetical approaches. Both are willing to offer new and even daring *peshaṭ* interpretations of biblical verses, interpretations that often fly in the face of traditional exegesis. But Rashbam and Ibn Ezra part company on some crucial interpretive issues,[9] including their willingness to identify literary patterns in biblical narratives. At least in that sense, Rashbam's way of reading the Bible appears much closer to our modern approach. This is so despite the ostensibly narrow nature of his background. Rashbam had, as far as we know, no literary training. He did not write poetry himself. Unlike Ibn Ezra, Rashbam probably had no secular education.

Even though Rashbam's commentaries often roundly rejected traditional midrashim, he was no religious radical. He was a talmudist, who believed in talmudic method and defended classical rabbinic exegetical methodology. He often writes that classical rabbinic *midrash halakhah* is a valid (perhaps the most valid) form of exegesis; it is, he argues, based on careful reading of the text, particularly the reading of *yitturim*, superfluities, in the text.[10]

Both Rashbam and Ibn Ezra accept *midrash* as valid, but Ibn Ezra attributes its validity to the chain of tradition[11] (thereby implicitly dismissing it as a form of exegesis), while Rashbam argues that *midrash* is a valid form of exegesis. *Midrash*, according to Rashbam, is not *peshaṭ*, but it is definitely exegesis. True, he limits his Torah commentary to *peshaṭ* and does not include therein specific explanations of how *midrash* works and how it differs from *peshaṭ*. But in his Talmud commentary he does from time to time show how a specific biblical passage can be interpreted in two ways—one understanding based on *peshaṭ* methodology and the second understanding based on the very close reading of *yitturim*.[12] Rashbam's Talmud commentaries further show just how seriously he takes rabbinic exegesis. Rashbam's definition of which rabbinic *midreshei halakhah* should be seen as originating in the Torah, (i.e., as being *de-'oraita*) is often considerably wider than that of his contemporaries. Various *derashot* that some medieval rabbis saw simply as examples of mnemonic devices (*'asmakhta'ot*) were understood by Rashbam as being true exegesis, and the resulting laws were then seen as having Torah-based validity.[13]

Rashbam, to be sure, has, like Ibn Ezra, many caustic comments for certain midrashic readings.[14] But while Ibn Ezra criticizes midrashic authors for making any comment at all about what he considers nonissues in the text,[15] Rashbam criticizes them for making the wrong comments, that is, for failing to notice the contextual reasons for the use of a certain word or phrase (and for bringing in an external explanation instead).

Despite Rashbam's sincere defense of traditional rabbinic exegesis, he developed his own alternative way of dealing with superfluities in the text. For a number of biblical passages, we can juxtapose the rabbinic approach to a specific *yittur* with Rashbam's literary approach to that same superfluity. We might label the rabbinic approach as the attempt to give referential meaning to the *yittur*, while Rashbam gives it rhetorical meaning. Two examples follow.

Both Rashi and Rashbam react to the alleged redundancy of the phrase (Exod 22:23), "I will kill you by the sword, and your wives will be widows and your children will be orphans." The text seems to provide the reader with unnecessary information, for if God kills a man, then we all know that his wife will be a widow and his children will be orphans. Rashi's approach (based on the Mekhilta[16]) assumes that the purpose of the redundancy must be to add some new meaning to the text; it must teach us some new fact that we did not know before—in this case that the husband will be dead but will be defined as missing in action, with all the painful religious and financial implications of such a determination. The meaning of the redundancy for Rashi is *referential*, because it refers the reader to new information.

Rashbam takes a very different approach, one that still finds meaning in the apparent redundancy, but, in this case, rhetorical meaning. For rhetorical reasons the text wants to emphasize through repetition that men who "mistreat any widow or orphan" (v. 21) will be punished by having their wives and children become widows and orphans. Now of course the reader ought to be able to figure out independently that if a man is killed, his wife will be a widow. The phrase "your wives will be widows and your children will be orphans" does not really teach us anything new; there is no referential meaning attached to it. But the added text, suggests Rashbam, helps to frighten the reader by making a connection between the sin and the poetically just punishment.

A second text, this time with legal ramifications—"Six days you shall work but on the seventh day you shall cease from labor; at plowing time and at harvest time you shall cease from labor" (Exod 34:21)—illustrates this same distinction. All classical commentators see a redundancy here. Since it is well known that work on the Sabbath is prohibited, why then should the text have to specify that it is forbidden "at plowing time and harvest time"? Rashi, following rabbinic traditions,[17] lists a number of new laws that we may learn from this alleged redundancy, again providing us with referential meaning. Rashbam in turn suggests a rhetorical purpose to the phrase: the time of year when there is most temptation to break the Sabbath rules would be "at plowing time and harvest time." Accordingly, the text must warn that the Sabbath is inviolable even then.

In these two examples, Rashbam, as in other places, explains certain biblical texts as attempts by the author to help the reader read the text more smoothly. Clearly that is a crucial element of his exegetical method. Much has been written about Rashbam's repeated use of the principle of literary anticipation, which argues that some biblical texts provide the reader with information that the reader does not need at that point in the narrative but will need at some further point.[18] Rashbam does not tire of telling us how anticipation is a common literary device used by the biblical author. Anticipation is, then, the prime example of Rashbam identifying a literary pattern in the text and showing how that pattern adds additional meaning—rhetorical meaning, not referential meaning—to the biblical text.

These examples of Rashbam's "literary" exegesis conform, more or less, to what we moderns expect of a commentator with literary sensitivity. But not all of Rashbam's comments with a literary direction are so easily understood and categorized. I would like to propose the thesis that Rashbam was among the first exegetes, perhaps the first, to identify many literary patterns in biblical texts without claiming that those patterns are meant to elicit any specific reader response, in fact without attributing any particular significance to those patterns. A few examples follow.

Rashbam is often given credit for having made the original discovery that the ten plagues, or at least the first nine of them, follow a literary pattern.[19] If one divides the nine plagues into three units of three, one notices that warnings are always provided for the first two plagues of each unit, but not for the third. This literary classification of the plagues was later developed and expanded by many other exegetes, both medieval and modern.[20]

However, Rashbam's "discovery" was not *his* discovery. We know that Rashbam was acquainted with *Midrash Leqaḥ ṭov* and his commentary is dependent on *Leqaḥ ṭov* on a number of occasions.[21] *Leqaḥ ṭov*'s commentary (to Exod 8:15) preceded Rashbam in identifying this literary pattern in the plagues narrative. But *Leqaḥ ṭov* also felt obliged to explain in an abstruse talmudic manner the significance of this pattern,[22] while Rashbam simply points out the pattern to his readers without attributing any particular significance to it.

Rashbam notes other literary patterns as well. For example, he discusses the use of chiasm by biblical authors, even in prose passages.[23] Rashbam is also generally given credit for teaching his grandfather, Rashi, about the phenomenon of ladder parallelism, verses on the pattern of (Gen 49:22) "*ben porat Yosef, ben porat 'alei 'ayyin.*"[24] In another example, Rashbam argues that a number of lists in the Bible are best understood if one assumes that the elements are not arranged chronologically but rather that a biblical text, like a mishnaic text, can be arranged in a *lo zo 'af zo* manner, listing first items of lesser importance and then moving on to the crescendo, to the more crucial and/or surprising items (the most innovative interpretation).[25] Finally, Simcha Kogut has argued in a recent book that Rashbam may have been aware of and may well have based a comment of his on the recently "discovered" literary phenomenon that biblical authors use inversion as a form of punctuation.[26] Yet never does Rashbam attempt to "do" anything with such literary analysis beyond pointing it out. Never does Rashbam suggest why chiasm is used at point A in the biblical text or why ladder parallelism is used at point B—that is, what purpose there might be in the author's use of those literary patterns, or what reader response these devices might be trying to elicit.

Rashbam was not the only Ashkenazic exegete concerned about literary patterns. The unusual nature of his approach becomes clearer when we compare his writings to those of some of his colleagues. For example, Rashi, Joseph Kara, and Rashbam are all sensitive to the fact that some questions in the Bible must be understood as rhetorical, not as informative. But Rashi and Kara explain why rhetorical questions are useful, that is, what purpose they serve in the flow of the narrative.[27] For Rashbam it is sufficient to say that that is the standard pattern.[28]

In a final example, Rashbam and his older contemporary, Joseph Kara, both react to the same apparent redundancy in the text of Exodus 19:

> (8) All the people answered as one, saying, "All that the Lord has spoken we shall do." *Then Moses brought back the people's words to the Lord.* (9) And the Lord said to Moses: "I will come to you in a thick cloud, in order that the people may hear. . . ." *Then Moses reported the people's words to the Lord.*

Rashbam and Kara offer interpretations that are similar but not identical. Both of them see the redundancy in these verses as similar to another redundancy in Judges 17:3–4. Both of them see the verses as describing only one instance of reporting by Moses, despite the repetition.[29] Both of them see the redundancy as being part of a literary pattern. Rashbam simply identifies that pattern, seeming to assume that the redundancy is thus explained.[30] Joseph Kara also sees the same pattern here but tries to explain its purpose: to teach that two events occurred at precisely the same time.[31]

When two friends and colleagues like Rashbam and Kara offer such similar interpretations, it seems likely that they discussed the issue together. Presumably one commentary is dependent on the other. Yet the small difference between their two approaches is significant. Kara sees the repetition of one verse after the other as teaching something, specifically that two actions occurred simultaneously. As far as Rashbam is concerned, there is no particular lesson or information conveyed by the doubling. It is a manifestation of a common literary phenomenon that Rashbam identifies many times in his Torah commentary. The alleged redundancy is in that case really repetition, repetition that is acceptable because it is part of an identifiable literary pattern.

Rashbam was not the only exegete to label literary patterns without discussing their significance. Many commentators, including at times Abraham Ibn Ezra, identify literary phenomena such as poetic parallelism without discussing their significance.[32] But I would argue that Rashbam does it far more often and far more consistently. I will try to explain why.

Rashbam developed his own literary method as a part of his general self-taught exegetical approach. He does not explain all the principles of his method. Accordingly, any theory put forward here is speculative. But perhaps his literary method is not so hard to understand when viewed as part of his general approach to reading a biblical text.

One of the most dominant features of Rashbam's pursuit of *peshaṭ* is that it often involves reading the text of the Bible in a manner that ignores the educational or edificatory purposes of the text. In Rashbam's exegesis he does not ask the most common question of religious commentators: "What can we learn from this text?" Rashbam consciously offers explanations that he knows are prosaic and perhaps even deflating. For example, Rashi sees significance and religious meaning in the fact that "the door or the doorpost" is the specified location for the ear-piercing ceremony of Exodus 21:6.[33] Rashbam counters with an explanation that has no "lesson" to it: piercing is best done against wood; doors and doorposts are usually made of wood.[34]

Rashbam wrote a biblical commentary that does not attempt to "teach" Judaism. Perhaps this is why his commentary never really caught on in traditional Jewish circles (and perhaps why it has some popularity in modern academic circles). The author of the one supercommentary on Rashbam quotes contemporaries who asked him why he even bothered to explain what Rashbam's commentary means: "What good has he done, what has he accomplished, what did he improve for us with this commentary of his on the Torah?"[35]

Yet Rashbam *does* feel that the Bible "teaches," that it uplifts and that it edifies. He feels, though, that the reader who is interested in the moral lessons of the Bible will have to read other books—midrashic works—to find such teachings. He also writes that the student of *halakhah* who wants to know what Jewish law says or which Jewish laws derive from which biblical verses will have to read other biblical commentaries to get that information.[36]

Rashbam has very circumscribed goals in his biblical exegetical works. He sets out to explain some aspects of what the biblical text means while ignoring others. Just as he omits from his commentary discussions of the text's religious or moral significance—even though such issues are crucial to him—he also sets for himself very limited goals when it comes to literary analysis.

Notes

1. In Ibn Ezra's longer commentary to Exodus 20: 1. See particularly the passage found in *Peirushei ha-Torah*, ed. A. Weiser 2: 127–31, or in Krinski, *Torah meḥoqeqei Yehudah* 2: 296–301. See also Ibn Ezra, *Sefat yeter*, 32 (paragraph 84).

2. For Kimḥi, see, e.g., commentary on Genesis 24:39. For ibn Kaspi, see, e.g., his *Mishneh Kesef*, *Tirat Kesef*, 111–12 and 124. For Kara, see, e.g., his commentary to Judges 13:12, Eppenstein's edition, 37–38.

3. In Greenberg, ed., *Parshanut ha-Miqra ha-yehudit*, 56.

4. See, e.g., the discussion of Moses Maimonides' attitude to poetry in Twersky, *Introduction to the Code of Maimonides*, 250–52. Many texts can be cited to prove Ibn Ezra's negative attitude specifically to liturgical poetry (*piyyuṭ*); see, e.g., the long excursus in the commentary to Ecclesiastes 5:1. See also the general discussion in Yahalom, *Sefat ha-shir*.

5. *Ḥiqqui shel hitḥarut*, a phrase first coined by Aḥad Ha-Am. See his *'Al parashat derakhim*, 1: 175.

6. Berger, "Judaism and General Culture," 72–84, 117–25.

7. See Lockshin, *Rashbam's Commentary on Exodus*, 219, n. 24, and Kanarfogel, *Jewish Education and Society*, 169–70, n. 37.

8. The works of Touitou (e.g., "*'Al shiṭato shel Rashbam*" and others show a lively interchange between Rashbam and Christian exegetes of his period; I argue here only that an approach to literary theory was not part of that interchange.

9. See my discussion in Lockshin, "Tradition or Context."

10. See, e.g., in his commentary to Genesis 1:1 and 37:2, and in the introduction to his commentary on Exodus 21.

11. See, e.g., his *Safah berurah,* 4b-6a, esp. "what the Rabbis say is [to be considered] true, because they received traditions" (5a).

12. See, e.g., Rashbam's Talmud commentary to Bava Batra 75b, s.v. *shalosh,* or to BB 121b, s.v. *'elai.*

13. See, e.g., Rashbam's commentary to BT Bava Batra 48b, s.v. *tinaḥ*, where he polemicizes at length against Rashi's teachers who had defined a law that the Talmud derived by analogy (*gezerah shawah*) as being solely of rabbinic origin. (In this approach, Rashbam follows the lead of Rashi, who made the point a number of times in his Talmud commentary; see, e.g., his commentary on BT Git. 33a, s.v. *be'ilat zenut.*) See also the dispute between Rashbam and his brother, Rabbeinu Tam, in Tosafot, Ḥagigah 18a, s.v. *ḥolo shel mo'ed.*

14. See, e.g., his commentary to Genesis 49:9, s.v. *mi-ṭeref,* and to 49:16, s.v. *dan.*

15. See, e.g., Ibn Ezra's introduction to his Torah commentary, *ha-derekh ha-revi'it* in *Peirushei ha-Torah,* 1:7–9. It is hard to imagine Rashbam belittling the midrashic method in the way that Ibn Ezra does there.

16. Mekhilta *Kaspa* 2, ed. Lauterbach, 3: 144. See also BT Bava Meṣi'a 38b.

17. BT Rosh ha-Shanah 9a.

18. See Lockshin, *Rabbi Samuel ben Meir's Commentary on Genesis,* 400–21, and the literature cited there on 400, n. 1. See also Malkiel, "'Eqron ha-haqdamot."

19. See his commentary to Exodus 7:26. See also, e.g., Greenberg, *Understanding Exodus,* 171: "That pattern was first sketched by Rashbam." Greenberg also notes there (n. 1) that it is possible to see this pattern reflected earliest well before Rashbam in the mnemonic of the tanna, R. Yehudah, *deṣakh 'adash be'aḥav* quoted in the Passover Haggadah.

20. See, e.g., Abarbanel's commentary to Exodus 7:26, and Greenberg, *Understanding Exodus.* See also some further sources cited in N. Sarna's *The JPS Torah Commentary: Exodus,* 38, and in Lockshin, *Rashbam's Commentary on Exodus,* 75, n. 23.

21. See David Rosin's introduction to Samuel ben Meir, *Perush ha-Torah,* xxix. The notes to my translations of Rashbam on Genesis and on Exodus point out many similarities between the commentaries which, perhaps, give evidence of borrowing by Rashbam.

22. "I asked myself about these three [plagues] why was there no warning about them. . . . This follows the principle that we learned in the Mishnah [Sanhedrin 9:5], 'When someone has been punished but still repeats his sin a second time, one puts him into a prison-cell and feeds him barley until his stomach bursts.'"

23. See Rashbam's commentary to Exodus 2:6, s.v. *we-hinneh,* where he discusses the chiasms both in that passage and in 1 Sam 1:5. See Lockshin, *Rashbam's Commentary on Exodus,* 24, nn. 19 and 21.

24. See Rashbam's commentary and my notes, there, and to Exodus 4:9.

25. See Rashbam's commentary and my notes to Genesis 49:25, to Exodus 16:24, and to Leviticus 19:11–12.

26. *Hippukh ha-seder 'oseh hefseq.* See Kogut, *Ha-Miqra bein ṭe'amim le-farshanut,* 88–89 and n. 44 there.

27. See Rashi's list of rhetorical questions in his commentary to Genesis 3:9. See also Joseph Kara's list of rhetorical questions in his commentary to Numbers 22:9 published by Abraham Berliner in *Peleiṭat soferim,* 22. There Kara explains at length the function of rhetorical questions: "This is the pattern: when one attempts to entrap someone through his own speech, one asks him a question [to which the answer is already known, simply] so that the person will answer. Once he answers, one can engage him on the topic and express one's own opinion on the subject."

28. See, e.g., Rashbam's commentary to Genesis 18:9, which discusses a number of rhetorical questions. Rashbam simply says of them: *ve-khol zeh derekh hatḥalat dibbur.* See also Touitou's "Perushim ḥadashim shel Rashbam la-Torah," 94. There Touitou identifies a MS comment on

the rhetorical question of Genesis 18:9 as Rashbam's. The comment reads: *ken derekh ha-Miqra le-dabber*.

29. See, e.g., the commentary of Rashi to verse 8 and to verse 9, where Rashi understands that the two phrases about Moses reporting to God mean that Moses reported on two separate occasions. Rashi's approach is the more common one in the Jewish exegetical tradition.

30. Rashbam labels this pattern *kolel we-'aḥar kakh mefaresh*, "a general statement followed by the details." See my discussion of that term in my notes to Rashbam's commentary to Exodus 19:8 and 2:15.

31. *'Otah sha'ah*. Kara's commentary on this passage in Exodus may be found in Grossman, "Mi-genizat Iṭalyah," 22–23. For further discussion of this passage, see Lockshin, *Rashbam's Commentary on Exodus*, 203–5, nn. 8–11.

32. *Kefel* (or *kafal*) *ha-'inyan be-millim shonot*. Concerning the understanding of this phenomenon by medieval exegetes, see Kugel, *Idea of Biblical Poetry*, On the general issue of sensitivity to literary issues see also Harris, "The Literary Hermeneutic," 171–203.

33. Rashi's explanation, following BT Qiddushin 22b, reads as follows:

In what way are the door and the doorpost different from all other objects in the home? The Holy One, blessed be he said: "The door and the doorpost were my witnesses in Egypt when I passed over the lintel and the two doorposts and I said (Lev 25:55), 'For it is to me that the Israelites are servants'; they are my servants, and not servants of servants. But this man went and acquired himself a master. Let him be pierced in their presence."

34. Many more examples of this phenomenon could be cited. Another striking one is the difference between Rashi and Rashbam in explaining the perhaps unusual choice of the caulking materials with which baby Moses' basket was sealed (Exod 2:3). For Rashi, the text teaches us something about Moses' righteousness; for Rashbam, it says something about how you keep water out of a basket. See Lockshin, *Rashbam's Commentary on Exodus*, 21, n. 11.

35. Introduction to Ashkenazi, *Qeren Shemu'el*. The text is cited in Lockshin, *Rashbam's Commentary on Exodus*, 396. There (395–99) I also discuss some of the issues raised here about Rashbam's exegetical goals.

36. Rashbam often makes this point. See, for example, his introduction to Exodus 21 or his introduction to Leviticus.

Bibliography

Ahad Ha-Am. *'Al parashat derakhim* (At a crossroads). 2d ed. 3 vols. Berlin, 1902.

Ashkenazi, Shelomoh Zalman. *Qeren Shemu'el*. Frankfurt, 1727.

Berger, David. "Judaism and General Culture in Medieval and Modern Times." In *Judaism's Encounter with Other Cultures: Rejection or Integration?* Ed. J. J. Schacter, 72–125. Northvale, N.J.: Jason Aronson, 1997.

Berliner, Abraham. *Peleiṭat soferim*. Mainz, 1872.

Greenberg, Moshe, ed. *Parshanut ha-Miqra ha-yehudit* (Jewish Bible exegesis). 2d ed. Jerusalem: Mosad Bialik, 1992.

——. *Understanding Exodus*. New York: Behrman House, 1969.

Grossman, Abraham. *Ḥakhmei Ṣarefat ha-rishonim* (Early Sages of France). Jerusalem: Magnes Press, 1995.

——. "Mi-'genizat 'Iṭalyah': seridim mi-peirush Rabbi Yosef Qara la-Torah" ("From the Italian Geniza"—remnants of the commentary of R. Yosef Qara on the Torah). *Pe'amim* 52 (Summer 1992): 16–36.

Harris, Robert A., "The Literary Hermeneutic of Rabbi Eliezer of Beaugency." Ph.D. diss., Jewish Theological Seminary of America, 1997.

Ibn Ezra, Abraham. *Peirushei ha-Torah*. Ed. Asher Weiser. 3 vols. Jerusalem: Mossad Harav Kook, 1976.

——. *Safah berurah*. Fürth, 1839.

——. *Sefat yeter*. Warsaw, 1895.

Kanarfogel, Ephraim. *Jewish Education and Society in the High Middle Ages*. Detroit: Wayne State University Press, 1992.

Kara, Joseph. *Peirushei Rabbi Yosef Qara li-Nevi'im rishonim*. Ed. S. Eppenstein. Jerusalem: Mossad Harav Kook, 1972.

Kaspi, Joseph Ibn. *Mishneh Kesef, Ṭirat Kesef*. Pressburg, 1915.

Kogut, Simcha. *Ha-Miqra bein ṭe'amim le-farshanut* (Correlations between biblical accentuation and traditional Jewish exegesis). Jerusalem: Magnes Press, 1994.

Krinski, Y. L., ed. *Ḥamishah ḥumshei Torah 'im peirush 'al 'Ibn 'Ezra Meḥoqeqei Yehudah*. 5 vols. 1906; reprint, Jerusalem, 1961/2.

Kugel, James. *The Idea of Biblical Poetry: Parallelism and Its History*. New Haven, Conn.: Yale University Press, 1981.

Lockshin, Martin, trans. *Rabbi Samuel ben Meir's Commentary on Genesis: An Annotated Translation*. Lewiston: Edwin Mellen Press, 1990.

——, trans. *Rashbam's Commentary on Exodus: An Annotated Translation*. Atlanta, Ga.: Scholars Press, 1997.

——. Trans. *Rashbam's Commentary on Leviticus: An Annotated Translation*. Providence: Brown Judaic Studies, 2001.

——. "Tradition or Context: Two Exegetes Struggle with Peshat." In *From Ancient Israel to Modern Judaism: Intellect in Quest of Understanding: Essays in Honor of Marvin Fox*. Ed. J. Neusner, E. Frerichs, and N. Sarna. Vol. 2, 173–86. Atlanta, Ga.: Scholars Press, 1989.

Malkiel, Orly. "'Eqron ha-haqdamot bĕfarshanut Rashbam 'al ha-Torah." Master's thesis, Hebrew University of Jerusalem, 1997.

Mekhilta de-Rabbi Yishma''el. Ed. J. Z. Lauterbach. 3 vols. Philadelphia: Jewish Publication Society, 1935.

Samuel ben Meir. *Peirush ha-Torah*. Ed. David Rosin. Breslau, 1881.

Sarna, Nahum. *The JPS Torah Commentary: Exodus*. Philadelphia: Jewish Publication Society, 1991.

Touitou, E. "'Al shiṭato shel Rashbam be-feirusho la-Torah" (Concerning the methodology of R. Samuel b. Meir in his commentary to the Pentateuch). *Tarbiẓ* 48 (1978–79): 248–73.

——. "Peirushim ḥadashim shel Rashbam la-Torah 'al pi ketav yad Winah 23" (New interpretations of Rashbam on the Torah according to MS Vienna 23). In *Meḥqarim ba-Miqra uve-ḥinnukh muggashim le-profesor Mosheh 'Arend*. Ed. Dov Rappel, 87–104. Jerusalem: Touro College Press, 1996.

Twersky, Isadore. *Introduction to the Code of Maimonides (Mishneh Torah)*. New Haven, Conn.: Yale University Press, 1980.

Yahalom, Joseph. *Sefat ha-shir shel ha-piyyuṭ ha'Ereṣ-Yisre'eli ha-qadum* (Poetic language in the early Piyyut). Jerusalem: Magnes Press, 1985.

7

Asceticism and Eroticism in Medieval Jewish Philosophical and Mystical Exegesis of the Song of Songs

ELLIOT R. WOLFSON

Eroticism, Asceticism, and Mystical Experience

At first blush it might appear that the title of this study brings together two themes of a mutually exclusive nature. Asceticism, conventionally understood, implies rigorous discipline of body and soul and the adoption of an austere lifestyle, which in some cases leads to the abrogation of desire, self-denial, and self-mortification. Eroticism, by contrast, entails the sense of ecstatic rapture that ensues from the inspired indulgence in matters of the body and the full embrace of the sensual. In the case of both asceticism and eroticism, moreover, there is a paradoxical confluence of life and death, but from opposite ends of the spectrum: asceticism is the negation of life that occasions a simulation of death, eroticism the affirmation of life even to the point of death.

When one probes more deeply, however, it becomes apparent that asceticism and eroticism are not necessarily oppositional. Indeed, the ascetic impulse manifest in pious devotion may itself be rooted in erotic desire, which is a recurring element in the phenomenology of religious experience.[1] Matters pertaining to the sacred can be depicted erotically because there is a presumption with respect to the sacred nature of the erotic. In the medieval setting of Judaism, Islam, and Christianity, this is enhanced by the common Platonic heritage according to which the intelligible realm is itself rendered in distinctively erotic language.[2] It is commonplace for historians of religion to emphasize, therefore, that the love of God is often expressed in the language of human sexuality. But the issue is not merely one of expression. The texture of intense religious experience frequently is marked by the tension between yearning and fulfillment.[3] As Georges Bataille put it, "The saint turns from the voluptuary in alarm; she does not know that his unacknowledgeable passions and her own are really one."[4] To be sure, in traditional communities, the erotic aspect of the saintly life is not fulfilled by the satiation of physical desire, but by union with the spirit. The celibate calling nevertheless elicits a response no less erotic than that aroused by carnal temptation for one in pursuit of sensual pleasure.

The confluence of eroticism and asceticism is especially prevalent in the realm of mystical religious experience.[5] As is well known, a central (if not defining) feature of mysticism cultivated within theistic traditions is the experience of communion of the individual soul with the personal God. Typically, such experiences are described in terms of love, betrothal, marriage, and consummation. The soul, which is feminized for both men and women,[6] expresses its desire for the divine, personified as the male bridegroom, through amorous images such as kissing, caressing, and copulation. It would be misleading to interpret these forms of erotic spirituality in the Freudian sense of sublimation. Mystics do not fit neatly into Freud's clinical category of the repressed subject who is ignorant of the libidinal force that he sublimates. On the contrary, mystics consciously appropriate modes of discourse from the realm of sensual love, for they are well aware of the amorous nature of religious experience. Therefore, we would do better to speak of the *transformation* of sexual energy rather than its displacement.

Allegorization of the Erotic in Medieval Jewish Exegesis

Medieval rabbinic exegesis of the Song of Songs presented an array of possible readings.[7] The midrashic orientation to the Song with a tendency toward historical allegory was preserved and expanded, particularly in the Ashkenazi tradition exemplified by Rashi.[8] In addition to this approach, philosophical and mystical interpretations of the Song abounded in the Jewish Middle Ages. In spite of the substantial differences between the philosophical and the kabbalistic perspectives on many doctrinal issues, with respect to the spiritualized understanding of the erotic images of the Song there is an important affinity between philosopher and kabbalist.[9] Indeed, the mystical conception of the union of the soul and God expressed in both theosophic and prophetic kabbalah (the two major trends of kabbalistic speculation that took shape in thirteenth-century Spain) is indebted to the philosophical interpretation of the Song as an allegorical depiction of the relationship of the female soul to the masculine God or to the Active Intellect.[10] By contrast, Scholem has argued that the Spanish kabbalah in its early period is to be distinguished from other forms of mysticism, especially that of Christianity, by the fact that man's relation to God is not portrayed in erotic images. In support of his claim, Scholem asserts that the interpretation of the Song as an allegorical depiction of the soul's yearning for union with the divine is lacking in kabbalistic sources until the sixteenth century.[11] Moshe Idel has argued that Scholem's view is valid with respect to theosophic kabbalah, but not in the case of ecstatic kabbalah.[12] As I will argue later, however, even in thirteenth-century theosophic kabbalah, one can find evidence for the allegorical interpretation of the Song as an erotic dialogue between the soul and God.

Brief allusions to the philosophical orientation are found already in Baḥya ibn Paquda's classical work of Jewish pietism, *Ḥovot ha-levavot* (Duties of the heart), which is clearly modeled on a Sufi paradigm. In particular, Baḥya cites from the Song in support of the notion that the pietistic ideal entails the all-consuming love of God, which is realized only in a state of contemplative isolation (*hitbodedut*).[13] Interestingly enough, in the introduction to his commentary on the Song, Abraham Ibn Ezra specifically rejects the philosophers (*'anshei meḥqar*) who interpret the biblical narrative as a reference to the union of the supernal, masculine soul and the female body as antithetical to the allegorical approach adopted by the Rabbis.[14] Ibn Ezra's remark is somewhat problematic inasmuch as in his own poetry as well as in his *'Iggeret Ḥai ben Meqiṣ*, an adaptation of Avicenna's *Ḥayy ibn Yaqẓān*,[15] he does apply philosophical allegory to verses from the Song, an approach that jibes with that taken in other parts of his scriptural commentary.[16] This comment, regardless of its sincerity, is clear evidence that by the twelfth century a philosophical allegory of the Song had taken its place alongside the allegorical interpretations of the Rabbis. Thus we find, for example, in the *Torat ha-nefesh* (Doctrine of the soul), falsely attributed to Baḥya, that the soul is identified explicitly as the female voice of the Song, Shulamit, because of her peaceful return from the world to her ontological source in the divine. The erotic content of the Song, therefore, relates to the desire and love of the rational soul for the Creator.[17]

The philosophical approach is attested as well in the works of Maimonides. For example, in the *Mishneh Torah*, Maimonides explicitly states that the entire Song of Songs is a parable (*mashal*) for the all-consuming love of the soul for God.[18] Along similar lines, in the context of explicating the ideal of the intellectual worship of God, Maimonides cites the verse, "I was asleep, but my heart was wakeful" (Song 5:2), to provide scriptural support for the idea that those inclined to prophecy experience the union of the rational soul and the divine,[19] an exegesis that is repeated by Abraham Maimonides in his treatise on Jewish Sufism, the *Highways to Perfection*.[20] In the continuation of the aforementioned passage from the *Guide*, Maimonides interprets the kiss mentioned in Song 1:2 as a reference to the comprehension that arises as a result of the passionate love (*'ishq*) for God,[21] which is followed by the experience of ecstatic death (related to the rabbinic trope of the death of the righteous by a kiss[22]), which is in fact deliverance from physical mortality and the limitations of the body.[23] Maimonides, therefore, appropriates the erotic symbolism to depict the contemplative ideal of union, the intellectual love,[24] which is also identified as true worship and the highest level of prophecy.

The philosophical reading is given its fullest expression in the commentaries on the Song composed in the thirteenth century by Joseph ibn Aknin and Moses ibn Tibbon. Ibn Aknin proposed three approaches to the book: *peshaṭ*, *derash*, and *sod*, which correspond respectively to the philological, homiletical, and philosophical. The three hermeneutical approaches are also related to the three human faculties—the natural, the animalistic, and the rational. The last approach, which is presented as the truly esoteric or internal meaning of the text, assumes that the erotic dialogue between bride and bridegroom relates to the desire of the human soul to become one with the Active Intellect.[25] The attainment of this state is clearly predicated on the liberation of the intellect from the subjugation of physical pleasures.[26] Nevertheless, erotic imagery is the most appropriate to characterize the longing of the soul for union with the Active Intellect even if there is no precise parallel between the contemplative and carnal forms of eros. Thus, to cite one example, in his interpretation of the kiss mentioned in Song 1:2, ibn Aknin writes, "Its explanation according to my approach is that the rational [soul] compares the dissemination of the lights of the [Active] Intellect upon her to the kisses of the mouth . . . and this is intellectual pleasure."[27]

In spite of some minor differences in interpreting certain images and phrases in the Song, Moses ibn Tibbon adopts the same hermeneutical approach as that of ibn Aknin. That is, he similarly affirms that the ultimate meaning of the Song is related to the "belief in the conjunction of the soul of man, that is, the rational [soul], with the Separate Intellect, for through this faith is the survival of the soul of man after death possible."[28] Ibn Tibbon accepts the standard medieval notion (which has its roots in antiquity) that the weaker party of any pair is depicted as feminine and the stronger as masculine. Thus, matter is configured as female and form male, the soul female and the intellect male, the intellect of man female and the Separate Intellect male.[29] In a state of potentiality, the soul is characterized as female, but when it is actualized it is male.[30] Commenting on the image of the kiss in Song 1:2, ibn Tibbon writes: "'Oh, let him kiss me' alludes to the fact that conjunction of the soul of man and the Separate Intellect is possible. . . . The conjunction of man with the Separate Intellect involves the intellect alone, for when he comprehends it, it is conjoined to him. The reality of the forms is in the intellect alone, for they are not matter so that the one is conjoined to the other, body to body."[31]

In a manner similar to the exegetical strategy prevalent in Christian authors, a resemblance explicable on the basis of the shared indebtedness to Aristotelian and Neoplatonic sources, the sensual images of the biblical text were applied figuratively by these Jewish exegetes to the contemplative desire of the human intellect for union with God (or the Active Intellect).[32] The philosophical orientation took root in the cultural climate of the golden age of Hispanic Jewry, reflecting the particular impact of Greco-Arabic philosophy. To appreciate the unique contribution of the Sephardic thinkers in formulating a philosophical-mystical interpretation of the Song, however, it is necessary to bear in mind that the new secular poetry composed by the Hispano-Jewish poets undoubtedly revived the erotic element in the literal reading of this biblical book. On the other hand, the attempt to combine Arabic love poetry and the rabbinic liturgical use of the Song also leads to the allegorization of the love poems.[33] More important, the same poets who utilized the erotic symbolism of the Song in their secular love poetry also applied a philosophical allegory to it, understanding the overtly erotic imagery as a figurative depiction of the rational soul's longing for union with God. The application of images culled from the Song to refer to the relationship between God and the soul shifted the focus from national eschatology to personal salvation.[34]

Ecstatic and Theosophic Elements in Kabbalistic Allegoresis

In the history of scholarship on medieval kabbalah, it is generally assumed that the individualizing interpretation[35] of the Song of Songs as an imaginative representation of the love of the soul for matters spiritual, which was cultivated by a rabbinic elite given to a kind of philosophical mysticism,[36] had its greatest impact on the prophetic kabbalah developed by Abraham Abulafia.[37] In a measure this is true insofar as Abulafia's mystical teaching is a unique blend of Maimonidean philosophy and ancient Jewish esotericism (principally mediated through the writings of the German Pietists).[38] Abulafia follows Maimonides in affirming the love of God as the apex of intellectual worship. The passionate relationship between the mystic and God is also portrayed by Abulafia in the erotic images of the Song, especially the symbol of the kiss. Abulafia relates the bridegroom and bride to the rational soul and the Active Intellect respectively, the erotic union of the two constituting the mystical significance of prophecy.[39] He even goes so far as to interpret the midrashic understanding of the Song in these terms. That is, on an exoteric level the Song is a parable about the community of Israel and God, but esoterically it alludes to the relationship of the rational soul and the Active Intellect.

The influence of the philosophical approach to the Song is evident in a passage in the *Ginnat 'egoz*, a late thirteenth-century work by Abulafia's disciple, Joseph Gikatilla, which combines Maimonidean thought and various forms of linguistic and numerical mysticism.[40] In line with the philosophical interpretation, Gikatilla describes the experience of prophecy as the separation of the rational soul from the body and its consequent conjunction with the intelligible world (*'olam ha-śekhel*), identified further as the angelic beings that are incorporeal light. Gikatilla relates these immaterial and translucent forms to the waters mentioned by Akiva in his warning to those who entered Pardes (according to the version of the legend in the Babylonian Talmud, Ḥagigah 14b) not to say "water, water" when they come upon the pure marble stones. "These are the waters," writes Gikatilla, "that are entirely the inner, intelligible, spiritual, subtle light. . . . Concerning these waters it says, 'Abundant waters cannot quench love' (Song 8:7). Love is not a corporeal matter that the waters could quench, but rather the waters are intelligible waters and the love is intelligible love."[41] *'Ahavah śikhlit*, a love that comes by way of intellect, commands the intense passion of the soul for the object of its longing. The Song expresses poetically the fervor of mind in its desire to be conjoined to the intelligible world of incorporeal light.

It would be wrong, however, to limit the impact of the philosophical interpretation exclusively to the trend of kabbalah cultivated by Abulafia and his followers. Indeed, there is ample evidence that other kabbalists in the formative period acknowledged the individualizing orientation with respect to the Song.[42] I do not wish to argue with the standard, and certainly valid, point of view that many kabbalists (early on and through the generations) have applied the erotic imagery of the Song to the masculine and feminine potencies of the divine.[43] Nevertheless, these very kabbalists did affirm a more personalistic and mystical stance when interpreting the Song.

The following remark from the earliest kabbalistic commentary on the Song by Ezra ben Solomon of Gerona illustrates this point:

> "Oh, let him kiss me with the kisses of his mouth" (Song 1:2): These are the words of the glory, which desires and yearns to ascend, to be conjoined and to be illuminated in the supernal light that has no image. It ascends in thought and in will, and thus it speaks in the third person. The kiss is a symbol for the joy of the conjunction of the soul in the source of life and for the abundance of the Holy Spirit. Thus it says, "of the kisses of his mouth," for each and every cause receives the thought and the increase from that sweet light and resplendent splendor. When he speaks with the glory, which is the gate to the entities, he speaks in the third person.[44]

The verse from the Song can be read in two ways, referring either to the intradivine relationship between the feminine and masculine glories or to the ecstatic encounter of the soul and the glory.[45] According to the first reading, the kiss signifies the aspiration of the lower, feminine glory (*Shekhinah*) to ascend and to be united with the upper, masculine glory (*Tif'eret*). By contrast, according to the second reading, the kiss is symbolic of the delight that the soul experiences when it is conjoined to the divine glory. In this case, then, the soul of the male mystic assumes the persona of the feminine lover and the divine glory that of the male beloved. The passage of Ezra attests that at a relatively early literary stage the feminization of the male mystic in relation to the masculine God is found in the symbolism of theosophic kabbalah and is not associated exclusively with ecstatic kabbalah.[46] Consistent with other mystical traditions, theosophic and ecstatic kabbalists portrayed the soul of the mystic as feminine in relation to the male deity. In particular, I would note that with respect to this reversal of gender roles, there is a striking phenomenological similarity between the kabbalah and Christian mysticism, for the latter is based in great measure on the appropriation of the erotic imagery of the Song to depict the soul's relationship to Christ: the male mystic assumes the voice of the female beloved and Jesus that of the male lover. According to the mystical exegesis of the Song in both traditions, the overtly heterosexual language of the biblical narrative is transmuted into a spiritualized homoeroticism.[47] As I will suggest at length in the conclusion of this essay, the homoerotic bond of the male kabbalist and the divine presence is predicated on the ascetic abrogation of carnal desire.

In the final analysis, the theosophic and ecstatic readings offered by Ezra cannot be separated, because the realm of divine potencies provides the ontological structure that occasions the mystical experience of union, an experience poetically rendered by the image of the kiss.[48] The kiss of the *Shekhinah* symbolizes the conjunction of the soul in the source of life and the consequent overflow of the Holy Spirit.[49] Thus, in the introduction to his commentary, Ezra refers to individuals who interpret the erotic imagery of the Song theosophically as the "true Sages of Israel" who "receive the face of the *Shekhinah*,"[50] in contrast to both those who take it literally and those who explain it allegorically. Ecstatic conjunction with the divine is an integral part of the theosophic hermeneutics.

The point is underscored in another kabbalistic commentary on the Song, composed by Isaac ibn Sahula somewhat later, in thirteenth-century Castile. Ibn Sahula is explicitly critical of ibn Aknin's philosophical interpretation of the Song as a dialogue between the rational soul and the Active Intellect. In spite of ibn Sahula's criticism, however, he was greatly influenced by ibn Aknin and indeed incorporated in his own commentary his allegorical interpretation as the "revealed way" (*derekh ha-nigleh*), which stands in contrast to the "hidden way" (*derekh ha-nistar*).[51] More important, the esoteric interpretation presented by ibn Sahula is not merely theosophical in nature. His kabbalistic orientation entails a mystical-ecstatic dimension, which shares much in common with the philosophical outlook, especially as it relates to the conjunction of the soul and the divine. Consider, for example, ibn Sahula's explanation of the title, *shir ha-shirim*, "song of songs":[52] in spite of ibn Sahula's rejection of ibn Aknin's philosophical allegory, he explains the mystical mechanics of the song, which underlie the book as a whole, in terms of a process that is very close in spirit (if not terminology) to the philosophical idea of conjunction. Indeed, ibn Sahula explicitly states that the soul of the one who hears the song is "escorted and conjoined to that which is above."[53] The theosophic interpretation, which is quantitatively more prevalent, cannot be understood properly without one's taking into account the mystical dimension.

The intersection of the two hermeneutical tracks is most evident in ibn Sahula's treatment of the image of the kiss related in Song 1:2. In a manner similar to that of Ezra, ibn Sahula presents two explanations, which I call the theosophical and the ecstatic. The symbolic meaning of the kiss is the "emanation of the spirit from its source," but this can be applied to the *Shekhinah* in relation to the potencies above her or to the soul in relation to the *Shekhinah*. The Song begins with the verse, "Oh, let him kiss me with the kisses of his mouth," "in order to arouse man so that he yearns for this supernal gradation . . . to provide him with the support to assist him in being conjoined to him in the manner of lovers who out of the abundance of their affection are conjoined to one another."[54]

The same claim can be made with respect to the interpretation of the Song found in the *Zohar*, the major kabbalistic anthology that surfaced in Castile in the latter decades of the thirteenth century and the beginning of the fourteenth. The theosophic reading of the Song as a symbolic narrative about the relationship of the male and female potencies of the divine is combined with the ecstatic rendering of the Song as a dialogue between the human soul (personified as the feminine) and the divine (imaged as male).[55] Thus, following the earlier examples of Ezra and ibn Sahula, the *Zohar* provides two concurrent explanations for Song 1:2[56] According to one line of interpretation, the one who utters the verse "Oh, let him kiss me with the kisses of his mouth" is the *Shekhinah*, designated by the technical expression "Community of Israel" (*keneset Yiśra'el*), and the one addressed is *Tif'eret*. In that case, the kiss denotes the conjunction of the *Shekhinah*, imaged as the feminine beloved, with *Tif'eret*, the masculine lover.[57] According to the second line of interpretation, the one uttering the verse is the human soul (or, more specifically in terms of the historical and literary context of zoharic literature, the soul of the male Jew) who addresses the *Shekhinah*. The kiss signifies the union of the lower spirit of the *ṣaddiq*, the righteous Jewish man, and the upper spirit of the divine, (*'itdabquta' de-ruḥa be-ruḥa*),[58] a union that is also represented by the kiss of death. In a manner consonant with Maimonides, the author of the zoharic passage assumes that the kiss of death signifies the passionate union of the soul and God, which is in fact the salvation from the death of body.[59]

The two interpretations in the *Zohar* cannot be isolated, for it is precisely the ecstatic union of the male mystic and the *Shekhinah* that promotes the unification of the latter and her masculine partner in the divine realm. Indeed, basic to the zoharic symbology is the view that the erotic impulse of the divine feminine to cohabit with the masculine is triggered by the arousal from below, which is brought about by the communion of the group of enlightened (*maskilim*) with the divine feminine.[60] The principle is stated clearly in one passage, which explicates the conjunction of David with the three patriarchs who constitute the divine chariot: "The desire of the female towards the male occurs only when a spirit enters into her and casts fluid corresponding to the supernal, masculine waters. Analogously, the Community of Israel is not aroused in relation to the Holy One, blessed be He, except by means of the spirit of the righteous who enter into her."[61] The interpretation of the metaphor of the kiss in the Song is a specific exegetical application of the larger ontological principle. Moreover, the erotic encounter with the *Shekhinah* on the part of the righteous souls inverts the gender attribution, for the male below is feminized and the female above masculinized.[62] Subsequently, I shall return to this reversal of gender roles prompted by the eros of the mystical experience of communion (*devequt*).

The theosophic reading, which is obviously central to the understanding of the Song in the *Zohar*,[63] cannot be separated from the psychological-ecstatic interpretation, nor can it be severed from the historical-allegorical sense, which, in fact, would have been understood by the medieval kabbalists as the *peshaṭ*, the contextual sense, of the Song. The socio-economic and political condition of Israel in this world reflects the ontological state of the divine above. The erotic yearning expressed in the Song aptly depicts the exile, which in its deepest symbolic sense alludes to the separation of the male and female aspects of the divine, the unification of which characterizes the redemption. I will here mention one passage that illustrates the point.[64] The erotic desire spoken by the female persona in the Song, "Upon my couch at night [I sought the one I love—I sought, but found him not]" (3:1), is applied by the *Zohar* to the divine feminine, the *Shekhinah*, which is identified further as the Community of Israel. The *Shekhinah* utters the words of longing before the masculine potency, for in the state of exile she is separated from him. The *hieros gamos* occurs within the spatial confines of the holy of holies of the Temple, but since in the time of exile the latter is not standing, there is no space wherein this union can be fully realized. Thus the feminine expresses her yearning to cohabit with the masculine, to inhabit the same space, nay to be the space wherein the phallic foundation is laid. Ever mindful of the standard medieval Christian triumphalist claim regarding God's rejection of Israel, the *Zohar* is quick to point out that even though the *Shekhinah* is in a lowly state, reflecting the depraved condition of Israel in exile, the Jews are still the only ones among the nations who can truly hear the word of God. The calling out by Israel in an effort to respond to the divine voice is correlated with the erotic longing expressed by the *Shekhinah* in relation to *Tif'eret*. Symbolically, the eroticism of the Song—marked by the ceaseless pull of attraction and push of deferment—must be interpreted in light of this theosophic dynamic.

According to other passages in the *Zohar*, the utterance of the Song celebrates not only the desire of the female for the male, which marks the temporal transition from exile to redemption, but the moment of consummation wherein the fragmentariness is overcome and the sense of integration is realized. The matter is expressed as follows in a passage from a fragment on the Song assigned to the *Midrash ha-ne'elam* section of zoharic literature: "In that moment, when everything was removed from the world, and the wife remained face-to-face with her husband, the Song of Songs was revealed."[65] Building upon the midrashic tradition that located the recitation of the Song by Solomon on the day of the dedication of the Jerusalem Temple,[66] the zoharic author interprets that historical moment in theosophic terms as a reference to the union of the masculine king in the feminine palace, a union that is also depicted by the symbolism of enthronement or that of the full moon illuminated by the light of the sun.[67] Thus, in one passage, the efficacy of the songs uttered respectively by Moses, David, and Solomon is distinguished in the following way: the song of Moses ascended to the heights but it did not descend, for the ultimate purpose of his song was to offer praise to the supernal King so that miracles would be performed in order to save Israel; the song of David was an attempt to adorn the Matrona and her maiden; the song of Solomon was aimed at bringing the Matrona under the bridal canopy to unite with her masculine consort. Whereas Moses united with the *Shekhinah* below so that there would be union in the terrestrial realm, Solomon at first facilitated the union above between the bride and the bridegroom in the canopy, and then he invited them to the Temple built below.[68]

The Elevation of the *Shekhinah* and the Transposition of Gender

The recitation of the Song signifies the moment of erotic coupling that occurs in both realms of being, but it is particularly the effect that this unification has on the *Shekhinah* that most engaged the imagination of the kabbalists of the *Zohar*. The mystical significance of the Song relates principally to the ontological transformation of the *Shekhinah*, which is portrayed in a number of different figurative tropes. For example, in one passage, the zoharic author describes the purification of the "lower point," that is, the *Shekhinah*, from all the other hymns that are gathered within the celestial palace that is called *zevul*. "And when it is purified from everything, it ascends above in the secret of the song, and it is called the 'Song of Songs,' and it rises above all those praises, and it is purified from them all." This process of purification (*berur*) is depicted, as is the female being prepared for her union with the male, a process that is also related exegetically to the account of the building of the Temple from the *'even shelemah*, the stones cut from the quarry (1 Kings 6:7). The cutting of the stones alludes symbolically to the mystery of the splitting of the primordial androgyne so that the female other could be constructed to provide the space in which the male could procreate and thereby extend himself.[69]

The ontological elevation of the status of the *Shekhinah* in relation to the Song is expressed in slightly different terms in another passage: "When Solomon built the Temple and the lower world was perfected in the manner of the upper world, all of Israel were righteous, and they ascended in several supernal gradations, and then the throne of glory ascended in joy with several delights and several ascensions."[70] The utterance of the Song at the time of the building of the Temple is associated with the ascent of the throne, which is one of the standard symbols employed by kabbalists to describe the *Shekhinah*. The elevation of the *Shekhinah* in the form of the ascending throne signifies the transformation of gender that follows her reunion with the masculine potency.[71] In one passage, this motif of the dedication of the Temple is marked by the elevation of the wisdom of Solomon, which signifies the *hieros gamos* of the King and the Matrona. The consequence of the union is the illumination of the face of the Matrona and the increase in her gradation (*darga*), which is celebrated in the utterance of the Song.[72] In another passage, the alteration in the ontological status of the *Shekhinah*, which is related exegetically to the verse "If you do not know, fairest of women, go follow the tracks of the sheep, and graze your kids by the tents of the shepherds" (Song 1:8), is represented as the transmogrification of the letter *yod* into the letter *he*, the opening of the female space (a "single dark point") to receive the male in coitus, as a result of which the female herself overflows to all sides and thereby sustains the beings beneath her.[73]

The esoteric meaning of the Song thus alludes to the gender transformation of the *Shekhinah* that follows the union of the female and male. In the process of her elevation and augmentation, the *Shekhinah* assumes the demiurgical characteristics of the upper female, *Binah*.[74] This is the implication of the metamorphosis of the *Shekhinah* from the diminished *yod* to the enlarged *he*, for *Binah* too is symbolized by the letter *he*. Indeed, the isomorphic relationship of *Binah* and the *Shekhinah* is captured succinctly by the fact that they correspond respectively to two occurrences of the letter *he* in the Tetragrammaton.[75] The extension of the point that was hidden signifies the transmutation of the *Shekhinah* from a passive receptacle to an active force that overflows. In overflowing to the lower world, the *Shekhinah* mirrors the activity of *Binah* in the upper world. The zoharic author claims that the Song celebrates the restitution of the *Shekhinah* to *Binah*, the eschatological union of Mother and Daughter through the ascent of the latter to the former, the lower world of the feminine to the upper world of the masculine.[76] This appears to be the symbolic import of the following statement, which attributes the explication of the Song to Elijah,[77] an attribution that undoubtedly carries messianic implications:

> When [*Shekhinah*] ascends, it ascends from gradation to gradation, and from crown to crown, until everything is united above. And this is the secret of "The Song of Songs of Solomon." The Song of Songs was decreed by the mouth of Elijah by means of the supernal authority. The "Song of Songs," the praise of praises to the King to whom peace belongs, for this is the place that desires joy, for no anger or judgment is there. The world-to-come is entirely joyous, and it gladdens everyone, and thus it dispenses joy and happiness to all the gradations. Just as the joy must be aroused from this world above, so the happiness and joy must be aroused from the world of the moon in relation to the supernal world. Consequently, the worlds exist in one pattern, and the arousal ascends only from below to above.[78]

According to this passage, the Song is directed to *Binah*, the "supernal world" or the "world-to-come," which is also identified as Solomon (*Shelomoh*), based on the rabbinic interpretation of the name as a reference to God who is the King to whom peace belongs (*melekh sheha-shalom shello*).[79] The rabbinic remark can be theosophically interpreted in this way, for *Binah* is the king whose creative potency is actualized in the phallic gradation (*darga*) of *Yesod*, designated as *shalom*, "peace" or "wholeness."[80] The "King" in this context does not refer to the sixth emanation or the masculine potency of *Tif'eret*, the divine son who emerges from the union of *Ḥokhmah* and *Binah*, the father and mother. On the contrary, the "King" is clearly *Binah*, who is called by this name on account of her demiurgical role vis-à-vis the seven lower *sefirot*. The shift in symbolism underscores the fact that the ultimate theurgical purpose of the Song is to arouse the joy of the *Shekhinah*, the "world of the moon," in relation to *Binah*, the "upper world," so that the two worlds may be aligned in one pattern.[81] Indeed, the soteriological significance of the Song lies precisely in the gender transposition of the *Shekhinah* occasioned by her restoration to *Binah*, the divine attribute that is depicted by a variety of eschatological images, including the world-to-come. In another passage, the image of the kiss offered at the beginning of the Song is interpreted as a reference to the union of *Binah* and *Malkhut*, the lower light igniting the upper light.[82] The application of the ostensibly heterosexual setting of the metaphor of the kiss to the intimate relationship between these two attributes can be rendered meaningfully only if one bears in mind the transformation of gender to which I have alluded. That is, *Binah* assumes the persona of King Solomon in relation to the *Shekhinah*, who is the Shulammite woman; the desire of the latter to receive the kiss of the former denotes the longing on the part of the lower world to be united with the upper world, a union that is the decisive sign of the redemption.

The members of the zoharic circle continued the older midrashic tradition that assigned messianic significance to the Song. In the kabbalistic context, however, the messianism is linked primarily to the ontological elevation of the *Shekhinah* to *Binah*. It is from this eschatological perspective, moreover, that we can understand the zoharic utilization of the view attributed to Akiva (Mishnah Yadayim 3.5) that the Song is the holy of holies in relation to the rest of scripture as well as the implicit claim that the Song is equivalent to all of Torah:[83]

> This Song is the song that contains all of the Torah, the song in relation to which the upper and lower beings are aroused, the song that is in the pattern of the world above, which is the supernal Sabbath, the song on account of which the supernal, holy name is crowned. Therefore it is the holy of holies. Why? Because all of its words are in love and in the joy of everything.[84]

The eros of the Song conveys not only the heterosexual bonding of the King and the Matrona, but also the restoration of the holy pair to the womb whence they emerged.[85] The consummation of desire, therefore, involves the eschatological re/turn, the retracing of the way back to the great Mother, the union of the lower world of the feminine (*Shekhinah*) and the upper world of the masculine (*Binah*).[86] When the *Shekhinah* ascends to be conjoined to *Binah*, the upper is contained in the lower, a process that is semantically marked by the completion of the name *YHWH 'Elohim*.[87] Here the historical allegorization attains its fullest articulation inasmuch as the Song is read as a figurative depiction of the drama in the divine realm that corresponds to events in time, culminating with the coming of messiah. The symbolic approach articulated in zoharic literature does not preclude or supplant the historical allegory of the earlier rabbinic-targumic tradition; on the contrary, the former enhances and deepens the latter.[88] Thus, in one passage, we read:

> On the day [of the dedication of the Jerusalem Temple] the Song was revealed and the *Shekhinah* descended upon earth. . . . On that day verily this Song was revealed, and by means of the Holy Spirit Solomon uttered the hymn of the Song, which is the principle of all the Torah, the principle of the entire account of creation, the principle of the mystery of the patriarchs, the principle of the exile of Egypt . . . the principle of the coronation of the supernal, holy name in love and in joy, the principle of the expulsions of Israel amongst the nations and their redemption, the principle of the resurrection of the dead until that day that is the "Sabbath unto the Lord" (Lev 25:4).[89]

The Song encompasses every aspect of the *Heilsgeschichte* of the Jews, including the messianic redemption, resurrection of the dead, and the eschatological world-to-come, which is described as the Lord's Sabbath. The ultimate rectification involves the unification of all things in the world-to-come, the attribute of *Binah*, which is the "supernal Sabbath" that transcends the division of Sabbath into night and day, expressive of the polarity of female and male. The "Sabbath unto the Lord," therefore, signifies the transcending of gender dimorphism that is characteristic of zoharic soteriology.[90]

The apocalyptic reading of the Song as the symbolic depiction of the ontological restoration of the *Shekhinah* to *Binah*, the lower female to the upper female, is expressed somewhat differently in another context: the Song begins in the third person, "Oh, let him kiss me with the kisses of his mouth," for the initiation of love entails the arousal of kisses in the one that is not seen, the concealed of the concealed (*setima de-khol setimin*), who is conjoined to the gradation that corresponds to Jacob, the sun (*Tif'eret*), which illumines the moon (*Shekhinah*) with the supernal lights that shine from the place of the hidden wine, the attribute of *Binah*, or the world-to-come.[91] According to this passage, the Song is a poetic encoding of the overflow of light from the first of the ten luminous emanations, "the concealed of the concealed," to the last, "the moon." In this context, the process is interpreted from above to below rather than from below to above. Nevertheless, the common denominator is the view that the Song in its innermost structure reflects the unification of the divine emanations, and particularly the union of the upper and lower female attributes, which is concurrently the sacred history of the Jewish people from creation to redemption.

This same thought is articulated in a somewhat different way in another zoharic passage wherein the content of the Song is related to the "supernal chariot," which is constituted by the four names *'Adonai*, *Ṣeva'ot*, *YHWH*, and *'Ehyeh*. The divine names correspond respectively to four kinds of splendor, an allusion to the four sefirotic emanations in ascending order: *Shekhinah*, *Yesod*, *Tif'eret*, and *Binah*. The "mystery of the four inscribed names of the four splendors" entails that "each splendor is contained in the other, and the desire of the one is to enter the other, so that one may be contained in the other. These four splendors are specified in their names as they are known."[92] The nature of the Song, which bespeaks the erotic pattern of the poetic word in general, is related to the desire of each splendor, to which corresponds a particular name of God, to be contained in the other. The eros for the other is here related to the impetus for unity in the divine realm, a unity that underlies the mystical import of the Song. The symbolic reading of the poem, therefore, imparts information about the "mysteries of the wisdom of the supernal, inscribed name," which is the Tetragrammaton. Indeed, the Song itself is that very name, which is an alternative way of expressing the equivalency of the Song and the Torah, given the identification of the mystical essence of the Torah as the name.[93] From this perspective, it is appropriate to speak of the Song as the "extreme point of zoharic intuition," for this part of Scripture is the holy of holies that is poetically envisioned as the "absolute interiority" of the divine edifice of the Torah.[94] Alternatively expressed, it is possible to view the Zohar as a commentary on the erotic mysticism celebrated in the Song.[95]

The intrinsic connection between the Song, the Tetragrammaton, and the erotic nature of the kiss as the union of the four spirits, which translates symbolically to the elevation of the lower world of the feminine (*Shekhinah*) to the upper world of the masculine (*Binah*),[96] is made explicit in the following interpretation of the opening verse of the Song, "Oh, let him kiss me with the kisses of his mouth" (Song 1:2):

> What did King Solomon perceive that he placed words of love between the supernal world and the lower world, and at the beginning of the poem of love he placed between them [the words] "Oh, let him kiss me with the kisses [of his mouth]"? Rather, it has been established and it is the case that there is no love, that is, conjunction of spirit with spirit (*devequt de-ruḥa be-ruḥa*), except through the kiss, and the kiss is through the mouth, the wellspring of spirit and its overflow. When the one kisses the other, these spirits are conjoined to these spirits, and they are one, and consequently there is one love. In the book of the first Rav Hamnuna the elder, it is said concerning this verse, the kiss of love divides into four spirits, and the four spirits are joined as one, and they are within the mystery of faith (*raza di-meheimanuta*), and they arise in the four letters, and these are the letters upon which depend the letters of the holy name (*YHWH*), and the supernal and lower beings depend on them, and the praise of the Song of Songs depends on them. And what are they? [The four letters of the word] *'ahavah* (*ahbh*), and they are the supernal chariot, and they are the union, conjunction,

> and perfection of everything. These letters are four spirits, and these are the spirits of love and joy of all the parts of the body that has no sadness at all. Four spirits are in the kiss, each one is contained in the other. When the one spirit is contained in the other and the other is contained in it, the two spirits become one, and consequently the four [spirits] are joined perfectly in one conjunction.[97]

The essence of the Song is thus related to the desire of the four spirits to be united in the one bond of love. These spirits are related to the four letters of the word *'ahavah*, which in turn are correlated with the four letters of the most sacred name, the name that signifies that which cannot be signified, the garment of Torah unveiled in its mystical core. The four spirits, which correspond to the four splendors, relate to four divine attributes, but also to the fourfold entity that is born from the union of the spirit/breath of the male and the spirit/breath of the female. Each gender contains the other in itself, the principle that is basic to the kabbalistic notion of androgyny. The conjunction of male and female thus yields the male in female and the female in male. Mathematically expressed, the twofold that is one becomes four.

In the zoharic commentary on the Song, the matter is expressed in somewhat different terms, related exegetically to the four spirits (*ruḥot*) that shall alight upon the shoot to grow out of the stump of Jesse (Isa 11:2) and to the breath (*ruaḥ*) of prophecy that comes forth from the four winds (Ezek 37:9): "The kiss of love is only through the mouth, the spirit is joined to the spirit, and each of them is comprised of two spirits, its spirit and the spirit of its counterpart. Thus the two are in the four spirits, and all the more so the male and the female in the conjunction of the four spirits together. The son that comes out from them, this is the breath that comes forth from the four winds, as it says, 'Come, O breath, from the four winds' (Ezek 37:9), this is the perfect spirit."[98] The eros of the kiss is thus associated with the emanative process by means of which the androgynous being emerges from the union of the spirits of the mouth, male and female. This androgynous being is the perfect spirit, which can be depicted as the son, but the son that contains the daughter as his sister, or as the breath of prophecy, the masculine voice articulated through feminine speech.[99]

Corresponding to the upper union of the breaths is the lower union of the genitals, but even with respect to this lower union the depiction embraces the symbolism of language to express the texture of the erotic experience. The point is accentuated in the description of the second splendor, *Ṣeva'ot* or the "living splendor" (*zohar ḥai*), which corresponds to the phallic *darga* (gradation) of *Yesod*. "His desire is to praise constantly the first splendor, which is called song (*shir*), and thus they are contained as one in a single bond without separation, with a complete desire. As a result, the all (*kola*) is called Song of Songs (*shir ha-shirim*)."[100] The plural of the expression *shir ha-shirim*, the "song of the songs," alludes to the mystery of the sacred copulation between the first and second splendors, *Shekhinah* and *Yesod*. The former is transformed by this union, a transformation that is encoded in the linguistic transition from the singular *shir* to the plural *shir ha-shirim*. The theosophic interpretation of the title of the scriptural book indicates that the mystical constitution of the Song is related to the holy union of male and female. The final attainment of that union, however, is realized only in the restoration of the various splendors to the fourth splendor, the "hidden splendor that is not visible at all" except by means of "contemplation of the heart" (*sukhlatenu de-libba*), "for the heart knows and contemplates it even though it is not seen at all."[101] The Song of Songs is thus contrasted with the song that Moses uttered at the splitting of the Reed Sea, for the latter is the "song of the feminine" (*Shekhinah*) whereas the former is the "song that ascends to the world of the masculine" (*Binah*).[102] The Song is identified with the eschatological moment wherein the feminine potency ascends to the world of the masculine and is thereby transformed. The inspiration for the Song, the augmentation of the wisdom of Solomon, derives from the source wherein the feminine is restored to the world of the masculine.

Spiritual Eroticism and Ascetic Renunciation in Kabbalistic Readings of the Song

By way of summation, we may conclude that the impact of the Hispano-Jewish philosophical orientation on the kabbalistic understanding of the Song of Songs was quite profound. The negative attitude toward bodily pleasure fostered an allegorical interpretation that replaced the literal eroticism of the text by a spiritualized eroticism related to the contemplative ideal of conjunction. Going beyond the philosophers and poets, however, the kabbalists intensified the nexus of asceticism and eroticism. In a separate study, I argued that the sacralization of human sexuality, which lies at the heart of kabbalistic myth and ritual, is dialectically related to the ascetic impulse.[103] In the kabbalistic tradition, carnal sexuality is celebrated only to the extent that it is transformed by the proper intentionality into a spiritual act.

To be sure, as Scholem already noted, kabbalah is to be contrasted with non-Jewish mysticism, and in particular the spiritual ideal of Christianity, since the kabbalists resisted a monastic ideal of abstinence, viewing marriage not as a concession to the weakness of the flesh but as a symbolic realization of the union of the masculine and feminine divine potencies. Scholem thus distinguished the ascetic dimension of Christian mysticism, which led to the transplanting of eroticism into the relation of man to God, from the affirmation of human sexuality on the part of the kabbalists, which was viewed as one of the central means to discover the mystery of sex within the divine.[104] While I would agree that the Jewish and Christian approaches to asceticism must be distinguished in light of the respective values placed on human sexuality and the engenderment of the divine image, my own research has led me to the conclusion that the medieval kabbalistic tradition does share something closer to the Christian orientation. For the kabbalist, as for his Christian counterpart, the corporeal body, which is correlated with the feminine, is problematic.[105] In particular, the symbolic reading of the Song, which is expressive of both theosophic and ecstatic elements, underscores the extent to which the kabbalists sought to augment, and in some measure displace, carnal sexuality with spiritual eroticism.[106] Functioning within the confines of normative *halakhah*, the kabbalists could not affirm celibacy as an absolute ideal, but they nevertheless boldly posited an austere lifestyle for themselves wherein the intensity of their contemplative regimen was linked to an erotic passion that demanded the abrogation of physical desire. The ascetic renunciation of carnal sexuality for the sake of spiritual eros anticipates the condition of the *eschaton*, which must be a retrieval of the primordial beginning.[107] If one presumes that an actual circle of mystics in Castile produced the narrative tales of the *Zohar*, a presumption that I think is well grounded, then it is possible to refer to an eschatological community of ascetic mystics who believed they were already living at the end of days.[108]

It lies beyond the scope of this study to provide a detailed account of the nexus between asceticism and redemption. Such an account will appear as part of a chapter on eroticism and asceticism in my forthcoming monograph on eros and the construction of gender in kabbalistic ritual and myth. For the purposes of this study, let me simply note that the ascetic dimension is highlighted in kabbalistic literature by the symbolic association of *Binah*, which is the world-to-come, and Yom Kippur, a day in which physical pleasures are prohibited. The kabbalistic symbolism thus intensifies the rabbinic depiction of the world-to-come as a state beyond sensual joyance. A particularly important passage in this regard is found in one of the later strata of zoharic literature:

> Therefore, on Yom Kippur . . . sexual intercourse is forbidden. There the sign of the covenant, which is the *yod*, is the crown on the Torah scroll (*taga ʿal sefer torah*) . . . as it has been established, "In the world-to-come there is no eating, drinking, or sexual intercourse. Rather the righteous sit with their crowns upon their heads."[109] Since there is no intercourse (*shimmush*) in this world with the crown (*taga*), the masters of the Mishnah established,[110] "anyone who makes use of the crown perishes" (*kol ha-mishtammesh be-taga ḥalaf*).[111]

In this context, the sexual abstinence required on Yom Kippur is linked explicitly with the feminine assuming the posture of the crown, a theme that I have analyzed in a number of studies.[112] For my immediate purpose, what is important to note about this passage is that the eschatological image of the righteous sitting with crowns on their heads is interpreted as a symbolic depiction of their celibacy. The elevation of the *Shekhinah*, which is designated as the sign of the covenant, the phallic marking of the *yod*, to the position of the crown on the scroll of Torah or on the head of the righteous attests to the transformation of the feminine into an aspect of the masculine. In the social plane, it is necessary for the kabbalist to separate from physical sex with his wife in order to be assimilated into the *Shekhinah* in her transformed posture as the crown of the male. This motif is linked exegetically in several zoharic passages to the verse, "O maidens of Zion, go forth and gaze upon King Solomon wearing the crown that his mother gave him on his wedding day, on his day of bliss" (Song 3:11). The interpretation of this verse in the *Zohar* underscores the convergence of the theosophic and the ecstatic elements, for the coronation of Solomon by his mother on the day of his wedding is applied simultaneously to an event within the Godhead and to the experience of the mystic vis-à-vis the divine presence.[113] Most important, that experience involves the assimilation of the male mystic into the feminine presence that has been transposed into the corona of the phallus. The overtly heterosexual images, therefore, must be decoded as a veiled allusion to the homoerotic bond between the male mystic and the reconstituted male androgyne in the divine realm. Insofar as the homoeroticism is (ideally) predicated on the abrogation of carnal sexuality, one must distinguish the homosocial texture of the mystical experience from homosexuality.[114] Indeed, the kabbalist who is bound to God experiences the life of the world-to-come, which is a plane of existence beyond physical eros and the concomitant gender bifurcation. Alternatively expressed, the Song celebrates the great Sabbath in which the division of Sabbath into night and day is overcome. By contrast, this great Sabbath, the world-to-come, is, according to the rabbinic idiom, the day that is entirely Sabbath.[115]

In some measure, the process of eschatological reparation unfolds each Sabbath. Thus, according to one relevant passage, which I have analyzed elsewhere at great length, the letters of the word *shabbat* (*shin bet taw*) are interpreted as a reference to the ascent of *Shekhinah* to *Binah*, for the letters *bet* and *taw* spell the word *bat*, "daughter," which symbolizes the *Shekhinah*, and the letter *shin* the three patriarchs or the fourth, fifth, and sixth emanations, *Ḥesed*, *Gevurah*, and *Raḥamim*. When the *bat* rises as a crown on the head of the *shin*, the chariot is completed by the unity of the four, and they in turn ascend to be united in the world-to-come, which is the "great Sabbath" (*shabbat ha-gadol*).[116] This is precisely the theosophic dynamic that the zoharic authors assign to the Song. Thus, in one passage, the four words of the first verse of the Song, *shir ha-shirim 'asher li-Shelomoh*, are related to the "perfect, holy chariot," which consists of the three patriarchs and David, that is, the central three *sefirot* of *Ḥesed*, *Gevurah*, and *Raḥamim*, conjoined with the *Shekhinah*.[117] Contained in the first verse, therefore, is the mystery of the entire Song, which relates to the elevation of the *Shekhinah* to form together with the patriarchs the holy chariot for King Solomon, that is, *Binah*, the king to whom peace belongs. The symbolic import of the Song is thus identical to the mystical meaning attributed to the Sabbath.

The nexus between the great Sabbath, the world-to-come, and Yom Kippur indicates that the eschatological vision is predicated on the ascetic renunciation that characterizes the holiest day of the Jewish calendar. In the rhythm of each Sabbath, night is the time for the sexual union of man and his wife, since this is the time of the *hieros gamos* above between the Holy King and the Matrona,[118] but in the progression of the day the sanctity of physical copulation gives way to the abnegation of sexuality, a state of purity that anticipates the holiness of the world-to-come, which is Yom Kippur.[119] The reading of the Song that emerges from the different literary settings of the *Zohar* suggests that the thirteenth-century kabbalists responsible for this work imagined that the celebrated love poem is an allusion to the very same transition from the currently acceptable observance of Sabbath, which features prominently engaging in carnal intercourse in an effort to facilitate the sacred union above, to the eschatological Sabbath, which involves a state of holiness that is predicated on the abolition of physical desire. The zoharic interpretation of the Song, therefore, embraces an erotic mysticism that affirms the ideal of ascetic eschatology, an ideal that is proleptically realized by the kabbalists in their pietistic fraternity principally through the communal study of the secrets of Torah.[120] No scriptural text afforded these kabbalists a better opportunity to express the homoerotic asceticism of their mystical piety than the Song of Songs, for this book is the holy of holies, the speculum through which the invisible glory could be seen and the ineffable name spoken.

Notes

1. For a representative list of studies that deal with the nexus of eroticism and asceticism, see O'Flaherty, *Asceticism and Eroticism in the Mythology of Siva*; Schimmel, "Eros—Heavenly and Not So Heavenly," 119–41; Kripal, *Kali's Child*; Wolfson, "Eunuchs Who Keep the Sabbath," 151–85.

2. See Rist, *Eros and Psyche*. On Plato's characterization of the rational soul in terms of the sexual images of the body, see Thornton, *Eros*, 210–12.

3. The point is beautifully conveyed in Bürgel, "Love, Lust, and Longing," 81–117.

4. Bataille, *Death and Sensuality*, 7.

5. See the poignant remarks regarding this matter in Scholem, *Major Trends*, 225–26. On the relationship of mystical experience and the language of passion in medieval Christendom, see Rougemont, *Love in the Western World*, 141–70.

6. See the description in Zaehner, *Mysticism Sacred and Profane*, 151. In the Middle Ages, the spiritual or rational is symbolically associated with the male and the material or imaginative with the female. See Bynum, *Holy Feast*, 216–17, 262. Yet, in relationship to the divine, the soul is feminized, an experience that was shared by men and women. Although it was not uncommon for women in medieval Christian society to take on a symbolic maleness in order to advance spiritually, it is also the case, as Bynum has argued, that basic images of women's religious experience were feminine in nature or at the very least androgynous. See *Holy Feast*, 28 and 291.

7. The range of exegetical strategies in reading the Song can easily be gauged from even a cursory glance at Walfish, "Bibliyografyah mu'eret," 518–71.

8. See Kamin, *Ben Yehudim le-Noṣerim*, 13–61. On the rendering of Rashi's historico-allegorical approach to the Song as the literal sense (*exposito historica*) in the thirteenth-century Latin commentary on the Song, see Smalley, *Study of the Bible*, 352–55; Signer, "Thirteenth Century Christian Hebraism," 89–100; and Kamin and Saltman, *Secundum Salomonem*. On Ashkenazi exegesis of the Song, see also Salfeld, "Das Hohelied bei den jüdischen Erklärern des Mittelalters," 150–60. On the historical approach to the allegorical reading of the Song, referred to as the concealed meaning (*nistar*), in contrast to the literal or revealed sense (*nigleh*), see Abraham b. Isaac ha-Levi Tamakh, *Commentary on the Song of Songs*, 39–42. I am deliberately ignoring the utilization of verses from the Song in the formulation of the mystical theosophy articulated by the Jewish Pietists of the Rhineland in the twelfth and thirteenth centuries, as we find, for instance, in their depiction of chariot speculation in terms of the image of the secret of the nut (*sod ha-'egoz*), which is derived from Song 6:11. See Abrams, *Sexual Symbolism*, and comprehensive bibliography cited by the author. In my various attempts at decoding the Pietistic esotericism, which involved the attribution of an erotic drama to the divine realm, I have noted the central role played by key passages from the Song. See Wolfson, *Along the Path*, 185–86, n. 364. See also Marcus, "The Song of Songs in German Hasidism," 181–89.

9. See, by contrast, Green, "The Song of Songs," 49. I do not think it is valid to speak (as Green does) of a "contraction of midrashic thinking" in medieval Jewish academies or of "philosophical theology" as a dominant mode of discourse. Most important, it is unlikely that medieval Jewish philosophers would have been scandalized by the "sacred eros" articulated in kabbalistic literature. On the contrary, the sacred eroticism so pronounced in the kabbalah is related to and in a measure derived from the idea of an intellectual eros that informed the medieval philosophical conception of conjunction (*devequt*). The contrast between the approach of Maimonides to the image of the kiss in the Song as a metaphor for the union between the rational soul and the Active Intellect, and the erotic spirituality of the kabbalistic symbolism (especially of the *Zohar*) is also drawn too sharply by Perella, *Kiss Sacred and Profane*, 75–83. By contrast, Rosenberg, "Ha-parshanut ha-filosofit le-Shir ha-shirim," 133–51, proposes a typological distinction between the philosophical exegesis of the Song as a figurative dialogue between the individual soul and the divine, on the one hand, and the kabbalistic exegesis that reads the Song as a description of the relationship of the male and the female attributes of the divine, on the other, but he readily acknowledges that the philosophical interpretation appears in works that would be classified as kabbalistic (p. 134).

10. See Vajda, *L'amour de Dieu*, 142, 144–45, 168–69, 179–80, 242–47, 254–55.

11. Scholem, *Major Trends*, 226.

12. Idel, *Kabbalah*, 206.

13. Baḥya, *Sefer Torat Ḥovot ha-levavot*, 10.1, trans. Qafiḥ, 412.

14. See Vajda, *L'amour de Dieu*, 115, n. 6.

15. The relevant passages are cited by Rosenberg, "Ha-parshanut ha-filosofit," 136–37.

16. See Scheindlin, *The Gazelle*, 49, 128–29.

17. *Les réflexions sur l'âme*, 35, 38, and 40; see also Rosenberg, "Ha-parshanut ha-filosofit," 137.

18. *Mishneh Torah*, Hilkhot Teshuvah 10.3.

19. *Guide of the Perplexed* 3.51. On the reappropriation of the language of eros in the thought of Maimonides (and other philosophical thinkers influenced by him) as the most compelling metaphorical expression to depict the intellectual conjunction of the soul and the divine, see Fishbane, *The Kiss of God*, 24–30; Gordon, "The Erotics of Negative Theology," 1–38.

20. Abraham Maimonides, *The Highways to Perfection*, 2:395.

21. Saadia Gaon, *Kitāb al-mukhtār fī al-amānāt wal-i'tiqādāt* 10.4, ed. Qafiḥ, 300–303, discusses those individuals who are dedicated to passionate love (*'ishq*), which serves as the model for their relationship to God. For the social and intellectual background to Saadia's use of this term, including the possibility that it is borrowed from Islamic mysticism, see Goitein, *A Mediterranean Society*, 5: 317–20. On the use of *'ishq* in Sufism to connote the passionate love of the soul for God, see Schimmel, *Mystical Dimensions of Islam*, 137; Massignon, *The Passion of al-Hallaj*, 1:340–43, 523 n. 64; 2:412; 3:102–104; Wafer, "Vision and Passion," 111, 122, 128 n. 4. On the discrediting of *'ishq* on the part of Islamic philosophers, see Giffen, *Theory of Profane Love Among the Arabs*, 64–65.

22. Babylonian Talmud, Bava Batra 17a; *Shir ha-shirim rabbah* 1.16, ed. Dunsky, 16. On the description of the kiss of death as the "union of the soul in the root," see *Zohar* 1:168a.

23. See Rawidowicz, *Studies in Jewish Thought*, 291–98. The influence of Maimonides is clearly discernible in Baḥya ben Asher's description in *Kad ha-Qemaḥ* of *ḥesheq*, intense desire, which he contrasts with *'ahavah*, love, in *Kitvei Rabbinu Baḥya*, ed. Chavel, 34–35: "The intense desire (*ḥesheq*) is the conjunction of thought (*devequt ha-maḥshavah*) to the great and powerful love, for the thought of the one who desires is not at all separated from that which is desired. . . . The book of the Song of Songs is based on this level of intense desire, as it begins 'Oh, let him kiss me with the kisses of his mouth' (Song 1:2), and the Rabbis, blessed be their memory, explained that all of scripture is holy, but the Song of Songs is the holy of the holies, for the desired goal of human beings is to conjoin thought to the holy of holies. The word 'kiss' (*neshiqah*) has the meaning of conjunction (*devequt*). . . . Concerning the one whose death is by the kiss of the *Shekhinah*, his body is pure and his soul is pure."

24. On the origin of this term in Plotinus, see Ivry, "Neoplatonic Currents in Maimonides' Thought," 125.

25. Ibn Aknin, *Hitgalut ha-sodot we-hofa'at ha-me'orot*, 18–19. See also Vajda, *L'amour de Dieu*, 144–45.

26. Ibn Aknin, *Hitgalut ha-sodot*, 14–15.

27. Ibid., 24–25.

28. Tibbon, *Perush 'al Shir ha-Shirim*, 8. See also 9, 11, 12.

29. Ibid., 9.

30. Ibid., 11.

31. Ibid., 14–15. See also Vajda, *L'amour de Dieu*, 179–80.

32. This allegorical approach was continued by subsequent philosophical and mystical authors. See, for instance, Narboni, *The Epistle on the Possibility of Conjunction*, 96 (English section), 128–29 (Hebrew section); Levi ben Gershom, *Commentary on Song of Songs*, xv–xxxi.

33. For a similiar process in Christian authors, see Wright, "The Influence of the Exegetical Tradition of the 'Song of Songs'"; Brückmann and Couchman, "Du 'Cantique des cantiques' aux 'Carmina Burana,'" 35–50.

34. My brief analysis of the use of the Song in medieval Hebrew poetry is indebted to Scheindlin, *The Gazelle*, 20–21, 37–41, 48–49. See also Vajda, *L'amour de Dieu*, 86, 91, 99, 115.

35. I have borrowed this term from McGinn, "The Language of Love," 217, who bases his own remarks on the formulation of Idel, "Sexual Metaphors and Praxis in the Kabbalah," 199–200.

36. This locution is derived from the work of David R. Blumenthal. See especially Ḥoṭēr ben Shelomo, *The Philosophic Questions and Answers*, ed. and trans. Blumenthal, 72–73. Blumenthal cites several examples from the so-called "eastern school of Maimonidean interpretation," Zekharya ha-Rofe and Sa'id ibn Da'ud, who interpreted the Song as affirmation of the ideal of conjunction typical of medieval philosophical mysticism.

37. Idel, "Sexual Metaphors," 200–201; idem, *Kabbalah*, 206.

38. See Scholem, *Major Trends*, 126, 138–39, 144, 383 n. 76; idem, *Ha-qabbalah shel Sefer ha-Temunah*, 87–90, 107, 127–28, 151–52, 161, 164; idem, *Kabbalah*, 54; Idel, *The Mystical Experience in Abraham Abulafia*, 16–17, 22–24; idem, *Kabbalah*, 98–101; idem, "The Contribution of Abraham Abulafia's Kabbalah," 124–25.

39. In addition to the studies of Idel cited in n. 38, see *Mystical Experience*, 180–84, 203–5; *Kabbalah*, 151. See also Fishbane, *Kiss of God*, 39–43.

40. See Blickstein, "Between Philosophy and Mysticism."

41. Gikatilla, *Ginnat 'egoz*, 280–81. It is of interest to note that in his later work on the symbolism of the *sefirot*, Gikatilla reaffirms the contemplative ideal of *devequt* that is consequent to the passionate love of God, but in that context it is related to knowledge of the names, which are interpreted in a theosophic way as a reference to the divine attributes. See Gikatilla, *Sha'arei 'Orah*, 1:47, 83.

42. This has been duly recognized by McGinn, "Language of Love," 217–18. However, McGinn, following Idel, contrasts the mystical orientation to the Song in the two branches of kabbalah, the ecstatic and the theosophic, on the grounds that in the former the mystic, like the Christian saint, is conceived of as female in relation to the masculine divine lover, whereas in the latter the mystic is male in relation to the female aspect of the Godhead. In my judgment, there is ample evidence that in the theosophic kabbalah itself there is a gender metamorphosis whereby the male mystic is feminized in relation to the divine. See Wolfson, "Eunuchs," 166–67.

43. See Vulliaud, *Cantique des cantiques*, 118–33, 183–85, 191–204, 219–25; Pope, *Song of Songs*, 153–79; Green, "Song of Songs," 48–63; and Mopsik, *Le Zohar: Cantique des cantiques*, 18, 20–21. The theosophic interpretation of the male and female personae of the Song is already implied in several sections of the *Bahir*. See Abrams, *The Book Bahir*, 141–43 (§§ 43–44), 203 (§ 117).

44. *Kitvei Ramban*, 2: 485.

45. To a degree this is implicit in Green's comment on this passage, "Song of Songs," 57: "The 'Glory' here is the devoted bride whose longings for union with her spouse also represent the longing of the worshipper's soul for reunion with God." Green does not, however, note the gender reversal implied in the application of the verse to the soul in relation to the divine potency.

46. The contrast between the theosophic and the ecstatic trends of kabbalah along these lines is the position adopted by Idel, "Sexual Metaphors," 206; *Kabbalah*, 209–10.

47. For an alternative approach, see Green, *Keter*, 161–62, n. 35.

48. See Ezra of Gerona, *Le commentaire*," 141–44.

49. The reading proffered by Ezra, which is reiterated by many other kabbalists, has a striking resonance with philosophical mysticism, particularly as it has been expressed in Sufi-influenced authors. For instance, see Fenton, "Daniel Ibn al-Mashita's 'Taqwim al-Adyan'," 79.

50. *Kitvei Ramban*, 2:480.

51. See Vajda, *L'amour de Dieu*, 233–35; Green, "Peirush Shir ha-shirim," 396–97; idem, "Song of Songs," 57.

52. Green, "Peirush Shir ha-shirim," 408–9. For more on the background of this passage, see Idel, *Mystical Experience*, 59–60.

53. Green, "Peirush Shir ha-shirim," 409.

54. Ibid., 410. See also Green, "Song of Songs," 57–58.

55. Vajda, *L'amour de Dieu*, 210.

56. *Zohar*, 2:124b.

57. On the use of the kiss to symbolize the union of spirits in the divine realm, see *Zohar*, 1:44b, 70a; 2:124b, 146a–b, 253b–254a, 256b; 3:287a; *Zohar ḥadash*, ed. Margaliot, 63c–64a.

58. *Zohar ḥadash*, 60c.

59. See *Guide* 3.51. In *Zohar*, 1:137a (*Midrash ha-Ne'elam*) the desire for the kiss expressed in Song 1:2 is interpreted as the yearning of the soul to derive sustenance and pleasure from the splendor of the *Shekhinah*. See, by contrast, Fishbane, *Kiss of God*, 38–39. Although Fishbane readily acknowledges that in the *Zohar*, as in the case of Ibn Sahula, there are two explanations to the kiss, the ecstatic and the hypostatic, he concludes that the "zoharic tradition of ecstatic death by divine kiss is not affected by philosophical notions or vocabulary, which distinguishes it from the Maimonidean reworking of the talmudic tradition, as well as from the mystical adaptation of Maimonides by Abraham Abulafia." It seems to me that the Maimonidean influence is evident in the relevant zoharic passages as well.

60. See Liebes, "Zohar we-'Eros," 67–115.

61. *Zohar*, 1:60b. The zoharic attitude is well captured in the brief remark of Gikatilla, *Sha'arei 'Orah*, 2:51: "This is the secret of the conjunction of the tenth emanation in the ninth without any doubt, for he who causes the Community of Israel to be united with the emanation of *Yesod* is himself conjoined to her, and she is conjoined to *Yesod*, and the two of them as one are conjoined to *YHWH*."

62. Wolfson, "Eunuchs," 166–69.

63. Vajda, *L'amour de Dieu*, 217–21, 223–28. The theosophic interpretation is the mythical basis for the ritual instituted by Safedian kabbalists in the sixteenth century to chant the Song every Friday evening, the time of the *hieros gamos* in the divine realm, which is facilitated by the sexual intercourse below between a man and his wife. See Benayahu, *Toledot ha-'Ari*, 350, n. 3; Hallamish, "Meqomah shel ha-qabbalah ba-minhag," 209, n. 170.

64. *Zohar*, 3:42a–b.

65. *Zohar ḥadash*, 62c. See ibid., 63d, 72b.

66. See Lieberman, "Mishnath Shir ha-Shirim," 119.

67. *Zohar*, 2:143a.

68. *Zohar*, 2:144b–145a.

69. *Zohar ḥadash*, 62b.

70. Ibid., 62d.

71. I have discussed this motif in more detail in Wolfson, *Circle in the Square*, 92–98.

72. *Zohar*, 3:74b.

73. *Zohar ḥadash*, 71b.

74. For a more elaborate discussion of this gender transposition, see Wolfson, *Circle in the Square*, 103–6.

75. *Zohar ḥadash*, 72b.

76. In zoharic terminology, *Binah* is the mother, but she is called *'alma di-dekhura*, the world of the masculine, in contrast to the *Shekhinah*, which is called *'alma de-nuqba*, the world of the feminine. Elsewhere the zoharic text expresses the idea that the Song relates concomitantly to *Binah* and *Shekhinah*, the two arrayments of the feminine (*tiqqunei de-nuqvei*), and thus it mim-

ics the account of creation (*ma'aśeh bereshit*) at the beginning of the Torah that begins with a *bet*. See *Zohar*, 1:240b; 3:290b.

77. On the significance of Elijah in the zoharic commentary on the Song, see Mopsik, *Le Zohar*, 8–10.

78. *Zohar ḥadash*, 62b. Ibid., 60c–d, the symbolic intent of the Song is said to be contained in its first letter, the *shin*, which represents the three patriarchs, or the three central emanations, that constitute the supernal chariot. The Song thus encompasses the mystical intent of the esoteric discipline of the account of the chariot (*ma'aśeh merkavah*).

79. BT Shevu'ot, 35b.

80. See *Zohar*, 1:29a; 2:5a, 100b, 127b.

81. See Wolfson, "*Tiqqun ha-Shekhinah*," 313–22; idem, "Fore/giveness On the Way," 153–69.

82. *Zohar*, 1:70a–b. A similar interpretation is presented in *Zohar ḥadash*, 64b, but in that context the emphasis is on the desire of the lower world, *Shekhinah*, to join the upper world, *Binah*.

83. It is also possible to interpret this older rabbinic idea in a theosophic way as a reference to the union of the Oral Torah and the Written Torah, which correspond respectively to *Shekhinah* and *Tif'eret*. That is, the Song is equivalent to the Torah in its entirety because the Song is about the relationship between male and female, which relate to the dual Torah. See *Zohar ḥadash*, 63d–64a; Gikatilla, *Sha'arei 'orah*, 1:86.

84. *Zohar*, 2:143b. For analysis of this passage, see Mopsik, *Le Zohar*, 13–14.

85. See Mopsik, *Le Zohar*, 22–23.

86. This idea is on occasion related exegetically by the zoharic authors to the expression *mi zot*, "who is this one," which is found three times in Song of Songs (3:6, 6:6, and 8:5). See *Zohar*, 1:10a; 2:126b.

87. *Zohar ḥadash*, 67a; and see parallel discussion in Gikatilla, *Sha'arei 'orah*, 2:51–56.

88. Thus, one finds strewn throughout the zoharic corpus exegetical applications of specific verses in the Song to moments in Israel's sacred history. For instance, see *Zohar*, 1:170a, 176b. Mopsik, *Le Zohar*, 15, has duly noted the appropriation in the *Zohar* of the historical-allegorical approach to the Song evident in the Targum.

89. *Zohar*, 2:143b–144a. The all-inclusive quality of the Song is affirmed as well in *Zohar*, 2:18b: "Thus it is written the 'song of songs' (*shir ha-shirim*), that is, the song of those archons (*śarim*) above, the song that comprises all the matters of Torah, wisdom, power, and strength, all that was and all that shall be, the song that the archons above sing."

90. See Wolfson, "Coronation of the Sabbath Bride," 301–43.

91. *Zohar*, 2:146b–147a.

92. *Zohar ḥadash*, 61d.

93. See Scholem, *On the Kabbalah and Its Symbolism*, 37–44; Tishby, *The Wisdom of the Zohar*, 283–84, 292–95, 1079–82; and Idel, "Tefiśat ha-Torah be-sifrut ha-Heikhalot," 23–84, esp. 49–58.

94. Lévy-Valensi, *La poétique du Zohar*, 94.

95. Vulliaud, *Le Cantique des cantiques*, 183; Mopsik, *Le Zohar*, 13.

96. See Wolfson, *Circle in the Square*, 89, 99, 103.

97. *Zohar*, 2:146a–b. See Liebes, "Zohar we-'Eros," 79.

98. *Zohar ḥadash*, 60d.

99. See Wolfson, *Circle in the Square*, 73–74.

100. *Zohar ḥadash*, 60d.

101. Ibid., 62a.

102. Ibid., 63a.

103. Wolfson, "Eunuchs Who Keep the Sabbath."

104. Scholem, *Major Trends*, 235.

105. The negative attitude toward the body and consequent need for an ascetic lifestyle in the zoharic corpus was already noted by Tishby, *Wisdom of the Zohar*, 764–65.

106. See Biale, *Eros and the Jews*, 101–20.

107. On the different approaches to the sexual nature of primal Adam prior to the expulsion from the Garden of Eden, see Safran, "Rabbi Azriel and Nahmanides," 75–106.

108. This is the conclusion articulated by Liebes, *Studies in the Zohar*, 1–84, but he does not emphasize the ascetic dimension of the messianic posture.

109. BT Berakhot, 17a.

110. Mishnah Avot 1:13.

111. *Zohar*, 2:116a (*Ra'aya meheimna*).

112. Wolfson, *Through a Speculum That Shines*, 342, 357–68; idem, "*Tiqqun ha-Shekhinah*," 322–29; idem, "Coronation," 332–41; idem, "The Engenderment of Messianic Politics," 203–58, esp. 230–47.

113. Wolfson, *Through a Speculum That Shines*, 363–64.

114. See earlier, n. 47.

115. BT Sanhedrin, 97a.

116. *Zohar*, 2:204a. For fuller discussion of this motif, see Wolfson, "Coronation," 314–16.

117. *Zohar*, 2:144a.

118. The linkage of Sabbath evening and carnal intercourse is found in rabbinic sources, particularly as it relates to the time for scholars to fulfill their marital obligations. The rabbinic idea has been appropriated by kabbalists as the cornerstone for their belief that the enlightened should engage in sex only on Sabbath eve (and a few other times, which are treated like the eve of Sabbath). For citation and discussion of some of the relevant sources, see Wolfson, "Eunuchs," 159–61. Goitein, *Mediterranean Society*, 5:312–13, notes that from the Genizah material one can conclude that the talmudic recommendation that scholars engage in sexual intercourse on Friday night was extended to the Jewish population more generally. Additionally, Goitein notes the conflict between this Rabbanite view and that of the Karaites, who regarded sexual intercourse as a desecration of the holiness of the Sabbath. On the connection between Sabbath observance and ascetic renunciation, which leads to a vision of God, see Valantasis, *The Gospel of Thomas*, 100–101.

119. See Wolfson, "Coronation," 325–32.

120. The kabbalists were able to achieve the ascetic ideal without rejecting the social institution of marriage and thereby ignoring the religious obligation to procreate. A similar phenomenon is attested in medieval Christian culture in cases where husband and wife both renounced sexual activity for the sake of a more intense pious devotion. See Elliott, *Spiritual Marriage*.

Bibliography

Abraham ben Isaac ha-Levi Tamakh. *Commentary on the Song of Songs*. Ed. Leon A. Feldman. Assen: Van Gorcum, 1970.

Abrams, Daniel, ed. *The Book Bahir: An Edition Based on the Earliest Manuscripts*. Los Angeles: Cherub, 1994.

———. *Sexual Symbolism and Merkavah Speculation in Medieval Germany: A Study of the Sod ha-Egoz Texts*. Tübingen: J. C. B. Mohr, 1997.

Alonso-Fontela, Carlos, ed. "El Targum al Cantar de los Cantares (Edición Crítica)." Ph.D. diss., Universidad Complutense de Madrid, 1987.

Astell, Ann W. *The Song of Songs in the Middle Ages*. Ithaca, N.Y.: Cornell University Press, 1990.

Baḥya ben Asher ben Ḥlawa. *Kitvei Rabbeinu Baḥya*. Ed. Charles B. Chavel. Jerusalem: Mossad Harav Kook, 1970.

Baḥya ben Joseph Ibn Paquda. *Sefer Torat Ḥovot ha-levavot*. Trans. Y. Qafiḥ. Jerusalem, 1973.

——, supposed author. *Les reflexions sur l'âme par Baḥya ben Joseph Ibn Pakouda*. Trans. Isaac Broyde. Paris, 1896.

Bataille, Georges. *Death and Sensuality: A Study of Eroticism and the Taboo*. New York: Walker, 1962.

Bell, Rudolph M. *Holy Anorexia*. Chicago: University of Chicago Press, 1985.

Benayahu, Meir. *Sefer Toledot ha-'Ari (Toledoth ha-Ari and Luria's 'Manner of Life' [Hanhagoth])*. Jerusalem: Ben Zvi Institute, 1967.

Beumer, Johannes. "Die marianische Deutung des Hohen Liedes in der Frühscholastik." *Zeitschrift für katholische Theologie* 76 (1954): 411–39.

Biale, David. *Eros and the Jews: From Biblical Israel to Contemporary America*. New York: Basic Books, 1992.

Blickstein, Shlomo. "Between Philosophy and Mysticism: A Study of the Philosophical-Qabbalistic Writings of Joseph Giqatila (1248–ca. 1322)." Ph.D. diss., Jewish Theological Seminary of America, 1983.

Boyarin, Daniel. *Intertextuality and the Reading of Midrash*. Bloomington: Indiana University Press, 1990.

——. "Shenei mevo'ot le-Midrash Shir ha-shirim" (Two introductions to the Midrash on the Song of Songs). *Tarbiẓ* 56 (1987): 479–500.

Brückmann, John, and Jane Couchman. "Du 'Cantique des cantiques' aux 'Carmina Burana': amour sacré et amour érotique." In *L'érotisme au moyen âge: études présentées au troisième colloque de l'Institut d'études médiévales*. Ed. Bruno Roy, 35–50. Paris: Éditions de l'aurore, 1977.

Bürgel, J. C. "Love, Lust, and Longing: Eroticism in Early Islam as Reflected in Literary Sources." In *Society and the Sexes in Medieval Islam*. Ed. Afaf Lutfi al-Sayyid-Marsot, 81–117. Malibu, Calif.: Undena Publications, 1979.

Buzy, T. R. Denis. "L'allégorie matrimoniale de Jahve d'Israel et la Cantique des Cantiques." *Revue biblique* 52 (1944): 77–90.

Bynum, Caroline Walker. *Holy Feast and Holy Fast: The Religious Significance of Food to Medieval Women*. Berkeley and Los Angeles: University of California Press, 1987.

Clark, Elizabeth A. *Ascetic Piety and Women's Faith: Essays on Late Ancient Christianity*. Lewiston, N.Y.: Edwin Mellen Press, 1986.

Clark, Gillian. "Women and Asceticism in Late Antiquity: The Refusal of Status and Gender." In *Asceticism*. Ed. Vincent L. Wimbush and Richard Valantasis, 33–48. New York: Oxford University Press, 1995.

Cohen, Gerson D. *Studies in the Varieties of Rabbinic Cultures*. Philadelphia: Jewish Publication Society of America, 1991.

Cohen, Martin S. *The Shi'ur Qomah: Liturgy and Theurgy in Pre-Kabbalistic Jewish Mysticism*. Lanham, Md.: University Press of America, 1983.

Constable, Giles. *Three Studies in Medieval Religious and Social Thought*. Cambridge: Cambridge University Press, 1995.

Cooper, Kate. *The Virgin and the Bride: Idealized Womanhood in Late Antiquity*. Cambridge: Harvard University Press, 1996.

Elliott, Dyan. *Spiritual Marriage: Sexual Abstinence in Medieval Wedlock*. Princeton, N.J.: Princeton University Press, 1993.

Ezra of Gerona. *Le commentaire d'Ezra de Gérone sur le Cantique des cantiques*. Trans. Georges Vajda. Paris: Aubier Montaigne, 1969.

Fenton, Paul B. "Daniel Ibn al-Mashita's 'Taqwim al-Adyan': New Light on the Oriental Phase of the Maimonidean Controversy." In *Genizah Research After Ninety Years The Case of Judaeo-Arabic: Papers Read at the Third Congress of the Society for Judaeo-Arabic Studies*. Ed. Joseph Blau and Stephan C. Reif, 74–81. Cambridge: Cambridge University Press, 1992.

Fishbane, Michael. *The Kiss of God: Spiritual and Mystical Death in Judaism*. Seattle: University of Washington Press, 1994.

Fulton, Rachel Lee. "The Virgin Mary and the Song of Songs in the High Middle Ages." Ph.D. diss., Columbia University, 1994.

Giffen, Lois A. *Theory of Profane Love Among the Arabs: The Development of the Genre*. New York: New York University Press, 1971.

Gikatilla, Joseph. *Ginnat 'egoz*. Jerusalem: Yeshivat ha-ḥayim weha-shalom, 1989.

——. *Sha'arei 'orah*. Ed. Joseph Ben-Shlomo. 2 vols. Jerusalem: Mosad Bialik, 1981.

Gilson, Étienne. *La théologie mystique de Saint Bernard*. Paris: Librairie Philosophique J. Vrin, 1986.

Goitein, Shlomo D. *A Mediterranean Society: The Jewish Communities of the Arab World as Portrayed in the Documents of the Cairo Geniza*. Vol. 5. Berkeley and Los Angeles: University of California Press, 1988.

Gordon, Peter E. "The Erotics of Negative Theology: Maimonides on Apprehension." *Jewish Studies Quarterly* 2 (1995): 1–38.

Gottlieb, Isaac B. "The Jewish Allegory of Love: Change and Constancy." *Journal of Jewish Thought and Philosophy* 2 (1992): 1–18.

Green, Arthur. *Keter: The Crown of God in Early Jewish Mysticism*. Princeton, N.J.: Princeton University Press, 1997.

——. "Peirush Shir ha-shirim le-R. Yiṣḥaq 'ibn Sahulah" (Rabbi Isaac Sahola's commentary on the Song of Songs)." *Meḥqerei Yerushalayim be-maḥashevet Yisra'el* (Jerusalem studies in Jewish thought) 6:3–4 (1987): 393–491.

——. "The Song of Songs in Early Jewish Mysticism." *Orim* 2 (1987): 49–63.

Hallamish, Moshe. "Meqomah shel ha-qabbalah ba-minhag (The place of Kabbalah in customs)." In Daniel Sperber, *Minhagei Yisra'el: meqorot we-toladot* (The rituals of Israel: sources and developments). Vol. 3, 173–225. Jerusalem: Mossad Harav Kook, 1994.

Hirshman, Marc. *A Rivalry of Genius: Jewish and Christian Biblical Interpretation*. Albany: State University of New York Press, 1996.

Hollywood, Amy. *The Soul as Virgin Wife: Mechthild of Madgeburg, Marguerite Porete, and Meister Eckhart*. Notre Dame, Ind.: University of Notre Dame Press, 1995.

Ḥoṭēr ben Shelomo. *The Philosophic Questions and Answers*. Ed. and trans. David R. Blumenthal. Leiden: E. J. Brill, 1981.

Ibn Aknin, Joseph ben Judah. *Hitgalut ha-sodot we-hofa'at ha-me'orot: Perush Shir ha-shirim*. Ed. and trans. A. S. Halkin. Jerusalem: Meqiṣe Nirdamim, 1964.

Idel, Moshe. "The Contribution of Abraham Abulafia's Kabbalah to the Understanding of Jewish Mysticism." In *Gershom Scholem's "Major Trends in Jewish Mysticism" 50 Years After*. Ed. Joseph Dan and Peter Schäfer, 117–43. Tübingen: J. C. B. Mohr, 1993.

——. *Kabbalah: New Perspectives*. New Haven, Conn.: Yale University Press, 1988.

——. *The Mystical Experience in Abraham Abulafia*. Albany: State University of New York Press, 1988.

——. "Rabbinism Versus Kabbalism: On G. Scholem's Phenomenology of Judaism." *Modern Judaism* 11 (1991): 281–96.

——. "Sexual Metaphors and Praxis in the Kabbalah." In *The Jewish Family: Metaphor and Memory*. Ed. David Kraemer, 179–224. Oxford: Oxford University Press, 1989.

——. "Tefiśat ha-Torah be-sifrut ha-Heikhalot we-gilguleha ba-qabbalah (The concept of Torah in Hekhalot literature and its metamorphoses in the Kabbalah)." *Meḥqerei Yerushalayim be-maḥashevet Yisra'el* (Jerusalem studies in Jewish thought) 1 (1981): 23–84.

Ivry, Alfred L. "Neoplatonic Currents in Maimonides' Thought." In *Perspectives on Maimonides: Philosophical and Historical Studies*. Ed. Joel L. Kraemer, 115–40. London: Littman Library of Jewish Civilization, 1996.

Jantzen, Grace M. "Mysticism and Experience." *Religious Studies* 25 (1989): 295–315.

——. *Power, Gender and Christian Mysticism*. Cambridge: Cambridge University Press, 1995.

Johnson, Penelope D. *Equal in Monastic Profession: Religious Women in Medieval France*. Chicago: University of Chicago Press, 1991.

Kamin, Sarah. *Bein Yehudim le-Noṣerim be-farshanut ha-Miqra* (Jews and Christian interpret the Bible). Jerusalem: Magnes Press, 1991.

Kamin, Sarah, and Avrom Saltman, eds. *Secundum Salomonem: A Thirteenth Century Latin Commentary on the Song of Songs*. Ramat Gan: Bar-Ilan University Press, 1989.

Keiser, Elizabeth B. *Courtly Desire and Medieval Homophobia: The Legitimation of Sexual Pleasure in Cleanness and Its Contexts*. New Haven, Conn.: Yale University Press, 1997.

Kimelman, Reuven. "Rabbi Yohanan and Origen on the Song of Songs: A Third-Century Jewish-Christian Disputation." *Harvard Theological Review* 73 (1980): 567–95.

Kripal, Jeffrey. *Kali's Child: The Mystical and the Erotic in the Life and Teachings of Ramakrishna*. Chicago: University of Chicago Press, 1995.

Leclercq, Jean. *The Love of Learning and the Desire for God: A Study of Monastic Culture*. Trans. Catherine Misrahi. New York: Fordham University Press, 1961.

——. *Le mariage vu par les moines au XIIe siècle*. Paris: Les Éditions du Cerf. 1983.

Levi ben Gershom. *Commentary on Song of Songs*. Trans. Menachem Kellner. New Haven, Conn.: Yale University Press, 1998.

Lévy-Valensi, Eliane A. *La poétique du Zohar*. Paris: Éditions de l'éclat, 1996.

Lieberman, Saul. "Mishnath Shir ha-Shirim." In Gershom Scholem, *Jewish Gnosticism, Merkabah Mysticism, and Talmudic Tradition*, 118–26. New York: Jewish Theological Seminary of America, 1965.

Liebes, Yehuda. *Studies in Jewish Myth and Jewish Messianism*. Trans. Batya Stein. Albany: State University of New York Press, 1993.

——. *Studies in the Zohar*. Trans. Arnold Schwartz, Stephanie Nakache, and Penina Peli. Albany: State University of New York Press, 1993.

——. "Zohar we-'Eros" (Zohar and Eros). *'Alpayyim* 9 (1994): 67–115.

Loewe, Raphael. "Apologetic Motifs in the Targum to the Song of Songs." In *Biblical Motifs: Origins and Transformations*. Ed. Alexander Altmann, 159–96. Cambridge, Mass.: Harvard University Press, 1966.

MacKendrick, Karmen. *Counterpleasures*. Albany: State University of New York Press, 1999.

Maimonides, Abraham. *The Highways to Perfection*. Trans. and ed. Samuel Rosenblatt. 2 vols. Baltimore: Johns Hopkins University Press, 1938.

Maimonides, Moses. *The Guide of the Perplexed*. Trans. Shlomo Pines with an introductory essay by Leo Strauss. Chicago: University of Chicago Press, 1963.

Marcus, Ivan G. "The Song of Songs in German Hasidism and the School of Rashi: A Preliminary Comparison." In *The Frank Talmage Memorial Volume*, Vol. 1. Ed. Barry Walfish, 181–89. Haifa: Haifa University Press, 1993.

Massignon, Louis. *The Passion of al-Hallaj: Mystic and Martyr of Islam*. Trans. Herbert Mason. 4 vols. Princeton, N.J.: Princeton University Press, 1982.

Matter, E. Ann. *The Voice of My Beloved: The Song of Songs in Western Medieval Christianity*. Philadelphia: University of Pennsylvania Press, 1990.

McGinn, Bernard. "The Language of Love in Christian and Jewish Mysticism." In *Mysticism and Language*. Ed. Steven T. Katz, 202–35. New York: Oxford University Press, 1992.

Miller, Patricia Cox. "'Pleasure of the Text, Text of Pleasure': Eros and Language in Origen's *Commentary on the Song of Songs*." *Journal of the American Academy of Religion* 54 (1986): 241–53.

Mopsik, Charles. *Le Zohar: Cantique des cantiques*. Paris: Verdier, 1999.

Naḥmanides, Moses. *Kitvei Ramban*. Ed. Charles B. Chavel. 2 vols. Jerusalem: Mossad Harav Kook, 1964.

Narboni, Moses. *The Epistle on the Possibility of Conjunction with the Active Intellect by Ibn Rushd with the Commentary of Moses Narboni*. Ed. and trans. Kalman P. Bland. New York: Jewish Theological Seminary of America, 1982.

O'Flaherty, Wendy Doniger. *Asceticism and Eroticism in the Mythology of Siva*. Oxford: Oxford University Press, 1973.

Perella, Nicolas J. *The Kiss Sacred and Profane: An Interpretative History of Kiss Symbolism and Related Religio-Erotic Themes*. Berkeley and Los Angeles: University of California Press, 1969.

Pope, Marvin A. *Song of Songs: A New Translation with Introduction and Commentary*. Garden City, N.Y.: Doubleday, 1977.

Rawidowicz, Shimon. *Studies in Jewish Thought*. Ed. Nahum N. Glatzer. Philadelphia: Jewish Publication Society of America, 1974.

Rist, John M. *Eros and Psyche: Studies in Plato, Plotinus, and Origen*. Toronto: University of Toronto Press, 1964.

Rosenberg, Shlomo. "Ha-parshanut ha-filosofit le-Shir ha-shirim—he'arot mavo" (Philosophical hermeneutics on the Song of Songs: introductory remarks). *Tarbiz* 59 (1990): 133–51.

Rougemont, Denis de. *Love in the Western World*. Trans. Montgomery Belgion. Princeton, N.J.: Princeton University Press, 1983.

Saadia ben Joseph. *Kitāb al-amānāt wal-i'tiqādāt = Sefer ha-Nivḥar be-'emunot uve-de'ot*. Ed. Y. Qafiḥ. Jerusalem: Sura Institute for Research and Publication, 1970.

Safran, Bezalel. "Rabbi Azriel and Nahmanides: Two Views of the Fall of Man." In *Rabbi Moses Nahmanides (Ramban): Explorations in His Religious and Literary Virtuosity*. Ed. Isadore Twersky, 75–106. Cambridge, Mass.: Harvard University Press, 1983.

Salfeld, S. "Das Hohelied bei den jüdischen Erklärern des Mittelalters." *Magazin für die Wissenschaft des Judenthums* 5 (1878): 150–60.

Saltman, Avrom. "'Aleksander Neqwam—Peirusho le-Shir ha-shirim weha-parshanut ha-yehudit" (Jewish exegetical material in Alexander Nequam's commentary on the Song of Songs). In *Ha-Miqra bi-re'i mefarshaw: sefer zikkaron le-Sarah Qamin* (The Bible in the light of its interpreters: Sarah Kamin memorial volume). Ed. Sara Japhet, 421–52. Jerusalem: Magnes Press, 1994.

Scheindlin, Raymond P. *The Gazelle: Medieval Hebrew Poems on God, Israel, and the Soul*. Philadelphia: Jewish Publication Society of America, 1991.

Schimmel, Annemarie. "Eros—Heavenly and Not So Heavenly—in Sufi Literature and Life." In *Society and the Sexes in Medieval Islam*. Ed. Afaf Lutfi al-Sayyid-Marsot, 119–41. Malibu, Calif.: Undena Publications, 1979.

——. *Mystical Dimensions of Islam*. Chapel Hill: University of North Carolina Press, 1975.

Scholem, Gershom. *Jewish Gnosticism, Merkabah Mysticism, and Talmudic Tradition*. New York: Jewish Theological Seminary of America, 1965.

——. *Kabbalah*. Jerusalem: Keter, 1976.

——. *Major Trends in Jewish Mysticism*. 3d rev. ed. New York: Schocken, 1954.

——. *On the Kabbalah and Its Symbolism*. Trans. Ralph Manheim. New York: Schocken, 1969.

——. *Ha-qabbalah shel Sefer ha-Temunah we-shel 'Avraham 'Abul'afiyah*. Ed. Joseph Ben-Shlomo. Jerusalem: Akademon, 1965.

Sells, Michael A. *Mystical Languages of Unsaying*. Chicago: University of Chicago Press, 1994.

Shir ha-shirim rabbah. Ed. S. Dunsky. Jerusalem: Devir, 1980.

Signer, Michael A. "Thirteenth Century Christian Hebraism: The *Expositio on Canticles* in Ms. Vat. lat. 1053." In *Approaches to Judaism in Medieval Times*. Vol. 3. Ed. David R. Blumenthal, 89–100. Atlanta, Ga.: Scholars Press, 1988.

Smalley, Beryl. *The Study of the Bible in the Middle Ages*. 1st pbk ed. Notre Dame, Ind.: University of Notre Dame Press, 1964

Thornton, Bruce S. *Eros: The Myth of Ancient Greek Sexuality*. Boulder, Colo.: Westview, 1997.

Tibbon, Moses ibn. *Perush 'al Shir ha-shirim*. Lyck, Prussia: Meqişe Nirdamim, 1874.

Tishby, Isaiah. *The Wisdom of the Zohar*. Trans. David Goldstein. 3 vols. Oxford: Oxford University Press, 1989.

Turner, Denys. *Eros and Allegory: Medieval Exegesis of the Song of Songs*. Kalamazoo, Mich.: Cistercian Publications, 1995.

Urbach, Ephraim E. "The Homiletical Interpretations of the Sages and the Expositions of Origen and the Jewish-Christian Disputation." *Scripta hierosolymitana* 22 (1971): 247–75.

Vajda, Georges. *L'amour de Dieu dans la théologie juive du moyen âge*. Paris: Librairie Philosophique J. Vrin, 1957.

Valantasis, Richard. *The Gospel of Thomas*. London: Routledge, 1997.

Vulliaud, Paul. *Le Cantique des cantiques d'après la tradition juive*. Paris: Éditions d'Aujourd'hui, 1975.

Wafer, Jim. "Vision and Passion: The Symbolism of Male Love in Islamic Mystical Literature." In *Islamic Homosexualities: Culture, History, and Literature*. Ed. Stephen O. Murray and Will Roscoe, 107–31. New York: New York University Press, 1997.

Walfish, Barry D. "Bibliografyah mu'eret 'al ha-parshanut ha-yehudit 'al Shir ha-shirim mi-ymei ha-beinayyim" (An annotated bibliography of medieval Jewish commentaries on the Song of Songs). In *Ha-Miqra bi-re'i mefarshaw: sefer zikkaron le-Sarah Qamin* (The Bible in light of its interpreters: Sarah Kamin memorial volume). Ed. Sara Japhet, 518–71. Jerusalem: Magnes Press, 1994.

Wolfson, Elliot R. *Along the Path: Studies in Kabbalistic Myth, Symbolism, and Hermeneutics*. Albany: State University of New York Press, 1995.

——. *Circle in the Square: Studies in the Use of Gender in Kabbalistic Symbolism*. Albany: State University of New York Press, 1995.

——. "Coronation of the Sabbath Bride: Kabbalistic Myth and the Ritual of Androgynisation." *Journal of Jewish Thought and Philosophy* 6 (1997): 301–43.

——. "The Engenderment of Messianic Politics: Symbolic Significance of Sabbatai Sevi's Coronation." In *Toward the Millennium: Messianic Expectations from the Bible to Waco*. Ed. Peter Schäfer and Mark R. Cohen, 203–58. Leiden: E. J. Brill, 1998.

——. "Eunuchs Who Keep the Sabbath: Becoming Male and the Ascetic Ideal in Thirteenth-Century Jewish Mysticism." In *Becoming Male in the Middle Ages*. Ed. Jeffrey J. Cohen and Bonnie Wheeler, 151–85. New York: Garland, 1997.

——. "Facing the Effaced: Mystical Eschatology and the Idealistic Orientation in the Thought of Franz Rosenzweig." *Journal for the History of Modern Theology* 4 (1997): 39–81.

——. "Fore/giveness On the Way: Nesting in the Womb of Response." *Graven Images* 4 (1998): 153–69.

——. *Through a Speculum That Shines: Vision and Imagination in Medieval Jewish Mysticism*. Princeton, N.J.: Princeton University Press, 1994.

——. "*Tiqqun ha-Shekhinah*: Redemption and the Overcoming of Gender Dimorphism in the Messianic Kabbalah of Moses Hayyim Luzzatto." *History of Religions* 36 (1997): 289–332.

——. "Weeping, Death, and Spiritual Ascent in Sixteenth-Century Jewish Mysticism." In *Death, Ecstasy, and Other Worldly Journeys*. Ed. John J. Collins and Michael Fishbane, 209–47. Albany: State University of New York Press, 1995.

Wright, Constance S. "The Influence of the Exegetical Tradition of the 'Song of Songs' on the Secular and Religious Love Lyrics in Ms. Harley 2253." Ph.D. diss., University of California, Berkeley, 1966.

Zaehner, R. C. *Mysticism Sacred and Profane: An Inquiry into Some Varieties of Praeternatural Experience*. Oxford: Oxford University Press, 1957.

Zohar ḥadash. Ed. Reuven Margaliot. Jerusalem: Mossad Harav Kook, 1978.

8

Typology, Narrative, and History

Isaac ben Joseph ha-Kohen on the Book of Ruth

BARRY D. WALFISH

Commentaries on the book of Ruth are relatively uncommon in both Jewish and Christian exegesis.[1] Of those extant, one of the most intriguing is that of Isaac ben Joseph ha-Kohen, written around 1400 and published in Sabbioneta, Italy, in 1551.[2]

Isaac lived in Spain, perhaps in the town of Jativa, Valencia, around the turn of the fifteenth century.[3] His only other extant works are commentaries on the books of Esther and Ecclesiastes, neither of which has ever been published. The commentary on Ruth has several remarkable features. The first is the means by which Isaac claims to have come to his understanding of the book's contents. The second is his use of typological exegesis. The third is the interweaving of this typology with the narrative plot line of the book of Ruth.

The Purpose of the Commentary

Like other late medieval exegetes, Isaac justifies his commentary by claiming that the previous commentaries did not deal with all the issues adequately.[4] He writes that he has been troubled by several aspects of the book, especially the advice given by an intelligent woman (Naomi) to her companion (Ruth) to uncover the feet of a great and noble man, "an action which, when made known publicly, would be perceived to be brazen and degrading to the honor of all women."[5] Boaz's reaction to her brazen act is also difficult to understand. Instead of chastising Ruth, Boaz praises her and does not rest until he marries her. Isaac simply cannot understand how such a book, which presumably condones immoral behavior and promiscuity, could have been included in the canon.

Isaac's discomfort is difficult to fathom. The book of Ruth was highly regarded in rabbinic literature and its characters effusively praised for their actions at every point in the story, including the sexually charged scene on the threshing floor.[6] For the Sages, the book of Ruth exemplifies, above all else, the quality of *ḥesed*, loving-kindness, as well as many other praiseworthy virtues, such as modesty, loyalty, and obedience.[7] Nevertheless, Isaac was obviously troubled by the book's contents and had been pondering its meaning for some time. Initially, he tried to clarify the book's meaning through speculation, but he found that he was incapable of attaining true insights. The author then claims that he received a nocturnal vision which rescued him from his dilemma:

> While I was enjoying sweet slumber, a human-like figure awakened me and instructed me: "Stand on your feet so that I can reveal to you precious secrets which are alluded to herein [i.e., in the book of Ruth]. . . . Know that this book was written by the Prophet Samuel with prophetic inspiration . . . and any such book has big roots and deep secrets. Sometimes these secrets concern metaphysical matters and sometimes they refer to things destined to befall an individual or individuals, or a nation or a number of nations. These matters are revealed to the prophets, who will allude to them cryptically and enigmatically as is required by the nature of the situation."[8]

What is revealed to our author is the second unusual feature of this commentary—a well-developed, richly nuanced typology, in which each character in the book is a type or figure (*mashal*) of a different actor in the drama of Jewish history, from the time of King David until the arrival of the Messiah. In this way, the narrative is raised to the level of prophecy.

The third unusual and distinctive feature of this commentary is the close link between the typology and the story line of the book of Ruth. The result is a skillfully woven fabric of typological, historical, and narrative threads, the likes of which have seldom if ever been seen in medieval exegesis, either Christian or Jewish.

The figurative story told in the book of Ruth begins with the Davidic dynasty and the time of the division into two kingdoms, and then alludes to the cause for the split, the First Temple period, the exile of the ten tribes, the Babylonian exile, the building of the Second Temple, the Roman dispersion, and finally the future coming of the redeemer, and the missions of Elijah and Michael.

The character identifications are not arbitrary, but, as is often the case in Christian typology, are based on linguistic allusions connected to the root meanings of their names.[9] Elimelech (= my God is king) is a figure (or type; Hebrew, *mashal*) for the Davidic dynasty in its heyday. Naomi (= pleasantness), his wife, is a figure for the Israelite nation and all that adhere to her faith, obeying the "pleasant" divine laws. Machlon and Chilion, Naomi's and Elimelech's sons, represent the time when there were two kingdoms in Israel. The name Machlon, which in its root alludes to illness (*maḥalah*), represents the Kingdom of Judah, whose strength was steadily sapped from the time of Rehoboam onward. The name also alludes to forgiveness (*meḥilah*), as was granted to Judah in the time of Hezekiah. The name of Chilion, representing the Kingdom of Israel, alludes both to his role as a vessel (*keli*) for renewal after the unsatisfactory reply of Rehoboam to the people (1 Kings 12:1–20), and also to his ultimate destruction (from the root *k-l-h*). Isaac notes that it is in the nature of prophetic revelation to attach many intentions to one word. Ruth is a figure for the tribes of Judah and Benjamin who cleaved to God and his anointed one, called Machlon; Orpah is a figure for the other tribes, who turned their backs (*'oref* = back of the neck) to the kingdom (of Judah) and committed idolatry. Boaz whose name means "in him is strength," is a figure for God. He is also called an acquaintance of Naomi's husband Elimelech (Ruth 2:1), which alludes to God's providence for David and Solomon.

Isaac then proceeds to give a verse-by-verse exposition of the biblical text, a summary of which follows.

Chapter 1: First Temple Period

"In the days when judges judged" (Ruth 1:1) refers to David's judgment to Mephibosheth that he and Ziba would divide the field [that he had originally given to Mephibosheth] (2 Sam 19:30). This act of betrayal sealed the fate of David's kingdom and was the reason for bringing about exile and poverty, and this is the antitype (*nimshal*) of the famine mentioned in 1:1.[10] As long as Elimelech was alive, the kingdom was united. When he died, his sons married Moabite women, which means that they worshipped idols. Orpah is mentioned first because she was the first to worship, followed by Ruth, who also did, but not as much. Jeroboam (= Chilion) and Israel (= Orpah) worshipped idols and caused the Judeans to be dragged into idolatry as well. This situation lasted the whole time of the First Temple, 410 years, alluded to in *ke-'eśer-shanim* (about ten years)(Ruth 1:4).[11]

Chapter 1:19–2:20: Second Temple Period

The deaths of Machlon and Chilion allude to the destruction of both of these kingdoms. After the destruction, Naomi, or the Israelite nation who had lost the two dynasties and the two kingdoms, returns to Bethlehem. This return alludes to the return of the Jewish people to the Land of Israel after the Babylonian captivity. When Naomi realized that she would not be restored to her former greatness, she told her daughters-in-law to go back. All her efforts to dissuade them refer to the sufferings of the exile. Naomi's statement that she was too old to remarry indicates that there was not much hope for a renewed kingdom. Orpah kisses Naomi and returns to her people. Her leaving is a figure for those Israelites who gave up and descended into idolatry—the ten tribes who were lost forever to the Jewish people. Ruth insists on staying with Naomi. Her response to Naomi and her insistence on cleaving to her is a figure for those who are strong in their faith and do not hesitate or falter because of their troubles. She thus represents to the remnant upon whom God had mercy and helped to return to Jerusalem in the days of Cyrus.

The reaction of the people on seeing Naomi and their asking *Ha-zot Na'omi?* (Can this be Naomi? 1:19) is a figure for the state of the Jewish people at this time—only a shadow of its former self. Naomi had left full, with all of her people, and had returned with only a small remnant. That remnant is Ruth, who is likened to a gleaner in the field.

The period of the harvest described in chapter 2 is a prefiguration of the early Second Temple period in which the Land of Israel is under Persian domination. The kings of Media and Persia are the reapers. Boaz, who symbolizes God, grants them prosperity. Ruth's diligence in gleaning is a figure for the Jewish people's industry in rebuilding the land. Boaz's exhortation to Ruth that she not glean in another field (2:8) is a warning to the people not to worship idols. And indeed there was very little idolatry in Second Temple times. Boaz's instructions to his lads to leave extra sheaves for Ruth to gather alludes to the kings of Persia helping the Jews rebuild the Temple. The sheaves (*'omarim*) in 2:15 refer to the Jews' enemies, and the instruction to allow Ruth to glean among the sheaves alludes to the success of the Hasmonean dynasty. Ruth's gleaning in the field till the evening (2:17) refers to the time up to the next exile. The reference to the harvest of both the barley and the wheat refers to both the bad times and the good during the Second Temple period. "She remained with her mother-in-law" (2:23) alludes to the return to exile after the destruction of the Second Temple.

Chapter 3:1–7: Mystical Contemplation and Union

At this point the story takes a detour into the realm of kabbalah and mystic contemplation. Naomi's search for a home where Ruth might be happy is a figure for the remnant of the Jewish people (Ruth) cleaving to God (Boaz) in an attempt to bring about the advent of the Messiah. The Jewish people were not completely sovereign during the Second Temple period but were in an intermediate state somewhere between success and degradation. Naomi gives Ruth advice on how to get close to Boaz, that is, God. All of Ruth's preparations are part of the process of repentance and removal of sins. The descent to the granary signifies the embarkation on a voyage of mystic contemplation. Ruth rises up through the levels of contemplation until she reaches God's feet.

The uncovering of Boaz's feet signifies that Ruth's repentance should have reached the divine throne. Isaac is aware of the difficulties in this analogy, in that the distinction between Ruth and Naomi is blurred, and he points out that both Ruth and Orpah are parts of Naomi. He finds support for this position in the *ketiv* (written) spellings in v. 3 (*we-yaradeti* [I will go down] and *we-shakhavti* [I will lie down]),[12] which indicate to him that Naomi is speaking for herself as well as to Ruth. Ruth did whatever Naomi told her to do and Boaz (God) ate and drank. Boaz (God), pleased with his food and drink, as if he had eaten of her sacrifices and drunk of her libations, is drawn by his desire to deal with Ruth's condition. Therefore, he descends by emanation until the last level which separates the divine from the human soul. This action is alluded to by the word *lishkav* (to lie), which is an anagram for *be-sekhel* (with intellect, i.e., through contemplation). This understanding of the text is affirmed for Isaac by the fact that it says that Boaz ate and drank after Ruth had gone down to the granary. According to the *peshaṭ* (contextual meaning) it should have been the other way around.[13] This, then, provides justification for seeing Boaz's actions as being in some way determined by those of Ruth. It is her initiative that brings about the mystical union. We have here an interesting demonstration of the interplay between different levels of interpretation.

Chapter 3:8–4:22: Redemption

The story now returns to the historical/typological plane and the focus shifts to the theme of redemption. The last chapter and a half of the book focus on the need to find for Ruth a husband who will redeem her and her husband's property and provide a namesake for her dead husband. The terms *go'el* and forms of the root *g-'-l* (redeem) figure prominently in this section and lend themselves readily to typological interpretation with respect to the final redemption of the people. "It came to pass at midnight" (Ruth 3:8) refers to the darkness of the exile. "The man trembled" recalls other times in history when God has felt compassion for Israel. He awakens to find the remnant of Israel (the woman, Ruth) pleading for mercy at his feet because he is a redeemer. Boaz (God) replies to her that "her latest deed of loyalty is greater than her first" (3:10). This refers to the behavior of the Jewish people in the different exiles. In the first exile among the Persians and the Medes, the enticements to idolatry were not that great and there were great leaders like Mordecai, Esther, and Daniel to help them withstand temptation. But in the second exile, that of Edom and Ishmael, the temptations were greater, since Christians and Muslims behave in some ways like Jews and imitate their laws.[14] Both religions have much to commend them and count many good people among their adherents. But still, Israel, that is, Ruth, was not tempted to follow them and learn their ways.

Isaac now introduces the concept of two types of redemption: remunerative (*gemulit*), to recompense the people for their good deeds, if they are deserving; and merciful (*raḥmanit*), offering them the ultimate reward even if they are not deserving.[15] Verse 3:13 is interpreted in this light. Boaz says to Ruth, "Spend the night here." The night refers to the exile. In the morning, when the time of redemption comes, *'im yig'alekh ṭov yig'al*, if you are worthy of being redeemed because of your merit (*ṭov*), well and good, the redemption will occur immediately on this basis. If not, then the redemption out of mercy will have to take effect. And this is what happens. She is not found worthy for immediate redemption. The close relative who can redeem (*go'el qarov*) refers to the righteous of Israel, whose good deeds could bring on the redemption. Boaz makes it clear to the redeeming relative that if he is unable to redeem, then he, Boaz, will (4:4). The redeemer answers that he will redeem, meaning that he can free Naomi from the yoke of oppression, that is, from the subjugation of Edom. This indeed came true when Muslims conquered the Land of Israel. For this small feat, the redeemer's power was sufficient.

Boaz replies that this is not enough but demands that the name of the deceased be called after his inheritance (4:5), that is, that independent rule should be restored to Israel by the Messiah. The redeemer replies that he does not have the power to do this, because for this the merits are lacking, and he drops out of the picture. The words he says, *ge'al lekha et ge'ulati* (you redeem my inheritance; 4:6), refer to the final end alluded to in the Book of Daniel.

"And Boaz took Ruth" (4:13) alludes to God providing for *Keneset Yis'ra'el* (The Assembly of Israel) by taking her as a wife. He made a union with her in such a way that resulted in a pregnancy, and she bore a son who is the redeemer who would lead the people. Only God gave Ruth this child—she wasn't worthy by virtue of her personal merit to produce a redeemer (an interesting christological allusion).

Upon the birth of the child, the women (an allusion to the nations of the world) say to Naomi, "Blessed is the Lord who has not withheld a redeemer from you" (4:14). This is an unusual turn of phrase. Rather than *lo hishbit* (not withheld), it could have said *natan lakh* (gave you) or *shalaḥ lakh* (sent you). It is used for something that is ready to be brought into action—an allusion that when the time of redemption comes, there will be no interference from on high. Here he refers to the verse, "I the Lord will speed it in due time" (*'Ani ha-Shem be-'ittah 'aḥishennah*) (Isa 60:22) and to the rabbinic gloss on this verse.[16] The ultimate redemption is destined to happen and would require an effort for it to be prevented. He finds in the name Oved, the son born to Boaz and Ruth, allusions to the restoration of the sacrificial cult (*'avodah*) in the Temple.

Isaac concludes his commentary by pointing out that all of these worthy allusions justify the inclusion of the book in the canon. He sees the interpretation of the book he has presented as a product of the prophetic soul which is above all the others. He thanks God for giving him this insight and offers a prayer for the speedy arrival of the Messiah.

The interpretation of the book of Ruth offered by Isaac has much charm and appeal. It offers an alternative deeper reading of the book on a level which the average Jew could comprehend, as opposed to a purely philosophical-allegorical or mystical[17] reading, which would have been beyond the grasp of all but the initiated.

Typology in Jewish Exegetical Literature

Typology, or figural interpretation, the term preferred by Erich Auerbach,[18] has traditionally been associated almost exclusively with the Christian understanding of the Hebrew Bible. It is characterized by the effort to establish symbolic connections between certain events, persons, or things in the Hebrew Bible (Old Testament) and other events, persons, or things in the New Testament, pertaining particularly to the life of Jesus. The purpose of this effort is to "strip the Old Testament of its normative character and show that it is merely a shadow of things to come."[19] What distinguishes this method from allegory is that both poles of the figure, the promise and fulfillment, or type and anti-type, are real historical events. Some have already been fulfilled in the life of Jesus, and others will be fulfilled in the second coming.[20] This type of exegesis, which originated with the Letters of Paul in the New Testament,[21] continued to be used in the works of the Church Fathers and remained popular in the Middle Ages[22] and in the modern period through the nineteenth century. With the rise of modern biblical criticism, it, like much of traditional Christian exegesis, fell into general disfavor.[23]

According to Amos Funkenstein, this method is relatively underused in Jewish exegesis.[24] However, recently Marc Saperstein has demonstrated that its use was not as peripheral as Funkenstein would have us believe and that it was especially popular in homiletical literature in the late medieval and early modern periods.[25] Sarah Kamin has also written about Rashi's use of the term *dugma* in his commentary on Song of Songs, a clear instance of typological exegesis, and one that Funkenstein seems to have overlooked.[26] The case of Rashi is probably the earliest occurrence of typology in medieval Jewish exegesis and seems to have been influenced by Christian use of this method. But, already in the midrash, parallels were drawn between events in the lives of the biblical patriarchs and the lives of their descendants in biblical times, and Judah Goldin has pointed out how the midrash interpreted biblical verses to show how they alluded to the messianic age, thus showing that every age could be paradigmatic of another, especially the messianic age.[27] Of course, there is nothing intrinsically Christian about the word *typology* itself. One of the original connotations of the word *typos* is that of "archetype," "pattern," or "model" capable of exact repetition in numerous instances. Another is "prescribed form or model to be imitated."[28] In this sense, then, figures or events in the Hebrew Bible can be understood, in a Jewish context, to model, prefigure, or serve as types of events in a later stage in Jewish history.[29] In the Middle Ages, the most famous proponent of this method was Moses ben Naḥman, or Naḥmanides (1194–1270), who used it extensively in his Torah commentary.[30] In a famous methodological statement in his commentary on Genesis 12:6, he states:

> I shall tell you a rule which applies in all the subsequent passages concerning Abraham, Isaac and Jacob, . . . "that everything which occurred to the fathers is a sign for the sons." Therefore the scriptures describe at length the travels and the well-digging and the other events, and one might think that they are superfluous and useless. But they are all there to teach about the future, because whenever something happens to one of the three patriarchs, one may understand from it that which has been predestined to befall his progeny. Know that whenever a divine decree goes from the potentiality of a decree to the actuality of a similitude [prefiguration, *dimyon* in Hebrew], it will be fulfilled no matter what. . . . And therefore God kept Abraham in the land [of Israel] and made for him similitudes (*dimyonot*) for everything that was destined to befall his progeny.[31]

In his commentary, Isaac makes a similar programmatic statement:

> Although the story of the book is true and everything told in it actually happened, it also is a *mashal* [figure or type] for something else which agrees with the *nimshal* [thing alluded to or antitype], for *whatever happened to the ancestors* [*lit. fathers*] *is a sign for the children* [*lit. sons*], and many things are alluded to in it, some of which are even today in the future, and some of which already occurred in the past, some time after the writing of the book.[32]

This statement reflects the influence of Naḥmanides (the wording of the key phrase is exactly the same) and other rabbinic statements of a similar nature.[33] Though Isaac ben Joseph uses the term *mashal* rather than the *dimyon* of Naḥmanides, his approach is very similar.[34] The main difference is Naḥmanides' stress on God's intention in guiding the actions of the Patriarchs in order that these actions might serve as similitudes for future events in the life of the people. In Isaac's commentary this intentionality seems to be lacking. Also apparent is a connection between typology and prophecy which is suggestive of the Christian use of prophetic allegory. It should be pointed out, however, that the relationship between type and antitype in Christian literature is quite different from that described in the works of Naḥmanides or Isaac ben Joseph. Christian typological exegesis uses the language of shadow and reality or promise and fulfillment. The Old Testament figures are shadows which are predictive of the reality in the New Testament and distinctly subordinate and inferior to it.[35] This is decidedly not the case with the Jewish exegetes, who had no interest in denigrating the Hebrew Bible. Isaac makes it especially clear that he is providing another level of meaning for the text which in no way undermines or detracts from the historical meaning.[36]

In his study of the symbolic exegesis of Naḥmanides,[37] Amos Funkenstein argues that typological exegesis was relatively scarce, peripheral, and unimaginative among Jewish exegetes. He gives several reasons to account for this situation.[38] One is that this method was predominantly Christian and had been used heavily and effectively by Christians in their appropriation of the Hebrew Bible for their own purposes.

Another reason is that Jews were never "compelled to demonstrate the unity-within-diversity of two or more successive revelations"; this need to demonstrate the concordance of the Old and the New Testaments was a constant imperative for Christians who engaged in this type of exegesis.[39]

Third, Funkenstein argues that for Naḥmanides, the theosophical had more appeal than the historiosophical, and the same deeds of the Patriarchs symbolized for him divine processes and powers as understood in the kabbalah, and therefore the mystical method dominated the typological in his exegesis.

The final reason concerns a major difference in worldview between Judaism and Christianity. Christianity has a distinct sense of progress within history, from the old to the new dispensation, of the development of the church militant and triumphant, progress both within and without, and an ever-widening mission to the nations of the world. Jews, according to Funkenstein, lack such a sense of progress and therefore also lacked the desire to show how events repeated themselves periodically on a higher level.

Funkenstein's analysis is not entirely persuasive. Marc Saperstein has already pointed to some of its shortcomings in his article cited earlier.[40] Isaac's commentary provides further grounds on which to challenge the validity of much of his argumentation. There is certainly no question that typological exegesis served an important purpose in Christian theology, in showing the adumbration of New Testament events in the Hebrew Bible. It is logical to assume that Jews would shy away from a method that was overtly christological. But there existed ample examples of the methodology in midrashic texts to give it sufficient legitimization.[41] If typology was used by Christians "to eliminate Jewish history and national characters from the Hebrew Bible, in order to make it acceptable to the Celtic and Germanic peoples,"[42] it could be used just as effectively to restore them, or to stress their essential Jewishness and historical immediacy. Indeed, Saperstein in his article makes a strong case for the centrality of typological exegesis in Jewish homiletical literature after Naḥmanides, beginning with Jacob ben Ḥananel Siqili of the fourteenth century. According to Saperstein, Jacob's sermons "reveal typology as a powerful tool for reading the patriarchal narratives as messianic texts.[43] Isaac's Ruth commentary is another outstanding example of the effectiveness of this methodology and, as was discussed earlier, it succeeds in reading the Ruth narrative as a messianic text.

Funkenstein's argument concerning the greater appeal of theosophy is a subjective one. It is difficult to determine why an exegete comments on some verses and not others, or uses a particular method in some places and not others. And of course, it should not be necessary to point out that these methods were not mutually exclusive, and several could be applied to the same verse if the exegete felt so inclined, as does Naḥmanides and his younger contemporary, Baḥya ben Asher. In any case, what may be true for Naḥmanides was not necessarily so for others. Isaac ben Joseph, for instance, was kabbalistically engaged but still chose to stress typology in his Ruth commentary.

Funkenstein's fourth reason is the weakest. Even in the Middle Ages, Jews had a sense of progress in history and felt that they were moving to an age in which conditions would change for them and the other nations and a new era would ensue—the Messianic Age. This longing for redemption is an ever-present theme in Jewish theological writing and becomes increasingly predominant in the late Middle Ages, as the political situation in Spain and elsewhere steadily deteriorates and Jewish communities are threatened with physical as well as spiritual destruction.[44]

Conclusion

To my knowledge, Isaac ben Joseph's commentary on the book of Ruth is the only medieval example of a complete commentary devoted almost exclusively to typological exegesis.[45] Isaac's typology is comprehensive and is sustained over the course of the entire book. Obviously well versed in kabbalah, he introduces a mystical level of interpretation at several points in his commentary without deviating too far from the typology. His emphasis on the redemption of the Jewish people is a reflection of his time, an age when the Jewish people in Spain were being persecuted and messianic ferment was high.[46] The commentary's claim of prophetic inspiration is also highly unusual. Isaac's commentary is a fine example of typological exegesis applied to a narrative text in a Jewish-messianic context. It provides important evidence from a different genre, that of commentary, to strengthen Saperstein's claim that typological exegesis played a central role in conveying the message that the biblical narratives "were not merely part of an ancient past, but that they bore a historical message for the present and the future."[47] Indeed this message is still being heard today.[48]

Notes

Dedicated to my teacher Prof. Moshe Greenberg on his seventieth birthday. My thanks to Marc Saperstein for his comments on an earlier draft of this essay.

1. See Walfish, "Annotated Bibliography," and Martel, *Repertoire*. Martel lists eighty-two commentaries and seventy-nine sermon collections. The early medieval Jewish exegesis was studied and much of it translated by Beattie, *Jewish Exegesis of the Book of Ruth*.

2. This commentary first came to my attention while I was gathering material for my doctoral dissertation on the medieval exegesis of the book of Esther. I brought it to the attention of Frank Talmage, who mentioned it briefly in his "Apples of Gold," 314 (reprint, 109). I have based my study of Isaac's commentary not on the printed edition, which is full of errors, but rather on one of the six extant MSS: New York, Jewish Theological Seminary of America, MS L1052, fols. 77r-87v (IMHM no. 24255) (henceforth MS J). This is a fifteenth-century Spanish MS written in a clear Sephardic cursive script.

3. The little that is known is summarized in the appendix of Walfish, *Esther*, 223–24.

4. Cf. Walfish, *Esther*, 5–7.

5. MS J, fol. 77r.

6. That the Sages recognized the sexual overtones in this scene is clearly seen in the following passage from Ruth Rabbah 6.1: "*And turned himself* (Ruth 3:8). She clung to him like ivy, and he began to finger her hair. 'Spirits have no hair,' he thought, so he said, '*Who are you?* (3:9), a woman or a spirit?' She answered, 'A woman.' 'A maiden or a married woman?' She answered, 'A maiden.' 'Are you clean or unclean?' She answered, 'Clean.' *And behold a woman*, purest of women, *lay at his feet*. . . ."

7. See Bronner, "Thematic Approach to Ruth in Rabbinic Literature."

8. MS J, 77r-v.

9. An example from the New Testament is the identification of John the Baptist with Elijah in Mark 9:9–13 and Matthew 17:9–13. Or see Origen's comment on the nature of the harlot Rahab: "Let us now see who this harlot is. Her name is Rahab, which means 'breadth.' What is this breadth but the Church of Christ which is made up of sinners and harlots. It is this breadth which receives the spies of Jesus (Joshua)." (In PG 12.839d; translated in Danielou, *From Shadows*, 249). Woollcombe, "Biblical Origins," 40, gives a more far-fetched example of Isaac, who carried the wood for his sacrifice, being portrayed as "a type of Simon of Cyrene, who carried the wood of the cross, on the grounds of an etymological similarity between the names of their children."

10. See BT Shabbat 56b, where the breakup of the united kingdom of David and Solomon is portrayed as punishment for David's act of betrayal, according to the principle of retributive justice (*middah ke-neged middah*).

11. *Shanim* in *gematria* = 400, plus 10 = 410.

12. I.e., the first person singular forms, as opposed to the *qere* forms, which are second person feminine singular. The *ketiv* (written) and *qere* (read) forms indicate places where the text is problematic and variants were suggested or recorded by scribes in ancient times. The *ketiv* form is the received text and the *qere* form is the variant which in the course of time became obligatory. See Tov, *Textual criticism*, 58–63, esp. 62–63.

13. See MS J, fol. 82v.

14. "Edom and Ishmael—one is poor and the other rich." This a gloss on *'im dal 'im 'ashir*, that Ruth was not tempted by the youths, "whether poor or rich." According to Isaac, the religion of Edom, i.e., Christianity, "attracts those who wish to live in poverty and submission, shunning bodily pleasures. Many priests come from them. Ishmael, on the other hand, follows the path of wealth and haughtiness and dedication to bodily pleasures" (MS J, fol. 83r-v). There are many comparisons between Christians and Muslims in Jewish literature of the late Middle Ages. See, e.g., the views of Abraham Saba, summarized in Walfish, *Esther*, 136–39, and Septimus, "Taḥat 'Edom." Simeon ben Ẓemaḥ Duran's *Qeshet u-magen* is a rare example of a Jewish polemic directed against both Christianity and Islam. See Mark Cohen, *Under Crescent and Cross*, 160–61. For Christianity as an imitation of Judaism, see Saperstein, "Sermons," 228 and 239, n. 12 (reprint, 61), citing Jacob Anatoli.

15. I am not aware of other sources that use this terminology. Marc Saperstein (personal communication) suggests it may be Ibn Tibbonide.

16. BT Sanhedrin 98a: "It is written: 'in due time' and it is written 'I will speed it.' If they have merit, 'I will speed it'; if they do not have merit, 'in due time.'" See also discussion by Saadia ben Joseph, *Book of Beliefs and Opinions*, 301.

17. Cf. *Midrash ha-ne'elam* on Ruth. English translation: *The Mystical Study of Ruth*, ed. and trans. Englander.

18. Auerbach, "Figura."

19. Ibid., 50.

20. Ibid., 53. Cf. Danielou, *From Shadows*, 52: ". . . the essence of typology lies in showing that it is history itself which is figurative rather than in replacing history with allegory."

21. E.g., 1 Corinthians 5:7, 10:6, 11, 15:21; Romans 5:12–14; Hebrews 9:11–10:17.

22. A very useful source for the numerous figurative interpretations of the Old Testament in Christian patristic and medieval literature is the index volume to Migne's *Patrologia Latina*. See esp., "Index de allegoriis Veteris Testamenti," in PL 219.123–127, and "Index figurarum V.T.," in PL 219.242–259.

23. But see, e.g., Lampe, "The Reasonableness of Typology."

24. Funkenstein, "Naḥmanides' Symbolical Reading of History"; expanded Hebrew version: "Parshanuto ha-ṭippologit shel ha-Ramban," 35–59, esp. 35.

25. Saperstein, "Jewish Typological Exegesis after Naḥmanides."

26. See Kamin, "Dugma."

27. See Goldin, "Of Midrash and the Messianic Theme," 359–60. Goldin cites a passage from *Pirqei de-Rabbi 'Eli'ezer*, ed. Mandelbaum, 105, in which a section from Isaiah relating to the messianic age is shown to hark back to the Exodus and the revelation at Sinai.

28. See Woollcombe, "Biblical Origins," 61.

29. See e.g., Gen. Rab. 40:6: "You find that everything written about Abraham is written about his children." Parallels are then given between verses referring to Abraham and those referring to Jacob or the Israelites in the Book of Exodus. In Tanḥuma Wa-yiggash 10, parallels are drawn between the life of Joseph and subsequent events in the history of the Jewish people in biblical times.

30. See articles by Funkenstein, and more recently, the chapter by Perani in Idel and Perani, *Naḥmanide esegeta e cabbalista*, 87–95.

31. Naḥmanides, *Peirushei ha-Torah*, 1:77.

32. MS J, fol. 77v.

33. Cf. Tanḥuma Lekh lekha 9: "R. Joshua of Sikhnin said: The blessed Holy One gave a sign to Abraham that everything that happened to him would happen to his children" (*'Amar R. Yehoshu'a de-Sikhnin: Siman natan lo ha-qadosh barukh hu le-'Avraham she-kol mah she-'ira' lo 'ira' le-vanaw*). See also Ramban to Genesis 26:29: "The sons performed deeds similar to those of their fathers" (*ukhe-ma'aśeh 'avot 'asu banim*). Also Baḥya ben Asher, *Beiur 'al la-Torah* 1:137 ad Genesis 12:6: "the fathers are a sign for the sons" (*ha-'avot siman la-banim*), and 1:238 ad Genesis 28:6: "the sons repeat the deeds of the fathers" (*ma'aśeh-'avot ya'aśu banim*). The most famous formulation of this concept is *ma'aśeh 'avot siman la-banim*, "the deed of the fathers is a sign for the sons," which apparently first appears in the talmudic commentary of Samuel Edels (1555–1629), *Ḥiddushei 'aggadot* Ḥagigah 5b, 'Avodah zarah 8b. Cf. Jonah Fraenkel, *Darkhei ha-'Aggadah weha-midrash*, 2:607 n. 59. Edels seems to imply that this adage is not his invention, so an earlier source may still come to light. The phrase also appears in Horowitz, *Shenei luḥot ha-berit*, Lekh lekha 4 and Wa-yishlaḥ 6. Horowitz (1565–1635) was a younger contemporary of Edels.

34. Very similar use of this word is made by the thirteenth-century philosopher and kabbalist Isaac Ibn Latif, who in the early version of his *Sha'ar ha-shamayim* (Gate of heaven), written before 1238, speaks of four methods of scriptural interpretation, one of which is the *mashal*, or philosophical-allegorical method. See Wilensky, "Isaac Ibn Latif," 219. Further research may reveal other examples of the use of this term, which differs from the terminology of Naḥmanides and from the *remez*, the more common term for philosophical allegory made famous in the *Zohar* and other kabbalistic writings as part of the acronym *pardes*. Isaac ben Joseph's use of *mashal* as type or figure can be seen as a variation of the more common usage. The word *mashal* is also used occasionally in midrashic literature and more generally in the Middle Ages to indicate a parabolic or allegorical sense. This is usually the case in Naḥmanides with some exceptions. See Wolfson, "By Way of Truth," 114, 124–25.

35. See, e.g., Danielou, *From Shadows*, 282–83, who quotes Origen on the Law of Moses. The Old Testament has been superseded, but the Church, rather than rejecting it, preserves it because it contains the type of Christ. Christians receive the Law of Moses when it is read to them by Jesus, who explains to them its spiritual significance. Thus the letter of the law as expressed in the Old Testament is a foreshadowing of the spiritual reality found in the New Testament.

36. In the case of Naḥmanides, we are faced with his intriguing statement that God kept Abraham and the other Patriarchs wandering in the Land of Israel in order to provide more opportunities for them to make figures (*dimyonot*) that prefigure events in the history of the nation. However, even here, there is no intention to denigrate or dismiss the historical meaning as being unimportant or shadowy. Rather, the purpose is to establish connections between the sacred text of the Jewish people and the subsequent history of that people which this text alludes to.

37. Others, such as Baḥya ben Asher, and Abraham Saba, use it on occasion. See Talmage, "Apples of Gold," 314, 346 n.7 (in the reprint: 109, 141 n.7).

38. See Funkenstein, "Symbolical Reading," 142–43.

39. Ibid., 142.

40. See Saperstein, "Jewish Typological Exegesis," 159–60, 169.

41. Ibid., 162.

42. See Auerbach, "Figura," 52.

43. On the other hand, Saperstein overstates his case when he claims that "typological exegesis remained 'peripheral and unimaginative' among Christian writers in the Middle Ages" ("Jewish Typological Exegesis," 169). See, for example, the recent critique of Auerbach's essay by Emmerson, "Figura and the Medieval Typological Imagination." Emmerson shows that Auerbach's and other

scholars' evaluations of typological exegesis depend too heavily on patristic sources. He points out that the apologetic motivations of early Christian exegetes give way in the Middle Ages to the practical concern for deriving moral lessons for the individual Christian. He describes the typological imagination of the Middle Ages as "neither schematic, nor circumscribed, but fluid and wide-ranging; it was not primarily concerned with justifying doctrine, but with celebrating the essential congruity discovered in superficially differing stories and applying their moral lessons to the lives of Christians. It was a lively imagination nourished by a multitude of amazing and varied *exempla*" (ibid., 42). Emmerson's conclusions are based on his analysis of two popular late-medieval illustrated books, the *Biblia pauperum* and the *Speculum humanae salvationis*. One can see here an obvious parallel with some of the homiletical sources cited by Saperstein, which also showed a concern for conveying social criticism and deriving practical lessons for the audience hearing the sermons (see Saperstein, "Jewish Typological Exegesis," 166). On the *Biblia pauperum*, see Labriola and Smeltz, *The Bible of the Poor*, and Henry, *Biblia pauperum*, which reproduce blockbooks with commentary. On the *Speculum humanae*, see Henry, *The Mirour of Mans Saluacioune* which is an edition of a Middle English translation of the *Speculum humanae*. Both of these works, which were probably intended for use as an aid to meditation (Henry, *Biblia pauperum*, 18), contain illustrations of Old Testament scenes juxtaposed with scenes from the New Testament depicting the life of Jesus. The richness of the typology in these works is quite striking. Interestingly, the book of Ruth does not figure in either of these works.

44. See Moshe Idel, introd. to Aescoly, *ha-Tenu'ot ha-meshiḥiyyot be-Yisra'el*, 16–28; Tishby, *Meshiḥiyyut*.

45. It should be pointed out that all the examples cited in Saperstein's article are taken from homiletical literature. In Rashi's Song of Songs commentary, *dugma* appears twenty times, but many verses are not interpreted in this way. See "Dugma," Kamin, 42, n.3. In any case, the Song of Songs is a collection of love poems which may have a few narrative elements but these are at best loosely connected.

46. The commentary of Abraham Saba, *'Eshkol ha-kofer 'al Megillat Rut*, written about a hundred years later, after the expulsion from Portugal, is also replete with references to redemption.

47. Saperstein, "Jewish Typological Exegesis," 170. As for his argument that no aspect of Naḥmanides' exegesis had greater impact on subsequent generations than his typological exegesis, this still needs to be substantiated by further research. Exegetes and homilists that use typology may be harking back to the rabbinic statements mentioned above. This could easily be the case for Shem Tov ibn Shem Tov (ibid., 168) and possibly for others as well.

48. Evidence that the typological imagination is alive and well even today can be seen in the recent *Templates of the Ages*, by David Cohen, which elaborates on a number of themes found in the midrash and in the Torah commentary of Naḥmanides. It is based on an earlier Hebrew work by the same author entitled *Ma'aseh 'avot siman la-banim*.

Bibliography

Auerbach, Eric. "Figura." In *Scenes from the Drama of European Literature*, 11–76. Minneapolis: University of Minnesota Press, 1984.

Baḥya ben Asher. *Bei'ur 'al ha-Torah*. Ed. Charles B. Chavel. 3 vols. Jerusalem: Mossad Harav Kook, 1976/77.

Beattie, D. R. G. *Jewish Exegesis of the Book of Ruth*. Sheffield: Sheffield Academic Press, 1977.

Bronner, Leila Leah. "A Thematic Approach to Ruth in Rabbinic Literature." In *A Feminist Companion to Ruth*. Ed. Athalya Brenner, 146–69. Sheffield: Sheffield Academic Press, 1993.

Cohen, David. *Templates for the Ages: Historical Perspectives Through the Torah's Lenses*. Trans. Sarah Cohen. Brooklyn, N.Y.: Mesorah, 1999.

Cohen, Mark. *Under Crescent and Cross: The Jews in the Middle Ages*. Princeton, N.J.: Princeton University Press, 1994.

Danielou, Jean. *From Shadows to Reality: Studies in the Biblical Typology of the Fathers*. London: Burns & Oates, 1960.

Emmerson, Richard K. "Figura and the Medieval Typological Imagination." In *Typology and English Medieval Literature*. Ed. Hugh T. Keenan, 7–42. New York: AMS Press, 1992.

Fraenkel, Jonah. *Darkhei ha-'aggadah weha-midrash* (The methods of the Aggadah and the Midrash). 2 Vols. Giv'atayim: Yad La-talmud, 1991.

Funkenstein, Amos. "Naḥmanides' Symbolical Reading of History." In *Studies in Jewish Mysticism*. Ed. Joseph Dan and Frank Talmage, 129–50. Cambridge, Mass.: Association for Jewish Studies, 1982.

——. "Parshanuto ha-ṭippologit shel ha-Ramban" (Naḥmanides' typological exegesis) *Ẓion* 45 (1979–80): 35–59.

Goldin, Judah. "Of Midrash and the Messianic Theme." In *Studies in Midrash and Related Literature*, 359–79. Philadelphia: Jewish Publication Society, 1988.

Henry, Avril, ed. *Biblia pauperum*. Aldershot, England: Scolar Press, 1987.

——, ed. *The Mirour of Mans Saluacioune: a Middle English Translation of Speculum Humanae Salvationis*. Aldershot, England: Scolar Press, 1986.

Idel, Moshe. Introd. to A. Aescoly, *ha-Tenu'ot ha-meshiḥiyyot be-Yisra'el* (Messianic movements in Israel), 16–28. Jerusalem: Mosad Bialik, 1987.

Idel, Moshe, and Mauro Perani. *Naḥmanide esegeta e cabbalista: studi e testi*. Firenze: Giuntina, 1998.

Isaac ben Joseph, ha-Kohen. "Perush Rut." New York, Jewish Theological Seminary of America, Library, MS L1052, fols. 77r-87v (IMHM no. 24255).

Kamin, Sarah. "Dugma be-feirush Rashi le-Shir ha-shirim" (Dugma in Rashi's commentary on Song of Songs). *Tarbiẓ* 52 (1983–84): 41–58. Reprint in: *Bein Yehudim le-Noṣerim*, 13–30. Jerusalem: Magnes Press, 1991.

Labriola, Albert C., and John W. Smeltz, eds. and trans. *The Bible of the Poor = Biblia pauperum*. Pittsburgh: Duquesne University Press, 1990.

Lampe, G. W. H. "The Reasonableness of Typology." In *Essays on Typology*, 9–38. London: SCM Press, 1957.

Martel, Gérard de. *Repertoire des textes latins relatifs au Livre de Ruth* (*VIIe-XVe s.*) Steenbrugis: In Abbatia S. Petri, 1990.

Midrash ha-ne'elam le-sefer Rut. English version: *The Mystical Study of Ruth: Midrash HaNe'elam of the Zohar to the Book of Ruth*. Ed. and trans. Lawrence Englander with Herbert Basser. Atlanta: Scholars Press, 1993.

Naḥmanides, Moses. *Peirushei ha-Torah*. Ed. Charles B. Chavel. 2 vols. Jerusalem, 1958–59.

Saba, Abraham. *'Eshkol ha-kofer 'al Megillat Rut*. Ed. Eliezer Segal. Bartfeld, 1907. Reprint, Jerusalem, 1980–81.

Saperstein, Marc. "Christians and Christianity in the Sermons of Jacob Anatoli." In *The Frank Talmage Memorial Volume*, Vol. 2 (= *Jewish History* 6). Ed. Barry Walfish, 225–42. Revised in "*Your Voice Like a Ram's Horn*": *Themes and Texts in Traditional Jewish Preaching*, 55–74. Cincinnati: Hebrew Union College Press, 1996.

——. "Jewish Typological Exegesis after Naḥmanides." *Jewish Studies Quarterly* 1(1993/94): 158–70. Reprint in: "*Your Voice Like a Ram's Horn*," 23–35.

Septimus, Bernard. "Taḥat 'Edom we-lo taḥat Yishma''el—gilgulo shel ma'amar" (Under Edom and not under Ishmael: the history of a saying) *Ẓion* 47(1982):103–11.

Talmage, Frank."Apples of Gold: The Inner Meaning of Sacred Texts in Medieval Judaism." In *Jewish Spirituality: From the Bible to the Middle Ages*. Ed. Arthur Green, 313–55. New York: Crossroad, 1986. Reprint in: *Apples of Gold in Settings of Silver: Studies in Medieval Jewish*

Exegesis and Polemics. Ed. Barry D. Walfish, 108–50. Toronto: The Pontifical Institute of Mediaeval Studies, 1999.

Tishby, Isaiah. *Meshiḥiyyut be-dor geirushei Sefarad u-Portugal* (Messianism in the generation of the expulsion from Spain and Portugal). Jerusalem: Merkaz Zalman Shazar le-hisṭoryah yehudit, 1984–85.

Tov, Emanuel. *Textual Criticism of The Hebrew Bible*. Assen: Van Gorcum, 1992.

Walfish, Barry. "An Annotated Bibliography of Medieval Jewish Commentaries on the Book of Ruth in Print and in Manuscript." In *The Frank Talmage Memorial Volume*. Vol. 1. Ed. Barry Walfish, 251–71. Haifa: Haifa University Press, 1993.

——. *Esther in Medieval Garb*. Albany, N.Y.: SUNY Press, 1993.

Wilensky, Sara O. Heller. "Isaac Ibn Latif–Philosopher or Kabbalist?" In *Jewish Medieval and Renaissance Studies*. Ed. Alexander Altmann, 185–224. Cambridge, Mass.: Harvard University Press, 1967.

Wolfson, Elliot R. "By Way of Truth": Aspects of Naḥmanides' Kabbalistic Hermeneutic." *AJS Review* 14 (1989): 103–78.

Woollcombe, K. J. "The Biblical Origins and Patristic Development of Typology." In *Essays on Typology*, 39–75. London: SCM Press, 1957.

9

The Method of Doubts

Problematizing the Bible in Late Medieval Jewish Exegesis

MARC SAPERSTEIN

Scholars of medieval Jewish exegesis have devoted considerable energy to various matters of content.[1] Surprisingly little attention has been given to questions of form: how the content of the commentary is organized and presented, what formal innovations are discernible within the medieval tradition. Of course, the commentary genre requires special formal characteristics—primarily, the organization of material in accordance with the order of verses in the text being expounded, and treatment of a relatively large percentage of the verses in the text. But within these parameters, there is opportunity for formal variation.[2]

The focus in this chapter will be on a structural model and exegetical technique widely associated with Isaac Abarbanel and Isaac Arama, who flourished at the end of the fifteenth century: beginning the discussion of a textual unit by raising a series of "doubts" (*sefeqot*), "questions" (*she'elot*), or "difficulties" (*qushyot*), which are resolved in the ensuing exegetical treatment. I shall refer to this hermeneutical technique as the "method of doubts," even though the technical term *sefeqot* is not always used. The origins of this form in Jewish literature, its prevalence in the generation of the expulsion,[3] and the cultural significance of this phenomenon have yet to be analyzed. Several generations ago, Jacob Guttmann claimed that Abarbanel learned this form from Christian scholastic writers, without indicating precisely what works Abarbanel might have used.[4] The possibility that Abarbanel, or Arama, may have taken the form from earlier Jewish writers seems hardly to have been considered.[5]

I therefore propose to explore this structure of exposition in three related genres of Jewish writing: biblical exegesis, sermons, and discursive philosophical texts, beginning with the late fifteenth century and moving back as far as the evidence allows. I shall then give some examples of a similar form in the same genres of Christian writing from antiquity and the Middle Ages.[6] The challenge will be to see where these two traditions might meet. In addition to the structure, I will examine the terminology, particularly the technical term *sefeqot*, and its Latin correlative *dubitatio* or *dubium*.[7] Finally, I will comment on the cultural significance of this exegetical mode, what I call the "problematizing" of the Bible by the exegete.

Generation of the Expulsion

The "method of doubts" is far more common in the generation of the Expulsion than has been recognized; I will provide just selected examples. Abarbanel incorporates the form into his first biblical commentary, that on the Early Prophets. In the introduction to this work, he states, "I have raised fifteen questions (*she'elot*) concerning the books [of the Prophets], which have recently occurred to me, questions our ancestors did not think of." After enumerating these questions, he justifies the importance of his method: Although some of the questions will be answered in a different place, "I have not refrained from mentioning them here, for the nature of the subject brought me to them, and it was necessary for the sake of thoroughness. Pay attention to everything I bring to your attention today, for the raising of doubts (*sefeqot*) that I have done, and the exposition of my thoughts and opinions about their solution, is not an empty matter for you." He then continues with the Book of Joshua: "I decided to proceed by asking at the beginning of every section six questions, based on the content of the verses and the nature of the subject to be investigated." He will not waver from the number six, no matter how complex or straightforward the biblical passage may be, whether the questions raise "profound doubt" or are simple to resolve. This technique "facilitates complete understanding and helps in remembering. I have chosen to set out the questions before the exegesis of the verses, for that in my judgment is a beneficial way to raise the matters, to generate disputation and expand investigation. Furthermore, the raising of questions frequently leads to deeper study of the verses, and to discovery within them of matters sweeter than honey."[8]

Abarbanel does not claim to be introducing a radically new element into Jewish biblical exegesis. The novelty appears to lie in the content of at least some of the questions, the use of a fixed number of questions for each section, and the presentation of the questions as an introduction to each exegetical unit. These formal decisions are justified pedagogically: they aid in remembering and lead to deeper understanding. By the time he came to write the Torah Commentary, he felt no need to explain his method at all. His commentary on Genesis begins by raising ten long and complex questions, ending, "These are the questions I thought of for this first section (*parashah*), and the verses of the section should be interpreted so as to provide a solution to all of them."[9] Similarly, after a general introduction to Deuteronomy, he continues, "The doubts that occur in this section (*seder*), after a cursory look at the verses . . . are fourteen." After enumerating them, he concludes, "These are the doubts I have seen fit to raise about the topics of this section (*seder*). Their solution will come with the exegesis of the section (*parashah*) and the [proper] understanding of the verses."[10]

Because the commentary on Deuteronomy uses the term *sefeqot* for the questions raised at the beginning of each section, while the other commentaries use *she'elot*, some scholars have suggested that the term *sefeqot* may reflect the influence upon Abarbanel by Isaac Arama or Joseph Ḥayyun.[11] But as we shall see, the term *sefeqot* was widespread in this generation, as well as earlier, and it usually seems to be interchangeable with *she'elot*, as indeed was the case for Abarbanel.[12] A manuscript sermon attributed to Abarbanel also uses this technique, but without any technical term for the questions at all.[13]

The same use of the method of doubts as an integral part of a contemporary Torah commentary can be seen in Isaac Caro's *Toledot Yiṣḥaq*.[14] Like Abarbanel, Caro divides the biblical material into unified sections based on content, almost invariably introducing each one with a statement such as, "In this section . . . " or "in these verses, there are [a specified number of] doubts." The solution to the "doubts" comes in the subsequent discussion of the verses. The absence of any explanation for this technique suggests that it was self-explanatory. Even a casual comparison reveals that many of Caro's questions are similar to those of Abarbanel.[15]

The raising of problems, usually called *qushyot*, is a dominant rhetorical device in many of Caro's recently published sermons. They may be answered immediately, or only after a long intervening discussion. One sermon begins with a rabbinic dictum, and then immediately continues, "One may raise a difficulty" (*we-yesh le-haqshot*). Six questions follow, each one developed in some detail. Then, "The answer to these difficulties [will come] when we first raise difficulties pertaining to chapter *Ḥeleq* [of tractate Sanhedrin]." Eleven such questions ensue. Then "It seems to me that to resolve all these difficulties we must make an introductory statement, in which the resurrection of the dead will be established as true. . . ." The eleven questions in the second set are addressed in the course of this discussion, and the original questions are addressed at the end of the discourse. Along the way, other problems are raised and resolved.[16] More intricate than the structural unit used in the biblical commentaries, this is a form that places considerable demands upon the listeners.

The method of doubts is every bit as crucial in Joel Ibn Shuaib's collection of sermons, *'Olat Shabbat*, where the section that raises and resolves *sefeqot* frequently constitutes a major component of the text, integral to the structure of the discourse. These doubts appear in a manner that reveals careful attention to the intricacies of construction. Instead of appearing in a constant, recurring common format, as in Abarbanel's commentaries, Ibn Shuaib's doubts are presented with frequent variation of form, though always with an eye to artistic balance.[17] This was obviously a preacher who spent considerable energy in crafting his material in what he must have thought to be an aesthetically appealing way. It is not the originality of the doubts (some of which are described as "well-known" or "famous", but rather the solution he provides and the format in which he presents them, that the preacher believed to be his special contribution.

Straddling the border between a homiletical and exegetical work is Isaac Arama's *'Aqeidat Yiṣḥaq*. In his introduction, Arama writes:

> And the homily (*perishah*) will proceed by first raising the doubts (*sefeqot*), both new and old, that occur in the simple meaning of the verses pertaining to the subject being studied (*derush*), and also in matters that are apparent from these verses, or that have been raised by previous interpreters. I shall arrange them first in the appropriate order, and then proceed to explain them so as to resolve them satisfactorily . . . consistent with what preceded it in the *derush*. In this way, I shall reconcile the verses properly, so that none of the doubts remain.[18]

This form is more complex than in the commentaries of Abarbanel and Caro, for the "doubts" appear in the middle of the discourse, as a transition between its two main sections. Sometimes they appear as if it were a routine procedure to "mention the doubts that fall in this section," concluding, "after the mention of these [fourteen] doubts, we will proceed to an explanation."[19] Occasionally, the project is introduced with greater fanfare: "This will be well explained when we look closely at his intent in this passage.

It is truly difficult to explicate, for its words appear to be jumbled, not following the order of the events, and it also includes matters that seem to be irrelevant. I have not seen any commentator who has paid attention to this." After specifying eight problems, Arama proceeds with a majestic sweep of the rhetorical wand: "The solution of all these doubts, sorting out their confusion, will be based on what I shall now say."[20]

Another contemporary, Shem Tov ben Joseph Ibn Shem Tov, begins an elaborate wedding sermon based on the verse "It is not good for the man to be alone" (Gen 2:18) with a formal disputed question: whether "human perfection is [best] achieved through solitary living, without the participation of another human being."[21] This completed, he launches a new discussion: "Before we speak about the companionship of a man and his wife, which is a divine association, we shall express the relevant doubts about this association." Specifying eight, the preacher continues, "Now we shall respond to the first doubt. . . . "[22] The second part of the sermon on *Noaḥ* is composed of nine "doubts" and their answers.[23] In the sermon on *Va-yiqra*, the method is applied to the rabbinic dictum cited at the beginning of the sermon: "Now after this, we should explicate the dictum. But first, it is appropriate to express doubts about it (*ra'ui le-sappeq bo*), for whoever does not express doubts does not know, and whoever does not know remains in irremediable blindness. Now first, one may express the doubt. . . ."[24] Four follow, and then their solution. This method is one of many rhetorical options in Shem Tov's preaching, justified by the claim that without it, knowledge remains incomplete.

Finally, we may note three manuscripts of unpublished sermons from the same period. The first, entitled "Qeṣat parashiyot," contains sermons by the important talmudist Isaac Aboab different from those in the published *Nehar Pishon*.[25] The sermon on *Ḥayyei Sarah* begins immediately with a series of eight questions, each introduced with the same word, "Furthermore." Then the answers begin; after three are discussed, the preacher states, "However, the rest of the questions will be resolved with the exegesis of the verses," which begins forthwith.[26] We see here how close the sermon may be to a commentary.

The second manuscript is entitled "Dover meisharim"; its author is known only by the name "Israel." Though most of his sermons do not use this method, he resorts to it on occasion. After a discursive introduction to a topic pertaining to the lesson *Noaḥ*, he continues, "Now we shall express doubts on this *parashah*," raising nine.[27] The next sermon, on *Lekh lekha*, has sections beginning *yesh le-sappeq* for both parts of the sermon, and the next one, on the same scriptural lesson, follows the same method, summarizing, "we shall explicate this *parashah* through the solution of these doubts."[28] Once he explains the purpose of the technique: "In raising doubts about a matter, it is not my intent to allow the doubt to remain in the mind of the listeners, heaven forbid, but rather that the matter become fully explicated."[29]

The third manuscript contains sermons from several different authors, including Isaac Abarbanel and Isaac Caro. We have already noted the use of questions in the sermon on Exodus 20:2 attributed to Abarbanel. The following sermon, labeled "Another on this lesson [*Yitro*]," begins, "My intent is to speak about the matter of the day [*Shavu'ot*]," using verses in Exodus 19–20. "But before this intent [is fulfilled], there are five difficulties to be raised. . . ." In a different sermon, on the lesson *Toledot*, the preacher begins his discourse immediately following an opening rabbinic dictum: "One may express four difficulties about this dictum. . . . To resolve these difficulties, it is necessary first to make an introductory statement."[30]

Enough examples have been given here to demonstrate that the method of doubts was by no means unique to Abarbanel and Arama; rather, it was widely prevalent in the exegetical and homiletical literature of Jews in the generation of the Expulsion. The cultural significance of this enterprise will be discussed later. Now we must look for the sources of the form.

Earlier Jewish Writers

The explanation given by Shem Tov—"whoever does not express doubts does not know"—is quite similar to Isaac Canpanton's justification, given a generation earlier, for raising "doubts" about talmudic passages being studied:

> Whenever you look closely at some topic or matter, just as you must undertake to look carefully at the linguistic formulation of the matter, so should you also look for problems to raise against it (*le-vaqqesh devarim le-haqshot ke-negdo*), first by raising the doubts (*le-hani'a ha-sefeqot*) pertaining to that matter or that formulation, and by knowing the fallacies and the problems that can occur in that topic, for that is the way to reach the truth, and to understand that matter fully.[31]

It is not entirely clear whether Canpanton in this passage means the formal raising of a series of questions and then resolving them all in the course of an extended discussion, or the intellectual exercise of conceiving problems, each of which may be addressed after it is raised. The formulation he uses, *le-hani'a sefeqot*, is unusual Hebrew that seems to be a technical term.[32] In a very similar passage, the Portuguese Rabbi Joseph Ḥayyun uses the same phrase, and then, shifting to the apparently synonymous term "questions," cites Aristotle as the source for the justification:

> One should ask questions about what he is studying, and raise doubts, in order to illuminate that matter, for as a result of the questions it will be fully clarified. After asking the questions, one should not leave them without an answer, but rather respond to them and set them straight. The Philosopher said, "It is good for the truth to raise difficulties about it (*she-taqsheh 'alaw*), so that it can better endure."[33]

And indeed, Ḥayyun does use various forms of this technique. His short treatise (*ma'amar*) on Numbers 32 begins, "There are questions on this section"—nine are provided—and ends, "This is what I thought about the solution of these doubts, praise be to God."[34] Similarly, a discussion of the blasphemer in Leviticus 24 begins, "I have seen fit to raise doubts (*le-hani'a sefeqot*) about this story, and they are of two kinds." Seven are given about the differences between this and the account of the wood-gatherer in Numbers 15, followed by their solution, then seven more about the passage itself, with answers after the first three, and then after each succeeding "doubt." At the end, "these are the two kinds of doubts that occurred to me in this story and their solution."[35] The affinities between this form and the questions in Abarbanel's commentary are obvious; some of the questions are quite close.[36] If we could imagine many of these treatments of the doubts in discrete biblical passages strung together, they would appear quite similar in form to the commentary of Abarbanel.

Joseph Ibn Shem Tov, identified by Abarbanel as his mentor,[37] flourished in the middle of the fifteenth century; he uses the method of doubts in some, though certainly not all, of his extant sermons. The clearest example comes in a discussion of the revelation at Mount Sinai, where he raises seven *sefeqot*, then proceeds to resolve them.[38] He begins a different sermon on repentance with two questions about David's sin, and continues, "The Sages of blessed memory already resolved these doubts (*sefeqot*)."[39] And after talking about several characteristics of the language of the Torah, he introduces an "answer that encompasses all these doubts."[40] There is no indication in these passages that Joseph believed he was doing anything new.

A group of sermons by a disciple of Ḥasdai Crescas (or perhaps a circle of his disciples), dating from the first quarter of the fifteenth century, contains a fine example of the homiletical use of the "disputed question."[41] Elsewhere, the preacher justifies the disputed question with the statement, "from out of intellectual give and take, the truth will sprout."[42] In one place, the terminology of doubts is used to refer to the raising of conceptual problems crucial to the philosophical enterprise. After setting forth a position on the problem of divine attributes taken by his mentor, Crescas, he expresses his own view, "not as one who disagrees, but as one who arranges and orders his doubts before his master, in order to learn how they can be resolved. I shall raise here six doubts. . . ." The preacher then notes that some of his "doubts" have already been raised by Crescas in *'Or 'Adonai*.[43]

Crescas himself used this terminology as part of this discursive masterpiece. The discussion of God's knowledge of particulars and divine providence is filled with "doubts" and their resolution. Speaking of divine providence, he notes that "the doubts that were set forth (*ha-sefeqot 'asher hiniḥu*) with regard to God's knowledge of things can also be set forth here"; he goes on to enumerate "doubts" arising from empirical observation, from rational analysis, and from biblical authority, before endeavoring to resolve them.[44] Similarly, after setting out his doctrine of prophecy, he raises a series of doubts about what he has said, and then proposes his solution.[45] The formal problematizing of belief is clearly a part of Crescas's method.

Dating from the last quarter of the fourteenth century is the homiletical-exegetical work identified by its editor as written by Joseph ben David of Saragossa, a student of Nissim ben Reuben Gerondi.[46] Beginning a discussion of Isaac's blessing of his sons, the author asserts that the passage contain matters that surprise (*min ha-temihah*):

> First, when Isaac wanted to bless his son, whom he loved . . . why did he withhold the blessing until Esau would prepare him a tasty dish and he might eat, in order to bless him (cf. Gen 37:4)? . . . Second, how could Rebecca advise Jacob to take the blessing deceitfully? . . . Third, how did Jacob say, "Perhaps my father will touch me" (Gen 27:12), without worrying that his father might recognize him somehow other than by touch? . . . Fourth, how did God agree that Isaac would intend his blessing for a different person? . . . Fifth, after Isaac realized that he had been deceived and knew that he had not blessed Esau . . . why did he confirm his blessing? . . .[47]

In the course of his exegesis that provides a solution to the problems, the author resorts to the technical term *safeq*: "Now with regard to the doubt we mentioned—how could a blessing be efficacious if it was not intended for the one blessed—the answer is. . . ." "With this the doubt we mentioned—after Isaac was 'seized with violent trembling' (Gen 27:33), how did he confirm the blessings?—disappears." "As for the doubt we mentioned—why did Rebecca and Jacob not worry that Isaac would recognize him by the quality of his voice?—the likely answer is. . . ."[48] Here is evidence for the formal method of doubts more than a century before the generation of the Expulsion.

This commentator's mentor was Nissim ben Reuben Gerondi. One of his sermons, dating from the third quarter of the fourteenth century, contains a passage relevant to this subject. Discussing Exodus 33, the aftermath of the Golden Calf episode, he raises one problem about a statement by Moses (33:15) that seems inappropriate, ending, "This is a great doubt that needs to be explicated. Similarly, there are many doubts pertaining to the interrelationship of [verses in the] the passage that need explication. The first doubt is . . . , the second doubt . . . , the third doubt. . . . In sum, this passage requires extensive explication." In the ensuing discussion of the passage, the exegetical problems are addressed, providing another example of this "method of doubts."[49]

A generation earlier, the work of the philosopher and exegete Levi ben Gershom (Ralbag), dating to the 1320s and 1330s, also reveals the method of doubts in its crystalized form. A good example is in the second book of *The Wars of the Lord*. After a preliminary discussion of knowledge about future events communicated through dreams, divinations, and prophecy, Ralbag continues: "There are many doubts (*sefeqot*) with respect to this type of communication. It is proper that we discuss them to the extent that we are able." Eight doubts are stated, and then each one is addressed in turn; some of them he describes as easily solvable, others as more difficult to handle.[50] This is the method of doubts applied to a conceptual problem.[51]

Ralbag's biblical commentaries also contain examples of this form that have not to my knowledge been appreciated by scholars. An example is the discussion of the Golden Calf episode (starting with Exod 31:18): "Rabbi Levi said, I have seen fit to mention a few doubts that occur in this narrative before I begin to explicate it, so that the explication, through which we shall emerge from these doubts, will be comprehensible to us. . . . Now these doubts can be resolved. . . . " After an extensive discussion of the stalling tactics Aaron used in the hope that Moses would return before the calf was made, he concludes, "Now this is what seems proper to us in the resolution of these doubts."[52]

Like the passage in *The Wars of the Lord*, this passage bears all the characteristics of the classic method of doubts. The problems are raised at the beginning, they are designated by the technical term, and they are resolved in the course of a conceptual-exegetical discussion of a series of verses (though without the marker, "With this, the first doubt is resolved"). We should also note the unusual introduction to the section, "Rabbi Levi said," a phrase that Ralbag ordinarily uses at the beginning of a work (for example, the Torah commentary, Joshua, *The Wars of the Lord*). It seems as if this were a separate unit, like the "*ma'amarim*" by Joseph Ḥayyun we encountered, written in an unusual form and incorporated into the commentary. There are other examples as well in Ralbag's exegetical oeuvre.[53]

We see then that the method of doubts can be traced back in an unbroken chain to the first half of the fourteenth century, appearing in the work of some of the most influential late medieval biblical commentators and preachers. Before this, the traces become less clear. I have not found a clear example of this technique in any thirteenth-century commentary or in any of the very few extant collections of sermons. We should note, however, two texts, one containing the form without the term *sefeqot*, the other with the technical term but without the precise form. The first is represented by the questions with which David Kimḥi introduces his comment on the third chapter of Genesis:

> One might ask (*yesh lish'ol*) about the matter of the snake's speaking to the woman how this was, and whether it occurred miraculously? . . . Furthermore, how the angel seduced the woman to transgress God's commandment? Furthermore, what is the relevance of the snake here, and why does it say that the snake was cunning? . . . And why did the angel not come to the man?[54]

The function of these questions is to introduce the difficulty and complexity of the passage, which requires a separate esoteric commentary, yet the questions are addressed and for the most part resolved in the ensuing exoteric discussion of the verses (33–34). While the form is not as neat as in Abarbanel or Ralbag, and the technical term *sefeqot* does not appear, it may be considered a rudimentary precedent for the later models.

The other example is a discursive work from the thirteenth century, Hillel of Verona's *Tagmulei ha-nefesh*. Discussing the Platonic doctrine of multiple souls, he notes:

> To this Aristotle attached doubts in the manner of questions (*sefeqot be-derekh she'elot*). They are: is every one of those souls that Plato mentions a unique soul in and of itself, according to Plato, or are they parts of one soul? And if you say that they are parts of one soul, are they different from each other in definition alone or also spatially, that is to say, is there a special vessel for each one? He goes on to say that some of these things are not difficult to accept, and some of them raise doubts.[55]

These are not precisely the "doubts" of our method—problems raised to be resolved in the course of an exegesis of the text—but rather objections that cast doubt on a position taken, which are not to be resolved. Hillel serves as a convenient transition to the non-Jewish material, in that he invokes both Aristotle and Thomas Aquinas, from whom the passage is taken.[56]

Non-Jewish Writers

Aquinas writes that Aristotle *dubitationem movet* (literally, sets in motion a doubt), and that some of Plato's views on this matter *dubitationem habent* (have or raise a doubt).[57] The relevant passage in Aristotle is *De anima* 413b13–26. But indeed, the origin of the form would appear to be the beginning of Book 2 of Aristotle's *Metaphysics*:

> In pursuing our science, we ought first to make a careful survey of the doubts which confront us at the outset. Among them would be the diverse ways in which others have dealt with our problems and in addition any points that may have been overlooked. To have stated well the doubts is a good start for those who expect to overcome them, for what follows is, of course, the solution of those very doubts, and no one can untangle a knot which he does not see.[58]

The Greek word *aporeia*, which recurs in this passage, underlies the Latin *dubitatio* and the Hebrew *safeq*. Aristotle sets out the method of doubts as the soundest approach to the discovery of understanding and truth. (His commentator, Alexander of Aphrodisias, paraphrased that it is by way of these points of doubt that the discovery of the sciences occurs.)[59] In the Latin text used by Thomas Aquinas, the passage reads, "Now for those who wish to investigate the truth it is worth the while to ponder these doubts well (*bene dubitare*). For the subsequent study of truth is nothing else than the solution of earlier problems (*solutio dubitatorum*)." Aquinas's own paraphrase speaks of "those subjects about which it is necessary to doubt (*dubitare*) before the truth is established.[60] After this introductory programmatic statement, Aristotle devotes the rest of Book 2 to formulating the numerous doubts or difficulties he will need to address.[61] The rest of the work is an attempt to provide solutions.

Aquinas also comments on the structural uniqueness of the *Metaphysics* with regard to the presentation of "doubts."

> Aristotle was accustomed, in nearly all his works, to set forth the doubts (*praemittet dubitationes*) that emerge before investigating and establishing what is true. But while in the other works Aristotle sets forth the doubts one at a time in order to establish the truth about each one, in this work he sets forth all the doubts at once (*simul praemittit omnes dubitationes*), and afterward in their proper order establishes the things that are true.[62]

We have here the basis for both an intellectual approach and a literary structure—raising a series of questions to be expounded in the course of a subsequent discussion—that characterize the Jewish material we have reviewed. What we need to trace now is the use of this form in an exegetical context. The issue is not the difficulties that arise out of a set of ideas, but those generated by a passage of text. And the solution is reached not through abstract argumentation, but through exegesis.

We begin to find this in the literature of the Church Fathers. Among his exegetical works, Augustine wrote *Quaestionum in Heptateuchum*. After an introductory justification of the technique, Augustine raises a series of questions about the biblical texts: How was Cain able to found a city (Gen 4:17) when the Bible has mentioned only his parents and the brother whom he killed? How could Methusaleh have continued to live after the flood (Gen 5:25)? How could the "angels" have cohabited with the "daughters of men" (Gen 6:4)?[63] And so forth. These are not simple questions with obvious answers; some of the questions are extensive, indicating apparent ways out of the conundrum that are not satisfactory. It is truly a problematizing of the biblical text. The same technique is used in his *Quaestionum Evangeliorum*.[64]

This form, however, was not common in medieval Christian exegesis. We do find something similar in the exegetical works of Honorius of Autun (Augustodun) (early 12th century), who wrote "Questions and Answers" on Proverbs and Ecclesiastes.[65] These are actually rather different, however, from the form being investigated here. Structurally, the answer comes immediately after each question. And conceptually, the questions are simplistic and the answers obvious. It is exegesis serving the purpose of catechism.[66] Similar to these are the *Quaestiones et decisiones in epistolas Pauli*, formerly attributed to Hugh of Saint Victor: the answer comes after each straightforward question, and the biblical text seems like an excuse for a catechetical exercise.[67]

Quite different is Abelard's articulation of the importance of raising problems and doubts for the pursuit of truth in the Introduction to his path-breaking *Sic et non*. After quoting Aristotle on the value of raising doubts about matters to be investigated, he continues, "For through doubting we come to inquiry and through inquiry we perceive the truth."[68] Abelard does not use the formal structure of raising a series of "doubts" in this work.[69] Rather, the entire work can be viewed as a problematizing of the Christian tradition, by juxtaposing apparently contradictory authorities on a panoply of important issues, in quest of a firm grasp on the ultimate truth.

Later in the twelfth century, the formal dialectical use of questions, including the more elaborate disputed question, made headway into scriptural study, despite considerable opposition.[70] By the thirteenth century, *quaestiones* became a staple of academic instruction, and collections of such questions became a prevalent form of scholastic writing.[71] But increasingly, the term *quaestio* came to mean the formal "disputed question," in which antithetical positions are fully sustained and then the conflict is resolved. It is perhaps because of this usage that some of the scholastic writers began to use the terms *dubitatio* and *dubium* for the question arising out of a problem in a text, which can be resolved without one's arguing its opposite. We have seen this use in Aquinas's commentary on Aristotle's *Metaphysics*. Bonaventure's *Commentary on the Sentences* is largely in the form of a series of disputed questions. But scattered throughout the work is a series of "*Dubia circa litteram magistri*," which begin with the following (or a similar) formulation: "*In parte ista sunt dubitationes circa litteram. Et primo. . . .*"[72] In his commentary on Ecclesiastes, he begins with a discursive comment (*postill*) on a passage from the biblical text, and then he frequently continues with a series of questions, introduced with one of the following phrases: "*Quaeritur de hoc quod dicit . . .* ," "*Sed dubitatio est de hoc quod dicit . . .* ," or "*Dubitari potest de hoc quod hic dicit. . . .*"[73] There seems to be no distinction in terminology: *quaestio* and *dubitatio*, *quaeritare* and *dubitare*, are used interchangeably, all referring to the disputed question. It should be noted, however, that where more than one question or doubt is raised, the answer almost invariably follows it immediately before the next question is entertained. Only rarely do we find a series of questions appearing before the answer is given.[74] It is not a precise model for the fully developed method of doubts we have seen in Jewish preachers and exegetes of a later period.[75]

The Latin sermons of John Wycliffe, delivered in the 1380s, provide an important example of homiletical problematizing. At the end of his Preface, he gives a succinct statement of the structure of his sermons: after treating the mystical sense of the passage, "secondly, following the custom of Augustine, I will address the doubts that can be taken up from the Gospel."[76] And indeed, Wycliffe regularly introduces the second part of his sermons with a phrase such as "*Circa hoc evangelium dubitatur*." Many of these *dubia* are in the form of the disputed question; they may be theological, historical, moral, or legal.[77] In some sermons only one "doubt" is discussed, in others, three. A recent study has shown that other contemporary English preachers as well raised "doubts" as an integral part of their preaching.[78]

John Gerson, chancellor of the University of Paris from 1395, was a renowned preacher. His sermons reveal the use of questions as a formal device, though not in the precise form sought here. In a French funeral sermon, Gerson raises twelve questions about Purgatory and the fate of the soul after death. A Christmas sermon contains twelve questions about the birth of Christ, and a sermon for Pentecost contains six questions appropriate to that occasion.[79] In each case, the answer is provided immediately after the question is posed. The questions are straightforward, and the answers fairly obvious. This is not an example of problematizing a tradition, but rather is like some of the twelfth-century commentaries, a form of catechetical teaching. Rather different are the questions in a Latin sermon on the circumcision of Christ delivered before Pope Benedict XIII. A long series of questions is placed rhetorically in the mouth of a personified *studiositas speculatrix*; each one is given a response from the speaker, but each response produces a further question. The questions are not of the sort that every Christian would be expected to know, but rather of the kind that might have been troubling to many listeners.[80] This passage indeed reflects a problematizing of tradition in preaching to an elite audience.

Many of Gerson's sermons, especially those delivered before the court of Charles VI, contain one or more series of questions, ranging from two to twenty-seven.[81] Most often, they are questions about doctrinal issues, but some are about biblical passages, such as the wedding at Cana.[82] While not a fixed part of the structure of each sermon, the questions are a common feature of Gerson's homiletical technique.[83]

The closest Christian model I have found is in a Commentary on Peter Lombard's *Sentences* by the Augustinian friar Gregory of Rimini, who taught at the University of Paris from 1341. In this work, the author does at times raise a series of "doubts," introducing them with a phrase such as "*Nunc movenda sunt quaedam dubia.*" Four problems are presented. Then each one is addressed in turn, with headings "Solution to the first doubt. . . . Solution to the fourth doubt."[84] The form is the same as that used by the Jewish writers, but the content of these questions is conceptual rather than exegetical, indeed highly abstract. Gregory of Rimini's "doubts" are quite similar to those cited previously in discursive works by Crescas or Ralbag; they are a step or two removed from the *sefeqot* in those biblical commentaries and sermons.

In short, the Christian material surveyed does not reveal an obvious model for the exegetical or homiletical use of the method of doubts that could serve as the source for the Jewish writers. Aristotle, perhaps Thomas Aquinas through his commentaries, provided justification for raising a series of conceptual questions (called by Aquinas *dubitationes*) that fully problematize a subject, and then setting out to answer them one by one, but neither Aristotle nor Aquinas used this method in an exegetical work. While many Scholastic authors incorporated "questions" into their commentaries, these were usually either simple rhetorical questions or complex disputed questions, not the series of "doubts" so common in Jewish literature. Indeed, the influence of Scholasticism on Christian sermons and biblical commentaries of the high and late Middle Ages appears to be less than was once assumed. Most Christian writers were careful to keep their genres distinct.[85] While there may indeed have been influence from Christian writings or preaching, the precise models leading to the Jewish form remain elusive.

Cultural Significance

Problematizing a tradition can be fraught with peril. When Abelard sets forth apparently contradictory positions held by earlier authorities on an array of doctrinal issues, the chaotic diversity of belief may impress the reader more than the attempted reconciliation. When Aquinas formulates his theology through an unending series of questions and presents seemingly cogent arguments to substantiate the antithesis of every position he ultimately affirms,[86] the reader may conclude that the arguments for the contrary position are as strong as their eventual refutation. (Indeed, Leon Modena later used the *Summa theologiae* in this way, citing the first part of Thomas's questions in support of his own attacks on doctrines such as the Trinity, the Incarnation, and the Virgin Birth.)[87]

The dangers of this approach in the Jewish context are expressed through a classic joke about the impact of Abarbanel's biblical commentaries on a certain pious Jew. Each Sabbath, returning home from the synagogue, he would eat a full, leisurely Sabbath meal with his family and then turn to study the weekly lesson with Abarbanel's commentary. After reading the "doubts" or "questions" that introduce each section, the man would doze off for a Sabbath nap, not awakening until it was already time to go to the synagogue for the afternoon prayer. Reading the "doubts" but never reaching the solutions, he became a heretic.[88]

I see three conceivable interpretations of the problematizing of Hebrew scripture in the late Middle Ages. First, it is possible that we have here a kind of duplicity, an effort by the writers to communicate an esoteric message: that the Hebrew scripture was indeed riddled with profound problems. In this reading, the "resolutions" are essentially a cover that allows the writer to express doubts without taking responsibility for them, by claiming that he has a solution for each one. The true purpose of the author was not to provide answers, but to express grave misgivings that, given the community in which he lived, could not be presented in any other way. This interpretation might be plausible if we had just one or two authors using this format. But we have seen that it is widely prevalent in the literature of the 1492 generation, and not uncommon during the 175 years before. To assume that each of the authors who used this technique was engaging in the same subversive enterprise—that each really believed that the doubts remained despite the answers presented—strains credulity.

Assuming, then, that the authors genuinely believed that, at least in most cases, they resolved the doubts they raised, a second possibility is that they were responding to problems already present in the minds of their readers. This explanation would suggest a broad skepticism in Spanish Jewry about the Bible, consistent with Yitzhak Baer's claim that the impact of extreme rationalism—"Averroistic" tendencies—had corroded and undermined the foundations of traditional Jewish belief, leaving large numbers of Spanish Jews with no effective resistance to the pressures toward apostasy.[89] In this view, the commentators and preachers would have been fighting a desperate rear-guard action to defend the Bible with their arguments that the manifold "doubts" in the text were only apparent, and could indeed be resolved.

In addition to the problems with Baer's thesis and his promiscuous use of the term "Averroist,"[90] there is a more basic problem with this reconstruction. The "doubts" addressed by the commentators and preachers are not fundamental philosophical problems about the nature of God and the revelation of scripture that might be generated by philosophical study. Most are problems that would not occur to the casual reader or listener; they derive from the devotion of considerable intellectual energy to a detailed and exhaustive study of the biblical text. Individuals whose commitment to traditional Jewish discourse had been subverted by immersion in philosophical texts would hardly have been likely to be bothered by the issues that are addressed by these commentators. It is therefore questionable whether the prevalence of the method of doubts in the generation of the Expulsion can serve as evidence that a widespread awareness of problems required a massive effort to hold down the fort.[91]

The third and most likely option is that the authors were exposing their audience to novel problems in the classical texts that most of these listeners and readers had not thought of themselves. But why, given the risks noted here, would they do this? I see two possible explanations. One is their own theoretical commitment to the proposition—going back to Aristotle's *Metaphysics*—that complete understanding of a philosophical truth, and by extension of a classical text, is impossible without an exploration of its full problematic. Jewish writers maintain this position not only in epigrammatic statements but also in developed arguments. For example, Joel Ibn Shuaib, in a confraternity sermon, cites Aristotle (apparently drawing from Aquinas's commentary on the *Metaphysics*) to justify his own use of *sefeqot*:

> First, in this manner, the person will come upon the way of logical demonstration. For the arguments that cast doubt upon something that is true are rhetorical, not true, as truth cannot be opposed to truth. Escape necessarily comes through knowledge of logical demonstration. This is similar to untying a knot: similarly, knowledge of logically cogent arguments comes upon the perfected after knowledge of the doubts.
>
> Second, one who does not know a matter in depth, with the doubts that can be raised about it, will come upon the truth only by chance. He will know the places that diverge from the straight path, going to a certain location, but he will not be able to guard himself from them, and he will rarely follow the straight path. . . .
>
> Third, one who investigates speculatively should be like a judge. Just as the judge should pay attention to the contradictory arguments of the contestants, deriving the truth by investigating both sides, so the one who investigates speculatively must have the opposing arguments before him, to derive from them the truth.[92]

Ibn Shuaib frequently justifies his use of "doubts" with phrases suggesting that they lead to a fuller knowledge of the biblical passage: "for when these doubts are resolved, many things in the *parashah* will be understood," or "so that [even] the uneducated people may know."[93] Such statements appear to indicate a sincere belief in the value of this method as an educational tool for the entire people.

The second explanation is that the exegetes and preachers were responding to a popular demand for this kind of discussion, that readers and listeners looked forward to the challenge of being confronted with puzzles and problems and then seeing how they could be resolved. A hint of this attitude may be found in the introduction to Arama's *'Aqeidat Yiṣḥaq*, where he describes Jews impressed by the level of Christian orators and demanding something similar from their own leaders. These Jews

> heard the [Christian] preachers and found them impressive; their appetites were whetted for similar fare. This is what they say: "The Christian scholars and sages *raise questions and seek answers* in their academies and churches, thereby adding to the glory of the Torah and the prophets. . . . Why should the divine Torah with all its narratives and pronouncements be as a veiled maiden beside the flocks of her friends and her students?[94]

As was noted previously, I could find no evidence that this method of doubts was a standard part of contemporary Christian preaching, although the warnings by Christian theoreticians against exploring complex disputed questions from the pulpit indicate that it must have been done. Nevertheless, the raising and resolving of doubts appears to have become a kind of convention among Jews of that generation. Among the various rhetorical tools at the disposal of Sephardic preachers, this method of doubts apparently became a favorite.

It has often been noted that many of Rashi's comments are responses to difficulties he perceived in the biblical text, and that to appreciate his exegesis properly one must reconstruct the question to which his comment is an answer. That is a very different approach to the exegesis of scripture from explicitly setting forth the "doubts" in every biblical passage before endeavoring to resolve them, and constructing a form of discourse in which the exegete is required to produce problems even if they are not apparent. In this approach, no statement from the Bible is accepted as self-evident or clear. Everything is shown to be more complex than anticipated. The reader or listener is expected to understand and appreciate this complexity, for only then will the eventual solution be valued.

As for the actual doubts raised, I have already noted a considerable degree of repetition and overlap, both between earlier and later writers and among contemporaries who could not have borrowed from each other. My guess is that an effort to correlate systematically the "doubts" or "questions" pertaining to the Pentateuch raised by Abarbanel, Isaac Caro, Isaac Arama, and Joel Ibn Shu'aib would reveal a high percentage of the same *sefeqot* appearing in two, three, or even four of these works. If so, there must have been a common tradition, transmitted in the Spanish schools, of specific problems for each scriptural lesson, indeed for each scriptural passage, which individual writers could draw upon, supplement, and adapt to their own purpose. Originality was expressed not so much in the doubts themselves, but in the formal variations with which they were presented, and in the solutions that were proposed.

The prevalence of this form in the literature of the Expulsion generation, and the unbroken tradition of its use for close to two centuries, cannot be documented in Christian texts. But even where we do find something akin to the "method of doubts" in Christian commentaries and sermons, this was in literature intended for a rather elite audience. The Jewish texts of the generation of the Expulsion, by contrast, were, if not fully "popular," intended for a wide reading public, while the sermons were appropriate for delivery to the entire congregation of listeners. There is not a hint that this method was restricted to the most educated and sophisticated Jews. It was not an esoteric method of discourse. All Jews were to be led through the thicket of a densely problematized scriptural tradition. Even if the solutions were not always fully satisfying, there was something of value in the questioning, in and of itself.

Notes

1. For example, the commentator's attempt to uncover the "simple meaning" (*peshaṭ*) of the biblical text as distinct from the mode of homiletical rabbinic interpretation (*derash*); the influence of grammatical studies; criteria for the commentator's use of rabbinic midrash; the impact of philosophical rationalism in understanding the Bible; allegorical interpretation; the distinctiveness of kabbalistic, symbolic exegesis; the use of biblical commentary as a vehicle for apologetical or anti-Christian polemical statements; the reflection of contemporary historical realities in the commentary. A detailed bibliography of works on these various topics is beyond the scope of this paper and can be found in other contributions to this volume.

2. For example, commentaries that include two, three, or even four different modes of interpretation, presented one after the other (Baḥya ben Asher) or having divided the biblical material into conceptual units, provide an "explanation of the words" followed by a series of "beneficial lessons" (*to'aliyyot*) pertaining to belief and conduct (Levi ben Gershom).

3. See recently Bland, "Issues," 52–58, on Isaac Caro's Torah commentary.

4. Guttmann, *Isaak Abravanel*, 6; cf. Segal, "R. Yiṣḥaq 'Abarbanel," 266. Guttmann actually refers in this context to the "disputed question" so prominent in scholastic literature, which is a related but distinct form. Cf. Urbach, *Ba'alei ha-Tosafot*, 527, drawing a parallel between the method of commentators on Roman law and the Tosafists in the importance placed on "doubt and question." The Tosafist literature, however, does not appear to provide any basis for the form we shall be discussing.

5. In her full-length study of Arama, Sarah Heller Wilensky refers to "the method of raising difficulties and solutions" in half a sentence, without any further comment on the sources or significance of this form: (Wilensky, *R. Yiṣḥaq 'Aramah u-mishnato*, 33). Recently, it has been suggested that Abarbanel derived the method from Isaac Canpanton's talmudic study: Shalem, "Ha-metodah," 120; Bentov, "Shiṭat limmud ha-Talmud," 67. This, however, leaves unresolved the origin of this method in Canpanton himself. Cf. also Bland, "Issues," 58, noting an "innovative trend in Jewish intellectual circles," which originated in Salonika after 1492 with the figure of Joseph Taitaẓak. By contrast, Frank Talmage wrote, "In Spain and Provence during the twelfth century, the *she'ilta* (*quaestio*) appears within the continuous commentary, as in Latin exegesis (the *she'ilta* reached the peaks of its development in the commentaries of Abarbanel in the sixteenth century)" (Greenberg, *Parshanut*, 108). But this statement, which appears to blur the distinction between the "disputed question" and the method of doubts in Abarbanel, refers to twelfth-century material that is not identified, and it is not clear to me what Talmage had in mind.

6. In this kind of investigation, it would be misleading to insist on an overly rigid differentation between genres. Sermons, especially in the "homily" mode (called in Hebrew *perishah*), could be extremely close to passages from a biblical commentary. For Christian material see Bataillon, "De la *lectio*," 559–75; Roberts, *Stephen Langton*, 95–108; Smalley, *The Study of the Bible*, 209–11. For Jewish material, see Saperstein, *Jewish Preaching*, 14, esp. n. 23, and 73–74, esp. n. 26.

7. I do not include here the use of this term in the classical texts of Jewish law, where *sefeqot* refers to people or things whose legal status is uncertain (e.g., M. Qiddushin 4.3; BT Shabbat 15b; BT Bava Meṣi'a 83b). I see no connection between this usage and that of the authors to be analyzed later. The use of *sefeqot* as a technical term in talmudic study at the end of the fifteenth century (see n. 5) is quite different: philosophical, rather than legal in nature.

8. Abarbanel, *Nevi'im* 1:12a-13a.

9. Abarbanel, *Torah* 1:12b.

10. Ibid., 3:8a, 11b.

11. For the influence of Arama, see Segal, "R. Yiṣḥaq 'Abarbanel," 266; for Ḥayyun, see Gross, *R. Yosef*, 146 n. 157. Both will be discussed later.

12. See, for example, Abarbanel on Zechariah 7:1 (*Nevi'im* 3:219a). In his Torah commentary *Toledot Yiṣḥaq*, Isaac Caro ordinarily uses the term "doubts," but sometimes he will use "questions" (e.g., 38b, 81b), and sometimes "difficulties" (*qushyot*) (e.g., 39a, 111b).

13. "Derashot" by various authors, fol. 87v, on the Ten Commandments. The questions bear some similarities, but are by no means identical, to the questions in Abarbanel's Torah commentary. The sermon is somewhat disappointing: a routine preaching exercise rather than a response to a special occasion. It does not provide clear evidence for either the use of sermonic material in the commentary, or the opposite.

14. On this work, see the recent discussion by Bland (n. 3). Sha'ul Regev characterizes this as "a book of sermons on the Torah," recast by the editor in the form of a commentary (Caro,

Derashot, 12), but unfortunately he does not compare the content of the "commentary" with the sermons he published.

15. For example, six of the eight "doubts" raised by Caro at the beginning of the lesson *Lekh lekha* (*Toledot Yiṣḥaq*, 20b) can be found among Abarbanel's more expansive "questions" on the same passage (*Torah* 1:186b–187b). Note that after raising two doubts at the beginning of *Ḥayyei Sarah*, Caro continues, "The *hakham* Rabbi Ephraim Caro, of blessed memory, my brother, responded to these doubts by saying . . . ," possibly reporting the content of a sermon by the author's brother (the father of the author of the *Shulḥan 'arukh*) in which the same doubts were discussed (*Toledot Yiṣḥaq*, 27a; cf. 40a).

16. Caro, *Derashot*, 69–93.

17. For examples, see Ibn Shuaib, 10b–c (*Noaḥ*) and 73c–d (*Yitro*), formally similar to Abarbanel, and the more complex forms in the sermons on Bereshit (3d–10a), *Lekh lekha* (13d–15c), *Wa-yera* (17c–19a), *Ḥayyei Sarah* (21c–24d), *Wa-yeḥi* (44b–46b), *Bo* (61c–62b), 44b-46b.

18. Arama, *'Aqedat Yiṣḥaq*, Introduction, 1: 9a.

19. Ibid., chap. 26 (*Wa-yishlaḥ*), 1:155a–b.

20. Ibid., chap. 91 (*'Eqev*), 3:25d–26a. Cf. also the commentary on the scroll of Esther, where the "doubts" are divided into two categories, substantive and linguistic: *Peirush Megillat Ester*, in *'Aqeidat Yiṣḥaq*, vol. 3. This commentary, printed in the standard editions of *'Aqedat Yiṣḥaq*, was apparently written by Isaac's son, Meir (Walfish, *Esther in Medieval Garb*, 226, although Walfish describes Isaac's own commentary in a similar manner: 8).

21. Shem Tov Ibn Shem Tov, *Derashot*, 5c.

22. Ibid., 6c, 6d.

23. Ibid., 8b–9a; cf. also *Lekh lekha*, the third part raising five questions about the first ten verses of the *parashah* and answering them: 9c–d.

24. Ibid., 39c.

25. Aboab, "Qeṣat parashiyot"; the longest sermon in this collection is published in Saperstein, "*Your Voice*," 293–365.

26. "Qeṣat parashiyot," fol. 3a, 3b. The second and fourth questions are the same as *sefeqot* brought by Caro, *Toledot Yiṣḥaq*, 27a. After one of his questions, Aboab states, "Others have spoken, you may look at their explanations."

27. "Dover meisharim," fol. 197a–b; on this work, see Saperstein, *Jewish Preaching*, index s.v. "Israel, author of 'Dober Mesharim,'" and "*Your Voice*," 253.

28. "Dover meisharim," fols. 202a, 206a.

29. Ibid., fol. 55a. Cf. the author's defense of his sermonic use of the "disputed question" form: Saperstein, *Jewish Preaching*, 395–96.

30. "Derashot" by various authors, fol. 89r, 16r–v. The raising of doubts or difficulties about the rabbinic dictum, as opposed to the biblical passage, would become increasingly common in the following century; see the example from Moses Almosnino in Saperstein, *Jewish Preaching*, 232–33 and a comparable passage in Solomon Levi, *Divrei Shelomoh*, 126b–c.

31. Canpanton, *Darkhei ha-gemara*, 13; cf. Gross, *R. Yosef*, 73.

32. It is actually the precise equivalent of the Latin *dubitationes movere*; see Thomas Aquinas, discussed later. The legacy of the Latin phrase remains in the English expression, "to move the question."

33. Gross, *R. Yosef*, 74. Cf. also the later formulation by Solomon Levi in *Divrei Shelomoh*, 205d, a sermon from 1573. Solomon, however, did not use the "method of doubts" as an integral part of his preaching. Cf. Davidson, *'Oṣar ha-meshalim* 50, n. 725: *mi-tokh ha-wiqquaḥ mitbarer ha-'emet*.

34. Gross, *R. Yosef*, 195–97. Note that not all questions in this passage are presented together; first two are given, then answers to both; other answers come immediately after the respective questions. The terms "doubts" and "questions" are used interchangeably.

35. Ibid., 198–201; cf. 222–23, raising two sets of doubts on the sin of Moses and Aaron at the waters of Meribah. The answers are given after all the doubts are raised.

36. E.g., Abarbanel, *Torah* 2: 149b, question 1 and Ḥayyun, in Gross, *R. Yosef*, 200 question 1; Abarbanel, *Torah* 2: 150a, question 6, and Ḥayyun, in Gross, *R. Yosef*, 200, question 4.

37. Abarbanel, *Torah* 2: 253b, on Exodus 25.

38. Joseph Ibn Shem Tov, "Derashot," fols. 72b–74a.

39. Joseph Ibn Shem Tov, "Derashot 'al ha-teshuvah," 188. Cf. 207: "the sages already resolved this doubt."

40. Ibid., 194.

41. See Saperstein, "*Your Voice*," 183, 200–207. On a different occasion, the preacher says he will give "the answer to this [question] in short, without points of possible arguments on each of the antithetical propositions, in order to avoid the burden of excessive time" ("Derashot" by disciple of Crescas, fol. 31a).

42. Ibid., fol. 13b (*mi-tokh ha-maśa we-ha-mattan tiṣmaḥ ha-'emet*). Cf. n. 33 in this chapter.

43. Ibid., fol. 14a.

44. Crescas, *'Or 'Adonai*, 2.2.2, (pp. 157–62).

45. Ibid., 2.4.3, (pp. 195–203).

46. Leon Feldman first published this work without an author's name and then republished it with the attribution to Joseph ben David (Jerusalem, 1973). Feldman assumes that it is a commentary, but the sections have structural affinities with the sermon, and there are internal indications of an occasion for preaching (see, e.g., 65, 132–37, 198). Cf. Saperstein, *Jewish Preaching*, 74, n. 26.

47. Joseph ben David, *Peirush 'al ha-Torah* (1973), 18–19. These questions should be compared with those of Abarbanel and his contemporaries—for example, the first question with Abarbanel's fourth, the second with Abarbanel's sixth, the third with Abarbanel's ninth, the fourth with Abarbanel's seventh, and the fifth with Abarbanel's twelfth (*Torah* 1:304b–305b).

48. Joseph ben David, *Peirush 'al ha-Torah* (1973), 20–21. Cf. 220: "There are also other doubts (*sefeqot*) that require explication," a passage taken from *Derashot ha-Ran* (see later), and 148–50.

49. Gerondi, *Peirush 'al ha-Torah*, 53. This passage is used by Nissim's disciple; see *Peirush 'al ha-Torah*, 220–21. Cf. also Nissim's eighth sermon (136, 137, 139), where he raises a series of "doubts," not clustered at the beginning of a discussion, but rather presented in an associative manner, the solution of one leading to the presentation of the next.

50. Levi ben Gershom, *Milḥamot ha-Shem* 2.6, (pp. 104–11); cf. idem, *The Wars of the Lord*, 2: 49–59, where the translation is the more idiomatic "problems." Cf. also 1.13, Hebrew, 89–90; English, 1: 223–24.

51. Note also that the introduction begins with a list of six "important and difficult questions (*she'elot*)," each one of which actually entails more than one such query (*Milḥamot*, 2, *Wars*, 1: 91). Then, "we have also appended to these questions two religious problems, fraught with doubt (*she'elot datiyot mesuppaqot me'od*)" (3, cf. 92). Gersonides also used the term *sefeqot* in his technical supercommentaries on Ibn Rushd; see Glasner, "Early Stages," 43–45.

52. Levi ben Gershom, *Peirush 'al ha-Torah*, 112b–c, 112d. The commentary by Nissim's disciple incorporates this passage without giving credit to Ralbag, introducing it with the phrase, "Now it is worthwhile to speak about some of the doubts that fall upon this matter"; Joseph ben David, *Peirush 'al ha-Torah* (1973), 215–16.

53. See his discussion of the two celestial lights in the creation story (Levi ben Gershom, *Peirush 'al ha-Torah*, 12a; cf. Gerondi, *Peirush 'al ha-Torah*, 38, referring to the first doubt and Ralbag's solution); his discussion of Isaac's blessing (Gerondi, op. cit., 35d–36a); his comments on Joshua 10:12, introducing the problem of the sun over Gibeon, and on Proverbs 30:4.

54. Kimḥi, *Peirushei Qimḥi* 33.

55. Hillel ben Samuel, *Tagmulei ha-nefesh*, 116.

56. A recently published manuscript letter, apparently by Hillel of Verona, may provide additional information about this form. The author asks that a friend send him a copy of Maimonides' commentary on the *Aphorisms* of Hippocrates. Continuing, he notes that he has "more than one hundred great 'difficulties' on Galen's commentaries" on the *Aphorisms*, and he hopes that "with careful study of Maimonides' commentary, the burden of [or, all] these difficulties will be resolved" (Richler, "Iggeret," 12). The passage is not entirely clear, but it appears that Hillel was referring to Maimonides' "doubts that occurred to me concerning the words of Galen" (*ha-sefeqot ha-mitḥadshim li be-divrei Galenus*); see Maimonides, *Pirqei Mosheh (bi-refu'ah)*, 323. (I am grateful to Tzvi Langermann for this reference.) Alternatively, Hillel could be referring to his own method of studying the medical text by composing a series of "difficulties," equivalent to "doubts" in other passages, and then attempting to resolve them with recourse to a commentary to which he did not yet have access. This method could indeed be applied to biblical passages. On the works in question, see Sarton, *History of Science*, 1: 379–81. The Maimonides passage cited raises the issue of the "method of doubts" in Arabic literature, which cannot be considered here. Since the Jewish writers considered worked in Christian Europe, and few knew Arabic, it seems more fruitful to explore the Latin literature.

57. *De unitate intellectus contra Averroistas*, 26–27.

58. *Metaphysics* 2.1.995a 24–29. I have followed the translation of Richard Hope in Aristotle's *Metaphysics*, 40, except for translating "doubts" where Hope has "difficulties," following Hope's own explication of the Greek term *aporeia* on 388.

59. Alexander of Aphrodisias, 88. See 87, n. 3 for the various meanings of *aporeia* in Alexander.

60. Thomas Aquinas, *Commentary on the Metaphysics of Aristotle*, 1:141–42; *Opera omnia*, 20: 308a.

61. For an enumeration of these fourteen problems and their solutions, see Aristotle's *Metaphysics*, trans. Apostle, 272–74.

62. Thomas Aquinas, *Commentary on the Metaphysics*, 143; *Opera omnia*, 20: 308b. The Latin verb used in this passage is *praemittere*. In the same passage, Aquinas uses two other phrases to characterize Aristotle's raising of conceptual problems: *ponit dubitationes* and *movet dubitationes* (20:309a), the precise equivalent of the Hebrew phrases *le-haniaḥ sefeqot* and *le-hani'a sefeqot*, which we have encountered. Despite the distinction in the usage of the verbs suggested by Blanche, "Le vocabulaire," 168–69, the material in Thomas's *Commentary*, especially in the passage just cited, suggests that the two terms were used by the author interchangeably. Cf. also Thomas Aquinas, *Commentary on the Posterior Analytics*, 30–31 (*Opera omnia*, 18: 145a) on 81b30–82b34.

63. PL 34.547–49.

64. PL 35, beginning 1321. Cf. also Jerome, *Hebraicae quaestiones*. For a full discussion of this form in Patristic literature, see Lagrange, La littérature patristique,"; for more recent treatments, see Kamesar, *Jerome*, esp. 82–96, and Jerome, *Saint Jerome's Hebrew Questions*, esp. 2–5. Kamesar notes a "long history" of this literature before Jerome, beginning with the sixth-century B.C.E. criticisms of Homeric poems (82).

65. Honorius of Autun, in PL 172.313–48.

66. E.g., "What does Solomon mean when he says, "In vain the net is spread in the eyes of every winged creature" (Prov 1:17)? . . . Who are the winged ones? The saints and elect of God, who have the wings of faith, hope, and love, as well as the other virtues." "What is the wisdom about which Solomon says, 'Wisdom cries aloud in the streets' (1:20)? Jesus Christ, who is the virtue of God and the wisdom of God." Cf. also Honorius's *Liber duodecim quaestionum*, PL 172.1177, where the twelve questions are listed together, separate from any exegetical context, and then answered one by one.

67. PL 175.431-634. For the spuriousness of the attribution to Hugh, see Smalley, *The Study of the Bible*, 97, n. 1. Cf. Spicq, *Esquisse d'une histoire*, 67.

68. "*Dubitando ad inquisitionem venimus, inquirendo veritatem percipimus*," immediately following the Aristotelian quotation "*Dubitare autem de singulis non erit inutile*" (Abelard, *Sic et non*, 103). Cf. Grabmann, *Die Geschichte*, 1: 203, 209.

69. Note the statement by A. Landgraf that "Gilbert de la Porrée and Abelard initiated this practice of introducing the *quaestio* into the scriptural commentary, a practice that would quickly become so strongly prevalent in their schools" (Landgraf, "Collections,"124). No evidence, however, is provided for Gilbert or Abelard, and the evidence for the schools is in manuscript (Landgraf, "Collections," 124, n. 21).

70. Cf. Spicq, *Esquisse d'une histoire*, 68-69: "Little by little, *Quaestiones* were inserted [into biblical commentaries] in order to resolve contradictions between two biblical texts or between two exegeses of the same text; aided by the influence of Aristotelian dialectic, reasoning takes a more and more considerable place in the structure of the *Quaestio*."

71. See, for example, the discussion by Baldwin, *Masters, Princes and Merchants*, 2: 96-101.

72. Bonaventure, *Opera theologica selecta*. These *dubia*, from a separate manuscript, were derived from the period of Bonaventure's studies in Paris, influenced by Alexander of Hales; they were interspersed with the text of the "Commentary on the Sentences" by the editors. See Bougerol, *Introduction to Bonaventure*, 100-105.

73. Bonaventure, *Opera omnia*, 6: 66, 57, 63. The same pattern is used in the commentary on John (e.g., ibid., 260). Cf. Smalley, *The Study of the Bible*, 276, and idem, *Medieval Exegesis of Wisdom Literature*, 43-45. Smalley concludes that Bonaventure's purpose in using this form was "to give the students some guidance on the type of problem which arose from the text and to sketch the lines for a solution" (45). For the influence of these *quaestiones* on subsequent commentators, see ibid., 49-51 (William of Tournai), 71 (William of Alton), 84-86 (John of Varzy).

74. For example, in the commentary on John (*Opera omnia* 6: 261, paragraph 69).

75. During the 1340s, the Carmelite monk John Baconthorpe wrote in Oxford a series of biblical commentaries, of which his postill on Matthew has survived. Smalley's description of this published work indicates that it contains series of *quaestiones*, for example: *Hec sunt tres difficultates* (another term corresponding to a term in Jewish sources), "*Sed tunc remanet difficultas. . . . Sed ex hiis sequitur alia difficultas. . . . Hic oritur quarta difficultas. . . .*" Smalley, in *Studies in Medieval Thought and Learning*, 316, 328-29.

76. Wycliffe, *Sermones*, 1: xiv: "*In dominicis sermonibus supposito sensu literali intendo breviter sensum misticum explanare et secondu more Augustini salutabo dubia que ex evangelio possent capi.*"

77. Ibid., 1: 3, 12-13, 240, 26, 40, 236. The early-sixteenth-century French preacher Michel Menot regularly devoted the second part of his sermons to a fully developed disputed question; see Gilson, *Les idées*, 135-36; Taylor, *Soldiers of Christ*, 62, 66.

78. Spencer, *English Preaching*, 45-46.

79. Gerson, *Six sermons français inédits*, 231-39, 82-84, 298-99.

80. Gerson, *Oeuvres complètes*, 5:70-73. For example, "What if Peter had wanted to defend his error by armed force, notwithstanding that he remained pope: would it have been permissible to repel force with force, whether by words, or by imprisonment, or finally by death itself? As Jerome and Augustine, both exceptional scholars, disagreed on this matter, must one of them be said to be a heretic?" (72).

81. See the many references in Mourin, *Six sermons*, 341-42.

82. Gerson, *Oeuvres complètes* 5:378-39; cf. also Mourin, *Six sermons*, 342, on the relationship between the scriptural reading and the questions in some of the sermons.

83. The technique of introducing "doubts" suggested in the *Ars praedicandi* written by the

contemporary Catalan Franciscan friar Francesc Eiximenis of Gerona is rather different from this, in that they are questions used to *introduce* the theme verse (which provides the answer to them) rather than questions arising from the verse. See Martí de Barcelona, *Francesc Eiximenis*, 335–36.

84. Gregory of Rimini, 1:381–88. Cf. also Biel, *Collectorium*, 1:22 ("*In articulo quarto movenda sint dubia circa praedicta et solvenda*"). Each of these "doubts," however, is answered after it is raised.

85. This point has been made recently by D'Avray, *Preaching of the Friars*, 7–8, 164–71, 242–43; he emphasizes the paucity of scholastic questions in thirteenth-century preaching. Cf. Thomas Waley's critique of preachers who incorporate *profundae materiae theologicae* into their sermons as if they were addressing "clerics in the schools" (a complaint that can be paralleled in Jewish sources): Charland, *Artes praedicandi*, 112, 344; see also Spencer, *English Preaching*, 46; Taylor, *Soldiers of Christ*, 33. On the important distinction between discourse of the academic and discourse of the pulpit, see Robert of Basevorn's *Forma praedicandi* (in Charland, *Artes praedicandi*, 238), and Thomas Illyricus (Taylor, *Soldiers of Christ*, 83; note her statement there that "Scholastic debates did not, for the most part, furnish material for popular preaching").

86. "It seems that God does not exist" (*Summa theologiae* 1.2.5). "It seems that to be good does not pertain to God" (1.6.1). "It seems that it was not fitting for God to become incarnate" (3.1.1). "It seems that the Mother of God was not a virgin in conceiving Christ" (3.28.1). "It seems that it was not necessary for Christ to suffer for the deliverance of the human race" (3.46.1).

87. See, for example, the long quotation from Thomas's argument that "it seems that Christ's Mother did not remain a virgin after His birth" (3.28.3), which Modena calls *sefeqot* (*Magen wa-ḥerev*, 60–61). He then goes on to rebut Thomas's answers to the doubts. It was for such reasons that Henry of Hesse warned that "the preacher should never in the pulpit frivolously or presumptuously put any belief to the test," and that "when the preacher brings up doubts and disputed questions in the pulpit, he should not retire without settling the point" (Caplan, *Of Eloquence*, 72, 73, and cf. the incident in Taylor, *Soldiers of Christ*, 186).

88. Cf. the more serious expression of the dangers of problematizing, particularly if the solution is not compelling, cogently articulated by Abraham ben David in his animadversions on Maimonides' *Mishneh Torah*, Hilkhot Teshuvah (Laws of Repentance) 5.5.

89. See references in Saperstein, "The Social and Cultural Context," 295, 310–12.

90. Ibid., 213, at nn. 121–24.

91. This is not to suggest that there were no philosophical problems discussed in sermons that genuinely vexed late medieval Spanish Jews. The efficacy of repentance and its reconciliation with divine foreknowledge and justice is an example; see Saperstein, *Jewish Preaching*, 395–98; idem, "*Your Voice*," 85–86, 296–97, 317–24.

92. Ibn Shuaib, *'Olat Shabbat*, 144a-b. Cf. Thomas Aquinas, *Commentary on the Metaphysics*, 1:142, paragraphs 340 and 342. Aboab gives a similar, though more succinct, defense of this type of argumentation in the sermon where he cites Thomas; Saperstein, "*Your Voice*," 86–87, n. 41.

93. Ibn Shuaib, *'Olat Shabbat*, 25c, 10b.

94. Arama, *'Aqeidat Yiṣḥaq*, introduction (my emphasis); see Saperstein, *Jewish Preaching*, 393 and n. 3.

Bibliography

Abelard, Peter. *Sic et non*. Ed. Blanche Boyers and Richard McKeon. Chicago: University of Chicago Press, 1976.

Aboab, Isaac. "Qeṣat parashiyot." Oxford, Bodleian Library, MS Hunt. 342 (Neubauer 952).

Abarbanel, Isaac. *Peirush 'al ha-Torah*. 3 vols. Jerusalem: Benei Arbel, 1964.

——. *Peirush 'al Nevi'im u-Khetuvim.* 3 vols. Jerusalem: Torah wa-Da'at, 1956–60.

Alexander of Aphrodisias. *On Aristotle's Metaphysics 2 & 3.* Trans. William Dooley and Arthur Madigan. Ithaca, N.Y.: Cornell University Press, 1992.

Anonymous. "Derashot" by disciple of Crescas. St. Petersburg, Russian National Library, MS Firk. Evr. I. 507.

——, by various authors, generation of the Expulsion. New York, Jewish Theological Seminary of America, MS 9856.

Arama, Isaac. *'Aqeidat Yiṣḥaq.* 3 vols. Warsaw, 1882.

Aristotle. *Metaphysics.* Trans. Richard Hope. New York: Columbia University Press, 1952.

——. *Metaphysics.* Trans. with commentaries by Hippocrates Apostle. Bloomington: Indiana University Press, 1966.

——. *Posterior Analytics.* Trans. Jonathan Barnes. Oxford: Clarendon Press, 1975.

Augustine of Hippo. *Quaestionum in Evangeliorum.* PL 35.1321–1364.

——. *Quaestionum in Heptateuchum.* PL 34.547–823.

Baḥya ben Asher. *Bei'ur 'al ha-Torah.* 3 vols. Ed. Charles B. Chavel. Jerusalem: Mossad Harav Kook, 1966.

Baldwin, John. *Masters, Princes and Merchants: The Social Views of Peter the Chanter and His Circle.* 2 vols. Princeton, N.J.: Princeton University Press, 1970.

Bataillon, Louis. "De la *lectio* à la *praedicatio*: commentaires bibliques et sermons au XIIIe siècle." *Revue des sciences philosophiques et théologiques* 70 (1986): 559–75.

Bentov, Ḥayyim. "Shiṭat limmud ha-Talmud bi-yshivot Saloniqah we-Turqiyah" (The method of Talmud study in the academies of Salonika and Turkey). *Sefunot* 13 (*Sefer Yavan* 3) (1971–78): 5–102.

Biel, Gabriel. *Collectorium circa quattuor libros Sententiarum*, Ed. Wilfred Werbeck. 4 books in 5 vols. Tübingen: Mohr, 1973–92.

Blanche, F. A. "Le vocabulaire de l'argumentation et la structure de l'article dans les ouvrages de Saint Thomas." *Revue des sciences philosophiques et théologiques* 14 (1925): 167–87.

Bland, Kalman. "Issues in Sixteenth-Century Jewish Exegesis." In *The Bible in the Sixteenth Century.* Ed. David Steinmetz, 50–67. Durham and London: Duke University Press, 1990.

Bonaventure. *Opera omnia*, 10 vols. plus Index. Florence: Quaracchi, 1893.

——. *Opera theologica selecta.* Ed. Pacificus M. Perantonus. 4 vols. Florence: Quaracchi, 1959.

Bougerol, J. Guy. *Introduction to the Works of Bonaventure.* Paterson, N.J.: St. Anthony Guild Press, 1964.

Boyarin, Daniel. "Meḥqarim be-farshanut ha-Talmud shel megoreshei Sefarad" (Studies in the Talmud exegesis of the Spanish exiles). *Sefunot* 2 (17) (1983): 165–84.

Canpanton, Isaac. *Darkhei ha-gemara.* Vilna, 1901.

Caplan, Harry. *Of Eloquence.* Ithaca, N.Y.: Cornell University Press, 1970.

Caro, Isaac. *Derashot R. Yiṣḥaq Qaro.* Ed. Sha'ul Regev. Ramat Gan: Bar Ilan University Press, 1995.

——. *Toledot Yiṣḥaq.* Riva di Trento, 1558.

Charland, Th.-M. *Artes praedicandi.* Paris and Ottawa: L'Institut d'études médiévales d'Ottawa, 1936.

Crescas, Ḥasdai. *'Or 'Adonai.* Jerusalem: Sifrei Ramot, 1990.

Davidson, Israel. *'Oṣar ha-meshalim we-ha-pitgamim* (Thesaurus of proverbs and sayings). Jerusalem: Mossad Harav Kook, 1979.

D'Avray, David. *The Preaching of the Friars.* Oxford: Oxford University Press, 1985.

Eisen, Robert. *Gersonides on Providence, Covenant and the Chosen People.* Albany: State University of New York Press, 1995.

Gerondi, Nissim ben Reuben. *Derashot ha-Ran.* Ed. Leon Feldman. Jerusalem: Mekhon Shalem, 1974.

——. *Peirush 'al ha-Torah.* Ed. Leon Feldman. Jerusalem: Mekhon Shalem, 1968.

Gerson, John. *L'oeuvre oratoire*. Ed. Palem Glorieux. Oeuvres complètes, 5. Paris and Tournai: Desclée, 1963.

——. *Six sermons français inédits de Jean Gerson*. Ed. Louis Mourin. Paris: J. Vrin, 1946.

Gilson, Étienne. *Les idées et les lettres*. Paris: J. Vrin, 1932.

Glasner, Ruth. "The Early Stages in the Evolution of Gersonides' *The Wars of the Lord*." *JQR* 87 (1996): 1–46.

Grabmann, Martin. *Die Geschichte der scholastischen Methode*. 2 vols. Berlin: Akademie-Verlag, 1956.

Greenberg, Moshe, ed. *Parshanut ha-Miqra ha-Yehudit* (Jewish Bible exegesis). Jerusalem: Mosad Bialik, 1983.

Gregory of Rimini. *Gregorii Ariminensis Oesa lectura super primum et secundum sententiarum*. Ed. A. Damasus Trapp and Venicio Marcolino. 7 vols. Berlin: Walter de Gruyter, 1979–87.

Gross, Abraham. *R. Yosef ben 'Avraham Ḥayyun: manhig qehillat Lisbon wi-yṣirato* (Rabbi Joseph ben Abraham Hayyun: leader of the Lisbon Jewish community and his literary work). Ramat Gan: Bar Ilan University Press, 1993.

Guttmann, Jacob. *Die Religionsphilosophischen Lehren des Isaak Abravanel*. Breslau: M & H Marcus, 1916.

Hillel ben Samuel, of Verona. *Sefer Tagmulei ha-nefesh*. Ed. Joseph Sermoneta. Jerusalem: Israel Academy of Sciences and Humanities, 1981.

Honorius of Autun (Augustodun). *Quaestiones et responsiones in Proverbia et in Ecclesiasten*. PL 172.313–48.

Hugh of Saint Victor, attributed. *Quaestiones et decisiones in epistolas Pauli*. PL 175.431–634.

Ibn Shem Tov, Joseph. "Derashot 'al ha-Teshuvah le-Rabbi Yosef 'Ibn Shem Ṭov" (Sermons on repentance by Rabbi Joseph Ibn Shem Tov). Ed. Sha'ul Regev. *'Asufot* 5 (1991): 183–211.

——. "Derashot." The Hague, Juynboll, MS 1 (Private collection housed in Leiden).

Ibn Shem Tov, Shem Tov. *Derashot*. Salonika, 1525; reprint, Jerusalem: Hebrew University, 1973.

Ibn Shuaib, Joel. *'Olat Shabbat*. Venice, 1577; reprint, Benei Beraq: Meir Morgenstern, 1973.

Israel, author of "Dover Meisharim." "Dover Meisharim." Oxford, Christ Church, MS 197.

Jerome. *Hebraicae Quaestiones in Libro Geneseos*. CCSL 72. Turnhout: Brepols, 1959.

——. *Saint Jerome's Hebrew Questions on Genesis*. Trans. C. T. R. Hayward. Oxford: Clarendon Press, 1995.

Joseph ben David, of Saragossa. *Peirush 'al ha-Torah meyuḥas le-talmid Rabbeinu Nissim b. R. Re'uven (ha-Ran)*. Ed. Leon Feldman. Jerusalem: Mekhon Shalem, 1970.

——. *Peirush 'al ha-Torah*. Ed. Leon Feldman. Jerusalem: Mekhon Shalem, 1973.

Kamesar, Adam. *Jerome, Greek Scholarship, and the Hebrew Bible: A Study of the Quaestiones Hebraicae in Genesim*. Oxford: Clarendon Press, 1993.

Kimḥi, David (Radak). *Peirushei Rabbi Dawid Qimḥi (Radaq) 'al ha-Torah*. Ed. Moses Kamelhar. Jerusalem: Mossad Harav Kook, 1970.

Kretzmann, Norman, Anthony Kenny, and Jan Pinborg, eds. *The Cambridge History of Later Medieval Philosophy*. Cambridge: Cambridge University Press, 1982.

Lagrange, M.-J. "La littérature patristique des "*Quaestiones et responsiones*" sur l'Écriture sainte." *Revue biblique* 41 (1932): 210–36, 341–69, 514–37; 42 (1933): 14–30, 211–29, 328–52.

Landgraf, A. "Collections de '*Quaestiones*' du XIIe siècle," *Recherches de théologie ancienne et médiévale* 7 (1935): 113–28.

Levi ben Gershom (Gersonides, Ralbag). *Milḥamot ha-Shem*. Berlin: L. Lames, 1923.

——. *Peirush 'al ha-Torah*. Venice: Bomberg, 1547. Reprint, New York: Jacob M. Shurkin, 1958.

——. *The Wars of the Lord*. Trans. Seymour Feldman. 3 vols. Philadelphia: Jewish Publication Society, 1984–99.

Levi, Solomon (Shelomoh le-Veit ha-Levi). *Divrei Shelomoh*. Venice, 1596; reprint edition, Brooklyn: Goldenberg Brothers, 1993.

Maimonides, Moses. *Pirqei Mosheh (bi-refu'ah)*. Trans. Nathan Ha-Me'ati. Ed. Süssmann Muntner. Jerusalem: Mossad Harav Kook, 1961.

Martí de Barcelona, P. "L'ars praedicandi de Francesc Eiximenis." *Analecta sacra tarraconensia* 12 (1936): 301–40.

Modena, Leon. *Magen wa-ḥerev*. Jerusalem: Meqiṣei Nirdamim, 1960.

Morteira, Saul Levi. "Derashot." 5 vols. Budapest, Rabbinical Seminary, MS 12.

Mourin, Louis, ed. *Six sermons français inédits de Jean Gerson*. Paris: J. Vrin, 1946.

Netanyahu, B. Z. *Don Isaac Abravanel*. Philadelphia: Jewish Publication Society, 1968.

Renan, Ernst. *Les écrivains juifs français du XIVe siècle*. Histoire littéraire de la France, 31, 351–789. Paris: Imprimerie Nationale, 1893.

Richler, Benjamin. "'Iggeret nosefet me-et Hillel ben Shemu'el 'el Yiṣḥaq ha-Rofe?" (An Additional Letter by Hillel ben Samuel to Isaac the Physician?). In *Mi-ginzei ha-Makhon le-Taṣlumei Kitvei ha-Yad ha-'Ivriyim* (From the archives of the Institute of Microfilmed Hebrew Manuscripts). Ed. A. David, 11–13. Jerusalem: Beit ha-Sefarim ha-Le'umi we-ha-'Universita'i, 1995.

Roberts, Phyllis. *Studies in the Sermons of Stephen Langton*. Toronto: Pontifical Institute of Mediaeval Studies, 1968.

Saperstein, Marc. *Jewish Preaching 1200–1800*. New Haven, Conn.: Yale University Press, 1989.

——. "The Social and Cultural Context." In *History of Jewish Philosophy*. Ed. Daniel H. Frank and Oliver Leaman, 294–330. Routledge History of World Philosophies, vol. 2. London: Routledge, 1997.

——. *"Your Voice Like a Ram's Horn": Themes and Texts in Traditional Jewish Preaching*. Cincinnati: Hebrew Union College Press: 1996.

Sarton, George. *A History of Science*. 2 vols. Cambridge, Mass.: Harvard University Press, 1959.

Scholem, Gershom. *On the Kabbalah and Its Symbolism*. Trans. Ralph Manheim. New York: Schocken Books, 1965.

Segal, M. Z. "R. Yiṣḥaq 'Abarbanel be-tor parshan ha-Miqra" (R. Isaac Abarbanel as a biblical exegete). *Tarbiẓ* 9 (1937): 260–99.

Shalem, Shim'on. "Ha-metodah ha-parshanit shel Rabbi Yosef Ṭaiṭaṣaq we-ḥugo" (The exegetical method of Rabbi Joseph Taitazak and his circle). *Sefunot* 11 (*Sefer Yawan* 1) (1971–78): 113–34.

Shalom, Abraham. *Neweh Shalom*. Venice, 1575.

Smalley, Beryl. *Medieval Exegesis of Wisdom Literature*. Atlanta, Ga.: Scholars Press, 1986.

——. *Studies in Medieval Thought and Learning*. London: Hambledon Press, 1981.

——. *The Study of the Bible in the Middle Ages*. New York: Philosophical Library, 1952.

Spencer, H. Leith. *English Preaching in the Late Middle Ages*. Oxford: Clarendon Press, 1993.

Spicq, Ceslas. *Esquisse d'une histoire de l'exégèse latine au Moyen Âge*. Paris: J. Vrin, 1944.

Taylor, Larissa. *Soldiers of Christ: Preaching in Late Medieval and Reformation France*. Oxford: Oxford University Press, 1992.

Thomas Aquinas. *Commentary on the Metaphysics of Aristotle*. Trans. John Rowan. 2 vols. Chicago: H. Regnery, 1961.

——. *Commentary on the Posterior Analytics of Aristotle*. Trans. F. R. Larcher. Albany, N.Y.: Magi Books, 1970.

——. "De unitate intellectus contra Averroistas." In *Aquinas Against the Averroists*. Ed. Ralph McInerny. West Lafayette, Ind.: Purdue University Press, 1993.

——. *Opera omnia*. 24 vols. in 25. Parma: P. Fiaccadori, 1852–70. *In libros posteriorum Analyticorum Aristotelis expositio*, 18 (1865); *In duodecim libros Metaphysicorum Aristotelis expositio*, 20 (1866).

——. *Summa theologica*. Trans. Fathers of the English Dominican Province. 3 vols. New York: Benziger Brothers, 1947–48.

Touati, Charles. *La pensée philosophique et théologique de Gersonide*. Paris: Éditions de Minuit, 1973.

Urbach, Ephraim. *Ba'alei ha-Tosafot* (The Tosafists). Jerusalem: Mosad Bialik, 1968.

Walfish, Barry. *Esther in Medieval Garb: Jewish Interpretation of the Book of Esther in the Middle Ages*. Albany: State University of New York Press, 1993.

Wilensky, Sarah Heller. *R. Yiṣḥaq 'Aramah u-mishnato* (The philosophy of R. Isaac Arama). Jerusalem and Tel Aviv: Mosad Bialik and Dvir, 1957.

Wycliffe, John. *Sermones*. Ed. Johann Loserth. 4 vols. London: Wyclif Society, 1887–90.

Yiẓhari, Mattathias. "Parashiyot." Parma, Biblioteca Palatina, MS 2365 (De Rossi 1417).

10

Introducing Scripture

The *Accessus ad auctores* in Hebrew Exegetical Literature from the Thirteenth through the Fifteenth Centuries

ERIC LAWEE

In his 1901 *General Introduction to the Study of Holy Scripture*, C. A. Briggs indicated that "Holy Scripture, as given by divine inspiration to holy prophets, lies buried beneath the rubbish of centuries." He then reassured his reader that modern biblical criticism was "digging through this mass of rubbish"—most notably "the débris of the traditional interpretations of the multitudinous schools and sects"—in search of "the rock-bed of the Divine Word."[1] If nowadays Briggs's analogy between archaeological exploration and historical-critical study of the Bible seems "hopelessly naive" (as "biblical bedrock has proven to be an elusive item, and far less adamantine than had been supposed"),[2] we might succumb momentarily to its intuitive appeal in order to ask whether the disjunction between modern biblical scholarship, viewed as a critically informed excavatory endeavor, and premodern exegesis, viewed as a producer of countless layers of "rubbish" that only obscured biblical *terra firma*, is so total as Briggs and his ilk reflexively presupposed.

Initially, it was questions of this sort that lay at the heart of the following investigation into the deployment in medieval Hebrew exegetical literature of various exordial *topoi* (*accessus ad auctores*) used in high and late medieval Christian schools and universities to introduce authoritative secular and sacred texts studied therein. As time-honored certainties concerning Hebrew scripture crumbled in the postmedieval period and as the need to probe questions of biblical authorship, dating, original historical setting and the like was felt with unprecedented intensity in "modernity," it was in "introductions" to the Hebrew Bible (or rather the "Old Testament") that biblicists typically sought to address such issues.[3] The hope in turning to medieval introductions was to illuminate, from an admittedly oblique angle, discontinuities and linkages between medieval and modern exegetical mentalities. The aim, to be clear, was not to certify a segment of premodern exegesis as (however this term be understood) "critical." Still less was the objective to redeem the medieval exegetical inheritance by showing that some of its makers could (to invert a medieval metaphor) be seen as dwarfs upon whose shoulders the giants of modern biblical scholarship might have stood.[4] (Such modernizing paradigms are at any rate currently unfashionable in North American medieval studies.)[5] The purpose was simply to chart the extent to which some southern European Jewish biblical commentators became familiar with

Latin prologue formats in order to assess whether such familiarity supplied an impetus for new turns in these exegetes' designs for reading Holy Writ, fructifying interpretive efforts which, in their own way, might be deemed acts of exegetical digging.[6]

With work underway, it soon became apparent that study of Jewish awareness of the *accessus* format and its impact would be partial and potentially distorting if conducted solely from the vantage point of medieval interests in issues pursued with increasing verve by early modern and modern biblicists. The history of the introduction as a "genre" of Jewish literature, in terms both of internal structural and substantive developments[7] and Arabic and Latin precursors and counterparts, made a claim to attention. Evidence of the influence of Arabic and Latin exegetical techniques and hermeneutic outlooks on Jewish exegetical habits and aims in disciplines beyond scriptural commentary (rabbinic exegesis, philosophic commentaries, and so forth) would provide important points of reference. Finally, Jewish use of Latin prologue formats, real or alleged, could be evaluated properly only in light of larger trends in medieval (southern European) Jewish awareness and appreciation of Christian learning. Thus it was that the initial focus on premodern "critical" approaches receded and the effort to chart exegetical options available to specific authors and to sketch different models of cultural transmission at work in their adaptations of Christian *modi interpretandi* expanded. The paper's theme became premodern historical-literary approaches to scripture in light of an as yet unwritten history of Jewish-Christian scholarly "creative symbiosis" in the late medieval period.[8]

This essay begins with aerial surveys of the genre of the introduction in earlier medieval Jewish exegetical literature and of the Latin *accessus* in its historical development. It then reconsiders what has been seen as an initial stratum of Jewish awareness of Latin prologue formats in thirteenth-century southern France, investigates the less ambiguous yield of a handful of Hebrew texts of Italian and Iberian provenance, and offers conclusions.

Jewish Prolegomena in the Muslim Sphere

The advent of the preface in medieval Jewish literature mainly reflects the stimulus of a generic form developed by Christian and Muslim writers working in the Muslim world. The *ṣadr* and *muqaddima* spurred Jewish scholars familiar with this form, Rabbanite and Karaite alike, to compose introductions, mostly in Judeo-Arabic, to a wide variety of exegetical and nonexegetical works, first in the Muslim East and later in Andalusian Spain. In the realm of biblical commentary, one thinks of the influential tenth-century Rabbanite theologian and exegete Saadia b. Joseph al-Fayyūmī, the twelfth-century itinerant Spanish scholar Abraham Ibn Ezra, and among Karaites, of Saadia's younger contemporary Japheth ben Eli, who authored the most extensive extant corpus of *ṣudūr* to Bible commentaries in the Judeo-Islamic sphere.[9] In their introductions to biblical books, and at times in treatments of a biblical book's opening verse or verses (or elsewhere), such commentators variously addressed issues of biblical authorship, genre, and literary style in addition to the substantive issues raised by the book on which they were commenting.[10] To be sure, such treatments were not inevitably characterized by independence from tradition or a spirit of free inquiry. Regarding the question of Job's authorship, for instance, Saadia opined that "although the text does not specify it, [talmudic] tradition explicates, stating that . . . it was Moses who set down this book of

Job at the mandate of God and published it to the nation. And this is the true account."[11] Similarly, when this same writer did break with rabbinic tradition over the Psalter's origins—the talmudic Sages having ascribed this book to multiple authors whose contributions were collected by David, in contrast to Saadia's view of David's exclusive authorship of the whole—his divergence reflected the demands of intrareligious (anti-Karaite) polemic[12] rather than the results of his impartial audit of Holy Writ. Still, figures like Abraham Ibn Ezra and the more obscure Andalusi exegete Moses Gikatilla, upon whom Ibn Ezra drew heavily, could, in their introductions and elsewhere, engage in subtle accounts of the authorship, editing, and prophetic status of biblical books.[13]

Northern European Developments

If one turns to Jewish exegetical literature written in northern Europe, one finds meager prefatory offerings where one finds them at all, be it in the French school associated with Solomon b. Isaac (Rashi) or the school of the "German Pietists." It is generally held that the beginnings to Rashi's Song of Songs and Zechariah commentaries constitute introductions; a more recent trend views his opening remarks in his commentary on the Torah in this light as well.[14] But these texts do not take up historical or literary questions. Also in northern France, Eliezer of Beaugency observed that Isaiah's opening verse is "in the language of a prologue" (the Hebraicized Latin *anprologus*), and brief introductory comments are found in the Torah commentary of Rashi's grandson Samuel ben Meir.[15] The prevailing practice among northern French Jewish exegetes, however, was to begin commenting on the opening verse of a biblical book without looking back.

A word is in order about the German exegetical school, study of which remains in its infancy, since texts emanating from it serve as reminders that piety and insights regarding the processes through which biblical books came into being are not mutually exclusive and that introductions are not the only place to seek for such insights. Judah the Pious's vibrant interest in the literary formation and authorship of biblical books and such subjects as the identification of nonbiblical scripturally referenced books are well known. So are his references to postexilic insertions into the Pentateuch.[16] No less impressive, however, is the overarching interpretive principle regularly invoked by an anonymous author of a Chronicles commentary (which remains in manuscript) that discrepancies between various biblical books reflect the incomplete and contradictory genealogical scrolls from which Ezra constructed Chronicles and the book that bears his name.[17]

This brief retrospective of mostly pre-thirteenth-century developments should suffice to indicate that neither the exegetical introduction nor reflection on questions of scriptural authorship and origins were inventions of the late Jewish Middle Ages. It remains to determine whether introductory formats developed in the Christian Middle Ages spurred or directed thinking about such questions by Jewish exegetes.

Latin Prolegomena

The stylized Latin prologue traces its origins to late antiquity.[18] It was, for instance, a classical rhetorical scheme that supplied the template for a form of *accessus* developed in Carolingian times.[19] By the early twelfth century a range of prefatory formats were in use, two of them (classified some fifty years ago by Richard Hunt as "types A and B") likewise based on ancient rhetorical practices. A third (classified as "type C" by Hunt) had its origins in the philosophic commentary tradition. Writers who used it characteristically identified a work's title, author, intention, subject matter (*materia*), usefulness (*utilitas*), arrangement (*ordo*), including the book's divisions if any, its mode of action (*modus agendi*), which could take in stylistic and structural features, and the part of knowledge (*pars philosophiae*) which the text served.[20]

In the thirteenth century another format came into vogue which, using scholastic terminology, varyingly supplanted and supplemented the "type C" prologue. Books were now understood in light of categories derived from recently recovered works of Aristotle. The book's "efficient cause" was its author, its material cause was its subject matter, its formal cause was the pattern that the author imposed on his materials—this took in both the author's "form of treatment," or *forma tractandi*, and the "form of the treatise," or *forma tractatus*, this being principally the text's ordering of parts—and its final cause was the book's ultimate purpose or "ultimate objective in a Christian society."[21] In a wrinkle on this approach, the turn-of-the-fourteenth-century Franciscan exegete Nicholas of Lyra argued in his prologue to the Psalter that allusion to this book's four causes could be glimpsed in part of Luke 7:16: "A great prophet has arisen among us."[22] For the investigation of Latin prefatory schemes in relation to Jewish practices, the "type C" introduction and Aristotelian prologue are salient.

Hebrew Exegetical Prolegomena in Southern France

Jewish cognizance of the Latin *accessus* has been traced to an Ecclesiastes commentary written in the early decades of the thirteenth century by Samuel ibn Tibbon, a southern French rationalist best known for his translation from Arabic to Hebrew of Maimonides' *Guide of the Perplexed*.[23] As it happens, in his introduction to his earlier *Guide* translation, ibn Tibbon had defined his task in terms of Aristotelian causes, with the translator as efficient cause, the original text as material cause, and so forth. This application is, however, doubtless reflective of the Greco-Arabic philosophic tradition in which ibn Tibbon was steeped, rather than of Latin sources, in which use of the Aristotelian scheme was still decades away[24] (though the "slippage" from *accessus ad auctorem* to *accessus ad commentatorem*,[25] or in this case *ad translationem*, evinced in ibn Tibbon's introduction and later Hebrew works of translation that invoke the fourfold Aristotelian scheme does have a parallel in the Latin tradition).[26]

What of the Ecclesiastes commentary? In its lengthy introduction ibn Tibbon relates that sages who have composed books of wisdom "from Aristotle down to today" have prefaced these with a prologue generally constructed around all or some of eight points, among these being the book's aim (*kawwanat ha-sefer*); its utility (*to'alto*); its "stamp," or title (*ḥotamo*); its division (*ḥaluqqato*); its "relation" (*yaḥaso*) to other branches of learning, associated discourses, and the like; its position (*madregato*); the mode of instruction (*min ha-limmud*); and the author's name.[27] At first a rough parallel with Latin prologue headings found in the "type C" format suggests itself and, indeed, some have tried to urge such a parallel.[28] Upon closer inspection, however, problems arise. To cite but two, ibn Tibbon's list lacks a heading corresponding to *materia,* and his headings *yaḥaso* and, to a lesser extent, *min ha-limmud* lack Latin parallels.[29] Far more to the point, these latter terms, along with most others mentioned by ibn Tibbon, appear in a number of works stemming from the commentary tradition on Greek writers that in its Arabic stratum, especially with respect to Aristotle, was well known to ibn Tibbon.[30]

Ibn Tibbon's presentation also possesses a point of contact with an earlier Jewish (in this case Judeo-Arabic) source: like Japheth ben Eli, ibn Tibbon postulates that introductions to the Solomonic books are to be found in their opening verses.[31] To illustrate, "the words of Qohelet, son of David, king in Jerusalem" supplies the book's title, its author's name, and its expository style—namely, "words" in or close to their simple sense rather than figurative or poetic speech like Proverbs and Song of Songs (whose discursive modes are likewise indicated in their opening verses).[32] Verse two discloses Ecclesiastes' method of study and intention. The former is mainly inductive syllogism (*ha-heqqesh ha-ḥippuśi*): examination of many particulars (hence "vanity of vanit*ies*"), all of which revealed vanity yields the universal conclusion that "all is vanity." Ibn Tibbon's reading of these verses may have been shaped by Japheth's, though ibn Tibbon has Solomon as his own book's introducer whereas Japheth posits a narrator-editor (*mudawwin*) who composed Ecclesiastes' first two verses.[33] Ibn Tibbon explains Proverbs' opening seven-verse pericope in like manner, mentioning earlier unnamed commentators who recognized the introductory nature of these verses but who failed to elaborate.[34] Why ibn Tibbon would have considered it natural that Ecclesiastes and Proverbs should have been introduced in the manner of Aristotelian writings and other ancient "books of wisdom" is clear: Solomon's writings were to him of this very sort, with, for example, Ecclesiastes' main theme being the possibility of the soul's duration and conjunction with the active intellect, that is, the possibility of immortality.[35]

As one whose family had fled to Christian Europe after the 1148 Almohade invasion of Muslim Spain, ibn Tibbon was aware of scholarly developments in Christendom. In one place he even remarked that "the true sciences are far better known among the nations . . . in whose lands we live than they are in the lands of Ishmael." At one point in the Ecclesiastes commentary, he supplies Latin glosses for philosophic terms that he invokes.[36] Yet if aware of Christian learning, ibn Tibbon was by no means immersed in it. The source of his conception of the scholarly foreword seems clearly to be Arabic rather than Latin,[37] though it is perhaps too early to rule out entirely the possibility of his familiarity with the Latin prologue.

The evidence is slightly more promising in the case of another Provençal Jewish scholar. In the introduction to the Proverbs commentary written by or at least ascribed to David Kimḥi the author writes that the name of anyone who composed a book should be made known "so as to inform the public whether he is sufficiently wise and competent in wisdom so that one may rely on the words that he has written." Translated into Latin, the statement would read that the *auctor*'s name should be given to confirm his prestige, and thereby his book's *auctoritas* (this being a motif central to Christian concern with the *nomen auctoris*).[38] The author adds that a work's intention should be indicated as well. Whereas Samuel ibn Tibbon, however, had found these points as well as Proverbs' title, didactic procedure, and usefulness addressed in the book's first seven verses, this author sees only a circumscribed one-verse introduction in which the author's name and intention are disclosed, along with an oblique suggestion of usefulness.[39]

Then too, the author finds the *accessus* supplied by Proverbs' scribe rather than by its author: "this is what the *sofer* who wrote [down] the words of this book intended. He said 'the proverbs of Solomon,' mentioning the author by name. . . ." The author possibly invokes the conventional Latin heading, *utilitas*, when he adds that the scribe "wrote that the intention of the book's author was to benefit people desirous of hearing his teaching . . . so as to attain the ultimate reward which is eternal life."

On the basis of these remarks, David Kimḥi's leading modern student has inferred Kimḥi's familiarity with the *accessus*.[40] But if one can reasonably surmise that Kimḥi's consciousness of stratification in biblical texts—attested elsewhere[41]—may have been sharpened by the Latin commentary tradition's distinction between a work's *auctor* and *scriptor* (as, on the terminological plane, his usages *meḥabber* and *sofer* [or "transcriber," *kotev*] may be partially owed to Latin counterparts),[42] the case for his awareness of the *accessus* is by no means clinched. The author-scribe distinction had, in the case of Proverbs, a scriptural basis (Prov 25:1) that had already left its mark on rabbinic discussion of the book's compilation.[43] Though Samuel ibn Tibbon had eschewed this distinction in understanding Proverbs' opening verses, he had invoked it in explaining Ecclesiastes' closing ones, the last six of which he viewed as additions by the book's collective scribes Hezekiah and his colleagues.[44] Again, with the textual evidence ambiguous, one is compelled to turn to contextual evidence for clarification. Like ibn Tibbon, Kimḥi inherited the fruits of a Spanish *paideia* but, though some possibility of his knowledge of Judeo-Arabic insights regarding biblical prefatory style cannot be denied,[45] he was less a product of a strictly Greco-Arabic education than was ibn Tibbon. His latinity, if any, is elusive but his strong consciousness of Christendom—evinced especially in sustained exegetical efforts to rebuff Christianity's claim to the mantle of *verus Israel*—is not in doubt. Minimally, both Kimḥi's rationale for the requirement to mention certain introductory points and his intellectual profile generally allow for his placement within a Christian context with greater assurance than ibn Tibbon's. Still, during the transitional decades following the forced removal of Jewish savants from Muslim Spain to Provence, the latter was a place where Jewish hermeneutic sensibilities could be shaped by both the Arabic and Latin commentary traditions such that questions of external stimuli often admit of no easy disentangling.[46]

To round out the foregoing, it should be mentioned that there is no apparent additional evidence of awareness of the Latin prologue among the closing generations of southern French Jewish biblical interpreters. In the preface to his Song of Songs commentary Samuel ibn Tibbon's son, Moses, discourses on literary forms of biblical texts, mentioning in passing the general "cause" (*sibbah*) of Solomon's song and the "intention of its name," but he does not structure his foreword around such categories. Though Moses was formed intellectually in a wholly Christian environment, he remained rooted in the Arabic learning favored by his father, as his ample body of Hebrew translations of Arabic works attests.[47] Similarly, Menaḥem Meiri manifests no familiarity with the Latin exordial format.[48]

Levi b. Gershom (Ralbag) presents an only slightly more complicated case. His introductions to and commentaries on the opening verses of Song of Songs and Ecclesiastes do make mention of the critical categories "author," "intention," "benefit," and the like. In his commentary on Song of Songs' opening verse, Levi even refers to these as "matters with which every author ought to begin, before taking up the subject matter of his book itself," having just taken note of these items (*ma'alato, to'alto, 'ofen ha-ma'amar bo,* and so forth) as he finds them expounded in the biblical book's introduction.[49] Given his extensive undertakings as an Averroës supercommentator, however, and Levi's ties to the tradition of Hebrew philosophic exegesis represented by Samuel ibn Tibbon and his ilk, a case for scholastic influence here is unwarranted, especially as Levi's links to Christian literature are not well attested even as his oral contacts with Christians are.[50]

Evidence from Italy

Late medieval Italy—which saw the main continuation of the Maimonidean-Tibbonide school of Hebrew philosophic biblical interpretation and Jewish engagement with medieval Christian philosophic (and in a few cases literary) works in a degree never seen before—offers the first certain instance of Jewish adaptation of the *accessus*, and a couple of doubtful cases as well.

One doubtful case occurs in a commentary of Zeraḥyah Ḥen, who worked in Rome in the late thirteenth century.[51] The introductions to his Proverbs and Job commentaries both take up issues of authorship, intention, and the like, but for present purposes it is the Proverbs commentary that makes a claim to attention.[52] Here Zeraḥyah discusses the name of this biblical book as well as its aim (*kawwanah*), ultimate purpose (*takhlit*), and multiple utility (*to'alotaw*).[53] What is more, he explains that the book's opening seven verses, authored in his view by Solomon, express "by way of introduction" the four things that "any author of a book in one of the areas of wisdom" must mention: the book's name, author's name, book's utility, and the "conditions (*tena'im*) in consequence of which the book was composed" (something like its final purpose). This final point is addressed in the expression "to understand proverb and epigram / the words of the wise and their riddles (Prov 1:6)," which imparts the truth (ever so critical to Maimonideans) that not all words of the prophets were intended in accordance with their literal sense alone, these words having an exoteric meaning of benefit to the vulgar (*he-hamon*) and an esoteric one useful to "men of wisdom."[54]

If, on the basis of such data, one could hardly argue for Zeraḥyah's familiarity with the *accessus*, his general intellectual profile only cements one's doubts on this score. Though produced in Italy, Zeraḥyah's writings reflect the closing period of his life after his arrival from Barcelona, where his "second language" was Arabic, as his ample corpus of Hebrew translations from Arabic indicates.[55] Since his acquisition of Latin is not assured and his works reflect relatively little Christian influence generally,[56] one cannot easily ascribe awareness of the *accessus* to Zeraḥyah on the basis of the evidence of his Job and Proverbs commentaries.

Another figure who offers a tantalizing but in the end unlikely case of Jewish awareness of the *accessus* is Immanuel of Rome. Immanuel is best known for his *maḥbarot* or cantos—which, in their indebtedness to Dante, evince a Jewish respect for Christian literary works not typically found elsewhere. Immanuel also produced a considerable body of biblical commentaries, beginning several of these works with introductions.[57] Furthermore, his commentary on Proverbs 1 commences by citing Samuel ibn Tibbon to the effect that "all of the commentators have concurred that this first pericope of seven verses is all introductory."[58] He then recapitulates nearly word for word ibn Tibbon's account of the putative Solomonic introduction to Proverbs as developed in the latter's Ecclesiastes commentary.[59] However, since Immanuel does not indicate his understanding of the origins of the structuring categories that he mentions, nothing conclusive can be drawn from his long exordial discourse and one is left only with more tenuous evidence that might suggest Immanuel's familiarity with the *accessus* even if he did not use it.[60]

Immanuel's younger cousin, Judah Romano, perhaps Italy's most profound Jewish student of Christian scholasticism, offers in his exegetical monograph concerning the Work of Creation a Jewish application of the four Aristotelian questions that unquestionably draws on Christian models.[61] The manuscripts of this work are many and diverge down to fundaments,[62] and so detailed analysis must await the establishment of solid textual foundations. By way of a general outline, it may be noted that Judah makes explicit at the outset the assimilation of literary works to artificial objects implicit in analysis of a book according to its Aristotelian causes:[63] he states that since a book's composition reflects an activity and since any activity has causes, it is incumbent upon one who undertakes a book's explanation—who thereby brings the book's intention from potentiality to actuality—to begin with an account of its causes.[64] He then treats the four causes of Genesis's opening pericope in more or less detail and in divergent ways, depending on the version one consults (the material cause of this pericope is either "existence" [*ha-meṣi'ut*][65] or "hidden";[66] its "final cause" is either "bestowal of the ultimate perfection" [*ḥaninat ha-shelemut ha-'aḥaron*][67] or, along with the pericope's efficient cause, "known"[68]). There is no doubt as to the pedigree of Judah's prefatory technique since the pericope's "formal cause" is said to be twofold, comprising the *ṣurat ha-be'ur* and *ṣurat ha-ma'amar*, Hebrew equivalents for *forma tractandi* and *forma tractatus*. The latter is said to comprise the division of the book or pericope into "identifiable parts" (*ḥalaqim yedu'im*). The former supplies the means through which the intellect receives *intelligibilia*: division, composition, syllogism, definition, allegory.[69]

Judah's awareness of Christian philosophy and exegesis did not grow out of collaborative activities with Christian savants as did, say, that of Jacob Anatoli, Samuel ibn Tibbon's disciple and relative who, as a physician at the court of Frederick II and collaborator with the Christian polymath Michael Scot, had an opportunity in Italy to "learn about Christianity directly while living and working in an environment of sophisticated Christian intellectuals."[70] Rather, it was Judah's energetic program of producing Hebrew translations of works of Boethius, Albert the Great, Thomas Aquinas, Giles of Rome (his favored scholastic), and other Latin writers that brought him into contact with Christian literary forms.[71]

Still, though Judah's latinity was such that even when writing in Hebrew he "seems to have thought in philosophical terms corresponding to Latin,"[72] a distance characterizes his relationship to the Christian scholars whom he admires. These, it would seem, he knew from books; few if any were contemporaries known to him personally. Thus in his monograph on the creation story Judah speaks of "the scholars of the nations" who are "not far from us in time and condition," "who are close to us in time and place," and so forth. Then, too, Judah remains conscious of the highly problematic character (at least for his readers, if not for himself) of his wholesale appropriation of teachings of Christians into his biblical scholarship.[73] And yet, seen in its larger context, his invocation of the Latin Aristotelian prologue may be seen as one of many signs of an apparent shift in medieval Jewish openness to Christian erudition as well as increasing Jewish interest in and mastery of languages of Christians, both Latin and vernacular. It is indicative of one aspect of the late medieval Jewish–Christian "creative symbiosis" mentioned at the outset that has yet to be described.[74]

Evidence from Iberia

The Jewish "Golden Age" in Muslim Spain that is often presented as the epitome of medieval Jewish-Muslim symbiosis has been amply researched, but the nature and extent of cross-traditional scholarly fertilization among Christians and Jews in late medieval Iberia awaits systematic exploration.[75] Turning specifically to forewords organized around prologue headings, one is led away from the famous Jewries of late medieval Spain to Portugal's unjustly neglected Jewish community, wherein biblical interpretation seems to have been a major focus.[76] It was by two biblical commentators born in Lisbon, Joseph Ḥayyun and his (presumed) student Isaac Abarbanel, that the *accessus* was deployed most fully in the Jewish Middle Ages.

In the case of Ḥayyun, Lisbon's leading rabbinic figure in the third quarter of the fifteenth century, three surviving introductions to commentaries on individual books attest to their author's innovative desire to introduce biblical books systematically by way of prologue headings. Ḥayyun's headings include the book's transcriber, original formulator, manner of speech, constituent parts, order (i.e., position in the canon), name, intention, and more. Ḥayyun also prefaced his interpretations of individual psalms with short introductions—an innovation also attested in his sole work devoted to exegesis of rabbinic texts—and he viewed the first psalm as a "prologue to the book" much as Nicholas of Lyra had before him.[77]

As in so many instances seen hitherto, the Christian genealogy of Ḥayyun's procedure is far from clearly demonstrable. Ḥayyun was aware, no doubt mediately, of segments of the Arabic philosophic tradition;[78] his latinity is not otherwise attested; there is no one-to-one correspondence between the patterns of his introductions and specific Latin prologue models; and many of the categories invoked in Ḥayyun's introductions, albeit not their methodical arrangement and topical invention taken as a whole, hark to a Maimonidean or even rabbinic hermeneutic frame of reference. Thus, Ḥayyun discusses the "manner of speech" or "grade of prophecy" employed in given biblical books,[79] perhaps echoing Latin concerns with the *genus prophetiae* granted to diverse biblical authors but more likely drawing on earlier Maimonidean exploration of this issue, as a prophetological work begun by Abarbanel in Lisbon when Ḥayyun may have been alive might further suggest.[80] Balancing these points is the fact that Ḥayyun collates many categories found in the Latin exordial tradition (*auctor, scriptor, ordo, titulis, intentio, utilitates*, and so forth) and the fact that his prologue-headings-based approach, with its heedful progression from topic to topic, is unprecedented in Ibero-Jewish exegesis. That Ḥayyun wrote slightly after the heyday of the *accessus* format in the medieval Latin tradition would present no difficulty. Such a time lag is readily understood for a Jewish writer, especially one working in the Iberian peninsula where Christian intellectual-literary "belatedness" is well-attested.[81] Of course, it is also possible that Ḥayyun used

Latin terms already absorbed into the Hebrew exegetical tradition unaware of their Christian origins. An example from elsewhere in his writings of this sort of unconscious absorption is his usage "to incite doubts," which he knew from Isaac Canpanton's *Darkhei ha-gemara*, which in turn seems to reflect the Latin *dubitationes movere*.[82]

Though Ḥayyun's prefatory efforts typically raised questions found in one or another earlier Hebrew text, and often as not provided conventional answers drawn from the rabbinic tradition to resolve them, the systematic character of his introductions and the range of categories that he invokes impart a fresh quality to his biblical introductions. This quality is less apparent in the commentaries themselves but examples can be found—for instance, Ḥayyun's concern with the ostensibly musical terminology that appears in superscriptions to Psalms. Biblical scholarship from the mid-sixteenth century on would evince a lively interest in Jewish antiquities such as Hebrew measures, coinage, architecture, clothing, and the like.[83] When, then, Ḥayyun makes one of the ten heads of his Psalms introduction "the instruments mentioned in this book" and also classifies musical references in the book's superscriptions, speculating briefly on their meanings and implications, one can feel, however fleetingly, that a transition from medieval to early modern biblical exegesis is on its way.[84]

This conclusion provides access to Isaac Abarbanel, a figure often depicted as the inventor of "Einleitungswissenschaft"[85] within the domain of Hebrew exegetical literature, though how little merit there is to this claim should by now be clear. Still, the impressive size and scope of Abarbanel's exegetical introductions cannot be gainsaid.

Elsewhere, I have argued that Abarbanel's exegesis marks a transition from medieval to postmedieval biblical scholarship.[86] This transition is most noticeable in his introductions, especially those to the commentaries on the books of Joshua, Judges, and Samuel (written in Spain in 1483–84). The "second investigation" of the general introduction to these commentaries comprises a most ample Aristotelian prologue. Among its striking elements is its innovative account of the "efficient causes" of the Former Prophets: on various literary and historical-chronological grounds, Abarbanel argues against time-honored rabbinic views concerning the authors of the books of Joshua and Samuel.[87] As notable, however, is Abarbanel's account of these books' formal cause, which suggests the sorts of novel insights that could emerge when the Aristotelian *accessus* was employed by a medieval exegete with budding Renaissance hermeneutic proclivities. After suggesting that one sign of the prophetic character of the books of the Former Prophets is their authors' awareness of past events otherwise unknown in Israel—a sort of backwards-acting prophecy—Abarbanel explains how this came about:

> These prophets undoubtedly found things that had been written in those [former] times in the books of chronicles referred to in the book of Kings. . . . Since these [sources] were scattered and disparate . . . and since there were in them things written according to wish rather than the truth and in some of them [also] extraneous matters . . . for this reason, God's spirit rested on these prophets and He commanded them to record all of these narratives fully and accurately. All of these documents were then gathered to them and God informed them through his prophecy of the completion of these events, their truth, their justification, and how to distinguish the true from the false and the essential from the extraneous.[88]

Here is one criterion "on the basis of which we know that the form of these books is prophetic," Abarbanel concludes.[89]

Passing over additional exegetical applications by Abarbanel of the stereotypical Aristotelian format,[90] there remains the issue of the source of his knowledge of this exordial format. Of his deep reading in Latin exegetical literature there is no doubt, as even the commentaries written in Spain on Joshua, Judges, and Samuel make clear. Within a dozen pages of these works Abarbanel may refer to the Vulgate's translation of a difficult word, praise the interpretation of the verse in which the word occurred, advanced by unnamed Christian commentators as "very fine"; reject, without a hint of interreligious disparagement, another interpretation of Christian scholars; and invoke positively the views of Christian theologians in the course of making a prophetological argument contra Maimonides.[91] But was it Christian exegetes who provisioned Abarbanel with the model for his exegetical forewords? Among Christian commentators Abarbanel was familiar with Nicholas of Lyra. What is more, though he does not mention him by name, he apparently read assiduously in the involved introductions of the supremely prolific mid-fifteenth-century Franciscan exegete Alfonso de Madrigal Tostado.[92] Precise parallels remain to be traced but seem probably forthcoming. To supply one concrete example, the "first investigation" in the introduction to Abarbanel's commentaries on the Former Prophets treats of the proper division of the constituent books of the biblical canon, a subject explored by Tostado in his introduction to his commentary on Joshua in like manner.[93]

It is hard to gauge Abarbanel's indebtedness to the *accessus* in producing insights that would lead Richard Simon to say in the seventeenth century that among "tous les Rabbins" Abarbanel seemed the one "dont l'on puisse le plus profiter pour l'intelligence de l'Ecriture."[94] The main question is how much to attribute such insights to formats and critical vocabulary known to Abarbanel from medieval Latin sources and how much to credit other "external" factors such as the stimulation of Abarbanel's incipient Spanish humanist environment. However this may be, it seems likely that the proliferation of historical and literary insights in Abarbanel's commentaries is one element which recommended them to the many Christian scholars who translated and studied his exegetical writings during the revival of interest in Hebraic writings in the Renaissance and centuries following.[95]

Conclusions

To consolidate, while throughout the Christian Middle Ages a variety of traditions of textual interpretation worked alongside each other, the high and late medieval periods saw the rise of modes of interpretation that, as partially exemplified in the Aristotelian prologue, seemingly had the effect of "focussing attention on the author of the book and on the reasons which impelled him to write."[96] For reasons that have become clear, equally well-demarcated patterns of development are not evident in the medieval Hebrew commentary tradition. First, chronologically, the existence of a sophisticated early and high medieval Judeo-Arabic stratum grounded in a multifaceted oriental scriptural hermeneutic means that linear depictions of the totality of the medieval Jewish exegetical tradition, and certainly "progressive" ones, fail. Second, no specific exordial formats were invoked *en bloc* by all or even most high or late medieval Jewish exegetes in any given scholarly center, in part because there were no institutionalized contexts of instruction, like the university or cathedral school, which could propagate uniform approaches that would increase attention to biblical authorship or style.[97] It may be that additional generalizations regarding differences between medieval Christian and Jewish introductions to biblical commentaries will emerge from further research. For instance, Latin prologues seem to possess a natural quality that Hebrew ones lack. Growing as they did out of oral lectures in the classroom, where some sort of introduction was invariably called for, the Latin prologues were an unremarkable outcome of their institutional origins. By contrast, Hebrew writers could be apologetic about their exordial forays, feeling that they were—or might be perceived by their readers to be—artificial or extraneous. After announcing his plan to discuss the Former Prophets' four causes, Abarbanel indicates he is "prefacing these words . . . inasmuch as they are beneficial and necessary for their [the books'] understanding." He implies that his reader may be doubtful of the need for such propaedeutics.[98]

What then can be said of medieval Jewish use of the *accessus ad auctores* as a contributor to "exegetical digging" of the sort mentioned at the beginning of this essay? The main finding of this investigation is that such use was relatively rare. But perhaps more to the point, one wonders to what extent the use of the organizing categories of any given prefatory format would have pointed an individual commentator's exploration of Holy Writ in fundamentally new directions. True, Aristotelian notions of efficient causality, with their allowance for the autonomy of intermediate causes working under an ultimate cause, seemingly transformed literary theory in the Latin sphere, producing reflections among Christian commentators on scripture's human dimension that prologue formats organized around different conceptual components had not. Still, stock forms ultimately remained media through which exegetical insights born of greater or lesser sophistication and intelligence were communicated. In other words, more than the form of the prologue, it was the "efficient cause" behind it, the mind of the individual interpreter, that determined how deep an introduction's exegetical insights would reach.

Notes

The research and writing of this essay was made possible by grants from the Social Sciences and Humanities Research Council of Canada and Memorial Foundation for Jewish Culture in support of a larger project on the transition from medieval to Renaissance Hebrew biblical scholarship. I should like to express my thanks for this generous aid.

1. (New York: Scribners, 1901), 531, as cited in Kugel, "Bible in the University," 155–56.
2. Kugel, "Bible in the University," 156–57.
3. For the "history of the discipline" of the modern Old Testament introduction see Childs, *Introduction to the Old Testament as Scripture*, 30–39. For "introduction" as a "technical term of long standing [by the time of the appearance of Childs' study]" see Brett, *Biblical Criticism in Crisis?* 62.
4. For the "dwarf standing on the shoulders of a giant" motif, see the ample secondary literature cited in Miller, *Poetic License*, 178–82 nn. 1, 5, 16.
5. See Freedman and Spiegel, "Medievalisms Old and New," 677–704.
6. For the digging metaphor used by the Victorines with respect to their quest for the "literal" foundation of scripture's spiritual senses, see Smalley, *Study of the Bible*, 196.
7. See now Attias, "L'âme et la clef."

8. For "symbiosis" as a critical category in the study of medieval Jewish-Muslim relations, see Wasserstrom, *Between Muslim and Jew*, 3-12. Obviously my invocation of this usage is designed to describe only a small segment of medieval Jewish-Christian interaction in the late Middle Ages and not its totality as has typically been the case with respect to the classical period (tenth to twelfth centuries) of medieval Jewish life under Islam.

9. For the "Arabic" model of biblical interpretation employed by Saadia and his Karaite counterparts and illustrative samples from their commentaries, including introductions thereto, see Drory, *Reshit ha-magga'im*, 110-17. I have learned a great deal from an unpublished paper of Daniel Frank entitled "Ṣadr al-Kitâb: Japheth b. Eli's Introductions to the Books of the Bible." I wish to thank him for supplying me with this paper and several other references found herein.

10. For detailed treatments of Saadia's and Japheth's treatment of the origins and authorship of the book of Psalms, see Uriel Simon, *Four Approaches*, 1-57, 71-111. For examples in English translation of prefatory remarks of Saadia and Japheth included in commentaries on the opening verses of biblical books, see, for the former, Saadia, *The Book of Theodicy*, 152, and for the latter, Bland, "The Arabic Commentary of Yephet ben 'Ali on the Book of Ecclesiastes," 142-47. For a possible rationale for Japheth's "infiltration" of his expositions on matters of genre, authorship, prophetic status, and the like into comments on a biblical book's opening verses, see Uriel Simon, *Four Approaches*, 72. For Saadia's introductions as "the most important and interesting feature" in his biblical exegesis see E. I. J. Rosenthal, "Saadya Gaon," 1:88. For Ibn Ezra's treatments of biblical authorship, which are scattered more diffusely throughout his commentaries, see Uriel Simon, *Four Approaches*, in the index under "R. Abraham ibn Ezra."

11. Saadia, *Book of Theodicy*, 152.

12. Uriel Simon, *Four Approaches*, 37-39.

13. For a celebrated example from "elsewhere," see Uriel Simon, "Ibn Ezra Between Medievalism and Modernism," 257-71.

14. Marcus, "Rashi's Historiography," 47-48.

15. For the former, see Eliezer of Beaugency, *Commentaries on the Later Prophets*, on Isaiah 1:1 (for the editor's strange interpretation of the origins of this usage, see p. CLI); for the latter, see Samuel b. Meir, *Perush 'al ha-Torah*, 3.

16. See Brin, "Qawwim le-ferush ha-Torah shel R. Yehudah he-Ḥasid," 220-25; Sarna, "The Modern Study of the Bible," 24. For basic orientation in the German exegetical school, see Wolfson, "The Mystical Significance of Torah Study in German Pietism," 43-77; Marcus, "Exegesis for the Few and for the Many: 1*-24*.

17. For this and other "critical" features of this commentary, see Ta-Shma, "Perush Divrei ha-yamim she-bi-khetav-yad Minkhin 5," 135-41. For connections between the critical vocabulary found in this work and that attested in the commentary on Ezekiel and the Minor Prophets published in Nicholas De Lange, *Greek Jewish Texts from the Cairo Geniza*, 165-294, see Steiner, "Beḥinot lashon," 51-54. For a fuller panorama of surprisingly bold trends in Jewish biblical scholarship in medieval northern Europe, see Ta-Shma, "Mashehu 'al biqqoret ha-Miqra be-'Ashkenaz," 453-59.

18. The classic study is Quain, "The Medieval *Accessus ad auctores*," 215-64.

19. Copeland, *Rhetoric, Hermeneutics, and Translation in the Middle Ages*, 66-76.

20. Hunt, "The Introduction to the 'Artes' in the Twelfth Century," 126-29; A. J. Minnis, *Medieval Theory of Authorship*, 15-28.

20. Minnis, "The *Accessus* Extended," 276. In general see Minnis, *Medieval Theory of Authorship*, 28-33. For ongoing use of the "type C" prologue, at times in combination with the scholastic system, see Copeland, *Rhetoric*, 109.

22. Minnis and Scott, eds., *Medieval Literary Theory and Criticism c. 1100–c. 1375*, 271-74. "Prophet" referred to the Psalter's "principal" and "instrumental" efficient causes, these being God and David respectively (the act of prophecy involving God's raising the mind of the prophet

to comprehension of divine knowledge). "Among us" referred to its final cause, promotion of "our salvation," and so forth.

23. See, e.g., Sermoneta, "He'aroteihem shel R. Mosheh ben Shelomoh mi-Salerno," 213–14 n. 2; Rivlin, "Shemu'el 'ibn Tibbon," 17–21. On Sermoneta's authority, this view subsequently made its way into a number of local studies (e.g., Rigo, "Un'antologia filosofica," 90). It had already achieved wide diffusion (albeit without documentation but with an ascription to Sermoneta) in Sirat, *A History of Jewish Philosophy in the Middle Ages*, 216. I was unable to consult Ruth Ben-Meir's forthcoming "The Introduction of R. Samuel Ibn Tibbon to His Commmentary to Ecclesiastes" (to appear in *Maimonidean Studies* 4) prior to completion of this chapter. Since its completion, the relevant text of ibn Tibbon has been published in a superb copiously annotated critical edition; see Robinson, "Samuel ibn Tibbon's *Commentary on Ecclesiastes*." As full findings from this essay could not be included in what follows, the reader is referred there for further details.

24. This point seems incontrovertible, Sermoneta's suggestion to the contrary ("He'aroteihem," 213, n. 2) notwithstanding. For ibn Tibbon's text, see Maimondes, Moses, *Sefer Moreh nevukhim*, 117. Note that ibn Tibbon did not preface all works of translation with an introduction of this sort; see Fontaine, *Otot Ha-Shamayim*, 3–5.

25. Copeland, *Rhetoric*, 193.

26. E.g., Averroës, *Commentarius in Aristoteles De arte rhetorica libros tres*, 1–4. Since this introduction could easily have been modeled on ibn Tibbon's invocation of the four Aristotelian questions, it need not reflect Latin influence as suggested in Lesley, "Hebrew Humanism in Italy," 167.

27. Samuel ibn Tibbon, "Perush Qohelet," Parma, Biblioteca Palatina, MS 272 (De Rossi 2182) (= film no. 13354 at the Institute of Microfilmed Hebrew Manuscripts of the Jewish National and University Library in Jerusalem [henceforth IMHM]), fol. 20v. (Robinson, "Samuel ibn Tibbon's *Commentary on Ecclesiastes*," 92 [Hebrew], 104–5 [English].)

28. For a (literally) graphic argument to this effect see Rivlin, "Shemu'el ibn Tibbon," 18–19.

29. The uphill struggle to match ibn Tibbon's categories to Latin ones is visible in the diagrammatic efforts referred to in n. 28.

30. Hadot, "Les introductions aux commentaires exégètiques," 99–122; Berman, "Ibn Rushd's Middle Commentary on the Nicomachean Ethics, 303, 306–8; Harvey, "The Hebrew Translation of Averroes' Prooemium," 72–73, n. 4 (with thanks to James T. Robinson for drawing my attention to this last reference). Based on his systematic study, Robinson was able to conclude far more authoritatively than was I that "Samuel borrowed the prooemium directly from Alfarabi and Averroes." See "Samuel ibn Tibbon's *Commentary on Ecclesiastes*," 84. (For ibn Tibbon's awareness of the Andalusi-Jewish *Commentary on Ecclesiastes* composed by Isaac ibn Ghiyyat in the eleventh century, which also treated the "eight things that someone beginning [a book] should know," see ibid.)

31. See the excerpt from Bland's dissertation referred to here in n. 10. Japheth refers here as elsewhere to the *ṣadr* of the biblical book. For another example of such reference see Japheth's commentary on the opening verse of Habakkuk in Livne-Kafri, "Sefer Ḥavaqquq," 81.

32. "Perush Qohelet," fol. 26r.

33. "Perush Qohelet," fol. 29v. (For ibn Tibbon's account of his coining *ḥippuś* to translate induction see ibid., 7v.) For the *mudawwin* in Japheth's exegesis see Uriel Simon, *Four Approaches*, 90–91. Two parallels are striking: the first concerns expository style (cf. ibn Tibbon's "words" in or close to their simple sense rather than proverbs or poetic speech like Proverbs and Song of Songs and Japheth's remark as in Bland, "Arabic Commentary," 2 [Arabic], 144 [English]); the second concerns ibn Tibbon's view that "son of David, king of Jerusalem" in Ecclesiastes 1:1 furnishes strong proof that Solomon is this book's author, David having had no other son who served as a monarch (cf. "Perush Qohelet," fol. 20r with Japheth's observation as in Bland,

"Arabic Commentary," 4 [Arabic], 145–46 [English; cf. Song of Songs Rabbah 1:1:10]). But note that ibn Tibbon may have encountered Japheth's ideas only mediately, as in this case where Abraham Ibn Ezra expounds the same opinion, perhaps on the basis of Japheth's insight. For Ibn Ezra's familiarity with Japheth and the uncertain case for such familiarity on the part of ibn Tibbon's colleague David Kimḥi, see Birnbaum, "Yefet ben 'Ali," 257–63.

34. "Perush Qohelet," 30r–33r. Verse 1 ("The proverbs of Solomon the son of David, king of Israel") relates the book's and author's names and its expository style, the next two verses ("To know wisdom . . .") the author's intention, the next three verses ("To give prudence to the simple . . .") the book's benefit for a variety of audiences, and so forth. Verse 7 (". . . the foolish despise wisdom and discipline") performs a prefatory function outside of the usual as Solomon seeks to forestall prospective objections to his enterprise by those (the majority in his day) who, ignorant of Proverbs, will doubt his book's utility and fail to grasp the sort of wisdom to which it serves as a goad.

35. "Perush Qohelet," fols. 17v–18r. For the Ecclesiastes commentary as the first in a series of philosophic commentaries on the three Solomonic books, see Ravitzky, "Mishnato shel R. Zeraḥyah," 30.

36. Samuel ibn Tibbon, *Ma'amar Yiqqawu ha-mayim*, 175; Ravitzky, "Mishnato shel R. Zeraḥyah," 55, n. 3.

37. For ibn Tibbon's critical vocabulary, see Robinson's "Samuel ibn Tibbon's *Commentary on Ecclesiastes*," nn. 113–119.

38. Talmage, ed., *Perushim le-sefer Mishlei le-vet Qimḥi*, 330; Hunt, "Introduction to the 'Artes,'" 127. (This paragraph, but not the next, has been revised to express caution about the work's authorship, a change that reflects Naomi Grunhaus's presentation on December 18, 2001, at the 33rd Annual Conference of the Association for Jewish Studies in Washington, D.C. entitled "The Commentary of R. David Kimhi to Proverbs: A Case of Mistaken Attribution?")

39. Cf. "Perush Qohelet," fols. 30r–32v with Talmage, *Perushim le-sefer Mishlei*, 330.

40. See the note in Talmage, *Perushim le-sefer Mishlei*, 329; but Talmage blurs the question of origins by including references to the Arabic versions of prologues to scholarly works.

40. Talmage, *David Kimhi*, 113–15.

42. Cf. Minnis, *Medieval Theory of Authorship*, 97, for the Latin terminology.

43. BT Bava Batra 14b: "Hezekiah and his colleagues wrote . . . Proverbs." For the semantic range of "write (*katav*)" in this formulation see Leiman, *The Canonization of Hebrew Scripture*, 163, n. 259.

44. "Perush Qohelet," fol. 9v.

45. Note Japheth ben Eli's suggestion that Ecclesiastes' opening reference to "king of Jerusalem" was included so that people "would realize that it is a discourse of Solomon" and hence would "study it and pay heed to his words, for it is the discourse of a Sage rich in ideas" (Bland, "Arabic Commentary," 146). For Kimḥi's possible familiarity with one of Japheth's commentaries (on Hosea), see Birnbaum, "Yefet ben Ali," as above n. 33.

46. Talmage, *David Kimhi*, 135–62. For interdiction by Bernard Gui of Kimḥi's Psalms commentary due to its anti-Christian content, see Albert, "L'image du chrétien," 120.

47. Sirat, *History of Jewish Philosophy*, 228–29. For the text see *Perush Shir ha-shirim*, 5–14. For discussion of the work see Kellner, "Communication or the Lack Thereof," 227–54.

48. See, e.g., Meiri's introduction to his Proverbs commentary (*Peirush ha-Me'iri 'al Sefer Mishlei*, 1–13), where one might expect to come upon signs of such awareness but where, in handling "bio-bibliographic" data in the book's opening verse, Meiri veers in a moral-homiletical direction.

49. I have used the forthcoming Hebrew edition of Menachem Kellner, kindly supplied to me in advance, for which my thanks. For the cited passage see Levi ben Gershom *Commentary on the Song of Songs*, 18.

50. See Kellner's annotation in *Commentary*, 114, n. 15: "Gersonides seems to be following Averroës here in his concern for proper introductions to books." For the introduction to the Ecclesiastes commentary see Ben Meir, "Perush Ralbag le-Qohelet," 2:1–3. For connections between this commentary and ibn Tibbon's, see Ben Meir, 1:179–97. For a (largely speculative) attempt to uncover scholastic awarenesses in Levi's writings see Pines, "Scholasticism after Thomas Aquinas," 5–13.

50. For his life and biblical commentaries see Ravitzky, "Mishnato shel R. Zeraḥyah," 68–81.

52. In the case of Job, Zeraḥyah argues for the allegorical nature of this book, in part on the basis of conclusions regarding authorship that he draws from the book's literary character: ". . . if Job and his friends were truly as the plain sense of the text presents them and not an allegory, individual differences of speech should have appeared among them besides the differences of opinion that appear among them. . . . Thus anyone familiar with books and the science of language must acknowledge that Job is stylistically uniform from beginning to end, and that a single author composed and invented it." See the critical edition of the Hebrew original of this passage and accompanying English translation in Greenberg, "'Iyov hayah 'o lo hayah," 8*, 11*.

53. *'Imrei da'at*, 1–3. This printed version is, however, deficient at various points as regards this passage; cf. Munich, Bayerische Staatsbibliothek, MS 792 (film no. 1621 at the IMHM), fols. 105r–v.

54. Ibid., 7–8 (correcting both the printed version and the manuscript referred to above on the basis of Hamburg, Staat- und Universitätsbibliothek, MS Levy 3/3 [film no. 1485 at the IMHM], fol. 152r, which reads *ha-nevi'im ki-feshuṭam* in place of *ha-nevi'im ha-rishonim*).

55. See for a summary Zonta, *La filosofia antica nel Medioevo ebraico*, 222–26.

56. In Sirat's formulation (*History of Jewish Philosophy*, 267), "the scholastic climate is less perceptible."

57. These await careful study. Murray Rosenthal's "The Haqdamah of Immanuel of Rome to the Book of Ruth," 169–84, is digressive and scant on analysis, but it does supply the Hebrew text of Immanuel's introduction to this biblical book along with an English translation. In this introduction Immanuel does not concern himself with questions surrounding the authorship and origins of the book, though he does find occasion to refer to books that have not come down from Jewish antiquity. For Immanuel's relation to Dante see Walfish, *Esther in Medieval Garb*, 231–33 and the bibliography cited there (305, nn. 6–7).

58. *Sefer Mishlei*, 2.

59. Cf. *Sefer Mishlei*, 2–6 with Samuel ibn Tibbon, "Perush Qohelet," 30r–33v. For additional borrowings from or parallels to ibn Tibbon's exegesis in the body of Immanuel's commentary, see Ravitzky, "*'Al meqorotaw shel peirush Mishlei le-'Imanu'el ha-Romi*," 726–39.

60. Aside from his knowledge of works of Dante—a writer who occasionally did use the *accessus* (Lesley, "Hebrew Humanism," 167)—in Latin and the vernacular (see n. 58, earlier, where reference is made also to Immanuel's familiarity with at least one of Dante's Latin works)—Immanuel may have understood various literary roles that he played in light of the roles often discussed in Latin *accessus* (*auctor, scriptor, compilator, commentator*). Such is the argument of Schechterman, "Filosofyah shel 'Imanu'el ha-Romi," 33–39, who remarks that this truth explains Immanuel's so-called borrowing from ibn Tibbon. On this understanding Immanuel was acting legitimately as a *scriptor* and *compilator* when reproducing ibn Tibbon's ideas. As the former, he would reproduce earlier work exactly as is (*nihil mutando*); as the latter he would add nonoriginal material (*addendo, sed non de suo*). See, e.g., the text of Bonaventure as in Minnis, *Medieval Theory of Authorship*, 94.

61. For bibliography regarding Judah see Rigo, "Un'antologia filosofica," 73–74, nn. 2, 3, 5; Rothschild, "Un traducteur hébreu qui se cherche," 159–60, nn. 1–2. For the work in question see Sermoneta, "Ha-peirush le-'farashat Bereshit'," 341–42.

62. The brief excerpt in Sermoneta, "Ha-'Issuq ba-'umanuyot ha-ḥofshiyot," 254–56, seems

to be based on Paris, Bibliothèque Nationale MS héb. 989/1, fol. 1r–v. I have used mainly this manuscript (= film no. 33990 at the IMHM), though it should be understood, that there is some reason to believe it may not have been the final one; see n. 67.

63. Lesley, "Hebrew Humanism," 167.

64. New York, Jewish Theological Seminary of America, MS Mic. 2362, fol. 1r (this section is missing from the above-cited Paris manuscript).

65. Ibid., fol. 2r.

66. Paris, Bibliothèque Nationale, MS héb. 989/1, fol. 1r. For the change from this version to the former, see the correction in Parma, Biblioteca Palatina, MS 2384 (= film no. 13249 at the IMHM), 2r–v. Other changes of this sort are reflected in the marginal and superlinear notes of the Parma manuscript as well.

67. Paris, Bibliothèque Nationale, MS héb. 989/1, fol. 1v.

68. JTS, MS Mic. 2362, fol. 2r.

69. Paris, Bibliothèque Nationale, MS héb. 989/1, fols. 1r–1v.

70. Saperstein, "Christians and Christianity in the Sermons of Jacob Anatoli," 226.

70. For the long and impressive list of translations by Romano of works by Thomas, see Sermoneta, "Jehudah ben Moseh Ben Dani'el Romano, traducteur de Saint Thomas," 231–62. For the preference for Giles over Thomas see ibid., 237, n. 4.

72. Sirat, *History of Jewish Philosophy*, 270.

73. Sermoneta, "Prophecy in the Writings of R. Yehuda Romano," 348 n. 15, 354 n. 30.

74. Consideration here of a fifteenth-century chapter in Italian Jewish-Christian interreligious intellectual stimuli in which Jewish use of the Aristotelian prologue is attested in the exegetical work of Yohanan Alemanno is omitted here as belonging to a post-medieval Renaissance milieu.

75. For a preliminary consideration, see Lawee, "Changing Jewish Attitudes Towards Christian Society."

76. Abraham Gross, *R[abbi] Yosef ben 'Avraham Ḥayyun*, 106–7. One text from Spain that does supply a link between a wider Christian environment and categories found in prologues of scripture is the apologetic tract of the fifteenth-century savant Joseph Albo, *Sefer ha-'Iqqarim*, ed. Husik, 3:217–45. It contains an elaborate rebuttal to a critique of the "law of Moses" structured by a Christian protagonist (real or fictive) around the four Aristotelian causes. In this case, however, the exegetical application of the Aristotelian causal scheme is secondary to Albo's interreligious theological concerns.

77. For his Esther introduction, see Walfish, *Esther in Medieval Garb*, 6–7. For the texts see Gross, *Ḥayyun*, 172–91. For his brief introductions to maxims in tractate 'Avot see ibid., 48. For the Psalter see *Perush Tehillim*, 3r. For Nicholas's view that the Psalter's editor (most likely Ezra) composed the first psalm "as a kind of prologue" to his collectio, see Minnis, *Medieval Literary Theory and Criticism*, 275–76. Nicholas nonetheless deemed Psalm 1 a psalm "in the true sense," unlike Ḥayyun, who denied it was "a psalm in itself."

78. See the citation of Farabi in the Song of Songs' introduction in Gross, *Ḥayyun*, 187.

79. Gross, *Ḥayyun*, 174 (for Psalms, with a citation from *Guide*, 2.45), 180 (for Esther), 184 (Song of Songs).

80. Cf. *Guide*, 2.45. Abarbanel (*Perush 'al Nevi'im rishonim*, 8) describes *Maḥazeh Shaddai* as a work in which he "investigated in extreme detail prophecy and the holy spirit and the distinction between the prophetic grade and the grade of the holy spirit," eventually concluding that "this investigation is very, very deep . . . and I have not found anything with respect to it except what Maimonides wrote in that chapter forty-five of part two [of the *Guide*]."

81. Curtius, *European Literature and the Latin Middle Ages*, 541. As best one can tell, scholarship thus far has done nothing to uncover the development of the Latin *accessus* in Iberia, preferring instead to concentrate on dominant and pioneering French and English centers.

82. See Marc Saperstein's chapter in this volume, 137–38, 148 n. 32.

83. Shuger, *The Renaissance Bible*, 34–35.

84. For follow-up on this interest in the Psalms commentary itself, see, e.g., *Perush Tehillim*, 8r, 22v. For concern with the meaning of Psalms superscriptions on the part of earlier medieval Jewish interpreters working within the Muslim sphere, see, e.g., Uriel Simon, *Four Approaches*, 224–57.

85. See the many examples cited, in keeping with his own such accreditation, by Ruiz in "Las introducciones y cuestiones de don Isaac Abrabanel," 708 nn. 3, 4, 5. For an indication of Ḥayyun's pride of place on this score see Gross, *Ḥayyun*, 48.

86. Lawee, "On the Threshold of the Renaissance," 283–319. See now Lawee, *Isaac Abarbanel's Stance toward Tradition*, 169–202.

87. See Lawee, "Don Isaac Abarbanel," 65–73.

88. *Perush 'al Nevi'im rishonim*, 8.

89. Ibid.

90. E.g. *Perush 'al Nevi'im u-Khetuvim*, 279.

90. *Perush 'al Nevi'im rishonim*, 171, 181, 184.

92. For a study of Tostado's general influence on Abarbanel (which does not treat the introductions) see Gaon, *The Influence of the Catholic Theologian Alfonso Tostado*. Tostado's massive exegetical output has hitherto received scant attention. The fullest treatment with which I am familiar is Gonzalo Maeso, "Alonso de Madrigal (Tostado) y su labor escrituraria," 143–85.

93. Cf. Abarbanel, *Perush 'al Nevi'im rishonim*, 3–5, with Tostado, *Commentaria in primam partem Iosue*, 1–2.

94. *Histoire critique du Vieux Testament*, 380.

95. The commentaries were studied assiduously by such Christian biblical scholars as Simon, Constantijn l'Empereur van Oppijck, Johann Buxtorf the younger, and yet others. The story of Abarbanel's role as a cross-cultural filter, receiving Hebrew and Latin exegetical techniques and traditions from the past and transforming and conveying them to later interpreters, remains to be told.

96. Smalley, *Study of the Bible*, 297.

97. For recent (and rightful) emphasis on the lack of institutional structures to sustain various Jewish "cultural" enterprises parallel to ones found in the Christian domain, where such institutional contexts did exist (this, in the case of philosophic study), see Saperstein, "The Social and Cultural Context," 296–306.

98. *Perush 'al Nevi'im rishonim*, 6. Abarbanel announces regularly that he has "seen fit to commence with . . . introductions" (ibid., 3, 162, 423). One might discern an apologetic tone in Ḥayyun's regular preamble to the preamble as well: "before I shall begin its [the Psalter's or Scroll of Esther's or Song of Song's] explanation I will preface with an explanation of related matters" (Gross, *Ḥayyun*, 172, 179, 183).

Bibliography

Abarbanel, Isaac. *Perush 'al Nevi'im rishonim*. Jerusalem: Torah Wa-Da'at, 1955.

——. *Perush 'al Nevi'im u-Khetuvim*. Tel Aviv: Sefarim Abarbanel, 1961.

Albert, Bat-Sheva. "L'image du chrétien dans les sources juives du Languedoc (XIIe–XIVe siècle)." In *Les Juifs à Montpellier et dans le Languedoc à travers l'histoire du Moyen Age à nos jours*, 113–27. Montpellier: Centre de recherches et d'études juives et hébraïques, 1988.

Albo, Joseph. *Sefer ha-'Iqqarim*. Ed. Isaac Husik. 5 vols. Philadelphia: Jewish Publication Society, 1930.

Attias, Jean-Christophe. "L'âme et la clef: de l'introduction comme genre littéraire dans la production exégètique du Judaïsme médiéval." In *Entrer en matière*, 337–58. Paris: Cerf, 1998.

Averroës. *Commentarius in Aristoteles De arte rhetorica libros tres*. Trans. Todros Todrosi. Ed. Jacob Goldenthal. Leipzig: Henricum Franke, 1842.

Ben Meir, Ruth. "Perush Ralbag le-Qohelet: nittu'aḥ we-ṭeqsṭ" (Ralbag's commentary on Ecclesiastes: analysis and text). Ph. D. diss., The Hebrew University of Jerusalem, 1994.

Berman Lawrence V. "Ibn Rushd's Middle Commentary on the Nicomachean Ethics in Medieval Hebrew Literature." In *Multiple Averroès*. Ed. Jean Jolivet, 287–321. Paris: Les Belles Lettres, 1978.

Birnbaum, Philip. "Yefet ben 'Ali and His Influence on Biblical Exegesis." *JQR* n.s. 32 (1941–42): 51–70, 159–74, 257–71.

Bland, Richard Murray. "The Arabic Commentary of Yephet ben 'Ali on the Book of Ecclesiastes." Ph. D. diss., University of California, Berkeley, 1966.

Brett, Mark G. *Biblical Criticism in Crisis? : The Impact of the Canonical Approach on Old Testament Studies*. Cambridge: Cambridge University Press, 1991.

Brin, Gershon. "Qawwim le-ferush ha-Torah shel R. Yehudah he-Ḥasid" (Studies in R. Judah the Pious' exegesis of the Pentateuch). In *Meḥqarim be-sifrut ha-Talmud, bi-leshon Ḥazal uve-farshanut ha-Miqra* (Studies in talmudic literature, in post-biblical Hebrew and in biblical exegesis). Ed. M. A. Friedman, Avraham Tal, and Gershon Brin, 215–26. Te'udah, 3. Tel-Aviv: Universitat Tel-Aviv, 1983.

Childs, Brevard S. *Introduction to the Old Testament as Scripture*. Philadelphia: Fortress, 1979.

Copeland, Rita. *Rhetoric, Hermeneutics, and Translation in the Middle Ages: Academic Traditions and Vernacular Texts*. Cambridge: Cambridge University Press, 1991.

Curtius, Ernst R. *European Literature and the Latin Middle Ages*. Trans. Willard R. Trask. New York: Pantheon, 1953.

De Lange, Nicholas. *Greek Jewish Texts from the Cairo Geniza*. Tübingen: J.C.B. Mohr, 1996.

Drory, Rina. *Reshit ha-magga'im shel ha-sifrut ha-yehudit 'im ha-sifrut ha-'arvit ba-me'ah ha-'asirit* (The emergence of Jewish-Arabic literary contacts at the beginning of the tenth century). Tel Aviv: Ha-Kibbutz Hameuchad, 1988.

Eliezer of Beaugency. *Commentaries on the Later Prophets I. Isaiah*. Ed. John W. Nutt. London: Joseph Baer, 1879.

Fontaine, Resianne. Otot *Ha-Shamayim: Samuel ibn Tibbon's Hebrew Version of Aristotle's Meteorology*. Leiden: E. J. Brill, 1995.

Freedman, Paul, and Gabrielle M. Spiegel. "Medievalisms Old and New: The Rediscovery of Alterity in North American Medieval Studies." *The American Historical Review* 103 (1998): 677–704.

Gaon, Solomon. *The Influence of the Catholic Theologian Alfonso Tostado on the Pentateuch Commentary of Isaac Abravanel*. Hoboken, N.J.: KTAV, 1993.

Goldstein, Bernard R. "Levi Ben Gerson's Astrology in Historical Perspective." In *Gersonide en son temps: science et philosophie médiévales*. Ed. Gilbert Dahan, 287–300. Louvain: Éditions Peeters, 1991.

Gonzalo Maeso, David. "Alonso de Madrigal (Tostado) y su labor escrituraria." *Miscelánea de estudios árabes y hebraicos* 4 (1955): 143–85.

Greenberg, Moshe. "'Iyov hayah o lo hayah: sugyah be-farshanut yemei ha-beinayim" (Job existed or did not: A chapter in medieval exegesis). In *"Sha'arei Talmon": Studies in the Bible, Qumran, and the Ancient Near East Presented to Shemaryahu Talmon*. Ed. Michael Fishbane and Emanuel Tov with the assistance of Weston W. Fields, 3*-11*. Winona Lake, Ind.: Eisenbrauns, 1992.

Gross, Abraham. *R. Yosef ben 'Avraham Ḥayyun: manhig qehillat Lisbon wi-yṣirato* (Rabbi Joseph ben Abraham Hayyun: leader of the Lisbon Jewish community and his literary work). Ramat-Gan: Bar-Ilan University Press, 1993.

Hadot, Ilsetraut. "Les introductions aux commentaires exégètiques chez les auteurs néoplatoniciens et les auteurs chrétiens." In *Les règles de l'interprétation*. Ed. Michel Tardieu, 99–122. Paris: Cerf, 1987.

Harvey, Steven. "The Hebrew Translation of Averroes' Prooemium to His Long Commentary on Aristotle's Physics." *Proceedings of the American Academy of Jewish Research* 52 (1985): 55–84.

Ḥayyun, Joseph. *Perush Tehillim*. Salonika, 1522.

Ḥen, Zeraḥyah. *'Imrei da'at*. Ed. Israel Schwarz. Vienna, 1871.

——. "Peirush 'Iyov." In *Tiqwat 'enosh*. Ed. Israel Schwarz. Berlin, 1868; reprint, Jerusalem: Makor, 1969.

Hunt, R. W. "The Introduction to the 'Artes' in the Twelfth Century." In idem, *The History of Grammar in the Middle Ages: Collected Papers*. Ed. G. L. Bursill-Hall, 117–43. Amsterdam: John Benjamins, 1980.

Immanuel ben Solomon of Rome. *Sefer Mishlei 'im perush 'Imanu'el ha-Romi, Napoli 1487 le-'erekh*. With an introduction by David Goldstein. Jerusalem: Jewish National and University Library and Magnes Press, 1981.

Kaspi, Joseph ibn. *Shulḥan kesef*. Ed. Hannah Kasher. Jerusalem: Mekhon Ben Tsevi, 1996.

Kellner, Menachem. "Communication or the Lack Thereof Among Thirteenth–Fourteenth Century Provençal Jewish Philosophers: Moses ibn Tibbon and Gersonides on Song of Songs." In *Communication in the Jewish Diaspora: The Pre-Modern World*. Ed. Sophia Menache, 227–56. Leiden: E. J. Brill, 1996.

Kugel, James L. "The Bible in the University." In *The Hebrew Bible and Its Interpreters*. Ed. William Henry Propp, Baruch Halpern, and David Noel Freedman, 143–65. Winona Lake, Ind.: Eisenbrauns, 1990.

Lawee, Eric. "Changing Jewish Attitudes Towards Christian Society: The Case of Spain in the Late Middle Ages." In *Facing In and Facing Out: Relations with Gentiles in the Eyes of Jewish Traditionalists*. Ed. Michael Brown, 2–15. Toronto: Centre for Jewish Studies at York University, 2001.

——. "Don Isaac Abarbanel: Who Wrote the Books of the Bible?" *Tradition* 30 (1996): 65–73.

——. *Isaac Abarbanel's Stance Toward Tradition*. Albany: State University of New York Press, 2001.

——. "On the Threshold of the Renaissance: New Methods and Sensibilities in the Biblical Commentaries of Isaac Abarbanel," *Viator* 26 (1995): 283–319.

Leiman, Sid Z. *The Canonization of Hebrew Scripture: The Talmudic and Midrashic Evidence*. Transactions of the Connecticut Academy of Arts and Sciences, 47. Hamden, Conn.: Archon, 1976.

Lesley, Arthur M. "Hebrew Humanism in Italy: The Case of Biography." *Prooftexts* 2 (1982): 163–77.

Levi ben Gershom. *Commentary on the Song of Songs*. Trans. and ed. Menachem Kellner. New Haven, Conn.: Yale University Press, 1998.

——. *Perush 'Iyov*. Ferrara, 1477.

Livne-Kafri, Ofer. "Sefer Ḥavaqquq (peraqim 'aleph, gimel) be-feirusho shel ha-parshan ha-qara'i Yefet ben 'Eli Ḥassan ben 'Eli ha-Lewi ha-Basri" (The book of Habakkuk (chap. 1, 3) in the commentary of the Karaite exegete Japheth b. Eli Hassan b. Eli ha-Levi ha-Basri). *Sefunot* 21 (1993): 73–113.

Maimonides, Moses. *Sefer Moreh ha-nevukhim*. Trans. Samuel ibn Tibbon. Ed. Judah Even-Shemu'el. Jerusalem: Mossad Harav Kook, 1981.

Marcus, Ivan G. "Exegesis for the Few and for the Many: Judah He-Ḥasid's Biblical Commentaries." *Meḥqerei Yerushalayim be-maḥashevet Yisra'el* 8 (1989): 1*–24*.

——. "Rashi's Historiography in the Introductions to his Bible Commentaries." *Revue des études juives* 157 (1998): 47–55.

Meiri, Menahem. *Peirush ha-Me'iri 'al sefer Mishlei*. Ed. Menachem Mendel Meshi Zahav. Jerusalem: 'Oṣar Haposkim, 1969.

Miller, Jacqueline T. *Poetic License: Authority and Authorship in Medieval and Renaissance Contexts*. New York: Oxford University Press, 1986.

Minnis, A. J. "The *Accessus* Extended: Henry of Ghent on the Transmission and Reception of Theology." In *Ad litteram: Authoritative Texts and Their Medieval Readers*. Ed. Mark D. Jordan and Kent Emery, Jr., 275–326. Notre Dame, Ind.: University of Notre Dame Press, 1992.

——. *Medieval Theory of Authorship: Scholastic Literary Attitudes in the Later Middle Ages*. 2d ed. Aldershot, England: Scolar Press, 1988.

Minnis, A. J., and A. B. Scott, eds. *Medieval Literary Theory and Criticism c. 1100–c. 1375: The Commentary-Tradition*. Oxford: Clarendon, 1988.

Pines, Shlomo. "Scholasticism after Thomas Aquinas and the Teachings of Ḥasdai Crescas and His Predecessors." *Proceedings of the Israel Academy of Sciences and Humanities* 1 (1967): 1–55.

Quain, Edwin A. "The Medieval *Accessus ad auctores*." *Traditio* 3 (1945): 215–64.

Ravitzky, Aviezer. "'Al meqorotaw shel peirush Mishlei le-'Imanu'el ha-Romi" (Immanuel of Rome's commentary on the book of Proverbs—its sources). *Qiryat sefer* 56 (1981): 726–39.

——. "Mishnato shel Rabi Zeraḥyah ben Yiṣḥaq ben She'alti'el Ḥen we-he-hagut ha-maimonit-tibbonit ba-me'ah ha-13" (The thought of R. Zerahiah ben Isaac b. Shealtiel Hen & the Maimonidean-Tibbonian philosophy of the 13th century). Ph. D. diss., The Hebrew University of Jerusalem, 1978.

Rigo, Caterina. "Un'antologia filosofica di Yehuda b. Mosheh Romano." *Italia* 10 (1993): 73–104.

Rivlin, Efraim. "Shemu'el 'ibn Tibbon" (Samuel ibn Tibbon). M. A. thesis, Tel Aviv University, 1969.

Robinson, James T. "Samuel ibn Tibbon's *Commentary on Ecclesiastes* and the Philosopher's Prooemium." In *Studies in Medieval Jewish History and Literature III*. Ed. Isadore Twersky and Jay M. Harris, 83–146. Cambridge: Harvard University Center for Jewish Studies, 2000.

Rosenthal, E. I. J. "Saadya Gaon: An Appreciation of His Biblical Exegesis." In *Studia Semitica*. Vol. 1, 86–96. Cambridge: Cambridge University Press, 1971.

Rosenthal, Murray. "The Haqdamah of Immanuel of Rome to the Book of Ruth." In *Approaches to Judaism in Medieval Times*. Vol. 2. Ed. David R. Blumenthal, 169–84. Brown Judaic Studies, 57. Chico, Calif.: Scholars Press, 1985.

Rothschild, J. P. "Un traducteur hébreu qui se cherche: R. Juda b. Moïse Romano et le *De causis et processu universitatis*, II, 3, 2 d'Albert Le Grand." *Archives d'histoire doctrinale et littéraire du Moyen Âge* 59 (1992): 159–73.

Ruiz, Gregorio. "Las introducciones y cuestiones de Don Isaac Abrabanel." In *Simposio biblico español*. Ed. N. Fernández Marcos, J. Trebolle Barrera, and J. Fernández Vallina, 707–22. Madrid: Universidad Complutense, 1984.

Saadia ben Joseph. *The Book of Theodicy*. Trans. and ed. L. E. Goodman. New Haven, Conn.: Yale University Press, 1988.

Samuel b. Meir. *Perush 'al ha-Torah*. Ed. David Rosin. Breslau, 1881.

Saperstein, Marc. "Christians and Christianity in the Sermons of Jacob Anatoli." In *The Frank Talmage Memorial Volume*. Vol. 2 (= *Jewish History* 6). Ed. Barry Walfish, 225–42. Haifa: Haifa University Press, 1992.

——. "The Social and Cultural Context: Thirteenth to Fifteenth Centuries." In *History of Jewish Philosophy*. Ed. Daniel H. Frank and Oliver Leaman, 294–330. London: Routledge, 1997.

Sarna, Nahum M. "The Modern Study of the Bible in the Framework of Jewish Studies." In *Proceedings of the Eighth World Congress of Jewish Studies. Division A, Bible and Hebrew Language*, 19–27. Jerusalem, 1983.

Schechterman, Deborah. "Filosofyah shel 'Imanu'el ha-romi le-'or peirusho le-sefer Bereshit" (The philosophy of Immanuel of Rome in light of his commentary on the Book of Genesis). Ph. D. diss., The Hebrew University of Jerusalem, 1984.

Sermoneta, Joseph. "He'aroteihem shel R. Mosheh ben Shelomoh mi-Salerno we-shel Niqolos mi-Yuvinaṣo le-Moreh nevukhim" (The comments on the *Guide of the Perplexed* by R. Moses b. Solomon of Salerno and Niccolo of Yuvinaṣo). *'Iyyun* 20 (1969): 211–40.

——. "Ha-'issuq ba-'umanuyot ha-ḥofshiyot ba-ḥevrah ha-yehudit be-'Iṭalyaḥ ba-me'ah ha-14" (The study of the liberal arts in Italian Jewish society in the fourteenth century). In *Ha-'ir we-ha-qehillah: qoveṣ harṣa'ot she-hushme'u ba-Kenes ha-sheneim-'asar le-'iyyun be-hisṭoryah* (The city and the community: lectures presented at the 12th Conference for the Study of History), 249–58. Jerusalem: Israel Historical Society, 1968.

——. "Jehudah ben Moshe ben Dani'el Romano, traducteur de Saint Thomas." In *Hommage à Georges Vajda: études d'histoire et de pensée juives*. Ed. Gérard Nahon and Charles Touati, 231–62. Louvain: Éditions Peeters, 1980.

——. "Ha-peirush le-'farashat Bereshit' le-r[abbi] Yehudah ben Mosheh ben Daniyel Romano u-meqorotaw" (The commentary on the Lesson Bereshit of R. Judah b. Moses b. Daniel Romano and its sources). *Divrei ha-Qongres ha-'olami ha-revi'i le-mada'ei ha-Yahadut* (Fourth World Congress of Jewish Studies papers). Vol. 2, 341–42. Jerusalem: World Union of Jewish Studies, 1968.

——. "Prophecy in the Writings of R. Yehuda Romano." In *Studies in Medieval Jewish History and Literature*. Vol. 2. Ed. Isadore Twersky, 337–74. Cambridge, Mass.: Harvard University Press, 1984.

Shuger, Debora Kuller. *The Renaissance Bible: Scholarship, Sacrifice, and Subjectivity*. Berkeley and Los Angeles: University of California Press, 1994.

Simon, Richard. *Histoire critique du Vieux Testament*. Rotterdam, 1685; reprint, Frankfurt am Main: Minerva, 1967.

Simon, Uriel. *Four Approaches to the Book of Psalms*. Trans. Lenn J. Schramm. Albany: State University of New York Press, 1991.

——. "Ibn Ezra Between Medievalism and Modernism: The Case of Isaiah XL–LXVI." *Supplements to Vetus Testamentum* 36 (1985): 257–71.

Sirat, Colette. *A History of Jewish Philosophy in the Middle Ages*. Rev. ed. Cambridge: Cambridge University Press, 1985.

Smalley, Beryl. *The Study of the Bible in the Middle Ages*. 1st paperback ed. Notre Dame, Ind.: University of Notre Dame Press, 1964.

Steiner, R. C. "Beḥinot lashon ba-peirush li-Yeḥezkel we-li-Terei 'asar she-ba-megilot ha-'ivriyot mi-Bizanṭyon" (Linguistic features of the commentary on Ezekiel and the Minor Prophets in the Hebrew scrolls from Byzantium). *Leshonenu* 59 (1995–96): 39–56.

Talmage, Frank E. *David Kimhi: The Man and the Commentaries*. Cambridge, Mass.: Harvard University Press, 1975.

——, ed. *Perushim le-sefer Mishlei le-vet Qimḥi* (The commentaries on Proverbs of the Kimhi family). Jerusalem: Magnes Press, 1992.

Ta-Shma, Israel. "Mashehu 'al biqqoret ha-Miqra be-'Ashkenaz bi-ymei-ha-beinayim" (Bible criticism in early medieval Franco-Germany). In *Ha-Miqra bi-re'i mefareshaw: sefer zikkaron le-Sarah Qamin* (The Bible in the light of its interpreters: Sarah Kamin Memorial Volume). Ed. Sarah Japhet, 453–62. Jerusalem: Magnes Press, 1994.

——. "Perush Divrei ha-yamim she-bi-khetav-yad Minkhin 5" (The commentary on Chronicles in MS Münich 5). In *Mi-ginzei ha-Makhon le-taṣlumei kitvei ha-yad ha-'ivriyim* (From the collections of the Institute of Microfilmed Hebrew Manuscripts). Ed. Avraham David, 135–41. Jerusalem: Beit ha-Sefarim ha-Le'umi weha-'Universita'i, 1996.

Tibbon, Moses ibn. *Perush Shir ha-shirim*. Lyck, Prussia: Meqiṣei Nirdamim, 1847.

Tibbon, Samuel ibn. *Ma'amar Yiqqawu ha-mayim*. Ed. M. L. Bisliches. Pressburg [Bratislava]: A. E. V. Schmid, 1837.

——. "Perush Qohelet." Parma, Biblioteca Palatina, MS 272 (De Rossi 2182) (IMHM no. 13354).

Tostado, Alfonso de Madrigal. *Commentaria in primam partem Iosue et Commentaria in secundum partem Iosue*. Venice, 1530.

Walfish, Barry Dov. *Esther in Medieval Garb: Jewish Interpretation of the Book of Esther in the Middle Ages*. Albany: State University of New York Press, 1993.

Wasserstrom, Steven M. *Between Muslim and Jew: The Problem of Symbiosis under Early Islam*. Princeton, N.J.: Princeton University Press, 1995.

Wolfson, Elliot R. "The Mystical Significance of Torah Study in German Pietism." *JQR* n.s. 84 (1993): 43–77.

Zonta, Mauro. *La filosofia antica nel Medioevo ebraico: Le traduzioni ebraiche medievali dei testi filosofici antichi*. Brescia, Italy: Paideia, 1996.

11

On the Social Role of Biblical Interpretation

The Case of Proverbs 22:6

ALAN COOPER

> We are commanded that our children know the commandments. And how will they know them, if we do not teach them?[1]

The entrance hall of my children's school in Cincinnati is adorned with a calligraphed rendering of the Hebrew text of Proverbs 22:6, a text that has served as a byword for Jewish educators for at least a thousand years: *ḥanokh la-na'ar 'al pi darko gam ki yazqin lo yasur mimmennu.*[2] The standard English translations range from the elegant literalism of the King James Version ("train up a child in the way he should go: and when he is old, he will not depart from it") to the charming gender-neutral rhyme of the New Revised Standard Version ("Train children in the right way, and when old, they will not stray"). A word-for-word translation of the first part of the verse would be somewhat less explicit than either of those: "train a lad [not necessarily a child] according to his way" ("the way he should go" and "the right way" are translators' glosses).

The three main terms in that part of the verse are notoriously ambiguous and therefore open to a wide range of interpretations. What does it mean to "train" (*ḥanokh*)? What is the nature of the "child" (*na'ar*)? What is the "way" (*derekh*) in which the child ought to be directed, and precisely what does "*his* way" denote? I intend to demonstrate that the manner in which the verse is interpreted—in other words, the various ways in which Jewish commentators have answered those questions—provides a litmus test for attitudes toward educational theory and practice.

The twin pillars of Jewish pedagogy are habituation and discipline: the inculcation of right thinking and behavior, and the chastisement of those who stray from them. These two principles are affirmed and expounded in a number of rabbinic, medieval, and modern prescriptive texts. Those halakhic prescriptions constitute a "pedagogical duty" (*miṣwat ḥinnukh*) that is imposed on the parents of young children.[3] Even before children are old enough to go to school, their parents are obligated to provide them with a grounding in Jewish practice, including various ritual observances as well as elementary instruction in the Hebrew language.

This parental responsibility is crystalized in a single *halakhah* in Joseph Caro's Code of Law, the *Shulḥan 'arukh* (OḤ 657.1): "As soon as small children know how to wave a lulav properly, their parents must buy them their own lulavim, in order to educate them in the performance of commandments." The Talmudic texts and commentaries underlying the *halakhah* list other religious duties that children are to undertake as soon as they are able—with parental instruction. The base text is M. Sukkah 3.15, which states that "a child who knows how to shake it must carry the lulav." This text might appear to be imposing an obligation upon the child, but as the *Shulḥan 'arukh* states, the real onus is upon the parents. Thus, for example, the expansion in Tosefta Ḥagigah 1.3:[4]

> As soon as children are weaned, they are required to sit in the sukkah. . . . When they know how to shake it, they must carry the lulav.[5] When they know how to wrap, they must wear *ṣiṣṣit* (fringes on their garments). As soon as they know how to speak, their parents must teach them the *shema'*, to read Torah, and to speak Hebrew. If they do not, the children might as well never have come into the world. . . .

"Knowing how" to do any of these things, obviously, is the consequence of having been taught. Despite the elliptical language of the text, the commandments of sukkah, lulav, prayer, study, *ṣiṣṣit*, and so forth are not understood to be imposed on small children. Rather, their observance of those commandments fulfills the pedagogical duty that is placed upon their parents.[6]

In addition to educating preschool children in the performance of commandments, parents also are required to reprimand them as necessary. One of the principal halakhic texts on the subject of reprimand provides a nexus between the genres of prescriptive and exegetical writing. Maimonides' *Hilkhot ma'akhalot 'asurot* (Laws of Forbidden Foods) 17.27–28 is one of a few places in his code of law, the *Mishneh Torah*, where he takes up the question of parental versus public responsibility for the reprimand of minor children who have committed breaches of Jewish law:[7]

> [27] In the case of small children who ate one of the forbidden foods, or who did prohibited work on the Sabbath, the Rabbinical Court is not responsible for reprimanding those who are not yet capable of understanding. This applies when the children acted of their own volition. Feeding children [forbidden food], however, is forbidden, even food that is only rabbinically prohibited. In like manner, it is forbidden to accustom a child to the profanation of Sabbath and Festivals, even with respect to the finer points of rabbinic prohibitions.[8]
>
> [28] Although the Rabbinical Court is not obligated to reprimand the children, their parents are obligated to scold and reprimand them in order to educate them in the way of holiness,[9] as it is written, "Train up a child in the way he should go," etc.

It is not difficult to infer Maimonides' interpretation of Proverbs 22:6 from his use of it as a prooftext. "Training" means disciplining; the "child" of the verse is a minor who is "not yet capable of understanding" (the Tosafists define such a child as 2–3 years old,[10] or what we would call a "preschooler," assuming normal development); and the "way" of the verse is the conduct prescribed by Jewish law, referring in the present case to the laws of *kashrut* and Shabbat.[11]

This interpretation narrowly restricts the meaning of the verse. There is no reason to confine "training" to discipline.[12] Taking the *na'ar* to be a toddler overdefines that term as well.[13] And the understanding of the "way" of the verse is problematic in several respects. In particular, it runs afoul of the third-person masculine singular pronominal suffix on *darko*, "his way." The natural antecedent of that suffix is the *na'ar*, and it is not easy to see how the "way of the *na'ar*" denotes "the way of holiness." Perhaps the implied antecedent of the pronominal suffix is supposed to be God, but that is just a guess.

As is commonly the case in the *Mishneh Torah*, an uncited midrashic interpretation underlies Maimonides' understanding of his prooftext.[14] The interpretation is found in the *Midrash Mishlei* (Midrash on Proverbs), which, according to Burton Visotzky, editor of the recent critical edition, dates from the ninth century:[15]

> Rabbi Eliezer said, "If you educate your children in words of Torah while they are yet young, they will continually grow up according to them, as it is said, 'when he is old, he will not depart from it.' It is like the tendril of a vine—if you do not train it when it is still young and moist, once it dries out you will be unable to do so."

The midrash contains all three elements of the interpretation that is implicit in Maimonides' use of the verse: the "way" of the verse is glossed as "words of Torah"; the *na'ar* is taken to refer to a young child; and the metaphor of the vine illustrates the kind of "training" that is involved.

Although Maimonides does not mention that metaphor per se, it figures prominently in many discussions of Proverbs 22:6. It encapsulates two widely shared assumptions about education: on the one hand, small children are pliable and easily disciplined; on the other hand, those who are not disciplined when they are young are likely to become intractable later on. A well-known thirteenth-century elaboration of the plant metaphor is in Jonah Gerondi's commentary on M. 'Avot 1.14. Gerondi is commenting on Hillel's famous rhetorical question, "if not now, when?" which he takes to mean that it is never too soon to undertake the task of self-improvement:[16]

> If not now—in the days of youth—then when? If one leaves it until old age, one will never be able to do it. In this regard, David said, "our children are as plants grown up in their youth" (Ps 144:12). When a seedling is still small, a person can train it so that it will grow into an upright tree, and it will not be crooked. But once it has grown up crooked, it is very difficult to straighten. And so too with children, when they are still small, it is easy to set them on the good path and turn them away from evil. But if they grow up in a bad way, it will be hard to set them straight, as it is written, "train up a child in the way he should go: and when he is old, he will not depart from it." . . .

The moral character of the child, like that of the seedling, seems to be neutral. (Immanuel of Rome, writing about half a century later than Gerondi, cites M. 'Avot 4.20, which likens the education of children to writing on a fresh sheet of paper.)[17] A seedling may indeed grow wild if it is not properly trained. That is not the case because it is evil, however, but because it is a plant. And the salient characteristic of the young plant, like that of the child, is not an inclination toward wildness, but receptivity to training.

The ultimate source for this view is undoubtedly Aristotle's *Ethics*, where the philosopher states that "the virtues are implanted in us neither by nature nor contrary to nature: we are by nature equipped to receive them, and habit brings this ability to completion and fulfillment." It is, therefore, "no small matter whether one habit or another is inculcated in us from early childhood; on the contrary, it makes a considerable difference, or, rather, all the difference."[18]

Jonah Gerondi takes up the particular receptivity of the child again in his Commentary on Proverbs.[19] He observes that children are incapable of self-discipline because their minds are insufficiently developed. Parents, therefore, are required to discipline them; without such discipline, the children might fall into bad habits that would be impossible to break later in life. As Gerondi puts it, "parents are obligated to assist [their children] in their intellectual development, improving their characters while they are young, lest they succumb to bad habits. It is when they are young that it is easiest to improve their characters," he continues, once again adducing the metaphor of the young plant.

The cultivation of bad habits in children, then, is not the product of their evil inclination, but of an unpropitious combination of their own callow ignorance with their parents' dereliction of pedagogical duty. According to Gerondi, in fact, bad habits are the fuel that feeds the evil inclination, and not the reverse. "When self-improvement is delayed," he writes in *Sha'arei teshuvah* 2.30, "the evil inclination grows stronger and hardens the heart, making self-improvement increasingly difficult."[20] As the saying goes, *ha-hergel 'al kol davar shilṭon*, "habit rules over everything."[21] In a sermon about the patriarch Isaac and his sons, Gerondi (quoting Prov 22:6) states that habituating children to right action is even the way of overcoming natural deficiencies of character, since "habit is second nature" (*ha-hergel ṭeva' sheni*).[22]

It is essential, therefore, for parents to cultivate good habits in their children, and that is what Gerondi takes to be the gist of Proverbs 22:6 (note that each time I use a form of the word "way" in my translation, it represents Gerondi's use of *derekh*, alluding to the language of the verse):

> Habituate children in the ways of virtue and correct conduct in accordance with their proclivities [lit. "according to the way on which they stand"]. In other words, begin by habituating them in improvement in those areas to which they are more receptive by nature. And thus habituate them in one area after another, in one way after another, in accordance with the receptivity of their intellects and natural faculties. One does not arrive at perfection in virtue all at once, but gradually, by means of one's intellect, and proceeding from that which is more congenial to one's nature to that which is farther from it. And that is the meaning of *'al pi darko*, "according to his way."

Like any good exegete, Gerondi wants to have his cake and eat it, too. The "way" of the verse, in his interpretation, is both the "way" of virtue and right conduct (as in the Midrash on Proverbs and Maimonides) and also the "way" of the child, which denotes the child's natural receptivity to instruction. Since this receptivity manifests itself differently in different children, each will require a different manner of instruction.

This notion that education should be tailored to the age and character of the individual child goes back to the tenth-century Arabic translation and commentary on Proverbs by Saadia Gaon; his rendering of *'al pi darko*, "according to his way," is *'alā qadri sinnihi*, "commensurate with his age [lit. 'his teeth']."[23] The same interpretation turns up regularly in Provençal literalist commentary. According to Joseph Kimḥi (twelfth century):[24]

> "Train children in the right way" means that when they are five you train them in the discipline appropriate for five-year-olds; when they are ten you train them in the discipline appropriate for ten-year-olds. And so also at each successive stage: "in the right way" means in accordance with their understanding and age [again, as in Saadia, "age" is denoted by "teeth": Kimḥi's *'al pi shinnaw* = Saadia's *'alā qadri sinnihi*].

A similar attitude seems to have been prevalent among the German Pietists.[25] Citing Ecclesiastes 12:1 and Proverbs 22:6, Judah he-Ḥasid (a generation younger than Joseph Kimḥi) writes that "since piety is difficult to attain at first, it is good to begin in youth."[26]

The beginning of piety is assiduous avoidance of worldly matters, which can be achieved only "if one has been trained from childhood. Parents, therefore, should train their children with respect to these things when they are small, so that when they get older they will not abandon or forsake them, as it is written, 'when he is old, he will not depart from it.'"[27]

Judah he-Ḥasid also admonishes teachers to let students' interests and abilities determine the course of instruction:[28]

> When one is teaching babies, and some are sharper than others, and their parents see that it does not make sense for all of them to be learning together, but that the sharper ones require their own teacher—[the teacher] should not be silent, but should say to the parents, "each group needs its own teacher," even though he will lose income by separating them. "Train up a child in the way he should go: and when he is old, he will not depart from it": if you see that children are more successful at Bible than at Talmud, do not press to teach them Talmud at that moment; if they understand Talmud, do not press to teach them Bible. Train them in what they are able to understand.

In a similar vein, Judah he-Ḥasid instructs the teacher to teach in a way that comports with the students' level of understanding, again citing the first half of Proverbs 22:6.[29]

To return to Provence, Joseph Kimḥi's interpretation is adopted by Menaḥem Meiri in the thirteenth century,[30] and by Joseph Naḥmias in the fourteenth.[31] In addition to citing Joseph Kimḥi, however, Meiri raises—for the first time, as far as I know—an alternative interpretation of Proverbs 22:6 that differs radically from those discussed thus far. "There are those who interpret the verse ironically," he writes, "as an unreal imperative intent upon negating rather than affirming the matter. It says 'train a child in its way,' in other words, habituate children to act according to their own nature and will, and do not discipline them, and know that if you do so, even when they are older they will not depart from it."

Meiri does not identify "those who interpret" the verse in this admonitory way. I have not yet found the interpretation in a commentary prior to Meiri's, and my tentative guess is that it arose in the academic or homiletical discourse of his own day. It turns up in the next generation in the Proverbs commentary of Levi ben Gershom:

> As for training children in the way that their own behavior and character leads them, thinking that they will acquire discipline when they get older, it will turn out to be impossible to divert them from that evil path; they will not depart from it of their own accord even in old age.[32]

Far from the relatively benign view of the child as unformed, ignorant, and receptive to training, this alternative interpretation presupposes that children are naturally inclined to evil and that only by strict discipline can they be turned aside from their natural course.

This dark view of the nature of the child finds its fullest expression in later homiletical writings, beginning in the fourteenth century. I will give two examples here, the first from the ethical treatise *Reshit ḥokhmah* (Beginning of Wisdom), completed in 1575 by the Safed kabbalist Elijah de Vidas. The famous chapter in the *Reshit ḥokhmah* entitled "The Upbringing of Children"[33] is now known to be derived from a fourteenth-century work, *Menorat ha-ma'or* (Illuminating Lamp) by Israel Al-Nakawa of Toledo.[34] Since the earlier work was not published until the twentieth century, de Vidas must have had access to it in manuscript. In any case, the views expressed in that chapter are often associated with de Vidas rather than Al-Nakawa.[35]

The way in which the chapter begins leaves no doubt about the direction in which it is headed. De Vidas cites Proverbs 29:17, "Discipline your son and he will give you peace," and comments that "if you discipline your son when he is small, . . . you will not have to worry about him turning out badly." Then he brings in Proverbs 19:18, "Discipline your son while there is hope," which he takes to mean that "even if you see that your son is stupid, do not think, 'of what use would discipline be?'" For there is always "hope" if the rod is applied diligently. And lest one worry about disciplining a child so much that he perishes under the rod, de Vidas observes that the alternative is to have him "turn out badly," commit some capital offense, and be put to death by the court. By the time he gets to Proverbs 22:6, de Vidas is in full flight. Here is his interpretation:

> If you train up children according to the way of children—and what is the way of children? not to study and not to pray, but to waste their time in pursuit of their evil inclinations, as Scripture says, "the inclination of the human heart is evil from youth" (Gen 8:21)—if you leave them on that evil path to follow the natural proclivities of youth, and you do not discipline them in order to bring them back to the good, then "even in old age [they] will not leave [the evil path]," for they will be utterly habituated to folly and will never be able to escape it. On the other hand, if you discipline them from youth, they will be inculcated with virtues that they will never be able to forsake. "Train up a child in the way he should go" is not a commandment but is to be compared with [Eccles 11:9], "Rejoice, young man, in your youth," which means "if, young man, you rejoice in your youth" by doing one thing and another, "know that for all these things God will call you to account."

The second text, which complements *Reshit ḥokhmah* and almost certainly was influenced by it, comes from the compendious *Shenei luḥot ha-berit* (Two tables of the covenant), the magnum opus of Isaiah Horowitz, which was compiled over a long period and completed in Jerusalem in 1623. One section of this enormous work is a discussion of important concepts of kabbalistic ethics in alphabetical order. The entry for the letter "daleth," *derekh 'ereṣ*, deals with the attainment of physical and spiritual perfection. Two sections of that entry are devoted to the upbringing of children:[36]

> It is well known that "a person is a wild ass at birth" (Job 11:12), and that "the inclination of the human heart is evil from youth" (Gen 8:21). That is why it is essential to habituate and train children in the virtues from the moment they begin to speak. . . . "Train children in the right way" means that parents should not withhold discipline even from earliest childhood, augmenting it daily to the extent that the child's intellect is able to bear it. Nor should the rod of chastisement be withheld, as it says, "He who spares the rod hates his son, but he who loves him disciplines him early" (Prov 13:24).[37]

Horowitz then supplies long lists of negative and positive qualities and admonishes parents to discipline their children with respect to both "constantly, every single day, even a hundred times a day."

This constant, vigilant disciplining, according to Horowitz, should begin when the child is two or three years old.[38] There are two reasons for making such an early start. The first, Horowitz writes, is that "what children are inculcated with in youth stays with them all their lives," and he cites Proverbs 22:6 once again. The second is that a parent who strictly disciplines a child from early youth will always command the child's respect. To achieve that goal, Horowitz states, parents must treat their children with "overt reproof and hidden love" (a reference to Prov 27:5). If parents treat their children too affectionately, the children most likely will cease to respect them when they grow up and will reject their teachings.[39] In conclusion, Horowitz reverts to the metaphor of the plant: it is easily trained when young, but impossible to straighten once it has grown crooked. Like Jonah Gerondi, he cites Psalm 144:12 in support of the metaphor.

In contrast to Gerondi, to whom children are basically unformed and malleable, de Vidas and Horowitz see them as recalcitrant, resistant to virtue, and inclined to evil. If Gerondi's view is reminiscent of Aristotle's, the alternative view evokes Plato's notion that children are devoid of self-control, dominated by "motley appetites and pleasures and pains," and "chock-full of rage and high spirit" from birth.[40] One would like to know what ideological and social factors might account for the dour view of the later authorities. I would, with all due diffidence, propose two such factors.

The ideological consideration has to do with the basic view of human nature. The giveaway, perhaps, is the use of Job 11:12 and Genesis 8:21 to assert the fundamentally evil character of people from birth, promulgating what amounts to a judaized version of the doctrine of Original Sin. Its pedigree in Jewish sources is traceable to a couple of talmudic references to the "contamination of the snake"[41] as filtered through both kabbalistic[42] and philosophical traditions of interpretation, and it emerges to prominence in late medieval Jewish thought, beginning in the thirteenth and fourteenth centuries.[43]

In Horowitz's view, Adam was created "completely good" and assumed his corruptible corporeal state only "because of the snake." Afterwards, in Horowitz's words, Adam "sired offspring and the offspring produced offspring. It all derived from a putrid drop. For the drop became putrid as a result of the contamination of the snake."[44] The ramifications of this view are obvious. Children are born in a state of evil, and their natural proclivities are evil as well. Only by dint of supreme effort can evil impulses be controlled. And even then, they cannot be eliminated but merely held in check.[45] Given this view of human nature, it is no surprise that Horowitz calls for extreme measures in the disciplining of children.

The second factor that accounts for his attitude, in all likelihood, is the social reality of his time. In another section of *Shenei luḥot ha-berit*, there is a lengthy diatribe against the presence of young children in synagogue, one that is obviously drawn from life. Horowitz introduces the section with the remark that "the chatter of children in synagogue is strictly prohibited." Then he transcribes a report on the behavior of children from the *Derekh ḥayyim* (Way of life) by his older contemporary, Menaḥem de Lonzano, who also lived in Jerusalem in the early 1620s, as follows:[46]

> Near the beginning of Ḥagigah [3a], we learn how R. Eleazar b. Azariah expounded the verse, "Assemble the people—the men, the women, and the children" (Deut 31:12). The men came to study, the women came to listen, and why did the children come? To provide reward to those who brought them. According to the Tosafists, this is the basis for bringing small children to synagogue. Menaḥem says: Nowadays there are children who come to synagogue to provide punishment to those who bring them. They come to profane the sanctity of the house of our God, to play there as if they were out in the street. They make merry (cf. Exod 32:6), they beat each other up, this one laughs and that one

cries, this one talks and that one shouts, they run hither and yon. Some of them even urinate in the synagogue, and then they all sing *mayim mayim*.[47] Sometimes one of the parents gives a child a book, which the child throws on the ground or tears into a dozen pieces (cf. 1 Kings 11:30). The end of the matter is that because of their stupid noise, the worshipers lose all concentration, and the heavenly name is profaned. The one who brings children like this to synagogue, far from being worthy of reward, ought to be worried about retribution!

This picture of chaos in the synagogue is confirmed independently by Moses Ḥagiz (1672–ca.1750). Ḥagiz was born in Jerusalem but spent much of his adult life in several different European communities, which gave him an excellent perspective on synagogue life. His ethical treatise *Ṣeror ha-ḥayyim* ("Bond of life") includes a diatribe against permissive parents.[48] Parents should be quick to discipline their children and should not indulge "indecent" behavior. Such behavior, he writes sarcastically, arises out of the "intelligence and wisdom of the child, who knows how to do evil and not how to do good." Parents who teach the child "according to his [that is, the child's] way" (*'al pi darko*) will be teaching the child "folly, mockery, and derision" instead of Torah.

Ḥagiz gives three examples of the impious behavior of children. Two of them, disrespect for holy books and bad table manners, are cited almost verbatim from an earlier work, Samuel Benveniste's *'Orekh yamim* ("Length of Days").[49] The third example is not found in Ḥagiz's source. "Parents bring children to synagogue to add even further confusion to the prayer service." The behavior of adults is bad enough: they sit around gossiping and singing along in competition with the cantor. On top of that, "the sin of the children is great. Because of them, practically no one prays. They urinate and defecate right in the synagogue, crying and causing consternation to those who are near them."

If these accounts of the behavior of children in synagogue are accurate—and I see no reason to doubt that they are—it is no wonder that pious authorities such as Horowitz were inclined to deal harshly with them! The children whose monstrous behavior Lonzano and Ḥagiz describe obviously were both uneducated and undisciplined, shortcomings for which one could not fail to hold their parents accountable.

I have used the interpretation of Proverbs 22:6 as a lens through which to view traditional Jewish attitudes about children and early childhood education. Two distinct attitudes have emerged. The primary view is traceable to the dawn of medieval Jewish commentary—the ninth-century Midrash on Proverbs and the tenth-century translation and commentary of Saadia Gaon—and ultimately to Aristotle's *Ethics*. In this view, the child is an undeveloped person characterized by particular receptivity to training. Around the end of the thirteenth century, an alternative view emerges, reminiscent of Plato's characterization of children (also women, slaves, and "the base rabble") in *Republic* Book 4. According to this view, the child is a bundle of untamed passions, naturally inclined to evil unless discipline is applied early and often.

The respective views are anchored in diametrically opposed interpretations of the biblical verse and are reified in dramatically different educational theories and practices. The earlier, more benign view stresses age-appropriate education suited to the child's affinities; the later view emphasizes strict discipline, including physical punishment—"overt reproof and hidden love," in Isaiah Horowitz's memorable formulation. It remains to be determined what particular ideological and social factors gave rise to the later view, but I have tentatively identified the Jewish adaptation of Christian anthropology and the actual conditions of synagogue life, respectively, as likely key factors.

The contrast between the two attitudes has penetrated the popular mentality; it is, for example, an important element in Chaim Potok's best-selling novel *The Chosen*. Although, as the novel suggests, the harsher attitude toward children survives to the present day in certain circles, the mainstream orthodox view was tempered considerably by the influence of Enlightenment and post-Enlightenment attitudes about childhood and child-rearing. I will conclude, then, with one sympathetic example of this latter-day approach à propos of Proverbs 22:6, from *Musar ḥokhmah* (Ethical wisdom) by the great nineteenth-century Polish scholar Malbim:[50]

> "Train up children the right way" is a commandment in two respects: First, when one educates children, one habituates them from youth to striving for perfection in ideas, as well as in deeds and virtues. For the habits that one acquires in youth make a profound impression that is preserved within the soul, and does not depart even in old age. Not so the education that one receives in maturity, the impression of which is not fixed within the soul, so that it departs with old age. Second, it is a commandment that education be "the right way" for each person, appropriate to his or her nature. With respect to ideas, some people have sharp minds, and others are more commonsensical but not so sharp. Each one should be taught in a manner befitting his or her ability. With respect to actions, some people are particularly talented, and pick up a given skill with ease. This will be discerned by the child's zeal for and application to a particular task. All should be taught the skill "the right way," that is, according to their talents and abilities, for then "when they are old, it will not leave them." Such is not the case with those who are educated in ways contrary to their natures.

Although in some respects Malbim could be our contemporary, the extent to which he echoes Jonah Gerondi's views of six centuries earlier is equally remarkable.

No matter how one interprets Proverbs 22:6, the gist of the verse is an obvious principle: there is nothing more fundamental to the perpetuation of Judaism than the education of children. The history of interpretation is an impressive record of the various ways in which committed and imaginative interpreters have used the genre of commentary to discover and rediscover that central tenet of the faith in the biblical text. The greatest commentators continue to fascinate us with the interplay between their worldview and the Bible's, or, to put it another way, with the way their intellectual horizons appear to converge with that of the authoritative text. The commentaries I have cited are clear examples of the intimate relationship between Jewish reading and Jewish living, vivid demonstrations of the social and cultural relevance of biblical interpretation.

Notes

1. Moses Naḥmanides (Ramban) on Deuteronomy 6:7, *Peirushei ha-Torah*, 2:372.
2. Simḥah Assaf's checklist of Jewish pedagogical writings includes eight books with the title *Ḥanokh la-na'ar*. See Assaf, *Meqorot le-toledot ha-ḥinnukh be-Yisra'el*, 4:278–80.
3. See my article, Cooper "Parental Responsibility," 19–30.
4. See also BT Sukkah 42a; Jerusalem Talmud Sukkah 4.15 (54a).
5. Rashi on BT Sukkah 42a: "so that they may be educated in these matters."
6. In a similar vein, see *Shulḥan 'arukh* OḤ 689.6: "It is a good practice to bring little boys and girls to the public reading of the Megillah." In this case, however, the *Bei'ur halakhah*,

following the *Magen 'Avraham*, insists that "little boys and girls" (*qeṭanim u-qeṭanot*) denote "children who already have begun their formal education, since those who are younger than that will only cause confusion." It is, nonetheless, a parental obligation to educate children in the reading of the Megillah, and eventually to bring them to synagogue for the public reading "in order to educate them" (*kedei le-ḥannekham*).

7. See also *Hilkhot shabbat* (Laws of Sabbath) 12.7, 24.11; *Hilkhot yibbum* (Laws of Levirate Marriage) 7.18; *Hilkhot 'evel* (Laws of Mourning) 3.12.

8. Cf. *Hilkhot shabbat* 24.11.

9. *Le-ḥannekho bi-qedushah*; cf. *Hilkhot 'evel* 3.12.

10. See Tosafot to BT Shabbat 121a.

11. Abraham Maimonides (Moses' son) extends this admonition to include oath-taking. People commit this "great sin," he writes, because they were not trained properly when they were small: "It is, therefore, proper to accustom them from youth to refrain from oaths—even true ones—and to forbid them in this matter just as one forbids them concerning forbidden foods, profanation of the Sabbath, and other prohibitions of the Torah: 'train up a child, etc.'" See Abraham Maimonides, *Sefer ha-Maspiq*, 306. For Moses Maimonides' strictures regarding oath-taking by children, see his *Hilkhot shevu'ot* (Laws of Oaths) 12.7–8.

12. The eleventh-century lexicographer Jonah Ibn Janaḥ glosses *ḥanokh la-na'ar* with "teach him and habituate him" (*'allimhu wa-darribhu* = *lammedehu we-hargilehu* in Judah Ibn Tibbon's twelfth-century Hebrew translation). See *The Book of Hebrew Roots*, 238; *Sefer ha-Shorashim*, 162. Maimonides himself glosses *meḥannekhin* with *yu'awwidūna*, "habituate," in his commentary on M. Yoma 8.2, rendered *melammedin*, "teach," in the standard medieval Hebrew translation (Vilna ed., 94b, on M. Yoma 8.4), but more accurately as *margilin*, "habituate," in the modern Hebrew translation of Yosef Qafiḥ (*Mishnah 'im peirush Rabbeinu Mosheh ben Maimon*, 2:263). The text there refers to getting youngsters accustomed to fasting on Yom Kippur a year or two before they are halakhically obligated to fast. Maimonides also appears to take *ḥanokh* to refer to habituation in his commentary on M. 'Avot 1.14 (Vilna ed., 6a). Cf. also, for example, Rashi and pseudo-Ibn Ezra on Proverbs 22:6; also Rashi's commentaries on Genesis 14:14 and BT Qiddushin 30a, respectively.

13. Compare BT Qiddushin 30a, where *na'ar* is taken to denote someone between the ages of sixteen and twenty-four—hardly a preschooler! Cf. Jerome, who renders *na'ar* by *adolescens*—unmarked with respect to age, as opposed to *puer*. The terms *puer* and *adolescens* correspond roughly to Hebrew *yeled* and *na'ar*, respectively—the first two of the "seven ages of man" in *Midrash Tadshe* 6 (Eisenstein, *'Oṣar midrashim*, 2:477). On the distinction between the two terms in traditional sources, see Wertheimer, *Bei'ur shemot ha-nirdafim*, 176–80. A modern scholar who argues that *na'ar* denotes an adolescent rather than a young child is Ted Hildebrandt, "Proverbs 22:6a: Train Up a Child?" 3–19. Hildebrandt suggests that the verse is about adolescents becoming responsible adults (precisely the point of the BT Qiddushin passage cited earlier).

14. See Greenberg, "The Uses of Scripture," 197–232; Isadore Twersky, *Introduction to the Code of Maimonides*, 143–64.

15. See Visotzky, *The Midrash on Proverbs*, 10. My translation is adapted from Visotzky, 97. For the Hebrew/Aramaic text, see his *Midrash Mishlei*, 152.

16. Vilna ed., 6a; cf. Gerondi, *Sha'arei teshuvah* (Gates of Repentance) 2.26 (ed. and trans. Silverstein), 114–17.

17. Immanuel of Rome, *Peirush Mishlei*, *ad loc.* (the commentary is unpaginated). Educating adults, in Immanuel's view, is like writing on a sheet of paper that has been written on and erased, or like writing on sand.

18. Aristotle, *Nicomachean Ethics* 2.1.1103a–b, cited in the translation of Ostwald, 33–35. Aristotle is mentioned explicitly in connection with Proverbs 22:6 in a sixteenth-century sermon by Judah Moscato. See Saperstein, *Jewish Preaching*, 262.

19. Gerondi, *Sefer Mishlei*, 272–73.

20. Gerondi, *Sha'arei teshuvah*, ed. Silverstein, 116–19.

21. See Davidson, *'Oṣar ha-meshalim we-ha-pitgamim*, 145, #2389.

22. *Derashot u-feirushei Rabbeinu Yonah Gerondi 'al ha-Torah*, 49. For the aphorism, see Davidson, *'Oṣar ha-meshalim*, 145.

23. *Version Arabe des Proverbes . . . de R. Saadia ben Iosef al-Fayyoûmî*, 124; *Mishlei 'im targum u feirush ha-Ga'on Rabbeinu Se'adyah*, 170. Similarly, Saadia's younger contemporary David ben Abraham Alfasi: "Train a lad (*al-ṣabīy*) according to his way (*'alā ṭarīqihi*) means train your child (*waladaka*) according to what is good for him at every age to the point that he attains what is necessary for him to attain, and then when he is old, he will not turn aside from it" (*Kitāb Jāmi' al-alfāẓ*, 1:564).

24. Talmage, *Peirushim le-sefer Mishlei*, 112.

25. See Kanarfogel, *Jewish Education and Society in the High Middle Ages*, 33–41.

26. Judah he-Ḥasid, *Sefer Ḥasidim*, 58 (§7).

27. Ibid., 60–61 (§10).

28. Ibid., 243 (§308).

29. Ibid., 521 (§983).

30. *Peirush ha-Meiri 'al Sefer Mishlei*, 215.

31. *Peirush 'al Sefer Mishlei le-Rabbi Yosef be-Rabbi Yosef 'Ibn Naḥmias*, 122. Although Naḥmias lived in Toledo, he was a disciple of the well-traveled Asher ben Yeḥiel, and northern influence is detectable on every page of Naḥmias's Proverbs commentary.

32. I am citing Levi's commentary from a standard Rabbinic Bible (*Miqra'ot gedolot*). Proverbs 22:6 is used as an epigram in a compilation of *to'aliyot* ("useful lessons") concerning the education of children that were culled from Levi's biblical commentaries. See *Sefer ha-De'ot we-ha-middot le-ha-Ralbag*, 39a–40a. Eli's sons (1 Sam 3:13), Samuel's sons (1 Sam 8:3), and Adonijah (1 Kings 1:6) serve as examples of children who turned out badly because they were not disciplined in their youth. Samuel himself, on the other hand, had been brought up properly: "he was already doing obeisance to the Lord when he was about two years old; his parents had commanded him to do so, in order to train him and accustom him (*le-ḥannekho ule-hargilo*) to the service of Exalted God" (see 1 Sam 1:28).

33. Elijah de Vidas, *Reshit ḥokhmah*, 290a-295b. The book was first printed in Venice in 1579, and there have been at least forty subsequent printings, as well as condensed versions.

34. Al-Nakawa, *Menorat ha-ma'or*, 4:117–48, esp. 120. Al-Nakawa's interpretation of Proverbs 22:6 is also cited in the late-fourteenth century *Menorat ha-Ma'or* by Aboab, ed. Ḥorev, 197, and in the late fifteenth or early sixteenth century *Sefer ha-Musar* ("Book of Ethics") by Judah Khalaṣ, ch. 7 (unpaginated).

35. See, for example, Assaf, *Meqorot*, 2:64–66; 3:87–88.

36. Horowitz, *Shenei luḥot ha-berit* (commonly known by the acronym *Shelah*), *Sha'ar ha-'otiyot: derekh 'ereṣ*, 1:285 (§§14–15).

37. Proverbs 13:24 is the subject of a famous homily at the beginning of Midrash Exodus Rabbah on the upbringing of children. See Cooper, "Parental Responsibility," 26–27.

38. Cf. Plato, *Laws* 7.793d–794a. A more direct source for Horowitz's view, however, is the ethical will of his father, Abraham b. Shabbetai Halevi Horowitz: "Start directing [your children] on the right path when they are young, for 'if not now'—in childhood—'when?' Even if they are only small children, two or three years old, it is incumbent upon parents to nurture and instruct them gradually. And they must not withhold the rod of discipline in order to bring them back to the good, for this is the meaning, in my opinion, of the verse, 'your children, like olive saplings around your table' (Ps 128:3): children are considered to be like olives in the sense that just as one crushes olives in order to obtain their oil, one disciplines one's children by scoldings and beatings until they bring forth purest olive oil" (apud Assaf, *Meqorot*, 1:64).

39. Cf. the statement by Horowitz's Polish contemporary, Isaac b. Eliaqim of Posen: "Parents must love their children with all their souls and their might [paraphrasing Deut 6:5], but must not reveal their love openly, lest the children neither fear nor obey them" (apud Assaf, *Meqorot*, 1:75).

40. *Republic* 4.431b–c, 441a–b, cited from *The Collected Dialogues of Plato*, ed. Hamilton and Cairns, 673, 683.

41. BT Shabbat 146a and BT Yevamot 103b. For general discussions of Jewish attitudes concerning original sin, see Cohon, "Original Sin," in idem, *Essays in Jewish Theology*, 219–72; Rembaum, "Medieval Jewish Criticism of the Doctrine of Original Sin," 353–82.

42. See, e.g., Tiqqunei Zohar 69 [100a], and Safran, "Rabbi Azriel and Nahmanides," 75–106.

43. See Schechterman, "Sugyat ha-ḥeṭ ha-qadmon," 65–90. See also, inter alia, Crescas (early fifteenth century), *'Or 'Adonai* 2.2.6, with Lasker, "Ha-Ḥeṭ ha-qadmon," 127–35 [Hebrew with English summary]; Ashkenazi (sixteenth century), *Ma'asei 'Adonai, Ma'asei Torah*, 85d, with Cooper, "An Extraordinary Sixteenth-Century Biblical Commentary," 129–50, esp. 136–37.

44. *Shenei luḥot ha-berit: Toledot 'Adam, Beit Dawid*, 1.89–90. See also Horowitz, *The Generations of Adam*, 227. I am citing Krassen's translation.

45. *Shenei luḥot ha-berit: Toledot 'Adam, Beit Dawid*, 1.92; trans. Krassen, 232.

46. *Shenei luḥot ha-berit: Ner miṣwah, Massekhet Tamid, 'Inyan Sefer Torah we-'Inyan Beit hakeneset*, 3.337–38. The *Derekh ḥayyim* consists of 315 lines of poetry (doggerel, actually) that are, in Lonzano's words, "replete with ethical admonitions" [*mele'im tokheḥot musar*]. The poetry is broken up by lengthy explanatory discourses. Lonzano's discussion of children in synagogue is preceded by four lines of verse which I would translate roughly as follows:

> Teach your offspring fear of God,
> And they will flourish like palm trees.
> Bring them to the house of God to sing in praise of God,
> But not to romp like drunkards,
> Like people who bring their children there to their shame,
> Depriving themselves of reward.
> Give them life by the Tree of Life;
> Do not kill them by the tree of worldly knowledge.

I have consulted the *Derekh ḥayyim*, which was first published in Constantinople in 1573, in the Venice, 1618 edition, where it is part four of Lonzano's composite work, *Shetei yadot*, 117a–b.

47. A popular song based on Isaiah 12:3. The word *mayim* ("water") is also a euphemism for "urine."

48. Moses Ḥagiz, *Ṣeror ha-ḥayyim*, 13b; also (with some omissions) in Assaf, *Meqorot*, 3:58–59.

49. Little is known about Benveniste, whose work was published in Venice in 1600. See Assaf, *Meqorot*, 3:16–19.

50. *Sefer Miqra'ei qodesh* [Malbim's collected commentaries on the Prophets and Hagiographa], 2:550.

Bibliography

Aboab, Isaac. *Menorat ha-ma'or*. Ed. Yehudah Ḥorev. Jerusalem: Mossad Harav Kook, 1961.

Alfasi, David ben Abraham. *Kitāb Jāmi' al-alfāẓ*. Ed. Solomon L. Skoss. 2 vols. New Haven, Conn.: Yale University Press, 1936–45.

Al-Nakawa, Israel. *Menorat ha-ma'or*. Ed. H. G. Enelow. 4 vols. New York: Bloch, 1929–32.

Aristotle. *Nicomachean Ethics*. Trans. Martin Ostwald. Indianapolis: Bobbs-Merrill, 1962.

Ashkenazi, Eliezer. *Ma'asei 'Adonai.* Warsaw, 1871; reprint, Jerusalem: 'Oṣar ha-Sefarim, 1986/87.

Assaf, Simḥa. *Meqorot le-toledot ha-ḥinnukh be-Yisra'el* (Sources for the history of Jewish education). 4 vols. Tel Aviv: Devir, 1925–47.

Cohon, Samuel S. *Essays in Jewish Theology.* Cincinnati: Hebrew Union College Press, 1987.

Cooper, Alan. "An Extraordinary Sixteenth-Century Biblical Commentary: Eliezer Ashkenazi on the Song of Moses." In *The Frank Talmage Memorial Volume.* Ed. Barry Walfish. Vol. 1, 129–50. Haifa: Haifa University Press, 1993.

——. "Parental Responsibility for the Jewish Upbringing of Small Children: Some Traditional Sources." *Central Conference of Americal Rabbis Journal* 43/2 (Spring/Summer 1996): 19–30.

Crescas, Hasdai. *'Or 'Adonai.* Ferrara, 1555.

Davidson, Israel. *'Oṣar ha-meshalim we-ha-pitgamim mi-sifrut yemei ha-beinayim* (Thesaurus of proverbs and sayings in medieval Hebrew literature). Jerusalem: Mossad Harav Kook, 1957.

Eisenstein, J. D. *'Oṣar midrashim* (Thesaurus of Midrashim). 2 vols. New York, 1915.

Gerondi, Jonah. *Derashot u-feirushei Rabbeinu Yonah Gerondi 'al ha-Torah.* Ed. Shemu'el Yerushalmi. Jerusalem: Wagshal, 1979/80.

——. *Sefer Mishlei 'im bei'ur . . . Rabbeinu Yonah Gerondi.* Jerusalem: Haskel, 1991/92.

——. *Sha'arei teshuvah.* Ed. and trans. Shraga Silverstein. Jerusalem: Feldheim, 1976.

Greenberg, Moshe. "The Uses of Scripture in Classical, Medieval Judaism: Prooftexts in Maimonides' Code." In *The Return to Scripture in Judaism and Christianity: Essays in Postcritical Scriptural Interpretation.* Ed. Peter Ochs, 197–232. New York: Paulist Press, 1993.

Ḥagiz, Moses. *Ṣeror ha-ḥayyim.* Wandsbeck, 1728.

Hildebrandt, Ted. "Proverbs 22:6a: Train Up a Child?" *Grace Theological Journal* 9 (1988): 3–19.

Horowitz, Isaiah. *The Generations of Adam.* Trans. Miles Krassen. New York: Paulist Press, 1996.

——. *Shenei luḥot ha-berit.* 5 vols. Jerusalem: 'Oz we-hadar, 1993.

Ibn Janaḥ, Jonah. *The Book of Hebrew Roots.* Ed. Adolf Neubauer. Oxford, 1875. Reprint, Amsterdam: Philo, 1968.

——. *Sefer ha-Shorashim.* Ed. Wilhelm Bacher. Berlin: Itzkowski, 1896.

Immanuel ben Solomon, of Rome. *Peirush Mishlei.* Naples, 1487.

Judah ben Samuel, he-Ḥasid. *Sefer Ḥasidim.* Ed. Reuven Margaliot. Jerusalem: Mossad Harav Kook, 1956/57.

Kanarfogel, Ephraim. *Jewish Education and Society in the High Middle Ages.* Detroit: Wayne State University Press, 1992.

Khalaṣ, Judah. *Sefer ha-Musar.* Constantinople, 1537.

Lasker, Daniel J. "*Ha-Ḥet ha-qadmon we-kapparato le-fi Ḥasdai Qreśqaś*" (Original sin and its atonement according to Ḥasdai Crescas). *Da'at* 20 (Winter 1988): 127–35.

Levi ben Gershom (Ralbag). *Sefer ha-De'ot we-ha-middot le-ha-Ralbag.* Ed. Yehiel Mahriaḥ. Warsaw: Orgelbrand, 1864/65.

Lonzano, Menaḥem de. *Shetei yadot.* Venice, 1618.

Maimonides, Abraham. *Sefer ha-Maspiq le-'ovedei ha-Shem* (*Kitāb Kifāyat al-'Ābidīn*). Ed. Nissim Dana. Ramat-Gan: Bar-Ilan University Press, 1989.

Maimonides, Moses (Rambam). *Mishnah 'im peirush Rabbeinu Mosheh ben Maimon: maqor we-targum.* Ed. Yosef Qafiḥ. 6 vols. Jerusalem: Mossad Harav Kook, 1963.

Malbim, Meir Leibush. *Musar ḥokhhma.* In Sefer *Miqra'ei qodesh.* 2 vols. Jerusalem: Mefareshei ha-Tanakh, 1957.

Meiri, Menaḥem. *Peirush ha-Meiri 'al Sefer Mishlei.* Ed. Menaḥem Mendel Meshi Zahav. 2d ed. Jerusalem: 'Oṣar ha-Poseqim, 1969.

Naḥmanides, Moses (Ramban). *Peirushei ha-Torah le-Rabbeinu Mosheh ben Naḥman (Ramban).* Ed. Ḥayyim Dov (Charles B.) Chavel. 2 vols. Jerusalem: Mossad Harav Kook, 1959/60.

Naḥmias, Joseph. *Peirush 'al Sefer Mishlei.* Ed. Mosheh Bamberger. Berlin: Meqiṣei Nirdamim, 1912.

Plato. *The Collected Dialogues.* Ed. Edith Hamilton and Huntington Cairns. New York: Pantheon, 1961.

Rembaum, Joel E. "Medieval Jewish Criticism of the Doctrine of Original Sin," *AJS Review* 7/8 (1982/83): 353–82.

Saadia ben Joseph. *Mishlei 'im targum u-feirush ha-Ga'on Rabbeinu Se'adyah ben Yosef Fayyumi.* Ed. Yosef Qafiḥ. Jerusalem: Ha-wa'ad le-hoṣa'at sifrei Rasag, 1975/76.

——. *Version Arabe des Proverbes . . . de R. Saadia ben Iosef al-Fayyoûmî.* Ed. J. Derenbourg and Mayer Lambert. Paris: Leroux, 1894.

Safran, Bezalel. "Rabbi Azriel and Nahmanides: Two Views of the Fall of Man." In *Rabbi Moses Nahmanides (Ramban): Explorations in His Religions and Literary Virtuosity.* Ed. Isadore Twersky, 75–106. Cambridge, Mass.: Harvard University Press, 1983.

Saperstein, Marc. *Jewish Preaching 1200–1800: An Anthology.* Yale Judaica Series, 26. New Haven, Conn.: Yale University Press, 1989.

Schechterman, Deborah. "Sugyat ha-ḥeṭ ha-qadmon we-ha-parshanut le-divrei ha-Rambam be-hagut ha-yehudit ba-me'ot ha-shelosh-'eśreh we-ha-'arba'-'eśreh" (The doctrine of original sin and Maimonidean interpretation in Jewish philosophy of the thirteenth and fourteenth centuries). *Da'at* 20 (Winter 1988): 65–90.

Talmage, Frank, ed. *Peirushim le-sefer Mishlei le-veit Qimḥi* (The commentaries on Proverbs of the Kimhi family). Jerusalem: Magnes Press, 1990.

Twersky, Isadore. *Introduction to the Code of Maimonides (Mishneh Torah).* Yale Judaica Series, 21. New Haven, Conn.: Yale University Press, 1980.

Vidas, Elijah de. *Reshit ḥokhmah.* Amsterdam, 1708.

Visotzky, Burton L., ed. *Midrash Mishlei.* New York: Jewish Theological Seminary of America, 1990.

——, trans. *The Midrash on Proverbs.* Yale Judaica Series, 27, New Haven, Conn.: Yale University Press, 1992.

Wertheimer, S. A. *Bei'ur shemot ha-nirdafim shel Torah, Nevi'im u-Khetuvim* (Explanation of synonyms in the Tanakh). Ed. J. C. Wertheimer. Jerusalem: Ktav Yad V'sefer, 1983/84.

PART II

MEDIEVAL CHRISTIAN EXEGESIS OF THE BIBLE

12

An Introduction to Medieval Christian Biblical Interpretation

JOSEPH W. GOERING

The Christian Bible is made up of two parts, the Old and the New Testaments, both of which were understood throughout the Middle Ages as the divinely revealed word of God. Broadly speaking, the Old Testament comprises the same books as the Jewish or Hebrew Bible. The New Testament adds the four Gospel accounts of the life, death, and resurrection of Jesus Christ, a history of the early Christian community (the Acts of the Apostles), twenty-one pastoral letters ascribed to the Apostles Paul, Peter, John, James, and Jude, and the Apocalypse of Saint John.

The earlier, and much the larger, part of this Christian Bible is the so-called Old Testament. Although it is virtually identical with the Hebrew Bible, sharing the same books and appealing to the same letter (founded, ultimately, on the same Hebrew text), something crucial has happened, for Christians, to transform these books of the Law, the Prophets, and the Writings into the Old Testament of the Christian dispensation. For Christian interpreters, the Hebrew scriptures have taken on new meaning in the light of the life, death, and resurrection of Jesus.

This transformation can be seen already in the Gospel accounts. Saint Luke, for example, includes at the beginning of his Gospel a telling incident in Jesus' life (Luke 4:16–30):

> When Jesus came to Nazareth, where he had been brought up, he went into the synagogue on the Sabbath, as was his custom. He stood up to read the scripture [i.e., the Hebrew Bible] and was handed a scroll of the prophet Isaiah. Unrolling the scroll, he found the passage where it was written: "The Spirit of the Lord is upon me, for he has anointed me; he has sent me to preach good news to the poor, to proclaim release for prisoners and sight for the blind, to send the downtrodden away relieved, and to proclaim the year of the Lord's favor." Jesus rolled up the scroll, returned it to the attendant, and sat down. The eyes of the synagogue were fixed intently on him, as he began to speak to them: "Today this passage of scripture sees its fulfillment, in your hearing."

In Luke's account the scandalous nature of this assertion was not immediately obvious; he says that the listeners "were surprised that such gracious words came from his lips. Is this not Joseph's son? they asked." But by the end of Jesus' earthly life there was no doubt that more was meant. Jesus was understood by many to be the Messiah and the

Anointed One who was sent by God to fulfill all that was taught in the Law and the Prophets. Henceforth the Hebrew "scriptures" would be understood by Christians as relating, both literally and also mysteriously, to this Christ.

Luke makes this idea perfectly clear at the end of his Gospel. He describes how Jesus appeared, after his death and resurrection, to two disciples on the road to Emmaus, a day's journey West of Jerusalem (Luke 24:13–35). The two disciples were desolate because the one whom they hoped would be the Messiah (i.e., the Christ, the Anointed One) had been crucified. Jesus says to them:

> "How foolish you are, and slow of wit to believe in all that the prophets have said! Was not the Messiah bound to suffer all this before entering into his glory?" *Then he began with Moses and all the prophets and interpreted for them what pertained to himself in every part of scripture* (emphasis added).

In this story of the encounter with the risen Christ, Christians found the warrant for interpreting every part of the Hebrew Bible christologically. They were guided in their interpretive activity by the teachings of the Apostles, whose writings constituted the New Testament, and in which the revelation of God's word in holy scriptures was completed.

One of the unusual characteristics of the early Christian communities is their insistence, seemingly from the outset, on the importance of unity.[1] Because of this it is impossible to understand later medieval developments and interpretations of scripture without taking into account those that went before. In the medieval view, the correct interpretation was that which has been held "everywhere, always, and by all" of the faithful (*quod ubique, quod semper, quod ab omnibus creditum est*).[2] No responsible medieval writer felt free to disregard or to disavow those who went before, and whose lives and opinions had been approved by the customs, usages, and judgements of the Church. Rather, medieval biblical interpretation continually returned to, and built upon, the work of earlier generations. Indeed, in the coherence of the old and the new it found a strong proof of its authenticity, and in incoherence, a *prima facie* intimation of error. Because of this medieval insistence on the unity and continuity of Christian exegesis across time and space, it will be well to sketch very briefly the broad outlines of its history.

The Patristic Age (the Age of the [Church] Fathers): First to Sixth Century

This period is played out primarily within the confines of the old Roman Empire which encircled the entire Mediterranean Sea. The "Fathers" or "Doctors" of the Church, as they came later to be called, can usefully be divided by language into those from the Eastern or Greek-speaking half of the Empire and those from the Western or Latin-speaking half. In the (Greek) East one thinks of Athanasius, John Chrysostom, Basil, Gregory of Nyssa, and Gregory Nazianzus. In the (Latin) West, Ambrose, Jerome, Augustine, and Popes Leo and Gregory the Great come especially to mind. These are, of course, only a few of the influential interpreters of the period,[3] but they are the authorities who continue to be studied most thoroughly, and under whose aegis the full range of catholic argument and interpretation is most clearly represented to later ages. The fate of lesser-known writers and of noncatholic or suspect writings is more complex. If these texts were thought to be of particular value and to add something important to the stock of interpretations, they tended to be adapted and copied in one form or another. Some even came to circulate under the name of one of the undoubted "Fathers," and some, like the extremely influential writings of (Pseudo-)Dionysius, which were probably composed in Syria in the sixth century, gained currency through their association with an undoubted Apostle and Saint. These patristic writings, in both Latin and Greek, were continually rediscovered and reintroduced into the mainstream of discussions in subsequent centuries.

The Central Middle Ages: Seventh to Eleventh Century

This period saw the rise and spread of Islam throughout much of the known world, the collapse of the unity of the Mediterranean empire of Rome, and the creation of a new version of that empire in the West (in what would come to be known as "Europe") under the Carolingian and Ottonian royal houses. When Charlemagne was crowned emperor by Pope Leo III in Saint Peter's Basilica on Christmas Day of the year 800, he looked out on a world whose horizons included the Baltic and North Sea as well as the Mediterranean coasts of Spain and Italy. To the East was the East Roman or Byzantine Empire, which continued to play an important role in the life and thought of Europe, and the lands of the (Central- and East-European) pagans who would soon be converted to Christianity. The centers of biblical interpretation in this period were no longer to be found concentrated in a few Roman cities, but were dispersed in monasteries and cathedral courts throughout the length and breadth of Europe.[4] The names and deeds of the exegetes active in this period are less familiar to most of us than they should be, and the rich biblical scholarship and ecclesial developments of these centuries have been much neglected until very recently. Now, however, some of the most interesting and important work is being done on this period, as can be seen in Abigail Firey's contribution to this volume.

The Scholastic Age: Eleventh to Fifteenth Century

The flowering of schools and universities as places for scholarship of all kinds is perhaps the most salient characteristic of this period of medieval biblical interpretation. It is within the context of revivals of learning in every field, from the recovery of Roman Law and legal science to the introduction of Aristotle's philosophical and scientific works, that scholastic exegesis finds its place. In this period, also, the Medieval Bible became a kind of textbook, accompanied by a scholarly apparatus. The ensemble included: (1) a relatively stable Latin text of the Old and New Testaments, divided for ease of study and teaching into the chapters that have remained the norm into our own day; (2) a standard body of accompanying commentary on the words and things mentioned in the text, drawn from the writings of the ancient Fathers and later commentators (the most common form of this critical apparatus was called the "Ordinary Gloss," *glossa ordinaria*); and (3) the Histories, drawn from a wide range of sources, including apocryphal and deutero-canonical writings, Jewish oral and written traditions, patristic commentaries, secular histories, and scientific and archaeological investigations. This medieval "school" Bible, comprising texts and glosses and histories, formed the common inheritance of the later Middle Ages, and shaped not only its thought and institutions, but also its art, literature, music, drama, and everyday life.[5]

Several essays in this volume explore the diverse ways in which medieval teachers and preachers exploited these resources, and they illustrate the range of play as modern scholarship begins to come to terms with medieval methods and principles of interpretation. Edward Synan (R.I.P.) provides an excellent summary of the received opinions of twentieth-century scholarship concerning the "four senses" of scripture. Other contributors add nuance and strike out in new directions. James Ginther reevaluates the traditional views concerning Robert Grosseteste (d. 1253) and his attitude toward the literal and spiritual senses. Robert Sweetman develops an innovative approach to the question of the literal and spiritual senses in his study of Thomas of Cantimpré (fl. 1260), and his distinction between a scholarly and a "performative" reading of scripture, the latter to be found in accounts of Thomas's work as an exorcist. John Boyle draws attention to a largely neglected aspect of scholastic commentary—the *divisio textus*—and illustrates brilliantly how it works as an interpretative tool. Édouard Jeauneau provides an original and thoughtful introduction to Thomas of Ireland's (d. ca. 1330) treatise on the three (spiritual) senses of scripture.

Within the five centuries (1000–1500) that I have labeled "scholastic," it is perhaps important to mark an internal division. Those writers and interpreters who flourished before ca. 1300, as diverse as were their backgrounds, training, and interests, all shared a common view that the Bible contained both a literal and a spiritual meaning, and that the important and difficult task of the interpreter *qua* interpreter was to elucidate and expound both in preaching and teaching.[6] Although this view continued to be espoused after 1300, the interpretative practices of some commentators shifted subtly but importantly. In the traditional interpretation, the literal or historical meaning of the text was that in which words signified things; the spiritual senses were those in which the things signified by the words in turn signified other things, whether through allegory or tropology or anagogy.[7] Perhaps it was the radical philosophical critique, generally associated with the terms "nominalism" or the *via moderna*, that questioned our ability to know things and privileged our knowledge of words, and thus made the older practice of spiritual interpretation seem untenable. Whatever the cause, one finds increasingly, after 1300, that the spiritual senses of scripture are derived from the "letter" (i.e., the text and its context) rather than from the "things" that the letter signifies, as in the older interpreters. The result of this shift is a gradual reduction in importance of the spiritual senses, as they come to be seen as mere rhetorical ornaments rather than as the bearers of the heart and soul of the biblical revelation. The fruits of this interpretive shift can be seen in several of the chapters in this volume, but especially in Alastair Minnis's study of "the devaluation of allegory" in William of Ockham.

The Modern Age

I will touch briefly here on two subsequent historical periods that were particularly important for creating the received opinion, both academic and ecclesial, of medieval exegesis, and thus for shaping our own view of Christian biblical interpretation in the Middle Ages.

First is the Renaissance and reform of the sixteenth century. The Protestant Reformation encouraged on the one side, a rejection of, and on the other, a muted embarrassment over, many elements of the medieval inheritance. Renaissance humanists and Reformation critics combined to call into question the traditional authority of medieval scholastic commentators, especially in law and theology. One type of interpretation came to dominate succeeding generations; this school of interpretation insisted on the stripping away from the authoritative texts (both the Bible and legal texts) all medieval accretions and apparatus, thus leaving individuals free to interpret the texts themselves in whatever way seemed most consonant with the new sensibilities.[8] Medieval authors might continue to be studied in the schools, and even occasionally invoked, but only as isolated figures and not as representatives of a common and unbroken tradition to which one was accountable, and which needed to be mastered in its entirety.

The last period to be considered here is the one that is just coming to an end. The study of the Bible in the nineteenth and twentieth centuries has been marked especially by scientific detachment and historical positivism (of both the materialist and the idealist variety). These characteristics can be seen clearly in the spectacular success story of modern biblical criticism. The nineteenth century saw the emergence, for the first time, of the Study of the Bible as an independent discipline, divorced from the ecclesiastical disciplines of law and theology, and following its own scientific principles and procedures. For the professionals in this field, medieval exegesis was important only as a source of contamination of the text—something that needed to be stripped away in order to discover the *ipsissima verba* and the true, historical meaning of the original. The interlocutors of the modern biblical critic are other, similarly trained scholars, and for the proper exercise of their task, they have nothing of value to learn from the medieval authors.[9] As a result, the study of medieval biblical interpretation disappeared almost entirely from the schools. Almost, but not quite.

By the middle of the twentieth century a few scholars had begun the task of studying critically the medieval contribution to biblical interpretation. How were they to respond to the challenge posed by the triumph of modern biblical criticism? The most popular response was to argue that there were, indeed, a few writers in the Middle Ages who shared something of the scientific values and approaches of the modern critic, and who pointed the way to the bright future of modern exegesis. One of the earliest and most influential of such arguments, for example, was that there were two fundamental types of medieval exegesis, represented respectively by the Antiochene and the Alexandrian "schools." The Antiochenes, the heroes of this story, were interested in the literal meaning of the text, in grammatical analysis, and in using the natural history and geography to illuminate and understand it, whereas the Alexandrians (under the influence of Philo and Origen) relied primarily on allegory and spiritual interpretations. The Antiochenes, we are told, "set out to correct the abuse of the allegorical method." They shifted the emphasis "back to earth, and to man on earth." And, most important, "Antiochene principles favoured the development of [modern] biblical scholarship."[10] The congeniality of this formulation is obvious, and its historical inaccuracy and implausibility seems not to have mattered to anyone. The two schools correspond neatly to the modern division between critical, human-centered scholarship, on the one hand, and obscurantist medieval piety on the other. Through championing of the former and discounting of the latter, at least a thin thread could be found in the Middle Ages which could be traced forward to the modern biblical scholar.

However attractive this approach may be, it is finally unsatisfying to all parties. It fails to provide any medieval texts or arguments (even those of the so-called "Antiochenes" and their scattered descendants) that can enter into the discussions of modern biblical critics, and, more important, it distorts the medieval evidence by forcing it into two divergent and opposing currents of thought: something that is largely alien to the medieval experience.

But what was that medieval experience? and how can we recover it more adequately? It is to address that question that scholars gathered in Toronto in 1997, with representatives of the other great interpretive traditions of the Middle Ages. The study of medieval biblical interpretation is still in its infancy. When it has been subjected for some time to the kind of searching and thoughtful consideration that one sees in these papers, we will be well on our way to recovering it as an important part of our intellectual inheritance.

Notes

1. This insistence on unity across time and space is seen already in the Gospel of John, in Jesus' repeated prayer for his disciples and for those who will follow after them, "that they might be one," *ut unum sint* (John 17: 11, 21, 22, 23, etc). The "Nicene" Creed (325 x 381) famously professes a belief in the "one, catholic and apostolic church." It is not difficult to see the latter profession as an attempt to instantiate the unity for which Jesus prayed.

2. This is the so-called "Vincentian Canon," a threefold test of catholicity, formulated by Vincent of Lerins (d. ca. 450).

3. For a critical introduction to the full range of writings and writers of this period, see Johannes Quasten, *Patrology*, 4 vols. (Westminster, Md.: Newman Press, 1950–86).

4. One can find a useful overview of this period in the *New Cambridge Medieval History*, v. 2. *c. 700–c. 900*, ed. Rosamond McKitterick (Cambridge: Cambridge University Press, 1995).

5. Still the best historical introduction to this period is the pioneering work of Beryl Smalley, *The Study of the Bible in the Middle Ages*, 4th ed. (Oxford: Basil Blackwell, 1984). The "Vulgate" or common Latin text of the Bible is widely available, and an English translation was made in the fifteenth and sixteenth centuries at Douay (1609) and Rheims (1582). The Ordinary Gloss is less readily available and has never been translated from the Latin; it is best consulted in the photostatic reprint of the Editio princeps, Strasbourg 1480–81, published in four volumes by Brepols of Turnhout (1992) with an introduction by Karlfried Froehlich and Margaret T. Gibson. The "Master of the Histories" was Peter Comestor (d. ca. 1179); his *Historia scholastica* can most easily be consulted in PL 198; there is no translation.

6. Beryl Smalley called this common view into question in *The Study of the Bible in the Middle Ages*, through her painstaking evocation of the importance of literal/historical exegesis, and her relegation of "spiritual" exegesis to a secondary and decorative (if not actually destructive) activity. Henri de Lubac articulates the common view in his monumental *Exégèse médiévale: les quatre sens de l'Ecriture*, 4 vols. (Paris: Aubier, 1959–64); volume one has appeared recently in English translation: *Medieval Exegesis: The Four Senses of Scripture*, trans. Mark Sebanc (Grand Rapids Mich.: William. Eerdmann, 1998).

7. Thomas Aquinas sums up the traditional view most succinctly: "The author of Holy Writ is God, in whose power it is to signify his meaning not by words only, as man also can do, but also by things themselves. So, whereas in every other science things are signified by words, this

science has the property that the things signified by the words have themselves also a meaning. Therefore the first meaning, whereby words signify things, belongs to the first sense, the historical or literal. That meaning whereby things signified by words have themselves also a meaning is called the spiritual sense. . . ." *Summa theologiae* 1.1.10c.

8. In law this type of interpretation became known as the *mos gallicus*, the "French style," as opposed to the more traditional *mos italicus*, the "Italian style." In the latter, the authoritative texts continued to be studied in the context of an unbroken tradition of commentary and scholarship.

9. This can be verified by reading any modern biblical commentary. I know of no instance where a modern biblical scholar has entered into serious engagement with any medieval interpretation of a text.

10. The quotations are all from Smalley, *Study of the Bible*, 14–15.

13

The Letter of the Law

Carolingian Exegetes and the Old Testament

ABIGAIL FIREY

"You force and compel me, dearest brother, Abbot Theodemir, and, as I would say, with a Peevish Soul rebuke me that for too long I ran wild and did not comply with your order for an exposition of Leviticus," wrote Claudius of Turin in 823 in the preface to his commentary *In libros informationum litterae et spiritus super Leviticum.*[1] With scarcely more enthusiasm, sometime between 822 and 829,[2] his contemporary Hrabanus Maurus began *his* preface to *his* commentary on Leviticus: "It is a hard task and one beyond my own powers that you have commanded me recently to undertake, that I should explain to you in the spiritual sense, in order, the five books of Mosaic Law."[3] While these remarks might seem to be mere prefatory *topoi*, one senses a certain sincerity, especially in light of the enthusiasm with which Hrabanus introduced his commentary on Exodus, which he described as a book that stood out in merit, in which almost all the sacraments of the present Church were instituted, fostered, and regulated.[4] The dread voiced by these authors as they confronted Leviticus seems all the more comprehensible in view of the scarcity of patristic commentaries on the third book of the Torah. The favored authorities of Carolingian intellectuals—Augustine, Gregory, Jerome, Ambrose—left no works dedicated specifically to detailed exegesis of this text, and so Hrabanus relied on Hesychius and Origen, the latter the only author mentioned by Cassiodorus as an interpreter of Leviticus in the description of his cabinets of biblical commentaries.[5] Not only was Leviticus addressed only intermittently by most patristic writers, but few exegetes chose to explore it systematically after Claudius and Hrabanus: the next major commentary appears to be that of Ralph of Flaix in the twelfth century.[6]

Why, then, within the space of at most seven years, did two leading Carolingian scholars find themselves compelled to publish commentaries on the difficult, substantial, often recondite, and usually neglected Priestly Code of ancient Israel? While it might appear that Hrabanus and Claudius were simply victims of social obligations and a highly systematized, programmatic approach to biblical studies in which commentators marched through the books of the Old Testament in sequence,[7] it may be suggested that their commentaries on Leviticus were composed in the context of a volatile cultural milieu, in which the topics of the Levitical prescriptions were subjects of current dispute, and in which the definition of the Christian community was as contested, often in the same terms, as it had been in late antiquity, in response to many of the same situations.

To support this initial suggestion that these two Carolingian commentaries on Leviticus were not merely academic exercises, it is useful to review briefly some evidence from sources somewhat outside the range of strictly defined biblical exegesis. Testimony from the seventh, eighth, and ninth centuries shows that in a variety of cross-cultural encounters, Christians referred to Old Testament ritual, dietary, and marital prescriptions as they attempted to cast a formulation of Christian identity in the midst of cultural diversity. For clerics trained to discern reality through a biblical lens, the Levitical prescriptions were a logical resource, but also a problematic filter.[8] The sources show a variety of responses, some of them inconsonant. In the northeastern European regions of Saxony in the mid-eighth century, the missionary Boniface attempted to assess the customs of the Frisians, Thuringians, Hessians, and Saxons, and sent letters to Bishop Daniel of Winchester and Pope Zacharias in which, like so many sojourners in foreign parts, he is startled by culinary options. "There are our struggles against . . . false priests and hypocrites, who are teaching new divisions and offering diverse errors to the people, some abstaining from the food that God created to be taken; some, feeding only on milk and honey, reject bread and other foods . . . ," he laments.[9] In 732 Pope Gregory III had instructed him "that people should eat as food wild or domestic horses is filthy and accursed"[10]; sixteen years later, Boniface was apparently still appealing to the papacy for clarification of dietary regulation, for Zacharias wrote to him, "About the birds, that is the jackdaws, crows, and storks. These are certainly to be advised against in the diet of Christians. And to eat of beavers, hares, and forest ponies is far worse. But, most holy brother, you are well versed in the sacred Scriptures concerning all these matters."[11]

Boniface's training in England may have exposed him to a particularly strong tradition of Christian dietary analysis. Theodore of Tarsus, bishop of Canterbury, had died scarcely twenty years before Boniface's first expedition to Frisia, and for twenty years before that (669–690 C.E.) had been commenting on the differences in diet between his fellow Greeks and the Romans.[12] Penitential traditions associated with Theodore elaborated dietary regulation according to Levitical principles, such as the proscription of consuming of strangled or suffocated animals, animals torn by beasts, and similar adaptations of the Levitical code.[13] Other early medieval penitential literature is rich in such reformulations of Levitical prescriptions.[14] Secular law, too, became a vehicle for transmission of these precepts, as Theodore's injunctions entered into the preface of Alfred's laws.[15] Beyond the penitential tradition, Levitical prescriptions entered into the broader traditions of canon law. The English Legatine synods of 786 adopted similar material, citing the Greek Christians as precedent.[16] The *Collectio canonum hibernensis*, usually dated to the late eighth or early ninth century, transmits the dietary canons of Theodore.[17] A Breton canon law manuscript of the same period, Orléans 221, transmits a text known as the *Liber ex lege Moysi*, which comprises excerpts from Leviticus, Numbers, and Deuteronomy, including the dietary laws.[18] The interest in Levitical or quasi-Levitical regulation is revealed, too, in late eighth-century papal correspondence. Not only did the Greek and Syriac popes Zacharias and Gregory III counsel Boniface, but Pope Hadrian, between 785 and 791, wrote to Egila, who was engaged in pastoral work in Spain, regarding the consumption of pork and meat suffocated in its own blood.[19]

Yet counter to this apparent incorporation of Levitical law in Christian practice are contemporary expressions of concern about Judaizing. Insular sources refer to charges of Judaizing. Bede makes several references to the supercession of Mosaic Law, although he is curiously reticent on the matter of diet.[20] In response to Boniface's complaints, Pope Zacharias in 745 convened a synod in Rome that condemned the priest Clement, "who, spurning synodal law, affirms on his own authority that he can be a bishop; imposing Judaism, he judges that it is right for a Christian, if he wishes, to marry the widowed wife of a dead brother."[21] Bishop Elipandus of Toledo in the early 780s reproved the rigorist Migetius for his dietary regulation.[22]

In these cases, it was the customs and practices of Judaism, rather than the fundamental confessional beliefs, that drew criticism. In other words, the outer boundaries of cultural definition were perceived as frangible, endangered. External signs represented the interior condition, and some cultural practices could not be disassociated from religious identity. These indications of mutated religious identity may have seemed particularly dangerous in an environment harboring different religious populations, and in which conversions were a real possibility. Bernhard Blumenkranz noted that Judaism in antiquity and the early Middle Ages was more proselytic than in other eras, and it would be helpful if the extant sources revealed more about the patterns, existence, or absence of Jewish missions in the late eighth century.[23]

The instance of conversion in the early ninth century most notorious among historians is that of Bodo, called Eleazar after his conversion.[24] Bodo seems to have been a deacon who moved at the heart of the court of Louis the Pious. In 839 he departed from France on the pretext of making a pilgrimage to Rome. When he reached southern Gaul, instead of proceeding to Rome, he diverted his entourage to Spain, where he and his nephew converted to Judaism and became members of the Jewish community in Saragossa. From there, he annoyed his former co-religionists by engaging in vivacious polemic: we are fortunate to have some surviving manuscript fragments of an exchange between Eleazar and the Christian Paul Alvarus.[25]

For present purposes, two points about Bodo's conversion seem particularly noteworthy. First, what his scandalized contemporaries recorded in their accounts of his conversion were the changes in the external signs: he was circumcised, he grew a beard, "wholly made a Jew in clothing," he wore the *cingulum* or *zonar* that was prescribed in Ummayad Spain as the sign distinguishing the non-Muslim population from the Muslim. (He also took a wife.)[26]

Second, it was in the realm of biblical exegesis that Eleazar waged his confessional campaign. In his analysis of language and text, he shows how the Carolingian promotion of scholarly biblical study bred its own challenges. Eleazar's criticism of Christian exegetes is that they do not know, or that they ignore, the letter of the text. His first definition of the letter is philological: he asserts that Christians, and more particularly Jerome, have embraced selective mistranslations of the Hebrew text, as, for example, when they translate the "young woman" who will bear the Messiah as "a virgin."[27] While he accepts Jerome's translation of the Psalms as faithful, he considers the translations of the other books false.[28] It appears that Eleazar reproved Christians reading the Bible in different senses. The Jews, he seems to argue, having one text, have one faith, but among the Christians he knew in the palace of the king of the Franks, there were fourteen catholics who represented different cults.[29] He then turns to the heart of his argument:

that Christians, who profess to recognize the Prophets and the Law, do not observe the Law. The Law which was written by the finger of God is the Law of which the Lord said in the book of Deuteronomy, 'Put in your heart and in your soul these words which I have said to you.'"[30]

Eleazar's words, as reconstructed by Bernhard Blumenkranz, that are intriguing to the textual historian: "I affirm that your authors, or rather your compilers, in the books in which you transmit your arguments, are in profound error."[31] In the following paean to the Lord's disposition of Israel among the nations, Eleazar quotes Ezekiel 36:26–28: "And I shall give you a new heart, and I shall put in you a new spirit: I shall take away the heart of stone from your flesh and I shall give you a heart of flesh. And I shall put my spirit among you, and I shall cause you to follow my ordinances, and that you observe and practice my laws. And you shall live in the land that I have given to your fathers, you shall be my people, and I shall be your God. . . ." "These passages led me to Judaize (*iudaizare*)," says Eleazar; "may they lead you to do likewise."[32]

Eleazar's rejection of the Christian faith, then, was expressed as rejection of a particular exegetical tradition, the tradition that was exemplified a decade earlier in the commentaries of Claudius and Hrabanus. The elements Eleazar adduced—the heart, the flesh, and the spirit—were construed differently by this pair of Christian exegetes.

Both Claudius and Hrabanus record a passage from Origen in their prefaces that melds the language of Christology with the language of exegesis to establish a deeper significance to the methods of scriptural interpretation:

> Because indeed you know well, just as in the last days the Word of God clothed in flesh proceeded from Maria [Hrabanus: *Maria virgine*] into the world, and what was seen in him was one thing, what was understood was another, for the aspect of the flesh appeared to all, but only to the few and the elect was knowledge of his divinity given. And so also when through the prophets or through the Lawgiver the Word of God was proffered to men, not without suitable garments was he proffered. For just as there he was covered with the veil of the flesh, so here he is covered with the veil of the letter: so that just as indeed the letter is seen as the flesh, so truly, hiding inside, the spiritual sense is perceived as divinity.[33]

By locating their discussion at the intersection of the language of theology and exegesis, Claudius and Hrabanus, following the trajectory established by Origen, extend their hermeneutic to a description of the world outside the text, to the relation of the flesh and the spirit, and the further relation of humanity to Christ. This approach effectively recasts the book about the signifiers of Judaism into a book about the mystery of the Incarnation and, in transforming one fleshly paradigm to another, approaches the critical point of distinction between the faiths, the acceptance of Jesus as Messiah. While exegesis of the patriarchal histories provided a past for Christians, and the prophets signaled the future now come, the Law described some present condition, and so its exegesis was neither a rehearsal of history nor an exposition of prefigurations, but rather an act of conversion.[34]

Yet the project of converting the text of Leviticus would present particular problems to the exegetes. Law, intended to be read literally, is difficult to allegorize. The "spirit" of the law is its intent, and upon this jurists can comment, but spiritualization of earthly prescriptions is no simple task. Second, the text of Leviticus, which is fully consistent in its literal reading, comprises a variety of modes of legislation, from ethical to ritual prescription, from care for the economically deprived to the prohibition of eating camels. Christian exegetes had to develop a rationale for accepting or adopting some precepts while rejecting, through transformation, others, all without seeming arbitrary, or even self-serving, in their interpretive stances.

Augustine had proposed a distinction between the laws and prescriptions of permanent value and the ceremonial law, limited in its duration. The words of the ceremonial law still had value, for not one word of scripture is without value, but (and here we recall the training of Hrabanus and especially Claudius in Augustinian scholarship) their significance is hidden; the New Testament of the Spirit is hidden within the Old Testament of the Flesh, the interior is hidden within the exterior; hence, he explained, the Mosaic law was written in stone, and the Gospel implanted in the heart.[35] Augustine's historical vision, however, and means of accounting for the continued existence of the Jewish community permitted further debate among some Christians with respect to Mosaic Law. In his exegesis of Paul's Letter to the Romans, Augustine distinguished between the children of the flesh and the children of the spirit: Christians are children of the Spirit, and Jews, although according to the flesh the sons of Jacob, had lost the inheritance of the covenant. "He who resembles Abraham is the son of Abraham; he who is far from Abraham's faith has lost the claim to descent from Abraham." In claiming that the ancient Israelites were the prefiguration of the Church, and that the Covenant had now passed to the Christian faithful, Augustine raised the possibility that Christians could identify themselves as the "true Jews" and, from that point of identification, reenter into the Mosaic rituals attendant upon subscription to the Covenant. In his *De cavendo Iudaismo* (letter 196), Augustine responded to the questions of whether Christians should call themselves Jews or Israelites, and, notably, whether they should observe Jewish dietary law.[36]

Hrabanus had embraced this account of the transfer of the covenant and referred to it upon numerous occasions in his writings, including his commentary on Leviticus.[37] Augustine's explanations, however, were in the context of conceptual, rather than textual, explication. Carolingian exegetes, when they undertook full verse-by-verse commentary, would have to be agile and flexible in their technique to progress through the sequence of regulations that varied in their degree of concord with, and deviation from, Christian premises and practices.

It is in the social prescriptions and in the regulation of outward signs that some of Hrabanus's varied exegetical strategies emerge most clearly.[38] Like the earlier seventh- and eighth-century readers of Leviticus who perceived it as a penitential code, so did Hrabanus, himself the author of two penitentials, read it as a penitential text. In his reading, however, the penitential associations of Leviticus are transferred from external acts to analysis of interior conditions, and he reframes the text around the same deadly sins that framed many early medieval penitentials. Thus the clean and unclean animals become emblems of sinful interior conditions, and in this symbolic bestiary we find the drunkard, the lecher, the miser, and so forth. Among the birds, "The hoopoe is a mournful animal, and it is one loving sorrow: it is, moreover, sadness that works death in the world, because it behoves him who loves God to rejoice always, to pray without intermission, to give thanks for all things, because joy is the fruit of the spirit."[39]

This rather charming approach to Leviticus as fable has, however, an aspect more disturbing to modern readers. Hrabanus does not simply convert the clean and unclean animals into human failings: continuing to follow Hesychius, he relates those failings back to the Jews. First, he suggests (repeatedly) that the question of whether or not one can eat certain animals is not intended literally: "If indeed," he argues, "'man does not live by bread alone, but in every word which proceeds from the mouth,' then just as bread is the nourishment of the body, so also the Law of God is the nourishment of the soul."[40] Hrabanus then proposes a second qualification of his lemma, "You may eat everything among the beasts which has a divided hoof and chews the cud" (Lev 11:13). "When he said this," argues Hrabanus, "he distinguished not beasts but the customs of men."

> And so there are those men in the world who "chew the cud," who carry ever in their mouths as if it were food the divine precepts; there are also those who divide the hoof, because, trusting in two Testaments, the Law and the Gospels, they stand on the firm step of innocence and justice. Just as the Jews indeed ruminate upon the words of the Law but do not divide the hoof, that is, because they do not receive the two Testaments, and do not place the steps of their faith on the Father and the Son, they are considered for this reason unclean. Heretics, also, although they divide the hoof, believing in the Father and the Son, and receiving two Testaments, but because they do not ruminate the doctrine of truth in their mouths, notwithstanding are themselves also unclean.[41]

Then, in the category of cud-chewing but undivided in hoof, Hrabanus comes to the camel.

> The camel is the Jew, swollen with pride, just as were the Scribes and Pharisees, to whom the Lord said, "straining out a gnat and swallowing a camel." Therefore the Scribes and Pharisees eat while ruminating, because they glory in meditation upon the letter of the law, and in the observance of the sabbath, and of purifications and sacrifices and other such things; they do not, however, in those things which are eaten by them, divide the hoof, and they do not distinguish the letter from the spirit, and on account of those things, their knowledge is unclean.[42]

A striking aspect in most of Hrabanus's explications is the interweaving of the textual and the customary. It is in the rejection of books that the Jews become unclean, the words in the mouth become the heretics' uncleanness. The word that nourishes is represented by the food that nourishes, because the Word was made flesh. In sum, this exegesis of Leviticus is not merely explication, disarmament, and endowment of new meaning, it is an intrinsically Christological and Messianic reading of the text.

It is this Christological aspect of their commentaries on Leviticus that marks both Hrabanus and Claudius as members of their generation. Carolingian jurists and exegetes had been considerably exercised over the Adoptionist controversy between the 780s and the 820s and had had to confront the paradox of Christ's simultaneous humanity and divinity. In their efforts to refute a heresy that emphasized his human nature, an emphasis that commentators explicitly noted as parallel to the Jewish refusal to recognize his divinity, the scholars around Hrabanus and Claudius worked to excavate biblical and patristic texts that supported the argument for the presence of divinity in the flesh.[43] Paradox, however, depends on the combination of seemingly opposite or irreconcilable qualities, and when the dichotomy of the Word and the Flesh became the frame for interpretation of Leviticus, literal and spiritual readings became opposed, rather than forming the spectrum of interpretation that they present in other biblical commentaries.[44]

Although Claudius was described with considerable animosity by Jonas of Orléans and Dungal as a partisan of his compatriot the Adoptionist Felix of Urgel, who was exiled to Lyons during Claudius's sojourn there, there appears to be no reason to construe the commentary on Leviticus as adumbrated by Adoptionist Christology.[45] Like Hrabanus, Claudius dwells upon the metaphysical intersections of the words of Scripture, the Word incarnate, and the mastication of the word in the mouths of those who hear the preached word, and thus his imagery delicately evokes the Word in the eucharistic Body chewed by the Christian faithful. In a passage almost certainly inspired by, if not drawn from Augustine, Claudius relates the word that is heard by the ruminating listener to food that is chewed, and the word that is forgotten to food that is swallowed without rumination. The scriptural locus to which the conceit is attached is "Desirable treasure rests in the mouth of the wise; but the foolish man swallows it" (Prov 20: 21): in one of the closest textual parallels, Augustine states explicitly that the treasure is like bread.[46]

In matters of faith, Claudius concurs with Hrabanus in reading carnal uncleanness as signifying defects in belief. He, too, cites the passage construing the ruminating and cloven-hooved animals as Christians, Jews, and heretics.[47] In parallel exegesis, when Hrabanus and Claudius interpret Leviticus 13, because both understand the leprosies to be monitored by the priest as signs of spiritual diseases, there is a similar parsing of the uncleanness as indicating the differences between Christians, Jews, and heretics: the leprosy of the head, which pertains in such a reading to the head of the Church, is the leprosy of Judaism and Christological heretics.[48] Similarly, the betrothed slave-woman bedded in Leviticus 19:20 is for both Hrabanus and Claudius Synagogue, enslaved by law until joined to the body of Christ.[49]

In his moral exegesis, that is, the hermeneutic that pertains to conduct and the condition of the individual soul, Claudius seems less prone than Hrabanus to use concrete metaphors that transfer the uncleanness to particular persons. Whereas Hrabanus constructs his exegesis around the psychological, Claudius's preference is for metaphysical analysis. Unlike Hrabanus, he chooses not to draw upon Hesychius for explication of the clean and unclean animals. Hrabanus extended the contrast between Jews and Christians, initiated in the general exegesis of the clean and unclean animals, by proceeding to the metaphor of the camel and the proud Jew; Claudius turns instead to the description of the camel that apparently isolates its twisting neck rather than its hump as the distinguishing feature: "What does the Law mean when it states: 'You shall not eat the camel'? From the example of an animal, it condemns a malformed life and one twisted by crimes."[50] Hrabanus pursues his theme further by continuing to draw on Hesychius for his explanation of the rock-badger. In his description of the unclean rock-badger,[51] Hesychius, through an elaborate philological exercise, equated the rock-badger (or rock-rabbit) of Leviticus 11:5, the *chirogrillus*, to the *erinaceus*[52] of Psalm 103, and quoted the Psalm as saying, "The rocks are a refuge for the badgers."[53] From this premise, he proceeded: "the rock-badger, moreover, is indeed weak, but rapacious and savage and they call him lethal, because indeed in every people, but especially among the people of the Jews, he is present. . . . How timid and weak the sons of the Jews be, the divine voice shows when it says, 'Woe to your fearful hearts and remiss hands.' Moreover, how much injustice and savagery are among them, hear Isaiah saying, etc. . . ."[54] Claudius, on the other hand, shows little interest in either the rock-badger, the hare, the pig, or the psychological vices they might represent: he merely notes their basic habits and uncleanness and then supplies a passage from Origen that reiterates his previous point that what matters is the resonance of the articulated word in the soul:

> There are those who are outside our religion, or those who are among us, who indeed part the hoof and so advance in their lives that they prepare their deeds for the coming age. For many both learn thus from the philosophers and believe there is a future judgement. For they are aware of the immortal soul and they confess a reward is owed to all good people. Some of the heretics do this, and inasmuch as they expect it, they have a fear of the future judgement and they temper their deed more cautiously as being liable to be examined in the divine judgement. But neither of these chews the cud nor recalls [Barkley: applies] the cud. For hearing what was written in the Law of God, he does not meditate upon it and recall [Barkley: apply] it with a keen and spiritual understanding. But when he hears something, he immediately either disdains or despises it and does not look for what valuable understanding is concealed in the more common words.[55]

Claudius reserves much of his moral exegesis for the later passages on leprosy, where he can excavate the dense descriptions of defects in the human flesh and relay them as signifiers of sinful interior conditions. This shift to examination of the universal experience of human disease tends to produce a commentary marked only lightly by religious distinction. In contrast, Hrabanus seems inclined to keep before the reader's eyes the fact that Leviticus is a Jewish text.[56]

Although Claudius seems less interested in the boundaries delineating either the historical or the present Jewish and Christian communities, in his reading of Leviticus he implicitly shares the project of Christian reclamation of the text from the Judaic tradition. The conversion of Jewish law to a Christian exposition of faith and morals became textually entangled in the continuing exploration of the mysterious relation of carnality and spirituality in Christian theology. Common to both Claudius and Hrabanus is the self-conscious, perpetual interweaving of the conceit of the spiritual meaning veiled by the letter, and the interior condition of the soul veiled in the flesh. The peculiar carnality of Leviticus, with its detailed description of flesh foods, diseases of the flesh, emissions of the male and female body, and even the status of enslaved flesh, provided both exegetes with rich material for their hermeneutic of the body as text and of the text as an ingestible, copulative, embodied word. Both interpreters resort to exegetical methods that intensified the carnality of the text so as to sanctify it.

The similarities and differences in their efforts may illuminate the environment of Carolingian biblical exegesis for scholars of Hrabanus's and Claudius's generation, and the extent to which that environment had changed from that known to Theodore and Boniface. In the world of Theodore, himself a philological and historical exegete,[57] and Boniface, Christians could follow Levitical prescriptions as sacral rituals that were readily and suitably adapted in a rural, tribal, and converting culture that still had a keen sense of the sacrality of the universe and the need for ritual negotiation of that universe.

While Theodore was developing ecclesiastical government among the barely Christianized Angles and Saxons, in Spain the Visigothic kings were enacting legislation restricting the rights of Jews, banning Jewish–Christian intermarriage, forbidding proselytizing, and prohibiting Jews from holding public office. There were also restrictions upon Jewish rituals and customs, including circumcision and dietary observances.[58] Collective memory of the seventh-century persecutions of the Jews in Spain must have penetrated the Carolingian realms, especially southern Gaul, where not only Visigothic personnel but also Spanish theological and legal texts circulated freely. What is not yet clear is in what form that memory survived transmission to Carolingian Gaul.

It would seem that the concern to delineate Jewish and Christian practices may have developed in an environment in which the social and political relations between Jewish and Christian communities were in a period of flux, and in which Christian intellectuals were negotiating with a proximate, apparently substantial, and possibly proselytizing Jewish population. In the Christian theological struggle to understand the flesh and its role in both the human condition and divine history, external signs presented a particular problem. The identification of the letter with flesh, in an environment in which Jews did give the text a literal reading and observed the outward signs in the flesh, caused some Christian exegetes to reject the letter overtly by decrying it as specifically Jewish, as the law that kills.[59] Allegorical exegesis of Levitical prescriptions set boundaries to Christian adoption of Jewish practices and delimited the Jewish and Christian communities by controlling the external signifiers of faith.

Hrabanus Maurus is the interesting point of juncture between the two traditions of adaptation and rejection of Jewish law. Hrabanus was the heir of Boniface in so many ways. He was a monk of Fulda, the monastery founded by Boniface, before becoming the bishop of Mainz, Boniface's episcopal see. Manuscripts of Theodore's commentaries on Leviticus were still being copied in the northeastern scriptoria that would have supplied his books.[60] Nevertheless, Hrabanus is a figure who shows the transition to the admired model of *Romanitas*, and he is departing from the world of Boniface and Theodore and entering into the new cultural configuration of later Carolingian Francia, with both its possibilities and dangers. In his commentary on Leviticus, the rhetoric of concrete images to distinguish Christian behavior from non-Christian behavior frequently leads Hrabanus to apparent anti-Judaic polemic. The important questions about his intent, and the understanding assigned to his text by an audience, remain unanswered and perhaps unanswerable. It may be noted, however, that both of his penitentials, although short, include chapters detailing the canonistic prohibitions of Jewish and Christian social mingling—over meals, in marriage, and in slave ownership.[61]

The Visigoth Claudius, on the other hand, is a salutary reminder of the variety of perspectives evident in even a closely circumscribed range of literary production. Before becoming bishop of Turin, he trained at Lyons, a site notorious among historians because of the anti-Judaic letters and treatises written by two of its prominent Carolingian bishops, Amulo and Agobard.[62] It is important, however, to recognize the evidence in Lyons for complex dynamics of negotiation and accommodation, as well as antipathy, with respect to the local Jewish community.[63] In his commentary on Leviticus, the voice of Claudius is one that minimizes the divergence of Jewish and Christian practices, and the relative absence of anti-Judaic polemic in this work suggests just how complex, varied, and unpredictable were Carolingian attitudes concerning Jews.

Surrounding both scholars was a vapor of discourse comprising apparently live concerns about judaizing, the lingering debate over the relation of divinity and humanity in Christ, the incipient and related controversy over the eucharist, and the polarization of the concrete and the abstract in the iconoclasm controversy. Ultimately, the differences between Hrabanus and Claudius may be less indicative of their historical circumstances than of their theological interests. Hrabanus was steeped in monastic ritual and asceticism, and he wrote penitentials: for him, external signs seem to have been particularly evocative.[64] Despite his rejection of the literal reading of the text's regulation of carnal practices, Hrabanus provides a reading that operates at a fairly immediate human level of psychology and identity. Claudius, whose predilection for Augustinian abstraction would eventually place him in a heterodox position in the iconoclasm controversy, and whose rejection of visual representation extended to ridding his new diocese of Turin of its images, directs interpretation to metaphysical experience of God, and the more abstract, intangible manifestations of the Word.[65]

Yet both Hrabanus and Claudius, through somewhat different approaches, circumscribe the external signs and gestures manifested by Christians and seem to represent an important transition to an altered appreciation of signs, a transition with implications for their sacramental value. Both offered an alternative to the earlier juridical sources, penitentials, and papal decretals, which had engaged the legalities of Leviticus on their own terms. Whereas Law can easily and seamlessly incorporate prescriptions from other codes, because of the nearly universal formulaic cast of proscriptions, it cannot, without commentary or gloss, adjust the meaning of those proscriptions. Thus, exegesis rather than law was the essential mode for realignment of the meaning of Leviticus. The rhetorical devices for mingling and then redistinguishing elements of the language of law, theology, and exegesis were thoroughly exploited in the Carolingian Levitical commentaries. Few canon law texts composed after the publication of Hrabanus's and Claudius's commentaries on Leviticus refer overtly to Levitical precedent.[66] Law, exegesis, and cultural experience all shifted in response to each other. It appears that perhaps largely through the persuasive force of a particular line of hermeneutical reasoning, practices that in some early medieval times and places were common to Jews and Christians became the marks that distinguished them. The commentaries of Hrabanus and Claudius may well mark an important stage in the development of the Christian perception of Jews as Other, in terms not only of doctrine, but also of culture.

Notes

1. "Cogis et compellis, carissime frater Theodemire abba, atque, ut ita dicam, stomachanti animo me reprehendis diu siluisse nec paruisse iussioni tue in expositione Levitici." Claudius's *Praefatio* is printed in PL 104. 615–20, and also was edited by E. Dümmler, in *MGH Epp.* 4: 602–5. Although Stegmüller, 2. 1951, reports two Carolingian manuscripts of the still unedited commentary (Rheims, Bibliothèque municipale, MS 74 and MS 124), the correct shelf-mark of the sole existing MS is 123. Michael Gorman has established that the reference to MS Rheims 74 is erroneous (personal communication, February 7, 1998); cf. Gorman, "The Commentary on Genesis of Claudius of Turin," 284 n. 28, 321. On the exegetical work of Claudius, see also Cavadini "Claudius of Turin"; Hablitzel, "Hrabanus Maurus und Claudius von Turin;" and Matter, "Theological Freedom."

2. These are the dates supplied in Stegmüller, 5. 7024; PL 108. 245–586 is annotated with a suggested date of 834 C.E.

3. "Arduum opus et ultra proprias vires me aggredi jampridem jussisti, ut quinque libros Mosaicae legis, quos Hebraei Torach appellant, sensu spiritali tibi per ordinem exponerem . . . ," PL 108. 246. Of the extensive literature on Hrabanus (see Spelsberg, *Hrabanus*), most pertinent to the present discussion are Blumenkranz, "Raban Maur et Saint Augustin"; Brunhölzl, "Zur qeisteqen Bedentung"; Hablitzel, *Hrabanus Maurus*; Le Maître, "Les methodes"; Reinelt, "Hrabeanus Maurus"; Reinelt; Rissel, *Rezeption*; Wenger, *Hrabanus Maurus*; and Wilmart, "Les allégories." The value of Reinelt's work is diminished by his lack of awareness of Wilmart's article.

4. "Inter caeteras Scripturas quas Pentateuchus legis continet, merito liber Exodi eminet, in quo pene omnia sacramenta quibus praesens Ecclesia instuitur, nutritur et regitur, figuraliter exprimuntur." PL 108. 9.

5. Cf. Cassiodorus, *Cassiodori Senatoris Institutiones* 1.9, ed. Mynors, 15. Origen's commentary (in Rufinus's translation) has been edited by Baehrens, *Homilien zum Hexateuch in Rufins Übersetzung*; the commentary of Hesychius of Jerusalem (as translated in the sixth century by a certain Jerome) is printed in PG 93. 787–1180. Late antique and early medieval commentaries on the Pentateuch or the Octateuch, did, of course, address Leviticus, but the book did not, of itself, draw interpreters in the way that Genesis or Kings did. Hrabanus's own account of the sources available intimates to his reader that the commentary of Hesychius has some primacy, and notes the difficulties of examining the diffuse references to Leviticus in the Fathers; he refers briefly to Jerome for a general commendation of his project (PL 108. 247).

6. Hrabanus's student Walafrid Strabo did compile an epitome of Hrabanus's commentary. On Carolingian biblical commentaries, see Contreni, "Carolingian"; Gorman, "Wigbod"; Riché, "Méthodes"; Laistner, Early Medieval Commentaries"; McNally, *The Bible*; and Smalley, *Study of the Bible*. Later commentaries are noted in Spicq, *Esquisse*.

7. The foundations for this prevailing perspective are set forth cogently by Contreni, "Carolingian," 1–6; other more or less explicit articulations of the same view surface intermittently in the scholarly literature.

8. This issue attracted considerable attention in the early part of this century; cf. Böckenhoff, "Die römische Kirche"; idem, *Speisesatzungen mosaischer Art*; Fournier, "De quelques infiltrations byzantines," 67–71. Recently, scholars applying anthropological analysis have revisited the regulations of the early medieval penitentials; see Meens, "Pollution," and Lutterbach, "Die Speisegesetzgebung."

9. "Sunt enim nobis . . . pugnae . . . per falsos sacerdotes et hypochritas, offerentes populis et docentes novas sectas et diversi generis errores: quidam abstinentes a cibis, quos Deus ad percipiendum creavit, quidam melle et lacte proprie pascentes se panem et ceteros abiciunt cibos." Boniface of Mainz, *Briefe* no. 63, ed. Tangl, 129.

10. "Inter ea agrestem caballum aliquantos adiunxisti comedere, plerosque et domesticum. Hoc nequaquam fieri deinceps sanctissime sinas frater; sed quibus potueris Christo iuvante modis per omnia compesce et dignam eis interdicito paenitentiam; immundum enim est atque exsecrabile." Ibid., no. 28, ed. Tangl, 50.

11. "In primis de volatilibus, id est de graculis et corniculis atque ciconiis. Quae omnino cavendae sunt ab esu christianorum. Etiam et fibri atque lepores et equi silvatici multo amplius vitandi. Attamen, sanctissime frater, de omnibus scripturis sacris bene compertus es." Ibid., no. 87, ed. Tangl, 196. Cf. Leviticus 11:13; Deuteronomy 14:11. In the absence of textual precedent, the pope sounds less confident: "Nam et hoc inquisisti: post quantum temporis debet lardas comedi. Nobis a patribus institutum pro hoc non est. Tibi autem petenti consilium praebemus, quod non oporteat eum mandi, priusquam super fumo siccetur aut igne coquatur; si vero libet, ut incoctum manducetur, post paschalem festivitatem erit manducandum," ibid., 198.

12. Cf. Böckenhoff, "Die römische Kirche," 191–204; Fournier, "Quelques infiltrations," 69–71.

13. The preferred edition is Finsterwalder, *Die Canones Theodori Cantuariensis*. The texts printed in F. W. H. Wasserschleben, *Die Bussordnungen der abendländischen Kirche*, 182–219, and in an annotated version in Haddan and Stubbs, *Councils and Ecclesiastical Documents*, 173–213 (including a concordance of the various editions). Cf. Charles-Edwards "Penitential of Theodore." Often the biblical referent in the early medieval texts prescribing dietary regulations is obscured by the partial, reduced replication of the Mosaic code in Acts 15:19: "Therefore my judgment is that we should not trouble those of the Gentiles who turn to God, but should write

to them to abstain from the pollutions of idols and from unchastity and from what is strangled and from blood" (trans. RSV). Sufficient evidence is in specific explications or explicit references to the texts of Leviticus, Numbers, and Deuteronomy to warrant a general description of the prescriptions as "Levitical." For example, when Theodore's text, "Aves, animalia et cetera si in retibus strangulantur, non sunt comedenda hominibus, nec quod accipiter oppresserit, si mortua inveniuntur: quia a quatuor capitulis precipimur in actibus apostolorum abstinere a fornicatione et sanguine et suffocato et idolatria" is transmitted in the *Scarapsus* of Pirmin (d. 753 C.E.), it is modified to read, ". . . animalia vel aves, que bestiae, vel canis, vel accipiter consumaverint, si mortua inveniuntur, quia in Livitico dominus ait . . . (Lev 17:14). Et quattuor capitula actus apostolorum preciperunt abstinere a fornicatione et suffocato et sanguine et idolatria." Pirmin, in Jecker, Heimat, 53; cf. 114–15; cf. Böckenhoff, "Die römische Kirche," 192–94. There is, however, scholarly debate over the extent of the Old Testament foundations for the medieval penitential prescriptions; see Lutterbach, "Speisegesetzgebung," 30–36; Meens, "Pollution," 5.

14. A survey of the references in McNeill and Gamer, *Medieval Handbooks of Penance*, yields the following: Penitential of Theodore 7. 3 (He who drinks blood . . .), 7. 6 (He who eats unclean flesh . . .), 7. 7 (If anyone accidentally touches food with unwashed hands, or if a dog, a cat, a mouse, or an unclean animal . . .), 7. 8 (If a mouse falls into a liquid), 7. 9 (The liquid in which the mouse or weasel is submerged . . .), 7. 10 (If birds drop dung . . .), 7. 11 (Unwittingly to absorb blood with saliva), 7. 12 (If one eats what is polluted by blood); Penitential of Cummean: 11. 12 (He who gives to anyone a liquor in which a mouse or weasel is found dead . . .), 11. 13 (He who afterwards knows that he tasted such a drink . . .), 11. 14 (But if those little beasts are found in the flour . . .), 11. 15 (He who with unfit hand touches liquid food . . .), 11. 18 (Whoever eats or drinks what has been tainted by a household beast, namely, the cat . . .); "The Irish Canons": 1. 12 (The penance for drinking blood . . .), 1. 13 (The penance for eating horseflesh . . .), 1. 14 (The penance for eating flesh which dogs have been eating . . .), 1. 15 (The penance for eating the flesh of a dead beast . . .), 1. 17 (The penance for drinking what has been contaminated by an eagle or crow . . .), 1. 18 (The penance for the illicit drinking of what has been contaminated by a cat . . .), 1. 19 (The penance for the illicit drinking of what has been contaminated by the carcass of a beast . . .), 1. 20 (The penance for the illicit drinking of what has been contaminated by the dead body of a mouse . . .); The Canons of Adamnon: canons 1–14 and 17–20 are all descriptions and definitions of clean and unclean animals and food; "An Old Irish Penitential": 1. 2 (Anyone who eats the flesh of a horse . . .), 1. 3 (Anyone who eats flesh which dogs or beasts have been eating, or who eats carrion . . .), 1. 4 (Anyone who drinks liquid in which there is a dead mouse . . .), 1. 5 (Anyone who drinks the leavings of a cat . . . ; Anyone who drinks or eats the leavings of a mouse . . .), 1. 12 (Anyone who gives another anything in which there has been a dead mouse or dead weasel . . .). For other citations; see Meens, "Pollution," and Lutterbach, "Die Speiseqesetzqebung" (who provides a scheme of classification).

15. Levison, *England and the Continent in the Eighth Century*, 101.

16. Haddan and Stubbs, *Councils*, 459 (cap. 19): "Equos etiam plerique in vobis comedunt, quod nullus Christianorum in Orientalibus facit; quod etiam evitate: contendite ut omnia vestra honesta et secundum Dominum fiant."

17. Herrmann Wasserschleben, *Die irische Kanonensammlung*, 217–18: Lib. LIV (*De carnibus edendis*) capp. 12, 13, 14 = Theod. *Poen*. 2. 11. 7, 8; 2. 11. 4; 2. 8. 7; 2. 11. 7, 1, 3, 2, 4.

18. Cf. Fournier, "Le *Liber ex lege Moysi*." The text is also found in MSS Cambridge, Corpus Christi College, 279; London, British Library, Cotton Otto E.XIII and Paris, Bibliothèque Nationale, MS Lat. 3182.

19. Böckenhoff, "Die römische Kirche," 206–7. The text of the letter is found in the *Codex Carolinus*, ed. Gundlach, MGH *Epp*. 3, Ep. 96, pp. 644–47. Fournier, "Quelques infiltrations," 70, notes that Hadrian was from a part of Italy exposed to Byzantine influence.

20. Bede, *Historia ecclesiastica* 3.25, ed. Colgrave and Mynors, 300–302: "Nec tamen hodie

clarescente per mundum evangelio necesse est, immo nec licitum, fidelibus vel circumcidi vel hostias Deo victimarum offerre carnalium." In the *Responsiones* of Gregory I to Augustine of Canterbury embedded in the *Historia ecclesiastica* 1.27 is a passage of exegesis on the unclean foods of the Mosaic law that, drawing upon the standard references to Matthew 15:1, Matthew 15:19, Timothy 1:15, concludes that *ei cibus immundus non est, cui mens inmunda non fuerit*, but the intent of the text is to clarify by analogy that a woman is not polluted by her menses. On the *Responsiones*, cf. Meyvaert, "Bede's Text of the *Libellus Responsionum*"; idem, "Les *Responsiones* de S. Grégoire le Grand"; idem, "Le *Libellus Responsionum* à Augustin de Cantorbéry."

21. "Alter autem hereticus, qui dicitur Clemens, contra catholicam contendit aecclesiam, canones ecclesiarum Christi abnegat et refutat, tractatus et intellectus sanctorum Hieronimi, Augustini, Gregorii recussat. Synodalia iura spernens, proprio sensu adfirmat, se—post duos filios sibi in adulterio natos sub nomine episcopi—esse posse legis christianae episcopum. Iudaismum inducens, iustum esse iudicat christiano, ut, si voluerit, viduam fratris defuncti accipiat uxorem." *Acta synodi Romanae*, 25 Oct. 745, Ep. 59 in *MGH Epp.* 1: 112. Cf. Boniface, *Ep.* 57: "[Clementem] . . . et tamen sacerdotium sibimet vindicabat, adfirmans hoc iustum esse iuxta traditionem veteris testamenti, ut defuncti fratris superstes frater ducat uxorem" (p. 105).

22. Elipandus to Migetius, in PL 96. 859–67 (cf. 865–66). Earlier Spanish examples are presented by Blumenkranz in *Juifs et Chrétiens dans le monde occidental 430–1096*, 62–63.

23. Blumenkranz, "Die christlich-jüdische Missionkonkurrenz," and Giese, "In Judaismum." There is evidence of some early ninth-century concern that Christians are preferring Jewish sermons to Christian ones (both Agobard and Amulo of Lyon complain; see Blumenkranz, *Les auteurs chrétiens latins*, 162, 199). It seems significant, too, that the text of the "Letter by Anna to Seneca," directed apparently to potential pagan proselytes to Judaism, although tentatively dated to the fourth century, should be preserved in a ninth-century manuscript; see Bischoff, *Anecdota novissima*, and Momigliano, "The New Letter by 'Anna' to 'Seneca.'"

24. Recent discussion of this episode can be found in Löwe, "Die Apostasie."

25. Blumenkranz, "Un pamphlet juif médio-latin de polémique antichrétienne."

26. On Bodo's *cingulum*, see Blumenkranz, "Du nouveau sur Bodo-Eléazar?"

27. Blumenkranz, "Un pamphlet," 406.

28. Ibid.

29. Ibid.

30. Ibid., 408: "[Quia dissolute vivitis, dicitis legem esse solutam. Non autem soluta est] lex que digito Dei scripta [est, lex de qua Dominus dicit] in libro Deuteronomio: Ponite hec verba mea in cordibus et in animis vestris." I have followed Blumenkranz's French translation of the Latin. Words in square brackets are supplied by Blumenkranz: cf. p. 403.

31. Ibid.: [Auctores vel potior] compilatores [vestros,] de quorum libris [argumenta trahitis], multum errasse [probo].

32. Ibid, 410, 412. "*Iste sententie me iudaizare coegerunt.* [*Utinam et vos cogant*]."

33. Origen, *In Leviticum Homilia* 1.1, ed. Baehrens, 280: "Sicut in novissimis diebus verbum Dei ex maria carne vestitum processit in hunc mundum et aliud quidem erat, quod videbatur in eo, aliud, quod intellegebatur—carnis namque aspectus in eo patebat omnibus, paucis vero et electis dabatur divinitatis agnitio—ita et cum per prophetas vel legislatorem verbum Dei profertur ad homines, non absque competentibus profertur indumentis. Nam sicut ibi carnis ita hic litterae velamine tegitur, ut littera quidem adspiciatur tamquam caro latens vero spiritalis intrinsecus sensus tanquam divinitas sentiatur." For Hrabanus, see PL 108. 247–48, for Claudius, Rheims MS 123, fol. 2r. As Baehrens notes, Origen was drawing on 2 Corinthians 3:14: "But their minds were hardened, for to this day, when they read the old covenant, that same veil remains unlifted, because only through Christ is it taken away. Yes, to this day whenever Moses is read a veil lies over their minds; but when a man turns to the Lord the veil is removed" (trans. RSV).

34. Cf. Lubac, *Exégèse médiévale*, 1:2, 522–36.

35. *De spiritu et littera* 17.29, cited by Blumenkranz, "Augustin et les juifs," 229.

36. Blumenkranz, "Raban Maur," 234, 236. The latter point became entangled with questions of Pelagian theology, which would also have been a matter of considerable concern to orthodox Carolingian exegetes, because of the ease with which ritual observances could be perceived as human works performed to obtain salvation.

37. Blumenkranz, *Les auteurs chrétiens*, 176 (with references).

38. The present discussion focuses on the social regulations of Leviticus because Hrabanus's exegesis of the section concerning sacrifices reveals his strategies less clearly. The idea of sacrifice is so laden with significance for Christians that prefigurational typologies of the sort used in exegesis of the Prophets to illuminate the role and identity of Christ are almost the only conceivable reading for a Christian exegete. A corollary is that Christian exegetes rejected or neglected any literal reading of the first section of Leviticus. Commentators as early as the first-century author of the Letter of Barnabas had resolved the initial problem that the text appears to mandate sacrifices by adducing citations from the prophets (Hrabanus cites Isa 1:11, Amos 5:25, Jer 7:21–22) to the effect that the Lord no longer wants such sacrifices: cf. Epistle of Barnabus 2:4–10. For most successive Christian commentators, no literal reading other than the historical was viable. (Hrabanus at times considered the possibility that readers might attempt a literal reading, and he offered firm guidance: "Ea quae ad faciem est interpretatio litterae omnino multis videtur esse ridicula"; "Haec quodammodo ad litteram videntur esse ridicula"; "prohibet a servitute legis litterae, et Judaicam doctrinam demonstrat inutilem. . . . Neque enim omnia quae nunc vetita sunt studentur, quippe cum non solum sint ridicula, sed etiam et noxia studentibus ea, quia. . . . Qui observat ventum, non seminat. . . .") An exception to this tradition is presented by Smalley, "An Early Twelfth-Century Commentator." This commentator's interest in the literal sense, evident also in the exegesis of Hugh and Andrew of Saint Victor, Smalley saw as a significant twelfth-century contrast to what she called the "old spiritualist tradition," where Levitical precepts "had no true literal meaning" (p. 90).

39. "Upupa lugubre animal amansque luctuum est: saeculi autem tristitia mortem operatur, propter quod oportet eum qui diligit Deum semper gaudere, sine intermissione orare, in omnibus gratias agere, quia gaudium fructus est spiritus." (PL 108. 357). The passage is drawn from Hesychius (PG 93. 910).

40. "Si enim 'non in solo pane vivit homo, sed in omni verbo quod procedit de ore Dei' (Matt 4), sicut panis nutrimentum corporis, sic et lex Dei nutrimentum est animae, ut pote rationalis rationali virtus et substantia." (PL 108. 351).

41. "Haec itaque munda esse dicit: 'Omne,' inquit, 'quod habet divisam ungulam et ruminat in pecoribus, comedetis.' Quod cum diceret, non pecora sed mores hominum discernebat. Denique hi homines mundi sunt qui ruminant, qui in ore semper portant quasi cibum praecepta divina, hi et ungulam findunt, quia duo Testamenta, Legis et Evangeliorum, credentes, se firmo gressu innocentiae justitiaeque statuunt. Item Judaei ruminant quidem verba Legis, sed ungulam non findunt, hoc est, quod nec duo Testamenta recipiunt, nec in Patrem et Filium fidei suae gressum statuunt, propterea immundi habentur. Haeretici quoque, licet ungulam findant, in Patrem et Filium credentes, et duo Testamenta recipientes, sed quia doctrinam veritatis in ore non ruminant, nihilominus et ipsi immundi sunt" (PL 108. 351–52). The passage is from Isidore of Seville, *Quaestiones de Veteri et Novo Testamento* (PL 83. 325–326); its antecedents are widespread, cf. Irenaeus of Lyons, *Adversus Haereses* 5: 8, ed. Harvey, 2: 340–41, Chromatius of Aquileia, *Tractatus in Mathaeum* 53, ed. Etaix and Lemarié, 464–65; Novatian, *De cibis iudaicis*, ed. Diercks, 94–95; following Isidore, Pseudo-Bede, *In Pentateuchum commentaria—Leviticus*, PL 91. 189–394; cf. col. 345. (See Gorman, "The Commentary on the Pentateuch," for arguments for the Pseudo-Bede tract's Spanish origin.) The image was also familiar to Bede, who describes the holy monk Caedmon as one who, "instructed in the whole course of sacred history . . . learned all that he could . . . and then, memorizing it and ruminating over it, like some clean

animal chewing the cud . . . . " *Historia ecclesiastica* 4. 24, ed. Colgrave and Mynors, 419. Cf. Illich, *In the Vineyard of the Text*, 54–57, for later medieval citations of the clean and ruminating reader.

42. "Camelus est Judaeus tumens per superbiam, quales Scribae sunt et Pharisaei, ad quos dicebat Dominus: 'Liquantes culicem, camelum autem glutientes' (Matt 23:24). Ergo Scribae et Pharisaei ruminantes comedunt, quia in legis litterae gloriantur meditatione, et in cultu sabbati, purificationisque et sacrificiorum, aliorumque similium; ungulam autem non dividunt, ea quae ab eis comeduntur, neque discernunt ab spiritu litteram, et propterea eorum scientia immunda est." (PL 108. 352–53). This passage, too, is from Hesychius (PG 93. 905).

43. For example, Beatus of Liébana, *Adversus Elipandum*, ed. Löfstedt, 135, comments, "Ecce et istos [hereticos] inuenimus similes Iudeorum, quia illi nudauerunt Christum et nudum eum imposuerunt in crucem et ibi mortuus pependit, et ipsa nuditas, crux et mors facit scandalum Iudeis, et dicunt: 'Non est Deus.' Hoc dicunt et isti heretici: 'Non est Deus.' Nudauerunt illi Christum uestimentis, nudant et isti fide. Illis fecit scandalum Christi nuditas, istis facit scandalum Christi humilitas."

44. Explicit rejection of literal readings comes primarily from Hrabanus's citations of Hesychius: "Ab omni fermento malitiae mundum esse fidelem vult, et propter nunc quidem prohibet a servitute legis litterae, et Judaicam doctrinam demonstrat inutilem" (PL 108. 457); "Haec quodammodo ad litteram videatur esse ridicula" (PL 108. 452); etc. Cf. Quasten, *Patrology III*, 489.

45. Jonas of Orléans, *De cultu imaginum* (PL 106. 307); Dungal, *Responsa* (PL 104. 466). Cf. Gorman, "The Commentary on Genesis of Claudius," 279, n. 4; Matter, "Theological Freedom," 52, 59 n. 2; Cavadini, "Claudius," 50, n. 52.

46. Thesaurus desiderabilis requiescit in ore sapientis; vir stultus glutit illum. Rheims MS 123, fol. 57. The Proverbs lemma is a non-Vulgate reading based on the Septuagint. Augustine, *Enarrationes in Psalmos*: "Qui autem thesaurus, idem et panis. Nam si non idem esset thesaurus et panis, non de ipso thesauro alibi scriptum esset: 'Thesaurus desiderabilis requiescit in ore' . . . "; elsewhere, on the lemma Et in lege eius meditabitur die ac nocte, Augustine comments, "Panem istum manducas una hora, et dimittis; panem illum verbi die ac nocte. Quando enim audis, aut quando legis, manducas, quando inde cogitas, ruminas, ut sis animal mundum, non immundum. Quod significat etiam sapienta per Salomon dicens: Thesaurus desiderabilis requiescit in ore . . . " *Enar. in Psalmos* 141, *Sermo ad populum*, cap. 1, ed. Dekkers and Fraipont, 2046; *Enar. in Psalmos* 36, sermo 3, cap. 5, 371. Not only in the *Enarrationes* did Augustine present the construct relating the Proverbs citation to the clean and unclean animals and the memory of what is heard: it is also in *Contra Faustum* 6.7, ed. Zycha, 295. In these latter two texts, Augustine, like Claudius, clarifies that animals are by nature clean, and their uncleanness signifies vice. Claudius's text resembles in many respects sermon 149 of Augustine, but that text is replicated almost verbatim in sermon 176 of Caesarius of Arles, which was likely available to Claudius as well; see Caesarius, *Sermones*, ed. Morin, 713–14. Augustine's sermon 149 is printed in PL 38. 800–807. Both sermons are on the text of the vision of Peter concerning the clean and unclean animals, reported in Acts 10. This scriptural text, which would seem to be central to the exegesis of Leviticus, appears to be given relatively scant attention in the Carolingian commentaries: in the present instance, when Claudius is citing exegesis attached to Peter's vision, the scriptural lemma is not mentioned, and the exegesis, independent of the Acts text, does not point to it. For later transmission of this reading of Proverbs 21:20 in Bernard of Clairvaux, cf. Illich, *In the Vineyard*, 56, n. 22.

47. Rheims MS 123, fol. 57v.

48. Hrabanus: "Lepra doctrina est falsa. Proinde leprosi non absurde intelliguntur haeretici, qui unitatem verae fidei non habentes, varias doctrinas profitentur erroris, veraque falsis admiscent, sicut et lepra veris falsisque locis humana corpora variando commaculat. Huius scilicet leprae

invenimus legislatorem sex species in homine posuisse: prima capitis et barbae. . . . In capite lepram portat, qui in divinitate Patris, vel in ipso capite, quod est Christus, peccat: 'Caput enim viri Christus est' (1 Cor 11:10). Hanc lepram Judaei habent, et Valentiniani, Marcionistae, Fabiani, Manichaei, Ariani, Sabelliani, Macedoniani, Anthropomorphitae, Priscilliani, Donatistae, Nestoriani, Eutychiani. . . ." (PL 108. 386). Cf. Claudius, Rheims MS 123, fol. 74r (excerpts), and Isidore, *Quaestiones*, in PL 83. 328, whom Claudius follows for subsequent commentary on the leprosies. Curiously, Claudius omits the references to the Nestorians and Eutychians, the Christological heretics adduced in Carolingian anti-Adoptionist polemic.

49. Hrabanus: "Neque enim praecepit in ancillas quaslibet, quanto magis desponsatas, delictum fornicationis admitti, sed ancillam desponsatam sive custoditam homini, Judaeorum dicit Synagogam, quae legi custodita est, nec despondi Christo priusquam moreretur, legis littera poterat. Unde et Paulus dicebat, 'ergo, fratres, et vos mortui estis legi per corpus Christi, ut sitis alterius qui ex mortuis resurrexit' (Rom 7:4). Ipse autem ancillam esse Judaeorum Synagogam haec dicens docuit, 'quia Abraham duos filios habuit, unum ex ancilla et unum de libera' (Gal 4: 22). 'Deinde quam voluit ancillam intelligi, exponens subdidit: quae sunt per allegoriam dicta. Haec enim sunt duo Testamenta, unum quidem ex monte Sina, in servitutem generans, quae est Agar. Sina autem mons est in Arabia conjunctus ei quae nunc est Hierusalem quae servi' (ibid.). Cum hac ergo si quis dormierit coitu seminis, id est, qui huius particeps effectus fuerit doctrinae, in tantum ut conjugatur ei et coeat cum ea, per legis videlicet conversationem. Quasi unum reperiuntur hi qui sibi conjugali consortio sociantur. Semen autem in doctorali verbo accipi debere multipliciter in hoc Levitico libro pridem demonstravimus. Quicunque ergo haec antequam per adventum Christi liberaretur fecerat, recte non moriebatur. Nam etsi secundum litteram et non secundum spiritum legem accipiebat, quemadmodum Judaeorum docet Synagoga, unde et ancilla juste nominatur, quia legislatoris intentionem ignorabat; servus autem, sicut dicit Christus, nescit voluntatem domini sui, et propterea delinquere dicebatur, remissionem necessariam habebat, quia Dominicum praeceptum non secundum Dominicam studebat voluntatem" (PL 108. 454). Cf. Claudius, Rheims MS 123, fol. 106v (abridged).

50. "Camelus ex eo quod ruminat mundus est; ex eo autem quod ungulas divisas non habet et tortuos est inmundus habetur, et non manducandum praecepit. Quid aliud significative innuit nisi ut per exemplum animalii damnet vitam informem et criminibus tortuosam?" (fol. 57v). Cf. Novatian, *De cibis* 3. 14; Origen, *In Leviticum Homilia* 7. 6 (p. 389); Isidore, *Quaestiones*, col. 326; Pseudo-Bede, col. 345. Hrabanus cites the phrase "de exemplo animalium, vitam damnat informem et criminibus tortuosam" with reference to the pelican (*PL* 108. 358).

51. Or rock-rabbit, depending on one's philological authority.

52. Known to Lewis and Short, *Latin Dictionary*, rev. ed. (Oxford: Clarendon Press, 1980) as a hedgehog.

53. Petrae refugium herinaciis; alt. Petrae hyracibus perfugium praestant.

54. "'Petra refugium erinaciis sive chirogrillis' (Ps 103:18): chirogrillis autem debile quidem, sed rapax et bestiale atque mortiferum dicunt, quod omni quidem plebeio, maxime autem Judaeorum inest populo. . . . Quantum autem timidi et infirmi filii Judaeorum sint, vox divina ostendit cum dicit, 'Vae cordibus trepidus et manibus remissis.' Quanta autem injustitia et feritas apud eos erat, audi Isaiam dicentem . . . " Hrabanus, in *PL* 108. 353; Hesychius, in *PG* 93. 906.

55. Origen, *In Leviticum Hom.* 7. 6; *Homilies in Leviticus* 1–16, trans. Barkley, 149. "Sunt alii qui extra religionem nostram sunt, vel ex his, qui nobiscum sunt, qui dividunt quidem ungulam et ita incedunt in viis suis, ut actus suos ad futurum saeculum praeparent. Multi ex philosophis sapiunt et futurum esse iudicium credunt. Immortalem namque animam sentiunt et remunerationem bonis quibusque positam confitentur. Hoc et hereticorum nonnulli faciunt et quantum exspectant, timorem futuri iudicii gerunt et actus suos tamquam in divino examine requirendos cautius temperant. Sed horum uterque non ruminat nec revocat ruminationem. Non enim ea,

quae in lege Dei scripta sunt, audiens meditatur ac revocat ad subtilem et spiritalem intelligentiam; sed statim ut audierit aliquid, aut contemnit aut despicit nec requirit, qui in vilioribus verbis pretiosus lateat sensus." Claudius, Rheims MS 123, fol. 57v–58r.

56. The references to Jewish identity, both of the figures within the text and of those who have interpreted it, are too numerous to register. Typical are, e.g., *Et de his quae sunt secundum legem Judaicam dogmatibus loquitur* (col. 383), *Quod ad sanctificationem et castitatem Judaeorum genus legislator trahens* . . . (col. 409), *Recte maximam diligentiam legislator exhibet, ut non solum in verbis turpibus, aut in fabulis Judaicis* . . . (col. 414), *Sic enim non solum non condemnari ex obveniente sibi virtute Judaicae litterae* . . . (col. 455), *Non solum ad Judaeos haec dicta sunt* . . . (col. 471), *Hic interrogandi sunt Judaei* . . . (col. 530), *Propter quod et Dominus Judaeis dicebat* . . . (col. 538), *Quia autem a Judaeis invenimus omnimodo haec secundum litteram impleta* . . . (col. 552), etc. Most result from Hrabanus's use of Hesychius.

57. Theodore tended to provide quite literal commentary on Leviticus, even when it might be fanciful in its own way; e.g., he explained that a griffin has hooked talons and a beak, whereas the allegorizing Origen said that it was ridiculous to provide literal exegesis for a creature that didn't exist. Lapidge and Bischoff, *Biblical Commentaries*, 364–65; Origen, *De principiis* 4. 3. 2, ed. Koetschau, 325.

58. Convenient and useful discussion, with references to the legal texts, is in Collins, *Early Medieval Spain*, 129–45.

59. 2 Corinthians 3:6.

60. Discussion of the manuscripts is in Lapidge and Bischoff, *Biblical Commentaries*, 275–95 (cf. 287–90).

61. *Poenitentium liber ad Otgarium*, cap. xxvi, *De Christianis qui cum Judaeis vescuntur, et quod Judaeis non liceat habere Christianos uxores vel concubinas, seu mancipium Christianum* (PL 112. 1397–1424; 1418–19); *Poenitentiale ad Heribaldum*, cap. xxvi, *De his qui se gentilibus vel Judaeis iunxerunt*; cap. xxvii, *De his qui cum Judaeis vescuntur* (PL 110. 467–92; 490).

62. Summation of the evidence and extensive older bibliography is most conveniently found in Blumenkranz, *Les auteurs chrétiens latins*.

63. It has been noted, for example, that both Agobard and Amulo enjoin Christians not to attack Jews or their property, but merely to limit fraternization (citations in Parkes, *Jew in the Medieval Community*, 29). The extent to which Agobard's actions were contested in the courts is also worth noting: it appears that Jews instigated legal proceedings against Agobard when fifty-three Jewish minors requested baptism: cf. Blumenkranz, "Deux compilations canoniques." An important component of the history of relations between Jews and Christians, all too often neglected, is the similar concern among Jews for proper segregation of the different communities: still useful is the brief but insightful study by Katz, *Exclusiveness and Tolerance*.

64. In the *Praefatio* to his *Poenitentiale ad Heribaldum*, Hrabanus cites a lengthy passage from Leviticus, immediately provides Pauline sanction with an equally long excerpt from the letter to the Galatians, and concludes by remarking, "Si enim iuxta historiam, legislator transgressoribus mandatorum Dei minatus est carnis mortem, et praesentis vitae terminum, quanto magis nobis iuxta mandatum Salvatoris, et evangelicam doctrinam formidanda est mors animae, et poena perpetua, quam illa quae finem quodammodo habuit! . . . Unde necesse est ut in praesenti vita, iuxta Apostolum, mortificemus membra nostra quae sunt super terram: hoc est, desideria carnis nostrae, et voluptates terrenas in nobis exstinguere contendamus . . ." (PL 110. 470).

65. I regret that I have been unable to consult Italiani, *La tradizione esegetica nel commento ai Re di Claudio di Torino*.

66. Fournier, "Quelques infiltrations," 75, n. 4, notes a letter that some have attributed to Hrabanus, urging repression of dietary prohibitions. He also observes that the enormously influential canon law collection of the mid-ninth century, the *Pseudo-Isidorian Decretals*, reproves dietary distinction (75, n. 5). As exceptions that continue to transmit dietary law, Fournier found

that the *De synodalibus causis* of Regino of Prüm provided material for the subsequent collections of Burchard of Worms and Ivo of Chartres; the Collections in Nine Books (Vat. lat. MS 1349) and Five Books, and even a citation of Gratian, preserve the memory of dietary law, although glossators of the last remarked, "*longa in contrarium utentium consuetudine*" (76).

Bibliography

Augustine of Hippo. *Contra Faustum*. Ed. J. Zycha. CSEL, 25,1. Vienna: F. Tempsky, 1889.

——. *De spiritu et littera ad Marcellinum*. Ed. C.F. Urba and J. Zycha. CSEL, 60. Vienna: F. Tempsky, 1913.

——. *Enarrationes in Psalmos*. Ed. E. Dekkers and J. Fraipont. 3 vols. CCSL, 38–40. Turnhout: Brepols, 1956.

——. *Sermo* 149. PL 38. 800–807.

Beatus of Liébana. *Adversus Elipandum*. Ed. Bengt Löfstedt. CCCM, 59. Turnhout: Brepols, 1984.

Bede the Venerable. *Historia ecclesiastica* = *Bede's Ecclesiastical History of the English People*. Ed. Bertram Colgrave and R. A. B. Mynors. Oxford Medieval texts. Oxford: Clarendon Press, 1969.

Bischoff, Bernhard. *Anecdota novissima: Texte des vierten bis sechzehnten Jahrhunderts*. Stuttgart: Hiersemann, 1984.

Blumenkranz, Bernhard. "Augustin et les juifs, Augustin et le judaïsme." *Recherches augustiniennes* 1 (1958): 225–41. Reprint in *Juifs et Chrétiens*.

——. *Les auteurs chrétiens latins du Moyen Âge sur les Juifs et le Judaïsme*. Paris: Mouton, 1963.

——. "Die christlich-jüdische Missionkonkurrenz (3. bis 6. Jahrhundert)." *Klio* 39 (1961): 227–33. Reprint in *Juifs et Chrétiens*.

——. "Deux compilations canoniques de Florus de Lyon et l'action antijuive d'Agobard." *Revue historique de droit français et étranger*, 4th ser., 33 (1955): 227–54, 560–82; reprint in *Juifs et Chrétiens*.

——. "Du nouveau sur Bodo-Eléazar?" *Revue des études juives* 112 (1953): 35–42. Reprint in *Juifs et Chrétiens*.

——. *Juifs et Chrétiens: Patristique et Moyen Âge*. London: Variorum, 1977. (Cited as *Juifs et Chrétiens*.)

——. *Juifs et Chrétiens dans le monde occidental, 430–1096*. Paris: Mouton, 1960.

——. "Un pamphlet juif médio-latin de polémique antichrétienne." *Revue d'histoire et de philosophie religieuses* 34 (1954): 401–13. Reprint in *Juifs et Chrétiens*.

——. "Raban Maur et Saint Augustin: compilation ou adaptation? à propos du latin biblique." *Revue du Moyen Âge latin* 7 (1951): 97–110. Reprint in *Juifs et Chrétiens*.

Böckenhoff, Karl. "Die römische Kirche und die Speisesatzungen der Bussbücher." *Theologische Quartalschrift* 88 (1906): 186–220.

——. *Speisesatzungen mosaischer Art in mittelalterlichen Kirchenrechtsquellen des Morgen und Abendlandes*. Münster, 1907.

Boniface of Mainz. *Epistolae* = *Die Briefe des heiligen Bonifatius und Lullus* (*S. Bonifatii et Lulli epistolae*). Ed. M. Tangl. *Monumenta Germaniae Historica. Epistolae*. Vol. 1. Berlin: Weidmann, 1916.

Brunhölzl, F. "Zur geistigen Bedeutung des Hrabanus Maurus." In *Hrabanus Maurus, Lehrer, Abt und Bischof*. Ed. H. Zimmermann and R. Kottje, 1–17. Mainz: Akademie der Wissenschaften und der Literatur, 1982.

Caesarius of Arles. *Sermones*. Ed. G. Morin. CCSL, 103–4. Turnhout: Brepols, 1953.

Cassiodorus. *Cassiodori Senatoris Institutiones*. Ed. R. A. B. Mynors. Oxford: Clarendon Press, 1937.

Cavadini, John. "Claudius of Turin and the Augustinian Tradition." *Proceedings of the Patristic, Medieval, and Renaissance Conference, Villanova University* 11 (1986): 43–50.

Charles-Edwards, Thomas. "The Penitential of Theodore and the *Iudicia Theodori*." In *Archbishop Theodore: Commemorative Studies on his Life and Influence*. Ed. Michael Lapidge, 141–74. Cambridge: Cambridge University Press, 1995.

Chromatius of Aquileia. *Tractatus in Mathaeum*. Ed. R. Etaix and J. Lemarié. CCSL, 9A. Turnhout: Brepols, 1974.

Claudius of Turin. *In libros informationum litterae et spiritus super Leviticum*. Rheims, Bibliothèque municipale, MS 123.

——. *Praefatio*. Ed. E. Dümmler. *Monumenta Germaniae Historica. Epistolae* 4: 602–5. Berlin: Weidmann, 1895; also in PL 104. 615–20.

Codex Carolinus. Ed. W. Gundlach. *Monumenta Germaniae Historica. Epistolae* 3: 644–47. Berlin: Weidmann, 1892.

Collectio canonum hibernensis. In *Die irische Kanonensammlung*. Ed. Herrmann Wasserschleben. Leipzig, 1885. Reprint, Aalen: Scientia Verlag, 1966.

Collins, Roger. *Early Medieval Spain: Unity in Diversity, 400–1000*. London: Macmillan, 1983.

Contreni, John. "Carolingian Biblical Culture." In *Iohannes Scottus Eriugena: The Bible and Hermeneutics*. Ed. Carlos Steel, James McEvoy, and Gerd Van Riel, 1–23. Leuven: Leuven University Press, 1996.

Dungal. *Responsa contra perversas Claudii Taurinensis episcopi sententias* (Ep. 9). Ed. E. Dümmler. *Monumenta Germaniae Historica. Epistolae* 4: 583–85. Berlin: Weidmann, 1895.

Elipandus. *Epistula ad Migetium* (Ep. 1). PL 96. 859–67.

Étaix, R., and J. Lemarié. "La tradition manuscrite des *Tractatus in Matheum* de saint Chromace d'Aquilée." *Sacris erudiri* 17 (1966): 302–54.

Finsterwalder, Paul Willem. *Die Canones Theodori Cantuariensis und ihre Überlieferungsformen*. Weimar: Hermann Böhlaus Nachfolger, 1929.

Fontaine, Jacques. "Isidore de Seville, pédagogue et théoricien de l'exégèse." In *Stimuli: Exegese und ihre Hermeneutik in Antike und Christentum (Festschrift für Ernst Dassmann)*. Ed. Georg Schöllgen and Clemens Scholten, 423–34. Münster: Aschendorff, 1996.

Fournier, Paul. "De quelques infiltrations byzantines dans le droit canonique de l'époque carolingienne." In *Mélanges offerts à M. Gustave Schlumberger*. Vol. 1, 67–78. Paris: Librairie orientaliste P. Geuthner, 1924.

——. "Le *Liber ex lege Moysi* et les tendances bibliques du droit canonique irlandais." *Revue celtique* 30 (1909): 221–34.

Giese, Wolfgang. "In Judaismum lapsus est: Jüdische Proselytenmacherei im frühen und hohen Mittelalter (600–1300)." *Historisches Jahrbuch* 88 (1968): 407–17.

Gorman, Michael. "The Commentary on Genesis of Claudius of Turin and Biblical Studies under Louis the Pious." *Speculum* 72 (1997): 279–329.

——. "The Commentary on the Pentateuch Attributed to Bede in *PL* 91.189–394." *Revue bénédictine* 106 (1996): 61–108; 255–307.

——. "Wigbod and Biblical Studies under Charlemagne." *Revue bénédictine* 107 (1997): 40–76.

Gregorius III (pope). *Epistola ad Bonifatium* (Ep. 28). Ed. M. Tangl. *Monumenta Germaniae Historica. Epistolae Selectae* 1: 49–52. Berlin: Weidmann, 1916.

Hablitzel, Johann Baptist. *Hrabanus Maurus: Ein Beitrag zur Geschichte der mittelalterlichen Exegese*. Freiburg, 1906.

——. "Hrabanus Maurus und Claudius von Turin." *Historisches Jahrbuch* 27 (1906): 74–85; 38 (1917): 538–52.

Haddan, A. W., and W. Stubbs. *Councils and Ecclesiastical Documents Relating to Great Britain and Ireland*. Vol. 3, The English Church, 595–1066. Oxford: Clarendon Press, 1971.

Hadrian (pope). *Epistola ad Egilam* (Ep. 96. in *Codex Carolinus*). Ed. W. Gundlach. *Monumenta Germaniae Historica. Epistolae* 3: 644–47. Berlin: Weidmann, 1892.

Hesychius of Jerusalem. *Commentarius in Leviticum*. PG 93. 787–1180.

Hrabanus Maurus. *Expositio in Leviticum*. PL 108. 245–586.

——. *Praefatio*. Ed. E. Dümmler. *Monumenta Germaniae Historica. Epistolae Selectae* 5: 396–97. Berlin: Weidmann, 1898.

——. *Poenitentiale ad Heribaldum*. PL 110. 467–92.

——. *Poenitentium liber ad Otgarium*. PL 112. 1397–1424.

Illich, Ivan. *In the Vineyard of the Text: A Commentary to Hugh's Didascalion*. Chicago: University of Chicago Press, 1993.

Irenaeus of Lyons. *Adversus Haereses. Sancti Irenaei episcopi Lugdunensis libros quinque adversus haereses*. Ed. W. W. Harvey. 2 vols. Cambridge: Cambridge University Press, 1857. Reprint, Ridgewood, N.J.: Gregg Press, 1965.

Isidore of Seville. *Quaestiones de Veteri et Novo Testamento*. PL 83. 201–657.

Italiani, Giuliana. *La tradizione esegetica nel commento ai Re di Claudio di Torino*. Florence: CLUSF (Cooperativa editrice Universita), 1979.

Jecker, Gall. *Die Heimat des hl. Pirmin des Apostels der Alamannen*. Münster in Westfalia, 1927.

Jonas of Orléans. *De cultu imaginum*. PL 106. 305–87.

Katz, Jacob. *Exclusiveness and Tolerance: Jewish–Gentile Relations in Medieval and Modern Times*. Oxford: Oxford University Press, 1961.

Laistner, M. L. W. "Some Early Medieval Commentaries on the Old Testament." *Harvard Theological Review* 46 (1953): 27–46; reprint in *The Intellectual Heritage of the Early Middle Ages: Selected Essays*. Ed. Chester G. Starr, 181–201. Ithaca, N.Y.: Cornell University Press, 1957.

Lapidge, Michael, and Berhard Bischoff. *Biblical Commentaries from the Canterbury School of Theodore and Hadrian*. Cambridge: Cambridge University Press, 1994.

Le Maître, Philippe. "Les méthodes exégètiques de Raban Maur." In *Haut Moyen-Âge: culture, éducation et société; études offertes à Pierre Riché*. Ed. M. Sot, 343–52. Paris: Éditions Publidix, 1990.

Levison, Wilhelm. *England and the Continent in the Eighth Century*. Oxford: Clarendon Press, 1946.

Löwe, Heinz. "Die Apostasie des Pfalzdiakons Bodo (838) und das Judentum der Chasaren." In *Person und Gemeinschaft im Mittelalter: Karl Schmid zum fünfundsechzigsten Geburtstag*. Ed. Gerd Althoff, Dieter Geuenich, Otto G. Oexle, and Joachim Wollasch, 157–69. Sigmaringen: Thorbecke, 1988.

Lubac, Henri de. *Exégèse médiévale: les quatre sens de l'écriture*. 4 vols. Paris: Aubier, 1959–64.

Lutterbach, Hubertus. "Die Speisegesetzgebung in den mittelalterlichen Bussbüchern (600–1200): Religionsgeschichtliche Perspektiven." *Archiv für Kulturgeschichte* 80 (1998): 1–37.

Matter, E. Ann. "Theological Freedom in the Carolingian Age: The Case of Claudius of Turin." In *La notion de liberté au moyen âge: Islam, Byzance, Occident*. Ed. George Makdisi, Dominique Sourdel and Janine Sourdel-Thomine, 51–60. Paris: Les Belles Lettres, 1985.

McNally, Robert E. *The Bible in the Early Middle Ages*. Westminster, Md.: Newman Press, 1959.

McNeill, John T., and Helena M. Gamer. *Medieval Handbooks of Penance: A Translation of the Principal Libri Poenitentiales*. New York, 1965. Reprint, with new introduction, New York: Columbia University Press, 1990.

Meens, Rob. "Pollution in the Early Medieval Pentitentials: The Case of Food Regulations in Penitentials." *Early Medieval Europe* 4 (1995): 3–19.

Meyvaert, Paul. "Bede's Text of the *Libellus Responsionum* of Gregory the Great to Augustine of Canterbury." In *England Before the Conquest: Studies in Primary Sources Presented to Dorothy Whitelock*. Ed. Peter Clemoes and Kathleen Hughes, 15–33. Cambridge: Cambridge University Press, 1971.

——. "Le *Libellus Responsionum* à Augustin de Cantorbéry: une oeuvre authentique de saint Grégoire le Grand." In *Grégoire le Grand: Chantilly, Centre Culturel Les Fontaines, 15–19*

Septembre 1982. Ed. Jacques Fontaine, Robert Gillet, and Stan Pellistradi, 543–49. Paris: Éditions CNRS, 1986.

——. "*Les Responsiones* de S. Grégoire le Grand a S. Augustin de Cantorbéry." *Revue d'histoire ecclésiastique* 54 (1959): 879–94.

Momigliano, Arnaldo. "The New Letter by 'Anna' to 'Seneca.'" *Athenaeum* n.s. 63 (1985): 217–19. Reprint in *On Pagans, Jews, and Christians*, 202–5. Middletown, Conn.: Wesleyan University Press, 1987.

Novatian. *De cibis iudaicis*. Ed. by G. F. Diercks. CCSL, 4. Turnhout: Brepols, 1972.

Origen. *De principiis*. Ed. Paul Koetschau. *Greicheschen christlichen Schriftsteller*, 22. Leipzig: J. C. Hinrichs, 1913.

——. *In Leviticum Homilia*. In *Homilien zum Hexateuch in Rufins Übersetzung: erster Teil: Die Homilien zu Genesis, Exodus und Leviticus*. Ed. W. A. Baehrens. *Greichischen christlichen Schriftsteller*, 29. Leipzig: J. C. Hinrichs, 1920.

——. *Homilies in Leviticus 1–16*. Trans. Gary Wayne Barkley. Washington, D.C.: Catholic University of America Press, 1990.

Parkes, James. *The Jew in the Medieval Community*. London, 1938. Reprint, New York: Hermon Press, 1976.

Pirmin. *Scarapsus*. In Jecker, ed., *Die Heimat des hl. Pirmin*.

Pseudo-Bede. *In Pentateuchum commentaria–Leviticus*. PL 91. 189–394.

Quasten, Johannes. *Patrology III: The Golden Age of Greek Patristic Literature*. Westminster, Md.: Newman Press, 1983.

Reinelt, Heinz. "Hrabanus Maurus als Exeget." In *Hrabanus Maurus und seine Schule: Festschrift der Rabanus-Maurus-Schule Fulda*. Ed. W. Böhne, 64–76. Fulda, Germany: Rindt-Druck Fulda, 1980.

Riché, Pierre. "Méthodes de l'exégèse carolingienne." In *Le Moyen Âge et la Bible*. Ed. Pierre Riché and Guy Lobrichon, 147–62. Paris: Beauchesne, 1984.

Rissel, M. *Rezeption antiker und patristischer Wissenschaft bei Hrabanus Maurus: Studien zur karolingischen Geistesgeschichte*. Bern: Herbert Lang, 1976.

Smalley, Beryl. *The Study of the Bible in the Middle Ages*. Oxford: Clarendon Press, 1948; 1st pbk ed. Notre Dame, Ind.: University of Notre Dame Press, 1964.

——. "An Early Twelfth-Century Commentator on the Literal Sense of Leviticus." *Recherches de théologie ancienne et médiévale* 36 (1969): 78–99.

Spelsberg, Helmut. *Hrabanus Maurus Bibliographie*. Fulda, Germany: Hessische Landesbibliothek, 1984.

Spicq, Ceslas. *Esquisse d'une histoire de l'exégèse latine au Moyen Âge*. Paris: J. Vrin, 1944.

Stegmüller, F. *Repertorium biblicum medii aevi*. 7 vols. Madrid: Matriti, 1940–61.

Theodore of Tarsus (Theodore of Canterbury). *Poenitentiale*. In Wasserschleben, *Bussordnungen*, 182–219.

——. *Poenitentiale*. In Haddan and Stubbs, eds., *Councils and Ecclesiastical Documents*, 173–213.

Wasserschleben, F. W. H., ed. *Die Bussordnungen der abendendländischen Kirche*. Halle,Germany, 1851. Reprint, Graz, Austria: Akademische Druck-und Verlagsanstalt, 1958.

Wasserschleben, Herrmann, ed. *Die irische Kanonensammlung*. 2d ed. Leipzig, 1885. Reprint, Aalen, Germany: Scientia Verlag, 1966.

Wenger, Luke. *Hrabanus Maurus, Fulda and Carolingian Spirituality*. Ph.D. diss., Harvard University, 1973.

Wilmart, André. "Les allégories sur l'écriture attribuées à Raban Maur." *Revue bénédictine* 32 (1920): 47–56.

Zacharias (pope). *Epistola ad Bonifatium* (Ep. 87). Ed. M. Tangl. *Monumenta Germaniae Historica. Epistolae Selectae* 1: 194–201. Berlin: Weidmann, 1916.

——. *Acta synodi Romanae*, 25 Oct. 745 (Ep. 59). Ed. M. Tangl. *Monumenta Germaniae Historica. Epistolae Selectae* 1: 108–20. Berlin: Weidmann, 1916.

14

The Four "Senses" and Four Exegetes

EDWARD SYNANT†

The four senses of scripture honored during the Middle Ages generated two memorable lines of verse, a distich, that would be cited by Nicholas of Lyra around the year 1330 as if well known to all his fourteenth-century readers. Those Latin lines may be rendered loosely as:

> The *letter* teaches what's been done; *allegory*—your belief;
> *moral*—what you ought to do; *anagogy*—where you'll get relief.[1]

These four senses of scriptural texts can be designated by various synonyms of the four terms mentioned. The literal sense is identified with the "historical" sense; allegory is the "Christological" sense; the moral sense is "tropological" (a term used by John Cassian as well as by Saint Jerome himself);[2] the anagogic is designated at times as the "eschatological" sense. These four senses, their possible synonyms included, dominated Christian biblical scholarship from patristic to early modern times. After three medieval witnesses to the "four senses," one postmedieval exegete will be adduced to account for the gap between the Middle Ages and our time: Jean Astruc seems to have transformed the problematic of "senses" into one of "sources."

Godfrey of Saint Victor

The first of the three medieval exegetes is Godfrey of Saint Victor, born ca. 1125 and died after 1194. As this name conveys, Godfrey was a canon and a professor at the Parisian convent dedicated to the memory of Saint Victor. As a colleague of Andrew, a canon of the same house who was given to consulting Parisian rabbis on the meanings of difficult Hebrew terms he encountered in the Bible, Godfrey was acutely aware of the Jewish presence in his corner of Christendom. In the course of setting out the conventional four senses of scripture, Godfrey accounted for dissent between Jews and Christians in their interpretations of the "Old" and "New" Laws and did this in catchy "Goliardic" verses.

Using the image of Wisdom as a stream coursing down a mountainside, Godfrey has given us a reasonably detailed account of his own twelfth-century education in the liberal arts (philosophy included) and in theology, the latter, clearly under the sign of Saint Augustine. Godfrey drank the waters of the liberal arts, first the *trivium*: grammar, rhetoric, and dialectic (the last heavily "philosophical"). From these preparatory disciplines he advanced to the arithmetic, geometry, music, and astronomy of the *quadrivium*. Equipped with all seven of those arts, Godfrey was ready for theology. Then as now, Christian theology was founded on holy writ. In Godfrey's day that meant mastering the traditional "four senses" of the biblical text, in his image, four "modes" of Wisdom's stream:

Very various this wave: four modes it's comprising;
Now it's patent, now profound, varied its devising;
Now more gracious to the taste, sweetness emphasizing;
Now it flows back up the hill, whence is its arising![3]

Lest we miss his reference to the four senses in his "four modes," he spelled out the way we might receive them in his next stanza:

Easily of HISTORY we can be persuaded;
ALLEGORY'S drowning tide—hard to be evaded!
By MORALITY'S good taste and use we are aided;
ANAGOGY with this earth scornfully is jaded.[4]

The scriptural lore he had been taught at Saint Victor's our versifier recognized as a patristic inheritance. Godfrey devoted verses to each of the four major Latin Fathers, implying that there were many more, for he announced: "We'll just name the better ones." They were presented under the image of "bridge-builders," *pontifices*, who link two river banks, which, for Godfrey, represented the two Testaments:

Those bridge-builders need indeed much enumeration;
Be hard-pressed to find the men for that computation!
Besides, it would mean delay—no procrastination!
We'll just name the better ones in a brief notation.[5]

His "brief notation" consists of two stanzas on Gregory the Great, one on Ambrose, and two on Jerome. As an Augustinian Canon, Godfrey gave the Bishop of Hippo more extensive mention: Augustine's views rated ten stanzas.

Godfrey made it clear that he intended the two banks of his river to represent the Jewish and the Christian scriptures, a river bridged by the Latin Fathers. Given that Godfrey's adult life included the years of the Second and Third Crusades, it is an oddity that he seems never to have mentioned Islam, neither here nor in his other writings of which we know.[6] On the other hand, he makes a precious addition to our evidence for an ecumenical attitude at Saint Victor with respect to Jews and Judaism. The Jewish People he located *within* the Augustinian "City of God"; he acknowledged the identity of the Lord of Israel with the Lord of Christians, and he diagnosed Jewish–Christian dissent, on one plane at least, as a result of "rites diverse":

Hence and thence, one City is composed by elision;
Tongue and people—they're the same, really no collision;
For one King they both campaign, one faith, without fission,
Though their rites diverse have made long-standing division.[7]

Despite his friendly presentation of Jews and of their Covenant, Godfrey was a convinced Christian who regretted the fact that Jesus of Nazareth was absent from His own People, the Jews:

> This part has a numerous, a large population,
> With great men whose power reins their wild agitation;
> Patriarch, Judge, Prophet, King—what administration!
> But the Lord is missing there—and so is elation.[8]

Scripture, interpreted according to the four senses, played a truly fundamental role in medieval theology, but no theologian could avoid the speculative developments of the mysteries of the Faith by the School. Godfrey found this last step rough going:

> In DIVINITY this drink, all the rest preceding,
> Prompt in use, from intellect ever is receding,
> Nor within my mind's embrace this truth was I leading:
> Namely, that "One God is Three," "Triune" as we're reading.[9]

Godfrey's solution was to devote himself to proclaiming the more "human" aspects of Christianity: Jesus of Nazareth, His work and sacrifice, along with moral doctrine in the Augustinian perspective of what "to use" and what "to enjoy":

> What goods "to enjoy" might be man's orientation,
> Meanwhile he can "use" the things that are God's donation.[10]

Thus, in his last line Godfrey announced:

> I shall publish these things to all who'll be believing.[11]

Saint Thomas Aquinas, O.P.

Brother Thomas Aquinas of the Order of Preachers, the "Dominicans," ca. 1225–74, like all qualified university theologians of his time, could be termed a "Master of the Sacred Page." At the *studium generale* of his Dominican Order at Cologne under the tutelage of Saint Albert the Great, Thomas had the equivalent of what a "bachelor of the Bible" would have learned under a university master at Paris or Oxford. After that predominantly scriptural training Albert recommended that Thomas go to Paris for his years as a "bachelor of the *Sentences*" of Peter Lombard. In his maturity Thomas produced an imposing series of biblical "Expositions," more intimately associated with his teaching in various Faculties of Theology than were his better known "Expositions" of Aristotelian and other philosophical works. The scriptural works of Thomas were a "Literal Exposition of Job," "Expositions of the Psalms of David," of "The Canticle of Canticles," of the "Prophets Isaiah and Jeremiah," on the "Lamentations of Jeremiah," a "Continuous Gloss" (the so-called "Golden Chain," *Catena aurea*, on Matthew, Luke, and John), as well as an "Exposition of the Epistles of Paul." In all of these he practiced what we shall find him to have preached on biblical interpretation.

As the premier scholastic theologian, Brother Thomas dealt with the Vulgate Latin Bible and he read it through the lens of the four senses. When, toward the end of his life, he began to put together his *Summa theologiae*, a work he intended for the use of "beginners" or "novices," who were easily confused by intricate arguments, in his opening section he set out the guidelines of theological discourse as he saw and practiced it. Of his ten introductory "Articles," the last two raise the scriptural issue:

> 9. "Whether sacred scripture ought to use metaphors?" This is to ask, is it appropriate that the Bible has used expressions to convey meanings other than the literal sense?
>
> 10. "Whether sacred scripture, under the single 'letter' has many senses?" We must note that this question is put in factual terms: Are there wider senses to be perceived beneath the literal expressions?[12]

It will not suprise us that Brother Thomas answered both questions affirmatively and that he gave reasons for his answers. The use of "metaphor" he accounted for by our psychosomatic nature: "it is natural for a human being to arrive at the intelligible through the sensible," implying that for the more intellectual, even a literal statement of faith can ground a spiritual insight; he did not think that would be effective with the less instructed. "It is suitable that sacred scripture . . . be proposed under corporeal similitudes so that the uninstructed might grasp it in this way at least, people who are not ready to grasp things that are of themselves intelligible."[13]

There is more to his position on the "senses" of scripture than this. First, in all human learning, theological learning included, words signify realities, things; this basic "first sense is 'historical' or 'literal.'" As author of sacred scripture, the holy One has the capacity to make the realities that are signified by words taken literally to signify in their turn yet other realities; this second level of significance is called a "'spiritual sense,' founded upon, and presupposing, the literal sense."[14]

Second, Brother Thomas held that a theologian can contrive valid arguments from the literal sense only, "not from 'allegory,'" that is, not from any nonliteral sense. This commonsensical attitude relegates the nonliteral senses of scripture to the art of the poet, to the exhortations of the preacher, to the meditation of the mystic.

His third assertion is less obviously true and this may be why he thought it right to adduce the support of Saint Augustine's authority in his *Letter Against Vincent*: "nothing necessary for the faith is contained under the 'spiritual' sense which scripture does not convey elsewhere through the literal sense."[15]

Fourth, Aquinas seems to have anticipated in a seminal way at least a distinction for which our next witness, Nicholas of Lyra, O.F.M., is often named as the originator. This is the distinction between one "literal" sense of a given text in the Old Law and a different "literal" sense of the same passage in the time of the New Law. In this perspective the total reality which is the Old Covenant—*Torah, Nevi'im, Ketuvim* (Legal instruction, Prophets, Writings)—proclaimed in advance the essentials of what is the New Covenant of the Gospel. For, as "The Apostle" says (Heb 7:11–14; along with all his world, Aquinas ascribed the Epistle to the Hebrews to Paul, an ascription already questioned by Origen):[16] "The Old Law is a figure of the New Law."[17]

Nor is this all; the next step is that, whatever is literal in the New Law adumbrates in its turn an aspect of the eternal glory to come, the burden of the so-called "anagogic sense." This Aquinas established by appeal to the *De ecclesistica hierarchia*, the author of which Saint Thomas venerated (once more erroneously, but with all his world) as that Dionysius, a member of the Athenian Areopagus, who had been converted to Christianity by the preaching of Saint Paul as recounted in Acts 17:34.[18]

As to the Jewish presence in Christendom, it must be said that Aquinas was less irenic on the plane of theology than Godfrey had been. Still, at a period when serious Christian theologians could propose that Jewish children be taken from their parents, baptized, and brought up as Christians (John Duns Scotus was to do so),[19] Thomas Aquinas defended the inviolable human right of parents, Jewish parents included, over the education of their children.[20] So too, this Neapolitan recommended that Jews not be forced into usurious practices by restrictive laws, but that they be required to support themselves (by normal occupations such as farming?) "as is done in Italy."[21]

Unlike Godfrey of Saint Victor, Brother Thomas did not ignore Islamic thinkers. He weighed and either adopted or rejected a number of their opinions. Aquinas opposed, for instance, the views of Avicenna and Averroës that one or both of the two "intellects" of Aristotelian psychology might be one for the whole human race.[22] Still, it does not seem tenable that, as is often claimed, his *Summa contra gentiles* was inspired by zeal to convert the Muslims of Spain to Christianity. The work is better adjudged to be a Christian theological case against any and all who deny, with arguments, positions essential to the Christian view of the cosmos and of our place within it.

For all the good sense of Thomas's approach to the use of biblical texts in his theological work, the fact that he knew neither of the two major biblical languages, Hebrew and Greek, remains a cruel limitation. Nor was he well informed on Jewish religious practice. On Paul's divergent procedure in circumcising Timothy but not Titus, Aquinas thought the variation was based on the fact that both parents of one were gentiles, whereas only one parent of the other was a gentile: "The decision of The Apostle was that those born of a Jewish parent on either side ought to be circumcised, but on no account ought those born of entirely gentile parents be circumcised."[23] From that single case of Paul's not having circumcised Titus, Aquinas deduced a general rejection of the Old Covenant and its supersession by the New Covenant: "Whence was given that decision by The Apostle on the compulsory nonobservance of the legal precepts is had in Acts 15[:28]."[24] It is obvious that Saint Thomas did not know the Jewish position that Judaism descends through the mother rather than through the father.

Even his expert knowledge of Aristotelian logic led Brother Thomas into strange exegesis of the rabbinically trained Paul. Saint Thomas was convinced that he had found in the same Epistle "a syllogism in the second figure."[25]

The short life of Saint Thomas Aquinas was bracketed between the birth and death of the enormously talented, if somewhat eccentric, Roger Bacon, O.F.M., ca. 1214–92. Had Roger enjoyed more success with his views on language and exegesis, Thomas might well have avoided the limitations noted. Both in Roger's *Opus maius* and in his *Opus minus* it is possible to find the suggestion that was to flower in a movement to found "trilingual" schools, but that flowering was to be only in Renaissance times, then far in the future.[26] In those schools it would be possible to acquire not only a formation in golden age Latin, but also in Greek and in Hebrew; it is pleasant for an old student of Lucien Cerfaux and Joseph Coppens to mention that one such school was founded at Louvain (Leuven).[27]

Unlike Saint Thomas Aquinas, the third major figure discussed here was remarkable for his control, not only of the Hebrew language, but even of Jewish exegesis, above all that of "Rashi," Rabbi Solomon ben Isaac, 1040–1105.

Nicholas of Lyra, O.F.M.

To the delight of versifiers, Nicholas of Lyra, O.F.M., identified by his birthplace, Lyre, (now Vielle-Lyre) in Normandy, provided them with a prefabricated pun on that stringed musical instrument, the lyre. Some admired him so much that they ascribed even their sanity—presumably in exegesis—to Nicholas:

> The man from Lyre his lyre not playing?
> At the moon we'd all be baying![28]

The alleged association of the work of Nicholas with Luther's innovations has small foundation, it would seem, but generated another play on his place of origin:

> Had Nicholas his lyre not played,
> Luther in no dance had swayed.[29]

This exegete had no need of rhymesters to make or break his reputation. From one perspective, often overlooked, Nicholas, although a Hebraist, was also a standard scholastic theologian, trained at Paris and so close to the thought of John Duns Scotus that certain disputed Questions of Nicholas have been printed in modern times among the works of the Subtle Doctor, Duns.[30] (May it not be thought an instance of "the old school tie" to note that Louvain's Cerfaux was described as chary on a certain type of "Thomism" and that he was, in fact, a "neo-Scotist.")[31] Although the major contribution Nicholas has made to exegesis is the immense and detailed *Postilla* on the whole Bible, the very size of this work makes it unsuitable for brief mention. Hence, a Question from among those confused with the work of Scotus has been chosen. This is Question VI: "Whether the final salvation of Solomon can be proved efficaciously from sacred scripture?" This brief component conveys significant aspects of this exegete's work, some of which are easily overlooked or forgotten. The technique of this Question indicates that Nicholas was a trained scholastic Master of the Sacred Page. That editors ascribed works of Nicholas to that scholastic of scholastics, the "Subtle Doctor," John Duns, bears witness to this fact. Beyond that mal-ascription, because Nicholas was concerned with the conversion of Jews to Christianity, he recognized that this could succeed only if it were based upon scriptures acceptable to them. This approach leads to a double reservation on his part.

First, in this very Question Nicholas expressed his allegiance to the Palestinian canon which is honored by Jews but which excludes certain books (designated harshly as "apocryphal," and less harshly as "deuterocanonical") which were and are accepted by the Roman Catholic Church. He noted that Saint Jerome had insisted upon that restricted canon (it excludes books and parts of books contained only in the Diaspora Septuagint). Nicholas did so, however, with an ingenious account of why those "deuterocanonical" books are read justifiably in church services: This is for their moral value only, not (as in this disputed Question would be the case) in order to determine doubtful matters of belief.[32]

Although he acknowledged explicitly the conventional "four senses" of scripture, Nicholas gave his reason for arguing theologically from the literal sense only in the language of technical logic: To argue from senses other than the literal would entail the "fallacy of equivocation and the fallacy of amphiboly."[33] Like Godfrey of Saint Victor and Thomas Aquinas, Nicholas clearly had mastered dialectic before proceeding to theology! Like Saint Thomas too, Nicholas held that theological argument can proceed from the literal sense only. In a mode parallel to his acknowledgement that deuterocanonical books are read legitimately in the Church, Nicholas did not read out of court the three other senses of scripture: He banished them from theology only, precisely because that discipline is "scientific"; in its fashion, theology is an extension of revelation itself. This exclusion from theology could well leave a role for those three figurative senses in homiletics, in hymns, and in that poetry of prayer, mysticism.

Now medieval theologians had trouble with Aristotle's paganism on more issues than the eternity of his world and its "motion": Aristotle had habitually defined "science" in a way that seemed at first sight to exclude theology from that category.[34] Theology, whether biblical or quranic, deals with singulars, with the holy One, not with a universal class of "gods"; there is but one Moses, one Jesus of Nazareth, and every Prophet is an individual. Science for The Philosopher, however, was "of the universal."[35] How, asked the theologians, could they secure scientific status for theology, "queen," as they saw her, over all other branches of learning?

In answer to that puzzle Nicholas here shifted the criterion of "science" from universality to certitude. Scientific knowledge is certain knowledge (*epistêmé* as opposed to *doxa*, mere "opinion") and certitude is achieved either through "faith" or through "experimental" cognition; theology is "scientific," thanks to the certitude of faith.[36] Sacred scripture, inasmuch as it is the major source of what is believed, has an authority that "excels any demonstration."[37]

The purpose of scripture is our salvation, our direction to an end beyond nature; this is the reason why all that is necessary for salvation is "expressly" present in scripture.[38] Here Nicholas argued for a noncommittal response to the dubiety posed by his "Question:" We cannot know whether Solomon was saved or not, and the reason is that knowledge of "the salvation or damnation of Solomon is not . . . necessary for our salvation." In the view of Nicholas, revelation is on a "need to know" basis.[39]

Only once in this Question did Nicholas make explicit use of his knowledge of Hebrew. When explaining that the book (known to the Church under the Greek title "Ecclesiastes") was written by Solomon, not out of a spirit of penitence, but after the fashion of a scholastic "Doctor explaining some doubtful issue,"[40] he transliterated the Hebrew name of the book as *Coheleth* and explained that this term means "preacher," *concionator*, as, of course, it does.[41]

Jean Astruc

My first intention was to conclude these remarks with a reference to Richard Simon (1638–1712), a *quondam* member of the Congregation of the Oratory,[42] as the exegete whose work might be seen to open the gap between the medieval concern with the four senses and our contemporary concern with sources, along with all that goes with them: archaeology, linguistics, ethnology, cultural history, *Formgeschichte*, and the rest. Simon was expert in oriental languages, and his crucial publications were two large volumes, one on the Old Testament and one on the New. Among Simon's admirers in the next generation was a practicing medical doctor, Jean Astruc (1684–1766), who was a hebraist as well as medical advisor to the king of France.

Astruc, although chosen here for the innovating role, no doubt would have supported the choice of Simon. In an anonymously published work, doubtless because Simon's had ended on the Index of Forbidden Books, Astruc recalled the suggestion by Simon that Moses seemed to have used a large number of preexisting written "memoirs" in composing the Pentateuch. This reference to Simon occurs in a footnote, footnote a, on page 7, of Astruc's 1753 publication. It refers to the seventh chapter of Simon's first volume, *Histoire critique du Vieux Testament*, where that pioneer had suggested a plurality of written sources behind the work of Moses, now seen as an "editor" as well as an "author."

Despite this, my reason for adducing Astruc is that it was he who saw, in the presence of two divine names in the first chapters of Genesis, *Elohim* and the "Tetragrammaton," solid grounds for assigning two sources to the first book of the Pentateuch. He made the suggestion in his *Conjectures sur les memoires originaux dont il paroit que Moyse s'est servit pour composer le livre de la Genèse*,[43] and his suggestion, enormously supplemented, has perdured to our own day. The two names Astruc noticed in the Book of Genesis (arising from distinct sources which he termed "A" and "B") have become "E," the "Elohistic," and "J," the "Jahwistic," components of the Pentateuch in the analysis of Julius Wellhausen (1844–1918), supplemented, to be sure, by "D," the "Deuteronomic" source, and "P," the "Priestly" codex. As for the scriptures of the Christian Covenant, the suggestion (by both Simon and Astruc) that "memoires" of diverse origin lie beneath the Pentateuch is surely an ancestor of the claim that traditions stemming from various early Christian communities underlie the first three Gospel accounts as they have come to us. The resemblances in those accounts are as puzzling as their diversities, and the sum of both constitutes our "synoptic problem." Is it too much to say that the "Q" of our contemporaries was already implicit in the work of Astruc? Without Astruc's dramatic reorientation of exegesis, a development of Simon's basic insight, it is hard to see how our contemporary scholarship on the origins and meaning of Holy Writ could have come to fruition. The credit for this—or, for more "fundamentalist" exegetes, the blame—seems to belong to that eighteenth-century medical practitioner Jean Astruc.

Notes

1. Nicholas has cited this distich in his *Postilla super totam Bibliam IV*, ii iii, (*Ad Galatas* 4:24) as:

> *Littera gesta docet, quid credas allegoria,*
> *Moralis quid agas, quo tendas anagogia.*

2. Cassian, "Conlatio" 14.8, *Conferences*, ed. Pichery, 2: 189, 190: "*Spiritalis autem scientiae genera sunt tria, tropologia, allegoria, anagoge . . .*"; Jerome, "*Secundum tropologiam autem omnes fines terrae . . . ,*" "*Tractatus de psalmo LXVI,*" ed. Morin, *Opera homiletica*, 39.169.

3. See Godfrey of Saint Victor, *Fountain of Philosophy*.

> Ista modis quatuor uariatur unda,
> Modo transuadabilis, modo sit profunda;
> Nunc sapore gratior, dulcis et iocunda,
> Nunc in altis refluit quo est oriunda. (line) 480

4. Planior istoria leuis transuadari,
Sed allegoria uix ualet enatari,
Sapida moralitas utilis potari,
Anagoge respuit terris immorari. 484

5. Sunt permulti siquidem pontis extructores
Quorum computatio uix enarratores
Inueniret, exigens moras longiores,
Paucos memorabimus excellentiores. 680

6. His other known works are the prose *Microcosmus*, ed. Delhaye, and a verse "Preconium Augustini," ed. Damon. Godfrey seems to have been both a teacher at Saint Victor and a successful preacher. For traces of this second activity as well as traces of what his editor calls two "musical productions," a paraphrase of the "Magnificat" and a "Marian complaint" which Delhaye counts as an ancestor of the *Stabat mater*, see Delhaye's companion volume to his edition just noted, *Le microcosmus*, 27, as well as Appendices J and K, 231–51.

7. Hinc et inde ciuitas una sola quidem,
Una lingua, populus unus est et idem,
Uni regi militant per eamdem fidem,
Sed diuersis ritibus dissident iampridem. 548

8. Sed hec quidem portio ciuibus repleta
Multis, et potentia magnatorum freta,
Patriarcha, iudex, rex hic est et propheta,
Sed absente Domino non uidetur leta. 568

9. Unus hic pre ceteris haustus est diuinus,
Usu quidem notior, intellectu minus,
Quem nec totum caperet mentis mee sinus:
Scilicet quod unus est Deus atque trinus. 788

10. Quibus homo factus est ad fruendum bonis
Uti quibus interim posset Dei donis. 812

11. Crediturus omnibus editurus eo. 836

12. "*Utrum Sacra Scriptura debeat uti metaphoris*," and "*Utrum Sacra Scriptura sub una littera habeat plures sensus*." *Summa theologiae* 1.1.9 and 1.1.10; "Ottawa" ed., 1: 8b.36–9b.39 and 9b.42–11a.11. Subsequent references are to the "Ottawa" edition.

13. "Est autem naturale homini ut per sensibilia ad intelligibilia veniat, quia omnis nostra cognitio a sensu initium habet . . . Convenit etiam Sacrae Scripturae . . . sub similitudinibus corporalium proponantur, ut saltem vel sic rudes eam capiant, qui ad intelligibilia secundum se capienda non sunt idonei." Ibid. 1.1.5 c.; 1: 9a.28–46.

14. ". . . auctor Sacrae Scripturae est Deus, in cuius potestate est ut non solum voces ad significandum accommodet, quod etiam homo facere potest, sed etiam res ipsas . . . Illa ergo prima significatio, qua voces significant res, pertinet ad primum sensum, qui est sensus historicus vel litteralis . . . sensus spiritualis . . . super litteralem fundatur et eum supponit." Ibid. 1.1.10 c.; 1: 10a.31–45.

15. ". . . ut dicit Augustinus in epistola *Contra Vincentium* . . . nihil sub spirituali sensu continetur fidei necessarium, quod Scriptura per litteralem sensum alicubi manifeste non tradat." Ibid. 1.1.10, Ad 1; 1: 10b.28–34.

16. See Eusebius of Caesarea, *Historia ecclesiastica* 6.25.11–14. On the Epistle to the Hebrews, Origen was reported to have held: ". . . the diction . . . better Greek . . . admitted by everyone . . . able to discern differences in style . . . the thoughts are The Apostle's . . . [but] who wrote the epistle, in truth God knows" (*tis dē ō grapsas tēn epistolēn, tō mēn altethēs theōs oīden*). Greek was unknown to Brother Thomas as to most western scholars of his day; Robert Grosseteste, the Bishop of Lincoln, and Roger Bacon, O.F.M., were conspicuous exceptions.

17. Thomas, *Summa theologiae* 1.1.10 c.; 1: 10a.46–49.

18. Ibid., 1: 10a.51–10b.8.

19. John Duns Scotus, *In Sent.* 4.9.1; Thomas Aquinas, *Opera omnia*, 16: 488a.

20. "Dicendum quod maximum habet auctoritatem Ecclesiae consuetudo . . . usus nunquam habuit quod Iudaeorum filii invitis parentibus baptizarentur. . . ." Thomas Aquinas, *Summa theologiae* 2–2.10.12; 3: 1466b.4–14; the point here is that Church practice takes precedence over Church personalities cited against the thesis Thomas here defends.

21. ". . . melius enim esset ut Iudeos laborare compellerent ad proprium uictum lucrandum, sicut in partibus Ytalia faciunt, quam quod otiosi uiuentes de solis usuris ditentur et sic eorum domini suis redditibus defraudentur." "*Epistola ad Ducissam Brabantiae*," in Thomas Aquinas, *Opera omnia*, Rome ed., 42: 376.83–88.

22. See his "*De unitate intellectus contra Averroistas*," a mildly misleading title, since he there dissented from Averroës and his followers, but other Muslim thinkers as well; ibid., 43: 289–314.

23. These instances of how alien Jewish internal customs and convictions were to Saint Thomas have been dealt with in my essay, Synan, "Some Medieval Perceptions." See Thomas Aquinas, *Ad Galatas* 2.1.63, Turin ed., 579.

24. Ibid., 2.1.61, Turin ed., 579.

25. Ibid., 3.4.140, Turin ed., 597.

26. See Bacon, "*Opus minus*," 332, and *Opus majus*, 1: 92.

27. Vocht, *History of the Foundation and the Rise of the Collegium Trilingue Lovaniense*. Cerfaux (1883–1968) taught at Louvain from 1928 to 1953, Coppens (1896–1981) from 1927 to 1967.

28. *Si Lyra non lyrasset,*
totus mundus delirasset.

Cited thus by Feret, *La faculté de théologie de Paris*, 3: 338, but see n. 34.

29. In general, the notion that Nicholas had influenced Luther has long been counted "absurd;" see J. Soury, *Bibliothèque de l'École des Chartes* 54 (1893): 738, cited by Smalley, *The Study of the Bible*, xvi. The possible influence of Nicholas on Luther's views of the Book of Genesis has been the object of a doctoral dissertation, by Kalita, "The Influence of Nicholas of Lyra on Martin Luther's 'Commentary on Genesis'"; Kalita has concluded that, under four possible headings (Hebrew language, rabbinic exegesis, the literal sense, and the interpretation of concrete texts), this influence was inconsiderable; this valuable study focuses the general remark of H. Denifle, O.P., on "scholastic" influence on Luther before 1530 in *Luther und Luthertum*, 1.1: 376: ". . . Thomas v. Aquin hat sie, wie wir oben gesehen, nur wissenschaftlich entwickelt; er sowohl, wie die übrigen Lehrer, und dazu die Glosse des Nikolaus von Lyra, haben jene Lehre der Nachwelt bis Luther vermittelt, und der Luther vor 1530 hat sie angenommen." Kalita cited (p. 36) a curious combination of two of the Latin plays on the name of Nicholas' birthplace cited earlier:

Si Nicholas non lyrasset,
Totus mundus delirasset,
Et Lutherus non saltasset.

30. See Glorieux, *La littérature quodlibetique*, 200, 201; there Glorieux lists three quodlibetal questions by Nicholas printed among the works of John Duns Scotus in his *Omnia opera*, 5: 328b–331a, 331a–334a, and 404a–417a; this last Question, "*Utrum per sacram Scripturam possit efficaciter probari finalis salus Salomonis?*" exemplifies several characteristics of the scholastic culture of Nicholas. First, it asserts the theological preeminence of biblical revelation over human rationalizing; second, it more than hints at his concern for the conversion of the Jews to Christianity by scriptural demonstrations based on texts acceptable to those prospective converts; third, it lists the "four senses" in a passage reminiscent of the two lines of verse given at the beginning

of this essay and cited in his *Postilla* by Nicholas. Last, it shows that Nicholas sided with Jerome (and the Rabbis of the Land) on the canon of the Old Covenant, but that he did so with a tactful approval of the Church usage that included their reading during religious services for their moral value.

31. ". . . réaction contre un certain thomisme–le néo-scotiste Cerfaux . . . ," Descamps, "Monseigneur Lucien Cerfaux," 45–57.

32. Duns Scotus, "Quaestio VI," in *Opera omnia*, 5: 405a/b, no. 3.

33. ". . . *si ex aliis sensibus sumeretur probatio, sequeretur quod in argumento semper esset fallacia aequivocationis et amphiboliae. . . .*" Ibid., 406, no. 4.

34. See the essays on this theme collected in Knuuttila, *Knowledge and the Sciences*; papers were given at the quinquennial conference of La société pour l'étude de la philosophie médiévale, held August 24–29, 1987, in Helsinki.

35. *Posterior Analytics* 1.31.87b25–39; *Metaphysics* 11.1.1059b25, 26; 11.2.1060b20, 21.

36. Duns Scotus, "Quaestio VI," in *Opera omnia*, 5: 411a, no. 13.

37. "*Scriptura sacra . . . cujus auctoritas tanta est, quod praecellit omnem demonstrationem. . . .*" Ibid., 404b, no. 3.

38. Ibid., 414a, no. 18.

39. Ibid., 414b, no. 19.

40. ". . . *per modum Doctoris determinantis quaestionem quamdam dubiam.*" Ibid., 415b no. 20.

41. ". . . *unde dicitur Hebraice* Cohelet, *quod interpretatur concinator.*" Ibid., 415 a/b, no. 20.

42. Simon, a Roman Catholic priest, was the author of two extensive volumes in which he argued that Moses had used a number of preexisting "mémoires" in composing the Pentateuch. He was expelled from the Congregation of the Oratory and his published works placed on the Roman Index. His theories had provoked the opposition not only of the Gentlemen of Port-Royale but that of Bossuet, bishop of Meaux, as well. Simon retired and died in obscurity, but Jean Astruc, a medical doctor, knew, admired and, it is here claimed, furthered the work of Simon with new, concrete evidence.

43. This small volume, printed anonymously at Brussels in 1753, carries on its title page a significant citation from Lucretius, *Rerum natura* 1.926, 927:

> Avia Pieridum peragro loca, nullius antè
> *Trita solo.*
>
> I wander the pathless places of the Muses, before by no one's
> sole [have they been] trodden.

Bibliography

Astruc, Jean. *Conjectures sur les memoires originaux dont il paroit que Moyse s'est servit pour composer le livre de la Genèse.* Brussels: Fricx, 1973.

Bacon, Roger. *Opus majus*. Ed. J. H. Bridges. 3 vols. Oxford: Clarendon Press, 1897–1900.

——. "Opus minus." In *Fr. Rogeri Bacon Opera quaedam hacternus inedita*. Ed. J. S. Brewer. London: Longman, Green, Longman and Roberts, 1859.

Cassian, John. *Conferences*. Ed. E. Pichery. 3 vols. SC, 42, 54, 64. Paris: Cerf, 1955–59.

Delhaye, Philippe. *Le microcosmus de Godefroy de Saint-Victor: étude théologique*. Lille: Facultés catholiques, 1951.

Denifle, H. *Luther und Luthertum in der ersten Entwickelung*. 2 vols. Mainz: Kirchheim, 1904–6.

Descamps, A. A. A. "Monsieur Lucien Cerfaux: ébauche d'un portrait." *Ephemerides theologicae Lovanienses* 45 (1969): 45–57.

Duns Scotus, John. *Opera omnia*. 26 vols. Paris: Vivès, 1891–95.

Feret, P. *La faculté de théologie de Paris et ses docteurs les plus célèbres*. 4 vols. Paris: A. Picard et fils, 1894–1897.

Glorieux, P. *La littérature quodlibetique*. Paris: J. Vrin, 1935.

Godfrey of Saint Victor. *The Fountain of Philosophy: A Translation of the Twelfth-Century Fons philosophiae*. Trans. E. A. Synan. Toronto: Pontifical Institute of Mediaeval Studies, 1972.

——. *Microcosmus*. Ed. Philippe Delhaye. Lille: Facultés catholiques, 1951.

——. "Preconium Augustini." Ed. P. Damon. *Mediaeval Studies* 22 (1960): 92–107.

Jerome. *Opera homiletica*. Ed. Germain Morin. CCSL, 78. Turnhout: Brepols, 1958.

Kalita, T. M. "The Influence of Nicholas of Lyra on Martin Luther's 'Commentary on Genesis'." S.T.D. diss., Catholic University of America, 1985.

Knuuttila, Simo, Reijo Työrinosa, and Stan Ebessen, eds. *Knowledge and the Sciences in Medieval Philosophy*. Helsinki: [s.n.] 1990.

Nicholas of Lyra. *Postilla super totam Bibliam*. 4 vols. Strassburg, 1492; reprint, Frankfurt am Main: Minerva, 1971.

Simon, Richard. *Histoire critique du Vieux Testament*. Rotterdam, 1685; reprint, Frankfurt: Minerva, 1967.

Smalley, Beryl. *The Study of the Bible in the Middle Ages*. Oxford: Clarendon Press, 1952.

Synan, E. A. "Some Medieval Perceptions of the Controversy on Jewish Law." In *Understanding Scripture: Explorations of Jewish and Christian Traditions of Interpretation*. Ed. Clemens Thoma and Michael Wyschogrod, 102–24. Mahwah, N.J.: Paulist Press, 1987.

Thomas Aquinas. *Ad Galatas*. Turin: Marietti, 1949.

——. *Sancti Thomae opera omnia*. 50 vols. Rome: Editori di San Tommaso, 1882–1992.

——. *Summa theologiae*. Rev. ed. 5 vols. Ottawa: Comissio Piana, 1953.

Vocht, Henri de. *History of the Foundation and the Rise of the Collegium Trilingue Lovaniense. 1517–1550*. 4 vols. Louvain: Bibliothèque de l'Université, Bureaux du Recueil, 1951–55.

15

Laudat sensum et significationem

Robert Grosseteste on the Four Senses of Scripture

JAMES R. GINTHER

Over forty years ago, Clarendon Press published, along with a number of other important essays, Beryl Smalley's assessment of Robert Grosseteste (ca. 1170–1253) as a biblical scholar.[1] It has become required reading for anyone interested in the writings of this thirteenth-century Oxford theologian who later became bishop of Lincoln. In her essay, Smalley made four preliminary conclusions concerning Grosseteste's exegesis, one of which was that Grosseteste "gave high priority in [h]is study to the spiritual exposition."[2] Smalley was a careful reader, and she did not make such a statement without good evidence. In his commentary on the Genesis creation story, the *Hexaëmeron*, Grosseteste explains the meaning of the light divided from the darkness:

> Allegorically the light of the Church is wise and spiritual prelates, who shine with the knowledge and love of truth and with the splendour of good works. The darkness is their subjects, wrapped in the darkness of ignorance and brutish and carnal. Light comes when the carnal sense of Scripture bursts forth into the spiritual sense.[3]

As a reformer, so Smalley argued, Grosseteste followed in the footsteps of twelfth-century theologians. He focused on spiritual exegesis since it provided vast resources for preachers of reform. And, since literal exegesis was hardly conducive to training students in moral theology, Grosseteste had little interest in this approach to sacred scripture.

In the forty years since, no one has questioned whether Grosseteste really was interested in spiritual exegesis alone. This reticence is curious in light of James McEvoy's 1975 edition and study of Grosseteste's commentary on Ecclesiasticus, which has only partially survived as comments on the first five verses of chapter 43. McEvoy noted in his introduction that the exposition was solely *ad litteram*, a supposedly unusual course for Grosseteste to take. Indeed, McEvoy suggested that "the reason why Grosseteste withheld himself from elaborating a full spiritual commentary on the text may have been his fear that, once started, he could not stop."[4] Such a supposition notwithstanding, McEvoy's study, at the very least, raises the question as to whether modern scholarship has a clear understanding of Grosseteste's treatment of the exposition of scripture.

The lack of clarity and precision concerning Grosseteste as a biblical expositor may be due to the paucity of relevant data. There are brief sightings of Grosseteste's theory of exegesis in his *Hexaëmeron*, as well as in his *De cessatione legalium*, which is his treatment on the relationship between the two testaments.[5] Nonetheless, scholars have yet to examine a text in which Grosseteste focuses primarily on his theory of biblical interpretation. Among Grosseteste's unpublished works, there is just such a text. What follows is an examination of this small work, which places it within the context of Grosseteste's other theological writings.

Dictum 19: Authorship and Date of Composition

The text in question is a sermon preached by Grosseteste before he became bishop of Lincoln, when he was teaching theology. It now survives as part of his *Dicta* collection and is listed as *Dictum* 19. The *Dicta* are a series of sermons and research notes that Grosseteste himself edited soon after he left Oxford for the episcopal chair in 1235.[6] *Dictum* 19 must be considered a sermon, and not one of Grosseteste's research notes.[7] It has all the classic features of a medieval sermon and even concludes with a reference to the endurance of the audience.[8] It reads like an inception sermon, in which the speaker is laying out his general perceptions of his teaching office as a *commendatio scripturae sacrae*. However, judgment should be reserved, since there is no explicit evidence either in the text or in its transmission that would indicate the specific circumstances of its presentation. It would appear that Grosseteste was preaching before an academic audience, or at least an audience familiar with the institutions of higher learning.[9] In the end, we may have to be satisfied with the descriptor *in scholis*, which applies to the entire *Dicta* collection.[10]

The sources employed by Grosseteste do not provide any helpful clues to the date of composition. The most commonly cited author is Augustine, who, not surprisingly, figures prominently in all of Grosseteste's theological pieces.[11] The other explicity cited writer is Cassiodorus, another common source for Grosseteste—although in this instance the citation is from the Psalms commentary of this early medieval thinker.[12] The only other work of Grosseteste to cite this work by Cassiodorus is his own exposition of the Psalter.[13] It would seem appropriate to argue that if Grosseteste began to read Cassiodorus's *Expositio Psalmorum* for the first time in preparation for his lectures on the Psalter, then *Dictum* 19 was written around the same time.[14] Moreover, if it is indeed Grosseteste's inaugural sermon, it would have preceded the commentary. Unfortunately, the date of the *Super Psalterium* has yet to be firmly established: it has been stated that the *terminus a quo* should be 1229, the year that Grosseteste was appointed lector in theology for the Oxford Franciscans.[15] While this preliminary conclusion is entirely reasonable, an earlier date cannot be ruled out until a critical edition is produced. Hence, at present nothing is gained, in terms of dating the sermon, by connecting *Dictum* 19 and the *Super Psalterium*. I would posit, provisionally, that *Dictum* 19 was written some time between 1229 and 1235, the period in which we are sure Grosseteste was involved in the teaching of theology. More precise dating will require further research.[16]

The sermon itself is a model of exposition, a careful analysis of a pericope from the prophet Ezekiel. The text comes from the second chapter, in which the prophet reports that a hand appeared before him with a closed scroll. The hand then opens the scroll, and Ezekiel notes that it was written on the inside and on the outside. Grosseteste focuses his explanation on three words from the text: the noun *liber* and the two adverbs *intus* and *foris*. In particular, he considers how one uses these adverbs to describe the book of scripture.

He first of all notes that sacred scripture enjoys a special place among books because it is written both externally and internally. It is written externally, like all other books, because the mode of communication is the forms of letters and words (*voces signantes*). It is also written externally when the historical sense is expressed in these forms. However, sacred scripture's superiority is based on the fact that it also has a meaning inscribed within it. The book is written internally when the historical meaning points to the tropological. Even more internal is the allegorical sense. Finally, the most intimate writing of the book is unfolded in the anagogical reading of supernal contemplation.[17] For the remaining portions of the sermon, Grosseteste explores what these four modes of exegesis mean. His discussion appears to be out of step with his initial description of the four senses. While he maintains some sense of progressing deeper into the text, from the literal to the anagogical, Grosseteste also describes each form of exposition as having its own external and internal feature.

The Secular Sciences and the Literal Sense

Grosseteste spends almost half the sermon on the problems of the literal sense. He begins by noting the need to understand the letters and words of the text. Equally important, however, is an understanding of the natural elements of the created world to which sacred scripture refers. Knowledge of creation is crucial for understanding the literal sense, for only in considering God's wondrous creation can the reader "ascend internally towards a recognition of the truth."[18] Grosseteste supplements this assertion with two passages from the Psalter which share a common notion. In both instances the Psalmist states that he has remembered the past works of God, and this memory leads him to further acts of meditation upon them.[19]

The first pericope from the Psalms (76:12–13) receives some attention in Grosseteste's *Super Psalterium*. He notes there that human beings gain understanding of the invisible things of God through creation itself. For Grosseteste, these *invisibilia* are three major attributes of the Trinity, namely, power, wisdom, and goodness.[20] They exist in the visible world which is like a "book written by the finger of God." In this way, the evidence of God's attributes is available to both the literate and illiterate alike, because this book does not require any formal education on the part of the reader. Grosseteste grants that the meaning of the book of nature may be misunderstood, since carnal man (*stultus et animalis homo*) will see but not grasp its meaning. Instead, it is spiritual man who not only reads the book of nature but also discerns the reasons behind its works.[21] Recalling the wonders of nature should lead to meditation, in which the spiritual reader grasps the meaning of the text of nature and understands the symbols employed.[22] Meditation was a medieval activity grounded in the exemplary act of reading.[23]

But medieval readers of scripture, like those in any age, did not come to the sacred text with a blank slate. Before most students could begin the study of theology at a medieval university, they were usually required to master the diverse subject matter of the trivium and quadrivium.[24] This circumstance raises the question about the utility of all this learning in the higher science of theology. If, after all, sacred scripture contains all that is necessary for salvation, why would one need to have a grounding in the arts in order to be an expositor of this sacred science?

In the opening sections of the work he wrote after this sermon, the *Hexaëmeron*, Grosseteste broaches this issue under the heading of the sufficiency of scripture. He states that in addition to all that is necessary for human salvation, the book of scripture embraces the entire contents of nature, because it describes the creation of the world. Moreover, it encompasses all that is necessary for life and knowledge. He supports this claim with a well-known citation from Augustine: "Whatever man has learned outside of this scripture, if it is harmful, then it is condemned in the text, if it is useful then it is found there."[25]

In *Dictum* 19, this citation causes Grosseteste some concern. This statement of Augustine may produce amazement in those who first learned the secular arts and then have come to study scripture: they will discover that much of what they have learned appears nowhere in the sacred text. Exactly what passage of scripture contains the theorems of geometry? Where does one read about the rules governing the circuit of the sun and moon? If one takes Augustine's precept to its logical conclusion, the absence of these items would seem to indicate that they have no use in the study of the Bible.[26]

Grosseteste's examples of these missing arts provide an appropriate test for the Augustinian model. It would be possible to argue that some secular learning is necessary for the study of scripture, such as grammar, rhetoric, and, if one pressed the point, even logic. Moreover, the study of the world of plants and animals could be deemed appropriate because of their inclusion in the text, especially the careful enumeration of living creatures in the creation narrative and elsewhere in scripture. The quadrivium, however, was a more complicated matter. The prophets and the apostles were not given to mathematical discourse nor were they interested in the mechanics of the universe, unless there was a need to talk about a blackened sun, a bloody moon, or falling stars. All the sciences that were at the heart of Grosseteste's intellectual life seemed inappropriate for the study of the Bible, because they were not found within the sacred text.

This situation creates a theological problem. If one accepts the proposition that truth is about the essence of creation, then one cannot deem one part of creation irrelevant to the study of theology. This point is based on two related theological assertions. First, as Augustine noted, all creation bears the stamp of the Creator and so has a role to play in the testimony to Him. Second, God stated that all he had created was good. It is through the predicate of goodness, Grosseteste argues, that one may deem a created thing useful, for if God can use evil for good, then clearly good things are established for a good use. This good use is the created thing's utility. Since truth is about the essence of creation, which means truth and essence are the same thing, and all essence is good, therefore all truth about creation must be useful. This truth is learned in the secular sciences, which means that these must be useful in the study of the sacred page.[27]

But this thinking did not solve the problem of the absence of these sciences from the biblical text. All this philosophical wrangling will not transform Ezekiel into Euclid. Perhaps, then, some sciences are to be excluded from theology. A possible solution was to speak of the misuse of learning, that is to exclude those sciences that masters abused.

Such a solution would have found more than one sympathetic ear. In his famous letter to the pope, Stephen of Tournai was more than happy to enumerate the various abuses of learning found at the Paris studium at the beginning of the thirteenth century: "The studies of sacred letters among us are fallen into the workshop of confusion, while both disciples applaud novelties alone and masters watch out for glory rather than learning. . . . The indivisible Trinity is cut up and wrangled over in the trivium, so that now there are as many errors as doctors, as many scandals as classrooms, as many blasphemies as squares."[28] It might be wise, in light of these abuses, simply to withdraw this useless learning from the divine science. But if that were done, Grosseteste states, that act could easily exclude all forms of secular learning from theology, since any form of inquiry is open to abuse. Such a solution would bring the reader of scripture no closer to understanding Augustine's statement.[29]

Grosseteste then presents his own position: that scripture does appear to contain the truth of all the sciences and, moreover, approves of them. However, they act as certain elements or properties of the text, not as the subject matter. To illustrate what he means, Grosseteste presents two biblical texts. The first is from the first epistle of John: "no lies come from truth" (1 John 2:21). Here the reader discovers a dialectical maxim, that falsehood does not follow from truth. Scripture differs from a text on logic in that the author adds something to it, namely, the *edificatio morum*, which can be rendered as "the edification of habitual thinking," as was done by Brian Stock in his latest monograph, *Augustine the Reader*.[30] Grosseteste solidifies his argument by investigating a second passage, this time from the Genesis narrative: "And God divided the light from the darkness" (Gen 1:4). He then connects this to a passage from Paul's second letter to the Corinthians, which serves to illustrate his point. The fact that God divided light from darkness helps the Apostle to explain why Christians and pagans could not commingle. The people of light cannot conjoin with the people of darkness because contrary things cannot be connected. Here again we see a principle of logic employed by scripture. However, says Grosseteste, the Apostle adds to the biblical text "something which pertains to the building of morals and something which advances towards the light of faith and the fervour of love." It is these added conditions, so to speak, which allow for the secular sciences to be employed in the exposition of scripture.[31]

This description immediately brings to mind Grosseteste's brilliant discussion of subalternated sciences in his commentary on the *Posterior Analytics*. A subalternated science is one whose first principles are based on the conclusions of another science, which Grosseteste calls the subalternating science. Grosseteste was the first scholastic thinker to work out how it was possible for such conclusions to "descend" into another science. His solution was to introduce the "added condition." "A subject is subalternated to another whose subject adds a condition onto the subject of the subalternating science, which condition does not totally derive from the nature of the subject of the subalternating [science], but is assumed from without."[32] For example, if we think about *perspectiva*, the science of optics, its first principles are drawn from the conclusions of the science of geometry, whose subject is magnitude. *Perspectiva* is a science subalternated to geometry, because it adds the condition of "radiance" to produce the subject matter "radiant magnitude."[33]

Such a short explanation does not do justice to this complex concept. However, it becomes apparent that in *Dictum* 19 Grosseteste is not presenting theology as subalternated in this sense. One of the major criteria in this schema is that the subalternating science, which supplies the first principles, must be a higher science. In building a relationship between the secular arts and exegesis, Grosseteste is not producing a replica of subalternation, since all the secular sciences he has in mind are lower on the scale of knowledge. In some respects subalternation is akin to taking books from the top shelf; what Grosseteste is presenting in *Dictum* 19 is equivalent to lowering a bucket into a well.

More important, the investigation of the secular sciences is not what the study of scripture entails. When Scripture is properly expounded, Grosseteste continues, it either instructs one's faith or builds up love. This is the purpose of the sacred science. The only way the secular sciences participate in this process is by helping further these goals. In this regard one may discover the truth of secular sciences in scripture, in that they unlock the sacred page and thus enhance the instruction of faith or the building up of love. The secular sciences are then study aids to the superior form of inquiry, the exposition of scripture.[34]

This would appear to be a rather lengthy route to follow in order to end up at yet another Augustinian coordinate: Grosseteste's arguments simply echo the famous image of *De doctrina christiana*, in which Augustine encourages his readers to plunder pagan learning for the sake of Christian erudition, just as the Israelites had plundered the Egyptians before leaving for the promised land.[35] Ultimately Grosseteste does not seek to move beyond the Augustinian model, but he does want to present a clear relationship between secular learning and the study of scripture. In doing so he establishes three things. First, he clarifies the legitimacy of pursuing the secular sciences, something he continued to do even after he began to lecture on theology in the schools.[36] The philosophical arguments presented in *Dictum* 19 reveal that this is more than just a pedagogical concern; it reflects a well-developed view of the essential features of creation. Second, the designation of these sciences as study aids prevents the possibility of the biblical text being overshadowed by scientific interests. The book of scripture is not a variation on the book of nature. The goal of biblical exegesis is to interpret the closed book in order to increase the reader's faith and love. Finally, Grosseteste establishes the importance of the literal exposition. The literal sense points to the fundamental role of creation in the revealing of biblical truth.[37] Grosseteste does not argue that real meaning is found only in the spiritual exposition of scripture: meaning begins with the literal sense. Grosseteste admits that this explanation is incomplete, and he relinquishes this point of controversy to wiser minds who can dissect the problem even further.[38]

Allegory and Morality: Human Psychology and the Reflexivity of Exegesis

If Grosseteste's treatment of the literal sense is unusual, his examination of the spiritual senses is even more curious. The traditional account of Grosseteste's exegesis, as has been already noted, insists that he focused mainly on the allegorical meaning. He had little time for the literal exposition and was more eager to press on to the spiritual understanding of the text. There is some truth in this depiction; it must be qualified, however, as can be seen by a brief focus on two other works from Grosseteste's days at Oxford, the *De cessatione legalium* and the *Super Psalterium*.

At the beginning of the former, Grosseteste presents one of the major problems in the Christian exegesis of Mosaic law. He points out that the mandates of circumcision and the observance of the Sabbath were to be obeyed in perpetuity. How, then, can Christians state they are no longer necessary? Grosseteste tests the waters with a number of possible solutions only to demonstrate their faults. One suggestion is that the Christian expositor may simply expound these texts mystically and can therefore avoid the problem of literal perpetual obedience. It would seem to be a correct path to take, since this was the major thrust of medieval exegesis of the Old Testament. However, Grosseteste pauses here to consider the implications of this approach, and he finds it inappropriate. A good teacher does not say one thing when he means another: "If something is signified in his words which is other than what he intends to teach, he is not the best teacher, but rather he is either unlearned or a deceiver." In this case, God as the author of scripture is the best teacher and he means what he says. Moreover, what he intended is exactly what he wishes masters in theology now to teach. Grosseteste's point is clear: spiritual interpretation must be drawn from a proper understanding of the author's original intent.[39]

There is a parallel approach in his exposition of the Psalms. In the prologue to the *Super Psalterium*, Grosseteste broaches the prophetic nature of the Psalter, focusing on the kind of revelation David and others received.[40] In the tradition of earlier commentators, and in unison with contemporary thinkers, Grosseteste states that the author of a Psalm did not receive his prophetic vision through any signs or corporeal images; rather, the Holy Spirit illuminated his mind to allow him to contemplate the truth directly. Unlike his predecessors, Grosseteste finds this form of prophecy problematic for the exegete. He asks: "If [these truths] are in the imagination (*in spiritu*) without any corporeal signs expressed, how can these songs speak allegorically?"[41] It is a question that does not appear to have caused any other medieval commentator concern. Yet for Grosseteste, it goes to the heart of his exegetical strategy for the Psalms, since it raises the question of whether an image or an event mentioned in the Psalms can be said to represent allegorically another person, event, or idea.

Grosseteste is quite willing to admit that in this category of prophecy authors of the Psalms far excel all others. However, this does not mean that allegorical interpretations based on figures and natural objects have no role to play in the Psalms. Indeed, each author may have seen in his mind the truth which had been illuminated by the Holy Spirit without any signs, but, because of the weakness of his audience, he may at times have veiled the truth with figures. Each author did this because on occasion an object that obstructs vision can actually aid the viewer. One of the early manuscripts of the *Super Psalterium* records an analogy of clouds which allow a person to see the sun, an object that one cannot behold directly. Each author of the Psalms may have been able to see the truth directly, Grosseteste concludes, but his audience could not.[42] The upshot of this approach to allegory is that it is highly dependent upon authorial intent.[43]

Connected to this approach to allegorical exegesis in the Psalms is the practice of reading the text prosopologically. This ancient Christian form of reading assumed that the Psalms were either about Christ or his mystical body, the Church. It was thus possible to read a Psalm in the person of Christ, or in the person of the Church. In monastic readings of the Psalms, it was suggested that not only did one read in the person of the Christ, or the Church, or even of David himself, but one became that person in the act of reading. In prosopological exegesis, the reader becomes the author.[44]

While Grosseteste embraces this method in his exposition of the Psalms, in *Dictum* 19 he pushes the reader's assimilation even further. He begins his treatment of the spiritual senses by stating that there are more excellent ways of expounding scripture. He writes: "Scripture is more excellent in the human mind than on dead parchment."[45] It is the transformative nature of sacred scripture that concerns Grosseteste. The reader becomes not the author but rather the text. The book of scripture in this second mode of exegesis is the human mind inscribed with the truths of this science. This is so because the human mind is impressed with each and every species presented in the text. Grosseteste supports this claim with two verses, which present God sitting in judgment reading from a text. That text is the human mind, which on the day of judgment will be opened for all to see.[46]

Here the human soul is a book that is inscribed both externally and internally. In becoming the text, the soul first begins to comprehend the written text externally through what Grosseteste calls the "cognitive gaze of the mind" (*aspectus mentis*). This is not the end of the process, though, because the text must also be written within. This is accomplished when the will of the reader, or what Grosseteste calls the *affectus mentis*, is transformed. The process cannot proceed in any other way, Grosseteste asserts, for we cannot love what we do not know. The process of reading and becoming the text does not end here, for this kind of reading is reflexive. The written text may transform the mind of the reader, but it will also lead to external works of love. In this way, the book of scripture may be read by one's observing the external works of the expositor of the sacred text.[47]

Almost a decade later, when lecturing at the University of Paris, John of La Rochelle would say virtually the same thing. Whereas other sciences are directed only toward an understanding of the truth, John writes in his introduction to scripture, the exposition of scripture is directed toward the teaching of virtue. Teaching a discipline with such an end means that the subject must touch the soul of the teacher. "A wise man," John observes, "first incorporates the sacred knowledge into his own life through good will and works, and that knowledge flows into others when he lectures or preaches."[48]

Grosseteste, however, takes this idea one step further, which is the third mode of exposition. If scripture transforms the disposition of the reader, this transformation must have an impact on how he interprets. These works, which are the product of reading, act as a light which illuminates the mind. What begins as external writing moves to the inscription of the text internally in the human soul, which in turns bursts forth into external works. Finally, these works affect the continued act of reading scripture. It is because of this reflexivity that scripture is compared to a wheel, an image Grosseteste may have drawn from Gregory the Great's *Homilies on Ezekiel*.[49] Moreover, it is possible to describe this process as an ethics of reading in that it transforms the disposition of the reader. This is the main reason why rendering the phrase *edificacio morum* as "the edification of habitual thinking" best captures Grosseteste's notion of exegesis. The exposition of sacred Scripture changes the state of the reader to such a great degree, that the distinction between reader and text almost disappears.[50]

This idea takes us far beyond the simplistic notion that allegory teaches Christians what to believe and the moral sense teaches them what to do. However, it is not the theoretical dimensions of reading *per se* that capture Grosseteste's interest. Exegesis is not about the deconstruction of the text, but rather about the reconstruction of the exegete. In this sermon, Grosseteste seeks to explain why scripture surpasses all other texts. Any other text does not illuminate the *aspectus mentis*, he says, but rather darkens it; it does not shape the will, but rather deforms it. It is scripture alone that elevates man beyond himself and toward God, causing him to live according to God's nature. No other text can accomplish this.[51]

Anagogy: Finding the Creator

Exhaustive as this process is, it does not end here. The ultimate key to the exposition of scripture is found not in the dynamic relationship between reader and text, but rather in that between reader and Creator. This is the final level of exposition: to understand that the book is inscribed externally and internally as the word and wisdom of God. In some respects we have come full circle, because Grosseteste notes that the external inscription of the wisdom of God is the stamp and form of all creation. Its internal writing is the very image and substance of the Father. This in fact is the aim of anagogical reading: to take the reader beyond the written text, beyond creation, beyond himself, and to focus his mind on the highest reality.[52] For this reason, Grosseteste interprets the hand that holds the book in the Ezekiel passage as the word of the Father which creates all things. It is the *rationes aeternae* which allows the expositor to open the book in the first place.[53]

This conclusion leads Grosseteste to consider two basic features of this key to exegesis. The first is that the exposition of scripture entails a search for wisdom in created reality. He cites a long passage from the book of Wisdom concerning the discovery of Wisdom and allows Augustine to guide the audience in understanding it. Augustine's remarks consider the danger of focusing solely on the created symbol without considering the deeper meaning behind it.[54] Grosseteste had echoed this concern elsewhere when he wrote that all creation is a mirror which reflects the unity of the Trinity.[55]

Second, the only way in which these hidden realities can come to the exegetical light of day is within the broader context of the Incarnation. For Grosseteste, this is the ultimate code breaker. All that is written in scripture, Grosseteste claims, is found in the Word made flesh. Indeed, this is the only reason one can proceed at all with any form of allegorical exposition at all. He notes the Augustinian rule that obscure biblical texts can be clarified by more explicit texts. Something said allegorically in one passage may be said explicitly in the literal reading of another passage. Grosseteste has in mind here the Gospels, where the life, death, and resurrection of Jesus are the keys to understanding the hidden realities of the Old Testament.[56]

Conclusion

I conclude with some observations on the theory of the four senses which emerges from Grosseteste's sermon. This study was undertaken with an awareness of the possible gap between theory and practice, between what medieval expositors say and what they actually do. Nevertheless, this kind of assessment of Grosseteste's works can be undertaken only when we have a clear understanding of both his theory and his practice. With the publication of the *Hexaëmeron* over a decade ago, and more recently his Galatians commentary, a picture of Grosseteste as a biblical exegete is beginning to emerge.[57] This image will be further focused once his commentary on the Psalms is published.[58] The aim of this present study is to provide the theoretical outlines of Grosseteste's exegesis, which will enable us to determine if there is any gap between his theory and his practice.

However even the conclusions of a comparative approach would have to be considered tentative, for there is a real danger in collapsing medieval exegesis into theories of the four senses. The exposition of scripture as a historical act has a number of components. It begins first with engagement with the text, but it makes use of a number of filters, such as patristic authorities, the *Glossa ordinaria*, the secular arts, liturgy, contemporary debates and commentaries, as well as theoretical approaches such as the four-senses model. Furthermore, exegesis also had an intended audience, and so, for example, in scholastic exegesis we must consider the variables of the rhetorical devices employed, as well as the desire to engage contemporary thinkers on certain subjects. In light of this highly complex historical construction, Grosseteste's theory of the four senses accounts for only one part of his exegetical program.

Nonetheless, some initial points can be made about Grosseteste's understanding of exegesis. First, this sermon establishes that Grosseteste embraced all four senses as essential to a proper understanding of sacred scripture. The literal sense encompassed not only an understanding of grammar, but also an appreciation of creation, in expounding of the text. Spiritual exposition drew the reader further into the text, only to transform his disposition and collapse the distinction between the written text and the human mind. That dynamic had a practical result in which the transformed behavior of the reader affected how he would continue to read scripture. Ultimately, the exposition of scripture took the reader beyond the text and focused his mind on the highest reality. The key to this whole system of exegesis lay in understanding creation as an exemplar of its Creator, and more important, the centrality of the Incarnation to the biblical narrative.

Grosseteste's treatment of the four senses is built upon the accepted epistemological premise that created things can signify eternal truths. He also understood that exposition entailed a certain strategy of reading, indeed an ethical one at that. Beyond this, however, was his conviction that the sacred text was a means to know God, a place where a reader encountered the eternal, life-changing realities of his Creator. The exposition of scripture was about living the Christian life, which was to lead the reader to discover within the confines of a temporally limited event—a written text—the eternal Word of God.

Notes

I am indebted to my colleague Dr. Hugh Pyper for advice concerning theories of textuality and reading, and to Mr. David Wiljer for his insightful comments on a previous draft of this chapter. All conclusions and errors, though, remain my responsibility.

1. Smalley, "The Biblical Scholar." The most recent biography of Grosseteste is Southern, *Robert Grosseteste*, although Stevenson, *Robert Grosseteste*, is still of some use. See also the discussion of Grosseteste's life and writings in Callus, "Robert Grosseteste as Scholar." Some of Callus's conclusions have been updated in McEvoy, *The Philosophy of Robert Grosseteste*, 3–48,

while others have been challenged by Southern, *Robert Grosseteste*, esp. 3-25, 63-82. Also indispensable is Thomson, *The Writings of Robert Grosseteste*.

2. Smalley, "The Biblical Scholar," 85.

3. Ibid. See Grosseteste, *Hexaëmeron* 2.9.2, ed. Dales and Gieben, 96-97: "Item allegorice lux ecclesie sunt prelati, sapientes et spiritales, qui lucent veritatis cognicione et amore et bonorum operum exteriori splendore. Tenebre vero sunt subditi tenebris ignorancie involuti et animales et carnales. Item lux fit, cum sensus carnalis Scripture erumpit in sensum spiritalem."

4. James McEvoy, "The Sun as *res* and *signum*," 56.

5. *Hexaëmeron* 1.1.1-1.2.2, ed. Dales and Gieben, 49-51; Grosseteste, *De cessatione legalium* 1.9.1-1.9.8, ed. Dales and King, 47-51.

6. On the *Dicta*, see Thomson, *Writings*, 214-32. This collection still awaits a detailed examination, and a critical edition would provide a better understanding of Grosseteste's theology and his time as a master of theology at Oxford. What complicates this matter even more is the muddled relationship the *Dicta* have with the manuscript transmission of Grosseteste's *Super Psalterium*. See Ginther, "The *Super Psalterium* of Robert Grosseteste," 66-68; and Streitz, "Robert Grosseteste: *Commentarius in Psalmos I-XXXVI*," where some of the relevant *Dicta* have been edited.

7. This *Dictum* is printed in Westermann, "An Edition," 107-19, although the transcription is marred by a number of infelicities. I have employed only one manuscript copy for this study: London, British Library, MS Royal 6.E.v, where the sermon is found on fols. 13va-14va. For a description of this manuscript, see Thomson, *Writings*, 11-12, and Warner and Wilson, *Catalogue of Western Manuscripts*, 1:155-157. My selection of this witness is based mainly on its availability in microfilm and not on any particular codicological or editorial feature. It should be noted that this is a deluxe manuscript from the mid-fourteenth century which contains many of Grosseteste's principal theological works.

8. *Dictum* 19, fol. 14va: ". . . et, ne in longum protraham sermonem, quamuis priuata reducit ad habitum, dimunita ad complementum completu sustinet, ne vergant in detrimentum."

9. Grosseteste makes reference to the teaching of theology: Ibid., fol. 13vb: "Dicat ergo vnusquisque professor huius sapiencie, eciam si sit eruditus omni sciencia Egipciorum, cum Moyse: 'Obsecro Domine, non sum eloquens ab heri et nudius tercius et ex quo locutus es ad seruum tuum, impedicioris et tardioris lingue sum' (Exod 4:10). Dicatque cum Ieremiae: 'A. a. a. Domine Deus, nescio loqui quia puer ego sum' (Jer 1:6)."

10. Thomson, *Writings*, 214, records Grosseteste's prefatory comments: "In hoc libello sunt 147 capitula quorum quedam sunt brevia verba que dum in scolis morabar scripsi breviter et incomposito sermone ad memoriam. Nec sunt de una materia nec adinvicem continuata: quorum titulos posui ut facilius quod vellet lector posset invenire. Spondent itaque plerumque plus aliqui tituli quam solvant capitula lectori. Quedam vero sunt sermones quos eodem tempore ad clerum vel ad populum feci." This appears as the colophon to the collection in the Royal MS (fol. 69ra).

11. For Augustine's influence on Grosseteste see McEvoy, *Philosophy of Grosseteste*, 51-68, and, Southern, *Robert Grosseteste*, 32-33, 183-84.

12. Grosseteste quotes from the prologue (*Dictum* 19, fol. 14ra): "Huic modo videtur consentire Cassiodorus super Psalmos, qui ex verbis Augustini asserit: 'Omnia diuersa scemeta secularium litterarum in sacris litteris inueneri, insuper et eius proprios modos in primis eloquiis quos gramatici siue rethores nullatenus attigerant.' Deinde ne ex proprio sensu hec videatur dicere, sic subiungit: 'Sicud dixerunt hec ante nos et alii doctissimi patres in Ieronymo, Ambrosio, Hillario, vt nequaquam nos presumptores huius rei, sed pedisseque, esse videamur. Sed dicit aliquis, nec partes ille sillogismo, nec nomina scematum, nec vocabula disciplinarum, nec alia huius nullatenus inueniuntur in Psalmis. Inueniunter plane in virtute sensuum, non in efficcione verborum, sicud enim vina in vitibus, messem in semine, frondes in radicibus, fructus in ramis, arboris ispsas sensu contemplamur in nucleis. Nam et de profundissima abisso deliciosus piscis

attingitur qui tamen ante capcionem suam humanis oculis non videtur.'" Cf. Cassiodorus, *Expositio Psalmorum*, praef.15, ed. Adriaen, 1:20.

13. Ginther, "The *Super Psalterium* of Robert Grosseteste," 89. A quick check of the *index auctorum* of Grosseteste's works edited to date reveals no citations from Cassiodorus's *Expositio Psalmorum*.

14. There is a strong connection between *Dictum* 19 and the comments on Psalm 76:12, which will be discussed shortly.

15. Southern, *Robert Grosseteste*, 118–19.

16. There is considerable dispute over the chronology of Grosseteste's theological career prior to his becoming the lector in theology to the Oxford Franciscans in 1229/30. According to the traditional view, Grosseteste was a master of theology at Oxford from ca. 1214 onward, and was Oxford's first chancellor around that same time. More recently, Southern, *Robert Grosseteste*, 63–82, argued that Grosseteste could not possibly have been such a master until 1225, after he had been ordained a priest. Southern was criticized in a review by James McEvoy (Review, 354–55). In the second edition of his biography, in 1989, Southern took the occasion to answer his critics (McEvoy being only one of them), laying out the historiographical background to his position. A satisfactory resolution still eludes scholars as some recent articles have argued that Grosseteste may have been in Paris in the 1220s: Goering, "When and Where Did Grosseteste Study Theology?"; and Schulman, "Husband, Father, Bishop? Grosseteste in Paris." Nonetheless, none of the evidence presented in these two last studies brings into question the dates of Grosseteste's lectorship in theology to the Franciscans at Oxford.

Since completing this essay, I have come to a firmer conclusion that this sermon is indeed Grosseteste's inception sermon and that it should be dated to 1229–30, when he became lector in theology for the Oxford Franciscans. The arguments and supporting evidence for this conclusion can be found in my "Natural Philosophy and Theology at Oxford in the Early Thirteenth Century."

17. *Dictum* 19, fol. 13va: "'Vidi, et ecce manus missa ad me, in qua erat inuolutus liber. Et expandit illum coram <me> qui erat scriptus intus et foris' (Ezek 2:9). Liber iste sacra scriptura, que statim ipso sue scripcionis mirifico modo suam ad scripturas ceteras ostendit prerogatiuam. Ceterarum namque scripturarum libri solum foris sunt scripti. Hic autem liber cum ceteris foris scribitur, dum per litterarum apices aut signantes voces historicus sensus exprimitur. Preter vero communionem cum ceteris prerogatiuam habet interne scripcionis, dum res signate litterarum apicibus et signa<n>tibus vocibus fuerunt. Iterum, signa res preter intenciones signancia scribitur intra, dum per historiam signatur tropologia. Scribitur adhuc interius cum signatur sensus allegoricus; scribitur autem intime dum superne contemplacionis panditur anagoge. Quapropter qua collacione se habent ad scripturas ceteras litterarum apices, signantes voces hac se habent ad istam. Quasi creaturarum species talis, que est ad legendum librum hunc quoad internam eius scripcionem, ignarus ordinis; et est creaturarum qualis <que> est ad legendos libros ceteros ignarus litterarum sil<a>barum et dictionum."

18. Ibid.: "Unde non immerito tanto opere nos ad consideranda mirabilia Dei exitat scriptura vt per ea, que foris cernimus, intus ad agnicionem veritatis ascendamus."

19. Ibid., fol. 13va–vb: "Vnde Psalmista quasi pro magno aliquo se iam et hoc fecisse commemorat et adhuc facturum promittit, dicens (Ps 76:12–13): 'Memor fui operum Dei, quia memor ero ab inicio mirabilium tuorum, et meditabor in omnibus operibus tuis et ad<in>uencionibus tuis exercebor.' Et alibi (Ps 142:5): 'Memor fui dieorum antiquorum meditatus sum in omnibus operibus tuis, et in factis manuum tuarum meditabor.'"

20. *Super Psalterium*, 76:12 (Bologna, Biblioteca dell' Archiginnasio, MS 983, fol. 46vb): "Inuisibilia Dei a creatura mundi per ea que facta sunt intellecta conspiciuntur. Tria sunt invisibilia Dei: potentia, sciencia et benignitas. Ab hiis tribus procedunt omnia, in hiis tribus consistunt omnia et per hec tria reguntur omnia. Potentia creat, sapientia gubernat et benignitas conseruat

que tria sunt. Quod cum tria sunt ineffabiliter in Deo vnum sunt: ita in operacione separari non possunt. Potentia per benignitatem sapienter creat [in marg.]; sapientia per potentiam benigne gubernat; benignitas per sapientiam potenter conseruat."

21. Ibid.: "Vniuersalis enim ille mundus sensibilis quasi liber quidam [*quedam* ms.] scriptus est digito Dei, hoc est in virtute diuina creatus et singule creature quasi figure quedam sunt non humano inuente placido, sed diuino arbitrio institute ad manifestandum, id est, quasi quodammodo significationem, Dei inuisibilem sapientiam. Quemadmodum autem si illiteratus que apertum librum videat aspicit et literas non cognoscit, ita stultus et animalis homo qui no percipit ea que Dei sunt invisibilibus istis creaturis foris videt speciem sed non intelligit rationem. Qui autem spiritalis est in omnia iudicare potest, et foris considerat pulcritudinem operis: intus concipit quam miranda sunt sapientia Creatoris et ideo nemo est cui aperta Dei mirabilia non sunt dum insipiens solam foris miratur speciem. Sapiens autem per id quod foris videt profundam tu<e>atur diuine sapientie cognicionem velut in vna eademque pictura alter colorem sue formacione signarum commendet." The motif of the book of nature also appears in Richard Fishacre's prologue to his commentary on the Sentences of Peter Lombard. See Long, "The Science of Theology according to Richard Fishacre," 80.

22. Super Psalterium, fols. 46vb–47ra: "Aliter vero laudat sensum et significacionem. Bonum est ergo assidue contemplari ad admirari opera diuina sed ei qui rerum corporalium pulcritudinem in vsum nouum vertere spiritalem. Nam et ideo scriptura tanto opere nos ad consideranda mirabilia Dei exitat vt per ea que cernimus, intus ad agnicionem veritatis ascendamus. Vnde psalmus: pro magno aliquo se iam et hoc fecisse commemorat et ad hoc facturum promittit aliquid dicens, Memor fui, etc. Nota quod hic tangit per memoriam firmam inuentorum et agnitorum retentionem per meditationem diligentem, nondum agnitorum inuestigationem per affeccionem voluntatis ductionem secundum veritatis agnitionem."

23. Carruthers, *The Book of Memory*, 156–88.

24. A mastership in Arts did not become a regulated prerequisite for theological study at Oxford until 1253, at which point it was introduced to prevent Thomas of York O.F.M. from incepting in theology. Grosseteste, however, in Dictum 19 writes as if an arts education was a standard step to theology in his time, though not necessarily in the form of a completed degree. See Catto, "Theology and Theologians, 1200-1320," 475–76, and Rashdall, The Universities of Europe in the Middle Ages, 3:68. Sheehan, "The Religious Orders, 1220-1370," 204, describes the response to Thomas of York's attempted inception as an enforcement of "a longstanding regulation."

25. Hexaëmeron 1.4.1, ed. Dales and Gieben, 54; Dictum 19, fol. 13vb: "Cum autem, vt dictum est, aliarum scripturarum complementa sunt sicud huius scripture elementa, patet quam vere, licet inopinabile, dicat Augustinus: 'Quod quicquid homo extra hanc scripturam didicit, si noxium est, in ista damnatur, si vtile est, in ea inuenitur. Et cum ista quisque inuenerit omnia, que vtiliter alibi didicit, multo habundancius inueniet, ea que nusquam omnino alibi, sed eciam istius termino scripture mirabili altitudine et mirabili humilitate discuntur.'"

26. Dictum 19, fol. 13vb: "Sed forte iste sermo mirabilis Augustini quosdam vertit in admiracionem, qui postquam seculares litteras didicerunt sacram scripturam consequenter pertransierunt. Nec in ea inuenerunt plurima que alibi vera didicerunt. Vbi [*Vt* ms.] enim inueniri potest in sacra pagina diametrum esse assimetrum coste aut aliquod de ceteris theorematibus geometrie? Aut vbi in ea inueniuntur canones quibus solis et lune sine defectu sumuntur? Defectus ceterarumque arcium conclusiones innumeras."

27. Ibid.: "Sed quomodo verum et maxime quod verum est de esse creature non de eius defectione potest esse intuile, cum omnis creatura testante verbo Christi gerat aliquod exemplar honesti significacioque mistica, vt dicit Augustinus: 'Ab omni creatura sumenda est'? Omnis eciam creatura bona ac per hoc vtilis. 'Vidit enim Deus cuncta que fecit et erant valde bona' (Gn 1:31). Quod si eciam Deus quolibet malo bene vtitur mandato amplius quodlibet [*vsi* expung.]

bonum ad vsum bonum ab ipso statuitur, ipseque vsus bonus eius est vtilitas. Non est ergo aliquod verum maxime de esse creature quod vtile non est quia verum et esse idem sunt."

28. Denifle and Chatelain, eds. *Chartularium universitatis Parisiensis*, 1:47–48; translation from Thorndike, *University Records and Life in the Middle Ages*, 23. See Ferruolo, *The Origins of the University*, 269–72.

29. *Dictum* 19, fol. 13vb: "Omne ergo verum de esse creaturarum maxime, quod in aliis scienciis addiscitur, vtile est vtiliterque addiscitur nisi forte veritate quem addiscit quis abutatur. Sed si propter abusionem diceretur inutilis erudicio, nec in ipsa theologia est veritas cuius non possit inutilis esse cognicio."

30. Stock, *Augustine the Reader*, 164. See also Jaegar, *The Envy of Angels*, 9–11.

31. *Dictum* 19, fol. 13vb: "Videtur igitur secundum predicta et secundum sermonem Augustini hec scriptura omni ceterarum scienciarum veritates vt elementa quedam continere propriaque quedam insuper adicere. Est enim hec scriptura panis de celo panis, habens in se omne delectamentum et omnis saporis suauitatem, vtpote verbum illud Johannis: 'Omne mendacium non est ex veritate' (1 John 2.21). Habet enim in se hanc maximam dialectice: ex vero non sequitur falsum, superadditque aliquid quod est edificacio morum. Similiter verbum istud: 'Diuisit lucem a tenebris' (Gen 1:4). et illud Apostoli que coniunctio lucis ad tenebras continet in se contraria (2 Cor 6:14), in eodem non conuenire quorum omni duorum alterum se habet per modum inuencionis et lucis, et relictum per modum tenebrarorum et priuacionis. Superadditque idem sermo aliquid quod pertinet ad primordia creacionis et aliquid quod prouehit ad lumen fidei et feruorem dileccionis."

32. Grosseteste, *Commentarius in libros analyticorum posterium* 1.18, ed. Rossi, 261: "Scientia autem est subalternata alii cuius subiectum addit conditionem super subiectum subalternantis, que conditio non est totaliter exiens a natura subiecti subalternantis, sed extra sumitur. . . ." Cited in Laird, "Grosseteste on the Subalternate Sciences," 154.

33. Laird, "Grosseteste on the Subalternate Sciences," 154–55.

34. *Dictum* 19, fols. 13vb–14ra: "Sed numquid per modum hunc inuenitur alicubi in sacra pagina diametrum esse assimetrum coste et huiusmodi et ceterarum arcium tales conclusiones? Innuere huius abnegatio contraria videtur Augustino. Huius autem affirmacio maior est quam capiat opinio et quam attingat hominis perscrutacio. Cum autem tota scriptura fideliter exposita aut fidem instruat aut edificet caritatem, non est verisimile in ea predicto modo contineri veritatem, nisi forte quis diceret quod quemadmodum natura facit quodlibet menbrum in corpore directe propter aliam necessitatem et insuper addit alicuius iuuamenti vtilitatem. Sic eciam scriptura sacra quolibet verbo suo intendit fidem aut caritatem et preter hoc in multis verbis suis, quasi iuuamenta quedam, omnium scienciarum aliarum continet omnem veritatem."

35. Augustine, *De doctrina christiana* 2.41.62, ed. Martin, 75–76. The first author to use this biblical allusion to argue for the Christian use of pagan learning was in fact Origen. See Crouzel, *Origen*, 158–59.

36. It is for this reason that he finds Cassiodorus's explanation, which he uses as the final statement of his own *solutio* to the problem, concerning the use of rhetoric in exegesis so useful. See above n. 12.

37. The Franciscan Roger Bacon later argued virtually the same position, although he saw the absolute necessity of mathematical analysis in literal exegesis. See Bacon, *Opus maius*, 175: "Cum igitur ostensum sit quod philosophia non potest sciri nisi sciatur mathematica, et omnes sciant quod theologia non potest sciri nisi sciatur philosophia, necesse est ut theologus sciat mathematicam. Caeterum Deus posuit res creatas in scriptura sua, qui solus novit potestatem creaturam quas condidit, nec potest falsum sentire, nec decet suam veritatem. Ergo cum omnes res a Deo et angelis et summis coelorum usque ad terminos eorum ponantur in scriptura . . . necesse est theologum scire re hujus mundi si textum sacrum debet scire.

"Praeterea nos videmus, quod sensus literalis stat in cognitione naturarum et proprietatum creaturarum, ut per convenientes aptationes et similitudines eliciantur sensus spiriuales. Nam sic exponunt sancti et omnes sapientes antiqui, et haec est vera et sincera expositio, quam Spiritus Sanctus docuit. Quapropter oportet theologum scire optime creaturas. Sed ostensum est quod sine mathematica sciri non possunt. Ergo mathematica omnino est necessaria sacrae scientiae." Cf. McEvoy, "The Sun as *res* and *signum*," 57–59.

38. *Dictum* 19, fol. 14ra: "Hanc tamen controuersiam sapientibus dirimendam relinquo et ad illud, vnde sermo cepit, redeo."

39. *De cessatione legalium* 1.2.4, ed. Dales and King, 9: "Quod si aliquis dictas auctoritates [i.e., mandates concerning circumcision and the keeping of the Sabbath] aliter exponat sive mistice, ut sic evadat predictas obiecciones, sic poterit ei obviari: optimus doctor tali sermone docet, quali evidentius signatur hoc quod vult docere audientem quam aliquid aliud. Si enim aliud evidentius signatur quam illud quod docere intendit, non est optimus doctor, sed magis aut imperitus aut deceptor. Et si optimus doctor per eundem sermonem velit docere plura, hoc de illis pluribus per suum sermonem signabit evidentius quod vult ad audiente intelligi cicius. Autor enim dictarum auctoritatum est doctor optimus; ergo quod per suum sermonem signatur evidentius, hoc vult a nobis per eundem sermonem intelligi cicius. Signatur autem per dictas auctoritates evidentissime quod custodia et celebracio sabati sit precepta ut sit perpetua, et signum perpetuum quo intelligendum est quod Dominus ipse est Deus. Et hoc igitur per dictas auctoritates voluit nos ipse legis autor docere."

40. A more thorough discussion of the commentary's prologue is Ginther, "The *Super Psalterium* of Robert Grosseteste," 143–66. The prologue has been edited in Streitz, "Grosseteste: *Commentarius in Psalmos*," 26–54.

41. Ginther, "The *Super Psalterium* of Robert Grosseteste," 157.

42. Ibid., 158–59. See Streitz, "Grosseteste: *Commentarius in Psalmos*," 46, where an alternative way of reading this part of the prologue is presented.

43. See Minnis, *The Medieval Theory of Authorship*, 73–117.

44. See Rondeau, *Les commentaires patristiques du Psautier*, esp. 1:17–21; Ginther, "The *Super Psalterium* of Robert Grosseteste," 126–66. While Grosseteste does not state directly that he has adopted the prosopological model of Psalms exegesis, it is implicit both by his registering of the prosopological Rules of Tyconius in the prologue (extant in the two earliest manuscripts of the commentary), and by his exegesis of many of the Psalms.

45. *Dictum* 19, fol. 14ra: "Excellencior enim est scriptura in mente viua quam in pelle mortua."

46. Ibid.: "Liber itaque iste mens est humana inscripta scripture sacre manente sciencia, in quo libro—quasi in scripte dictiones—singule sunt species specierum menti impresse. Omnis namque anima eciam propter cuiuscumque noticie inscripcionem libri accipit nominacionem secundum quod propheta dicit: 'Iudicium sedit et libri aperti sunt' (Dan 7:10), que librorum apercio ipsa est manifestacio consiliorum. De qua ait Apostolus: 'Nolite ante tempus iudicare, quoad vsque veniat Dominus, qui illuminabit abscondita tenebrarum et manifestabit consilia cordium' (1 Cor 4:5)."

47. Ibid.: "Anime autem due sunt partes, aspectus videlicet et affectus quorum aspectus est velud exterior quia nichil in affectum peruenit quod prius aspectui non occurrit: nichil enim amatur nisi prius cognoscatur. Quod ergo per cognicionem in aspectum describitur quasi in libro foris depingitur, si vero eadem inscripcio se profundauerit, in affectum scilicet amorem scientis configurauerit. Iam liber est scriptus foris et intus. Taliter humane menti inscribenda est sacre pagine sciencia vt per medium aspectus profundet intimum affectus, vt sit liber scriptus non solum foris sed eciam intus. Hec enim sic in intimum affectus profundata inscripcio conformat hominem Deo faciensque deiformem [*difformem* ms.] restituit honori deperdito, quia is est verus honor hominis reformacio ymaginis sui conditoris. Cum autem hec interna descripcio prorumpit

per lucem operum in manifesto que se exerit legendam vi exteriorum operum quasi quibusdam litteris. . . ."

48. Delorme, "Deux leçons d'ouverture de cours biblique," 350: "Sapiens enim prius sibi incorporat sacram scientiam per voluntatem bonam et operationem, quam aliis legendo influat . . . per praedicationem."

49. Gregory the Great, Homiliae in Hiezechihelem prophetam 1.6.2, ed. Adriaen, 67–68. I am indebted to Ms. Anna Kaltsoyannis, a doctoral candidate in the Department of Theology and Religious Studies, University of Leeds, on this point.

50. Dictum 19, fol. 14ra: ". . . quid aliud est nisi tercio modo totus homo liber scriptus foris et intus? Hec itaque scripcio libri quasi ab eodem in illud est quedam redicio, quasi a forinseca descripcione in aspectu protenditur in affectum, indeque erumpit in lucem forinsecorum operum. Ipsaque itidem lux operum amplius reilluminat aspectum expressiusque et formacius inscribit prius inscriptum. Et forte propter hanc in se reuolucionem, hec scriptura rotis comparatur: nec roti quibuscumque sed in quibus est spiritus vite; nec stature humilis sed excelse altitudinis, quia nimirum ipsa sic rotata a viuificante spiritum vita est viuificata. Cumque a philosophis diffinatur vitam esse reciprocum spiritum quod in hiis rotis vite diffinicio site, ostendit protracta reciprocacio."

51. Ibid., fol. 14ra–rb: "In hiis autem iterum scripcionum modis qualiter hec scriptura supereminet scripturis ceteris ostenditur. Nulle enim scripture cetere sic in intimum affectus debent se profundare totumque hominem sibi configurare, quia nulla est alia que affectum perfecte ordinat suppremeque pulcritudini confortat. Immo si qua alia sic, per affectum in aspectum penetrat, non illuminat aspectum sed obtenebrat; non affectum format sed deformat. Cumque hec sola scriptura menti sic inscripta hominem supra se vsque ad Deum eleuet eique adherere faciens vnum spiritum efficiat hominemque secundum Deum viuere faciat. Omnisque alia scriptura non potest hominem vel ad se elevare vt per eam, saltem secundum hominem, viuat, plus quam viuere secundum Deum excedit viuere secundum hominem plus quoque quam deformitas recreacionis excedit speciam condicionis. Patenter est hec scriptura ad alias omnes superioris ordinis, et hoc est quod comparatur rotis excelse altitudinis."

52. A point that Grosseteste, almost two decades later, further elaborates in his commentary on the *Mystical Theology* of Ps-Dionysius: Il Commento di Roberto Grossatesta al "De mystica theologia" 1.4, ed. Gamba, 35–36: "In anagogia enim nondum videtur Deus nude et incircumvelate, sed in ea speculamur ipsum in omnibus creaturis quas in quibusdam vestigiis ipsius, et in creaturis inferioribus quasi in quibusdam vestigiis minus formatis, et in creaturis superioribus quasi in vestigiis formatioribus, et in summis quasi in formatissimis. Et propter hoc in anagogia videtur solum locus ubi stetit, inquantum est locus sue stationis, et summa et divinissma vias et intellecta inquantum talis, id est inquantum eius loca sunt quidam interiores mentis sermones non prolocutivi ipsius Dei in se sed suppositorum ipsi, inquantum per ea manifestatur eius presentia nuda in se superexcedens omnem summitatem omnis et summe et sanctissime creature."

53. Dictum 19, fol. 14rb: "Preter dictos modos interne et forinsece inscripcionis non incongrue accipitur libers scriptus est intus et foris ipsum verbum et sapiencia Dei patris. De quo Psalmista ait: *In libro tuo omnes scribentur* (Ps 138:16). Qui intus scribitur, dum patris est ymago et substancie eius figura foris scribitur, dum creaturarum est exemplar et forma in cuius incircumscriptum lumen cura contuentes oculi non defigant irreuerberatum contuitum. Ante huius libri ostensionem ad eiusdem inspeccionem innuit propheta se pergatum habere visum. Quid est enim quod dicit: 'Vidi,' nisi separato affectu ab amore transitorium sublimato que aspectu supra nubula fantasmatum corporalium in serenum quod super hoc lucet mentis aspectum defixi, 'et ecce manus missa ad me?' Quid est *manus missa* nisi verbum patris per quod facta sunt omnia? Verbum inquantum a patre dicitur: manus eo quod per ipsum omnia pater operatur. In hac manu bene dicitur liber esse quia in Verbo, per quod facta sunt, omnia descripte sunt factorum omnium raciones eterne. Liber autem inuoluitur dum factorum non facte raciones in secreto Verbo Patris

absconditur. Idem quoque liber expanditur dum in factorum speciebus eterne racionis velud in exemplis exemplaria dinoscuntur."

54. Ibid.: "Audi videntem eundem librum expansum. Ipse est philosophus qui ait: 'Clara est et que numquam marcessit, sapiencia, et facile videtur ab hiis qui dilexerunt illam et inuenitur ab illis qui querunt illam; preoccupat qui se concupiscunt, nec se illis prior ostendat; qu de luce vigilauerit ad illam, non laborabit; assidentem enim illam in foribus suis inueniet. Cognitare ergo de illa, sensus est consummatus et qui vigilauerit propter illam, cito erit securus, quoniam dignos se ipsa circuit querens, et in viis se illis ostendit hillarem et in omni prouidencia occurit illis' (Wisd. of Sol. 6:13–17). Vt enim ait Augustinus exponens hunc locum: 'Quomodo te verteris vestigiis quibusdem que operibus suis impressit. Sapiencia loquitur tibi et te in exteriora relabentem ipsis exteriorum formis, intro reuocat vt quicquid te delectat in corpore videas esse iniuriosum et queras, vnde sic et in teipsum redeas atque intelligas te id quod attingis sensibus corporis proprie aut eciam improprie non posse, nisi apud te habeas quasdam pulcritudinis leges ad quas referas pulcra sentis interius.'"

55. Dictum 60, in Gieben, "Traces of God in Nature," 153. See also Super Psalterium, 76:12 (fol. 47ra): "Item, possunt intelligi per opera ipse creature per mirabilia ab inicio ipse raciones eterne rerum creandarum non quod raciones ille habeant inicium, sed quod fuerent cum omni inicio sicut dicitur, 'In principio erat verbum' (John 1:1); non quod habent principium sed quod fuit presens cum omni principio et ita illa sine inchoacionis principio. Est itaque talis ordo vocatus in hiis versibus, vt primo sit agnicio creaturarum per quas fit assensus ad invisibilia Dei ad ipsas videlicet creaturarum increatas ad eternas raciones que conspicienda sunt."

56. Dictum 19, fol. 14rb-va: "Aliter quoque liber hic inuolutus expanditur dum verbum in principio apud Deum, caro factum manifestatur. De huius libri inuolucione loquitur Ysaiae: 'Vera tu es Deus Israel absconditus saluator' (Isa 45:15). De eiusdem manifestacione Baruch ait: 'Post hec in terris visus est et cum hominibus couersatus est' (Bar 3:38). In manu eciam missa sacre scripture liber continetur quis in verbo incarnato tocius scripture est consummacio, vt enim ait Augustinus. Multitudo paginarum sacre scripture hoc habet breue quia 'oportebat Christum pati et resurgere id est a mortuis tercia die' (Luke 24:46). Hic liber in veteri testamento sub figurarum vmbris inuoluitur. In nouo autem refulgente luce veritatis expanditur. Inuoluitur eciam in omnibus verbis allegoricis et expanditur in verbis nudis, non per allegoriam dictis quia teste beato Augustino: 'Nichil fere de allegoricis obscuritatibus eruitur quod non planissime alibi dictum reperiatur.'" Cf. Grosseteste, De cessatione legalium 1.9.2–4, ed. Dales and King, 48–49.

57. Grosseteste, *Expositio in epistolam sancti Pauli ad Galatas*, ed. McEvoy. Also included in this volume are the remains of Grosseteste's general gloss on the Pauline epistles (ed. R. C. Dales, 179–231).

58. An edition is under way with Joseph Goering, James Ginther, and Elizabeth Streitz collaborating.

Bibliography

Augustine of Hippo. *De doctrina christiana*. Ed. J. Martin. CCSL, 31. Turnhout: Brepols, 1962.

Bacon, Roger. *Opus maius*. Ed. J. H. Bridges. Oxford: Oxford University Press, 1897.

Callus, Daniel. "Robert Grosseteste as Scholar." In *Robert Grosseteste, Scholar and Bishop, Essays in Commemoration of the Seventh Centenary of his Death*. Ed. D. A. Callus, 11–69. Oxford: Clarendon Press, 1955.

Carruthers, Mary. *The Book of Memory: A Study of Memory in Medieval Culture*. Cambridge: Cambridge University Press, 1990.

Cassiodorus. *Expositio Psalmorum*. Ed. M. Adriaen. 2 vols. CCSL, 97–98. Turnhout: Brepols, 1958.

Catto, J. I. "Theology and Theologians, 1200-1320." In *The History of the University of Oxford, Volume I: The Early Oxford Schools*. Ed. J. I. Catto, 471-517. Oxford: Clarendon Press, 1984.

Crouzel, H. *Origen*. Trans. A. S. Worrall. Edinburgh: T. & T. Clark, 1989.

Delorme, F. M. "Deux leçons d'ouverture de cours biblique données par Jean de la Rochelle." *La France franciscaine* 17 (1933): 345-60.

Denifle, H., and A. Chatelain, eds. *Chartularium universitatis Parisiensis*. 3 vols. Paris: Delelain, 1887-89.

Ferruolo, Stephen C. *The Origins of the University: The Schools of Paris and their Critics, 1100-1215*. Stanford, Calif.: Stanford University Press, 1985.

Gieben, Servus. "Traces of God in Nature according to Robert Grosseteste: With the Text of the Dictum *Omnis creatura speculum est*." *Franciscan Studies* 24 (1964): 144-58.

Ginther, James R. "Natural Philosophy and Theology at Oxford in the Early Thirteenth Century: An Edition and Study of Robert Grosseteste's Inception Sermon (*Dictum* 19)." *Medieval Sermon Studies* 44 (2000): 108-34.

——. "The *Super Psalterium* of Robert Grosseteste (ca. 1170-1253): A Scholastic Psalms Commentary as a Source for Medieval Ecclesiology." Ph.D. diss., University of Toronto, 1995.

Goering, Joseph. "When and Where Did Grosseteste Study Theology?" In *Robert Grosseteste: New Perspectives on His Thought and Scholarship*. Ed. J. McEvoy, 17-51. Instrumenta Patristica, 27. Turnhout: Brepols, 1995.

Gregory the Great. *Homiliae in Hiezechihelem prophetam*. Ed. M. Adriaen. CCSL, 142. Turnhout: Brepols, 1972.

Grosseteste, Robert. *De cessatione legalium*. Ed. R. Dales and E. King. Auctores Britannici Medii Aevi, 7. London: British Academy, 1986.

——. *Commentarius in libros analyticorum posterium*. Ed. P. Rossi. Florence: Olschki, 1980.

——. *Il Commento di Roberto Grossatesta al* "De mystica theologia" *del Pseudo-Dionigi Areopagita*. Ed. U. Gamba. Milan: Società editrice, 1942.

——. *Dictum* 19. London, British Library, MS Royal 6.E.v., fols. 13va-14va.

——. *Expositio in epistolam sancti Pauli ad Galatas*. Ed. J. McEvoy. CCCM, 130. Turnhout: Brepols, 1995.

——. *Hexaëmeron*. Ed. R. Dales and S. Gieben. Auctores Britannici Medii Aevi, 6. London: British Academy, 1982.

——. *Super Psalterium*. Bologna, Biblioteca dell' Archiginnasio, MS 983.

Jaegar, C. Stephen. *The Envy of Angels: Cathedral Schools and Social Ideals in Medieval Europe, 950-1200*. Philadelphia: University of Pennsylvania Press, 1994.

Laird, W. R. "Robert Grosseteste on the Subalternate Sciences." *Traditio* 43 (1987): 147-69.

Long, R. James. "The Science of Theology according to Richard Fishacre: Edition of the Prologue to his *Commentary on the Sentences*." *Mediaeval Studies* 34 (1972): 71-98.

McEvoy, James. *The Philosophy of Robert Grosseteste*. Oxford: Clarendon Press, 1982.

——. "The Sun as *res* and *signum*: Grosseteste's Commentary on *Ecclesiasticus* ch. 43, vv. 1-5." *Recherches de théologie ancienne et médiévale* 41 (1974): 38-91.

——. Review of *Robert Grosseteste: The Growth of an English Mind in Medieval Europe* by R. W. Southern. *Bulletin de théologie ancienne et médiévale* 14 (1987): 353-58.

Minnis, A. J. *The Medieval Theory of Authorship*. 2d. ed. Philadelphia: University of Pennsylvania Press, 1984.

Rashdall, Hastings. *The Universities of Europe in the Middle Ages*. Ed. F. M. Powicke and A. B. Emden. 3 vols. Oxford: Oxford University Press, 1936.

Rondeau, Marie-Joseph. *Les commentaires patristiques du Psautier (IIIe-Ve siècles)*. 2 vols. Orientalia Christiana Analecta, 219-20. Rome: Pontificium Institutum Studiorum Orientalium, 1982-85.

Schulman, N. M. "Husband, Father, Bishop? Grosseteste in Paris." *Speculum* 72 (1997): 330-46.

Sheehan, Michael W. "The Religious Orders, 1220-1370," In *The History of the University of*

Oxford, Volume I: The Early Oxford Schools. Ed. J. I. Catto, 193–221. Oxford: Clarendon Press, 1984.

Smalley, Beryl. "The Biblical Scholar." In *Robert Grosseteste, Scholar and Bishop: Essays in Commemoration of the Seventh Centenary of his Death*. Ed. D. A. Callus, 70–97. Oxford: Clarendon Press, 1955.

Southern, Richard W. *Robert Grosseteste: The Growth of an English Mind in Medieval Europe*. Oxford: Clarendon Press, 1986. 2d ed. Oxford: Clarendon Press, 1989.

Spatz, Nancy. "Evidence of Inception Ceremonies in the Twelfth-Century Schools of Paris." *History of Universities* 13 (1994): 3–19.

Stevenson, Francis. *Robert Grosseteste: Bishop of Lincoln*. London: Macmillan, 1899.

Stock, Brian. *Augustine the Reader: Meditation, Self-Knowledge and the Ethics of Interpretation*. Cambridge, Mass.: Harvard University Press, 1996.

Streitz, Elizabeth M. "Robert Grosseteste: *Commentarius in Psalmos I-XXXVI*." Ph.D. diss., University of Southern California, 1996.

Thomson, S. H. *The Writings of Robert Grosseteste*. Cambridge: Cambridge University Press, 1940.

Thorndike, Lynn. *University Records and Life in the Middle Ages*. New York: Columbia University Press, 1944.

Warner G. F., and J. Wilson. *Catalogue of Western Manuscripts in the Old Royal and King's Collections*. 4 vols. London: British Museum, 1921.

Westermann, Edwin J. "An Edition, with Introduction and Notes of *Dicta* 1–50 of Robert Grosseteste, Bishop of Lincoln, 1235–1253." Ph.D. diss., University of Colorado, Boulder, 1942.

16

Beryl Smalley, Thomas of Cantimpré, and the Performative Reading of Scripture

A Study in Two *Exempla*

ROBERT SWEETMAN

Beryl Smalley and the Four Senses of Scripture

Thomas Aquinas sums up a general commitment among medieval readers of the Scriptures to the multiplicity of true meaning inherent within the biblical text. He writes: "Since the author of sacred scripture is God, who comprehends all things in his intellect at once, it is not unfitting . . . if one discovers in the one text of Scripture plural senses in continuity with the literal sense."[1] *Prima facie*, such a commitment seems impressively precocious in an academy increasingly sensitive to the situatedness of human intellect and the consequent, hermeneutically generative play of forces upon the reader and the meaning she is able to see.[2] On the other hand, when Thomas Aquinas turns to the three spiritual senses, many modern readers become uneasy. Such readers find it hard to imagine that Christ and his Church (allegorical sense), the healthy configuration of the human soul (moral sense), and the shape of our deepest hope (anagogical sense) are somehow intrinsic levels operating intentionally if below the literal surface of the biblical text.[3] Such an expectation seems "irrelevant, indeed freakish, and of interest only to the historian."[4] Medieval exegetical practice vis-à-vis these spiritual levels of meaning only increases skepticism. The resulting bemusement is well represented by the late Beryl Smalley's response to Philo's allegorical readings of the Septuagint:

> The rules for constructing allegories . . . bewilder by their number and their complexity. The line between reality and imagery seems to be melted. Reading Philo, one has the sensation of stepping "through the looking glass." One finds, as did Alice, a country governed by queer laws which the inhabitants oddly regard as rational. In order to understand medieval Bible study one must live there long enough to slip into their ways and appreciate the logic of their strict, elaborately fantastic conventions.[5]

What bothers Beryl Smalley, as I read her, is the opaqueness or privacy of spiritual exegesis. The "logic" of such reading is as hidden as the spiritual levels it purportedly brings to light. One cannot reconstruct, much less predict, the outcome of such reading, not at least until one has spent time with the reader and his friends, has gotten to know their texts well enough to intuit the intentions operating within. Such knowledge is less a matter of rule-based, reproducible or public scholarly analysis as it is a kind of personal knowing driven by other human functions than the analytical function constitutive of schooled learning. Smalley acknowledges that such personal knowing is possible; she claims to have acquired some measure herself. Moreover, she acknowledges, however grudgingly, that medieval spiritual exegesis had its appropriate uses.[6] Nevertheless, it is clear that she felt her scholarly interest truly piqued only when the "logic" of the exegete was placed front and center.[7] She appreciated medieval exegesis when it was easily accessible to her and when it conformed to logic as it is habitually applied by the scholar in the scholarly analysis of texts.

What she found difficult, then, about the spiritual senses of scripture is not that they existed per se, but that they were, for so much of the Middle Ages, given scholarly status, even priority, indeed, that examination of the spiritual senses of the scriptures was held to be the very end of scholarly study. By contrast, she reverses these medieval assumptions in her pioneering history of the study of the Bible. Her interest and historiographical vantage point was the literal sense and of the use of logical tools to establish its meaning.[8] Consequently, she dispensed with attention to the spiritual senses as soon as she decently could.

The latter move was not invulnerable to criticism, and she acknowledged the legitimate force of these criticisms in subsequent editions of her history.[9] Moreover, she responded by delineating an approach to the spiritual senses that would allow her to give them their due.[10] However, I do not cite the example of Beryl Smalley in order to exhume her intellectual bones, so to speak, and burn them. I acknowledge, as did her most consequential critic, that her oeuvre is indispensable to the study of scriptural exegesis in the Middle Ages.[11] Rather, I cite her history in order to understand better where she stood in telling the story as she did.

Here, I am particularly interested in her claim that study of the Bible underwent a crucial turning in the twelfth century, which she associated with the Augustinian canons of the monastery of Saint Victor in Paris. I am interested in her sense that the Victorine tradition breathed new life into a properly scholarly treatment of the text of scripture, by which she meant a treatment that focused upon the scripture's literal or historical sense and that used logical analysis to bring out its meaning, a treatment that had been largely eclipsed during the early Middle Ages in favor of spiritual exegesis. She saw this turning confirmed and built upon in the thirteenth century among the friars and the *studia generalia* they established in close proximity to Western Europe's nascent universities.[12] In what follows, Smalley's story will be examined in the light created by John Van Engen's recent account of the twelfth-century establishment of the scriptures as theological school text and by the thirteenth-century Dominican of Louvain Thomas of Cantimpré's reading practice as recorded in an autobiographical *exemplum* he included in his *Bonum universale de apibus* or "Book of Bees."[13] We begin with Thomas of Cantimpré and his reading practice, for it provides us a way of viewing the developments that John Van Engen describes in ways that affect the meaning of Beryl Smalley's history.

Exemplum 1: Thomas of Cantimpré as Performative and Scholarly Reader of the Scriptures

Recently, I had occasion to analyze a curious *exemplum* in which Thomas of Cantimpré used an episode of his *cura mulierum* to illustrate the power of demons to possess the souls of Christians, even those who lived a seriously religious life.[14] This analysis is suggestive in the present context and so will reward careful attention. Here is the *exemplum*:

> In the same land [Brabant], I saw another woman, one rich and of excellent life, who was possessed by a demon. I visited her at the request of a religious priest. We found her undisturbed by demonic torment. She was able to speak coherently as if of sound mind. I secretly repeated three times that verse of the Canticle of Moses found in Deuteronomy which goes, "You have abandoned the God who produced you and have forgotten the Lord your Creator." In this I acted in accordance with what I had heard from a certain holy man, and so as to call forth the demon who had possessed the woman. Directly, the woman's face and lips began to grow pallid and the two veins in her neck began to swell until they were as thick as thumbs. I then addressed the demon, "Why, O worst of all beings, have you dared to take possession of this woman?"
>
> The demon answered, "She had such compassion for her dead husband that she credited to him in aid of his soul all the good which she did in this life. Thus, an opportunity presented itself to me and I entered directly 'an empty vessel.'"
>
> I addressed him again, "You are lying, O most wretched of beings, for her giving, since it was mediated by charity, would only accrue to her account."
>
> He chuckled, saying, "I am a liar. Therefore, it is small wonder that I am lying."
>
> I responded forthwith, "Is she so beautiful that she recalls the heavenly home which you have lost?"
>
> He answered, "Heaven is infinitely more beautiful than what she can possibly call to mind."
>
> I then said, "Do you wish to return to that place, if you are able?"
>
> And he said, "Would that I could undergo every imaginable punishment from now until the Judgment Day, [and merit thereby to return]."
>
> I responded, "And I promise you upon danger of losing the salvation promised me if I am lying that you can regain glory if only you say this: 'O Lord God, I have sinned; forgive me.'"
>
> Straightaway, the woman's neck began to contort, and the demon called out in a horrible voice, "O Lord . . . O Lord. . . ." And when he had sounded these words over and over again with great clamor and could not proceed further (for I knew that it was not possible for him to profess that God was his Lord and confess that he had sinned and to beg to be forgiven), he finally added, "Lord God of Margaret (for that was the possessed woman's name), I am offended to have to profess [You], God, as my Lord."
>
> Then I said, "O most unfortunate of all creatures, pride has crushed you and has cast you from Heaven; inexpiable pride does not permit you to return."
>
> Thwarted, the demon fell silent without delay, and, even still, he did not leave the woman for a few days.[15]

The exorcist of this narrative is, of course, none other than Thomas of Cantimpré. In other words, he narrates his own textual *persona* via this *exemplum* (among others). Moreover, this *persona* is formed in large measure by means of remembered texts. In this *exemplum* such texts construct or perform Thomas as an exorcist, as is clear from an examination of the rite of exorcism.

The rite, as promulgated by Benedict XIV, is divided into three chapters.[16] The first chapter assembles twenty-one articles in which exorcists are admonished to right action in the performance of the rite. Something like this early modern compilation of *admonitiones* must have already accompanied the rite in Thomas of Cantimpré's day, for the *exemplum* cited conforms to the strictures articulated in a number of them.[17] The *admonitio* found in the fifth article warns the exorcist to be vigilant in the face of demonic arts and deceptions; in particular it warns that demons try to make their victims appear free of demonic vexation.[18] The *admonitio* of the next article further elaborates the demonic penchant for hiding itself as if relinquishing the demoniac's body and exhorts the exorcist not to cease the rite until he has observed the "signs of liberation."[19] In this *exemplum* Thomas does, in fact, find the woman, Margaret, quiescent, as if in her right mind, and refuses to be taken in.[20]

The *admonitiones* published in articles fifteen to seventeen and article twenty are also reflected in Thomas's story. Article fifteen lists the kinds of questions exorcists are to restrict themselves to. They are to ask after the number and name(s) of the possessing spirits, as to when the spirit(s) entered the demoniac, the reasons why, and the circumstances surrounding demonic entry.[21] Article sixteen admonishes the exorcist to command with authority, great faith, and humility and to be swift to follow up the advantage when he observes the demon in torment, a torment manifested in somatic phenomena convulsing the body of the possessed. Swelling of body portions is specifically mentioned.[22] Article seventeen admonishes exorcists to keep track of those words that spark demonic response.[23] Article twenty advises the exorcist to use the words of scripture above all.[24]

The ways in which these articles come to expression in the *exemplum* are clear enough, as we shall see. Thomas is single-minded in his pursuit of the demoniac's liberation. Moreover the questions he asks at the beginning of his inquiry reflect the prescribed list.[25] The demon is spurred to create swelling contortions in the body of its host, and the spur is provided by scriptural words that had previously been observed to effect the desired demonic response.[26] Finally, Thomas wastes no time in pressing his advantage, once he is aware of it.[27]

The most telling and complex allusion of all, however, refers to the text of the rite of exorcism itself. In the prayer which constitutes the heart and soul of the rite the offending demon is abjured to give way to Christ "in whom you find nothing of your works, who has despoiled you, who has destroyed your kingdom, who has bound you captive, and who has overturned your vessels."[28] The first three clauses of the passage list major achievements of Christ's *triduum* (the time between crucifixion and resurrection): the Old Testament saints were led out of hell, the kingdom of hell was laid waste, the devil was enchained. The fourth clause, then, ought also to be associated with the infernal events of Christ's harrowing of hell.[29] One must imagine him upsetting, in righteous anger, the bulging containers of Hades' treasuries. In addition, however, the overturning of hellish vessels has a secondary scriptural association: Christ's cleansing of the temple and the overturning of the tables of the money changers. Now, the term "vessel" (*vas*) also occurs in Thomas's story. The demon explains its entry into its victim by calling her an "empty vessel" (*vas vacuum*). This comment might have been safely passed over in silence but for the fact that her putative emptiness was the result of spiritual money changing, that is, the woman's investment of her spiritual goods on her husband's behalf. Consequently, in a complex allusion, the demon of Thomas's *exemplum* itself refers to the rite of exorcism and its coming defeat in and through Christ's overturning of its "vessel," that is, the freeing of its victim.

Once we have established the exorcistic elements within Thomas's narrative *persona*, however, we confront a difficulty which suggests that these textual elements are appropriated not *verbum pro verbo* but *sententialiter*, or according to the sense.[30] That is, just as texts construct Thomas as a person or character in his narrative, so his character and actions construct the meaning of those same texts. We read that the "demoniac" in question was a woman of excellent life (*honestam*) and was nevertheless possessed by a demon (*possessam a daemone*). But how could a demon possess a person who lived a preeminent life?

It should be noted that this is not the only story of the demon possession of virtuous women within the "Book of Bees." The dissonance between the presence of active virtue and demonic power to command is even more intense in the story immediately preceding this one. There the possessed woman is identified as a Cistercian nun, one who was *religiosam valde et vita puram*, "intensely religious and pure in life."[31]

Theologians of the thirteenth century were at one in emphasizing the limits of demonic power with respect to human beings.[32] All demonic activity took place, according to them, under the watchful forebearance of God. Demons were permitted wide powers with respect to the world of bodies, in keeping with their spiritual natures. They were, however, impotent to change human nature. Consequently, they stood before the human will as before what was simultaneously their greatest obstacle and their greatest hope, for it was a Janus-like entity, conduit to as well as adamant guardian of the inner recesses of the human person.

Since demons were helpless in the face of sustained repudiation, they perforce acted in stealth. They wheedled and coaxed, hoping to recruit willing compliance with their suggestions. But in the cited *exemplum* and its immediate predecessor, whatever Thomas may have meant by *mulierem honestam* and *monialem vita puram*, he does not seem to have imagined the women as having voluntarily opened the citadel of their souls to demonic occupation (*possessio*). The question then returns: Is the Thomas of this *exemplum* in fact an exorcist? It returns because it is not at all clear how Thomas understands the demon possession of exemplary women.

In the first of the two *exempla* the word "possession" is never actually used. Rather, the demon is said to have been hiding within the nun in question: *in ea latebat*. The demon clearly had a distressing level of control over her body, for Thomas describes how it responded to an hour's worth of what he laconically calls the "words of salvation." The woman's body began to bark like a dog with mouth agape and neck contorted. It turned away from all sources of light and began to blaspheme. Consequently, it would appear that in this story the phrase *in ea latebat* indicates that the demon had access to the nun's body without a corresponding access to the inner recesses of her person.

The second *exemplum* speaks of some of the same somatic manipulations just described. One thinks in particular of the demon's ability to contort its host's neck. Indeed, in the first segment of the story the woman's jugular veins swell unimaginably whereas in the third segment her neck is again said to have been contorted as the demon struggled with the invitation to confess before God. Here too demonic access to the woman's body seems clear.

The demon in this *exemplum*, however, would also seem to have had access to the inner recesses of its host's person, for she is explicitly identified as possessed in the course of the narrative. Thomas uses two words to indicate possession: *possessa* (twice) and *obsessa* (once). The words are, of course, perfect participles derived from the verbs *possidere* and *obsidere*. In classical usage, the verbs shared a semantic field of military meaning.[33] *Possidere* indicated the military occupation of what had been assaulted and captured, while *obsidere* indicated a laying siege to what one hoped to capture. While the latter verb maintains its classical significance in medieval usage, the former verb expands. While it can be and is used in its classical sense, *possidere* also comes to be used as a synonym for *obsidere*.[34] In other words, these verbs, when used interchangeably, denote a laying siege to what one hopes to capture. Since, in the present story, Thomas of Cantimpré uses their passive participles interchangeably, they are best viewed as synonyms.

Consequently, the virtuous woman of this *exemplum* is possessed not in the sense that the demon has gained access to the inner recesses of her being, but rather in that the demon is laying siege to her spiritual core. It is not yet victorious, and, given the woman's mode of life, is not likely ever to be so. In this story, then, demon possession has another meaning altogether. It indicates a pestiferous and malicious plaguing, an invidious nuisance-making. It constitutes a distinct species of the genus "temptation," a genus that is itself subject to misunderstanding, particularly regarding the temptation of saints (and, in medieval tellings, of Jesus).[35]

Temptation in its generic sense indicates something broader than the attempt to allure and entrap, the common experience of the ordinary or mediocre faithful. It indicates rather quite simply the attempt to make life difficult. Medieval demons tempt the saints (as they were understood to have tempted Jesus) not because they really hope that the saints (or Jesus) will be defeated by the difficulties placed before them. Rather, demons tempt out of sheer cussedness. Why should the saints have it easy? Demonic "crucifixion" of a saint may only serve to make her more Christ-like. Nevertheless, it also causes her suffering and pain. The enormous effort expended in causing such ineffectual, even counterproductive pain may seem vain and wasted. And so it is. But, it is a vanity and a waste entirely fitted to the kind of beings demons were believed to be.

At this point it is clear that Thomas's citations of the rite of exorcism and his allusions to the scriptures perform him exorcistically. In other words, the Thomas we meet in the *exemplum* can be understood only in terms of the texts he has taken into himself or ingested, to use the medieval metaphor, via the ruminative acts of memorization (*lectio*) and meditation (*meditatio*).[36] This mode of reading can also be called "performative." By such reading and under the aphorism "you are what you eat," he can be said to have *become* the texts he ingested. In short, he approached scripture and the rite of exorcism as one open to their shaping or formative power.

The *exemplum* shows that Thomas expected these texts to provide him words and sentences to be used subsequently to order his experience of life. In keeping with this *exemplum*, the very phrasing of the texts he ingested were expected to bedevil him; they were, so to speak, to possess him, moving him, as it were, by suggestion. That is, they were to guide him in his actions. However, once internalized, these texts were to be performed. Thus it is in Thomas's practice of *cura mulierum* that the meaning of the rite of exorcism and the passages of scripture it incorporated are established.

This "performative" reading is, as we shall see, far from the scholarly mode of reading which Smalley so valued in the Victorine and mendicant traditions of the twelfth and thirteenth centuries, friar though Thomas may have been. It is concerned with the literal sense of the rite of exorcism and of the scripture it contains, yet it is close in mode to the *lectio divina* of the monk and nun, if lacking monastic predilection for the spiritual senses. Monastic *ruminatio* too, as Jean Leclercq described it, was an internalization of sacred texts such that their spiritual senses conferred meaning upon subsequent experience of life.[37] Of course, Thomas's performative reading is not only distinct from monastic *ruminatio* in its focus upon the literal sense of the text to hand, it is also noncontemplative, for it is active, motivated by his pastoral apostolate.

Already we are positioned to say something about Smalley's historiographical focus. Medieval concern with the literal historical level of scriptural interpretation is not what matters most to her. She is really interested in the scholarly mode of reading the scriptures. Her interest is so finely honed that she gives short shrift to all other approaches to the text. While she admits her shortcomings vis-à-vis approaches to the scripture's spiritual senses, her identification of scholarly reading and examination of the literal historical sense blinds her to the widespread existence of interest in the literal historical sense of scripture that is performative rather than scholarly. Indeed, even when she does acknowledge instances of performative reading directed at the scripture's literal sense, she does not recognize them as reading or study at all. Consider the following passage.

> In the history of Bible studies, this dwindling of *lectio* has its positive side. The old allegories and moralities were fading before an intense realization of the literal meaning. The aim of St. Francis was to imitate Christ as 'literally' as possible. He told the novice who wanted a psalter that he too had been tempted to desire books; so he prayed to know God's will from the first text of Scripture that his eye should light on; it was: *to you it is given to know the mysteries of the kingdom of Heaven: but to them in parables* [Matt 13: 11,13], which he took as a command to poverty and simplicity. By a wonderful reversal, the *mystery* of the elect means to St. Francis, not the mystical, but the strictest literal understanding of Scripture. Similarly, in their meditations, the friars seek to share in the sufferings of Christ. The ideal is not new, but it gains ground in the thirteenth century. Reading is giving way to devotions, which signifies a more historical approach to Scripture. What is evoked by the crib, the rosary, the crucifix, is the Gospel in its literal sense.[38]

I agree that the example of Saint Francis and of devotional aids such as the crib, the rosary, and the crucifix represent a focus upon the Bible's literal sense. Smalley understands them to be a spillover effect of scholarly focus upon study of the literal sense. But such an interpretation misses the point. Saint Francis's example does not indicate scholarly focus upon the literal sense. It is itself a performative reading of the Gospel. His life, in its entirety, is an exegesis of the Gospel according to its literal sense. Moreover, the devotional props Smalley lists are also profitably understood as reading aids. They are mnemonics created to facilitate a devotion which is itself a performative reading of the scriptures according to the literal sense; it is *lectio divina* under a new dispensation.

This sharpening of Smalley's focus in *The Study of the Bible in the Middle Ages* already legitimates our attention to Thomas of Cantimpré's autobiographical *exemplum*. But his performative reading of the rite of exorcism is not the only trace of his reading practice we encounter in the *exemplum*. Examination of this second trace allows us to specify further the distinctive shape of scholarly reading.

The first segment of the *exemplum* ends when the vexing demon makes its presence known in and through its manipulation of the woman's body. The second segment begins when Thomas asks the demon the reason it has come to "possess" the woman.

The demon responds in characteristically demonic fashion with a sophism. Its reply centers upon the woman's suffrages on her husband's behalf. She invested her goodness to her husband's spiritual profit.[39] As the demon has it, her investment of her merits elsewhere renders her empty of merit and, thus, open to any demon willing to fill her void. The demon's argument hinges upon the properties of physical natures also being proper to *spiritualia*. To be sure, if merits are like coins or other physical media of exchange, their investment elsewhere entails their actually being elsewhere. Moreover, the movement of capital from investment to return necessarily takes time. Consequently, if merits are like coins, there would be a vacuity, that is, a window of opportunity to an enterprising spirit.

Merits, however, are spiritual things.[40] As such, they are not constrained by time and space. They can exist in more than one place simultaneously, and the movement of spiritual capital from investment to return is instantaneous. The demon's argument, while cunning in its way, falls short of true intelligence. To the trained scholastic eye, it is patently fallacious, and Thomas sees the fallacy instantly.

The demon cheerfully admits its lie and adds cheek by framing its admission as an allusion to the words of John 8: 44. The citation of scripture provides Thomas a complex piece of information. While it reveals the characteristically deprecating and devious demeanor of his opponent, paradoxically it also gives warrant to the demon's self-identification. All things being equal, a demon's disposition is simply incredible. Since it is a liar, how can it be believed? Scripture, however, can always be believed; it can be cited perversely but it cannot itself lie. As a result, Jesus' identification of the Devil as a liar and the father of lies transforms the demon's word into what can be believed.

This exchange teaches Thomas much about his foe. He has now measured his opponent and is prepared to wrest control of the interchange so as to effect the woman's release. He embarks on a new line of inquiry. He asks whether the woman's beauty conjures up memories of heaven, whether the spell of such reminiscence spurs the demon to the assault. The demon denies the charge implied in Thomas's question. However, since, as was already noted, the demon is a liar, its denial functions only to confirm Thomas's guess. He presses his advantage, asking whether the demon regrets its loss of bliss. The demon admits that it would gladly undergo any and all imaginable punishments if it could thereby return to heaven. But this reply puts Thomas in a delicate hermeneutical situation.

How is he to understand this admission? Is it a lie or the naked truth? In this instance, Thomas views the demon as telling the truth, but willy-nilly in confusion, in an inadvertent way appropriate to an inveterate liar. We are fortunate in being able to reconstruct the criteria by which Thomas establishes the truthfulness of this demonic admission. His criteria are textual, rooted in scholarly reading, as can be seen by an examination of a strikingly similar demonic admission found in Caesarius of Heisterbach's *Dialogus miraculorum*. Again, I cite the pertinent passage *in extenso*:

> One demon said to another, "O wretched one, why did we hurry so from eternal glory when we sided with Lucifer?"

> The other replied [in amazement], "Why are you doing this?" And then when the first demon persisted with what almost amounted to words of penitence, it added, "Be silent! This penitence comes too late; you cannot return." . . . This same evil spirit[, however,] when questioned . . . concerning [the possibility] of returning to glory, responded in my hearing with a word which strongly contradicted what he had said earlier. For now he said, "Were there to be erected between heaven and earth an iron and fiery column, inlaid with the sharpest edges and with blades, I would wish to shinny up it and slide down it from now until Judgment Day, even had I flesh whereby I suffered horribly, if only I could return to the glory I once had."[41]

Caesarius's story shares much with Thomas's. Both assume a huge demonic longing for heaven and a wistful desire to earn readmittance by their own efforts. Moreover, both express the conviction that such a demonic return cannot take place. These parallels urge consideration of the nature of the relationship between the two stories.

It is possible, of course, that all similarities are coincidental and point to nothing more than a broad demonological consensus which both compilers appropriate in their own separate ways. Such a possibility is, however, unlikely. Thomas knows Caesarius's *Dialogus*.[42] Consequently, it seems far more likely that Thomas has read Caesarius of Heisterbach's account of demons conversing nostalgically about heaven and that his own narrative therefore echos Caesarius's.

But one must still ask how Thomas is using his source. Nothing could be simpler than to say that Thomas is cribbing from Caesarius. The problem, however, is that he claims his story to be autobiographical. If he is cribbing from a work as widely known as Caesarius's[43] and passing vicarious experience off as his own, he undermines his whole treatise, for he explicitly founds its credibility on his and his circle of acquaintances' narrative trustworthiness.[44] Cribbing from what is the equivalent of a "best seller" is, at the very least, egregiously dull-witted. I suggest a different scenario.

Thomas has read Caesarius's story and believes it to illumine the demonic mind. He appropriates the tale's lesson, however, to his own ends. Whereas Caesarius presents his story as an example of demonic self-contradiction, a variation on the theme of demon as liar, Thomas sees it as revealing an exploitable demonic weakness. Thomas's *exemplum*, then, shows his putting the lesson into practice. He plays on demonic longing for heaven so as to sow the seeds of doubt and hesitation. In so doing he brings about precisely the contradictory confusion Caesarius's story illustrates.

What is significant in this trace of Thomas's reading is that it is scholarly. That is, he reads a monastic work designed to confirm Cistercian novices in their religious calling as a source of scientific (i.e., logically accessible and hence reproducible or public) information about demons, for it is information he needs above all as he casts about for a way of easing the burden of temptation for his pastoral charge. In other words, he comes to the text and acts upon it such that a work of spiritual formation exhibits the properties of a scientific *tractatus de daemonibus*. In this way, he effects it meaningful in a specified context by controlling for all concerns which, while native to the text to hand, fall outside the logic of present need.

Moreover, his reading of John 8:44 is in the same mode. It too is a source of scientific information which helps Thomas gain the measure of his demonic foe. The function of neither the passage in the context of John's Gospel nor of its eighth chapter is germane. Moreover, it is not a passage he is reading so as to order the subsequent shape of his life. Rather, his reading enables a conceptual judgment, an act, if you will, of logical control.

We do well, however, to look more closely at how Thomas's performative and scholarly readings are alike and differ. Both kinds of reading bespeak the reader's existential priority with respect to the text he is reading, and in both the reader affects the meaning of his text. While Thomas the scholar acts upon a text and discovers within a work of spiritual direction the lineaments of a scientific treatise *de daemonibus*, Thomas the pastor appropriates the rite of exorcism and its incorporation of scripture, establishing its meaning analogically within a concrete situation of demonic temptation. Thus, in both his performative and scholarly readings, he exceeds his textual engagement and exercises agency with respect to the present meaning of the text(s) to hand.

These forms of reading differ, however, in the way Thomas relates to texts. As performative reader, Thomas approaches his text in such a way that his essential subjectivity is on the line.[45] He enters into a reciprocal relationship with the text in the sense that the text forms his subjectivity even as he appropriates it. Moreover, this reciprocity is not symmetrical. Thomas approaches the rite of exorcism or passages of scripture as subject in a second sense; he subjects himself to the text such that it "performs" him. By contrast, Thomas as scholarly reader, because he prescinds from all concerns outside of the logical horizon of present scientific need, cannot be subject to the text in this way. Indeed, by definition, such a reader can approach a text only in the imperative mode.[46]

It is in the imperative mode that Thomas of Cantimpré finds within the Gospel of John and Caesarius of Heisterbach's *Dialogus miraculorum* an exploitable weakness in the spiritual eminence of his demonic foe. It is a discovery Thomas comes to (*inventio*) after the logic of scholarly need reframes the meaning of Caesarius's *exemplum*. Thomas uses the weakness he has "invented" to create a moment of confusion and uses it to deflate the demon so that it is diminished, too diminished to maintain its grip on its victim. He does so by promising the demon that heaven is within its grasp if it would only make contrite confession. He adds weight to his appeal by pledging his own salvation as surety. The demon's efforts to confess end in failure and defiance. Its failure gives Thomas the occasion to intone the grim reality of its spiritual predicament. Faced with the magnitude of its folly, the demon indeed shrinks and grudgingly, over the course of days, loosens its grip on the woman. It must be said, however, that Thomas is honest enough to record something of his disappointment and wonder at the length of time the woman's liberation still took. But in fact there is no need to wonder; the reason lies to hand: why should the saints have it easy?

In sum, Thomas of Cantimpré's *exemplum* preserves traces of both performative and scholarly reading. This finding suggests further sharpening of focus to identify the circumstances that attend his reading in these ways. We have noted that in this *exemplum* Thomas reads performatively when reading for ecclesiastical performance. In other words, he reads performatively with a view to a certain active practice (individual and communal) of faith. It must be admitted that Thomas also reads in a scholarly mode because he wishes to act, even to act pastorally; his is not a contemplative soul given to slow rumination upon texts for the subtle flavors released by unhurried mental mastication. Nevertheless, there is this difference. In contrast to his reading for ecclesiastical performance, Thomas reads in a scholarly mode when he needs to distinguish one set of things (demonic attributes of superior being and power) from another (exploitable attributes at the exorcist's disposal), that is, when he must make a logical determination of what something is or is not. Thus, it would seem that these two modes of reading respond to the contours inherent within two distinguishable modes of human life and endeavor: the cultic practice of faith and the contemplative science of analysis and composition. In this *exemplum*, Thomas brings both modes of reading together to effect performance of a single pastoral act.[47]

This analysis of Thomas's performative and scholarly reading reidentifies the primary point of interest in Beryl Smalley's *The Study of the Bible in the Middle Ages*. It raises the prospect that what Smalley was in fact chronicling in her account of the Victorine renewal of emphasis upon the literal historical level of scripture was the emergence of a new emphasis on a scholarly approach to scripture. This claim is confirmed and deepened by a second *exemplum*, in this case a modern piece of historical writing.

Exemplum II: John Van Engen and the Establishment of the Bible as School Text

John Van Engen has recently described a twelfth- and thirteenth-century pattern of change which effected the transformation of the Bible into a university textbook, in fact, *the* textbook of the new science of theology. In his view, this transformation took place in two stages: a first stage, about 1050–1200, in which masters and their students sought "an adequate form whereby to transform divine truth into a university discipline and Holy Scripture into a university textbook"; and a second stage, 1225–1275, in which were developed new "forms of interpretation and application after textbook knowledge of Scripture became the norm and theology a recognized 'science.'"[48]

> The situation he describes for the beginning of his first stage is, by now, familiar enough: . . . monks . . . meditate on Scripture and sing the psalms; . . . canons . . . read daily an office comprised largely of scriptural passages; . . . priests . . . read the prescribed Gospel and Epistle texts; . . . deacons . . . carry the holy book in procession, . . . kiss and incense it at the altar. . . .[49]

Van Engen contrasts this list of scriptural uses to the role that the scriptures come to play in the university setting. The list itself contains several examples of performative reading in our sense of the term: reading in which the meaning of the biblical text is established by the communal practice of faith. The formation of the first universities and the insertion of the Bible into university curricula, however, produced a different attitude toward the scriptural page. Scripture was now "brought into the dusty streets," so to speak. There it was explained word by word, its difficult passages argued over in the same way that teachers of the liberal arts handled books written by pagan authors.[50]

But how was this transformation effected? By what hermeneutical operations did the scriptures come to be conceived of not only as authoritative for the practice of faith, but as a humanly or logically accessible, rational whole? Van Engen points out that medieval theologians came to focus on an intelligible *intentio auctoris*, the intelligibility of which was guaranteed by the nature of the author, God. Since God was the author of the scriptures, its puzzles and apparent contradictions were conceived to be open to conceptual resolution. Ultimately, there could be nothing absurd or useless about even the most jumbled and chaotic textual phenomena, for the finely chiseled singularities presented in the scriptures signified even as they were, in some sense, universal states of affairs. Indeed, it was this universality present within scriptural singularities that "could yield the nodal points of . . . a science."[51] Logical analysis of the scriptures, beginning *verbum pro verbo*, was, then, about the determination of meaning and about the ordering of such significant matter into what was conceptually prior and posterior. Moreover, such an approach was extended beyond the literal historical level of the text to transform the allegorical level as well. Van Engen makes the point that the *Sentences* of Peter Lombard assume the position they do within the curriculum of theological studies because they hold within them *in nuce* the allegorical sense of the scriptures.[52]

Given the significance of the differences distinguishing performative and scholarly approaches to texts, one might reasonably expect there to have been resistance to this transformation. And Van Engen does speak of "some conservatives" who saw in the new study of the scriptures "a profaning of the divine Word."[53] Still, he goes on to say, there was surprisingly little reaction of this kind. Twelfth-century students appear, on the whole, to have followed lectures in both the arts and the scriptures "with little sense of crossing important boundaries."[54]

Van Engen's article makes two things clear. First, he shows how central the role of scientific or logical method was in the transformation of the Bible into a school text of theology. He does so by pointing out the synchronicity of the Bible's establishment as a university school text and the transformation of theology from a "discipline" of contemplative thought instituted as a religious practice to a science along the lines suggested by Aristotle's newly rediscovered *Posterior Analytics*. Such an Aristotelian science was constituted by a rational field of claims about a genus of reality, claims generated inferentially from primary claims (*principia*) accepted as sure, whether because they were intuited as such or because they were appropriated from a higher science. Theology in this new conception was a science that took its primary claims from a higher science, namely, God's science inasmuch as it was revealed to human beings. The repository of this humanly accessible divine science was, of course, the scriptures. They came to function, consequently, as the storehouse of *principia* from which the science of theology was to be inferred. As such, they constituted the necessary introduction to the science of theology, and so became the textbook for that science's study.

Second, Van Engen suggests that the scholarly reading of scripture associated with the scientific study of theology at the universities extends beyond the literal sense, at least as far as the allegorical of the spiritual senses. This view surely provides us the key to understanding not only the place of the study of the *Sentences* in theological studies but also of the *Sentence* commentary in the establishment of teaching mastery. By means of such commentary the bachelor of the *Sentences* demonstrated mastery by examining and providing a logical exposition of the *intentio* manifest in the order of the text and its theological content. Allegorical intention, then, was also susceptible to the logic of *divisio textus*.

Van Engen's article only strengthens our reidentification of the primary focus of Beryl Smalley's history: the emergence of the scholarly study of the biblical text. This is an important moment in the history of Christian thought. It is to her great credit that she was able to describe its institutional setting and pattern as well as she did, for, constantly, her identification of scholarly study and the literal historical sense of the text ill served her. I have already raised the ways in which it blinded her to the existence of performative readings which had the literal sense as their focus. Van Engen's article also makes clear how that same identification blinded her to scholarly study of the spiritual senses. Indeed, she was unable to see that *Sentence* commentaries were a form of biblical studies at all.

Since it has proven to be so problematic, one wonders again what prompted Smalley's identification of scholarly exposition with focus upon the literal historical sense. To what did she compare the couplet literal sense/scholarly exposition? Scholarly exposition, as we have seen, was constituted by logical analysis of the *intentio* underlying the text. The text's *intentio*, in turn, constituted the text's literal level as such. Thus scholarly exposition was to literal sense as a sign to its signified. Moreover, that which was signified was the text's *intentio* or intelligible core.

Smalley, of course, contrasted the literal sense to the spiritual senses; she contrasted scholarly exposition to monastic *lectio divina*. In a passage chronicling what she saw as the withering of *lectio divina*, Smalley wrote, "The spiritual exposition was doomed to artificiality as soon as it ceased to give an outlet to religious feeling."[55] From this statement we can infer that Smalley took up the nexus of scholarly exposition and the literal sense identified with logical *intentio* and contrasted it with the nexus of *lectio divina* and the spiritual senses identified as the outlet of feeling. That is, she identified *lectio divina* and the spiritual senses of scripture with the irrational aspects of human consciousness. Feeling stood in relation to *intentio* as a not-A to its A. But, as her description of Saint Francis makes clear, literal historical exposition was also a legitimate outlet for religious feeling. Moreover, Van Engen's article shows that spiritual exposition could itself be a rigorously scholarly use of logical analysis to discover and expound a logical *intentio*.

Performative and scholarly approaches to texts are, as was seen in Thomas of Cantimpré's reading practice, irreducible, for they were intended as really distinct human functions. If university study of the scripture was structured as a scholarly endeavor which addressed the literal and allegorical senses of the text, university theology masters such as Thomas Aquinas acknowledged that there were other senses intrinsic to the biblical text which were not determinable via scholarly analysis. As he put the matter, all spiritual senses flowed from the literal sense, but the moral and the anagogical senses' connection to the literal was mediated by the allegorical.[56] Thus, while the *intentio* of scripture was doubled (i.e., accessible at both the literal and allegorical level), that same *intentio* in its spiritual mode pointed to but could not be accessed through the moral and anagogical senses.

Nevertheless, these same masters understood the latter senses as the fruit and perfection of scholarly analysis. Preaching, for example, which engaged the scriptures in their moral sense, above all, was conventionally termed the roof of the theological house of studies and yet was given scant place within the theology curriculum.[57] This fact has puzzled historians.[58] But the examination here of Thomas of Cantimpré's *exemplum* suggests that the puzzlement can be resolved. University study was bounded by scholarly reading of the biblical text, that is, reading in which one examines the text's logical *intentiones*. The resulting science was speculative and thus worthwhile in and of itself. But it also provided information (logical judgments) that could subserve practical religious ends (pastoral care, mysticism etc.).

What I am suggesting, then, is that the moral and anagogical senses of scripture are profitably understood as relating to the literal and allegorical senses as logically underdetermined projections directed toward practical ends: as the bridge between speculative science and concrete action. As a consequence, I am also suggesting that medieval theologians were equally clear that the perfection of scholarly theory and praxis could be established only performatively: for example, in the pastoral act of preaching, in the experiential communion of the mystic, or in the obedience of the ordinary faithful. Indeed, medieval theologians saw no dichotomy separating scholarly exposition of the literal and allegorical senses, indication of the moral and anagogical senses they suggest, and the performative reading of all scriptural senses we encounter in preachers, the religious, pastors, mystics, and so on. I offer in confirmation the conclusion of the text of Peter the Chanter cited earlier:

> The Christian religion is concerned with faith and a moral pattern of living (*bonis moribus*). *Lectio* and *disputatio* intend toward faith, preaching toward moral living. Thus, once the roof of preaching has been set in place as shelter for us and our neighbours against the raging and rain, against the hail and whirlwind of the vices, a meeting hall will be constructed within the palace of the most high king in which one will discern the presence of laws and justice.

Peter understands faith as intellectual assent to truths. Theological study of scripture allows for precise formulation of those truths. Preaching is of a different order; it intends itself toward right living. It concerns itself with praxis and as such points toward secure life in the Church and the pattern of law by which that life is ordered. One almost sees here a claim that theology's perfection in preaching is the condition of possibility for the ordered institutional life of the Church which is the proper object of the canonist, consequently that it is canon law that constitutes the apex and perfection of Christian science.

Whatever the case, it is the productive synergy between scholarly and performative readings of the biblical text that Smalley cannot comprehend via her simplistic opposition of scholarly, literal logicality and unscholarly spiritual feeling. But here again Thomas of Cantimpré shows the way. Just as in his *cura mulierum* he combined scholarly and performative readings to facilitate the heart's ease of a much afflicted spiritual charge, so the university exegete assumed that logical determination of the biblical text's literal and allegorical meanings in no way precluded insight into the latter's moral and anagogical import, nor the performative authority of that text on all its hermeneutical levels. For the university master, too, the scriptures maintained an authority that invited the reader's submission, a submission whereby the text was to inscribe itself upon the reader's subsequent understanding and practice of life.

Notes

1. Thomas Aquinas, *Summa theologiae* 1.1.10.resp. "Cum sacrae scripturae auctor deus sit, qui omnia simul suo intellectu comprehendit, non est inconveniens . . . si etiam secundum litteralem sensum in una littera Scripturae plures sint sensus."

2. For a richly nuanced account of this sensitivity as it functions within the history of continental philosophy since Hegel, see Caputo, *Radical Hermeneutics*.

3. *Summa theologiae* 1.1.10.resp. "Hic autem sensus spiritualis trifariam dividitur. Sicut enim

dicit Apostolus . . . lex vetus figura est novae legis: et ipsa nova lex, ut dicit Dionysius . . . est figura futurae gloriae: in nova etiam lege, ea quae in capite sunt gesta, sunt signa eorum quae nos agere debemus. Secundum ergo ea quae sunt veteris legis, significant ea quae sunt novae legis, est sensus allegoricus: secundum vero quod ea quae in Christo sunt facta, vel in his quae Christum significant, sunt signa eorum quae nos agere debemus, est sensus moralis: prout vero significant ea quae sunt in aeterna gloria, est sensus anagogicus."

4. The phrase comes from the preface to the third edition of Beryl Smalley's *The Study of the Bible in the Middle Ages*, vii.

5. Ibid., 5.

6. For example, discussing Gregory the Great's *modus disserendi* in his *Moralia in Job* she writes: "To us this is a most annoying system. Everything in St. Gregory's teaching is attached, however loosely, to the thread of the text, which precludes any attempt at coherence or logical arrangement. But if we take a series of two or three homilies, or one of the thirty-five books of the *Moralia*, we can see how suitable it was for educational purposes. In two or three addresses, or hours of study, St. Gregory's hearers or readers would get a series of lessons on doctrine, prayer and ethics, in a well-arranged and carefully varied time-table" (ibid., 34).

7. I am using logic here and throughout this essay not in the narrow sense of a structure of correct inference but rather in the broad focus upon language and its various structures which characterized "logic" as the complete trivium in the twelfth century or as a rough and ready synomym of *Philologie* as it is understood in the German academy even to this day.

8. The preface to the third edition sets out a historiographical context for her frustration. There she declares that her intent had been to tell the story of how biblical scholarship as she understood it to exist today came into being. Thus, the basic plot line of her story can be summarized as "the medieval study of the literal historical sense and the story of how it came into more prominence" (ibid., vii).

9. Ibid., viii–ix.

10. Smalley, "Use of the 'Spiritual' Senses of Scripture," 44–63.

11. Lubac, *L'exégèse médiévale*, 2: 662.

12. Smalley treats these two episodes of her history in *Study of the Bible*, 83–110, 264–355. For a more precise understanding of the relationship between Dominican and secular *studia generalia* than was available to Smalley, see Mulchahey, *First the Bow is Bent*, 352–78.

13. I will be citing the text of the *Bonum universale de apibus* as one finds it in the edition of Colvenère [Henceforth *B.U.* book, chapter, part, and page]. For the biography of Thomas of Cantimpré, see DeBoutte, "Thomas van Cantimpré zijn opleiding te Kamerijk," 283–99; idem, "Thomas van Cantimpré als auditor van Albertus Magnus," 192–209; Debroux, "Thomas de Cantimpré"; and Grzebian, "Penance, Purgatory, Mysticism and Miracles." For the *Bonum universale de apibus* or "Book of Bees" and its several intents see Murray, "Confession as a Historical Source," 275–322; Platelle, "Le recueil des miracles de Thomas de Cantimpré," 469–98; but especially Sweetman, "Dominican Preaching in the Southern Low Countries 1240– 1260," and idem, "Visions of Purgatory," 20–33. The article in question is Van Engen, "Studying Scripture in the Early University," 17–38.

14. Sweetman, "Thomas of Cantimpré, Performative Reading and Pastoral Care," 133–67.

15. *B.U.* 2.57.67.591–93: "Vidi et aliam in eadem terra mulierem divitem et honestam possessam a daemone. Quam cum, rogante religioso presbytero, visitarem, invenimus eam a vexatione daemonis quiescentem, et sensate loquentem ut sanam. Tunc occulte, nullo advertente, versum cantici Moysi in Deuteronomio, secundum quod a sancto quodam viro audieram, tertio repetivi, ad provocandum daemonium in obsessa: 'Deum, qui te genuit dereliquisti, et oblitus es Domini creatoris tui.' Nec mora, mulier pallere coepit labijs atque vultu, et duae venae in collo eius ad grossitiem pollicis intumescere. Tunc ego: 'Quare (inquio), pessime, vexare feminam presumpsisti?' Et daemon: 'Mortuo (inquit) viro suo compassa, in subsidium animae illius contulit quidquid boni fecerat in hac vita, et

ex hoc nacta occasione, vas vacuum mox intravi.' Cui ego: 'Mentiris, miserrime, ex hoc enim quod dedit, mediante caritate, cumulatum est bonum eius.' Et ille cum cachinno: 'Mendax, inquit, sum, nec mirum si mentior.' Mox ego: 'Estne illa tam pulchra, ut dicitur caelestis patria, quam perdidisti?' Et respondit: 'In infinitum pulchrior, quam dicatur.' Et ego: 'Vellesne redire ad illam, si posses?' Et ille: 'Vellem, inquit, ut possem, et me usque in diem iudicij omnia excogitata supplicia pati oporteret.' Cui dixi: 'Et ego promitto tibi in periculum promissae salutis meae, si mendax inveniar, illam perditam gloriam recuperare te posse, si tantum hoc dixeris: "Domine Deus meus peccavi, ignosce mihi."' Et mox ille, contorto collo, exclamat horrifice: 'Domine, Domine.' Cumque hoc saepius cum clamore valido personaret, nec ultra in verbis procederet. (Impossibile enim sciebam illi, ut Deum suum Dominum recognosceret, et se peccasse fateretur, atque sibi precaretur ignosci) tandem subiunxit: 'Domine Deus Margaretae (sic enim obsessa mulier vocabatur) Deum recognoscere suum Dominum indignatus.' Tunc ego: 'O infelicissime omnium creaturarum, superbia elisit te, et celo depulit. Te redire inexpiabilis superbia non permittit. Nec mora, confusus obmutuit, et post paucos dies, non tamen tunc, feminam dereliquit.'"

16. *Rituale romanum*, 326–47.

17. As a result, I refer to the first *capitulum* of the early modern *Rituale romanum* when working with *admonitiones* addressed to the exorcist, but to the text of the tenth-century Romano-Germanic Pontifical when referring to the rite itself. See, in this regard, Vogel and Ilze eds., *Le pontifical romano-germanique du dixième siècle*, 193–204, esp. 199–204.

18. *Rituale* 1.5.326: "Advertat, quibus artibus ac deceptionibus utantur daemones ad exorcistam decipiendum: solent enim ut plurimum fallaciter respondere, et difficile se manifestare, ut exorcista diu defatigatus desistat; aut infirmus videatur non esse a daemonio vexatus."

19. *Rituale* 1.6.326: "Aliquando postquam sunt manifesti, abscondunt se, et relinquunt corpus quasi liberum ab omni molestia, ut infirmus putet se omnino esse liberatum: sed cessare non debet exorcista, donec viderit signa liberationis."

20. *B.U.* 2.57.67.591: "Quam cum . . . visitarem, invenimus a vexatione daemonis quiescentem, et sensate loquentem ut sanam."

21. *Rituale* 1.15.327: "Necessariae vero interrogationes sunt, ex. gr. de numero et nomine spirituum obsidentium, de tempore quo ingressi sunt, de causa, et aliis hujusmodi. Ceteras autem daemonis nugas, risus, et ineptias exorcista cohibeat. . . ."

22. *Rituale* 1.16.327: "Exorcismos vero faciat ac legat cum imperio, et auctoritate, magna fide, et humilitate, atque fervore; et cum viderit, spiritum valde torquere, tunc magis instet et urgeat. Et quoties, viderit obsessum in aliqua corporis parte commoveri, aut pungi, aut tumorem alicubi apparere, ibi faciat signum crucis, et aqua benedicta aspergat, quam tunc in promptu habeat."

23. *Rituale* 1.17.327: "Observet etiam ad quae verba daemones magis contremiscant, et ea saepius repetat."

24. *Rituale* 1.20.328: "Dum exorcizat, utatur sacrae Scripturae verbis potius quam suis, aut alienis."

25. *B.U.* 2.57.67.591–593: "Quare (inquio), pessime, vexare feminam praesumpsisti?"

26. Ibid.: "Tunc occulte, nullo advertente, versum cantici Moysi in Deuteronomio, secundum quod a sancto quodam viro audieram, tertio repetivi, ad provocandum daemonem in obsessa. . . . Nec mora, mulier pallere coepit labijs atque vultu, et duae venae in collo eius ad grossitiem pollicis intumescere."

27. One thinks, in particular, of Thomas's exchange with the demon about heaven.

28. *Le pontifical romano-germanique*, 200–201. ". . . in quo nihil invenisti de operibus tuis: qui te expoliavit, qui regnum tuum destruxit, qui te victum ligavit, et vasa tua diripuit: qui te projecit in tenebras exteriores, ubi tibi cum ministris tuis erit praeparatus interitus."

29. The classic telling of Christ's harrowing of hell can be found in *The Gospel of Nicodemus*, ed. Kim.

30. For the distinction between "word for word" and "according to the sense" in late antique and medieval hermeneutics, see Copeland, *Rhetoric, Hermeneutics and Translation in the Middle Ages*, 9–62.

31. *B.U.* 2.57.66.590–591: "Vidi in Brabantiae partibus in monasterio Cisterciensi monialem quamdam religiosam valde et vita puram, quam cum visitarem et eam, ut poteram, consolarer, subito daemon pessimus, qui in ea latebat, per horam verba salutis ferre non valens, coepit latrare ut canis et hianti ore et collo contorto, eversisque luminibus blasphemare. Cui dixi: 'O miserrime, qui Dei laudibus cum bonis angelis insistere noluisti, nunc canum latratus et bestias imitaris.'"

32. For an overview of medieval views about the Devil see Russell, *Lucifer*, esp. 159–207. Many of the formulations that follow, however, are drawn from the oeuvre of Saint Bonaventure as surveyed in Sweetman, "When Popular Piety and Theological Learning Conjoin," 4–18.

33. See the discussions of *obsideo* and *possideo* in Lewis and Short, *A Latin Dictionary*, 1243 and 1403.

34. Cf. Du Cange, *Glossarium mediae et infimae latinitatis*, 6: 430.

35. See, in this regard and with respect to what follows in the subsequent paragraph, the patristic discussions of Luke 4:1–13 (the temptation of Jesus) compiled by Aquinas in his *Catena aurea*, 61–66. This commentary is full of the language of being filled and being empty in which emptiness is associated with vulnerability to demonic vexation.

36. I am, of course, playing on that famous reader of the twelfth century, whose voracious appetite for books lay behind his traditional moniker, Peter Comestor or "the Eater." What I am suggesting is that "eating books" should not be mistaken for a simple hyperbole indicating that some, like the author of the *Historia scholastica*, were widely read. Rather, "eating" here refers to the discipline of literary ingestion (*lectio et meditatio*) described by Mary Carruthers in *The Book of Memory*.

37. See Leclereq, *L'amour des lettres et le désir de Dieu*.

38. Smalley, *Study of the Bible*, 284–85.

39. This religious project in which one person's acts are invested in another's welfare is well studied in Carpenter, "A New Heaven and a New Earth," especially its third chapter, "Spiritual Charity and Vicarious Suffering in the *Mulieres Religiosae*."

40. For the notion of merit as understood by Thomas Aquinas, see Argus, "Divine Self-Expression Through Human Merit," esp. 338–43; and also Wawrykow, *God's Grace and Human Action*.

41. Caesarius of Heisterbach, *Dialogus miraculorum*, 5.10.290: "Daemon daemoni dicebat: Miser, ut quid consentiendo Lucifero sic de gloria aeterna ruimus? Ad quod alter respondit: Quare fecisti? Cumque ille adhuc quasi poenitudinis verba proferret, alter subiunxit: Tace, poenitentia ista nimis est sera, redire non poteris. . . . Idem spiritus malignus de reditu ad gloriam, sicut superior, interrogatus, verbum sermoni eius valde contrarium audiente me respondit: Si esset, inquit, columna ferrea et ignita, rasoriis et laminis acutissimis armata, a terra usque ad coelum erecta, usque ad diem iudicii, etiam se carnem haberem, in qua pati possem, me per illam trahere vellem, nunc ascendendo, numc descendendo, dummodo redire possem ad gloriam in qua fui."

42. Thomas's early modern editor marks eighteen *exempla* which recall either in part or *in toto* stories recorded previously in Caesarius's *Dialogus miraculorum*. In nearly all cases, the corresponding narratives relate in ways similar to the ways discussed in this essay. Some seem to relate as different redactions of a common narrative tradition. This, for example, seems to be the best explanation of the resonances between *D.M.* 6.22 and *B.U.* 2.7.4.150–52. Others seem to relate in the manner that the two narratives presently under discussion relate, namely, Thomas uses Caesarius's narrative as a source of information. In one case, however, the relationship is more direct. In *D.M.* 21.2, Caesarius tells the story of a certain Count Louis who is a tyrant in

life. Facing death, Louis arranges to have his corpse clothed in the habit of the Cistercian Order. His machinations are to no avail. A colleague describes his fate in rich, ironic tones. His soul is received as a novice in the infernal order, so to speak, in which it takes on the discipline of that school of the Devil's service. In *B.U.* 1.3.5.16, Thomas also tells of a worldly sinner who seeks and is granted his dying wish to be buried, in this case, in a Dominican habit. We are not told of the otherworldly outcome, but Thomas does take the occasion to defend the practice against the disapproval of other, pastorally flint-hearted Orders who see the practice as spiritually vain. It is hard to avoid the impression that Thomas's *exemplum* is designed among other things to act as a response to and criticism of Caesarius's. Of course, Caesarius is reflecting the Cistercian position on these things; the Cluniacs, obviously, thought otherwise.

43. See the list of manuscripts of the *Dialogus* published in Meister, *Die Fragmente der Libri VIII Miraculorum*, xxi–xxiv. It should be noted that Caesarius's story is itself a stock telling. However, he never claims it to be anything else since he never enters into his own text, so to speak. All narration occurs via his fictive voices of experienced monk and novice.

44. See in this regard, Sweetman, "Thomas of Cantimpré, *Mulieres Religiosae*, and Purgatorial Piety," 606–28.

45. The contrast between "existential" and "essential" invoked at this point adapts the metaphysical distinction identified and argued for by Gilson in *Being and Some Philosophers*. The distinction, as I have appropriated it, implies that what is of the essence, so to speak, exists within a broader and deeper existential horizon. Thus, the essential self is not a Self such as Descartes, Kant, or Husserl posited—that is, it is not a First Thing. Rather, from this vantage point, it would appear that the essential self is the determinate posture or attitude that a concrete human person assumes under a certain conceptualizable aspect. Consequently, it comes to seem that Descartes, Kant, and Husserl, each in his own way, hypostasizes the essential self of scholarly reading and raises it up to the level of metaphysical principle.

46. It is by dint of this imperative approach, this commanding posture, that the scholarly reader insulates himself albeit willy-nilly from any essential change. Why this must be so can be illustrated as follows. If scholarly reading assumes that the text to hand has an intrinsic order that is logically representable, it proceeds at least in principle in terms of the binary mode constitutive of logical analysis (i.e., division and composition). Thus the scholarly reader asks questions of texts to which they answer "yes" or "no." For example, the scholar might ask a text whether it exhibits a given motif, say, the jaws of hell. If the text replies "yes," he might go on to ask whether the motif is represented in conformity with classical descriptions of Hades. If it answers "no," he might further ask whether its representation owes its divergence from classical models to the language of biblical apocalyptic. And so on. In such an approach it is obvious that the text's impact upon the scholarly reader is controlled. It can only really confirm or refute the scholar's guesses or hypotheses. The honest scholar goes where the text leads, to be sure, but only grudgingly, preferring rather to have it go where he wills, especially when looking to uncover what lies hidden between the text's lines. It is the paradigmatic character of this description that substantiates the claim that the scholarly reader goes to texts not to be interrogated but to interrogate.

47. I sketch out the some of the implications of this priority of the performative in Sweetman, "Thomas of Cantimpré, Performative Reading and Pastoral Care," 150–54.

48. Van Engen, "Studying Scripture," 22.

49. Ibid.

50. Ibid.

51. Ibid., 33.

52. Ibid., 34–36.

53. Ibid., 22.

54. Ibid.

55. Smalley, *Study of the Bible*, 284.

56. *S.T.* 1.1.10. resp. "Secundum vero quod ea quae in Christo sunt facta, vel in his quae Christum significant, sunt signa eorum quae nos agere debemus, est sensus moralis: prout vero significant ea quae sunt in aeterna gloria, est sensus anagogicus."

57. See in this regard the formulation of Peter the Chanter found in his *Verbum abbreviatum*, edited by Baldwin in *Masters, Princes and Merchants*, 2:63 n.22. "In tribus autem consistit exercitium sacrae scripturae: in lectione, disputatione et praedicatione, cuilibet istorum inimica est prolixitas, mater oblivionis et noverca memorie. Lectio ergo primo iacitur quasi stratorium et fundamentum sequentium ut ex ea omnia amminicula quasi ex quodam fonte ceteris duabus propinentur. Supponitur secundo structura vel paries disputationis. . . . Tercio erigitur tectum predicationis ust qui audit dicat: veni, et cortina cortinam trahat. Post lectionem igitur sacre scripture et dubitabilium disputationum inquisitionem et non prius est predicandum. Religio vero christiana est de fide et de bonis moribus. Lectio et disputatio ad fidem referantur, predicatio ad mores. Sic apposito tecto predicationis quod et nos et proximos nostros defendet ab estu et a pluvia et a grandine et a turbine vitiorum, constructum erit consistorium palatii summi regis in quo leges et iura discernet."

58. See, for example, the curt remarks of Goering about the activities of the twelfth-century master of theology William de Montibus in *William de Montibus*, 34.

Bibliography

Argus, Michael. "Divine Self-Expression Through Human Merit According to Thomas Aquinas." Ph.D diss., University of Toronto, 1990.

Baldwin, John. *Masters, Princes and Merchants: The Social Views of Peter the Chanter and His Circle*. 2 vols. Princeton, N.J.: Princeton University Press, 1970.

Caesarius of Heisterbach. *Dialogus miraculorum*. Ed. J. Strange. 2 vols. Cologne, 1851.

Caputo, John. *Radical Hermeneutics*. Bloomington: Indiana University Press, 1987.

Carpenter, Jennifer. "A New Heaven and a New Earth: A Study of the *Vitae* of the *Mulieres Religiosae* of Liège." Ph.D. diss., University of Toronto, 1997.

Carruthers, Mary. *The Book of Memory: A Study of Memory in Medieval Culture*. Cambridge: Cambridge University Press, 1991.

Copeland, Rita. *Rhetoric, Hermeneutics and Translation in the Middle Ages: Academic Traditions and Vernacular Texts*. Cambridge: Cambridge University Press, 1991.

DeBoutte, A. "Thomas van Cantimpré als auditor van Albertus Magnus." *Ons geestelijk erf* 58 (1984): 192–209.

——. "Thomas van Cantimpré zijn opleiding te Kamerijk." *Ons geestelijk erf* 56 (1982): 283–99.

Debroux, A. "Thomas de Cantimpré (v. 1200–1270): L'homme et son oeuvre écrite; essai de biographie." Mémoire de license, Université Catholique de Louvain, 1979.

Du Cange, C. *Glossarium mediae et infimae latinitatis*. New ed. 10 vols. Paris: Librairie des sciences et des arts, 1937–38.

Gilson, Etienne. *Being and Some Philosophers*. Toronto: Pontifical Institute of Mediaeval Studies, 1952.

Goering, Joseph. *William de Montibus (c. 1140–1213): The Schools and the Literature of Pastoral Care*. Studies and Texts, 108. Toronto: Pontifical Institute of Mediaeval Studies, 1992.

The Gospel of Nicodemus. Ed. H. C. Kim. Toronto: Pontifical Institute of Mediaeval Studies, 1973.

Grzebian, Thomas W. "Penance, Purgatory, Mysticism and Miracles: The Life, Hagiography, and Spirituality of Thomas of Cantimpré (1200–1270)." Ph.D diss., University of Notre Dame, 1990.

Leclercq, Jean. *L'amour des lettres et le désir de Dieu: Initiation aux auteurs monastiques du moyen âge*. Paris: Editions de Cerf, 1957.

Lewis, Carleton T., and Charles Short. *A Latin Dictionary*. Oxford: Clarendon Press, 1975.

Lubac, Henri de. *L'exégèse médiévale: Les quatre sens de l'écriture*. 4 vols. Paris: Aubier, 1959–64.

Meister, A. *Die Fragmente der Libri VIII Miraculorum des Caesarius von Heisterbach*. Rome: Spithöven, 1901.

Mulchahey, M. Michèle. *"First the Bow is Bent in Study . . .": Dominican Education Before 1350*. Toronto: Pontifical Institute of Mediaeval Studies, 1988.

Murray, A. "Confession as a Historical Source in the Thirteenth Century." In *The Writing of History in the Middle Ages: Essays Presented to Richard William Southern*. Ed. R. H. C. Davis and J. M. Wallace-Hadrill, 275–322. Oxford: Clarendon Press, 1982.

Platelle, Henri. "Le recueil des miracles de Thomas de Cantimpré et la vie religieuse dans les Pays-Bas et le Nord de France en XIIIe siècle." In *Actes du 97e Congrès national de sociétés savantes, Nantes 1972, Section de philologie et de l'histoire jusqu'à 1610*, 469–98. Paris, 1979.

Rituale romanum. Boston: Benziger, 1975.

Russell, Jeffrey Burton. *Lucifer: The Devil in the Middle Ages*. Ithaca, N.Y.: Cornell University Press, 1984.

Smalley, Beryl. *The Study of the Bible in the Middle Ages*. 3d ed. Oxford: Basil Blackwell, 1983.

——. "Use of the 'Spiritual' Senses of Scripture in Persuasion and Argument by Scholars in the Middle Ages." *Recherches de théologie ancienne et médiévale* 52 (1985): 44–63.

Sweetman, Robert. "Dominican Preaching in the Southern Low Countries 1240–1260: *Materiae Praedicabiles* in the *Liber de natura rerum* and *Bonum universale de apibus* of Thomas of Cantimpré." Ph.D. diss., University of Toronto, 1989.

——. "Thomas of Cantimpré, *Mulieres Religiosae*, and Purgatorial Piety: Hagiographical *Vitae* and the Beguine 'Voice.'" In *"In a Distinct Voice": Medieval Studies in Honor of Leornard Boyle, O.P.*. Ed. Jacqueline Brown and William P. Stoneman, 606–28. Notre Dame, Ind.: University of Notre Dame Press, 1997.

——. "Thomas of Cantimpré, Performative Reading and Pastoral Care." In *Performance and Transformation: New Approaches to Late Medieval Spirituality*. Ed. Mary A. Sudyam and Joanna E. Zeigler, 133–67. New York: St. Martin's Press, 1999.

——. "Visions of Purgatory and Their Role in the *Bonum universale de apibus* of Thomas of Cantimpré." *Oons geestelijk erf* 67 (1993): 20–33.

——. "When Popular Piety and Theological Learning Conjoin: St. Bonaventure on Demonic Powers and the Christian Soul." *Fides et historia* 23 (1991): 4–18.

Thomas Aquinas. *Catena aurea in quatuor evangelia*. Ed. P. Angelico Guarienti. 2 vols. Turin: Marietti, 1953.

——. *Summa theologiae*. 5 vols. Ottawa: Comissio Piana, 1953.

Thomas of Cantimpré. *Bonum universale de apibus, sive, Miraculorum exemplorum memorabilem sui temporis libri duo*. Ed. G. Colvenère. Douai: Bellaci, 1627.

Van Engen, John. "Studying Scripture in the Early University." In *Neue Richtungen in der hoch- und spätmittelalterlichen Bibelexegese*. Ed. Robert E. Lerner and Elisabeth Müller-Luckner, 17–38. Schriften des Historischen Kollegs, 32. Munich: Oldenbourg, 1996.

Vogel, Cyrille and, Reinhard Ilze, eds. *Le pontifical romano-germanique du dixième siècle: Le text II (nn. xcix–cclviii)*. Vatican City: Biblioteca Apostolica Vaticana, 1963.

Wawrykow, Joseph P. *God's Grace and Human Action: Merit in the Theology of Thomas Aquinas*. Notre Dame, Ind.: University of Notre Dame Press, 1986.

17

The Theological Character of the Scholastic "Division of the Text" with Particular Reference to the Commentaries of Saint Thomas Aquinas

JOHN F. BOYLE

The scholastic division of the text is an interpretive technique whose idea is rather simple. Starting with the text as a whole, one articulates a principal theme, in the light of which one divides and subdivides the text into increasingly smaller units, often down to the individual words. A scholastic division of the text has at least three essential characteristics. First, the interpreter articulates a theme that provides a conceptual unity to the text and the commentary as a whole. Second, the division penetrates at least to the level of verse; it does not simply articulate large blocks of the text. And third, because the division begins with the whole and then continues through progressive subdivisions, every verse stands in an articulated relation not only with the whole but ultimately with every other part, division, and verse of the text.

Consider, by way of example, Saint Thomas Aquinas's commentary on the Gospel according to Saint John (see appendix). Thomas begins by stating the principal point—the unifying theme—of the Gospel: to "show the divinity of the incarnate Word."[1] In view of this intention, Saint Thomas divides the Gospel into two parts: in the first, Saint John presents the divinity of Christ (chap. 1), and in the second he manifests that divinity through those things Christ did in the flesh (chaps. 2–21). These two parts are in turn further divided. For example, the second part—the manifestation of Christ's divinity through what he did—is divided into two parts: how Christ manifests His divinity in those things he did while living in the world (chaps. 2–11), and how Christ manifests his divinity in his death (chaps. 12–21). The manifestation of divinity while living in the world is again divided into two parts: manifesting his dominion over nature (chap. 2), and manifesting the effects of grace (chaps. 3–11). This latter is divided into spiritual regeneration (chaps. 3–4) and spiritual benefits conferred on those divinely regenerated (chaps. 5–11). These spiritual benefits are, in turn, threefold: spiritual life (chap. 5), spiritual food (chap. 6), and spiritual teaching (chaps. 7–11). Each of these sections is further divided and subdivided to the point that Saint Thomas can comment sometimes word by word on a given verse. The Marietti edition of Saint Thomas's commentary provides a full schematic outline of the division, which fills some thirty-seven pages.[2]

I do not know the first instance of a scholastic division of the text, although it appears to be a product of the thirteenth century; it is in full flower by the middle of the thirteenth century as manifest in the skillful use of it by such figures as Saint Bonaventure, Saint Albert the Great, Hugh of Saint Cher, and, of course, Saint Thomas Aquinas.

As a technique for interpreting texts, it is not limited to Sacred Scripture. Saint Bonaventure and Saint Thomas use it, not with such refinement to specific phrases, in their commentaries on Peter Lombard's *Liber sententiarum*. Nor is the division of the text limited to the science of theology. Saint Thomas uses the same technique in his commentaries on the works of Aristotle. Indeed, the division of the text is not limited to the interpretation of another's work: Saint Thomas uses a modified form of it as a guide to the reading of his own *Summa theologiae*. So too do the author/compilers of the *Summa fratris Alexandri*.

As for how the scholastic theologians understand the technique of division, either in practice or in theory, I know of no explicit discussion of it. Here the strictly hermeneutical question as such simply does not engage them. Certainly for the scholastic doctors of the mid-thirteenth century it is not a required form. That they choose to use it suggests they see some particular value to be had in it. As theologians, they presumably see some theological value to its use.

Which brings me, at last, to the two questions I would like to consider. First, what are the theological implications of this technique? And second, what are its theological limitations?

The principal and obvious implication suggested by the use of the scholastic division of the text is the unity of the text—by which I mean here a given book of the Bible. The text holds together. What holds the text together, however, is more than simply the material fact of its human author; what gives the Gospel according to Saint John unity is not simply that Saint John wrote it. For the scholastic division of the text to work, the unity must be an intrinsic conceptual unity; there must be a unifying idea in the light of which the whole can be seen and, still more important, each part can be understood.

This striving for conceptual unity in whole and part is of potential value to the theologian in at least two ways. In a famous article of his disputed questions *De potentia*, Saint Thomas addresses the question of how to read the first chapter of Genesis in the light of certain claims made by reason. He also confronts the reality of multiple literal interpretations of the text. Among the principles he articulates for evaluating an interpretation of a passage of scripture is that the circumstance of the letter be preserved (*salva circumstantia litterae*).[3] This would seem to mean, at least minimally, that the interpreter must be attentive to the context of the lemma in question. The thoroughgoing contextualization of the letter provided by a scholastic division of the text could then be a particularly fruitful means of safeguarding the circumstance of the letter.

Second, for a theologian such as Saint Thomas who understands the theological enterprise as the articulation of the ways in which revealed truths—indeed all truths—stand in relation one to another,[4] the scholastic division provides a way in which such a theological task can be undertaken in the very reading of scripture itself. It is not simply a matter of breaking the text down into component bits, but of seeing how its parts stand in relation one to another. This synthetic task is as much a part of the scholastic enterprise as is division and distinction; indeed, distinction is in service of unity. For the scholastics, the division of the text is precisely a means to arrive at ways of seeing the fundamental unity of revealed truth.

In this light, it is notable that the effort to articulate the intrinsic conceptual unity of the text extended beyond individual biblical books. Saint Thomas subjects the corpus of the epistles of Saint Paul as a whole to a division of the text. The central unifying idea is the mystical body of Christ, divided and subdivided according to each of the epistles.[5] Or again, Saint Bonaventure will suggest a division of Proverbs, Ecclesiastes, and the Song of Songs taken as a whole.[6] In theory at least, the whole of scripture could be subject to such a division. I know of no one who actually accomplished such a division; nonetheless, we have general divisions of the Old Testament and the New Testament, which suggest just such a way of thinking about the whole, in principle at least, if not in practice.[7] In this case, the unity is in no way based upon a unifying human author but solely upon the unifying divine author.

If one takes the technique seriously, it has decisive implications for how one is to read such commentaries. Those who study scholasticism commonly lament how the scriptural commentaries are so disappointing; they seem limp or thin or simply pedestrian. While scholars are initially eager to use the scriptural commentaries of the great scholastic doctors, when they turn to them, they are all too often disappointed and return to the systematic works with sadness in their hearts, suspecting that the doctors did not, after all, take scripture seriously enough. For example, the broad-minded thomist, interested in the sacrament of the Eucharist, but not satisfied simply with reading the *Summa theologiae*, turns to Saint Thomas's commentary on the bread of life discourse in the sixth chapter of the Gospel according to Saint John. The commentary is relatively short, moving quickly from phrase to phrase. Having made a brief foray into Saint Thomas's commentary he returns, disappointed, to his appointed task. He might return to the scriptural commentaries, but only for periodic footnote filler; the commentary itself is not likely to inform his thinking on Saint Thomas.

The problem is in looking simply to the commentary on specific verses. The genius of the scholastic division of the text is that every lemma has a context, or better, a set of nested contexts. It never stands alone. The comments presume all that has come before, and indeed, what comes after. The skilled commentator need not say as much at the particular lemma, because he has already said so much getting there.

Let us return to the example of the bread of life discourse in John 6. An appreciation of Thomas's interpretation requires minimally (see appendix) that one appreciate that this chapter is in the context of spiritual food as a spiritual benefit conferred on those divinely regenerated, which in turn is part of Christ's manifestation of his divinity through those things he did while living in the world.

Thus such commentaries must be read as a whole. The division of the text not only presumes a conceptual unity, but produces a commentary that itself must be understood as a whole. The division of the text is a guide to the biblical commentary as well as to the biblical text. It is a practical point, if not exactly a theological one, for those of us who would undertake the study of these monstrous commentaries.

Thus the most powerful and obvious characteristic of the scholastic division of the text is the articulation of a principle of unity of the text and then the situation of all the parts within that unifying principle. This technique is used principally, however, to elucidate the literal sense of scripture. The scholastics are generally agreed upon what the literal sense of scripture is: the thing signified by the words.[8] In this, Scripture is like any other literary work: words signify things. They may signify directly or through metaphor or any number of other literary figures and devices. All of this is a matter of the literal sense. It is not my intention to attend to the complexities and vagaries of scholastic literal interpretation, but rather to note that the scholastic division of the text as an interpretive technique is used principally, I am inclined to say exclusively, in the literal interpretation of scripture.

In the actual interpretation of the literal sense, however, the articulation and application of the division are rather more of an art than a science. This is especially true in articulating the intermediate divisions of the text. Medieval interpreters of scripture are strikingly comfortable with differing literal interpretations of a given passage; so too they seem quite comfortable with differing divisions. Beginning with the same unifying theme, Saint Bonaventure and Saint Thomas divide the Gospel according to Saint John in quite different ways with no attendant need to establish the exclusive truth of one division over the other.[9] This is so perhaps because such divisions were not understood as definitive but rather as illuminative. The division of the text provides insight into a text presumed to be rich, mysterious, multivalent, and ultimately inexhaustible.

As well, the scholastic division of the text orders and weighs particular passages in relation to one another. For example, in Saint Thomas's division, the second chapter of John manifests Christ's divinity by showing His dominion over nature. This is obvious enough in the miracle of turning water into wine at the beginning of the chapter. But what of the cleansing of the Temple which follows it? Saint Thomas looks to the discourse concluding the cleansing, in which Christ speaks of his resurrection, which resurrection will itself be an instance of his dominion over nature. The cleansing of the Temple provides the occasion for the announcing of the future miracle, and thus it is fittingly understood in relation to Christ's dominion over nature.

The variety of divisions brings to light a foundational understanding of literal authorship for medieval interpreters of Sacred Scripture. The literal sense is concerned in part with authorial intention, but that intention is twofold: divine and human. While both Saint Thomas and Saint Bonaventure in their commentaries on the Gospel according to Saint John begin with the intention of the human author, they have no difficulties with differing literal interpretations or divisions—at least in principle—since such diversity might have been intended by the human author under divine inspiration, and even if not, is embraced within the intention of the divine author. While the conceptual unity of the scholastic division of the text requires authorial intention, it need not require a univocal intention or a solely human author. With regard to the scholastic division, the particulars of the divisions, and perhaps the very possibility of such divisions, presume both human and divine authorship with regard to the literal sense.

That the scholastic division is an essentially literal interpretive method does not mean that commentaries built upon a scholastic division are without consideration of the spiritual or mystical senses of scripture. These commentaries do contain much in the way of mystical interpretation. The mystical, however, does not provide the overarching interpretive framework; it is the literal that provides the overarching framework, which in turn is the context for the mystical interpretation of a particular passage. Thus, the literal sense is necessarily established first in the division of the text, and thereby the basis of the mystical interpretation is also established. Such practice brings to life the important medieval principle, so dear to Saint Thomas, that the mystical should be founded on the literal.[10]

Consider Saint Thomas's treatment of the healing of the paralytic at the pool of Bethesda in the fifth chapter of the Gospel according to Saint John. Like all miracles, it is a sign. But of what? Within Saint Thomas's division, chapter 5 treats of the spiritual life as one of the benefits conferred by Christ on those divinely regenerated as part of the larger division of those things which manifest Christ's divinity while he lived in the world. In healing the paralytic, Christ literally conferred on him a new life. As a sign however, it immediately points to a mystical meaning: the conferring of new spiritual life in baptism. Thus, the literal division all the more firmly grounds a mystical interpretation of the passage.

Modern historiography of medieval exegesis, at least in the English-speaking world, has been especially interested in claiming a relevance for medieval exegesis precisely because it had not always and everywhere abandoned the literal sense. By literal sense, what was meant tended to be the modern critical project (hence Beryl Smalley's telling distinction between theologians and biblical scholars[11]). In the effort to find moderns in medieval garb, modern students of medieval interpretation have latched onto a few select figures, such as Saint Thomas, with their emphasis on the literal sense, as exceptional scholars in the Middle Ages and as notable precursors of our modern exegetical masters. Miss Smalley subsequently retracted, or at least significantly modified, her own praise for Saint Thomas, noting that he never fully appreciated the literal wholly apart from the mystical.[12] Without speaking to their status as precursors, I would suggest that such study has rather misconstrued the scholastics and their work. Indeed, when one considers what these figures understood by the literal sense, one can see that not simply Saint Thomas but many of his contemporaries are engaged in precisely literal interpretation; indeed, such is demanded by the use of the scholastic division of the text. The appearance of mystical interpretation within such commentaries is not a lapse, but an instance of building the mystical upon the literal.

Let us now turn to the second question, what are the theological limitations of the technique? Not all commentaries on scripture from this period are built upon a division of the text. Such a technique cannot do everything, and interpreters did not always use it. What are its limitations?

First, as is implied above, it is not a fruitful tool for sustained mystical interpretation. Scholastic interpreters agree on a fundamentally twofold division of the senses of scripture: literal and mystical (or spiritual—the name varies, but the reality does not). If the literal sense of scripture pertains to the things signified by the words, the mystical sense pertains to things that are signified, in turn, by the things signified by the words.[13] Thus, for example, the word "Jacob" signifies the patriarch; the patriarch himself signifies the rational soul. The former pertains to the literal sense, the latter to the mystical. For these theologians, God, as creator and provident Lord of creation, has invested things, persons, and events with intrinsic multivalent signification. In the investigation of those things signified by the words of scripture, the theologian discovers their still deeper realities in the economy of salvation. This mystical sense is usually divided into three specific senses which need not concern us here; indeed, while particular theologians may disagree on precisely how to carve up the number and character of mystical senses, they all agree on the existence of the mystical sense and how it stands in distinction from the literal sense.

The scholastic division of the text is not a fruitful tool for sustained mystical interpretation. The critical term here is "sustained." By this, I mean a commentary in which the whole—the conceptual unity that is the subject of the division—is mystical, not simply some part. I know of no such commentary. The reason for such a general absence appears obvious enough: few books would sustain such an interpretation as a whole. The most likely candidate is the Song of Songs. In its case, however, the difficulty is in establishing the literal sense in the first place. Much of what moderns critically dismiss as fanciful, or sympathetically classify as mystical, was treated by many medieval theologians as literal. Thus a christological reading of the Song of Songs within a scholastic division of the text would not necessarily signal a sustained mystical interpretation.

Nonetheless, widespread use of the scholastic division on the mystical level would be surprising from the very character of the mystical sense as so clearly enunciated in the scholastic period: things signify things. In order to get at the mystical thing, one must first get at the foundational literal thing. A sustained division of the text would require a division to cover both. It would seem more practical, one might even say more fitting, that the unifying division be on the literal level and that the mystical be drawn from that. Indeed, grounded in the literal sense, it could be drawn frequently and consistently, without being tied to an overarching mystical division. Such is precisely the technique of Saint Thomas in his Gospel commentaries.

Let me note one further area of possible limitation. In his Commentary on the Book of Job, Saint Thomas does not use the scholastic division of the text. The commentary is explicitly a literal one—concerned with Job and his circumstance. At the outset, Saint Thomas concedes the mystical ground to Saint Gregory the Great. His decision not to use the division of the text is thus not related to the particular sense of scripture he is investigating. Saint Thomas sees a theme to the book—divine providence—and that theme governs his commentary. Thus his decision not to use the division of the text does not arise from a lack of conceptual unity to the book. Saint Thomas's reading of Job is as a long extended dialectical argument. He carefully articulates the various steps and missteps in the argument. In Saint Thomas's hands it rather takes on the character of a narrative dialogue. Why not use the scholastic division here? Perhaps the scholastic division is not particularly useful in articulating the give and take of a narrative argument; the literal interpretation of the text is not served by a scholastic division of it.

In conclusion, the scholastic division of the text as a method employed by the doctors of the high Middle Ages is not without its theological character. Certainly for those who were masters of theology, the commenting on scripture was their primary task. In their choice to use or not use the scholastic division, they help us who would study them better understand their tasks as theologians entering into that deep and shrouded mystery that is sacred scripture.

Appendix: Saint Thomas Aquinas's Division of the Gospel according to Saint John

The Gospel according to Saint John principally intends to show the divinity of the incarnate Word

I. Presents the divinity of Christ, chap. 1
   - A. Shows the divinity of Christ, 1.1–1.13
     - 1. Considers the divinity of Christ 1.1–1.5
       - a. With regard to divine nature 1.1–1.2
       - b. With regard to divine power or operation 1.3–1.5
         - i. With regard to all things 1.3–1.4a
         - ii. With regard to all men 1.4b-1.5

2. Considers the incarnation of the Word 1.6–1.13
   a. The witness: John the Baptist 1.6–1.8
   b. The coming of the Word 1.9–1.14

B. Sets forth the manner in which Christ's divinity is made known, 1.14–1.51

II. Manifests the divinity of Christ by what he did in the flesh, 2.1–21.25
   A. How Christ manifests his divinity in those things he did while living in the world, 2.1–11.57
      1. In his dominion over nature, chap. 2
      2. In the effects of grace, 3.1–11.57
         a. Spiritual regeneration, 3.1–4.54
            i. In relation to the Jews, chap. 3
            ii. In relation to the gentiles, chap. 4
         b. Benefits conferred on those regenerated 5.1–11.57
            i. Spiritual life, chap. 5
            ii. Spiritual food, chap. 6
            iii. Spiritual teaching, 7.1–11.57
               aa. Its origin, chap. 7
               bb. Its power, 8.1–11.57
      3. Illuminative, 8.1–9.41
         a. By word, chap. 8
         b. By miracle, chap. 9
      4. Life giving, 10.1–11.57
         a. By word, chap. 10
         b. By miracle, chap. 11
   B. How Christ showed his divinity in his death, 12.1–21.25
      1. Christ's passion and death, 12.1–19.42
         a. Causes and occasion of Christ's death, chap. 12
         b. Preparation of the disciples, 13.1–17.26
            i. How he informed them by example, chap. 13
            ii. How he comforted them in word, 14.1–16.33
            iii. How he strengthened them by prayer, chap. 17
         c. passion and death, 18.1–19.42
            i. Passion at the hands of the Jews, chap. 18
            ii. Passion at the hands of the gentiles, chap. 19
      2. The resurrection, 20.1–21.25
         a. Manifest to the women, 20.1–20.18
         b. Manifest to the disciples, 20.19–21.25

Notes

1. Thomas Aquinas, *Super Evangelium s. Ioannis lectura* 1.1, 7. This is hardly a novel understanding of this Gospel; it is a commonplace for the Fathers and for medieval interpreters alike.
2. Ibid., 505–42.
3. Thomas Aquinas, *Quaestiones disputatae de potentia* 4.1, 2:105.
4. Cf. Weisheipl, "The Meaning of *Sacra Doctrina*," 49–80.
5. Thomas Aquinas, *Super epistolas s. Pauli lectura*, prologus, 1:3.
6. Bonaventure, *Commentarius in Ecclesiasten*, in *Opera omnia*, 6:5.
7. See Thomas Aquinas, *De commendatione et partitione sacrae Scripturae*, in *Opuscula theologica* 1:435–39. Another example, from the Franciscan John of La Rochelle, can be found in Delorme, "Deux leçons d'ouverture de Cours Biblique," 345–60.

8. Cf. Thomas Aquinas, *Summa theologiae*, 1.1.10. The fullest study of the senses of scripture as understood in the Middle Ages is Lubac, *Exégèse médiévale*.

9. Bonaventure, *Commentarius in Evangelium Ioannis*, in *Opera omnia*, 6:246. This is but one instance of many in which the great scholastic doctors overlap in their work.

10. Thomas Aquinas, *Summa theologiae*, 1.1.10.

11. Smalley, *Study of the Bible*, xv–xvi.

12. Smalley, *The Gospels in the Schools*, 265–66.

13. Thomas Aquinas, *Summa theologiae* 1.1.10.

Bibliography

Bonaventure. *Commentarius in Ecclesiasten*. In *Opera Omnia*. Ed. PP. Collegii a S. Bonaventura. Vol. 6. Quaracchi: Collegium S. Bonaventurae, 1895.

——. *Commentarius in Evangelium Ioannis*. In *Opera Omnia*. Ed. PP. Collegii a S. Bonaventura. Vol. 6. Quaracchi: Collegium S. Bonaventurae, 1895.

Delorme, F. M. "Deux leçons d'ouverture de Cours Biblique données par Jean de la Rochelle." *France franciscaine* 16 (1933): 345–60.

Lubac, Henri de. *Exégèse médiévale: les quatre sens de l'écriture*, 4 vols. Paris: Aubier, 1959–64.

Smalley, Beryl. *The Gospels in the Schools, c. 1000–c. 1280*. London: Hambledon Press, 1985.

——. *The Study of the Bible in the Middle Ages*. 1st pbk ed. Notre Dame, Ind: University of Notre Dame Press, 1964.

Thomas Aquinas. *De commendatione et partitione sacrae Scripturae*. Ed. R. A. Verardo. In *Opuscula theologica*. Vol. 1. Turin: Marietti, 1954.

——. *Quaestiones disputatae de potentia*. In *Quaestiones disputatae*. Ed. M. Pession. 2 vols. Turin: Marietti, 1949.

——. *Summa theologiae*. 5 vols. Ottawa: Commissio Piana, 1953.

——. *Super epistolas s. Pauli lectura*. Ed. R. Cai. Turin: Marietti, 1953.

——. *Super Evangelium s. Ioannis lectura*. Ed. R. Cai. Turin: Marietti, 1952.

Weisheipl, James A. "The Meaning of *Sacra Doctrina* in *Summa Theologiae* I, q. 1," *The Thomist* 38 (1974): 49–80.

18

Thomas of Ireland and his De tribus sensibus sacrae scripturae

ÉDOUARD JEAUNEAU

The Thomas of Ireland who is the subject of this essay has been confused with two others, both Thomases and both from Ireland: a Franciscan and a Dominican. The Franciscan lived in the convent of Aquila, in the Abruzzi (Italy); he died in 1270. The Dominican, probably originating in Palmerston in County Kildare (Ireland), was a friar at Winchester in 1371. He became prior of his order in England (1393–96) and then prior of the Dominican convent of London (1397–1407). "The last known reference to him is in 1415."[1] The third Thomas of Ireland was neither a Franciscan nor a Dominican, but a secular cleric. After he received his early training in Ireland, he went to Paris, where he became a fellow of the Sorbonne (June 9, 1295). He was a master of arts. He also studied theology, although in this field he does not seem to have advanced beyond the degree of bachelor.[2] The date of his death is unknown: "after 1316 and before 1338."[3] It is exclusively with this last Thomas that this chapter will deal.

The works of Thomas of Ireland include a large compilation called *Manipulus florum*, and a trilogy of small treatises. *Manipulus* means a sheaf, or gleaning, and so the *Manipulus florum* is a sheaf, or handful of flowers which Thomas gleaned in his reading in the Library of the Sorbonne. In other words, it is an anthology "of some 6,000 extracts from the writings of the Fathers and doctors of the Church, along with acceptable ancients."[4] The purpose of such an anthology was to provide preachers with an abundance of useful quotations. This work has been carefully studied by Richard and Mary Rouse in volume 47 of the series *Studies and Texts* of the Pontifical Institute of Mediaeval Studies (Toronto).

The trilogy consists of the following treatises: (1) *De tribus punctis religionis christianae*,[5] (2) *De tribus hierarchiis*,[6] and (3) *De tribus sensibus sacrae scripturae*.[7] The first treatise explains the three main points of Christian religion, which are (1) a firm belief in the articles of faith, (2) a strict adherence to the Ten Commandments, and (3) a careful avoidance of the seven deadly sins. The second treatise develops the doctrine of the three hierarchies: (1) the supercelestial (Holy Trinity), (2) the celestial (the angels), and (3) the subcelestial (the Church Militant). The third treatise shows how any passage of sacred scripture may be interpreted according to three senses: allegorical, tropological, and anagogical. It is on this third treatise that attention will be focused here.

The *De tribus sensibus sacrae scripturae* is a clear and lucid account of the traditional doctrine of the multiple senses of holy scripture. The theme is not new, but the approach is original. Since it remains unpublished, the *De tribus sensibus sacrae scripturae* has been neglected by historians of medieval exegesis. Had it been edited, surely Cardinal Henri de Lubac would have used it in his remarkable *Exégèse médiévale: Les quatre sens de l'écriture.*[8]

There is a discrepancy between the title of de Lubac's book and that of the treatise of Thomas of Ireland. De Lubac reckons four senses, while Thomas of Ireland reckons only three. Hence the title: "On the three senses of sacred scripture." This detail is not a major issue, however. Thomas actually enumerates four senses of holy scripture, but the title of his treatise reflects his formal preference for the number three. The treatise is part of a trilogy, and each piece of this trilogy is itself divided into three parts. The first treatise deals with the three points of Christian religion, the second with the three hierarchies. This third treatise, then, must also have a threefold division. Thomas himself remarks at the end of the *De tribus sensibus sacrae scripturae* that the three senses may correspond to the three hierarchies, namely the anagogical sense to the supercelestial hierarchy, the allegorical sense to the celestial hierarchy, the moral sense to the subcelestial hierarchy.

Now, how can the four senses be reduced to three? Very easily. Holy scripture may be read either according to the literal (or historical) sense, or according to the spiritual sense. Thomas of Ireland does not ignore the literal sense, but he chooses to deal mainly with the "spiritual" or "mystical" sense, which is threefold: allegorical, tropological, and anagogical. Therefore his treatise deserves its title: "On the Three Senses of Sacred Scripture."

This treatise nevertheless begins with a clear division of the four senses, immediately followed by overt praise for them. Thomas formulates the fourfold division of the senses of holy scripture as follows. In every book of the Bible, he says, we must examine four points: (1) the facts that are narrated (historical meaning of the text); (2) what these historical facts prefigure (allegorical meaning); (3) what they command us to do (tropological or moral meaning); and (4) the eternal rewards which they signify (anagogical meaning).[9] Here is how Thomas of Ireland himself extols the four senses:

> The four senses of sacred scripture are like the four rivers flowing from a place of delights to irrigate the paradise of the Scriptures. This is the paradise of which John of Damascus speaks in Book 4, Chapter 9:[10] "Let us knock at the very beautiful paradise of the scriptures, the fragrant, most sweet and lovely paradise which fills our ears with the varied songs of divinely inspired spiritual birds, which touches our heart, comforting it when grieving, calming it when angry, and filling it with everlasting joy."[11]

Number four is a sacred number.[12] It pervades the book of nature with its four elements; it is not surprising that it also pervades the book of scripture. In the passage just quoted, the four senses were compared to the four rivers of paradise. They can be compared also with the four wheels which Ezekiel saw in his first vision (Ezek 1). These four wheels were carrying the four living creatures.[13] And so do the four senses: history, tropology, allegory, and anagogy are the four wheels of holy scripture. To them the words of Ezekiel apply: "the spirit of life was in the wheels."[14]

Another vision, which occurred to Ezekiel in the valley of dry bones,[15] gave Thomas of Ireland the occasion for an interesting allegory. The spirit of the Lord brought Ezekiel in the midst of a valley full of bones. Ezekiel prophesied twice in this valley. After his first prophecy, the bones were covered with flesh and skin, "but there was no spirit in them." Then Ezekiel is commanded to prophesy a second time. "He said to me: 'Prophesy to the spirit, prophesy, O son of man, and say to the spirit: Thus saith the Lord God: Come, spirit, from the four winds and blow upon these slain and let them live again.' And I prophesied as he had commanded me, and the spirit came into them, and they lived, and stood upon their feet, an exceeding great army." The four winds, by whose agency the breath of life returns to the corpses in the valley of dry bones, symbolize the four senses of holy scripture. Such a comparison reveals clearly a principle of medieval Christian exegesis. In order to read the scriptures fruitfully, one must read them according to the four senses: they are the four winds by which the breath of life is blown upon the sacred text. Otherwise, our reading runs the risk of finding in holy scripture no more than slain corpses, nay merely dry bones. However, Thomas of Ireland develops his allegory with meticulousness, a meticulousness better appreciated in his time, perhaps, than in our own. Each of the four senses of holy scripture is compared to each of the four cardinal winds.[16]

The literal sense is compared to the wind that comes from the West (Occidens), for "the letter killeth" (littera occidit).[17] This explanation, however ingenious it may be, rests on a grammatical error: Thomas has confused two verbs: *occido -cidi -casum* (short "I"), meaning "to fall down," and *occido -cidi -cisum* (long "I"), meaning "to kill." The moral sense is like the wind that comes from the South (*Meridie*): it blows sweetly. The allegorical sense is similar to the north wind (*Aquilo*): its subtlety allows it to penetrate deeply into the sacred scriptures. The anagogical sense is compared to the wind that comes from the East (Oriens), because the anagogical sense ushers us into the House of God. Indeed, in the eschatological Temple of Ezekiel, which stands for the House of God, the door is situated in the East.[18]

Having established the doctrine of the four senses, Thomas of Ireland, as a good teacher would, gives concrete examples. He chooses a verse from holy scripture to which the theory of the four senses may apply. It is taken from the book of Proverbs (9:1): *Sapientia aedificauit sibi domum; excidit columnas septem* (Wisdom has built her house; she has set up seven pillars). From this single verse Thomas manages to extract a multiplicity of meanings. He plays with it as a juggler would: under his skillful fingers a host of tropological, allegorical, and anagogical considerations gush forth. In fact, his treatment of the literal meaning is quickly done away with: it hardly fills one of the forty-one columns that make up the *De tribus sensibus*. The literal meaning of Proverbs 9:1 tells us no more than what we read in 1 Kings 7: 1–2: "Solomon was building his own house thirteen years, and he finished his entire house." Solomon was famous for his wisdom. Hence his house is the house of Wisdom. In the book of Kings, however, the house of Solomon is said to have had forty-five pillars and not seven, as we read in the book of Proverbs. Such a difficulty does not detain Thomas for long. The forty-five pillars of the book of Kings can be distributed in seven categories according to the material from which they were made: gold, cedar, silver, bronze, iron, marble, and acacia.

Now that he has disposed of the task of expounding the literal sense, Thomas can freely apply his skill to the other three senses. We cannot follow him in all the twists and turns of his commentary, but I will give just a few examples of his method. First, it is necessary to be aware not only that any passage of holy scripture must be interpreted according to each of the three spiritual senses, but also that for each of these three senses a multiplicity of interpretations are possible. This principle of medieval exegesis was elegantly described by John Scotus Eriugena: "There are many ways, indeed an infinite number, of interpreting the scriptures, just as in one and the same feather of a peacock and even in one and the same point of a tiny portion of the same feather, we see a marvelously beautiful variety of innumerable colours."[19] Whether Thomas of Ireland knew these lines or not, his exegesis is a perfect illustration of the method described by Eriugena.

If we examine Proverbs 9:1 from the point of view of the moral sense, we may find at least three interpretations of it. First, the house of Wisdom is interpreted as representing the soul of any of the faithful. In that house are seven pillars, which are the basic virtues of a Christian life: three theological and four cardinal virtues. Faith is the foundation of the house, Hope its walls, Charity its roof. According to another moral (or tropological) interpretation, the house of Wisdom is a symbol of the cloister, in which men and women live a religious life. At the foundations of this house is voluntary poverty. The two walls are obedience and chastity; the roof is brotherly charity. Such a house must be built with the pavement of humility, with the fireplace of charity, with the door of mercy, with the windows of truth, with the cement of concord, and with the paint of honesty. The seven columns of this house are the seven rules which, according to Saint Bernard, must be observed in a cloister: scanty food, rough clothing, continuous fasting, long vigils, manual labor, rigorous discipline, and fervent devotion.

For a modern reader, the most striking of the three moral interpretations of Proverbs 9: 1 is probably the third. Here I quote Thomas himself:

> According to the moral sense one can say that the house which the Wisdom of God the Father has built is the University of Paris. The foundations of this house are the Faculty of Arts. The two walls, which sustain and protect both our health and our possessions are the Faculties of Medicine and Law. The roof, which covers and completes the whole building, is Theology. *Wisdom set up seven pillars*, [Proverbs 9:1] namely the seven liberal arts, from which the university takes its name. For the number seven stands for the universe. It was a mystical and sacred number under the Old Law.[20]

Having established the University of Paris on solid biblical foundations, Thomas is eager to connect it with Athens:

> The city of Athens, which was the first mother of studies, was divided into three sections, that of Mercury, that of Mars, and that of the sun, for the citizens designated the various districts by the names of the gods they worshipped. The district of the city inhabited by the merchants and others was dedicated to Mercury, who is called the god of the merchants. . . . The area where the princes and the nobles resided was dedicated to Mars, the god of war. The section where students and those devoted to philosophy dwelt was dedicated to the sun, who is the god of wisdom.[21] For, just as the sun surpasses all the stars, so wisdom prevails over all the arts and all the virtues.
>
> Saint Dionysius, the greatest philosopher of Athens, after he saw a miraculous eclipse the day of the passion of Christ, became a convert. . . . He came then to the kingdom of France, and brought with him two flowers from Greece, namely philosophy and military skill, to which he himself added a third flower, the Christian faith. This threefold flower

> is represented by the *fleur-de-lis*, which the king of France bears on his coat of arms, and it is composed of three petals: the one on the right designates philosophy and wisdom, that on the left, military glory, that in the middle faith. . . .
>
> Saint Dionysius came to Paris in order to make this city the mother of studies after the manner of Athens. The city of Paris is, like Athens, divided into three sections: one, that of the merchants, working men and others, is called the Great Town (*magna uilla*); that of the nobility, where the Royal Court and the Cathedral are situated, is called the City; that of students and colleges is called the University. The studies were first transferred from Greece to Rome, then from Rome to Paris at the time of Charlemagne, around the year 800. The school of Paris had four founders, namely Hrabanus, Claudius, Alcuin, master of king Charles, and John, who is named the Scot but was born in Ireland.[22]

Of course, the Athens that served as the model for the building of the city of Paris was not the prechristian Athens, since its ambassador to Paris was a bishop, and not any common bishop, but Dionysius the Areopagite, converted by Saint Paul in the year 51. Yet Jerusalem, where, according to the literal sense, the house of Wisdom was first built, and Athens, "the mother of studies" and ancestress of the University of Paris, represent two different cultures. It may seem odd, even sacrilegious, to derive the University of Paris from both, particularly for those, whose opinion I do not share, who see Christian wisdom and Greek philosophy as two irreconcilable entities. However, Thomas of Ireland was not an antiquarian, content with analyzing, describing, and classifying things of former times. Like many others in the Middle Ages, he was thinking for his own time, with a vivid sense of progress, based probably on the conviction that God reveals himself in History.

> In the holy scriptures, those who come after interpret those who went before: successors expound their predecessors. Whatever was obscure in the Law and the Prophets, Christ has explained in the Gospels. Whatever Christ left obscure in the Gospels, the Apostles have clarified in their epistles and other writings. Whatever the Apostles left obscure, the Fathers, Augustine, Jerome and others have explained in their books. What the Fathers left still obscure, modern doctors expose every day in their lectures and papers. The Holy Spirit wants no one to be idle.[23]

The progress of knowledge evoked here by Thomas of Ireland may remind us of the famous dictum of Bernard of Chartres: we (moderns) are like dwarfs who, seated on the shoulders of the giants (the ancients), can see further than they.[24] The two themes, however, are different, and to confuse them would lead us to misinterpret both Bernard of Chartres and Thomas of Ireland. Bernard of Chartres was teaching Latin grammar. It was appropriate for him to compare his pupils to dwarfs and the ancients (Cicero, Virgil, etc.) to giants. It would be inappropriate, of course, to say that the prophets were giants and Christ a dwarf seated on their shoulders!

Now, in regard to the allegorical sense, the verse of the book of Proverbs—"Wisdom has built her house; she has set up seven pillars"—may apply either to the Church Militant or to the Blessed Virgin Mary. Here is how Thomas of Ireland develops the theme of the Church Militant as the house of Wisdom. In this house, the seven pillars are the seven sacraments, on which the Church is founded. The foundation of this house is baptism, without which nothing can be built. The two walls supporting the house are confirmation and the Eucharist. The roof which covers everything is penance. The windows which provide the house with light, both corporeal and spiritual, are the sacraments of matrimony and holy orders. The door of this house is extreme unction, through which one passes from the terrestrial house to the house of the Church triumphant.

According to the anagogical sense, the verse may apply to the Church triumphant. Of such a house our Savior said: "In my Father's house there are many mansions."[25] King David also spoke of this house: "Blessed are they that dwell in thy house, O Lord: they shall praise thee for ever and ever."[26] The seven pillars of this house are the seven categories of the inhabitants of the celestial city. The first pillar, which is made of gold, is that of the angels; the second, made of cedar, is that of the patriarchs; the third, made of silver, is that of the prophets; the fourth, made of bronze, is that of the apostles; the fifth, made of iron, is that of the martyrs; the sixth, made of marble, is that of the confessors; the seventh, made of acacia, is that of the virgins. I will spare the reader the sophisticated considerations in which Thomas indulges in order to justify the attribution of a given pillar to a given category of the blessed.

Thomas goes on to describe the celestial spheres, quoting pell mell Basil of Caesarea, *Glossa ordinaria*, Bede, Augustine, Avicenna, Ptolemy, al-Farghani, and Rabbi Moses (i.e., Maimonides).[27] After this rapid excursion in the field of astronomy, Thomas returns to spirituality, his own field. And he concludes with a quotation from Maimonides:[28] "It makes no difference whether one is at the center of the earth or, supposing that this were possible, in the highest part of the ninth heavenly sphere. Nearness to the Creator amounts to knowing him; and distance from him amounts to ignorance of his ways."[29]

More than three centuries before Thomas of Ireland, Eriugena spoke along the same lines: "It is not by a movement of the body, but by a disposition of the mind that one draws further from or closer to God."[30] Now, such an idea is not so rare that Thomas and Eriugena each could not have found it by himself. However, since they chose to support it with authorities, it is perhaps worthwhile to note that, while Eriugena relied on Augustine,[31] Thomas of Ireland called upon Maimonides. In fact, Thomas and John Scotus, both Irish, lived in very different worlds: in the time that separates them, contacts between Judaism, Christianity, and Islam had been established. This tradition has endured and thrives into the present.

Notes

1. Rouse and Rouse, *Preachers, Florilegia and Sermons*, 94.
2. Rouse and Rouse, *Preachers*, 95.
3. Rouse and Rouse, *Preachers*, 96.
4. Rouse and Rouse, *Preachers*, 117.
5. The *De tribus punctis religionis christianae* is contained in more than 120 manuscripts. It was published in 1476 by Conrad Fyner in Hesslingen (Hain, Incunable 13854). For the manuscripts of the three small treatises, see Rouse and Rouse, *Preachers*, 246–50.
6. Only eight manuscripts of the *De tribus hierarchiis* are known, among which is Paris, Bibiothèque Nationale de France [BNF], MS Lat. 15966, fols. 10–14. The work is unpublished.
7. The *De tribus sensibus sacrae scripturae* is contained in three manuscripts. I have examined two of them only: Paris, BNF, MSS Lat. 15966, fols. 6–10 (ca. 1319); Lat. 16397, fols. 11–17v (ca. 1316).
8. Lubac, *Exégèse médiévale*.
9. In all this, Thomas of Ireland is indebted to another Thomas, namely Thomas Aquinas: *Summa theologiae*, 1a,1,10.

10. John of Damascus, *Expositio fidei* (*De fide orthodoxa*) 90.2; ed. Kotter, 209–10; PG 94.1176B; Latin versions of Burgundio and Cerbanus, ed. Buytaert, 336; English: Chase, John of Damascus, *Writings*, 374.

11. "Hii sunt quatuor sensus sacrae scripturae ueluti IIIIor flumina egrediencia de loco uoluptatis ad irrigandum scripturarum paradisum, de qua dicit Damascenus, li(br)o IIII, c.IX: Pulsemus in optimum paradisum scripturarum qui odoriferus, qui speciosissimus, qui omnimodis intellectualium deiferarum uolucrum cantalenis circumsonat aures nostras, qui cor nostrum tangit, contristatum consolatur, iratum substernit et leticia sempiterna replet." (Paris, BNF, MS Lat. 16397, fol. 11ra).

12. "Quaternarius enim numerus est misticus et figuralis in lege. Vnde Prosper li(br)o IIIo de uita contemplatiua dicit: Quaternarium numerum perfectioni sacratum pene nullus ignorat." (Paris, BNF, MS Lat. 16397, fol. 11va).

13. Ezekiel 1:20.

14. "Historia ergo docet factum, tropologia faciendum, allegoria credendum et anagogia sperandum. Vnde hiis IIIIor quasi IIIIor rotis tota uoluitur sacra scriptura. Istae sunt IIIIor rotae quas uidit Ezechiel in uisione, quibus deferebantur animalia plena oculis ante et retro, et spiritus uitae erat in rotis, sicut dicitur Ezechiel(e) Io." (Paris, BNF, MS Lat. 16397, fol. 11va).

15. Ezekiel 37:1–14.

16. "Hii sunt IIIIor uenti quibus perflantibus super interfectos uenit spiritus super eos et qui mortui fuerant reuixerunt sicut dicitur Ezech(iele) XXXVII. Primus, scilicet literalis, oritur ab occidente: litera enim occidit, sicut dicit apostolus II Cor. III. Secundus, scilicet moralis, oritur a meridie, qui dulciter et suauiter perflat. Tertius, scilicet allegoricus, oritur a septemtrione, qui uelut aquilo prae nimia subtilitate penetrat. Quartus, scilicet anagogicus, oritur ab oriente, qui introducit ad portam domus domini orientalem." (Paris, BNF, MS Lat. 16397, fol. 11va).

17. 2 Corinthians 3:6.

18. Ezeziel 47:1–2.

19. Eriugena, *Periphyseon, Liber Quartus* 749C; ed. Jeauneau, 19.

20. "Moraliter etiam potest dici quod Sapientia dei patris aedificavit sibi domum, id est uniuersitatem parisiensem, cuius fundamentum est facultas artium, duo parietes sustentantes et saluantes bona tam naturae quam fortunae sunt iura et medicina, tectum omnia cooperiens et perficiens est theologia. Et excidit in ea columpnas vii, id est septem artes liberales, a quibus universitas dicitur. Septenarius enim est numerus uniuersitatis et erat misticus et sacratus in lege." (Paris, BNF, MS Lat. 16397, fol. 12va).

21. By "the god of wisdom" Thomas means probably Apollo, identified with the sun.

22. Paris, BNF, MS Lat. 16397, fols. 13rb–13vb. For the Latin text, see Jeauneau, *Translatio studii*, 52–54.

23. "In scripturis enim semper posteriores exponunt priores et sequentes declarant precedentes. Nam quicquid obscurum erat in lege et prophetis Christus explanauit in euangeliis. Quicquid uero Christus dimisit obscurum in euangeliis apostoli declarauerunt in suis epistolis et aliis opusculis. Quicquid autem isti reliquerunt obscurum sancti patres Augus(tinus) Iero(nim)us et alii exposuerunt in suis libris. Sed quicquid isti reliquerunt adhuc obscurum cotidie doctores moderni in suis lectionibus et determinationibus exponunt, quia spiritus sanctus nullos uult esse ociosos." (Paris, BNF, MS Lat. 16397, fol. 12r).

24. Jeauneau, "Nani gigantium," 79–99.

25. John 14:2.

26. Psalms 83:5.

27. Paris, BNF, MS Lat. 16937, fols. 16r–17v.

28. "Rabi Mossei Aegyptii Dux seu Director dubitantium aut perplexorum . . . summa accuratione Reuerendi patris Augustini Iustiniani O.P. Nebiensis Episcopi recognitus" (*Venundatur ab Iodoco Badio Ascensio*, 1520), 1. 18. Maimonides, *The Guide of the Perplexed*, 45.

29. "Sed Rabi Moyses, parte prima libri sui, cãpitulõ xviii, dicit notabile uerbum. Si, inquit, possibile esset quod aliquis homo esset in summo noni celi, non esset propinquior deo nec remotior, quam ille qui esset in centro terrae, quia appropinquatio ad creatorem est in cognitione eius, et elongatio ab eo ignorancia uiarum ipsius." (Paris, BNF, MS Lat. 16937, fol. 17v).

30. Eriugena, *Periphyseon, Liber Quintus*, PL 122. 871D, 984A. Idem, *Commentarius in euangelium Iohannis* 1.31.10–11, PL 122. 310A.

31. Augustinus, *De musica* 6.13.40, PL 32.1185; *Confessiones* 1.18.28, ed. Verheijen, 15.11–12, PL 32.673; *De trinitate* 7.6.12, ed. Mountian, 266.150–52, PL 50.946.

Bibliography

Augustine of Hippo. *De musica*. PL 32. 1081–1194.

——. *Confessiones*. Ed. Luc Verheijen. CCSL, 27. Turnhout: Brepols, 1981.

——. *Confessiones*. PL 32. 659–868.

——. *De trinitate*. Ed. W. J. Mountian. CCSL, 50. Turnhout: Brepols, 1968.

——. *De trinitate*. PL 42. 819–1098.

Eriugena, John Scotus. *Commentarius in euangelium Iohannis*. Ed. É. Jeauneau. Sources chrétiennes, 180. Paris: Cerf, 1972.

——. Commentarius in euangelium Iohannis. PL 122. 297–347.

——. *Periphyseon, Liber Quartus*. Ed. É. Jeauneau and trans. John J. O'Meara. Scriptores Latini Hiberniae, 13. Dublin: Dublin Institute for Advanced Studies, 1995.

——. *Periphyseon, Liber Quintus*. PL 122. 859–1022.

Jeauneau, Édouard. "Nani gigantium humeris insidentes." *Vivarium* 5 (1967): 79–99. Reprint in Jeauneau. *Lectio philosophorum*. Amsterdam: Hakkert, 1973.

——. *Translatio studii: The Transmisson of Learning A Gilsonian Theme*. The Étienne Gilson Series, 18. Toronto: Pontifical Institute of Mediaeval Studies, 1995.

John of Damascus. *Expositio fidei (De fide orthodoxa)*. Ed. B. Kotter. Die Schriften des Johannes von Damaskos, vol. 2 = Patristiche Texte und Studien, 12. Berlin: Walter de Gruyter, 1973.

——. *Expositio fidei*. PG 94. 732–1228.

——. *Expositio fidei* (Latin versions of Burgundio and Cerbanus). Ed. E. M. Buytaert. St. Bonaventure, N.Y.: The Franciscan Institute, 1955.

——. *Writings*. Trans. Frederic H. Chase, Jr. New York: Fathers of the Church, 1958.

Lubac, Henri de. *Exégèse médiévale: les quatre sens de l'écriture*. 4 vols. Paris: Aubier, 1959–64.

Maimonides, Moses. *The Guide of the Perplexed*. Trans. with introduction and notes by Shlomo Pines. Chicago: University of Chicago Press, 1964.

Rouse, Richard H., and Mary A. Rouse. *Preachers, Florilegia and Sermons: Studies on the "Manipulus florum" of Thomas of Ireland*. Studies and Texts, vol. 47. Toronto: Pontifical Institute of Mediaeval Studies, 1979.

Thomas of Ireland. "De tribus sensibus sacrae scripturae." Paris, Bibliothèque Nationale, MS Lat. 15966, fols. 6–10; MS Lat. 16397, fols. 11–17v.

19

Material Swords and Literal Lights

The Status of Allegory in William of Ockham's *Breviloquium* on Papal Power

A. J. MINNIS

At Luke 22:38, the disciples are presented as saying to Jesus, "Lord, behold, there are two swords." And he replies to them, "It is enough." The next verses recount how the group goes to the Mount of Olives, where a multitude, led by the chief priest and elders, comes to arrest Jesus. The disciples ask, "Lord, shall we strike with the sword?" and one of them does just that, cutting off the right ear of the high priest's servant. But Jesus miraculously heals the wound. The somewhat cryptic statement affirming the existence of two swords is unique to Luke's Gospel, but all the other Gospels have versions of the subsequent narrative. Mark and John omit the miracle of healing; John identifies the sword-wielder as Saint Peter, the rock on which Christ is to build his Church; while Matthew has Jesus command, "Put up again thy sword into its place: for all that take the sword shall perish with the sword."

In patristic exegesis the undrawn and drawn swords are often interpreted as signifying, respectively, spiritual and temporal, or ecclesiastical and lay, power. During the Middle Ages Luke's remarks about them became a battle-ground on which many issues relating to *regnum* and *sacerdotium* were fought out. My purpose is to consider certain aspects of William of Ockham's contribution to the debate which raise general hermeneutic issues, centering on the extent to which sound doctrine can rest on spiritual interpretation as opposed to literal declaration. Here exegesis and politics intersect crucially, with potentially very serious consequences. How could a theory of power be justified by textual meaning which was attained by a type of reading which, in Ockham's day, was being called in question? If the theologians were reconsidering and to some extent devaluing allegory (at least in certain contexts), where did this activity leave the politicians, both ecclesiastical and secular, as they bandied about the allegorical sense of Luke 22:38 in urging their competing claims?

The significance of the "two swords" doctrine was debated from time to time in the early Middle Ages; generally speaking, it was interpreted in terms of harmonious cooperation between Church and State.[1] However, controversy flared in the eleventh century. Opponents of the eleventh-century Gregorian reforms accused Gregory VII of having unlawfully seized the secular sword; his supporters countered with the argument that both swords were rightfully under papal control, kings being deemed to be, in a sense, ministers of Saint Peter. In 1150 Bernard of Clairvaux built on this argument in urging a new crusade, Pope Eugenius III being assured that both swords were Peter's; therefore the Church should take the lead in urging military action to reclaim the Holy Land. And in Bernard's *De consideratione* (1145) it is asserted that "both the spiritual and the material sword belong to the Church; but while the former is unsheathed by the Church, the latter is unsheathed for the Church."[2] The basic point here is that the secular arm should function on behalf of the Church and to its benefit, not that the Church itself should maintain or directly command an army. This doctrine came to have wide currency in the thirteenth-century schools. When such dissident thinkers as Marsiglio of Padua and William of Ockham came to formulate their own views on papal power, they had to spend much time wrestling with *De consideratione*.

What really brought the issue into focus in the fourteenth century, however, was Pope Boniface VIII's bull *Unam sanctam* (of November 18, 1302), which declared that "it is entirely necessary to salvation for every human creature to be subject to the Roman Pontiff." In Boniface's formulation, the notion of the secular arm functioning on behalf of the Church has hardened into advocacy of the unequivocal subordination of the secular to the spiritual, of kings to popes.

> We are taught by the words of the Gospel that within this Church and in her power there are two swords: namely, a spiritual and a temporal. For when the apostles said "Here are two swords" . . . the Lord did not reply that this was too many, but enough. Certainly, he who denies that the temporal sword is in the power of Peter has ill understood the words of the Lord when he said, "Put up your sword into its sheath." Both, therefore, are in the power of the Church: that is, the spiritual sword and the material. But the latter is to be wielded on behalf of the Church and the former by the Church: the one by the priest, the other by the hands of kings and soldiers, though at the command and by the permission of the priest. And the one sword must be under the other, and temporal authority subject to the spiritual power. . . .[3]

That pronoucement prompted, so to speak, a major secular backlash from the king of France, Philip the Fair, who had been in dispute with the papacy since 1296 over the right of princes to tax the clergy within their realms and subsequently over the issue of clerical immunity from the jurisdiction of secular courts.[4] Philip's chief minister, Guillaume de Nogaret, urged the Estates General to take steps for Boniface's removal. The pope was subsequently charged with "usurpation of the papal office, adultery, blasphemy, fornication, heresy, homicide, masturbation, simony, sodomy and, to cap it all, neglecting to fast during lent."[5] Not relying on the force of moral recrimination alone, Nogaret assembled a band of men to kidnap the pope. In September 1303 the papal palace at Avignon was looted and Boniface captured, but his followers soon rescued him. A broken man, the pope returned to Rome to die. The French continued to uphold "the custom of France" and to resist any implication that their king's power in his own land was in some way dependent on the power of the papacy. A few years later a Frenchman became pope. Clement V moved the papacy to Avignon, where it was to remain until 1377, under what Petrarch termed the "Babylonian captivity." Philip the Fair's triumph could hardly have been more complete.

The next major skirmish between Church and State was a far more equivocal affair. It involved a notable English visitor to Avignon in the mid-1320s, William of Ockham.[6] Ockham had been asked by Michael of Cesena, the minister general of his order (or some other high-ranking Franciscan), to investigate issues relating to the poverty of Christ with reference to recently issued papal bulls. Michael was convinced that the notion that Christ and the apostles had given up all right to material things was a "Catholic truth" which had been affirmed in earlier papal doctrine; it was, moreover, at the very center of the ideals of the Franciscan Order.[7] Pope John XXII became a special target; Ockham came to hold the view that the pope had fallen into heresy in, for example, stating that any allowable use of such standard consumables as food and clothing involved a legal right to such things. This turned out to be a bad career move for Ockham. In 1328 he was obliged to flee from Avignon, in the company of Michael and other Franciscans, to seek the protection of Ludvig of Bavaria, who had been excommunicated by John XXII in 1324 for refusing to submit his election as Roman emperor (in 1314) to papal judgment. Ockham himself was excommunicated in 1328; while he was never explicitly and unequivocally condemned as a heretic, this would seem to be implicit in a clause in John's bull *Quia quorundam* of 1324. Ockham's *Breviloquium de principatu tyrannico super divina et humana*, was one of a series of tracts Ockham produced during his exile in Munich between 1332 and his death (in 1347?).[8] Ockham died unreconciled with the Church. His protector, Ludvig, had proven to be a far less effective opponent of papal power than Philip the Fair.

The Allegory of Papal Authority: Ockham's Attack

The argument of the *Breviloquium* depends heavily on the Bible as a source of authority for what should be believed about the nature of papal power (Ockham's objective being to determine firm limits for the pope's secular power). This issue leads him into extensive discussion of the ambiguities and complexities of language as used in scripture and by several of its saintly interpreters. "It cannot be shown that the Empire is from the pope" by words of scripture which are allegorically interpreted to that end, he declares, citing two passages as crucial cases in point: "See, here are two swords" (Luke 22:38) and "God made two great lights, a larger one to rule the day and a lesser one the night" (Gen 1:16). It is perfectly permissible to adduce "a mystical sense of scripture that is not contrary to the truth" for purposes of "edification and exhortation (*edificatio et exhortatio*)," he freely admits.[9] However, if that particular meaning "is not in divine scripture explicitly in itself or in something which implies it, it should not and cannot be adduced to prove and confirm disputable and doubtful things about which Christians disagree." Ockham then offers two examples of mystical senses that are explicitly confirmed elsewhere in scripture:

> For the mystical sense (*sensus misticus*) of the statement in Genesis that Abraham had two sons, one by a maid servant and one by a free woman, which is explicit (*expressus*) in Galatians, chapter 4, can be adduced to prove contentious points; similarly the mystical sense of the things written in Genesis about King Melchisedech, which is explicit in Hebrews, chapter 7, can be adduced to prove doubtful points. But a mystical sense not explicit in sacred scripture can never be adduced in this way, except in so far as it rests on another scripture or on evident reason.[10]

The fundamental principle here involved is no doubt familiar to most of us from the relevant statement in Saint Thomas Aquinas's *Summa theologiae* or Nicholas of Lyra's reiteration in his *Postilla litteralis*. From the literal sense alone can any argument be drawn, and not from the things said *secundum allegoriam*, as Saint Augustine remarks in his letter to Vincent the Donatist;[11] but this causes no confusion, since "nothing necessary for faith is contained under the spiritual sense that is not openly conveyed through the literal sense elsewhere."[12] In Ockham's application, the principle has come to mean a devaluation of those allegorical senses that are not expressed literally elsewhere in scripture.

Ockham then roundly attacks those who "try to prove whatever they please by mystical senses which they invent (*fungunt*)." Since they "want such proof accepted as beyond doubt," he will prove by authority and reason that such a mystical sense—presumably he means such an invented mystical sense—need not be accepted. His first authority is Saint Augustine's letter to Vincent the Donatist, specifically the source passage to which Thomas Aquinas referred in the passage from his *Summa* which was quoted earlier.

> Blessed Augustine says to Vincent: "Who would dare, without the greatest impudence, to interpret in his own favour something expressed in allegory, unless he had manifest testimonies whose light would illumine the obscurities?" From these words we gather that one disputing with another should not adduce an allegorical sense unless it is explicit in scripture, because if it cannot be proved explicitly by scripture his opponent will say that it can be as easily despised as approved.[13]

Further arguments are then offered, beginning with the statement that a mystical sense not explicit in divine scripture cannot have greater authority than certain biblical books (Judith, Wisdom, Ecclesiasticus, etc.) which, on the authority of Saint Jerome, are deemed to be less suitable for use in proving contentious points. Here Ockham's point seems to be that if we are to be careful with such books, how much more care should we exercise with mystical senses "which anyone invents (*fingit*) according to the strength of his own wit." There follow a series of points which allege the authority of Saint Augustine. First, the fact that certain mystical senses are included in the teaching of bishops and others who interpret scripture is in itself insufficient warrant for their veracity, for the testimony of such people is open to error, as Saint Augustine himself admitted when he noted that there are faults in many of his own books. Second, a person's sanctity and learning are not in themselves sufficient proof that what he has said is true. One always needs the assurance that comes from canonical authors or likely reasons. Then again, bishops' letters can rightly be refuted "by the wiser words of someone perhaps more expert in the matter, by the weightier authority and more learned prudence of other bishops, and by councils." Finally, the writings of those who were not the authors of holy scripture "must be distinguished from the authority of the canon." Therefore, with all due respect, it is perfectly possible to disagree with them. From all this, concludes Ockham, "we manifestly gather that the teaching of those who lived after the writers of canonical scripture is not so authoritative that nothing in it can be criticized; and consequently mystical senses that they have drawn from the scriptures to support contentious points need not be accepted."

Two major objections are then addressed. The first is that Augustine and other saints prove many things through mystical senses which are not explicit in scripture. Second, "the decretals of the Roman pontiffs can and should be adduced to demonstrate contentious points—yet in these many things are proved through mystical senses." Ockham answers the first of these with an appeal to the pleasure which fitting mystical interpretation can give:

> whenever a truth is certain first through sacred scripture or evident argument, it is permissible afterwards to adduce mystical senses in favour of that certain truth—to delight those who know the truth, many of whom are delighted when they see that mystical senses of the words of scripture can be fitted to the truth. . . .[14]

Could Ockham have in mind Saint Augustine's profession of pleasure in the allegorical sense of the Song of Songs? "I contemplate the saints more pleasantly when I envisage them as the teeth of the Church" (*De doctrina christiana*, 2.6.7).[15] Ockham adds that the production of mystical interpretations discourages the opponents of the truth, "who grieve that that such senses can be fitted to the truth which they deny." In short, here we are dealing with the provocation and exploitation of certain emotional responses rather than with proof of the type that is achieved through disputation "among experts (*inter peritos*)." Pleasure is not the same as proof.

Ockham answers the second objection, which posits the papal authorization of certain allegories, with the blunt statement that those popes who proceed in a correct Catholic manner, "seeking to enact, not their own, but God's justice, never try to prove anything, especially anything known to relate to faith and to divine law, by means of mystical senses, except in so far as they are supported by canonical scriptures or clear arguments." If they do otherwise, then such proofs as they offer should not be credited, for they are the results of an attempt to draw scripture to support "the conclusions they dream up or desire, conclusions that scripture conflicts with or does not suggest." "No matter how much authority the pope has," declares Ockham, "the truth must always be preferred to him, especially a truth known to relate to a divine law." But who is to take the enormous step of judging whether a pope's assertion is true or false, orthodox or heretical? When a pope offers an opinion that is "against things every Christian is bound to believe explicitly" or asserts something that is contrary to what is found explicitly in the Bible, Ockham responds, then anyone "ought to judge that he has erred." Moreover, if he were to err against things that expert theologians are bound to know, then it is up to such experts to judge him. In other words, the fact that a pope has affirmed a certain mystical sense need not, of itself, mean that such a sense is to be believed; other factors have to be considered. The pope's scriptural exegesis is subject to the same checks and balances as those that apply to lesser mortals. We cannot accept the truth of a certain mystical sense just because the supreme pontiff happens to believe it.

Ockham's review of hermeneutic principles having been completed, he proceeds to focus on his two crucial test-passages, beginning with Luke 22:38, "See, here are two swords."[16] It cannot be proved from this verse that "the pope has both temporal and spiritual powers," he declares, "because the mystical sense in which it is said that the two swords signify these two powers, namely temporal and spiritual, is not explicit in any part of scripture whatever." Here Ockham is applying the principle that "a mystical sense not explicit in sacred scripture can never be adduced" in an argument "except in so far as it rests on another scripture." If a doctrine is not expressed literally anywhere in scripture, its mystical expression lacks foundation and cannot have any weight in an argument. But what should be said concerning a kind of signification so obvious that it may be deemed explicit and therefore satisfy the criterion of explicitness which is necessary for viable argument from scripture?

> Perhaps someone will say that in scripture it is explicit (*expresse*) that a sword signifies power, since it is said: "He does not carry a sword for nothing" (Rom 13:4); therefore the two swords fittingly designate two powers, and none but the temporal or material power and the spiritual; therefore those words can be explained thus.[17]

This objection can be answered in three ways:

1. *In scripture swords do not always signify power.* While in scripture a sword does indeed on occasion signify power, elsewhere it signifies something else—the Word of God, as in Ephesians 6:17, where the Apostle refers to "The sword of the spirit, which is the Word of God." Therefore, Ockham declares triumphantly, he could as easily say that the two swords of Luke 22:38 "signify the word or preaching of the New and Old Testaments." That is how Saint Ambrose interprets the text: "May not one perhaps be the sword of the New Testament, the other of the Old Testament, by which we are armed against the ambushes of the devil? And then he says, 'It is enough,' as though nothing is lacking to anyone fortified by the teaching of both Testaments." We need not accept either interpretation, Ockham concludes, either Ambrose's or the one that regards the two swords as signifying the two powers in question. Further proof is needed for that supposition.

Now, Ockham could have said: but surely Ambrose's interpretation is the more correct, since it is based on a mystical sense which *is* rendered explicit elsewhere in scripture, namely in Saint Paul's literal statement that the sword of the spirit is the Word of God. But such is not Ockham's strategy; at this point he is concerned rather to emphasize the proliferation of possible readings.

2. *These swords need not signify the temporal and spiritual powers in particular.* Another answer is that, even if the two swords are understood as signifying two powers, it does not follow they they should be understood as signifying the temporal and spiritual powers in particular, "especially since one of those swords was no more material than the other, nor one more spiritual." In other words, there is nothing in the text of scripture that distinguishes between the two swords. Therefore they could be read as signifying two spiritual powers. Ockham offers two alternatives: "the power of preaching and the power of working miracles, or good life and sound doctrine, by which the apostles were to vanquish the demons and convert many unbelievers to the Catholic faith." By the same token, they could be understood to signify two temporal powers, "namely, pure authority and mixed."[18]

3. *Even if the two swords signified those two powers in particular, his opponents' doctrine of papal power does not follow.* "Even if the two swords signified" the temporal and spiritual powers, "it could nevertheless not be inferred from this that the pope regularly had both, or that the Empire was from the pope." For it is nowhere stated that Peter had those two swords, or any other individual, for that matter. "It is not likely that some one person carried both; more likely two persons did." Therefore, if the two swords do indeed signify the temporal and spiritual powers, it can be inferred that one person had the temporal power while another person had the spiritual power, "because two persons, not one, carried the two swords."

From all this, Ockham concludes, it would seem that the words "See, here are two swords"[19] were "said of two material swords," rather than of one sword that was material and another that was spiritual. They "were not spoken enigmatically (*enigmatice*) or in parable (*parabolice*) or figuratively (*figurate*) or improperly (*improprie*)": which I take to mean that Ockham is affirming that each material sword signified nothing other than a material sword. However, taken "improperly"—that is, not understood in accordance with the "proper," direct, and specific meanings of words[20]—the swords can signify any two kinds of power whatever: any two temporal powers, any two spiritual powers, or any combination of powers one of which is temporal and the other spiritual, including the case in which one power is just "and the other unjust or tyrannical," since, Ockham continues, "all these sorts of powers were to exist in the Church militant."

Here, then, Ockham seems to be imposing an important curb on the possible proliferation of interpretations of the two powers here in question: they must be powers which came to exist in a Church which was, as far as the original speakers of the words were concerned, a thing of the future. But those imposed limits yet allow him to indulge in some allegorization of his own. The two swords could even signify legitimate pontifical power and usurped pontifical power, he declares, "because in the Church militant there were to be some legitimate pontiffs, like true shepherds entering by the door [John 10:1], and some thieves and robbers not entering by the door, or at first entering by the door but afterwards turned by heretical wickedness and tyrannical cruelty into the nature of thieves and robbers, cruelly afflicting, corporeally, spiritually, or in both ways, Catholics and those who walk in simplicity." Ockham proceeds to name some guilty parties, including (of course) Popes John XXII and Benedict XII.

Clearly, Ockham is not one to pass up a mystical reading of his text when it is in his own polemical interest to do so. His championship of the literal sense could therefore be said to be selective, even opportunistic. However, what Ockham does not do is try to suggest that his own allegory has some sort of special status within the other possible spiritual readings of Luke's account. And it could be said that he himself has provided us with a principle which we could apply to his own case: "whenever a truth is certain first through sacred scripture or evident argument, it is permissible afterwards to adduce mystical senses in favour of that certain truth." Ockham would probably have claimed that his interpretation of the two swords as two types of pontifical power, the legitimate and the usurped, met that condition for truth. For him the *sensus litteralis* of "See, there are two swords" is stable and secure. Had he thought otherwise, he would have seriously undermined the premise which supports the main thrust of his attack, namely that his opponents' case rests on a mystical sense of scripture, which lacks explicit and literal statement elsewhere in scripture, and therefore it need not be accepted.

At long last we have come to the two literal lights promised in the title. Ockham now moves on to devalue the allegorical reading of Genesis 1 which held that the sun and the moon signify the pontifical and the kingly power respectively, the former being superior to the latter.[21] This interpretation "is merely (*solummodo*) mystical or allegorical," he declares, "and there is no mention of it" (i.e., no explicit or literal statement of the doctrine) "in the whole of scripture." But Ockham is not content to leave the matter there. He proceeds to demonstrate that the allegorical sense in question does not fit the facts very well; indeed, "that mystical sense is against the thesis of those who bring it forward, more than for it." "In respect of its substance the moon is not from the sun but from God alone, from whom the sun is also." Therefore the empire and the priesthood, while they come from the same ultimate source, are themselves different; it certainly cannot be argued that the Empire derives its essence and essential power from the priesthood. Moreover, the moon has certain virtues and power of its own, "namely over the waters and humours," which it does not have from the sun; it could therefore be suggested that "the empire has virtue and power of its own, and not from the priesthood." Ockham sums up by saying that all the imagery (*similitudo*) under discussion can prove ("if it can prove anything") is that, just as the moon is a lesser light than the sun and receives some light from it, so the empire is less—in the sense of having lesser dignity and being less noble—than the priesthood. "Even the power of a simple priest is nobler than the imperial power," Ockham declares; "it is nobler to serve the altar at the consecration of the body and blood of Christ than to rule in temporal matters." His entire discussion of material swords and literal lights is then brought to a triumphal conclusion: "Intelligent Christians who love truth and justice" cannot believe that the empire can be "shown to be from the pope" by "mystical senses of words of scripture."

Precedents and Provocations: Marsilius of Padua, Giles of Rome, John of Paris

Ockham's interest in material swords and literal lights now may be related to the relevant discussions of several of his predecessors, beginning with a fellow dissident who enjoyed the protection of Ludvig of Bavaria, Marsilius of Padua. In his highly influential *Defensor pacis*, a work that Ockham certainly knew, Marsilius argued that Christ denied of himself not only the "drawing of the material sword, but also the judgment and command as to its being drawn," and any interpretation that denies this fact is "not in harmony with the meaning of scripture (*intentio scripture*)."[22] The Saints agree, he continues, that "Christ was speaking metaphorically (*locucio metaphorica*) when to his disciples' words, 'Behold, here are two swords,' he replied, 'It is enough.'" "It is apparent that Christ's words had a mystical meaning (*sensus misticus*)," Marsilius continues, and this is also clearly indicated by Matthew 26 and John 28, "when, on being defended by the sword, he said to Peter: 'Put up again thy sword into its place,' or, 'into the sheath,' wherein he showed that he had not commanded the apostles to defend him by such swords, but rather he had been speaking mystically (*mistice fuisse locutum*)." Moreover, it is in this mystical sense that Saint Ambrose interprets the aforesaid words of Christ, when he writes of the two swords as the Old and New Testaments—an interpretation also cited by Ockham, as was already noted. Marsilius then delivers a swinging attack on his opponents' exegetical methods:

> Now by those priests who strive and strain with all their might, although wrongly, to usurp secular governments, wandering expositions of scripture (*peregrinas exposiciones scripture*) are gladly accepted when such expositions seem to savour of their current opinion and perverted emotions (*opinionem corruptam et affectionem perversam*). But if Christ's words be taken literally (*literaliter*), they are not in opposition to our view, for the material sword is not rulership or the judgment of secular acts; and if Christ's words be taken metaphorically (*secundum metaphoram*), then what he entrusted to Peter or any other apostle cannot signify (*significare*), according to Christ's own view, secular rulership or judgment,

> as has been clearly proved by Bernard elsewhere . . . and as we have indubitably shown through scripture. . . .[23]

In short, the literal sense must be respected in this case; if on the other hand it is supposed that Christ was speaking metaphorically, then his meaning can be elucidated by other passages of scripture, wherein metaphorical expression was not used. And the resultant evidence contradicts the view that the Church possesses both sacred and secular authority. There is much here that is in the same spirit as Ockham's analysis, although Ockham's discussion of the hermeneutic issues involved is more substantial.

It is possible that, to some extent at least, both Ockham and Marsilius were reacting to the hermeneutical attitudes and methods of Giles of Rome, a figure once alluded to by Marsilius as an "idle dreamer." Giles' *De ecclesiastica potestate* (1301–2), a work dedicated to Boniface *VIII*, faces the problem of the different interpretations of the two swords by highlighting the hermeneutic principles involved. Crucial to his analysis is the distinction between *res* and *figura*, the thing itself and its figurative significance:

> It must be known . . . that when we discuss the two swords mentioned in the Gospel, we may consider them either in terms of *res* or in terms of *figura*. If we wish to consider them in terms of reality (*res*), both were material: that which Peter drew and also that which was undrawn and which remained in the sheath. But if we wish to consider them in terms of figure (*figura*) it is not inconsistent to say that, viewed under different aspects, one and the same thing may represent (*figurare*) opposites, as the lion figures both Christ and Belial when it is said, "The lion of the tribe of Judah has conquered" (Rev 5:5); yet it represents the devil when it is said, "Your adversary the devil is like a roaring lion" (1 Peter 5:8). So also in the matter before us: the drawn sword can sometimes be taken to figure the material sword and sometimes the spiritual, and the undrawn sword can sometimes be taken to figure the one sword and sometimes the other.[24]

In short, at the level of *res*, or what might be called the literal sense, there is no confusion—we are dealing with two material swords. But at the level of figure, different senses are perfectly possible, including senses that appear to conflict sharply with each other.

Giles then attempts to rationalize and categorize those possible figurations by appealing to two crucial concepts which the text raises, use and appearance.The two swords can be considered in two ways: either with reference to use ("since the Apostle made use of the drawn sword and they did not make use of the undrawn"), or with reference to appearance ("since the drawn sword was visible because it was drawn, and the undrawn sword, as such, was not visible, but was hidden and concealed in a sheath"). Giles seems perfectly happy to accept that some Saints have taken one interpretative line, and others another. However, he is sensitive to an apparent anomaly in the interpretation of the drawn sword as the spiritual sword. If this is the case, why is Peter subsquently forbidden to strike with it, since "the spiritual sword is entrusted and given to the Church" in order that it may do just that: "strike and punish with it"? Giles declares that the drawn sword may be taken as either the spiritual sword or the material sword, and he applies to both interpretations the distinction between *secundum rem* or *secundum figuram*:

> If it is the spiritual sword which is represented by the drawn sword, Peter was forbidden to punish with that sword not in terms of *figura* but in terms of *res*. For although the drawn sword thus figured the spiritual sword, it was itself nonetheless a thing of iron (*res erat ferrum*), and was an iron and material sword.[25]

Here Giles seems to be postulating figurative meaning in respect of the sword's significance (it is the spiritual sword, meaning divine power) and meaning *secundum rem*—what may be deemed literal sense—in respect of the command not to use the sword. Presumably he means that Peter was forbidden to use a material sword in the service of his spiritual power.

If, on the other hand, the drawn sword is taken as representing the material sword (i.e., secular or earthly power), then Peter was forbidden to strike with that both literally and figuratively.

> But if this drawn sword represents or signifies the material sword, then Peter was forbidden to strike with that sword, or rebuked [for doing so], in both [senses]: in terms of *res*, because it was itself a material sword, and also in terms of *figura*, because it is here assumed that it also represented the material sword.[26]

Literally, Christ forbade his follower to assist him with such specific material means; Peter was not allowed to fight with that particular sword. Figuratively, "because it is here assumed that it also represented the material sword," Christ forbade the use of secular or earthly power in general to his Church.

This discussion is symptomatic of Giles's sometimes bewildering mingle of *res* and *figura*, of his quick movement from literal to allegorical sense and back again. There was, to be sure, nothing unusual about that method in the exegesis of his time; my point is rather that the *tour de force* aspect of his reading of the two swords is all too obvious and could easily have provoked strong reactions. It may well have provoked John of Paris, the author of *De potestate regia et papali*[27] and a staunch supporter of Philip the Fair. A note of caution should be struck here, however, since John and Giles may have written their treatises contemporaneously. But there is no doubt of John's utter opposition to many of the views expressed in *De ecclesiastica potestate*, or of the marked difference in their hermeneutics. The *De potestate* has much in common with Ockham's *Breviloquium*, particularly its questioning not just of specific allegorical interpretations but of the truth-claim of allegorical interpretation itself. Indeed, there are so many similarities in their treatments that it need not be doubted that John's discussion was a major influence on Ockham's. But there are also significant differences, as I hope to show.

It seems obvious that Ockham owes his literal lights to John of Paris. John summarizes his opponents' reading of Genesis 1:16 ("God made two lights") as follows: "one light is the sun and this symbolizes the pope; as the sun rules the day, so the pope rules spiritual matters. The other light, the moon, rules the night and so the emperor or king rules temporal matters. But the moon cannot rule the night except by the light it borrows from the sun. It follows then that the authority of the emperor and of kings in temporal affairs comes to them from the pope."[28] John's own response is that "this is a mystical exposition of the text," and according to Pseudo-Dionysius a mystical reading cannot be accepted (*mystica theologia . . . nihil arguit*) unless a proof is found from some other passage of scripture, because mystical exegesis does not proceed by proof "(*mystica theologia non est argumentativa*)."[29] In Ockham this is more dismissively described as "merely" a mystical or allegorical sense, and although the authority of Pseudo-Dionysius is not cited, the point that mystical exegesis does not deliver proof is maintained. (In any case the quotation in question is a highly selective citation of the Pseudo-Dionysian letter, which John probably obtained from Aquinas's *Sentences* commentary.)[30] John asserts that, even if we allow a mystical interpretation (*mystica expositio*) of this text, this particular one lacks authority in that "it is not that given by the saints; their reading tended the other way"; the contrary interpretation of Isidore is then cited to substantiate that point. Ockham omits that, but he was certainly influenced by what John says next, viz. that if we grant "our opponents' interpretation" it would seem that "their arguments" do not actually support their case.

> For although the moon can only light up the night through illumination it receives from the sun, yet the moon has a virtue proper to itself, given to it by God, which it does not receive from the sun, by which it can cause cold and wet, the very opposite of what the sun causes. Thus each has its own quality, and so in our case: the prince has instruction about the faith from pope and church whilst still having his own proper distinct power which he does not receive from the pope but from God directly without intermediary.[31]

Ockham's next moves, however, take him far beyond John's position. On the one hand, the Englishman affirms the higher dignity of the priesthood over the imperial power, and on the other he warns "intelligent Christians" that they should not believe what a pope has to tell them about the mystical senses of scripture (cf. pp. 295–296). While John was prepared to challenge certain interpretations of Boniface VIII—at considerable risk to himself, as it turned out—he certainly did not go so far as to posit general skepticism about papal authority in the control and manipulation of allegorical sense.

Ockham was also influenced by John of Paris in his treatment of the interpretation of the two swords, but here he diverges from his forebear far more markedly. "There is nothing here except a certain allegorical reading (*quedam adaptatio allegorica*) from which no convincing argument can be drawn," John declares concerning his opponents' allegorical reading of scripture, and cites both Pseudo-Dionysius (as already mentioned in respect of the "two lights" allegory) and "Augustine in his *Letter to Vincent*," here summarized as saying that "allegory is insufficient to prove any proposition unless some clear authority can be produced from another source to substantiate it."[32] However, whereas Ockham proceeded to present a general devaluation of allegory in the sphere of expert discussion, John is content to move quickly into a critique of the specific mystical sense which his opponents have offered. He believes he can offer better ones, including the two swords as figures of the Old and New Testaments (Ambrose's interpretation, as noted by Giles of Rome and William of Ockham). Another possible reading, with the two swords referring to the sword of the word and the sword of impending persecution, reveals an interest in the condition of the early Church, which in Ockham's discussion is regarded as defining the parameters for viable allegorical readings of the scriptural passage in question.

Thus far John's discussion has denied that the two swords have anything to do with the issue of temporal power. Now he concedes that this issue may indeed be involved and, having granted part and parcel of his opponents' argument, proceeds to punch holes in it. While in the case of the two lights John's objection rested on the different natural properties of the referents (the sun and moon), in this case it rests on the failure of the allegory to fit the text sufficiently well. Let us assume that the two swords signify the spiritual and temporal powers. The problem then arises that, while the text says those swords were actually there, it does not say that both of them are to be Peter's or indeed any other Apostle's—simply that the two swords exist. John does not pursue the implications of that subversive thought; that was left to Ockham, who declared that "It is not likely that some one person carried both [swords]; more likely two persons did." Where Ockham was to offer subversive literalism, John offers an allegorical interpretation in opposition to that of his opponents. This rests on the assumption that only one of the two swords was Peter's, namely, the drawn sword which he subsequently used against the high priest's servant. This is taken to represent spiritual, not temporal, power. Peter did not touch the secular sword because it was not his. He *did* touch the spiritual sword which was the only one the Lord said was his, "and yet he was not to unsheathe it immediately. Hence he was told: 'Put up thy sword into the scabbard,' for certainly an ecclesiastical judge ought not to use his spiritual sword precipitately for fear it might be despised. . . ." In short, if it be granted that the mystical meaning of the two swords is the two powers, such an approach supports Jean's position because, although there were two swords, "Peter was given only one for himself." This interpretation is reinforced by a series of scriptural passages which speak of one sword rather than two.[33]

What is missing from John's account is the sharp focus on the status of allegory which is such a major feature of Ockham's *Breviloquium*; although John is fully aware of two crucial prooftexts about allegory not being conducive to proof, it is left to Ockham to spell out the implications of that thought for exegesis of those scriptural passages that were taken as figuring the temporal and the spiritual powers. The result may advisedly be called a devaluation of allegory, at least within the elite sphere of the *periti*, those expert theologians whom Ockham often calls upon as an authoritative source of specialist knowledge. Where so many of Ockham's forebears were, in the context of their discussions of the two swords, eminently capable of criticizing one allegorical interpretation but then seeking to cap it with another, in the *Breviloquium* the view is maintained with remarkable consistency that only an allegorical meaning that is confirmed by an explicit statement made elsewhere in scripture can "be adduced to prove and confirm disputable and doubtful things about which Christians disagree." And that is the business of the *periti*. Other types of allegory are relegated to the sphere of *edificatio* and *exhortatio*, but perhaps "relocated" is a better word than "relegated," for a mystical sense which "is not contrary to the truth" can assuredly serve a useful function in building up and encouraging the faith. It may not be able to prove anything in disputation "among experts," but it can move—in other words, it has a rhetorical function (using that term in a broad sense). Allegory, then, can arouse emotion, give pleasure to those who take delight in seeing how "mystical senses of the words of scripture can be fitted to the truth" (cf. p. 296).

The importance which the allegorical sense retained within the area of exhortation and edification—in both theory and practice—is no small matter, and its significance should not be underestimated: the *periti* could agonize about the value of specific allegories and on occasion about the status of allegory in general, but this hermeneutic method maintained considerable status in Catholic doctrine designed for mass consumption. Those who were most vocal in professing the importance and primacy of the literal sense—such as the great Franciscan Bible scholar Nicholas of Lyra (ca.1270–1340) and his Spanish "spiritual descendant" Alfonso de Madrigal (ca.1410–55)[34]—were perfectly happy to compile moral interpretations of scripture for preaching and for private reading. And we have already noted that Ockham himself was ready and willing to demonstrate that he can allegorize scripture with the best of them (the best of them being the saints whose spiritual senses he found most supportable), providing that the epistemological status of what he was doing was abundantly clear. Allegory and logical process were, it would seem, quite capable of peaceful coexistence, despite the occasional skirmish and grand profession of principle.

Allegory and Authorial Intention: Dante and Wycliffe

These general impressions may be substantiated further by reference to an educated lay reader of our key biblical texts—the Italian poet of paradise, purgatory, and hell, Dante Alighieri. In his *De monarchia* (dated variously as 1307/8 and 1310/11) Dante prefaces his refutation of the allegorical reading of the "two great lights" of Genesis 1:16 as temporal and spiritual power with the statement that "one can make two kinds of error when dealing with the mystical sense: either looking where it does not exist, or taking it in some inadmissible way."[35] The refutation itself rests on the demonstration of major logical absurdities in his opponents' position. Then he moves on to consider the "two swords" of Luke 22:38, attacking the argument that here the two powers are represented by demolishing the allegorical interpretation on which it rests. This view must be "utterly rejected," Dante declares, because that response "would have been at odds with Christ's intention (*intentio*), and because Peter as was his habit answered unreflectingly, only considering the surface of things (*rerum superficiem*)." Christ's intention was to advise each and every one of his followers to have a material sword: anyone who did not have one should buy one, in view of the persecution and contempt which the disciples would face after his death. When Peter, misunderstanding the point, declared that they had two swords among them, Christ, rather than rebuking him, said that those two would be enough: "If each of you cannot have one, two will suffice." Dante then demonstrates that "Peter was in the habit of speaking without reflecting" with an arsenal of biblical quotations, concluding that "when he spoke of the two swords he was answering Christ" with a simple intention (*intentione simplici*) and no deep meaning.

The *Cambridge History of Medieval Political Thought* describes Dante's treatments of Church and state power as "amateurish";[36] in my view they should rather be regarded as fresh and somewhat unusual yet well informed, for Dante seems to be aware of many aspects of the previous debate, even if no clear source can be alleged. His attack on the status of allegory in the chosen passages is certainly not without precedent, as this chapter has shown, and his use of the principle of authorial intention has clear parallels in the arguments of John of Paris, Marsilius, and Ockham. More generally, Dante's interest in the personality and human fallibility of a major biblical authority figure is very much in line with major developments within the history of scriptural exegesis, these being features discussed at length in my *Medieval Theory of Authorship: Scholastic Literary Attitudes in the Later Middle Ages*. Finally, Dante is like his earlier-mentioned contemporaries in one other major respect: he too is prepared to indulge in allegorical reading when it suits him. If these words of Christ and Peter are to be understood figuratively (*typice*), he adds, "they are not to be made to bear the meaning those people claim," but rather the sense intended by Matthew (10:34–35) when he quotes Christ as saying that he came "not to send peace, but a sword." Then comes the allegory: "Jesus began both to do and teach" (Acts 1:1), and Peter's statement that the disciples had two swords may be interpreted as meaning that "they were ready both for the words and for the actions by means of which they would bring about" what Christ wished.[37] Through allegory the Apostle who spoke "unreflectingly" has been reread and reinstated.

The situation that has emerged may be summed up as follows. The *Breviloquium* affords little if any evidence for the now discredited view of Ockham as the *enfant terrible* who dealt a powerful blow to the great Thomistic synthesis of the thirteenth century with his subversive nominalism. The truth is far less sensational. One did not have to be a nominalist to call in question the validity of allegory—or, better, *certain* allegorical interpretations—in discussion of papal power. Witness John of Paris, Marsilius, Dante—the list could easily be expanded. It could perhaps be said that aspects of Ockham's nominalist approach made his critique far more ruthless and rigorous than the others, summarized in this essay. But there is another, more obvious reason for Ockham's position—discretion had been thrown to the winds on the day that he sought the protection of Ludvig of Bavaria. Clearly, it is dangerous to make sweeping generalizations about the status of allegory within the thought of any of the individuals here considered.

The relevant views of John Wycliffe, proto-protestant or arch-heretic (depending on one's point of view), afford a fascinating case in point. In his *De potestate papali* (written ca.1379) Wycliffe offers a literal reading of Luke 22.[38] The sense of the text, he argues, is that Peter and hence the Church should not wield the secular sword, this point being made within an argument that seeks to affirm the independence of secular power.[39] To this extent at least, Wycliffe and Ockham have something in common. And yet Wycliffe was a fierce critic of certain opinions of the "doctors of signs," as he termed his nominalist opponents, and his hermeneutic in general was quite accommodating of allegory. For Wycliffe, the fact that the Bible was the expression of the divine intention meant that all its senses (including the allegorical) were from God, and all its parts had equal authority.[40] These Neoplatonic realist attitudes are very far from the mind-set of William of Ockham. In respect of Luke 22, then, the "literalism" of Ockham and Wycliffe functions and flourishes within contrasting ideologies.

This picture is rich and complex. Modern scholars should be true to the letters of the individual texts. We must respect the different, diverse, and often paradoxical ways in which medieval Christian thinkers expressed their reverence for the Word.

Notes

1. Robinson ("Church and Papacy," 303) notes that the "classic interpretation" of the two swords "as the material sword of secular coercion and the spiritual sword of excommunication appears in papal letter of the ninth century." See further, Lecler, "L'Argument des deux glaives."

2. Robinson, "Church and Papacy," 303–4. Cf. Luscombe and Evans, "The Twelfth-Century Renaissance," 317–21, which includes discussion of the implications of the "two swords" doctrine in the dispute between Saint Thomas Becket and King Henry II of England.

3. Trans. Tierney, *The Crisis of Church and State, 1050–1300*, 188–89. On the sources of the ideas here expressed in the thought of Hugh of Saint Victor and (as amplified by Giles of Rome) of Bernard of Clairvaux, see the cogent summary in Watt, "Spiritual and Temporal Powers," 401–2.

4. In Dyson's judgment, "it is reasonable to say that Boniface's error of judgment in publishing *Unam sanctam* lay not so much in the immoderate nature of its content as in his ex-

tremely poor timing." See Giles of Rome, *Giles of Rome on Ecclesiastical Power*, trans. Dyson, 210.

5. *Giles of Rome on Ecclesiastical Power*, xii.

6. On the possible reasons for Ockham's presence at Avignon see Kynsh, "Biographical Rectifications," 61–91.

7. The following remarks are indebted to A. S. McGrade's succinct summary in the introduction to William of Ockham, *A Short Discourse on the Tyrannical Government*, trans. Kilcullen, xvii.

8. I have used the edition by Scholz, *Wilhelm von Ockham als politischer Denker*, and drawn on the translation by Kilcullen (see n. 7), hereafter referred to as McGrade and Kilcullen.

9. *Breviloquium*, 5. 3, ed. Scholz, 171; trans. McGrade and Kilcullen, 133–34. The contrast between things said by way of *edificatio et exhortatio* and statements with a higher scriptural and/or scientific truth-claim is of course a commonplace of late medieval thought. I am certainly not suggesting any kind of originality in Ockham's understanding of these notions, but rather drawing attention to the effective way in which he enlists them in this attack on his opponents' deployment of allegorical exegesis.

10. Ibid., ed. Scholz, 171; trans. McGrade and Kilcullen, 134.

11. Epist. 93. 8; PL 33.334.

12. Thomas Aquinas, *Summa theologiae* 1a.1.10, Blackfriars ed., vol. 1, ed. Gilby, 39.

13. *Breviloquium*, 5. 3, ed. Scholz, 171–72; trans. McGrade and Kilcullen, 134.

14. *Breviloquium*, 5. 4, ed. Scholz, 174; trans. McGrade and Kilcullen, 136.

15. If so, no doubt Ockham noted with special approval the remark Augustine makes at the end of that disquisition, to the effect that hardly anything may be found in the obscure places of scripture "which is not found plainly said elsewhere." But Ockham was concerned to put the plain truth first and the allegory second: "whenever a truth is certain first through sacred scripture or evident argument, it is permissible afterwards to adduce mystical senses in favour of that certain truth. . . ." For an interesting thirteenth-century use of Augustine's invocation of the pleasure principle, see Minnis, "Medium and Message," 215–16.

16. *Breviloquium*, 5. 5, ed. Scholz, 176–78; trans. McGrade and Kilcullen, 139–41.

17. Ibid., 5.5, ed. Scholz, 177; trans. McGrade and Kilcullen, 139.

18. Indeed, Ockham could have reinforced his argument with the point that such interpretations—which depend on the similarity rather than difference between the two swords—are more appropriate to the extent that they are more consonant with the text of scripture, wherein no distinction is made between the two swords and therefore it may be assumed that they are identical. Both are material swords, and therefore they are capable of being interpreted spiritually in any way that respects that similarity rather than introducing difference. Perhaps he thought that point was sufficiently obvious. Or, more likely, he felt that his argument here would not be helped by the suggestion that some mystical senses are more acceptable than others—he is reserving that point for later.

19. These being words which, Ockham explains, in their literal sense and "according to their first meaning" (*ad litteram et secundum primum intellectum*) can, as is generally true of literal senses, be adduced in proof of contentious points.

20. On the contrast between "proper" and "improper" speech see Courtenay, "Force of Words and Figures of Speech"; Minnis, "*A leur faiz cousines*."

21. *Breviloquium*, 5. 6, ed. Scholz, 179–80; trans. McGrade and Kilcullen, 141–42.

22. *Defensor pacis* 2.26.24, ed. Scholz, 564; trans. Gewirth, 397.

23. *Defensor pacis* 2.28, ed. Scholz, 567–68; trans. Gewirth, 400.

24. Giles of Rome, *De ecclesiastica potestate*, ed. Scholz, 138–39; trans. Dyson, 134. I have made several alterations to Dyson's translation here, to preserve Giles's technical language.

25. Ibid., 2.15, ed. Scholz, 140; trans. Dyson, 135.

26. Ibid.

27. I have used the edition included in Leclercq's study, *Jean de Paris et l'ecclésiologie du XIIIe siècle*, 173–260.

28. *De potestate* 11; ed. Leclercq, 202; trans. Watt, 131.

29. *De potestate* 14; ed. Leclercq, 218; trans. Watt, 165.

30. Cf. Pseudo-Dionysius, *Epistola* 9.c.1; cf. Thomas Aquinas, *Comm. in I Sent.* 11.1.1, in *Scriptum super libros sententiarium*, 1:276–80.

31. *De potestate* 14; ed. Leclercq, 218; trans. Watt, 165–66.

32. *De potestate* 18; ed. Leclercq, 232; trans. Watt, 196.

33. In his subsequent discussion John addresses the fact that in Luke 22:38 two swords are actually referred to, and so the question may be asked: in what sense did they belong to the Apostles? One is the property of the Apostles and their successors in itself, i.e., the spiritual sword. The "other is authorized to be theirs as occasion warrants because it is not incompatible with their calling and was going to be theirs in the future, given to them *by the grant and permission* of princes." That phrase is crucially important—the Church can request rather than order action by the secular authorities, and it is up to the prince to decide whether or not that request will be granted. For this view John manages to enlist the support of Saint Bernard (read very partially, of course): "Bernard says expressly, 'at the request of the priest and the command of the emperor' and not 'by his own hand or at his command,' because here he has no authority to command or compel, but only to intimate. Command is only if the emperor wishes it."

34. See Minnis, "Fifteenth-Century Versions of Literalism."

35. Dante, *De monarchia* 3.4, ed. Shaw, 109.

36. Watt, "Spiritual and Temporal Powers," 412–13.

37. Ibid., 3.9, ed. Shaw, 127.

38. Wycliffe, *Tractatus de potestate papae*, ed. J. Loserth, 122–23; cf. 138.

39. Wycliffe argues that the pope should not judge in secular affairs; priests do not need civil dominion (Ibid., 85, 101). The clergy should rely on divine authority and have nothing to do with civil power (115). Christ forbade his disciples to take the sword (cf. John 18). The causes of Saint Peter's primacy did not consist in secular glory but in the opposite: humility and mildness (136). Bernard's *De consideratione* is interpreted as saying that the pope should exercise secular rule or maintain his primacy by force (138).

40. Cf. *Tractatus de potestate papae*, 113.

Bibliography

Courtenay, W. J. "Force of Words and Figures of Speech: The Crisis over *Virtus Sermonis* in the Fourteenth Century." *Franciscan Studies* 44 (1984): 107–22.

Dante Alighieri. *De monarchia*. Ed. and trans. Prue Shaw. Cambridge: Cambridge University Press, 1995.

Giles of Rome. *De ecclesiastica potestate*. Ed. Richard Scholz . Weimar: H. Böhlaus Nachfolger, 1929.

——. *Giles of Rome on Ecclesiastical Power: The* De ecclesiastica potestate *of Aegidius Romanus*. Trans. R. W. Dyson. Woodbridge: Boydell Press, 1986.

John of Paris. "De potestate." In *Jean de Paris et l'ecclésiologie du XIIIe siècle*. Ed. J. Leclercq. Paris: J. Vrin, 1942.

——. *On Royal and Papal Power*. Trans. J. A. Watt. Toronto: Pontifical Insititute of Mediaeval Studies, 1971. A translation of *De potestate*.

Kynsh, George. "Biographical Rectifications Concerning Ockham's Avignon Period." *Franciscan Studies* 46 (1986): 61–91.

Lecler, Joseph. "L'Argument des deux glaives." *Recherches de science religieuse* 21 (1931): 299–339; 22 (1932): 151–77, 280–303.

Leclercq, Jean. *Jean de Paris et l'ecclésiologie du XIIIe siècle.* Paris: J. Vrin, 1942.

Luscombe, D. S., and G. R. Evans. "The Twelfth-Century Renaissance." In *Cambridge History of Medieval Political Thought, c.350–c.1450.* Ed. J. H. Burns, 306–38. Cambridge: Cambridge University Press, 1988.

Marsilius of Padua. *Defensor pacis.* Ed. Richard Scholz. Hanover: Hahn, 1933.

——. *Defensor pacis.* Trans. Alan Gewirth. Mediaeval Academy Reprints for Teaching, 6. Toronto: University of Toronto Press, 1980.

Minnis, A. J. "*A leur faiz cousines*: Words, Deeds and Proper Speech in Jean de Meun and Chaucer." In *Medieval Heritage: Essays in Honour of Tadahiro Ikegami.* Ed. Masahiko Kanno, et al., 31–63. Tokyo: Yushudo Press, 1997.

——. "Fifteenth-Century Versions of Literalism: Girolamo Savonarola and Alfonso de Madrigal." In *Neue Richtungen in der hoch- und spätmittelalterlichen Bibelexegese.* Ed. Robert Lerner, 163–80. Schriften des Historischen Kollegs, Kolloquien, 32. Munich: R. Oldenbourg, 1996.

——. "Medium and Message: Henry of Ghent on Scriptural Style." In *Literature and Religion in the Later Middle Ages: Philological Studies in Honor of Siegfried Wenzel.* Ed. R. Newhauser and John A. Alford, 209–35. Binghamton, N.Y.: Medieval and Renaissance Texts and Studies, 1995.

Pseudo-Dionysius. *Opera omnia.* Venice: A. Zatta, 1755.

Robinson, I. S. "Church and Papacy." In *The Cambridge History of Medieval Political Thought, c. 350–c. 1450.* Ed. J. H. Burns, 252–305. Cambridge: Cambridge University Press, 1988.

Thomas Aquinas. *Scriptum super libros sententiarum.* 4 vols. Paris: P. Lethielleux, 1929.

——. *Summa theologiae.* 61 vols. Cambridge: Blackfriars, 1964–76.

Tierney, Brian. *The Crisis of Church and State, 1050–1300.* Englewood Cliffs, N.J.: Prentice-Hall, 1964.

Watt, J. W. "Spiritual and Temporal Powers." In *The Cambridge History of Medieval Political Thought, c. 350–c. 1450.* Ed. J. H. Burns, 367–423. Cambridge: Cambridge University Press, 1988.

William of Ockham. "Breviloquium de principatu tyrannico super divine et humana." In *Wilhelm von Ockham als politischer Denker und sein* Breviloquium de principatu tyrannico. Ed. Richard Scholz. Leipzig: K. W. Hiersemann, 1944.

——. *A Short Discourse on the Tyrannical Government.* Trans. John Kilcullen. Introd. A. S. McGrade. Cambridge: Cambridge University Press, 1992.

Wycliffe, John. *Tractatus de potestate papae.* Ed. J. Loserth. London: Trübner, 1907.

PART III

MEDIEVAL EXEGESIS OF THE QUR'ĀN

20

An Introduction to Medieval Interpretation of the Qur'ān

JANE DAMMEN MCAULIFFE

Commentary on the Qur'ān, as both activity and achievement, has proven to be a remarkably stable enterprise over the long centuries of its production. In an academic world where intellectual fads rise and fall with ever-increasing frequency, the stability of this tradition runs counter to expectations that reward novelty and innovation. Yet stability does not mean a lack of vitality. The tradition of qur'ānic exegesis, or *tafsīr al-Qur'ān* to use its Arabic term, continues to occupy a prominent place within contemporary Muslim intellectual life. Its medieval antecedents are studied and taught in university classrooms worldwide and they form the basis and background for the flourishing publication of new works of commentary.

I experienced the classroom vitality of this discipline a few years ago when I spent a semester at the University of Jordan in Amman, auditing both graduate and undergraduate classes in their Faculty of Religious Law (*Kulliyyat al-Sharī'a*). I went to Jordan because I wanted to encounter contemporary qur'ānic studies in a Muslim academic context. The University of Jordan offered a large number of courses grouped under the general rubric of the "sciences" of the Qur'ān (*'ulūm al-Qur'ān*). Students in the program at the Kulliyat al-Sharī'a could take several semesters of qur'ānic exegesis as well as several semesters of recitation and memorization. The program included specialized courses on the Qur'ān's interpretation, its stylistics, its narratives, its verses with legal implications, the doctrine of its inimitability, and the rhetorical structures that support this doctrine. More advanced students could study classical exegetical methodology, work through specialized topical or thematic studies, and even analyze, largely for purpose of refutation, some of the assertions made by Orientalist scholarship.

Clearly an analogy can be drawn with programs of biblical studies as these are pursued in religiously related institutions, such as Jewish yeshivahs and Christian seminaries, or within secular research universities. While allowing for quite significant differences of emphasis and approach, such institutions share an appreciation of biblical studies as a multifaceted endeavor. This is also the case with Muslim academies such as the Kulliyyat al-Sharī'a, which mounts a full range of offerings in the field of qur'ānic studies and its many subdisciplines. An awareness of this fact may help readers who are not specialists in Islamic studies to view the contemporary study and production of qur'ānic interpretation as comparable in variety and sophistication to the studies of Jewish and Christian scriptures within European and American institutions of higher education. While the continuity between modern and medieval modes of discourse may differ among these three forms of scriptural studies—those of the Hebrew Bible, the New Testament, or the Qur'ān—each represents a multifaceted academic endeavor with a hierarchy of professional formation and certification.

The Chronology and Classification of Commentary

Qur'ānic exegesis (*tafsīr al-Qur'ān*), then, constitutes a major subdiscipline of the qur'ānic sciences which can be understood and described as both a literary genre and an academic discipline. Before its formal characteristics as a genre are presented, it is worth remarking upon its size, both chronological and physical, and its linguistic scope. Taken as a whole, the extant commentaries on the Qur'ān represent a large and sustained range of literary output from at least the ninth to the twentieth centuries with certain seminal works that predate even that span. In addition to being long in time, the genre of commentary is large in size. Virtually all of the major commentaries are multivolume works. Printed editions of ten, twenty, or even thirty volumes are not uncommon. The frequently cumulative nature of this genre accounts for much of its magnitude. Further, the linguistic scope of the commentary tradition exhibits an equally impressive expanse. While most of the classical production was penned in Arabic, commentaries have been written in many of the languages of the worldwide Muslim community: Persian, Turkish, Urdu, Malay, Javanese, Swahili, and others.

Muslim exegetical works, especially full-scale commentaries, ordinarily manifest a fairly standard format, particularly in their present, printed forms. First of all, this format follows the textual order of the Qur'ān: it begins with the first chapter (*sūra*) and continues to the last. Within this order, the segments of interpretation incorporate the complete text of a verse or a designated section of it. In some editions, the text portion under discussion is presented as a continuously running header. In others, it is set off typographically within the body of the commentary. Some of the most recent editions print all of the qur'ānic text in red, whether it is set off or incorporated within the sections of commentary. In whatever form it is presented, the qur'ānic text, unlike its surrounding commentary is ordinarily printed with fully marked vocalization. Such current printing conventions represent a standardization of more varied presentation mechanisms in the centuries-long manuscript history of exegetical works.

In the longest and most traditional commentaries, these exegetical are further segmented and associated with named authorities, thus graphically demonstrating the reality of multivalent readings of the text. Of course, the range of interpretations offered is subject to the selection and restriction exercised by the individual commentator (*mufassir*). The authorities that he cites define and demarcate the exegetical lineage within which he writes. Further, it is in the very process of selection, organization, presentation, and assessment of this material from one's exegetical predecessors that the individuality and originality of the particular commentator demonstrates itself. The late Norman Calder, who was to have been a participant in the conference that generated this volume, has captured this feature in a particularly felicitous manner:

> The qualities which distinguish one *mufassir* from another lie less in their conclusions as to what the quranic text means than in their development and display of techniques which mark their participation in and mastery of a literary discipline. Just as the skill of, say, a football player can be recognized only in relation to a complex body of rules (variously constituted by such things as white lines on grass or a complex and developing off-side rule) so too the literary skills of a *mufassir* must be assessed not in terms of the end product (the Qur'ān explained) but in terms of their skillful participation in a rule-governed activity.[1]

As an academic discipline, qur'ānic commentary is taught chronologically and that chronology is, in turn, recapitulated hermeneutically. Muḥammad Ḥusayn al-Dhahabī's *al-Tafsīr wa-l-mufassirūn* (Commentary and Commentators), which was submitted as a thesis to al-Azhar University in 1946,[2] is still the standard text, although many others have since been published that model themselves upon it or are drawn extensively from it. Chronological segmentation in such surveys ordinarily begins with the age of the Prophet and his Companions. Actually, Muḥammad himself is not the reputed source of much of the material that is attributed to this period. And that material itself tends to be rather succinct and simple, consisting of brief responses to posed questions or lexical glossing where a term is considered to be difficult or obscure. Some of the most prominent names associated with this period are 'Abdallāh b. Mas'ūd (d. 32/652) and Ubayy b. Ka'b (d. 42/662), to whom early codices are attributed, as well as 'Abdallāh b. 'Abbās (d. 68/687), who is frequently characterized as the "father" of qur'ānic exegesis.[3]

While "Companions" (*Ṣaḥāba*) is the term for those that the Islamic tradition has deemed to be the Prophet's closest associates, "Successors" (*Tābi'ūn*) is the name given to the leading religious figures of the generation that followed. Consequently, the next, normal segmentation in the Muslim history of qur'ānic commentary is that devoted to the Successors. Not unexpectedly, given the rapid diffusion of Islam, this period represents a broader geographical spread, with clearer identification of particular geographic centers, such as the Arabian Ḥijāzī cities of Mecca, Medina, and developing urban environments in southern Iraq and elsewhere. Some of the most noted commentators of this period are Sa'īd b. Jubayr (d. 95/714), Mujāhid b. Jabr (d. 104/722), al-Ḍaḥḥāk (d. 105/723), Ḥasan al-Baṣrī (d. 110/728), Qatāda (d. 118/736), and al-Kalbī (d. 146/763). Fred Leemhuis's essay in this volume, drawing upon some of these early authorities, demonstrates how later commentaries echo the exegetical debates of earlier generations.

A much longer time span is captured under the rubric of the "age of collecting/compiling" (*tadwīn*), and its principal product can be seen as both a summation and a starting point. That "product" is the qur'ānic commentary of Abū Ja'far b. Jarīr al-Ṭabarī (d. 310/923), *Jāmi' al-bayān 'an ta'wīl āy al-Qur'ān*.[4] This massive work, which is still regularly reprinted and can be found in virtually any large bookstore in the Muslim world, is an encyclopedia of the exegetical reports extant in the late ninth century, a vast compilation of the interpretive tradition (*ḥadīth*, pl. *aḥādīth*) then in circulation. Each of these *ḥadīth* enshrines something Muḥammad or his Companions is reported to have said or done, such as how one should pray, how divorce should be regarded, or how a particular word or phrase in the Qur'ān can be explained. Further, in al-Ṭabarī's commentary, and in others of the same type, each of these *ḥadīth* is prefaced with the names of those who have passed this particular record of thought or action down from one generation to the next (*isnād*). Herbert Berg, with particular concentration on *isnād* analysis, asks whether it is possible to assess the historical reliability of such exegetical *ḥadīth*.

In its earliest stages, commentary (*tafsīr*) was probably not a separate genre but simply one part of this growing mass of *ḥadīth*. According to classical Muslim sources, it was only after several generations and the exponential accumulation of such material that efforts at categorization and classification emerged. Al-Ṭabarī's commentary, therefore, represents a final, summative stage in a multigenerational process. The sheer quantity of exegetical information that he compiled, arranged, and ordered has made his commentary an exemplar for all subsequent centuries of what Muslim historians of the genre have come to call "interpretation by the received report or tradition" (*al-tafsīr bi-l-ma'thūr*).

The designation *al-tafsīr bi-l-ma'thūr* is balanced in the classical and contemporary accounts of Muslim exegetical history by that of the other major category of predominantly Sunnī *tafsīr*, *al-tafsīr bi-l-ra'y*, which is used to connote interpretation by informed, personal opinion. The phrase itself is not a self-designation employed by a particular group or lineage of exegetes; rather it is a categorization or even an evaluation that is made, with varying degrees of opprobrium, by those who privilege commentary that is based primarily on traditional reports. Islamic sources about the history of interpretation ordinarily list works in this category of *al-tafsīr bi-l-ra'y* because they have a certain dogmatic or doctrinal orientation and frequently include, as in the case of the major twelfth-century work by Fakhr al-Dīn al-Rāzī (d. 606/1210), much theological and philosophical speculation.[5]

Almost by definition, there is a classical category of exegetical works that fall within the scope of *al-tafsīr bi-l-ra'y*, those produced by Muslim "mystics" or Ṣūfīs. Ṣūfism, a mode of Muslim thought and practice that transcends the usual distinction between Sunnī and Shī'ī Islam, generated an extensive, eclectic literature of qur'ānic interpretation. In general, however, it was less marked by the transmission of accumulated exegetical *ḥadīth* and more concerned with discerning levels or layers of meaning that are not immediately accessible to the spiritually uninitiated. The chapters by Gerhard Böwering and the late Hava Lazarus-Yafeh explore this phenomenon. Böwering examines the interface between hermeneutical reflection by Ṣūfī commentators and their actual exegetical practice. Lazarus-Yafeh ponders the reluctance of this group of exegetes to employ full-fledged allegory and relates this to the prohibition of figural representation in Islam. A feature noted by both of these authors is that Ṣūfī commentators often concentrate on particular qur'ānic words, phrases, or verses which become the focus of mystical contemplation or which support an understanding of various forms of Ṣūfī spiritual formation.

A type of commentary that scholars frequently described in sectarian terms is that generated by the Shī'ī community. Shī'ī Islam, which currently accounts for about ten to fifteen percent of the Muslim world, ordinarily traces its genesis to disagreements about the legitimate line of political and spiritual succession from the prophet Muḥammad. Just as Shī'ism in thought and practice does not manifest great differences with Sunnī Islam, so too Shī'ī commentary does not usually exhibit significant methodological variance from Sunnī commentary, and there is a good deal of overlap between the exegetical literature of these two sectarian divisions.

Perhaps the principal line of distinction between the two can be found in the sources and authorities cited. While here, too, there is much overlap, Shī'ī commentaries supplement their attestation of exegetical authorities with reference to a lineage of religious leaders known as the Imāms. Because the Imāms are believed to provide ongoing, infallible guidance to the community, they constitute an important locus of exegetical insight. Additionally, the Shīʿī need to confirm succession to Muḥammad within his family line puts a different reading on certain passages in the Qur'ān, as does the desire to find esoteric meanings in the text.

The study of qur'ānic commentary, then, is frequently structured along diverse but intersecting lines—the chronological divisions, the sectarian separations of Sunnī, Shīʿī, and Ṣūfī; and the content categorizations of *al-tafsīr bi-l-ma'thūr* and *al-tafsīr bi-l-ra'y*. When Muslim scholars adopt the chronological perspective, however, they can proceed both historically and hermeneutically. To codify their exegetical methodology, classical Muslim scholars used both time and accessibility to the Prophet as the key factors. Classical qur'ānic hermeneutics, therefore, recapitulates this exegetical chronology, with its division into the time periods of the Prophet, then his Companions, then their Successors, as it presents the proper methodology for interpretation of the Qur'ān. The codification presented in the later medieval period by scholars like Ibn Taymiyya (d. 728/1328) and his student Ibn Kathīr (d. 774/1373) has found its way into most contemporary textbooks on this topic.[6]

The fourfold process approved by Ibn Taymiyya offers a discreet methodological idealization of exegetical steps. In the order in which they should be followed, these are (1) interpreting the Qur'ān by the Qur'ān, (2) interpreting it by the *sunna* of the prophet Muḥammad, (3) interpreting it by the statements of his Companions, those of his own generation who had direct access to him, and (4) interpreting it by the statements of the Successors, those of the next generation whose access to the Prophet's statements was mediated through one or more of the Companions.[7] As is immediately obvious, this is a hermeneutical hierarchy, arranged in decreasing order of probative value. It reflects not so much an actual working process, at least in this rigidly sequential format, as a means of assessing and establishing the comparative worth of particular exegetical views.

Varieties of Exegetical Material

Another way of viewing the total accumulation of exegetical material, and one that has recently become popular with Western scholars, is to do so by literary form. To put this method in more contemporary terminology, it is to interject a form-critical perspective to the study of qur'ānic interpretation. This is by no means a new exercise in the history of scholarship on the Qur'ān. Attention to different kinds of exegetical material, whether narrative or legal or linguistic, has characterized this discipline from its classical period. Some modern scholarship, however, has coupled chronology to form criticism with the assertion that genre emergence proceeded sequentially in the formative period of qur'ānic interpretation. One British scholar, for example, has postulated a typological analysis of the major forms of exegetical material: haggadic (paraenetic, narrative), halakhic (legal), masoretic (linguistic, grammatical), rhetorical (stylistic excellence), and allegorical (exoteric or allusive).[8]

This typology grows out of an attempt to trace the origins and textual development of the earliest forms of Muslim literature, particularly the Qur'ān and commentary (*tafsīr*)—

including the factors of both abrogation (*al-nāsikh wa-l-mansūkh*) and contextualization (*asbāb al-nuzūl*) and the biography of Muḥammad (*sīra*) and the statements and actions attributed to him (*ḥadīth*) and to understand these as analogous to Jewish and Christian scripture in being the end result of an extended historical process. Whether or not its chronological argument can be verified, such a typology functions as a very helpful way to classify and categorize the varieties of exegetical material. An interest in the *Sitz im Leben* of qur'ānic and *tafsīr* material remains an active concern in current scholarship on the Qur'ān. Angelika Neuwirth's essay develops a microanalytical approach to the connection between text and *tafsīr* through an analysis of early textual material dealing with the religious status of Jerusalem.

Questions Posed by the Commentators

Seen from a yet different perspective, the varieties of exegetical material constitute responses to the questions that the Qur'ān's interpreters repeatedly put to the text. Here are some of the issues to which commentary on the Qur'ān regularly addressed itself: What circumstances prompted a particular revelation or to what situation was it directed? Muslim scholars classify questions of this sort under the rubric of "occasions of revelation" (*asbāb al-nuzūl*), and the attempts to answer this kind of query often take the form of short or extended narratives. Traditional Muslim scholarship finds the sum total of such narratives to be a rich source for the history of the life of Muḥammad and of his early community.

In a related fashion the early commentators sought to identify all individuals and groups to whom the Qur'ān makes allusion. Who is intended, they would ask, by designations such as "the people of the book" (*ahl al-kitāb*) or "the men of the heights" (*aṣḥāb al-a'rāf*) or by the many pronouns whose referent is unclear? The suggested responses to such attempts at identification were also added to the storehouse of orthodox history. Gerald Hawting's essay explores this connection between exegetical identification and historical veracity with a focus on the term *mushrikūn*, a term that is usually glossed as 'idolaters.'

Another frequent question is: Does the verse have any variant readings, that is, differences in the consonantal structure or vocalization of words? According to the widely accepted Muslim view of the early codification of the text, versions with slight differences of wording and pronunciation circulated for years, both orally and in the truncated Arabic script of the first Islamic generations. Eventually, traditional accounts of this textual history tell us, both a restriction on the scope of acceptable linguistic variation for the Qur'ān and a more accurate written representation of it were achieved. In a spirit of textual inclusiveness, the scholarly community of medieval Islam finally canonized a recognized range of variants, a range that was felt to compromise neither uniformity of sense nor sacrality of origin. This range, in turn, was reflected in the exegetical tradition when commentators took note of these canonical variants and the classical authorities who substantiated them. The exegetical tradition, particularly in some of its earlier works, also records the continuing existence of noncanonical variants, and text-critical scholarship on the Qur'ān continues to hope that an exhaustive search of early Islamic sources may some day result in a critical edition of the qur'ānic corpus. Continuing advances in computer technology and searchable text files have certainly augmented these hopes.

The commentators also interrogated the qur'ānic text about stylistic and rhetorical concerns such as these: Are there apparent linguistic or grammatical anomalies that require explanation? Are there semantic ambiguities created by syntactical structures that permit more than one way of reading a passage? The chapter by Stefan Wild demonstrates how such a situation affects Q 3:7, a key verse in intra-qur'ānic exegesis. To continue this line of questioning: Does a correct understanding of a particular passage involve the implied insertion or transposition of words or phrases? As the Qur'ān was itself considered to be the lodestone of grammatical purity in Arabic, such discussions often involved justifying an unusual or idiosyncratic qur'ānic usage as against the expected morphological structures of classical Arabic. In a similar fashion, commentators were alert to words that fell outside the commonly accepted corpus of Arabic vocabulary. While efforts to explain this phenomenon varied, Andrew Rippin's essay notes that the category "foreign word" could be employed as a useful exegetical mechanism. Put more positively, this area of grammatical and stylistic exegetical inquiry would ask: Are there particular features of a given pericope that exemplify the claim for the Qur'ān's miraculous inimitability? How does this verse, or group of verses, manifest the unparalleled rhetorical power and linguistic beauty with which God endowed the Qur'ān?

Still another subject to which commentators regularly applied themselves was the possible legal implications of a specific verse or *sūra* segment. In fact, multivolume commentaries are devoted to this particular topic. While the proscriptive and prescriptive passages of the Qur'ān do not account for a large portion of the text—the usual estimate is about 500 of the more than 6,000 qur'ānic verses—they are obviously of great significance as they must guide the divinely mandated behavior of the believers. Consequently, extended attention has been paid to these verses in exegetical works but also in legal works. The migration of qur'ānic exegesis beyond the boundary of the commentary genre is the subject of my own essay in this volume. The Qur'ān was so central to the intellectual life of medieval Islam that its verses and their interpretation appear in virtually all forms of Islamic literature.

Among the further questions that this subcategory of qur'ānic material entails are those of abrogation and applicability. The Qur'ān itself makes references to the concept of sequentiality within the revelatory process, the notion that some parts of the revelation supersede or abrogate others. This topic, known as "the abrogating and the abrogated" (*al-nāsikh wa-l-mansūkh*), is a complicated one within the "qur'ānic sciences" (*'ulūm al-Qur'ān*) and has implications for the relation between the Qur'ān and the codified accounts of the Prophet's words and actions (*ḥadīth*). The issue of applicability is also complex, and it too straddles the boundary between exegetical and legal literature. Its motivating query is: Is this verse or verse-group of general or of restricted relevance? Did it apply only to a situation in the past? Does it concern only a limited group of the believers? Or must it be the concern of each and every observant Muslim?

The Continuity of Qur'ānic Commentary

Mention of these many questions with which Muslim commentators have approached the qur'ānic text prompts a query that takes us beyond the chronological confines of the present volume. Yet it should be posed because it provides much of the justification for continuing to pay attention to medieval scriptural exegesis produced within the Muslim world. The question is, of course, this: What is the relation of medieval qur'ānic commentary to modern and contemporary qur'ānic commentary? The short answer is that the latter stands, in large measure, as a direct continuation of the former. It is true that much contemporary commentary on the Qur'ān is marked by an increased interest in and emphasis upon current social, political, and ethical concerns. It is also true that some twentieth-century works speak in a reformist voice which may deny the importance of much of the massive interpretive edifice constructed in the classical period. Yet it must also be noted that present-day qur'ānic studies within a Muslim scholarly environment and present-day qur'ānic commentary have not sustained the rupture of the Enlightenment that so radically recast these same exercises within the milieu of biblical scholarship. In the main, contemporary qur'ānic commentators still want to position themselves as worthy and qualified heirs to the medieval exegetical tradition, especially to what is understood to be its summative, classical period, its "Golden Age."

Publication data can also attest to the continuing vitality of that tradition and to the abiding interest that contemporary Muslim scholars have in the works of their medieval predecessors. A quick stop at a good-sized book shop anywhere in the Muslim world will demonstrate the truth of this claim. The commentaries of al-Ṭabarī, al-Zamakhsharī, Fakhr al-Dīn al-Rāzī, Ibn Kathīr, and al-Qurṭubī are regularly stocked. If a trip to Cairo or Kuala Lumpur is not on your travel itinerary, then spend a few minutes checking some of the exploding number of websites devoted to Muslim literature that have appeared in the last few years. Once again, the continuing appeal of medieval commentary on the Qur'ān will be readily apparent.

These texts, and others like them, continue to attract the attention of Western scholars as well. Several major conference publications that have been published within little more than a decade attest to this interest. All three volumes have made significant contributions to this field and all three were edited by scholars who have also contributed to the present volume.[9] The articles in those volumes present a broad range of scholarship on the Qur'ān and its interpretation. Scanning their tables of contents offers a good sense of the scope of contemporary academic work within Euro-American universities on the Qur'ān and its centuries of interpretation. While studies that focus upon the contemporary period are well represented, much of the attention is directed toward the formative and the classical or medieval period of Islamic thought and culture.

These two periods, and the relation between them, remain of predominant concern in Western academic scholarship on the Qur'ān. I use the word "Western" here with the usual disclaimer that it is an imperfect descriptive, as imperfect as the attempt to distinguish between "Muslim scholarship" and "Western scholarship" in the present period. The rapidly mounting Muslim populations in Europe, North America, and elsewhere, as well as the increasing numbers of Muslim scholars in the educational institutions of these diaspora areas, continue to blur this distinction. Nevertheless, no new terminology has gained wide currency that captures the different perspectives and presumptions that have characterized these two scholarly approaches to the Qur'ān.

While much of this introduction has presented the world of traditional Muslim scholarship on the Qur'ān in its many forms and varieties, these concluding remarks concentrate upon the scholarly context from which the articles in this volume emerge. Certain questions have sparked particular attention in the academic milieu of qur'ānic studies during the last several decades, and these continue to preoccupy scholars in the field and to motivate much of its most interesting production. One example: Are the qur'ānic text, in its canonical form, and qur'ānic commentary actually two separate, sequential categories of material? Or in a related mode: How did exegetical material first surface and circulate? And what is the relation of both the Qur'ān and its early commentary to other forms of Islamic self-expression, such as legal development or historical reflection or liturgical activity? The effort to recapture the earliest strata of exegesis prompts the inquiry: Can proto-commentaries be constructed from the comprehensive works of the post-ninth century? Mining another vein, some scholars are asking: How porous are the boundaries between what could be termed Islamic versus non-Islamic materials? Can reciprocal influences be tracked within the sibling literatures of Judaism, Christianity, and Islam? You will find echoes of all of these queries in the pages that follow, pages that prove the abiding attractiveness of the medieval scriptural exegesis generated by the Muslim world.

Notes

1. Norman Calder. "Tafsīr from Ṭabarī to Ibn Kathīr: Problems in the Description of a Genre, Illustrated with Reference to the Story of Abraham," in *Approaches to the Qur'ān*, ed. G. R. Hawting and Abdul-Kader A. Shareef (London: Routledge, 1993), 106.

2. Muḥammad Ḥusayn al-Dhahabī, *al-Tafsīr wa-l-mufassirūn*, 2 vols. (Cairo: n.p., 1976).

3. Claude Gilliot, "Portrait 'mythique' d'Ibn 'Abbās" *Arabica* 32 (1985): 127–84.

4. Abū Ja'far Muḥammad b. Jarīr al-Ṭabarī, *Jāmi' al-bayān 'an ta'wīl āy al-Qur'ān* [up to Q 14:27], ed. Maḥmūd Muḥammad Shākir, 16 vols., 2d ed. (Cairo: n.p., 1954–69). See also id., *Jāmi' al-bayān 'an ta'wīl āy al-Qur'ān*, ed. Aḥmad Sa'īd 'Alī et al., 30 vols. (Cairo: n.p., 1373–77/1954–57; reprint, Beirut: n.p., 1984).

5. For an introduction to major figures of both medieval and modern qur'ānic exegesis, see the first part of my *Qur'ānic Christians: An Analysis of Classical and Modern Exegesis* (New York: Cambridge, 1991).

6. Jane Dammen McAuliffe, "Qur'ānic Hermeneutics: The Views of al-Ṭabarī and Ibn Kathīr," in *Approaches to the History of the Interpretation of the Qur'ān*, ed. Andrew Rippin (Oxford: Clarendon Press, 1988), 46–62.

7. Jane Dammen McAuliffe, "Ibn Taymiyyah's *Muqaddimatun fī uṣūl al-tafsīr*," in *Windows on the House of Islam: Sources on Spirituality and Religious Life*, ed. John Renard (Berkeley: University of California Press, 1998), 35–43.

8. H. Hirschfeld, *New Researches in the Composition and Exegesis of the Qoran* (London: Royal Asiatic Society, 1902); John Wansbrough, *Quranic Studies. Sources and Methods of Scriptural Interpretation* (Oxford: Oxford University Press, 1977).

9. Rippin, ed., *Approaches*; Hawting and Shareef, eds., *Approaches to the Qur'ān*; and Stefan Wild, *The Qur'an as Text* (Leiden: Brill, 1996).

21

Discussion and Debate in Early Commentaries of the Qur'ān

FRED LEEMHUIS

In verse 119 of *sūrat al-Nisā'*, the fourth sūra of the Qur'ān, Satan is quoted as having said about the pagans, "I will lead them astray, and fill them with fancies, and I will command them and they will cut off the cattle's ears: I will command them and they will alter God's creation (*fa-la-yughayyirunna khalqa-llāhi*)."[1]

On the face of it, this passage seems to have a rather straightforward meaning: Satan will command his followers, the pagan polytheists, to do unnatural things and the believers will be able to recognize them, whether these unnatural acts consist in maiming cattle or in other abnormal activity against God's creation. Nevertheless, what precisely was meant by "altering God's creation" apparently gave rise to vehement debate in the early period of qur'ānic commentary. At least such is the attestation of al-Samarqandī (d. 373/983)[2] some two and a half centuries later. He tells us:

> 'Ikrima said: "It is castration." Thus it is also transmitted from Ibn 'Abbās and Anas ibn Mālik. From Sa'īd ibn Jubayr it is transmitted that he said: "It is God's religion (*dīn Allāh*)." Thus it is also transmitted from aḍ-Ḍaḥḥāk and Mujāhid. It was told to Mujāhid that 'Ikrima said: "It is castration." Whereupon he said: "What is the matter with him, God curse him, because he knows that it is not castration." They then told this to 'Ikrima, who said: "It is God's nature (*fiṭrat Allāh*)."[3]

In the *Tafsīr* of al-Ṭabarī (d. 311/923), which was written about half a century earlier, we find Mujāhid even more outspoken:

> Al-Qāsim b. Abī Bazza said: "Mujāhid said to me: "Ask 'Ikrima about it." So I asked him and he said: "It is castration." Mujāhid said: "What is the matter with him, God curse him, for, by God, he knows that it is not castration." Then he said: "Ask him." So I asked him and 'Ikrima said: "Don't you listen to the word of God: *[So set thy face to the religion, a man of pure faith-] God's original (fiṭrat Allāh) upon which he originated mankind. There is no changing God's creation (khalq Allāh). That, surely, is God's religion.* (Q 30:30)?" I then reported this to Mujāhid, who said: "What is the matter with him, may God put him to shame."[4]

The point in this debate is basically a simple "it is, it isn't" argument. In both views the clue for the right interpretation is found in the words of Q 30:30 which are quoted in the report by al-Ṭabarī. The argument is whether the words *fiṭrat Allāh* and *khalq Allāh*, which here are apparently used as synonyms, are to be taken literally as denoting "nature" or "the natural order" in general, that is, "nature as God has created it," or metaphorically as "the original God-given innate religious nature of man." ʿIkrima expressed the first view and Mujāhid the latter.

Such differences of opinion between these early authorities form the warp and woof of al-Ṭabarī's and al-Samarqandī's commentaries. What is quite amazing, however, is the reported vehemence and abuse with which the arguments of both pupils of Ibn ʿAbbās, the "father of qur'ānic exegesis" were put forward. Curiously enough, this kind of debate seems to be almost entirely absent in the extant early *tafsīrs*, although later commentaries report these early differences of opinion in abundance. According to these later reports, the early commentators did not mince words about their opponents, as another example may show.

Here the question is about the precise identity of "on the ramparts are men" (*wa-ʿalā l-aʿrāfi rijālun*) in Q 7:46, where traditionally the word *aʿrāf* is taken to denote the limbo between paradise and hell. A number of early commentators held the view that these were either men whose good and bad deeds were in balance or men who had been killed in holy war but who had gone to war against the will of their fathers. Al-Samarqandī tells us:

> It was reported of Ibn Abī Mijlaz that he said: "They are the angels." That was reported to Mujāhid and he said: "Abū Mijlaz lies, God—exalted is he—has said: *on the ramparts are men.*" But then Abū Mijlaz said: "[I am right] because the angels are not female, but they are the servants of the Merciful. God has said: *And they [the unbelievers] have made the angels, who are themselves servants of the All-merciful, females*" (Q 43:19).[5]

Many later Qur'ān commentators, like al-Ṭabarī and al-Samarqandī, considered these debates about the meaning of many passages in the word of God as revealed to the Apostle of Islam as having really occurred among the founders of qur'ānic commentary. They not only extrapolated them from the enormous mass of traditions that they collected and presented in their commentaries, but they even quoted trustworthy traditions that reported these discussions and debates. And, of course, these discussions also helped to expound their own points of view more effectively.[6]

Nevertheless, other commentators apparently shrank from the idea that the trustworthy early commentators could have been at loggerheads. They tried to harmonize the reported conflicting opinions, as al-Naḥḥās (d. 338/950) did on the debate about "altering God's creation."[7] He reports the two different opinions as such but states that actually both opinions are reported from Ibn ʿAbbās as well as from ʿIkrima and then goes on to say, "These statements are not conflicting, because they refer to the performance of actions." To support this view he, interestingly enough, quotes the famous al-Ṭabarī, who lived one generation before him. However, the quotation is incomplete and suggests a more harmonizing tendency than we find in al-Ṭabarī's commentary. Admittedly, al-Ṭabarī also shows a harmonizing tendency, but at the same time he explicitly expresses his opinion that the interpretation as "God's religion" had to be preferred and that those who held that it applied only to castration and tattooing were wrong.[8]

This tendency to harmonize the conflicting interpretations of early authorities appears to have grown stronger with time.[9] And maybe rightly so. Perhaps too much attention had been attached to these early conflicts, as reported in much later sources.

The early sources themselves, of course, long remained silent, because they were no longer independently accessible.

In the last ten years, however, our firsthand knowledge of the early exegesis of the Qur'ān has been greatly improved because a number of early commentaries have now been edited.[10] With Claude Gilliot,[11] this stage before the introduction of grammatical considerations into qur'ānic exegesis should perhaps more appropriately be labeled proto-exegesis. It is to this early stage of qur'ānic exegesis that these later commentators referred. From these early commentaries, the history of the proto-exegesis of the Qur'ān can be reconstructed with somewhat more certainty than was possible before.

In broad outlines this history may be sketched as follows:[12] The beginnings of qur'ānic exegesis were rather modest. We may take for granted that the generation that first heard the revelation understood its meaning and needed only marginal guidance for its interpretation. The fact that, over time, the text of the Qur'ān required more and more interpretation was, among other things, due largely to the fact that the holy text itself had been instrumental in the establishment of a society and a linguistic community that had become quite different from the society in which the Qur'ān was revealed. Thus the qur'ānic message could be considered a co-instrumental factor in generating new interpretations of its text.

If we look carefully at the source material, it becomes clear that probably the earliest exegetical activity involved providing synonyms for words whose meaning was no longer entirely clear and that it took place in the process of teaching the proper way to recite the text. Some of these oral glosses occasionally found their way into the recitation itself, which, notwithstanding the promulgation of the vulgate text, was apparently not yet entirely fixed everywhere. This state of affairs must have gone on for quite some time. For instance, Mujāhid (d. 104/722), who lived at the end of the first Islamic century and to whom much important exegetical activity is ascribed by the Islamic tradition, is nevertheless known by his epithet *al-muqrī*, "the teacher of recitation."

The stores of such explanatory glosses gradually grew and were recorded, probably in lists. Tradition reports that Mujāhid himself came with his *alwāḥ* or "tablets" to his teacher, Ibn 'Abbās, by whose command he wrote down what was explained to him. Thus, writing became an important means of preserving the ever-growing store of explanations. Because of the lack of independent source material, we do not know exactly how orally transmitted glosses made in the process of recitation training evolved into an independent exegetical discipline, one that depended upon the collection and correct transmission of written material.

Nevertheless, although much is still not clear, there is sufficient evidence to support the reconstruction presented here, although other scholars have held different views. Sezgin,[13] on the basis of later reports, maintained that written commentaries had already been composed in the first generation after Muḥammad, and Wansbrough[14] proposed a later and different development on stylistic and typological grounds. In addition to arguments for my view that I have expounded elsewhere,[15] additional arguments for this reconstruction of the history of early *tafsīr* were recently advanced by Claude Gilliot.[16]

We also have reports about early opposition to qur'ānic exegesis, but most likely these should be taken as opposition to the use of exegesis for undermining political authority. This is probably one of the motives behind the general disapproval of the so-called *tafsīr bi-l-ra'y*, or exegesis that is based only on the exercise of one's own reasoning. Thus we find, for instance, that the exegetical work of people like 'Ikrima, who had Khārijī tendencies, and Muḥammad b. al-Sā'ib al-Kalbī, who leaned to Shī'ism, were discredited, notwithstanding the fact that they were considered to be important pupils of Ibn 'Abbās himself.

Another type of *tafsīr*-activity that was frowned upon by authorities at the beginning of the second Islamic century was the so-called *tafsīr al-qawm* or what could be called popular exegesis, in the sense of uncontrolled storytelling without mention of sources. Such exegesis was liable to originate from the wildest fantasies. It may be said in passing that the one important example of such a *tafsīr* that has survived and been published, that of Muqātil b. Sulaymān, is an interesting source for an early popular Islam which, perhaps, at the time of its composition was not yet divorced from orthodoxy.

Despite all attempts to the contrary, orthodoxy could not eradicate the popular stories; they kept coming back as illustrations for the qur'ānic lectionary, but increasingly attached by a reliable chain of transmitters to a trustworthy authority, so that the wilder flights of imagination were at least temporarily banned. However, on the basis of the material we now have at our disposal, a supposed general opposition to qur'ānic exegesis as such apparently did not exist.

In what I consider to be the mainstream of qur'ānic commentary, the number of glossed words and passages gradually increased for about two or three generations but remained embedded in a living, not yet fixed tradition. This means that not only was the store of explanations guarded and transmitted by the successive generations who belonged to a specific tradition, but also that it was supplemented with new material considered to be in accordance with what each generation had been taught. In this respect it is irrelevant whether separate lists of explanatory glosses to the Qur'ān were already in circulation earlier, because if so, they certainly were not seen as finite. From the available sources, we can infer that a number of such circles of transmission must have existed in the latter half of the first and the beginning of the second Islamic century. They cherished comparable but not identical stores of exegetical material, consisting mainly of lexical and paraphrastic glosses to the Qur'ān.

In the first half of the second/eighth century individual authors started to compose books that contained their store of qur'ānic interpretations, whether these were mainly from one traditional circle, as in the case of the pupils of Ibn Abi Najīḥ, who had been the pupil of Mujāhid, or from different circles, as in the case of Sufyān al-Thawrī. They knew, of course, where the material they recorded came from, and so one generation later their pupils had no problem transmitting their material according to the rules that had now become firmly established: proper *isnāds*, chains of transmitters, were added to the individual comments that were recorded. And so within one or two generations the character of *tafsīr* changed. Around the middle of the second Islamic century the first step to an independent branch of learning was taken: to fix the different traditional stores of qur'ānic commentary in writing. One generation later the next step gave it respectability by making it adhere to the rules of the game of traditionalist learning.

Once this last step was taken, the way was open to the inclusion of all kinds of material, such as juridical and narrative, that was trustworthily transmitted from one authority. But also permitted was inclusion of material that conflicted with the view of another, provided it had also been trustworthily transmitted. Even conflicting views of the same authority, but with different lines of transmission, could be recorded.

In the available sources which go back to the middle of the second Islamic century, of course, outright discussion and debate do not occur, because these sources consist mainly of redactions of the paraphrastic material which had been recorded from the early stages of qur'ānic exegesis. They still were not much more than authenticated lists of synonyms, short explanations, and occasionally a few illustrative stories.

So the question remains: How can we know if later reports about such early discussion and debate reflect a historical reality? Or, to put it differently: Since the firsthand sources which date back to the middle of the second Islamic century by their nature do not, except for the odd exception, record discussion and debate, should the reports about early debates be considered nothing more than a *topos*, employed to introduce the arguments of earlier authorities into the debates that were going on in the late third and the fourth Islamic centuries?

In one of the earlier commentaries, that of 'Abd al-Razzāq al-Ṣan'ānī (d. 211/827), the debate between Mujāhid and 'Ikrima is, exceptionally, already recorded, albeit much more succinctly: A tradition from al-Qāsim b. Abī Bazza is transmitted in which he reports that Mujāhid ordered him to ask 'Ikrima about "altering God's creation." "He said: 'It is castration.' Then I reported this to Mujāhid and he said: 'He is wrong; *and they will alter God's creation*, he said, [it means] God's religion.'"[17]

This tradition from al-Qāsim b. Abī Bazza occurs in the context of an enumeration of six traditions which give an explanation of the phrase in question. Four are, in the customary form of the early *tafsīr* sources, only synonyms and two are somewhat more elaborate. This presentation of the six traditions, however, does not appear to be random.

The first one is on the authority of 'Abd al-Razzāq's master Ma'mar, who is normally the only authority from whom he records a *tafsīr*. This tradition, which goes back to Qatāda (d. 117/735), gives *dīn Allāh* "God's religion" as the equivalent of *khalq Allāh* "God's creation." Then a tradition going back to al-Rabī' b. Anas is mentioned which gives *al-khiṣā'* "castration" as equivalent. Next there is a tradition going back to a certain Shubayl, who had heard Shahr b. Ḥawshab (d. between 100/718 and 112/730)[18] reading the passage *and they will alter God's creation* and then saying, "Amongst that is castration." Shubayl then consulted Abū al-Tayyāḥ (Yazīd b. Ḥumayd al-Ḍuba'ī), who asked al-Ḥasan about castration of small cattle and he said, "There is no objection to it."

This one is followed by the previously-mentioned tradition about Mujāhid's denial of 'Ikrima's opinion which is backed up by another one, on al-Qāsim's authority, but through a different intermediary stating the same. The series is finished with a tradition on the authority of Sufyān al-Thawrī and on the final authority of Ibrāhīm (b. Jarīr al-Bajalī, d. around 120/738) stating again that "God's creation" means "God's religion."

Obviously, this sequence is well ordered: The opinion of 'Abd al-Razzāq's master is given, then the conflicting opinion is introduced. This conflicting opinion is weakened by the third tradition and invalidated by the fourth, the fifth, and the sixth. The sequence bears all the marks of a clever briefing for debate.

From the same locus in the *tafsīr* of Sufyān al-Thawrī, who lived one generation before 'Abd al-Razzāq, it becomes clear what the probable reason is for our finding there two traditions stating the same thing—that it is "God's religion," instead of only one. And certainly in Ādam b. Abī Iyās' redaction of Warqā' b. 'Umar's edition of Mujāhid's *tafsīr* the function of the added traditions[19] is enlightening.

Not only Mujāhid's opinion as transmitted by Warqā''s master 'Abdallāh b. Abī Najīḥ is given, but Warqā', just like his contemporary Sufyān, added another one on the final authority of Ibrāhīm (al-Naja'ī) stating the same opinion as that of his contemporary Mujāhid. Then one generation later Ādam again added two more traditions. One contradicts the opinion of Mujāhid and one confirms it. Ādam did the same as his contemporary 'Abd al-Razzāq: he arranged the traditions in a sequence that created the sense of an ongoing debate. This is how he did it:

He started with a tradition on the final authority of Ibn 'Abbās stating that this passage is about the castration of cattle (*ikhṣā' al-bahā'im*). This is followed by two traditions stating that the passage is about changing God's religion: the one Warqā' added and another one which Ādam himself introduced on the same final authority. The sequence—and thus the presumed debate—is culminated with the same opinion transmitted from Mujāhid according to the regular chain of transmitters in this *tafsīr*. But this one, the proposed "knockout," has a nice twist. Mujāhid is reported to have said that "creation" (*khalq*) is here synonymous with "the original innate religious nature of man" (*fiṭra*) which is synonymous with "religion" (*dīn*). Thus the interpretation is linked to Q 30:30, where the context clearly favors this equation.

Needless to say, in the same early *tafsīr* the identical sequence, somewhat more succinctly stated, is found in connection with the interpretation of Q 30:30, with the slight difference that there the castration argument is transmitted by Ādam on the final authority of 'Ikrima. (Probably the whole argument had to do with the application of inheritance law,[20] but this issue does not concern us here.)

Many similar examples of presenting the case for a certain interpretation may be found in the available commentaries of the middle and late second century of Islam. Sometimes the discussion apparently occurred within a group adhering to the same tradition, as, for example, in the commentary on Q 2:237 in Warqā's edition of *Tafsīr Mujāhid*[21] about the question of who decides on the remission of payment of half the dowry to the wife in case of a divorce before the consummation of a marriage. In the Qur'ān this decision is given to the person "in whose hand is the knot of marriage." According to the transmitted opinion of Mujāhid, this is the bride's *walī* or guardian. Warqā' apparently disagreed, and to prove his point he adduced a tradition from al-Shu'bī that the decision rests with the husband.

'Abd al-Razzāq's master Ma'mar apparently had the same problem, although he recorded from Mujāhid the opposite view that it was the husband and from al-Ḥasan that it was the guardian of the wife. From Muqātil's *tafsīr*[22] we know that the real argument was probably about the permissibility of the payment of less than half the dowry, in which case the *walī* was the one to permit it, or more than half, in which case the husband was the one to decide.

In most cases, however, arguments are added that run against the opinions of the followers of other schools. By the middle of the second Islamic century, apparently the need to be prepared for what one could call "cross-platform debate" was distinctly felt. In his edition of Mujāhid's *tafsīr*, Warqā' added some eighty traditions in order to stress a point, and in his redaction Ādam added more than three hundred. In the commentaries of Sufyān and 'Abd al-Razzāq we find the same phenomenon. In these three *tafsīrs* the additions are often clustered around the same verses, such as Q 2:197, 237, 282; Q 4:6, 43, 119; Q 7:40, 46; Q 9:3; Q 11:5; Q 12:110; Q 14:25, 28; Q 17:16, 110;

Q 22:28; Q 24:3; Q 32:21; Q 51:17; Q 53:11. All seem to concern passages whose meanings were open to discussion or debate. Sometimes the added traditions simply give alternatives to the transmitted explanation of a qur'ānic simile, as is the case with Q 7:40: "Those that cry lies to Our signs and wax proud against them—the gates of heaven shall not be opened to them, nor shall they enter Paradise until the camel (*al-jamal*) passes through the eye of the needle." Sufyān only mentions a tradition from Ibn 'Abbās that the word *al-jamal* here means a hawser or thick rope, Ādam adds to the same explanation of Mujāhid a tradition that it actually does mean a camel, and 'Abd al-Razzāq gives two traditions affirming that a real camel is meant, one of them being on the authority of Sufyān, in whose own *tafsīr* only the meaning of hawser is mentioned.[23]

Often the purport of the discussion may be understood only from later sources, as in the case of Q 2:197. In Warqā''s edition of Mujāhid's commentary[24] we find Mujāhid's view that the passage "the Pilgrimage is in months well-known" means, "Shawwāl, Dhū l-Qa'da and ten days of Dhū l-Ḥijja" to be corroborated from a different authority, and in Sufyān al-Thawrī's commentary[25] the same opinion is mentioned thrice. From al-Ṭabarī's commentary[26] we learn that quite a few early authorities held the view that the whole of the month of Dhū l-Ḥijja belonged to the pilgrimage, the interpretation maintained in the school of which 'Abd al-Razzāq was a representative. It also becomes clear from al-Ṭabarī that the dispute actually was not about the duration of the *ḥajj*, but about the period in which the *'umra*, the lesser pilgrimage, could be undertaken as separate from the *ḥajj*: during nine months only or during nine months plus the last twenty days of Dhū l-Ḥijja.

In the later sources the different exegetical opinions that were discussed are nearly always put in the mouths of the early authorities of the formative period of qur'ānic commentary. We may conclude from the available sources that at least by the middle and late second century of Islam, editors and redactors of qur'ānic exegesis not only were transmitting the material from their masters, but were also considering views that deviated from those that prevailed in their own schools, either for their own edification or to augment the authority of the views of their schools through confrontation with dissenters, thereby arming their pupils for debate.

Whether or not actual debate was going on in an earlier period among, for example, the pupils of Ibn 'Abbās, as is reported by al-Ṭabarī and al-Samarqandī, cannot be conclusively proven from the earliest independent sources at our disposal. But if debate took place, these early authorities probably did not do it face to face. That, at least, may be inferred from al-Ṭabarī and al-Samarqandī's presentations of the debate on the meaning of "God's creation," (*khalq Allāh*) but also already from 'Abd al-Razzāq's commentary.

The apparent briefings for debate in the early sources clearly suggest, however, that even at an early stage the different, more or less independent circles of *tafsīr* probably interacted rather indirectly. Whether this was already the case before the second half of the first century of Islam is still open to debate.

Notes

1. Translation of qur'ānic quotations is according to Arberry.

2. Recently his *tafsīr* was published in Beirut: *Tafsīr al-Samarqandī*. According to Sezgin (GAS 445–50), the remark by Schacht (*EI*, new ed., 1:137a) that this *tafsīr* was printed in Cairo

in 1310/1892–93 is erroneous. The Beirut edition seems to be the first complete one, although a partial edition, edited by 'Abd al-Raḥīm Aḥmad al-Zaqqa, was published in Baghdad in 1985–86.

3. *Tafsīr al-Samarqandī*, 1:398.

4. *Tafsīr Ṭabarī*, ed. Shākir, 8:216–17; ed. Beirut, 4:282.

5. *Tafsīr al-Samarqandī*, 1:543.

6. As such they appear be a *topos*. At least the above-mentioned examples bear in their structure a clear similarity to the *topos* of Ṣabīgh b. 'Isl and others who kept on asking questions about ambiguous passages of the Qur'ān or about the precise definition of the division of spoils. Cf. Leemhuis, "Origins and Early Development of the *tafsīr* Tradition," 16–18, and Gilliot, "Les débuts de l'exégèse coranique," 84–85.

7. al-Naḥḥās, *Ma'ānī l-Qur'ān al-karīm*, 2:195–97.

8. *Tafsīr al-Ṭabarī*, ed. Shākir, 8:222–23; ed. Beirut, 4:285.

9. See, e.g., al-Dhahabī, *al-Tafsīr wa-l-mufassirūn*, 1:142–48.

10. The following are available in more or less critical editions: Mujāhid b. Jabr, *Tafsīr Mujāhid*; idem, *Tafsīr al-imām Mujāhid ibn Jabr*; Sufyān al-Thawrī, *Tafsīr al-Qur'ān al-karīm*; al-San'ānī, *Tafsīr al-Qur'ān*; and Muqātil b. Sulaymañ, *Tafsīr*.

11. Gilliot, "Les débuts."

12. See also Leemhuis, "Origins and Early Development," and idem, "The Koran and Its Exegesis."

13. GAS, 19.

14. Wansbrough, *Quranic Studies*, 119–246.

15. Leemhuis, "Origins and Early Development," 19–22.

16. Gilliot, "Les débuts."

17. al-Ṣan'ānī, *Tafsīr*, 1:173.

18. See *EI*, new ed., 7:576a.

19. *Tafsīr Mujāhid*, ed. al-Sūratī, 1:174–75; ed. Abū l-Nīl, 292–93.

20. See *EI*, new ed., 2:931–32, s.v. "*fiṭra*."

21. *Tafsīr Mujāhid*, ed. al-Sūratī, 1:110; ed. Abū l-Nīl, 238.

22. *Tafsīr Muqātil*, 1:200. Actually Muqātil held the view that the decision about not wanting to receive half the dowry was to be taken by the divorced wife herself, and the decision of paying the whole dowry by the husband.

23. *Tafsīr Sufyān al- Thawrī*, Rampur ed., 70; Beirut ed., 112; *Tafsīr Mujāhid*, ed. al-Sūratī, 1:236; ed. Abū l-Nīl, 336–37; al-Ṣan'ānī, *Tafsīr*, 2:228–29.

24. *Tafsīr Mujāhid*, ed. al-Sūratī, 1:101; ed. Abū l-Nīl, 228.

25. *Tafsīr Sufyān al-Thawrī*, Rampur ed., 22–23; Beirut ed., 62–63.

26. *Tafsīr al-Ṭabarī*, ed. Shākir, 4:114–21; Beirut ed., 2:267–71.

Bibliography

Arberry, Arthur J. *The Koran Interpreted*. London: Oxford University Press, 1964.

al-Dhahabī, Muḥammad Ḥusayn. *al-Tafsīr wa l-mufassirūn*. 3 vols. Cairo: Maktabat Wahba, 1416/1956.

Gilliot, Claude. "Les débuts de l'exégèse coranique." In *Les premières écritures islamiques = Revue du monde musulman et de la Méditerranée* 58 (1990): 82–100.

Leemhuis, Fred. "The Koran and Its Exegesis: From Memorizing to Learning." In *Centres of Learning: Learning and Location in Pre-Modern Europe and the Near East*. Ed. Jan Willem Drijvers and A. A. MacDonald, 91–102. Leiden: E. J. Brill, 1995.

———. "Origins and Early Development of the *tafsīr* Tradition." In *Approaches to the History of the Interpretation of the Qur'ān*. Ed. A. Rippin, 13–30. Oxford: Clarendon Press, 1988.

Mujāhid b. Jabr. *Tafsīr al-imām Mujāhid b. Jabr*. Ed. Muḥammad 'Abd al-Salām Abū l-Nīl. Cairo: Dār al-Fikr al-Islāmī al-Ḥadītha, 1989.

——. *Tafsīr Mujāhid*. Ed. 'Abd al-Raḥmān al-Ṭāhir b. Muḥammad al-Sūratī. Islamabad, 1976. Reprint, Beirut: Al-Manshūrāt al-'Ilmiyya, n.d.

Muqātil b. Sulaymān. *Tafsīr Muqātil ibn Sulaymān*. Ed. 'Abdallāh Maḥmūd Shiḥāta. 5 vols. Cairo: al-Hay'a al-Miṣriyya al-'Āmma lil-Kitāb, 1979–89.

al-Naḥḥās, Abū Ja'far. *Ma'ānī l-Qur'ān al-karīm*. Ed. Muḥammad 'Alī al-Sābūnī. 6 vols. Mecca: Jāmi'at Umm al-Qurā, 1988–89.

al-Samarqandī, Abū al-Layth Naṣr b. Muḥammad b. Aḥmad b. Ibrāhīm. *Tafsīr al-Samarqandī al-musammā Baḥr al-'ulūm li-Abī l-Layth Naṣr b. Muḥammad b. Aḥmad b. Ibrāhīm al-Samarqandī*. Ed. 'Alī Muḥammad Mu'awwaḍ, 'Ādil Aḥmad 'Abd al-Mawjūd, and Zakariyya 'Abd al-Majīd al-Nūtī. 3 vols. Beirut: Dār al-Kutub al-'Ilmiyya, 1413/1993.

al-Ṣan'ānī, Abd al-Razzāq. *Tafsīr al-Qur'ān lil-imām 'Abd al-Razzāq b. Hishām al-Ṣan'ānī*. Ed. Muṣṭafā Muslim Muḥammad. 3 vols. Riyadh: Maktabat al-Rushd, 1410/1989.

Sezqin, Fuat. *Geschichte des arabischen Schrifttums*. Vol. 1, Leiden: E. J. Brill, 1967.

al-Ṭabarī, Abū Ja'far Muḥammad b. Jarīr. *Tafsīr al-Ṭabarī al-musammā Jāmi' al-Bayān fī Tafsīr al-Qur'ān*. 12 vols. Beirut: Dār al-Kutub al-'Ilmiyya, 1412/1992.

——. *Tafsīr al-Ṭabarī: Jāmi' al-bayān 'an ta'wīl al-Qur'ān*. Ed. Maḥmūd Muḥammad Shākir and Aḥmad Muḥammad Shākir. 16 vols. to date. Cairo, 1955–69.

al-Thawrī, Sufyān. *Tafsīr al-Qur'ān al-karīm lil-imām Abī 'Abdallāh Sufyān b. Sa'īd b. Masrūq al-Thawrī al-Kūfī*. Ed. Imtiyāz 'Alī 'Arshī. Rampur: Maktabat Riḍā, 1965. Reprint, Beirut: Dār al-Kutub al-'Ilmiyya, 1403/1983 (without some of the indices).

Wansbrough, J. *Quranic Studies: Sources and Methods of Scriptural Interpretations*. Oxford: Oxford University Press, 1977.

22

Weaknesses in the Arguments for the Early Dating of Qur'ānic Commentary

HERBERT BERG

Medieval and even modern exegeses of the Qur'ān are heavily indebted to the commentary purporting to come from the first three centuries of Islam. At an early stage many Muslim exegetes attempted to limit the scope of possible meanings of the Qur'ān by demanding that exegesis be based on the received tradition, and not on personal opinion. Thus, most early and medieval qur'ānic exegesis comes in the form of *ḥadīths*—the same form that dominates Islamic legal and historical writings. A *ḥadīth* is a report of something Muḥammad, his Companions, or other early prominent Muslims said or did. Each *ḥadīth* comes with a chain of transmitters (the *isnād*) that demonstrates the authenticity and indicates the provenance of the report (the *matn*) to which it is attached. While Muslim scholars usually accept that some *matns* were fabricated by the unscrupulous and were supplied with equally fabricated or modified *isnāds* (the chains of transmitters which are meant to guarantee authenticity) to project them back upon respected Muslims of the past, they also maintain that most of these fabrications have been identified by the rigorous examination of their *isnāds*.

Skepticism regarding the authenticity of *ḥadīths* as a whole was first expressed by Ignaz Goldziher when he suggested that they do "not serve as a document for the history of the infancy of Islam, but rather as a reflection of the tendencies which appeared in the community during the maturer stages of its development."[1] For many Islamicists, Joseph Schacht's work on legal *ḥadīths* provided conclusive proof for Goldziher's claim.[2] Together Goldziher and Schacht seem to undermine the very foundation upon which Muslim law and history as well as qur'ānic interpretation have been built. Nabia Abbott, Fuat Sezgin, and Mohammad Azami, however, have each argued for a continuous written and oral transmission of *ḥadīths*—a process which for them guarantees the authenticity of the transmitted material.[3] Because their challenges to Goldziher's and Schacht's skepticism rests largely on ascription, their attempt to salvage some or all of the purportedly historical information contained in *ḥadīths* is unconvincing. Other scholars have sought an intermediate position between Goldziher and Schacht on the one hand, and Abbott, Sezgin, and Azami on the other. Each of these scholars sees the arguments of Goldziher and Schacht as compelling, but each also attempts either to push the date from which *ḥadīths* become reliable into the early decades of Islam (in the cases of

G. H. A. Juynboll and Harald Motzki) or to circumvent the issue of authenticity (in the cases of Fazlur Rahman and Gregor Schoeler).[4] Clearly, the debate over the authenticity of Islamic texts, most of which rely on *ḥadīths* or at least *isnāds* is far from over. And its critical importance to the study of the first two centuries of Islam was definitively demonstrated by John Wansbrough when he pushed Goldziher's skepticism to its logical, albeit extreme conclusion.[5]

Whether this same skepticism should apply to exegetical *ḥadīths* is also unresolved. This genre of *ḥadīths* has some unique characteristics which might suggest that they are inherently more reliable. First, qur'ānic commentary rarely comes in the form of tradition from the Prophet. With the notable exception of the renowned 'Abd Allāh b. 'Abbās (d. 67–68/686–88) most qur'ānic exegetes were not even counted as Companions, according to their *isnāds*. By Schacht's own guideline, "The more perfect the *isnād*, the later the tradition,"[6] exegetical *ḥadīths* should be more reliable since they have shorter *isnāds*. Moreover, Juynboll suggests that it is likely most *ḥadīths* were put into circulation by Successors and Successors to the Successors (that is, the third and fourth generations of Muslims).[7] This idea too is in accord with what most *isnāds* of exegetical *ḥadīths* claim. Second, there were no schools of *tafsīr* in the same way as there were schools of law that were in active competition with each other. Thus, the strong rivalries that forced legal scholars to discover corroborating *ḥadīths* appear to have had much less influence on exegetes and the transmitters of *tafsīr*.

Wansbrough, however, believes that exegetical *ḥadīths* are not a unique genre of *ḥadīths*. They have the same origin as historical *ḥadīths* and legal *ḥadīths*, the origin of the latter having been well described by Schacht. According to Wansbrough: "That Shāfi'ī's stringent standards with regard to prophetical *ḥadīths* were not applied in the fields of history and exegesis is an impression derived from a wholly artificial classification of their contents. The substance of history, of exegesis, and of law was identical."[8] The uniqueness of exegetical *ḥadīths* has been further undermined by Claude Gilliot. Noting the hagiographical nature of the biographical reports, Gilliot demonstrates that a mythic status developed around Ibn 'Abbās with respect to qur'ānic commentary.[9] It would seem that eventually Ibn 'Abbās and his students came to be seen as the proper source for exegetical *ḥadīths* in the same way that Muḥammad and his Companions did for legal *ḥadīths*. Perhaps this happened in response to the 'Abbāsid revolution, as Fred Leemhuis suggests,[10] or as part of the proliferation of Companion *isnāds*, as Wansbrough suggests.[11] Also Gilliot points out that exegetical traditions, at least those of al-Ṭabarī, also participate in the definition and elaboration of an orthodoxy and orthopraxy, and *isnāds* function to emphasize the continuity of these beliefs and practices. That is to say, *isnāds* "prove" that Islam as it was defined in the eighth and ninth centuries had always been thus.[12] Taken together, the myth of Ibn 'Abbās and the ideological importance of *isnāds* suggest a scenario in which the production of *isnāds* in *tafsīr* material might have been much the same as that of *isnāds* in other genres of *ḥadīths*—even if there were no competing schools of *tafsīr*.

Even prior to the work of Wansbrough and Gilliot, some scholars saw the implications of Goldziher's and Schacht's claims and set out to prove the general reliability of exegetical *ḥadīths*. The dissertations of Heribert Horst[13] and Georg Stauth[14] are the earliest works to address the authenticity question. Although Horst completed his dissertation in 1951 and Stauth his in 1969 and neither has been published in complete form, they are still regularly adduced as evidence in support of authenticity. Scholars who have used Horst include Georg Stauth himself, Nabia Abbott, Fuat Sezgin, Isaiah Goldfeld, Harald Motzki, and Kees Versteegh.[15] Those who cite Stauth include Motzki, Versteegh, and Leemhuis.[16] All of these scholars, in turn, are cited by others, and when combined may give the impression that a consensus has emerged about the authenticity of early exegetical *ḥadīths*. The influence of Horst and Stauth therefore demands that their works be examined more critically than they have. Had their dissertations been published, surely numerous reviews would have scrutinized their methods before their results were so readily accepted. Because of methodological problems, I will argue that the use of either of these works to support the authenticity of early exegetical *ḥadīths* is largely unwarranted.

Heribert Horst

Heribert Horst was the first to study the *isnāds* of the exegetical *ḥadīths* of al-Ṭabarī's *Tafsīr*. His source-analytical method relies primarily on accepting at face value the information presented in *isnāds*. Horst surveys the approximately 37,000 *ḥadīths*[17] in the *Tafsīr* to determine the frequency of each different *isnād*. He discovers that 11,364 *isnāds* are cited but once, 859 are cited twice, 295 three times, and so forth. Thus, *over* a third of the *isnāds* appear but once, while only ninety-one appear more than fifteen times, and of these, only twenty-one appear more than one hundred times.[18] Horst then examines these twenty-one *isnāds* in detail. He identifies each of the transmitters along with the main variations of each *isnād* and notes that even the most frequently cited *isnāds* are not uniformly or continuously distributed through the *Tafsīr*.[19] From this study, Horst draws several conclusions. He asserts that al-Ṭabarī had several qur'ānic commentaries from older authorities in written form at his disposal, including at least one transmission of the *tafsīr* of Mujāhid b. Jabr (d. 104/722) and several from Ibn 'Abbās.[20] Horst observes that many of the *isnāds* appear for only part of the Qur'ān. Since it is improbable that al-Ṭabarī would neglect a possible source—for he was even willing to put contradictory *ḥadīths* side by side—Horst reasons that many of the manuscripts were available to the compiler only in incomplete form.[21] Although there are reasons to doubt Horst's conclusions about al-Ṭabarī's sources,[22] his conclusions regarding early exegesis are more relevant and problematic.

Horst notes that the *isnāds* he examined are generally very short. The oldest transmitter/exegete is Ibn 'Abbās. The next oldest authorities are the students of Ibn 'Abbās, namely Mujāhid and al-Ḍaḥḥāk (both of whom are considered Successors of Successors, that is, third generation), and the others are from the fourth to the sixth generations.[23] Thus, very few of the exegetical *ḥadīths* adduced by al-Ṭabarī claim to come from Companions. This fact, Horst suggests, implies significant differences between legal and exegetical *ḥadīths*: (1) The "prophetic" rule promulgated by al-Shāfi'ī for legal *ḥadīths* did not extend to exegetical *ḥadīths* even in al-Ṭabarī's time. In fact, the vast majority of the *isnāds* in al-Ṭabarī's *Tafsīr* do not extend back beyond the year 100/719, half a century after the death of most Companions. And (2), since this date is the time given by Schacht for the beginning of the use of the *isnāds*, the exegetical *ḥadīths* adduced by al-Ṭabarī are more trustworthy by far than the legal *ḥadīths* contained in the six canonical collections, partly because of the written transmission of exegetical materials. Horst even ventures to date the origin of the largest part of the qur'ānic exegetical traditions as 80 A.H. to 130 A.H.[24] He concludes: "After careful assessment, a minimum of half of all *isnāds* in al-Ṭabarī's *Tafsīr* go back to the first half of the second century, and there is no ground on which to doubt the authenticity of this portion of the traditions, which is not to say that *ḥadīths* whose *isnāds* date from the earlier period are therefore untrustworthy."[25] This conclusion by Horst has been embraced by many scholars as constituting the definitive analysis of al-Ṭabarī's sources and early qur'ānic exegesis. This acceptance is somewhat unjustified, however, for Horst's study is methodologically unsound.

Horst examines those *isnāds* that appear in the *Tafsīr* at least one hundred times. Of the 13,026 different *isnāds* in al-Ṭabarī's *Tafsīr*, twenty-one different *isnāds* covering 15,700 *ḥadīths* are investigated. While this sample represents a substantial portion of the *ḥadīths* (44 percent), it does not represent a significant number of the *isnāds* (less than two-tenths of a percent).[26] More important, although Schacht admits that the introduction of the use of *isnāds* is relatively early, the implication is not that the appended traditions are more reliable. The date of introduction marks the beginning of *isnād* fabrication. Al-Shāfi'ī's insistence on the presence of a sound *isnād* spurred the proliferation of *ḥadīths* and the manufacture of *isnāds*. The very presence of *isnāds* in exegetical *ḥadīths* suggests al-Shāfi'ī's influence in the realm of qur'ānic commentary. That *isnāds* are not extended back to Muḥammad may well be due to the association of exegesis with Ibn 'Abbās and others as its proper source. Therefore, Horst's distinction between legal and exegetical *ḥadīths* is obviated. Most problematic is Horst's circular argument. He relies on the information contained in *isnāds* to prove their reliability. Evidence drawn from ascriptions is unconvincing to those skeptical of them. As a result, while Horst's study may be an interesting exercise, it cannot support its claims about the early exegetical activities of Companions such as Ibn 'Abbās and his purported students, such as Mujāhid.

Georg Stauth

Unlike Horst, who examines only *isnāds*, Stauth examines the *matns* of exegetical *hadīths*. In so doing, Stauth attempts to wrestle with the conflicting claims of Goldziher and Sezgin. The issues on which the two are at odds concern the validity and accuracy (and hence the authenticity) of the *isnād* system, the existence of theological literature during the Umayyad period, and the written/oral transmission of literature during this period. On the basis of similar content in the various "recensions," he concludes that *isnāds* serve as a fairly good indicator of the provenance and chronology of early exegetical *ḥadīths*.

More specifically, Stauth compares the *tafsīr* of Mujāhid b. Jabr as found in the independent *Tafsīr* attributed to him[27] and as found in the *Tafsīr* of al-Ṭabarī. This analysis is supplemented by a comparison of the al-Ṭabarī transmissions with those contained in the *Tafsīrs* attributed to Sufyān al-Thawrī[28] and 'Abd al-Razzāq—Ma'mar b. Rāshid.[29] Stauth recognizes that the sources for al-Ṭabarī's *Tafsīr* are hypothetical, but accords, in the manner of Sezgin, enough trust in *isnāds* to allow a comparison of the transmissions of the material from Mujāhid. Most of the material in the purportedly independent *Tafsīr* has the *isnād* 'Abd al-Raḥmān—Ibrāhīm—Ādam—Warqā'—Ibn Abi Najīḥ—Mujāhid. Even though, according to the *isnāds*, the bulk of the *ḥadīths* originated with Mujāhid and the last non-Mujāhid material was introduced by Ādam ibn Abī Iyās,[30] for the sake of clarity and parallelism, I will refer to this work as the *Tafsīr* of Ibn Shādhān, the first transmitter of the material not to appear in the individual *isnāds*.[31] Using the work of Horst, Stauth selects four prominent transmissions from Mujāhid found in al-Ṭabarī's *Tafsīr*, three of which share the same student of Mujāhid (namely, Ibn 'Abī Najīḥ), and one of which also shares with Ibn Shādhān's *Tafsīr* the transmitter Warqā'. See table 1. By selecting these particular transmissions from Mujāhid, Stauth hopes to examine whether the contents have changed after 150/767 (using the two Warqā'—Ibn Abī Najīḥ—Mujāhid transmissions), and to what extent the "text" changed after 120/737 (by comparing all five transmissions).

There are 1,730 *ḥadīths* in Ibn Shādhān's *Tafsīr* that cite Mujāhid (using *isnād* 1 of Diagram 1), and there are approximately 1,700, 1,021, 680, and 1,800 *ḥadīths* in al-Ṭabarī's *Tafsīr* that cite Mujāhid (using *isnāds* 2, 3, 4, and 5 of Diagram 1). From all these *ḥadīths* Stauth selects a mere thirty-six qur'ānic lemmata for which Mujāhid *ḥadīths* are adduced in both *Tafsīrs*. Stauth's comparison of the contents of the selected *ḥadīths* yields several observations. The three Ibn Abī Najīḥ—Mujāhid transmissions in al-Ṭabarī's *Tafsīr* (*isnāds* 2, 3, and 4) agree more with each other than with the corresponding transmission (*isnād* 1) in Ibn Shādhān's *Tafsīr*, which is also an Ibn Abī Najīḥ—Mujāhid transmission. This finding, for Stauth, implies that the three underwent more redactional work. Even the extent of the variation between the Ibn Jurayj transmission (*isnād* 5), whose *isnād* shares only Mujāhid (and not Ibn Abī Najīḥ) with the others transmissions, largely corresponds to the variation between the Ibn Abī Najīḥ transmissions themselves. That is, the *matns* attached to *isnāds* 2, 3, 4, and 5 have more in common with each other than with that attached to *isnād* 1, even though *isnāds* 1, 2, 3, and 4 share more transmitters than do *isnāds* 2, 3, 4, and 5. And so Stauth concludes that all four transmissions in al-Ṭabarī's *Tafsīr* must have differed more than they do now and were harmonized to some extent in the compiler's own time.[32] Stauth, having ignored the fact that the *Tafsīr* of Ibn Shādhān, who died after 424/1032, is over a century later than that of al-Ṭabarī,[33] is forced to invent a hypothetical redactor.[34] Why the *Tafsīr* of Ibn Shādhān is thought to be immune from redactional activity is not clear. That the apparently separate transmissions of Mujāhid's material in al-Ṭabarī's *Tafsīr* were redacted rather than the one in Ibn Shādhān's seems less plausible. Moreover, if a redactor were necessary to explain Stauth's observation, the seventy-two-year gap between Ibn Shādhān and 'Abd al-Raḥmān certainly leaves room for one.

After an additional comparison between the Mujāhid-transmissions in the *Tafsīrs* attributed to Sufyān al-Thawrī and 'Abd al-Razzāq—Ma'mar and the *Tafsīrs* of Ibn Shādhān and al-Ṭabarī,[35] Stauth also suggests that the materials of the various transmissions have a common source, an *Urtext*. The material does differ in terms of content, at times significantly, but it is fundamentally in accord. This text is presumed to date from 120/737.[36] However, Stauth suggests that the transmitters of it had a relatively free approach to this *Urtext*, and so it cannot be reconstructed on the basis of these later works. In this regard, Stauth is at odds with Sezgin. As for when the variations were introduced, he concludes, using the evidence of the *isnāds*, that little variation was introduced after 150/767 and that most of it occurred in the preceding three

Table 1. "Recensions" of Mujāhid's *tafsīr* used by Stauth

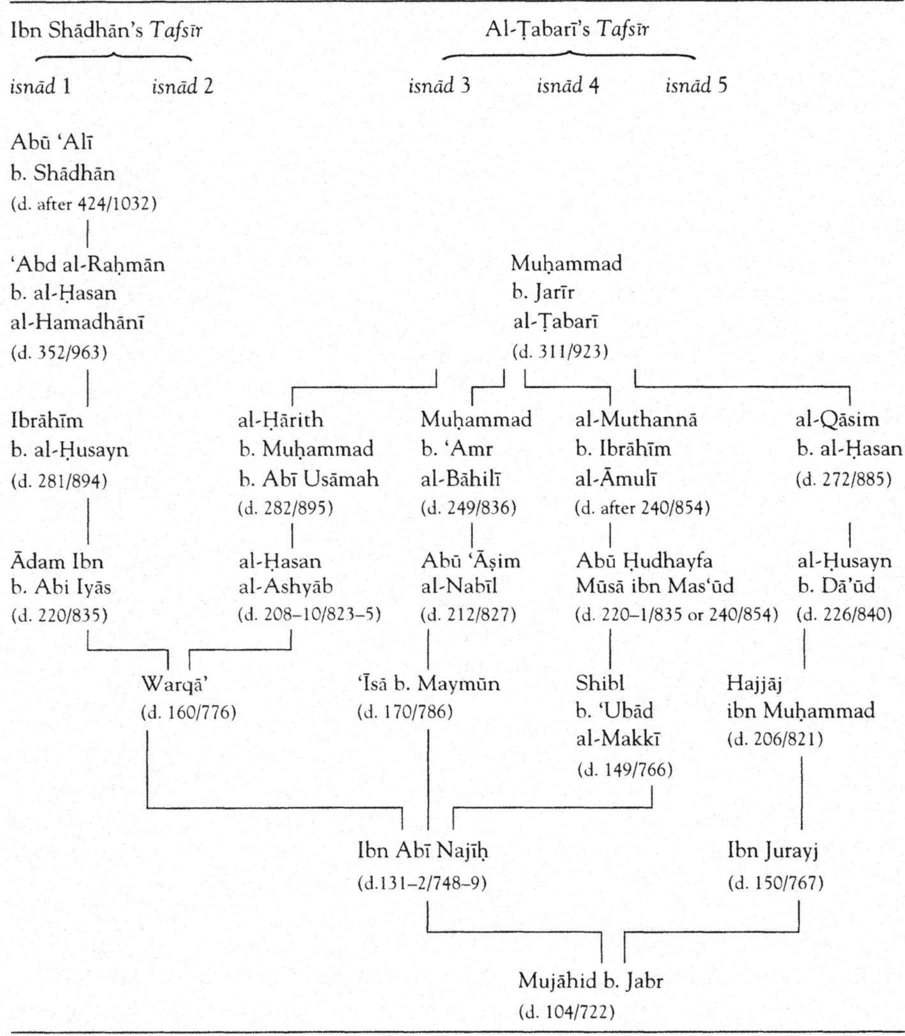

There are several suspiciously large gaps between the death dates of some of the transmitters. The seventy-two years between the death of Ibn Shādhān and 'Abd al-Raḥmān, the sixty-nine years between 'Abd al-Raḥmān and Ibrāhīm, the eighty-seven years between al-Ṭabarī and Muḥammad b. 'Amr, the seventy years between al-Ḥārith and al-Ḥasan, and the sixty-nine years between Abū Ḥudhayfa and Shibl make the claims of direct transmission very suspect.

decades. However, the evident variations, such as the differences in the poems cited, suggest to Stauth that the *Urtext* must have been larger than the sum of its preserved parts.[37] That these differences could not be attributed to fabrication is a suggestion not entertained by Stauth and so his only option is to posit the existence of a more substantial *Urtext*. Whether the transmissions from the *Urtext* were oral or written cannot be unequivocally determined, maintains Stauth, but the parallel passages are often so identical (though not word for word) that even before 150/767 written transmission cannot be precluded.[38] Finally, Stauth concludes that the doubts raised by Goldziher and Schacht concerning the fictive nature of *isnāds* do not apply to exegetical *ḥadīths*, thus vindicating the work of Horst, Abbott, and Sezgin. As for the applicability of Sezgin's method for investigations of the *isnād*, Stauth suggests that "the results endorse the methods."[39]

However, there are problems with Stauth's method and assumptions that undermine his description of the transmission history of Mujāhid's *Tafsīr*. The first is of relatively minor importance and can be readily dismissed. It involves the role assigned al-Qāsim b. Abī Bazza (d. 124/741). Stauth manufactures the date 120/737 because he uses a report by Ibn Ḥajar, which claims that al-Qāsim b. Abī Bazza wrote a book that contained all of Mujāhid's *Tafsīr*.[40] For Stauth, this is independent evidence for his hypothetical *Urtext*.[41] Stauth does not subject the report to any scrutiny. Leemhuis, who examines Ibn Shādhān's *Tafsīr* as well, also questions Stauth's argument that al-Qāsim's *Urtext* served as a basis for all the transmissions from Mujāhid.[42] Leemhuis agrees that the transmission from Ibn Abī Najīḥ—Mujāhid, such as that found in Ibn Shādhān's and al-Ṭabarī's *Tafsīrs*, achieved written fixation around the middle of the second century A.H.[43] However, he disagrees with their ascription by Stauth to a text by al-Qāsim. He says, "It is a flaw in Stauth's reasoning, and in fact conflicts with his other conclusion that this work cannot be reconstructed."[44]

The second and more significant problem is Stauth's circular argument. A Sezginian reconstruction of sources can hardly be used to vindicate the methods of Sezgin. That is not to say that Stauth attempts to reconstruct Mujāhid's *Tafsīr*. Rather he assumes that the *isnāds* going back to him convey reliable information about how the material to which they are attached was transmitted. He is thus reconstructing the "recensions" of Mujāhid's *Tafsīr*. In essence, as table 1 indicates, Stauth is relying on the common-link theory proposed by Schacht.[45] The common-link theory refers to a transmitter who appears in all the *isnāds* of a group of similar *ḥadīths*. The *isnāds*, because they converge on this one person, seem to indicate that this common transmitter is the earliest possible source for the *ḥadīths*. The theory presupposes that the information in the *isnāds*, at least above the common link, is reliable, while that below may not be. Stauth has taken the apparently related materials in Ibn Shādhān's *Tafsīr* and in al-Ṭabarī's *Tafsīr* and concluded that Mujāhid, as the common name in the *isnāds*, is the original source for those materials. However, three compelling arguments for not trusting the information extracted from an apparent common link have been formulated since Stauth's application of the theory.

First, the similarity of the materials may be the product of dispute and mutual *isnād* criticism. As Norman Calder argues, the production of a common link results, not from a common source, but from a convergence at the level of Companions and the Successors because of the common respect for these generations.[46] Later generations of tradents could be attacked as being unreliable in the hope of undermining the reliability of the *ḥadīths* which it was claimed they had transmitted, but the earliest generations of transmitters were sacrosanct. The common respect for Ibn 'Abbās, his companions (that is, the presumed students of Ibn 'Abbās including Mujāhid), and their successors in the realm of exegesis may explain the appearance of common links and so, again, the need for "recensions" to explain similarities is obviated.

Second, the similarity in the content of the *matns* observed by Stauth may not indicate a common source at all. It may simply reveal that the "spread of *isnāds*"[47] occurred.

As Michael Cook suggests with respect to *ḥadīths* in general, *isnāds* may have been fabricated in order to skip contemporaries, to assign teachings to one's own teacher, or to remove the charge of being "isolated." This proliferation of *isnāds* results in a common link.[48] Thus, if the common link has been artificially constructed in this manner, then there are no "recensions" to compare. Cook points out that though Stauth will come to conclude that Schacht's thesis of the fictive nature of *isnāds* is false—based in part on his assumption of the existence of the *Urtext* of al-Qāsim b. Abī Bazza—Stauth provides evidence in favor of the thesis. That is, if tradents such as Ibn Abī Najīḥ use the text of al-Qāsim without citing him, then this is a case of the spread of *isnāds*.[49] Even if one dismisses the role of al-Qāsim suggested by Stauth, the missing transmitter between Ibn Shādhān and 'Abd al-Raḥmān as well as others indicates that the spread of *isnāds* continued well into the fifth/eleventh century. Thus, the similarities between the Mujāhids of al-Ṭabarī's *Tafsīr* and between them and the Mujāhid of Ibn Shādhān's *Tafsīr* might well be due to inexact plagiarism and *isnād* fabrication.

Third, even Juynboll, who champions the use of the common link, notes that most *ḥadīths*, even those of a legal nature, do not display a common-link pattern. Instead, most exhibit what he terms a "spider pattern." That is, it first appears that there is an early common link, the Prophet, a Companion, or a Successor, but upon closer observation almost all the fanning out occurs in single strands—no transmitter having more than one or two alleged students (see table 2). Juynboll suggests that these spiders should be interpreted as having developed not downward, but upward: "The later transmitters/collectors invented single strands bridging the time gap between themselves and a suitably early, fictitious or historical, [person]."[50] Juynboll notes that it is impossible to draw conclusions about the chronology, provenance, or authorship of these spiders. Table 1, if inverted, already displays the spider pattern, and when the other Mujāhid-transmissions found in al-Ṭabarī's *Tafsīr* are added, the pattern becomes even more obvious.[51]

Table 2. The "Spider Pattern" of Juynboll

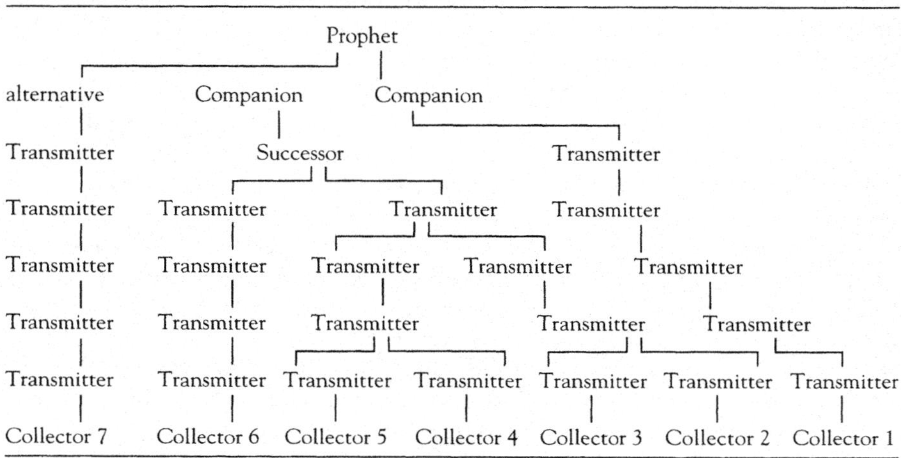

Adapted from Juynboll, "Nafi'," 215.

Thus, there seem to be several theoretical reasons for doubting Stauth's methodology for reconstructing the recensions of Mujāhid's *Tafsīr* and, because of these later theoretical objections to the common-link theory, Stauth may have been unaware of the need to compare the Mujāhid *ḥadīths* of his study with other exegetical *ḥadīths* from the selected passages. Such a comparison would have told Stauth how much the observed similarity is dependent upon *isnāds*. That is, often the similarities he observed between the various Mujāhid transmissions are present even in non-Mujāhid transmissions, suggesting perhaps that a consensus of sorts had formed about the exegesis of a certain passage and then various *isnāds* were subsequently fabricated to retroject these opinions. For example, the *ḥadīths* cited for the exegesis of Q 14:5 (Stauth's example XX) all contained the same gloss (*bi-ni'am*, or some minor variation of it), with the exception of one. While it is true that every *ḥadīth* ascribed to Mujāhid contains a similar expression, so do all the other *ḥadīths*. On the basis of content alone, thirteen *matns* seem to come from a related source, whereas two, one of which is attributed to Mujāhid, seem to have separate sources. The *isnāds*, of course, belie such a conclusion. Similarly, in seventeen of the thirty-six qur'ānic passages used by Stauth, at least some *ḥadīths* with non-Mujāhid *isnāds* use the same or similar wording in their exegesis.[52] Differences consist largely in the use of synonyms or different prepositions and pronouns. That these similarities are not simply restricted to single words, but extend to longer passages which even seem to mimic structure, is evident from the selection of *ḥadīths* from Stauth's examination of Q 108:3 (example XXXV). Each *matn* begins by identifying al-'Āṣ b. Wā'il as the subject of the verse and is followed by a paraphrase of the verse as the words of al-'Āṣ in which the object of his hatred is explicitly identified as Muḥammad. Each *matn* ends with a restatement and elaboration of the second half of the verse, in which the two *matns* ascribed to Mujāhid are more alike than that ascribed to Qatāda, but not definitively so. In addition, there are other examples in which key words, phrases, and concepts of the *ḥadīths* in Ibn Shādhān's *Tafsīr* occur in *ḥadīths* with non-Mujāhid *isnāds* in al-Ṭabarī's *Tafsīr*. Stauth himself uses this more flexible interpretation in order to argue that the *ḥadīths* with Mujāhid *isnāds* from the two *Tafsīrs* have a common source. His examination of Q 16:106 is one of the eight that exhibit these parallels.[53] Just as in the two *matns* ascribed to Mujāhid, that ascribed to Qatāda contains the phrases "some of the people of Mecca," "making the *hijra* to Medina," "companions," "written correspondence," "leaving [Mecca]," and the unbelievers or Qurashīs "caught up to them." Had the Qatāda-*matn* also been attributed to Mujāhid, by Stauth's standards it would seem to support the assertion that all three were derived from the same source.[54]

Nevertheless, eleven of Stauth's examples do seem to definitively support his assumptions that the material ascribed to Mujāhid in Ibn Shādhān's *Tafsīr* is related to the corresponding material in al-Ṭabarī's *Tafsīr*, though even of these, two examples are based on the comparison with a single word and two others have no non-Mujāhid *ḥadīths* with which to compare. The impact of the similarities among the remaining seven examples might be said to be reduced because of Stauth's selection, for it is possible to find Mujāhid *ḥadīths* in one of the *Tafsīrs* for which there are no corresponding *ḥadīths* in the other[55] and for which there are significant differences between the corresponding *ḥadīths*.[56]

However, I am not trying to suggest that Stauth's selection process is responsible for his observations, nor am I even trying to suggest that the Mujāhid *ḥadīths* in Ibn

Shādhān's and al-Ṭabarī's *Tafsīrs* are unrelated. In fact, it is clear that they are related. Rather, I have tried to show that on methodological grounds Stauth's analysis cannot resolve the Goldziher–Sezgin debate. Stauth is not using a comparison of the contents of these *ḥadīths* to evaluate the authenticity of their *isnāds*, but is assuming the authenticity of the *isnāds* in the manner of Sezgin. His comparison of the contents of the *ḥadīths* in question evaluates the correlation between the names supplied in the *isnāds* and the variation of those contents—a very different evaluation indeed. From a skeptical point of view, Stauth merely examines the degree to which the names in *isnāds* were assigned to the exegetical material in a random fashion. Ironically, therefore, Stauth's observation that there are more similarities between the materials in al-Ṭabarī's *Tafsīr* with the three Ibn Abī Najīḥ-Mujāhid *isnāds* than between the materials in al-Ṭabarī's *Tafsīr* and Ibn Shādhān's *Tafsīr* with the Warqā'—Ibn Abī Najīḥ—Mujāhid *isnāds* might well suggest that the names in the *isnāds* do not have as strong a correlation to the contents of their *ḥadīths* as Stauth assumes. Rather, they suggest that there is a correlation between the collectors, such as Ibn Shādhān and al-Ṭabarī (or for Stauth, the hypothetical redactor just prior to al-Ṭabarī) and the contents of the *ḥadīths* they record.[57]

Conclusions

Both Horst and Stauth set out to prove that exegetical *ḥadīths* are immune from the doubts raised by Goldziher and Schacht about all *ḥadīths*. Both failed to recognize the full and logical implications of a skeptical approach to the value of *isnāds*. As a result, the conclusions of Horst and Stauth are based on circular arguments. Horst relied exclusively on information drawn from *isnāds* in order to draw his conclusion that the data they contained was reliable. Stauth's circular argument is less obvious. He adopts the Sezginian methodology of analysis in order to antedate *ḥadīths* ascribed to Mujāhid in Ibn Shādhān's *Tafsīr* and al-Ṭabarī's *Tafsīr*. Having reconstructed these transmissions, Stauth then uses them to reach conclusions which substantiate Sezgin's methodology of reconstruction. Stauth's questionable selection process, his reliance on the al-Qāsim report, his use of the common-link theory, and his failure to use a control group further undermine his attempt to refute some of Goldziher's and Schacht's arguments concerning the fictive nature of the exegetical materials that employ *isnāds*.

Such a methodological critique of Horst and Stauth is necessary, for even though the more skeptical Stauth concluded that Mujāhid's *tafsīr* could not be reconstructed, it is a possibility too tempting for many scholars to resist, if one accepts, as Stauth argues, that the material attributed to Mujāhid largely reflects what he actually said. Versteegh's recent reconstruction of early grammatical terminology from later compilations of purportedly early qur'ānic exegesis provides an excellent example of the subtle pervasiveness of this temptation.[58] Even Stauth himself is lured into reconstructing the "recensions" of Mujāhid's *Tafsīr*. Without such a critique, it is hardly surprising that one scholar argues with regard to Ibn Shādhān's *Tafsīr*: "In my opinion the possibility that the manuscript would be nothing more than an abstract of Ṭabarī's *Tafsīr* may be disregarded. Not only did the text of the manuscript probably reach its present form at approximately the time that Ṭabarī composed his *Tafsīr*, but also it would imply unnecessary *isnād* forgery."[59] Another states, "One look at the edition of Muǧāhid's *Tafsīr*—

and the same conclusion applies to the *Tafsīr* of Sufyān al-Thawrī (d. 161/778)—suffices to show that these so-called commentaries are nothing more than a collection of quotations from later commentaries relating to individual verses without any internal cohesion."[60] Of course, in favor of the latter view are the large gaps in the dates of transmitters. These gaps imply that some manipulation or fabrication of *isnāds* took place: it seems that at least a few transmitters saw *isnād* forgery as necessary.

The arguments that I have presented do not necessarily imply that similarity in the content of *matns* cannot tell us anything. Yet there are other, very plausible theories that account for similarities that do not suggest that *isnāds* are reliable—in fact quite the opposite: they presuppose the large-scale fabrication of *isnāds*. Similarity signals authenticity for some scholars, fabrication for others. For the former, the suggestion of the latter is simply a product of hyperbolic skepticism. Be that as it may, the arguments of Horst and Stauth do not allay, nor even address those doubts, and so their conclusions must remain provisional and cannot be adduced as proof of the authenticity of early exegetical *ḥadīths*.

Notes

1. Goldziher, *Muslim Studies*, 2:19.
2. Schacht, *The Origins of Muhammadan Jurisprudence*.
3. Abbott, *Studies in Arabic Literary Papyri II*; Azami, *On Schacht's* Origins of Muhammadan Jurisprudence.
4. Juynboll, *Muslim Tradition*; Rahman, *Islam*, 43–67; Schoeler, "Die Frage der schriftlichen oder mündlichen Überlieferung"; Motzki, "The *Muṣannaf* of 'Abd al-Razzāq al-Ṣan'ānī."
5. Wansbrough, *Quranic Studies*, and idem, *The Sectarian Milieu*.
6. Schacht, "A Reevaluation of Islamic tradition," 147. Schacht states that "the backward growth of *isnāds* . . . is identical with the projection of doctrines back to higher authorities . . . and extends well into the literary period." Schacht, *Origins*, 165. And so the examination of *isnāds* also allows one to date the *ḥadīths* to which they are attached, for they have a tendency to grow backwards.
7. Juynboll, *Muslim Tradition*, 70–74.
8. Wansbrough continues: "The frequently adduced view that the text of revelation was easily understood by those who had witnessed its first utterance, as well as by their immediate successors, but by later generations could not be, is in my opinion not merely ingenuous, but belied by the many stories of early efforts towards the interpretation of scripture associated with the figures of 'Umar b. Khaṭṭāb and 'Abdallāh b. 'Abbās. Whatever the reasons for production of those stories, it seems hardly possible that at the beginning of the third/ninth century the Muslim community had to be reminded of what it had once known. *Tafsīr* traditions, like traditions in every other field, reflect a single impulse: to demonstrate the Hijazi origins of Islam" (*Quranic Studies*, 179).
9. Gilliot, "Portrait 'mythique' d'Ibn 'Abbās." See also Gilliot's brief summary of Ibn 'Abbās as the mythical ancestor of Muslim exegesis in his "Les débuts de l'exégèse coranique," 87–88.
10. Leemhuis, "Origins and Early Development of the *tafsīr* Tradition," 25.
11. Wansbrough, *Quranic Studies*, 158.
12. Gilliot, *Exégèse, langue, et théologie en Islam*, 281.
13. Horst, "Die Gewährsmänner im Korankommentar aṭ-Ṭabarī." Horst's results are presented in summary form in his "Zur Überlieferung in Korankommentar aṭ-Ṭabarīs."
14. Stauth, "Die Überlieferung des Korankommentars Muǧāhid b. Ǧabrs."
15. Stauth, "Die Überlieferung," ix and *passim*. Abbott states, "The early and subsequently widespread use of *tafsīr* works so copiously and specifically documented directly from some of

the earliest representative sources is reflected collectively and indirectly in Horst's painstaking and valuable analysis of the *isnāds* of Ṭabarī's *Tafsīr*." Abbott, *Studies II*, 101. She also draws conclusions about the existence of early *tafsīr* works on the basis of Horst, ibid., 101–2 and 111–12. Sezgin makes similar claims but goes even further. He adduces Horst as evidence for the existence of particular manuscripts from early exegetes. *GAS* 27, 29, 31, 32, 33, 34, 37, 79, and 91. Goldfeld claims, "The exhaustive *Isnād* study of H. Horst of *Jāmi' al-Bayān* by al-Ṭabarī attests to five of the seven versions of *Tafsīr* Ibn 'Abbās discussed up to now." Goldfeld, "The '*Tafsīr* or [*sic*] Abdallah b. 'Abbās," 130. Motzki states, "The source-analytical works of Heribert Horst, Georg Stauth, Fuat Sezgin, and others suggest that Goldziher and especially Schacht viewed the *isnād* too skeptically and that they generalized too quickly from single observations." Motzki, "The *Muṣannaf*," 2. Motzki also attempts source analysis on legal *ḥadīths* modeled on the work of Horst, Stauth, and Sezgin. Versteegh, *Arabic Grammar and Qur'ānic Exegesis in Early Islam*, 61.

16. For Motzki's thoughts on Stauth, see note 15. Versteegh, *Arabic Grammar*, 57. Leemhuis praises both Stauth's analysis and most of his conclusions. Leemhuis, "Origins," 19 and 22, n. 57. See also Leemhuis, "Ms. 1075 Tafsīr of the Cairene Dār al-Kutub," 177, in which he states that he considers his own paper "to be a reference to Stauth's comprehensive study, which deserves to be published on a wider scale."

17. Horst, "Die Gewährsmänner," 3. This figure is considerably lower than the 38,397 found in al-Ṭabarī's *Tafsīr*, even if one discounts the 150 *ḥadīths* found in al-Ṭabarī's introduction. al-Ṭabarī, *Tafsīr al-Ṭabarī*, 1:31–88 and 12:753.

18. See Horst, "Die Gewährsmänner," 6–8, and idem, "Zur Überlieferung," 292.

19. For example, the Bishr b. Mu'ādh—Yazīd b. Zuray'—Sa'īd b. Abī 'Arūba—Qatāda b. Di'āma-*isnād* appears throughout the commentary, with a lacuna from Q 22:1 to Q 27:80. Horst, "Die Gewährsmänner," 9–10. In the remaining chapters of his dissertation, Horst first gives a brief biography of each of the transmitters appearing in the one hundred most frequently cited *isnāds*. The biography includes years of birth and death, geographical location, intellectual interests, theological inclinations, teachers and students, if known. Horst relies primarily on Dhahabī's *Tadhkirat al-ḥuffāẓ*, Ibn Ḥajar's *Tahdhīb*, Ibn Nadīm's *al-Fihrist*, and Ibn Sa'd's *al-Ṭabaqāt* for this information. He then provides similar information for the main teachers of al-Ṭabarī (or more precisely, those whom al-Ṭabarī cites most frequently).

20. The manuscripts would have included those of 'Alī b. Abī Ṭalḥa (via 'Alī b. Dā'ūd), Muḥammad b. Sa'd (via a family *isnād*), a *tafsīr* from Mujāhid, a commentary from 'Abd al-Raḥmān b. Zayd b. Aslam, and a work of Ibn Isḥāq (perhaps his *Kitāb al-maghāzī*). This Muḥammad b. Sa'd is not the famous secretary (d. 230/845) of al-Wāqidī (d. 207/822) and author of the al-Ṭabaqāt al-kubrā as assumed by Horst, "Zur Überlieferung," 294, and "Die Gewährsmänner," 30. This informant is Muḥammad b. Sa'd Abū Ja'far al-'Awfī (d. 276/888). See al-Khaṭīb al-Baghdādī, *Ta'rīkh Baghdād aw Madīnat al-Salām*, 5:321–23, and Fück, "Ibn Sa'd," in *EI*, new ed. 3:922–23.

21. Horst, "Zur Überlieferung," p. 307. In addition, a shaykh might have limited himself to a certain subject, and this possibility, Horst suggests, could also account for the irregular occurrence of certain *isnāds*. Horst concludes that al-Ṭabarī did not exhaust all the sources available in his time, but just the admittedly enormous materials he encountered on his journeys. Horst, "Die Gewährsmänner," 62–64. This fragmentary nature of the appearance of many of the *isnāds* is due to the nature of the transmission: students traveled from shaykh to shaykh and knew only that part of a shaykh's commentary for which they were in attendance. The notes they did record often served only as mnemonic aids.

22. Horst's conclusion that al-Ṭabarī's sources were primarily in written form cannot be so readily accepted and needs to be reexamined in light of the greater skepticism about the authenticity or even existence of such sources during this earlier period. For example, Gilliot suggests that al-Ṭabarī remodeled written sources so that they appeared as oral sources. Gilliot, "La Sourate

al-Baqara," 89–98. Moreover, al-Ṭabarī's *Tafsīr* itself may not have been fixed in written form originally. Norman Calder observes:

> Between loose redactions on the one hand and the authorial control on the other, lies the world of organizing authorship. The *Tafsīr* of al-Ṭabarī (the *Jāmi' al-Bayān*) shows some features of organic growth (the untidy accumulation of hadith material bundled under Quranic lemmas and rarely subject to even that basic redactional process which brings Prophetic material to initial position) and some features of authorial control (the structured arguments and interpretations which provide an intellectual frame for the hadith). It is perhaps a text, initially a product of organic growth, finally so much controlled by its editor as to warrant classification as an authored book. *Studies in Early Muslim Jurisprudence*, 194.

That the publication of the *Tafsīr* was not as straightforward as normally assumed is also evident from the presence of *ḥadīths* that cite Muḥammad b. Jarīr (al-Ṭabarī) as part of their *isnāds*. See, for example, the first *ḥadīth* adduced for Q 2:31. Al-Ṭabarī, *Tafsīr*, 1:251.

23. Horst, "Die Gewährsmänner," 64–65.

24. Horst, "Die Gewährsmänner," 65–67.

25. Horst, "Zur Überlieferung," 306–7.

26. These calculations are based on Horst's own figures in his "Zur Überlieferung," 291–92, which, as was stated earlier in note 17, are somewhat inaccurate.

27. This *Tafsīr* is available in a few editions. A recent edition, which is used in this chapter, is Mujāhid b. Jabr, *Tafsīr*, ed. Muḥammad 'Abd al-Salām Abū al-Nīl.

28. Abū 'Abd Allāh Sufyān al-Thawrī, *Tafsīr*, ed. Imtiyāz 'Alī 'Arshī. For evaluations of this *Tafsīr* see Lecomte, "Sufyān al-Tawrī"; Gilliot,"Les débuts de l'exégèse coranique," 89; and Versteegh, "Grammar and Exegesis," 207. These authors do not place as much faith in its early date and/or authenticity as does Stauth.

29. This *Tafsīr* has not yet been published. It is preserved in two manuscripts. Sezgin, *Geschichte*, 1:99 and 1:290. See also Versteegh, *Arabic Grammar*, 42.

30. Only 1,730 of the 2,130 exegetical traditions in the *Tafsīr* go back to Mujāhid through this *isnād*. The remainder branch off the tradents to other authorities. Stauth, "Die Überlieferung," 78–99.

31. Abū 'Alī al-Ḥasan b. Aḥmad b. Ibrāhīm b. al-Ḥasan b. Muḥammad b. Shādhān (d. after 424/1032) is the first transmitter to appear only in the title pages of the fascicules. According to these title pages, he transmitted this material to Abū l-Faḍl Aḥmad b. al-Ḥasan b. Khayrūn (d. 488/1095). The preserved manuscript has its first three fascicules transmitted by Abū Manṣūr Muḥammad b. 'Abd al-Malik b. al-Ḥasan b. Khayrūn (d. 539/1144) and the other five by Abū al-Su'ūd al-Mubārak b. Khayrūn b. 'Abd al-Malik b. al-Ḥasan b. Khayrūn (d. After 541/1146). The final transmitter and author of the manuscript is Muḥammad b. Aḥmad b. Muḥammad b. 'Alī b. Aḥmad b. 'Amr b. al-Ḥasan b. Ḥamdī (d. after 544/1149).

32. Stauth, "Die Überlieferung," 156–89.

33. The colophon gives the actual date of the manuscript as 544/1149. Mujāhid, *Tafsīr*, 763.

34. This redactor is not likely to have been al-Ṭabarī himself, according to Stauth. His argument for this conclusion is the oft-repeated one that adduces the considerable amount of contradictory materials included by al-Ṭabarī. This argument asks rhetorically why he would include all this conflicting material if he were willing to redact the material into a more suitable form. One is to conclude that al-Ṭabarī must be considered simply a compiler. However, given that al-Ṭabarī seems to have manipulated his sources and attempted to define the limits of the debate on at least some issues, one could more easily envision al-Ṭabarī as a redactor of his material, despite (or perhaps, because of) the presence of contradictory material. See, for example, Powers, "The Islamic Law of Inheritance Reconsidered," 71 and Gilliot, *Exégèse*, 276 and 281.

35. Stauth examines ten and eight qur'ānic passages for the *Tafsīrs* attributed to Sufyān al-Thawrī and 'Abd al-Razzāq–Ma'mar, respectively. Only one of these eighteen passages is the same as the thirty-six qur'ānic passages of the earlier comparison.

36. Stauth, "Die Überlieferung," 208–22.

37. Ibid., 223-26.

38. Ibid., 228.

39. Ibid., 229. Stauth adds that his results also demonstrate the limits of the method: Sezgin was too optimistic about reconstructing the original works from later sources.

40. Ibn Ḥajar, *Tahdhīb al-tahdhīb*, 8:270.

41. Perhaps, Stauth was influenced by Abbott, who states: "Qāsim b. Abī Bazzah of Mecca (d. 124/742) is said to have been the only one who heard all of the *Tafsīr* from Mujāhid and made a complete copy of it. His fellow pupil 'Abd Allāh b. Abī Najīḥ (d. 132/749–50) heard only part of it from Mujāhid but copied the whole from Qāsim's book. All other transmitters of Mujāhid's *Tafsīr*, according to Yaḥyā b. Sa'īd al-Qaṭṭān and Ibn Ḥibbān, made copies from Qāsim's manuscripts but omitted his name and transmitted on the authority of Mujāhid. The list of such transmitters includes Laith b. Abī Salīm (or Sulaym; d. 143/760) and the well-known Ibn Jurayj and Sufyān b. 'Uyainah." *Studies II*, 98.

42. Leemhuis, "Ms. 1075," 177.

43. Leemhuis, "Origins," 21.

44. Ibid., 22, n. 57.

45. Schacht, *Origins*, 171–75.

46. Calder, *Studies*, 236–37.

47. Schacht uses this expression to refer to the process by which *isnāds* were invented for a particular *ḥadīth* to obviate the charge that it was "isolated" and therefore not well attested. *Origins*, 166.

48. Cook, *Early Muslim Dogma*, 107–16.

49. Ibid., 204, n. 39.

50. Inverted from Juynboll, "Nāfi'," 214–15.

51. For example, Stauth's Example XX ("Die Überlieferung," 167) contains *ḥadīths* with the *isnāds* given in Diagram 1 plus the following *isnāds*: Yaḥyā b. Ṭalḥa al-Yarbū'ī–Fuḍayl b. 'Iyāḍ–Layth–Mujāhid; Isḥāq b. Ibrāhīm b. Ḥabīb b. al-Shahīd–Yaḥyā b. Yamān–Sufyān–'Ubayd al-Muktib–Mujāhid; Aḥmad b. Isḥāq–Abū Aḥmad–Sufyān–'Ubayd al-Muktib–Mujāhid; Aḥmad –Abū Aḥmad–'Abthar–Ḥaṣīn–Mujāhid; al-Ḥasan b. Muḥammad–Shabābah–Warqā'–Ibn Abī Najīḥ–Mujāhid; and al-Ḥasan ibn Yaḥyā–'Abd al-Razzāq–al-Thawrī–'Ubayd Allāh or someone else–Mujāhid. al-Ṭabarī, *Tafsīr*, 7:417–18.

52. These include examples I, III, IV, IX, X, XI, XIII, XIV, XVII, XIX, XX, XXII, XXVI, XXVIII, XXXII, XXXV, and XXXVII. See Stauth, "Die Überlieferung," 158–73. See also Mujāhid, *Tafsīr*, 196, 198, 204, 212–13, 214, 216, 291, 351–52, 356, 358, 410, 410, 426, 538, 737, 757, and 761, respectively; and al-Ṭabarī, *Tafsīr*, 1:170, 1:214–15, 1:351–52, 1:566–69, 1:604, 2:35–37, 4:260–61, 6:180–81, 6:262–63, 6:288–90, 7:417–18, 7:428–30, 7:659–61, 10:428–30, 12:631–32, 12:724–26, and 12:746–48, respectively.

53. These include examples VII, VIII, XVIII, XXI, XXIV, XXV, XXVII, and XXXVI. See Stauth, "Die Überlieferung," 161–73. See also Mujāhid, *Tafsīr*, 207, 212, 356, 410, 426, 426, 534, and 761, respectively; and al-Ṭabarī, *Tafsīr*, 1:410–11, 1:545–46, 1:267–68, 7:426–28, 7:647–49, 7:651–54, 10:124–25, and 12:746–48, respectively.

54. A more elaborate version of this story with the same keywords and phrases is adduced by al-Ṭabari with an Aḥmad b. Manṣūr– . . . –Ibn 'Abbās-*isnād*. Al-Ṭabari, *Tafsīr*, 7:653–54.

55. For example, al-Ṭabari adduces a Mujāhid-*ḥadīth* for Q 11:77 (*Tafsīr*, 7:81) and Ibn

Shādhān does not. And Ibn Shādhān provides one for Q 103:2 whereas al-Ṭabari does not. Mujāhid, *Tafsīr*, 747.

56. See, for example, the phrase *yatlūnahu ḥaqq tilāwatihi* of Q 2:121, for which Ibn Shādhān cites Mujāhid's exegesis as *ya'malūna bihi ḥaqq 'amalihi*. Mujāhid, *Tafsīr*, 212–13. Al-Ṭabari adduces several Mujāhid-*ḥadīths*, some of which also gloss the qur'ānic phrase with *ya'malūna bihi ḥaqq 'amalihi* and some of which gloss it with *yattabi'ūnahu ḥaqq ittibā'ihi* in accordance with most other exegetes. Al-Ṭabari, *Tafsīr*, 1:567–69. It is odd that al-Ṭabari treats both explanations as synonymous, but not *yaqra'ūnahu ḥaqq qirā'atihi*. Perhaps al-Ṭabari attempted to harmonize discrepancies, as was his wont, or refused to accept that Mujāhid-*ḥadīths* could be at variance with each other.

57. Leemhuis points out that Ibn Shādhān's *Tafsīr* has only one *ḥadīth* with the Warqā'—Ibn Abī Najīḥ—Mujāhid-*isnād* from the beginning of Q 68 to the beginning of Q 77. For Leemhuis this lacuna is compelling evidence that Ādam b. Abī Iyās was a reliable transmitter. The most obvious explanation for the missing *ḥadīths*, according to Leemhuis, is the loss of four pages of the manuscript used by Ādam when he compiled the *Tafsīr*. This explanation implies that exegetical *ḥadīths* with the Ibn Abī Najīḥ—Mujāhid-*isnād* must have achieved a fixed written form during the lifetime of Warqā', the transmitter listed in the *isnād* between Ādam and Ibn Abī Najīḥ. Therefore, the latest possible date for this written fixation would be 160/776, the date of Warqā''s death. This date closely corresponds to that given by Stauth and Leemhuis. Leemhuis, "Origins," 20–21.

Missing folios are not the only plausible explanation for the absence of exegetical *ḥadīths* ascribed to Mujāhid via this *isnād* for this portion of the Qur'ān. But even if it were, Leemhuis's conclusion is predicated on the assumption that the earliest part of the *isnād* is reliable. Since it is precisely this assumption that is problematic, the implication he draws from it is also problematic. One could just as readily assume that the early portion of the *isnād* has been fabricated and that the earliest collection of the *Tafsīr* was produced by Ibn Shādhān. In this case, the missing folios might come from a manuscript produced as late as 352/963 (and then only if one trusts the later portion of the the *isnād* provided by Ibn Shādhān). That date puts the production of these *ḥadīths* with the Warqā'—Ibn Abī Najīḥ—Mujāhid-*isnāds* well after those adduced in al-Ṭabari's *Tafsīr*. And this theory might account for any observed similarities as well.

58. Versteegh, *Arabic Grammar*, *passim*.

59. Leemhuis, "Ms. 1075," 173.

60. Versteegh, "Grammar and Exegesis," 207.

Bibliography

Abbott, Nabia. *Studies in Arabic Literary Papyri II: Qur'ānic Commentary and Tradition*. Chicago: University of Chicago Press, 1967.

Azami, Mohammad Mustafa. On *Schacht's* Origins of Muhammadan Jurisprudence. Riyadh: King Saud University, 1985.

———. *Studies in Early Hadith Literature: With a Critical Edition of Some Early Texts*. 3rd ed. Indianapolis: American Trust Publications, 1992.

Calder, Norman. *Studies in Early Muslim Jurisprudence*. Oxford: Clarendon Press, 1993.

Cook, Michael. *Early Muslim Dogma: a Source-Critical Study*. Cambridge: Cambridge University Press, 1981.

Fück, Johann W. "Ibn Sa'd." *EI*, new ed. 3: 922–23.

Gilliot, Claude. "Les débuts de l'exégèse coranique." *Revue du monde musulman et de la Méditerranée* 58 (1990): 83–100.

——. *Exégèse, langue, et théologie en Islam: l'exégèse coranique de Tabari (m. 311/923)*. Paris: Librarie Philosophique J. Vrin, 1990.

——. "Portrait 'mythique' d'Ibn 'Abbās." *Arabica* 32 (1985): 127–84.

——. "La Sourate al-Baqara dans le Commentaire de Ṭabarī (Le développement et le fonctionnement des traditions exégètiques à la lumière du commentaire des versets 1 à 40 de la sourate)." Ph.D. diss., Université Paris-III, 1982.

Goldfeld, Isaiah. "The '*Tafsīr* or [*sic*] Abdallāh b. 'Abbās." *Der Islam* 58 (1981): 125–35.

Goldziher, Ignaz. *Muslim Studies*. Ed. S. M. Stern, trans. C. R. Barber and S. M. Stern. 2 vols. London: Allen and Unwin, 1971.

Horst, Heribert. "Die Gewährsmänner im Korankommentar aṭ-Ṭabarī: Ein Beitrag zur Kenntnis der exegetischen Überlieferung im Islam." Ph.D. diss., Rheinische Friedrich-Wilhelms-Universität zu Bonn, 1951.

——. "Zur Überlieferung in Korankommentar aṭ-Ṭabarīs." *Zeitschrift der deutschen morgenländischen Gesellschaft* 103 (1953): 290–307.

Ibn Ḥajar al-'Asqalānī, Shihāb al-Dīn Abū l-Faḍl Aḥmad b. 'Alī. *Tahdhīb al-tahdhīb*. 12 vols. Beirut: Dār al-Kutub al-'Ilmiyya, 1415/1994.

Juynboll, G. H. A. *Muslim Tradition: Studies in Chronology, Provenance and Authorship of Early ḥadīth*. Cambridge: Cambridge University Press, 1983.

——. "Nāfi', the *mawlā* of Ibn 'Umar, and his position in Muslim *ḥadīth* Literature." *Der Islam* 70 (1993): 207–44.

al-Khaṭīb al-Baghdādī, Abū Bakr b. 'Alī b. Thābit b. Aḥmad b. Mahdī al-Shāfi'ī. *Ta'rīkh Baghdād aw Madīnat al-Salām*. 14 vols. Cairo and Baghdad: Maktabat al-Khānijī and al-Maktabat al-'Arabiyya, 1349/1931.

Lecomte, Gérard. "Sufyān al-Tawrī: Quelques remarques sur le personage et son œuvre." *Bulletin d'études orientales* 30 (1978): 51–60.

Leemhuis, Fred. "Ms. 1075 Tafsīr of the Cairene Dār al-Kutub and Muǧāhid's *Tafsīr*." In *Proceedings of the Ninth Congress of the Union Européene des Arabisants et Islamisants, Amsterdam, 1st to 7th September 1978*. Ed. Rudolph Peters, 169–80. Leiden: E. J. Brill, 1981.

——. "Origins and Early Development of the *tafsīr* Tradition." In *Approaches to the History of the Interpretation of the Qur'ān*. Ed. Andrew Rippin, 13–30. Oxford: Clarendon Press, 1988.

Motzki, Harald. "The *Muṣannaf* of 'Abd al-Razzāq al-Ṣan'ānī as a Source of Authentic *aḥādīth* of the First Century A.H." *Journal of Near Eastern Studies* 50 (1991): 1–21.

Mujāhid b. Jabr Abū al-Ḥajjāj. *Tafsīr*. Ed. Muḥammad 'Abd al-Salām. Cairo: Dār al-Fikr al-Islāmī al-Ḥadītha, 1410/1989.

Powers, David S."The Islamic Law of Inheritance Reconsidered: A New Reading of Q. 4:12b." *Studia islamica* 55 (1982): 61–94.

Rahman, Fazlur. *Islam*. 2d ed. Chicago: University of Chicago Press, 1979.

Schacht, Joseph. *The Origins of Muhammadan Jurisprudence*. Oxford: Clarendon Press, 1950.

——. "A Reevaluation of Islamic Tradition." *Journal of the Royal Asiatic Society of Great Britain and Ireland* n.v. (1949): 143–54.

Schoeler, Gregor. "Die Frage der schriftlichen oder mündlichen Überlieferung der Wissenschaften im frühen Islam." *Der Islam* 62 (1985): 201–30.

Sezgin, Fuad. *Studies in Early Hadith Literature: With a Critical Edition of Some Early Texts*. 3rd ed. Indianapolis: American Trust Publications, 1992.

Stauth, Georg. "Die Überlieferung des Korankommentars Muǧāhid b. Ǧabr's: Zur Frage der Rekonstruction der in den Sammelwerken des 3. Jh.d.H. benutzten frühislamischen Quellenwerke." Ph.D. diss., Universität Gießen, 1969.

Sufyān al-Thawrī, Abū 'Abd Allāh. *Tafsīr*. Ed. Imtiyāz 'Alī 'Arshī. 1930. Reprint, Beirut: Dār al-Kutub al-'Ilmiyya, 1403/1983.

al-Ṭabarī, Abū Ja'far Muḥammad b. Jarīr. *Tafsīr al-Ṭabarī al-musammā Jāmi' al-bayān fī ta'wīl āy al-Qur'ān*. 30 vols. in 12. Beirut: Dār al-Kutub al-'Ilmiyya, 1992.

Versteegh, C. H. M. *Arabic Grammar and Qur'ānic Exegesis in Early Islam*. Leiden: E. J. Brill, 1993.

——. "Grammar and Exegesis: The Origins of Kufan Grammar and the *Tafsīr Muqātil*." *Der Islam* 67 (1990): 206–42.

Wansbrough, John. *Quranic Studies: Sources and Methods of Scriptural Interpretation*. Oxford: Oxford University Press, 1977.

——. *The Sectarian Milieu: Content and Composition of Islamic Salvation History*. Oxford: Oxford University Press, 1978.

23

The Scriptural "Senses" in Medieval Ṣūfī Qur'ān Exegesis

GERHARD BÖWERING

Muslims understand the Qur'ān to be a divine message in which each individual word has been divinely chosen and conveyed to the Prophet at a particular moment of his life. According to general Muslim belief, the divinely communicated words, though understood as mediated by an intermediary agent, a holy spirit or the angel Gabriel, were recorded after the Prophet's death in such perfectly faithful fashion that they represent God's dictation word for word. Every letter of the holy book of the Qur'ān is believed to be the direct utterance of God, reproduced with absolute accuracy.

As a sacred book recording divine revelation, the Qur'ān is widely understood by Muslims to have a significant meaning because God certainly meant what he explicitly said. Since early Islamic times, however, the Qur'ān has also been understood as being *dhū wujūh*, as possessing many "faces" or aspects. This multifaceted character of the Qur'ān is manifested in the many different types of verses it contains, such as those setting forth legal regulations, doctrinal statements, ethical premises, or practical rules. It is also apparent however in the fact that many individual verses can each be read and interpreted in a variety of ways. Taking this *dhū wujūh* character of the Qur'ān as the focus of his *Die Richtungen der islamischen Koranauslegung*, Ignaz Goldziher illustrated major trends of Qur'ān interpretation with a considerable degree of documentation and sophistication.[1] As is shown by Goldziher's study of the major sources of qur'ānic exegesis, as well as by other important Qur'ān commentaries that have come to light since the compilation of his groundbreaking work three quarters of a century ago, many of these trends of interpretation are based on a specific selection of qur'ānic verses. Commentators segregate certain passages from the text as a whole and interprete them in isolation from neighboring verses so as to undergird a particular, tendentious or even partisan point of view.

In such a way Ṣūfism, Islamic mysticism, developed its own approach to qur'ānic exegesis and formed its own body of Qur'ān commentary.[2] The well-known foundation of the Ṣūfī approach to exegesis is the distinction of two levels of meaning: *ẓāhir*, the outer literal meaning, and *bāṭin*, the inner hidden meaning of the qur'ānic text. The terms *ẓāhir* and *bāṭin* are derived from a lexical pair which the Qur'ān itself uses to contrast opposites, as when God describes himself as the Outward and the Inward who lavishes outer and inner blessings on humanity or when a person's outer and inner sins are set against each other.[3] The Qur'ān however, never applies this pair of terms to contrasting levels of the interpretation of scripture. These two levels of meaning, more over, are quite distinct from the divisions into categories or classes of verses, for which the Qur'ān explicitly makes provision, such as by separating clear, univalent from obscure, polyvalent verses, *muḥkamāt* from *mutashābihāt*,[4] and by distinguishing permissable food from forbidden food and lawful conduct from unlawful, *ḥalāl* from *ḥarām*.[5] The theory of "abrogation" (*naskh*) in the case of both qur'ānic verses and *ḥadīth* statements was also developed with reference to a pair of contrasting terms inspired by the qur'ānic mentions of "inscription" (*nuskha*) and God's recording of human actions.[6] Explicitly based on the qur'ānic references to God's act of abrogating a revelation by proposing a better one (Q 2:106) and to his abolishing a satanic insinuation (Q 22:52),[7] this pair eventually emerged in the post-qur'ānic terminology of *nāsikh* and *mansūkh* that seemed to imply that God actually altered qur'ānic regulations he had previously announced and that the Prophet had changed practices to which he had earlier adhered.

The Ṣūfī distinction of *ẓāhir* and *bāṭin*, however, is not only applied to particular words and verses of the Qur'ān, it is also understood as a twofold reading of the qur'ānic text as a whole. As such it hinges on the belief that beneath the surface of the literal sense of the Qur'ān, an inner hidden meaning can be unearthed in the inexhaustible depth of the divine word. Qur'ānic support for such a belief is illustrated by the verses, like "if the sea were ink for (writing) the words of my Lord, the sea would be spent before the words of my Lord are exhausted,"[8] and "and if all the trees in the earth were pens, and the sea, with seven more seas to replenish it, (were ink), the words of God could not be exhausted."[9] In the Ṣūfī view, each verse of the Qur'ān as well as the qur'ānic text as a whole, may be understood as including this multilayered depth of divine meaning hidden underneath the literal meaning. But it is this hidden and inner meaning of the Qur'ān, this *bāṭin*, that became the focal point of Ṣūfī exegesis of the Qur'ān.

For the Ṣūfīs this *bāṭin*, as the inexhaustible level of meaning contained in the divine word of the Qur'ān, had its counterpart in the spiritual knowledge the Ṣūfīs acquired through introspection into the inner emotions stirring their souls. They called this inner knowledge *'ilm al-bāṭin* and perceived it as a divine gift granted to them after intense ascetic effort and psychic discipline. Possessed by an elite of mystics who were granted the inner sight of and insight (*baṣīra*) into the realities, hidden within their souls, *'ilm al-bāṭin* was acquired in two principal ways: intuition and extrasensory perception. In his *Risāla fī 'ilm al-bāṭin wa-l-ẓāhir* the famous Ḥanbalī scholar Ibn Taymiyya (d. 728/1328) expressed these with a pithy definition. "Knowledge of the *bāṭin* can be knowledge of inner things, such as knowledge of intuitions and moods existing in the heart, or it can be knowledge of extrasensory things of which prophets were apprised. Knowledge of the *bāṭin* can also be understood as knowledge hidden from the understanding of the majority of the people."[10]

While the early Shī'a understanding of inner psychic knowledge (*'ilm al-bāṭin*), as an initiation into a body of secret knowledge, was inspired by the thought of the radical Shī'a (*ghulāt*) of second/eighth century Kufa,[11] the Ṣūfī notion of *bāṭin* can be traced back to the refined study of the soul in the circle of Ḥasan al-Baṣrī (d. 110/728)[12] and the teachings of his mystic disciple 'Abd al-Wāḥid b. Zayd (d. about 150/767).[13] On the basis of statements attributed to these early ascetics and mystics of Basra, Ḥārith al-Muḥāsibī (d. 243/857) expounded a more systematic instruction anchored in the Ṣūfīs' examination of conscience and the psychological awareness of their spiritual experiences.[14] Muḥāsibī's teachings became an essential building block of the mystical and moral theology eventually found in the handbooks of Ṣūfism, from Abū Naṣr al-Sarrāj (d. 378/988), Abū Bakr al-Kalābādhī (d. 380/990), Abū Ṭālib al-Makkī (d. 386/996), and Abū Sa'd al-Kharkūshī (d. 406/1015)[15] to Abū l-Qāsim al-Qushayrī (d. 465/1074), Abū l-Ḥasan al-Hujwīrī (d. 465/1073 or 469/1077), Abū Ḥāmid al-Ghazzālī (d. 505/1111), and Abū Ḥafṣ 'Umar al-Suhrawardī (d. 632/1234).[16] This predominant emphasis within Ṣūfī moral and mystical theology was accompanied by the significant development of Ṣūfī hagiographical accounts, such as the works of Abū 'Abd al-Raḥmān al-Sulamī (d. 412/1021) and Khwājā 'Abdallāh Anṣārī-i Harawī (d. 481/1089),[17] that traced characteristic specimens of Ṣūfī teachings to their respective authors. In addition to such Ṣūfī theology and hagiography, both of which were accorded normative Sunnī approval, there emerged, however, two other currents of Ṣūfī teaching that were suspect in the eyes of Sunnī orthodoxy: Ṣūfī philosophical thought as exemplified in the writings of al-Ḥakīm al-Tirmidhī (d. ca. 300/910)[18] and Ṣūfī Qur'ān commentary, beginning with the exegetical activity of Sahl al-Tustarī (d. 283/896).[19]

What came to be known as the *ḥadīth al-ikhlāṣ* encapsulates the core of Ṣūfī teaching on the inner knowledge of the soul as traced to the circle of Ḥasan al-Baṣrī. Ṣūfīs cherished this as a *ḥadīth qudsī*, a non-qur'ānic word of God revealed to Muḥammad by mediation of the angel Gabriel. Documented in an anonymous Ṣūfī source from the fourth/tenth century Ṣūfīs understood the *ḥadīth al-ikhlāṣ* to express the gist of their inner knowledge (*'ilm al-bāṭin*).[20] Al-Qushayrī quotes it together with a chain of transmitters (for which the *'Awārif al-ma'ārif* supplies a missing link),[21] on the authority of Abū 'Abd al-Raḥmān al-Sulamī—'Alī b. Sa'īd al-Thaghrī—Aḥmad b. Muḥammad b. Aḥmad Zakarīyā l-Taghlibī—'Alī b. Ibrāhīm al-Shaqīqī—Muḥammad b. Ja'far al-Khaṣṣāf—Aḥmad b. Bashshār al-Ṣayrafī—Abū Ya'qūb al-Sharīṭī—Aḥmad b. Ghassān—Aḥmad b. 'Alī l-Hujaymī—'Abd al-Wāḥid b. Zayd—Ḥasan al-Baṣrī—Ḥudhayfa b. al-Yamān (d. 36/656)—the Prophet Muḥammad—Gabriel: "I asked the Lord of Glory, 'What is sincere devotion [to God] (*ikhlāṣ*),' and he replied, 'It is a secret (*sirr*) from my secret which I have deposited in the heart of those of my servants whom I love.'"[22] This divine secret deposited in the heart of the mystics and interpreted as the essence of the experience of God in the inner recesses of their souls, eventually connected with the Ṣūfī interpretation of the Qur'ān that sought to discover the inner depth of meaning hidden in the divine word of the qur'ānic text. In a nutshell, the *bāṭin* of the soul was linked with the *bāṭin* of the Qur'ān in Ṣūfī exegesis.

Although virtually each verse or qur'ānic phrase was understood as opening vistas to the infinite variety of divine meanings embedded in the unfathomable depth of the Qur'ān, it became a characteristic feature of the Ṣūfī exegetical approach to concentrate upon keynotes within selected passages of the Qur'ān. These keynotes, frequently short phrases from a particular verse, are chosen as the focal point of the commentary. Whether taken up in isolation from their contextual environment or in connection with it, these keynotes awaken associations in the mind of the interpreter that spring from the mystical matrix of a Ṣūfī world of ideas. The process of the spiritual encounter between the qur'ānic keynotes and the mystical associations achieves a level of synthesis which makes it impossible to discern where "exegesis" ends and "eisegesis" begins, and where the discovery of the interpreter's own existence disappears in the revelation of the divine word. To bring to light the depth of meaning, either uncovered in the word of the Eternal Speaker or discovered in the soul of the mystic, clusters of figurative expressions, such as allusions, metaphors, symbols, and allegories, were required to reflect the various shades and facets of meaning that cannot be captured in one single definitive expression.[23] To a large degree, these figurative expressions constitute the Ṣūfī language of Qur'ān interpretation and give witness to its particular exegetical approach, as will later be shown here by two examples.

Ṣūfism developed this hermeneutical approach in its own body of Qur'ān commentary, a literature that may be divided into two different types of works, both following the pattern of running commentaries on a large number of selected verses of the Qur'ān. One type, diligently collecting a wide spectrum of the earliest layers of *bāṭin* commentary and representing the richest strand of this literature, was compiled by Abū 'Abd al-Raḥmān al-Sulamī (d. 412/1021) in two separate Qur'ān commentaries: his major work, *Ḥaqā'iq al-tafsīr*,[24] and the subsequent minor work, *Ziyādāt ḥaqā'iq al-tafsīr*.[25] They were both later copied widely in Rūzbihān al-Baqlī's (d. 609/1209) *'Arā'is al-bayān*,[26] and by Shams al-Dīn al-Daylamī (d. 598/1193) in his *Taṣdīq al-ma'ārif*, also known as *Futūḥ al-Raḥmān fī ishārāt al-Qur'ān*, (the latter is extant in manuscript only).[27] The other type of commentary literature, incorporating both *ẓāhir* and *bāṭin* elements, counts Abūl-Qāsim al-Qushayrī's (d. 465/1074) *Laṭā'if al-ishārāt*[28] and Abū Ḥafṣ 'Umar al-Suhrawardī's (d. 632/1234) *Nughbat al-bayān*[29] among its most representative sources. In part parallel to the latter type of Arabic Ṣūfī commentary, albeit somewhat later in origin, is the Persian Ṣūfī exegesis beginning with Rashīd al-Dīn al-Maybudī's (d. 530/1165). His *Kashf al-asrār*,[30] also incorporates *ẓāhir* and *bāṭin* elements, though in a framework of three exegetical categories (*nawbat*), separating the *ẓāhir* level from the *bāṭin* level by an intermediate level of interpretation. Principal subsequent stages of medieval Ṣūfī commentary in Arabic can be identified, on the one hand, in the collective Qur'ān commentaries of Najm al-Dīn al-Kubrā (d. 618/1221), Najm al-Dīn al-Rāzī (d. 654/1256), and 'Alā' al-Dawla al-Simnānī (d. 736/1326),[31] and, on the other hand, in the Qur'ān commentaries influenced by Ibn al-'Arabī (d. 638/1240) and exemplified by 'Abd al-Razzāq al-Qāshānī's (d. 730/1330) commentary.[32]

Commonly Ṣūfī commentaries on the Qur'ān include their authors' reflections on the method of Ṣūfī Qur'ān interpretation, usually in the introductions of their works. Two major issues predominate in such reflections, the process of qur'ānic revelation and the interpretation of qur'ānic content. The first issue is shared with non-Ṣūfī commentaries, while the second manifests an exegetical method specific to the Ṣūfīs. The fundamental question about the actual process of divine revelation forced the exegate to deal with the piecemeal character of the qur'ānic revelation: "and a Qur'ān we have divided, for you to recite it to humankind at intervals, and we have sent it down successively."[33] The conflict between the Qur'ān as a book existing in the presence of God in its entirety as source of all revelation, *kitāb*, and as the actual communication of revelation in stages, *furqān*, was already highlighted by the objection Muḥammad's adversaries raised in the Qur'ān: "Why has the Qur'ān not been sent down upon him all at once (*jumlatan wāḥidatan*)?"[34] A *ḥadīth* statement reported on the authority of Ibn 'Abbās (d. 68/687–88), the traditional father of qur'ānic exegesis,[35] was used by Ṣūfī exegetes to blunt the antinomy by linking a single revelation of the divine book with its piecemeal communications to the Prophet. God sent down the Qur'ān to the lowest heaven at one and the same time in its entirety (*wāḥidatan jumlatan*) but revealed it piecemeal to the Prophet over a period of about twenty years.[36]

This idea was linked by the Ṣūfī exegetes with the qur'ānic reference to a "guarded tablet" (*lawḥ maḥfūẓ*).[37] Since the Qur'ān included references to the tablet preserved in heaven, and depicted Gabriel as the envoy of revelation,[38] Ṣūfī exegetes could use this *ḥadīth* to provide the environment and imagery for the process of revelation. In the view of Ṣūfī exegetes, God, seated on his throne, fixed his sight on the heavenly writ of the Qur'ān, preserved in a tablet of emerald, and beckoned the angels, sending them as his envoys to Gabriel, the angel of revelation, who communicated each divine message to the Prophet, five times five verses at a time.[39]

The solution of "five times five verses at a time," a scenario elaborated with many modifications by yet another *ḥadīth*, also made it possible to account for the great variety of subject matter, the varying clarity of individual verses, and the different types of literary form observed in the Qur'ān. As attributed to Ibn 'Abbās, "God sent down the Qur'ān five times five verses at a time, five self-explanatory, five metaphorical, five prescriptive, five prohibitive, and five parabolic verses."[40] This fivefold distinction, however, provided neither a rationale for the interpretation of the Qur'ān as a whole, nor a consistent interpretive method for each of its verses taken singularly or in particular reflections. Rather, the Ṣūfīs found the necessary rationale in two statements, one coined by Sahl al-Tustarī and the other attributed to Ja'far al-Ṣādiq (d. 148/765).[41] According to both of these crucial statements, each qur'ānic verse was susceptible to interpretation in a fourfold manner, an exegetical expansion that came to be identified as four so-called "senses" of scripture.

Sahl al-Tustarī states that "each verse (*āya*) of the Qur'ān has four meanings, an outer meaning, *ẓāhir*, an inner meaning, *bāṭin*, a norm, *ḥadd*, and an anagose, *maṭla'/muṭṭala'*."[42] This literal translation of the statement includes lexical difficulties of which Sahl al-Tustarī is aware, since he adds an explanation that justifies the identification of *ẓāhir*, *bāṭin*, *ḥadd*, and *maṭla'/muṭṭala'* with the technical terminology of four senses of scripture: a literal, an allegorical, a moral or tropological, and an anagogical sense. He says, "The outer (literal) sense is the recitation (*tilāwa*) and the inner (allegorical) sense the understanding of the verse (*fahm*). The normative (moral) sense defines what is declared lawful and unlawful by the verse and the anagogical (transcendent) sense is the command of the heart over the meaning intended by it (*al-murād bihi*) as understood from the vantage point of God (*fiqhan min Allāh*)."[43]

The core statement itself is developed from a prophetic *ḥadīth*, related by both a Kufan and a Basran line of transmission. The Kufan transmission can be traced back, via Abū l-Aḥwaṣ ('Awf b. Mālik b. Naḍla l-Jushamī),[44] to 'Abdallāh b. Mas'ūd (d. 32/652).[45] The Basran chain of transmitters, as quoted by Abū Ḥafṣ 'Umar al-Suhrawardī on the authority of his own master and uncle Abū l-Najīb 'Abd al-Qāhir al-Suhrawardī (d. 563/1168), has its earliest links in Abū 'Ubayd al-Qāsim b. Sallām al-Baghdādī (d. 224/838), who transmits on the authority of Abū Muḥammad Ḥajjāj b. Minhāl al-Anmāṭī (d. 216–17/831–32)—Abū Salama Ḥammād b. Salama al-Barī (d. 167/784)—Abū l-Ḥasan 'Alī b. Zayd b. Jud'ān al-Qurashī (d. 131/748–49)—al-Ḥasan al-Baṣrī—the Prophet. However, Abū Ḥafṣ 'Umar al-Suhrawardī states that Abū 'Ubayd understood this saying as identical with the one transmitted by Ibn Mas'ūd, and that Ḥajjāj b. Minhāl undergirded his transmission with another of Ibn Mas'ūd's sayings which was similar in content. In literal translation the *ḥadīth* states: "No verse of the Qur'ān was sent down that would not have a "back" (*ẓahr*) and a "belly" (*baṭn*). Each word (*ḥarf*) has a "horizon" (*ḥadd*) and each horizon has "dawn" (*maṭla'/muṭṭala'*)."[46]

On the authority of 'Alī the statement is phrased slightly differently: "There is no verse of the Qur'ān that would not have four meanings (*ma'ānī*): an outer meaning (*ẓāhir*), an inner meaning (*bāṭin*), a moral meaning (*ḥadd*), including the precepts concerning what is lawful and unlawful, and an anagogical meaning (*maṭla'/muṭṭala'*), that is, what God intends to disclose through it to his servant."[47] A key to the understanding of this *ḥadīth* in its oldest ascription to Ibn Mas'ūd, however, may be found in al-Sulamī's quotation of another variant as related by Ibn Mas'ūd also on the authority of Abū l-Aḥwaṣ with the following chain of transmitters: Abū 'Abd al-Raḥmān al-Sulamī—'Abdallāh b. Muḥammad b. 'Alī b. Ziyād al-Daqqāq—Muḥammad b. Isḥāq b. Ibrāhīm al-Thaqafī (d. 313/925)—Isḥāq b. Ibrāhīm al-Ḥanẓalī—Abū l-Naḍr Jarīr b. Ḥāzim b. 'Abdallāh al-Baṣrī al-Jahḍamī (d. 170/876)—Wāṣil b. Ḥayyān (= Abū Hudhayfa Wāṣil b. 'Aṭā' al-Ghazzāl, d. 132/748–49?)—Ibn Abī l-Hudhayl—Abū l-Aḥwaṣ—'Abdallāh b. Mas'ūd—the Prophet: "The Qur'ān was sent down according to seven ways of reading (*aḥruf*), [its passages] each of their verses has a back and a belly, and each word (*ḥarf*) has a horizon and a dawn."[48] This version of the prophetic *ḥadīth* clearly refers to the "lectiones" (*aḥruf*, plural of *ḥarf*), the ways of reading the Qur'ān, and establishes a link between *ḥarf* as word and as "lectio."[49]

The *ḥadīth* not only includes difficult terms, it also combines two seemingly separate assertions. First, it states that each qur'ānic verse (*āya*) has an outer meaning, a *ẓahr*, literally a "back, outside or surface," and an inner meaning, a *baṭn*, literally a "belly, inside, or depth." Second, it links with this image the idea that each word (*ḥarf*) of the Qur'ān has a norm, a *ḥadd*, literally a "boundary" or a "horizon" of its intended meaning, and an anagoge *maṭla'/muṭṭala'*, literally a "dawn" or a point of ascending from the horizon of the intended meaning to a higher understanding of the passage.

By blurring the distinction between *āya* and *ḥarf*, Sahl al-Tustarī transforms the *ḥadīth* into a statement that collapses the two separate assertions into a composite declaration of the fourfold meaning of each qur'ānic verse. In fact, however, he effectively reduces the four levels of meaning to two by linking the literal and moral meaning in contrast with the combined allegorical and anagogical meaning. For he equates the *bāṭin* and *maṭla'* levels, making them the domain of the mystic elite, the "select," *khāṣṣ*, whereas he grants the common people, *'āmm*, access only to the combined literal and moral meaning.[50] Somewhat later al-Junayd (d. 297/910),[51] who counted Sahl al-Tustarī among his teachers, also distinguishes a fourfold sense of the qur'ānic text and asserts that "the word of God (*kalām Allāh*) has an outer meaning (*ẓāhir*), an inner meaning (*bāṭin*), an actual (*ḥaqq*), and a mystical meaning (*ḥaqīqa*).[52]

In Ṣūfī Qur'ān commentaries, Ja'far al-Ṣādiq is also on record with a statement concerning a four-point pattern of qur'ānic exegesis. "The Book of God is based on four things: the literal expression (*'ibāra*), the allegorical allusion (*ishāra*), the mystical symbols (*laṭā'if*), and the divine realities (*ḥaqā'iq*)."[53] This statement, too, combines two separate assertions, one applied to the distinction between the common people and the mystical elite, and the other to that between saints and prophets. For Ja'far al-Ṣādiq assigns comprehension of the literal expression to the common people and grants the mystics access to the allegorical allusion, while he reserves the *laṭā'if*, the mystical symbols, literally the subtleties, for the friends of God (*awliyā'*) and privileges the prophets (*anbiyā'*) with penetration of the *ḥaqā'iq*, the divine realities.[54] An anonymous gloss, cited in al-Sulamī's *Ḥaqā'iq al-tafsīr*, explains that the literal expression is meant to be listened to, the allegorical allusion is to be understood, while the subtleties are the object of contemplation, and the realities lead to self-surrender.[55] Ja'far al-Ṣādiq is also, however, on record in Ṣūfī Qur'ān commentaries with statements that emphasize a sevenfold or ninefold pattern of qur'ānic exegesis. In one of his sayings he differentiates seven types (*anwā'*)—*taṭrīf, taklīf, ta'ṭīf, tashrīf, ta'līf, takhwīf*, and *takfīf*[56]—and in another he enumerates nine aspects (*awjuh*) of the Qur'ān: *ḥaqq, ḥaqīqa, taḥqīq, ḥaqā'iq, 'uhūd, 'uqūd, ḥudūd, qaṭ' al-'alā'iq*, and *ijlāl al-ma'būd*.[57]

Grappling with the legitimacy of the four senses of scripture, Ḥārith al-Muḥāsibī (d. 243/857) identifies the literal meaning with the recitation of the Qur'ān (*tilāwa*), and the hidden, metaphorical meaning with the interpretive insight into the Qur'ān (*ta'wīl*). Yet neither those who merely recite the Qur'ān nor those who possess insights into its interpretation reach the limit of interpretation (*ḥadd*). This limit or norm is reached by the *ṣiddiqūn*, the sincere and accomplished mystics who alone possess the greatest possible insight into the depth of the Qur'ān. They understand the full meaning of the qur'ānic verses the way God himself understands them. For most Ṣūfīs this understanding constitutes a transition from the human interpretation of the Qur'ān to God's very own understanding of its meaning. In the general Ṣūfī view this step is taken when one reaches the anagoge, the so-called point of transcendency (*maṭla'/muṭṭala'*). For some Ṣūfīs such as al-Muḥāsibī this point defines not a mode of legitimate interpretation, but a line of transgression. Humans who try to overstep it go beyond the barriers established by God and fall into the trap of reading their own whims, fancies, and imaginations into a qur'ānic verse, ultimately falsifying its divinely intended meaning.[58]

These fourfold patterns of Qur'ān interpretation attributed to Sahl al-Tustarī, Ja'far al-Ṣādiq, and, with modifications, other Ṣūfīs as well, are not, however, systematically employed in the interpretation of qur'ānic verses throughout their commentaries, which are extant in substantial parts. In fact, there is not a single qur'ānic verse or keynote to which the fourfold pattern has been applied in a rigorous fashion. Rather, most authors consistently differentiate between a twofold meaning, a literal and a hidden allegorical sense, with primary emphasis on the hidden, allegorical meaning of the Qur'ān. On the other hand, some Ṣūfī authors expanded these twofold and fourfold patterns by creating additional categories of qur'ānic interpretation and assembling them in manifold ways, particularly in patterns of seven or twelve. Yet it was chiefly the fourfold pattern that attracted Western scholarly attentions, from Ignaz Goldziher through Louis Massignon to Josef van Ess, likely because of its suspected similarity to the four senses of scripture that emerged in biblical interpretation.

Encapsulated in the classical adage of medieval Christian exegesis—*littera gesta docet, quid credas allegoria, moralis quid agas, quo tendas anagogia*—and extensively studied in Henri de Lubac's *Exégèse médiévale*,[59] the analogy between the two is tempting, though untenable, if seen as directly and historically linking Islamic hermeneutics with the principles of biblical exegesis developed in the Jewish tradition and in Christian patristic exegesis. It is quite possible, however, that the early Ṣūfīs had some inkling of Christian and Jewish exegesis through contact with these cultures and with Christian and Jewish converts to the Muslim faith. Such contacts may well have facilitated the transmission of elements of the Jewish-Christian exegetical legacies into the Islamic environment. One may even feel inclined to see the exegetical distinction between *ẓāhir* and *bāṭin* as stimulated by the distinction between the literal and allegorical senses of scripture in the Alexandrian school, inspired by Philo of Alexandria (d. 45–50 C.E.) and elaborated in the Christian context by Origen (d. 254 C.E.). Origen, however, distinguishes three levels of meaning—somatic, psychic, and pneumatic—corresponding to his theory of body, soul, and spirit. Against the concept of *allegoria*, dominant in the Alexandrian school, the Antiochene school, remembered by Theodore of Mopsuestia (d. 428 C.E.), emphasized *theoria*, the discernment of intuitive and prophetical vision, as including both literal and metaphorical senses of scripture. Eventually, however, the doctrine of the four senses of scripture—historical, allegorical, tropological, and anagogical—emerged in the Latin tradition in Cassian (d. 435 C.E.), Augustine (d. 430 C.E.), and the sixth-century writings of Pseudo-Dionysius.[60]

Both the differentiation between literal and spiritual senses widely used in Jewish biblical hermeneutics and in Christian patristic exegesis, as well as the four senses of scripture developed in the Latin tradition, may be the ultimate roots of the Islamic distinctions between *ẓāhir* and *bāṭin* and the definition of a fourfold meaning of the Qur'ān (including literal, allegorical, moral or tropological, and anagogical senses). The acronym *PaRDeS*, however, employed as a mnemonic device for a fourfold exegesis of the Bible in medieval Judaism, including *peshaṭ* (literal meaning), *remez* (metaphorical interpretation), *derash* (homiletical interpretation), and *sod* (esoteric interpretation), can be confidently traced only as far back as Moses de Leon, who wrote his *Sefer ha-Pardes* in about 1290.[61] Although this fourfold pattern of exegesis echoes older Jewish precepts of biblical hermeneutics, both in form and in content, it has been difficult to push it back to Philo, or for that matter to link it with earlier Christian or Muslim hermeneutical precepts in clear lines of historical dependence. Yet the hermeneutical similarities are striking, especially if Ja'far al-Ṣādiq's methodological distinction of exegetical principles is compared with the Jewish tradition and Sahl al-Tustarī's with the Christian patristic tradition.[62] Demonstrable historical dependence, however, remains as yet unproven. Nowhere, moreover, do Ṣūfī Qur'ān commentaries consciously reflect such traces of historical continuity or dependence. The overriding attention of the Ṣūfī authors is directed to the central questions of Islamic mysticism, such as those surrounding the mystical vision of God and the recollection of the divine presence in prayer. These two basic themes will now be illustrated by clusters of characteristically Ṣūfī Qur'ān interpretation in order to exemplify the somewhat abstract methodological considerations discussed so far.

The prototype of the Ṣūfīs' mystical theophany is Muḥammad's vision of God as based on Q 53:1–18 and its parallels, passages that actually refer to two separate visions. Q53:1–18 reads:

> By the Star when it plunges, your comrade is not astray, neither errs, nor speaks he out of caprice. This is naught but a revelation revealed, taught him by one terrible in power, very strong; he stood poised, being on the higher horizon, then drew near and suspended hung, two bows'-length away, or nearer, then revealed to his servant that he revealed. His heart lies not of what he saw; what, will you dispute with him what he sees? Indeed, he

saw him another time by the Lote-Tree of the Boundary nigh which is the Garden of the Refuge, when there covered the Lote-Tree that which covered; his eye swerved not, nor swept astray. Indeed, he saw one of the greatest signs of his Lord.[63]

The various facets of interpretation linked with the Ṣūfī commentary on this passage demonstrate the way in which the Ṣūfīs translate the aurality of the Qur'ān as recited scripture into visual imagery. It further demonstrates the wide range of their exegetical flexibility. The following four examples of classical Ṣūfī exegesis highlighting Muḥammad's vision of God from different perspectives—the foretaste of the beatific vision, the primordial vision of preexistence, the vision as a spiritual journey of the soul, and the vision portrayed by the symbolism of love in secret communion—bridge the gulf between humanity and the Transcendent in a partially allegorical and a partially anagogical sense.

In the first of these, Abū Bakr al-Wāsiṭī (d. 320/932)[64] focuses on the uniqueness of Muḥammad's vision, understanding it as a breakthrough to eternity that anticipates the beatific vision in the world to come. The Prophet stands in the presence of the Transcendent at the Lote-Tree of the Boundary with his gaze fixed on the concealed God hidden behind veils. As the veils are lifted, all of Muḥammad's qualities, including self-consciousness, are effaced, and he is drawn into the vision God has of himself. Concluding his account, al-Wāsiṭī stresses, "In reality, it was God's essence witnessing his own essence, even though the accounts of Muslim tradition state that Muḥammad witnessed God."[65]

Rather than hearkening to an eternity beyond resurrection, in the second example Sahl al-Tustarī[66] traces the vision back to preexistential times when Muḥammad witnessed God at the dawn of creation in an act of primordial adoration during the unfathomable eon preceding Adam. When God resolved to fashion the cosmos and the human race, so Sahl al-Tustarī explains, God shaped Muḥammad from his own light as his first creation and had him bow down in prostration before the veil of divine majesty. From this light of Muḥammad (*nūr Muḥammad*), God fashioned a column of light, crystal-clear in its translucency. Not unlike the cosmic logos of Hellenistic speculation, this remained in the presence of God for a hundred thousand years before the beginning of creation, receiving the revelation of the divine mystery at the Lote-Tree of the Boundary and witnessing God face to face in the theophany of his attributes. Only after Muḥammad had stood as a column of light for a hundred thousand years in primordial adoration of God did God create Adam from the light of Muḥammad and the clay of divine glory.

The third interpretation, that of Ibn 'Aṭā' al-Adamī (d. 309/922)[67] interiorizes Muḥammad's vision as a spiritual journey to the innermost stages of the soul, a journey that paradoxically reaches the farthest horizon of nearness to God. Combining Muḥammad's vision at the Lote-Tree of the Boundary with the theme of the Prophet's night journey and ascension to heaven, Ibn 'Aṭā' states that "Muḥammad set out with his soul (*nafs*), traveled by night with his spirit (*rūḥ*), and was driven on by his inmost being (*sirr*)."[68] With Muḥammad sustained by God in his heart, his intellect, and his glance, sanctified by the lights of prophethood and fortified by the vision of the divine realities, his soul is firmly fixed in the station nearest to God. "Muḥammad beheld the Real One (*al-ḥaqq*), apprehending something of him without any mediation and without any human support. The Real One dealt with his servant in the (fullness of) reality and made him real, installing him where there is no station, addressing him, and revealing to him what he revealed."[69]

The fourth example, as drawn for the mystical Qur'ān interpretation attributed to Ja'far al-Ṣādiq, understands Muḥammad's vision as a meeting of lover and beloved, one establishing an exclusive domain of intimacy and awe. There is no space for a third party in this personal encounter with God nor is anyone else aware of the secrets God communicates in confidential conversation. A poignant segment of the commentary reads:

> The Real One inclined toward him with the affection of a lover for his beloved, and he communicated with him in secret as a lover converses with his beloved. They kept things hidden and did not divulge their secret to anyone else. No one knows that revelation except the One who revealed it and the one who received the revelation. No one knows what he beheld except the One who showed it and the one who beheld it. The lover drew near to the beloved, becoming his confidant and intimate.[70]

These highly esoteric interpretations of Muḥammad's vision at the Lote-Tree of the Boundary near the garden of paradise are clearly allegorical in character and anagogical in their allusions to the beatific vision, the primordial covenant, the spiritual journey of the soul, and the symbolism of God and his prophet as lover and beloved. To supplement and support their spiritual exegesis, the Ṣūfī commentators employ a method of synthetical interpretation that draws other, seemingly related, qur'ānic verses into the commentary on the particular passage. They use regiments, such as the verse pointing to the Prophet's night journey, the famous light verse, or the verse alluding to the purification of Muḥammad's heart[71] to bolster their exegesis of the primary passage, detecting an inner affinity even when, as in some cases, the linkage seems rather tangential.

The second theme to be examined, that of the recollection of the divine presence in prayer, can best be approached from the idea of the primordial covenant between God and the human race as this is rediscovered within the soul of the mystic by a process of anamnesis during the practice of *dhikr*, Ṣūfī recollection.[72] Two figures central to the Ṣūfī circle of Baghdad, al-Junayd and Ruwaym (d. 303/916),[73] depended loosely on Sahl al-Tustarī in developing this connection through a synthetical interpretation that amalgamates Q 7:172–73 and Q 79:15–25. The first passage reads, "And when your Lord took from the children of Adam, from their loins, their seed, and made them testify touching themselves, 'Am I not your Lord (*alastu bi-rabbikum*)?' They said, 'Yes, we testify'—lest you [i.e., humankind] should say on the Day of Resurrection, "As for us, we were heedless of this," or lest you say, "Our fathers were idolaters aforetime, and we were seed after them. What, will you then destroy us for the deeds of the vain-doers?[74]'" The second passage reads, "Have you received the story of Moses? When his Lord called to him in the holy valley, Ṭuwā: 'Go to Pharaoh; he has waxed insolent. And say, "Have you the will to purify yourself, and that I should guide you to your Lord, then you shall fear?"' So he showed him the great sign, but he cried lies, and rebelled, then he turned away hastily, then he mustered and proclaimed, and he said, 'I am your Lord, the Most High!' So God seized him with the chastisement of the Last World and the First."[75]

Ṣūfī exegesis traces the first passage back to preexistence and completely reverses the ordinary interpretation of the second passage. In preexistence, before the beginning of time and prior to God's creation of Adam as his viceroy on earth, the entire future human race, embryonically enshrined in their biological ancestor as Adam's seeds, is taken by God from the back of Adam. Spiritually extracted as sperm or light particles from the loins of their forefather, they are summoned by God to testify to his oneness and lordship. As God asks them, "Am I not your Lord?" they answer "Yes" thereby assuming the contractual obligation to profess monotheism once born into earthly existence. Intuitively perceiving God's testimony about himself in preexistence, they bear witness to him as the one and only Lord. The offer of divine testimony and its acceptance by the future human race not only constitute the primordial covenant between God and humanity, but at the same time endow individual human beings with intellect in their first self-conscious act.

Once born, virtually all human beings have the capacity to recall and reactualize their preexistential past in the secret of their souls, created by God as the locus of his intimate colloquy with each human, but only Ṣūfī mystics ever actualize this potential. The concentrated introspection of the mystic comprehends this colloquy as a soliloquy of God's self-revelation, manifesting himself in the soul of the mystic through the qur'ānic words, "I am your Lord, the Most High (*anā rabbukum al-a'lā*)."[76] These were the very words God uttered in his primordial self-revelation, and the mystic hears them as echoing in the secret of his inmost being (*sirr al-nafs*). Were this secret publicly divulged, its revelation would obliterate the distinction between prophets and saints or neutralize the purpose of prophethood, the essence of which is the summons to monotheism.

At one point, however, God revealed this inmost secret to Pharaoh, the symbol of unbelief in the Qur'ān. Hearing the qur'ānic words of Pharaoh's blasphemous proclamation of his own divinity, "I am your Lord, the Most High," the mystic ironically perceives the actual essence of belief flowing from Pharaoh's tongue of unbelief. In his exercise of Ṣūfī recollection (*dhikr*), the mystic remembers, as if by anamnesis, the moment in preexistence when God affirmed his oneness and lordship for human consciousness. This anamnosis is confirmed by the words of Ruwaym: "Humanity heard its first *dhikr*, when God addressed them (in preexistence), 'Am I not your Lord?' This *dhikr* was secreted in their hearts even as its occurrence was secreted in their intellects. So when they heard the *dhikr* (reciting the Qur'ān in the exercise of Ṣūfī recollection), the secret things of their heart appeared, and they were ravished: When the secret things of their intellects appeared and God informed them of this, they believed."[77]

After these forays into the realm of esoterics, the flight into eternity, the return to the primordial past, the journey of the soul, and exegesis turned into eisegesis, what can be said in conclusion? Medieval Ṣūfī interpretation of the Qur'ān demonstrates a great measure of reverence for the word, the revealed word of God recorded in the Qur'ān. Reading the book of God, rather than the book of nature, as the source of their inspiration, and neutralizing the prophets as mediators between humanity and God, the Ṣūfīs turn their attention singlemindedly to the Qur'ān and assign the role of mediator solely to the divine word. Unflinching in their monotheism and unrestricted in their interpretation of God's word, they seem unconcerned by the subjectivity of their exegetical method and the variegated nature of their hermeneutics. In fact, they show a preference for synthetic interpretation that intertwines disparate verses of the Qur'ān creating oft-repeated thematic relations and collapsing their commentary into a combined narrative of interpretation.

Demonstrating another characteristic form of exegesis, however, their use of analytical interpretation largely determines the actual selection of qur'ānic verses for commentary. Such analytical interpretation transforms those episodes that relate God's interaction with his prophets into prototypes of mystical experience. It also isolates telling references to God's nature and action, or values verses in which God speaks about himself in the first person. Whenever God says, *Anā*, "I am," permitting no rival to his claim for unicity and oneness, mystical Qur'ān interpretation attains its singular spiritual sensitivity. The mystical exegesis of qur'ānic expressions, such as "Am I not your Lord?" or "I am your Lord, the Most High!" dissolve the distinct identities of the human self and God, leaving only the ultimate and absolute *Anā*, called "God" as the object of faith, but "I" as the subject of mystical experience. The final truth of Islamic mysticism—that there is only One Who can truly say, "I"—is expressed in the ecstatic utterances of the Ṣūfīs, such as "I am He" or "I am the Real" (*anā l-ḥaqq*), secured in the innermost reaches of the soul through insight into the allegorical and anagogical meaning of the Qur'ān.

Notes

1. Goldziher, *Richtungen*.

2. Massignon, *Essai*; Nwyia, *Exégèse coranique*; Ateş, *Işârî Tefsîr Okulu*; Böwering, *Mystical Vision*; Lory, *Commentaires ésotériques*.

3. Q 6:120; 31:20; 57:3 [cf. Isa 44:6; 48:12]; 57:13 [cf. Matt 25:1–13]. See Paret, "Sure 57,12f"; cf. Q 6:151; 7:33.

4. Q 3:7; for *muḥkamāt* see also, Q 11:1; 22:52; 47:20; and for *mutashābihāt* see also Q 2:25 (with reference to the fruits of paradise); Q 6:99 and 6:141 (with reference to earthly fruits); Q 39:23 (with reference to revealed messages, cf. the commentary on Q 15:87, in Paret, *Der Koran*, 279–80).

5. Q 16:116; cf. 2:168; 5:87–88 (see Rivlin, *Gesetz im Koran*, 72–78; Gräf, *Jagdbeute*, 56); Q 8:69 (with reference to lawful booty at the battle of Badr); Q 10:59; 16:114.

6. Q 7:154 (*nuskha*); 45:29 (*nastansikhu*); cf. Jeffery, *The Foreign Vocabulary of the Qur'an*, 279–80; Horovitz, *Jewish Proper Names*, 80–81.

7. Q 2:106 (*nansakh*); Q 22:52 (*yansakhu*); cf. 16:101. See Burton, "*Naskh*," *EI*, new ed. 7:1009–12. Wansbrough, *Quranic Studies*, 192–202; Burton, *Sources of Islamic Law*; Versteegh, *Arabic Grammar*, 71–74. A paradigmatic example of "abrogation" of a particular qur'ānic verse is Q 4:10–11 abrogating the chronologically earlier verse Q 2:180, with regard to specific rulings about inheritance, or the claim that "the stoning verse" had been omitted from the definitve text of the Qur'ān.

8. Q 18:109; for an extensive Ṣūfī commentary on this verse, cf., e.g., al-Suhrawardī, *'Awārif al-ma'ārif*, Beirut ed., 24–25; Cairo ed., 1:162–63; Gramlich, *Gaben der Erkenntnisse*, 39.

9. Q 31:27 (see also Strack and Billerbeck, *Kommentar zum Neuen Testament*, 2:587; Haeuptner, *Koranische Hinweise*, 99–100).

10. Ibn Taymiyya, *Risāla fī 'ilm al-bāṭin wa-l-ẓāhir*, 230.

11. For a short account of the meaning of *'ilm al-bāṭin* in Shī'ism and Ṣūfism, see Radtke, "*Bāṭen*," in *EIr*, 3:859–61, and Halm, "*Bāṭenīya*," in *EIr*, 3:861–63.

12. Abū Sa'īd Ḥasan b. Yasār al-Baṣrī, born in Medina in 21/642, belonged to the class of Muḥammad's followers (*tābi'ūn*) and became famous as a deeply religious personality and eloquent preacher at Basra during Umayyad times. He holds a crucial place in the development of early Islamic theology, (cf. Ess, *Theologie und Gesellschaft*, 2:41–121 and 4:1057) and inspired the early developments of Ṣūfism; only fragments of his qur'ānic commentary are extant; cf. Ritter, "Ḥasan al-Baṣrī," *EI*, new ed., 1:247–48.

13. 'Abd al-Wāḥid b. Zayd's circle of disciples was the first to organize a Ṣūfī lodge (*ribāṭ*) in 'Abbādān. Cf. Meier, *Abū Sa'īd-i Abū l-Ḥayr*, 303–4; Böwering, *Mystical Vision*, 47–48, 303–304. 'Abd al-Wāḥid b. Zayd died in about 150/767 or shortly thereafter, but not in 177/793, as is generally assumed; cf. Ess, *Theologie und Gesellschaft*, 2:97.

14. Abū 'Abdallāh al-Ḥārith b. Asad al-Muḥāsibī, a highly renowned theologian and mystic during the first century of 'Abbāsid rule, was born in Basra but was active mainly in Baghdad, where before the year 230/845 he wrote a short treatise on qur'ānic exegesis, *Kitāb fahm al-Qur'ān*; cf. Ess, *Gedankenwelt des Ḥāriṯ al-Muḥāsibī*; idem, *Theologie und Gesellschaft*, 4:195–209, 1080; Arnaldez, "Muḥāsibī," *EI*, new ed., 7:466–67.

15. al-Kalābādhī, *Kitāb al-ta'arruf*; idem, *The Doctrine of the Ṣūfīs*, trans. Arberry; Abū Naṣr al-Sarrāj, *The Kitāb al-luma' fī l-taṣawwuf*; idem, *Pages from the Kitāb al-luma'*, ed. Arberry; Gramlich, *Schlaglichter über das Sufitum*; Abū Ṭālib al-Makkī, *Qūt al-qulūb*; Gramlich, *Die Nahrung der Herzen*; al-Kharkūshī, *Tahdhīb al-asrār*; cf. GAS 1:670; Arberry, "Khargushi's Manual of Sufism."

16. Abū l-Qāsim al-Qushayrī, *al-Risāla*, with continuing pagination; Gramlich, *Sendschreiben al-Qušayrīs über das Sufitum*; al-Hujwīrī, *Kashf al-maḥjūb*; idem, *The Kashf al-Mahjūb*, trans. Nicholson; al-Ghazzālī, *Iḥyā' 'ulūm al-dīn*; Gramlich, *Muḥammad al-Ġazzālīs Lehre*; al- Suhrawardī, *'Awārif al-ma'ārif*; Gramlich, *Die Gaben der Erkenntnisse des 'Umar as-Suhrawardī*.

17. al-Sulamī, *Ṭabaqāt al-ṣūfīya*; cf. Böwering, al-Sulamī, *EI*, new ed., 9:811–12; Anṣārī-i Harawī, *Ṭabaqāt al-ṣūfīya*.

18. Radtke, *Drei Schriften des Theosophen von Tirmiḏ*.

19. al-Tustarī, *Tafsīr al-Qur'ān al-'aẓīm*; Böwering, *Mystical Vision*.

20. Radtke, ed., *Adab al-mulūk*, 34.

21. The missing link is Aḥmad b. 'Alī al-Hujaymī; cf. al-Suhrawardī, *'Awārif al-ma'ārif*, 225; Gramlich, *Gaben*, 81, 195; see also Radtke, ed., *Adab al-mulūk*, 34.

22. al-Qushayrī, *al-Risāla*, 2:443; Gramlich, *Sendschreiben*, 295–96.

23. cf. Böwering, *Mystical Vision*, 135–37.

24. Abū 'Abd al-Raḥmān al-Sulamī's *Ḥaqā'iq al-tafsīr* is extant in its entirety in a great number of manuscripts cf. Böwering, "The Qur'ān Commentary of al-Sulamī," 51–53. Extracts were published by Massignon, *Essai*, 359–412; Nwyia, "Le Tafsīr mystique"; reprinted in Zay'ūr, *al-Tafsīr al-ṣūfī li-l-Qur'ān*, 125–212; Nwyia, "Sentences de Nūrī"; Nwiya, *Trois oeuvres inédites de mystiques musulmans*, 23–182. The recent publication of *Tafsīr al-Sulamū*, 2 vols., Beirut 1421/2001 represents a transcription of ms. Iotih 261 (600 a.h., 316 ff.).

25. al-Sulamī, *Ziyādāt ḥaqā'iq al-tafsīr*; cf. Böwering, "The Major Sources of Sulamī's Minor Qur'ān Commentary."

26. Rūzbihān al-Baqlī, *'Arā'is al-bayān wa-ḥaqā'iq al-Qur'ān*.

27. cf. Böwering, "Deylamī, Šams-al-Dīn," in *EIr*, 7:341–42.

28. al-Qushayrī, *Laṭā'if al-ishārāt*; for the somewhat complex situation of al-Qushayrī's activity as a Qur'ān commentator, see Böwering, review of *Das Sendschreiben*, by R. Gramlich.

29. Abū Ḥafṣ 'Umar al-Suhrawardī's (d. 632/1234) *Nughbat al-bayān* is extant in manuscript only.

30. al-Maybudī, *Kashf al-asrār wa-'uddat al-abrār*; cf. Sharī'at, *Fihrist-i Tafsīr*; Corbin, *Histoire de la philosophie islamique*, 22.

31. For the intricate attribution of the Qur'ān commentary by Najm al-Dīn al-Kubrā, Najm al-Dīn al-Rāzī, and 'Alā' al-Dawla al-Simnānī to these three authors, see Meier, "Stambuler Handschriften"; Ateş, "Üç müfessir bir tefsīr"; Shpall, "A Note on Najm al-Dīn al-Rāzī"; Elias, *The Throne Carrier of God*, 203–12; cf. also Corbin, *The Man of Light in Iranian Sufism*, 61–131.

32. al-Qāshānī, *Tafsīr al-Qur'ān al-karīm*; Lory, *Les commentaires ésotériques du Coran*; cf. Chodkiewicz, *Un océan sans rivage*.

33. Q 17:106; see Horovitz, *Jewish Proper Names*, 72–74; Jeffery, *Foreign Vocabulary*, 225–29; Paret, "Furqān," *EI*, new ed., 2:949–50.

34. Q 25:32.

35. 'Abdallāh b. al-'Abbās, a cousin of Muḥammad, commonly referred to as Ibn 'Abbās, died in 68/687 or, according to others, in 69/688 or 70/689. He was given the epithets of the

great doctor (*ḥabr*) of the community and the ocean (*baḥr*) of knowledge who was "the interpreter (*tarjumān*) of the Qur'ān"; cf. Veccia Vaglieri, "'Abd Allāh b. al-'Abbās," *EI*, new ed. 1: 40–41. The problems surrounding the Qur'ān commentary attributed to Ibn 'Abbās have been discussed by 'Salqīnī, *Ḥabr al-umma 'Abdallāh b. 'Abbās*, and by Goldfeld, "The Tafsīr of 'Abdallāh b. 'Abbās"; cf. also Rippin, "Ibn 'Abbās's al-Lughāt fi l-Qur'ān"; idem, "Ibn 'Abbās's Gharīb al-Qur'ān;" Gilliet, "Portrait mythique." The extant works, entitled *Tafsīr Ibn 'Abbās*, are by and large the redaction of Muḥammad b. al-Sā'ib al-Kalbī (d. 146/763), who transmits on the authority of 'Alī b. Abī Ṭalḥa al-Hāshimī (d. 120/737), that were collected by Abū Ṭāhir al-Fīrūzābādī (d. 817/1415), *Tanwīr al-miqbās min tafsīr Ibn 'Abbās*; cf. *GAS*, 1:25–28.

36. al-Tustarī, *Tafsīr*, 5.

37. Q 85:22 (*fī lawḥ maḥfūẓ*), to which may be compared the parallel passages, Q 56:78 (*fī kitāb maknūn*) and Q 80:13–16 (*fī ṣuḥuf mukarrama*). *Lawḥ* can mean two things in the Qur'ān: a "plank," such as Noah's ark made of planks (*dhāt alwāḥ*, 54:13), or a "tablet" of writing material, such as the tablets of Moses (*al-alwāḥ*, 7:145, 150, 154). In context, one can read Q 85:21–22 in two ways: (1) "Verily it is a glorious Qur'ān, in a guarded (*maḥfūẓin*) tablet," which refers to the tablet safely kept in heaven, or (2) "Verily it is a Qur'ān, glorious, preserved (*maḥfūẓun*) on a tablet," which would refer to the preservation of the Qur'ān against alteration. The first way of reading the passage is widely understood in connection with Q 97:1–5 with its reference to the night of the decree (*laylat al-qadr*). Furthermore, the linkage of Q 85:21–22 with Q 97:1–5 is interpreted in the Qur'ān commentaries either as a reference to the first revelation of Muḥammad (cf. Wagtendonk, *Fasting in the Koran*, 82–122), or as the descent of the Qur'ān from that tablet, which is above the seventh heaven, to the lowest. In this perspective the tablet as the original copy of the Qur'ān is identical with the archetypal book of the Heavenly Writ (*umm al-kitāb*, Q 3:7, 13:39, 43:4); cf. Wensinck, "Lawḥ," *EI*, new ed., 5:698.

38. Q 2:97–98; 66:4.

39. al-Tustarī, *Tafsīr*, 5.

40. Ibid., 6.

41. Ja'far al-Ṣādiq was born in Medina in either 80/699 or 83/703, the son of Muḥammad al-Bāqir (d. 114/732 or 117/735), the fifth Shī'a *imām*, and of Umm Farwa, a great-granddaughter of Abū Bakr (d. 13/634). Shortly before the revolt of his uncle Zayd b. 'Alī in 122/740, Ja'far was recognized as the sixth Shī'a *imām*. He neither played an active political role during the transition from Umayyad to 'Abbāsid rule nor supported the unsuccessful revolt of Ibrāhīm b. 'Abdallāh in 145/762. Except for some time spent in Kufa during his later years, Ja'far al-Ṣādiq lived and worked quietly as a scholar in Medina, where he died in 148/765; cf. Hodgson, "Ja'far al-Ṣādiq," *EI*, new ed., 2:374–75; Halm, *Shiism*, 29–31; al-Dhahabī, *Siyar a'lām al-nubalā*, 6:255–70; idem, *Ta'rīkh al-islām*, 9:88–93 (for years 141–60).

42. al-Tustarī, *Tafsīr*, 3; for an analysis of *ḥadd* as "boundary" and "delimitation", cf. B. Carra de Vaux, F. Schacht and L. M. Goidron, "*Ḥadd*," *EI*, new ed., 3:20–22, and Ess, *Theologie*, 2, 596f, 3, 288f, and 5, 72 and passim.

43. Ibid; for an analysis of *maṭla,ᶜ* see D. King, "Maṭlaᶜ," *EI*, new ed., 6:839–40.

44. He lived at Kufa and transmitted from Ibn Mas'ūd and 'Alī b. Abī Ṭālib; cf. Ibn Sa'd, *al-Ṭabaqāt al-kubrā*, 6:181–82; al-Baghdādī, *Ta'rīkh Baghdād*, 12:290–91.

45. 'Abdallāh b. Mas'ūd was a famous Companion of the Prophet and an early convert to Islam. He was in the small group of Muslims who emigrated from Mecca to Abyssinia but returned to follow Muḥammad to Medina. He took part in the battle of Yarmūk in 13/634 and settled permanently at Kufa in 21/642, where he was renowned as a reader of the Qur'ān until his death in 32/653; cf. Vadet, "Ibn Mas'ūd,"*EI*, new ed. 3:873–75.

46. al-Suhrawardī, *'Awārif al-ma'ārif*, Beirut ed., 25; Cairo ed., 1:163; Gramlich, *Gaben der Erkenntnisse*, 39; cf. Goldziher, *Richtungen*, 215; Ess, *Gedankenwelt*, 209.

47. al-Sulamī, *Ḥaqā'iq al-tafsīr*, introduction (manuscript reference).

48. al-Sulamī, *Ḥaqā'iq al-tafsīr*, introduction (manuscript reference).

49. In general terms, *ḥarf* literally means "edge" (of a sword), "border," or "letter" (of the alphabet). There may be good reasons to translate *ḥarf* as "Satz" (Weiss) or "Ausdruck" (Goldziher), or possibly as "passage, phrase," as strongly argued by Weiss, "Die arabische Nationalgrammatik und die Lateiner," 363–64; cf. Goldziher, *Richtungen*, 215. In fact, *ḥarf* designates any small element of speech that can be pronounced, whether it is a sound, a letter (i.e., a consonant or a consonant plus vowel), a particle, a word, or a phrase; cf. Fleisch, "Ḥarf," *EI*, new ed., 3:204–5, Fischer, "Zur Herkunft," 135; Dichy, "Grammatologie de l'Arabe I," 111; Versteegh, *Arabic Grammar*, 103–4. The translation of *ḥarf* as "lectio" is justified on the basis of *ḥarf* as the singular of *aḥruf*, "lectiones," ways of reading the Qur'ān; cf. Gilliot, "Les sept Lectures." The translation of "passage" is also implied, however, in a statement by Wahb b. Munabbih (d. 114/732), who, according to a quotation by Aḥmad b. Ḥanbal in al-Nasafī, *al-Radd 'alā l-bid'a*, 105, says, "Abraham, the friend of the All-merciful said, O Lord, I have read a passage (*ḥarf*) in the pages (*ṣuḥuf*), the interpretation of which I ignore." Finally, it may not be stretching the point to translate "*ḥarf*" as "word" rather than "letter" in the various renderings of the prophetic *ḥadīth* quoted above, because the earlier grammarians did not differentiate between *ḥarf* and *kalima* but used *ḥarf* in the sense of "word" (cf. Fischer, "Zur Herkunft," 139). With regard to the Ṣūfī use of the term *ḥarf* one could argue that Ṣūfī exegesis tends to understand *ḥarf* as a letter of the alphabet, because of the importance it assigns to the symbolic interpretation of individual letters and the well-known acronyms of the Qur'ān (*al-ḥurūf al-muqaṭṭa'a*); cf. Schimmel, *Mystical Dimensions of Islam*, 411–25.

50. cf. Böwering, *Mystical Vision*, 139.

51. Abū l-Qāsim b. Muḥammad b. al-Junayd al-Khazzāz al-Qawārīrī al-Nihāwandī (d. 297/910), the famous organizer of the Ṣūfīs at Baghdad, was recognized as a master in formulating allusions that gave eloquent expression to intricate mystical experiences and ideas; cf. Abdel-Kader, *The Life, Personality and Writings of Al-Junayd*; Arberry, "al-Djunayd," *EI*, new ed., 2:600.

52. al-Sulamī, *Ziyādāt al-ḥaqā'iq*, paragraph 3.

53. The Arabic text of this passage is found in the introduction to al-Sulamī's *Ḥaqā'iq al-tafsīr* as cited by Nwyia, "Le Tafsīr mystique," 186.

54. Ibid.

55. al-Sulamī, *Ḥaqā'iq al-tafsīr*, introduction (manuscript reference).

56. al-Sulamī, *Ziyādāt al-ḥaqā'iq*, paragraph 6.

57. al-Sulamī, *Ziyādāt al-ḥaqā'iq*, paragraph 4.

58. Ess, *Gedankenwelt*, 209–13.

59. Lubac, *Exégèse médiévale*; cf. also Dobschütz, "Vom vierfachen Schriftsinn"; Caplan, "The Four Senses."

60. Cassian, *Collationes* 148, pp. 404–5; Augustine, *De utilitate credendi*, chapter 3; for Pseudo-Dionysius, see Völker, *Kontemplation und Ekstase*, 106.

61. See Bacher, "L'exégèse biblique dans le Zohar"; Scholem, "Meaning of the Torah," 32–86, esp. 50–65; Heide, "PARDES"; cf. also Lazarus-Yafeh, 143–60.

62. Some groundbreaking observations on this point are made by Goldfeld, "The Development of Theory on Qur'ānic Exegesis in Islamic Scholarship."

63. Q 53:1–18, cf. Arbeny, *The Koran Interpreted*, 2, 244.

64. Abū Bakr Muḥammad b. Mūsā al-Wāsiṭī (d. 320/932), a native of Farghāna also known as Ibn al-Farghānī, belonged to the circle of companions that formed around al-Junayd (d. 298/910) and Abū l-Ḥusayn al-Nūrī (d. 295/907–8) of Baghdad. He left the city as a young man, however, long before al-Junayd's death, maintaining with the latter a correspondence on Ṣūfī topics as he searched for a new home. Driven out of many towns for his mystical teachings, al-Wāsiṭī first found temporary quarters in Abīward but finally settled at Marw in Khurasān. There

he was favorably received by the populace and enjoyed lecturing to large audiences, including a small group of disciples led by Abū l-'Abbās al-Sayyārī (d. 342/953–54). Cf. al-Sulamī, *Ṭabaqāt al-ṣūfiyya*, ed. Pedersen, 302–7; ed. N. Shurayba, 302–6; al-Qushayrī, *al-Risāla al-qushayriyya*, 1:140–41; Majd al-Dīn al-Ḥusayn b. Naṣr al-Ka'bī Ibn Khamīs al-Mawṣilī, *Manāqib al-abrār wa-maḥāsin al-aḥyār*, Istanbul, Topkapi Sarai, MS Ahmet III, 2904, fols. 166v–168r.

65. al-Sulamī, *Ḥaqā'iq al-tafsīr*, London, British Library, MS Or. 9433 (dated 564/1168–69), fol. 318r; Istanbul, Fatih MS 261 (dated 600/1203–4), fol. 269r; Alexandria, Baladiyya MS 1018b (dated 795/1392–93), fol. 248r; al-Baqlī al-Shīrāzī, *'Arā'is al-bayān fī ḥaqā'iq al-Qur'ān*, 2:286–87.

66. Abū Muḥammad Sahl b. 'Abdallāh al-Tustarī, probably born in 203/818 at Tustar in Khūzistān, emerged with a teaching of his own after Dhū l-Nūn al-Miṣrī's death in 245/860 and gathered a group of disciples, prominent among them Abū 'Abdallāh Muḥammad b. Sālim al-Baṣrī (d. 297/909). Expelled from his hometown for political or doctrinal reasons, Sahl al-Tustarī took up residence in Baṣra, where he became embroiled in religious controversy until his death in 283/896; cf. Böwering, "Sahl al-Tustarī," *EI*, new ed., 8:840–41.

67. Abū l-'Abbās Aḥmad b. Muḥammad al-Adamī, known as Ibn 'Aṭā' (d. 309/922), a Ḥanbalī Ṣūfī of Baghdad, was at first a companion of al-Junayd, then became a close friend of al-Ḥusayn b. Manṣūr al-Ḥallāj (d. 309/922) and a rival of Abū Muḥammad al-Jurayrī (d. 311/924), who was al-Junayd's successor as leader of the Ṣūfi circle of Baghdad. Ibn 'Aṭā' experienced life as a profound tragedy, losing his wife, his ten sons, and all his possessions under violent circumstances, perhaps when their caravan was ambushed on a pilgrimage to Mecca. Ibn 'Aṭā' is said to have compiled a book on Qur'ān interpetation, *Kitāb fī fahm al-Qur'ān*, which was transmitted by Abū 'Umar 'Alī b. Muḥammad al-Anmāṭī and, though lost today, may have served as the basis for the many statements al-Sulamī incorporated into his Qur'ān commentaries. An outspoken man who engaged in divisive controversy with other Ṣūfīs, Ibn 'Aṭā' so enraged the vizier publicly that the latter had Ibn 'Aṭā' brutally beaten to death, with his teeth knocked out. Cf. al-Sulamī, *Ṭabaqāt al-ṣūfiyya*, ed. Pedersen, 260–68; ed. Shurayba, 265–272; al-Dhahabī, *Siyar a'lām al- nubalā'*, 14:255–56; idem, *Ta'rīkh al-islām*, 23:247–48 (years 301–20). Gramlich, *Abu l-'Abbās b. 'Atā'*, 1–10; al-Baghdādī, *Ta'rīkh Baghdād*, 12, 73.

68. Nwyia, *Trois oeuvres inédites*, 75–76.

69. Nwyia, "Le Tafsīr mystique," 222–23.

70. Ibid., 223.

71. Q 17:1; Q 24:35; Q 94:1, respectively.

72. cf. Böwering, "Dekr," *EIr*, 7:229–33.

73. Ruwaym b. Aḥmad b. Yazīd (d. 303/916), a Ṣūfī of Baghdad, was a disciple of al-Junayd and was known as a reader of the Qur'ān and a scholar of religious law.

74. Q 7:172–73.

75. Q 79:15–25.

76. Q 79:24.

77. Kalābādhī, *Kitāb al-ta'arruf*, 126–27; idem, *Doctrine*, trans. Arberry, 166–67.

Bibliography

Abdel-Kader, Ali Hassan. *The Life, Personality and Writings of Al-Junayd*. London: Luzac, 1976.

Anṣārī-i Harawi, Khwājā 'Abdullāḥ. *Ṭabaqāt al-ṣūfiya*. Ed. 'Abd ul-Ḥayy-i Ḥabībī-i Qandahārī. Kabul: Anjumān-i Tarīkh, 1340.

——. *Ṭabaqāt al-ṣūfiya*. Ed. Muḥammad Surūr Mawlā'ī. Tehran, 1362.

Arberry, A. J. "al-Djunayd." *EI*, new ed., 2:600.

——. "Khargushi's Manual of Sufism." *BSOAS*, 9 (1937): 345–49.

Arnaldez, R. "Muḥāsibī." *EI*, new ed. 7: 466–67.

Ateş, Süleyman. "Üç müfessir bir tefsīr." *Ilâhiyât Fakültesi Dergisi* 18 (1970): 85-104.
——. *Işârî Tefsîr Okulu.* Ankara: Üniversitesi Bas_mevi, 1974.
Augustine of Hippo. *De utilitate credendi.* Ed. J. Zycha, 1-48. CSEL 25. Vienna: F. Tempsky, 1891.
Bacher, W. "L'exégèse biblique dans le Zohar." *Revue des études juives* 22 (1891): 33-46, 219-29.
al-Baghdādī, Abū Bakr Aḥmad b. 'Alī al-Khaṭīb. *Ta'rīkh Baghdād.* 14 vols. Beirut: Dār al-Kitāb al-'Arabī, n.d.
al-Baqlī, Rūzbihān. *'Arā'is al-bayān wa-ḥaqā'iq al-Qur'ān.* 2 vols. Cawnpore, 1301/1884. Reprint (lithograph), Lucknow, 1915.
Böwering, Gerhard. "Dekr." *EIr,* 7: 229-33.
——. "Deylamī, Šams-al-Dīn." *EIr,* 7: 341-42.
——. "The Major Sources of Sulamī's Minor Qur'ān Commentary." *Oriens* 35 (1996): 35-56.
——. *The Mystical Vision of Existence in Classical Islam.* Berlin: Walter de Gruyter, 1980.
——. "The Qur'ān Commentary of al-Sulamī." In *Islamic Studies Presented to Charles J. Adams.* Ed. W. B. Hallaq and D. P. Little, 51-53. Leiden: E. J. Brill, 1991.
——. Review of *Das Sendschreiben al-Qušayrīs über das Sufitum,* by Richard Gramlich. *Orientalia* 58 (1989): 569-72.
——. "Sahl al-Tustarī." *EI,* new ed. 8: 840-41.
——. "al-Sulamī." *EI,* new ed. 9: 811-12.
Burton, John. "*Naskh.*" *EI,* new ed. 7: 1009-12.
——. *The Sources of Islamic Law: Islamic Theories of Abrogation.* Edinburgh: Edinburgh University Press 1990.
Caplan, Harry. "The Four Senses of Scriptural Interpretation and the Medieval Theory of Preaching." *Speculum* 4 (1929): 282-90.
Cassian, John. *Collationes.* Ed. Michael Petschenig. CSEL 13. Vienna: C. Geroldus, 1886.
Chodkiewicz, Michel. *Un océan sans rivage.* Paris: Editions du Seuil, 1992.
Corbin, Henri. *Histoire de la philosophie islamique.* Paris: Gallimard, 1964.
——. *The Man of Light in Iranian Sufism.* Boulder, Colo.: Shambhala, 1978.
al-Dhahabī, Shams al-Dīn Abū 'Abdallāh Muḥammad b. Aḥmad. *Siyar a'lām al-nubalā'.* 25 vols. Beirut: 1401-5/1981-85.
——. *Ta'rīkh al-islām wa-wafayāt al-mashāhīr al-a'lām.* Ed. 'Umar 'Abd al-Salām Tadmūrī. 41 vols. to date. Beirut, 1407-/1987-.
Dichy, J. "Grammatologie de l'Arabe I: Les sens du mot *ḥarf* ou le labyrinthe d'une évidence." In *Studies in the History of Arabic Grammar II.* Ed. K. Versteegh and M. G. Carter, 111- 28. Amsterdam: J. Benjamins, 1990.
Dobschütz, E. von. "Vom vierfachen Schriftsinn: Die Geschichte einer Theorie." In *Harnack-Ehrung: Beitrag zur Kirchengeschichte,* 1-13. Leipzig: J. C. Hinrichs, 1921.
Elias, Jamal J. *The Throne Carrier of God.* Albany: State University of New York Press, 1995.
Ess, Josef van. *Die Gedankenwelt des Ḥāriṯ al-Muḥāsibī.* Bonn: Selbstverlag des Orientalischen Seminars der Universität Bonn, 1961.
——. *Theologie und Gesellschaft im 2. und 3. Jahrhundert der Hidschra.* 6 vols. Berlin: Walter de Gruyter, 1991-97.
al-Fīrūzābādī, Abū Ṭāhir. *Tanwīr al-miqbās min tafsīr Ibn 'Abbas.* Cairo: Muṣṭafā al-Bābī al-Ḥalabī, 1370/1951.
Fischer, W. "Zur Herkunft des grammatischen Terminus *ḥarf.*" *JSAI* 12 (1989): 135-45.
Fleisch, H. "Ḥarf." *EI,* new ed., 3: 204-5.
al-Ghazzālī, Abū Ḥāmid. *Iḥyā' 'ulūm al-dīn.* 4 vols. Cairo: Muṣṭafā al-Bābī al-Ḥalabī, 1358/1939.
Goldfeld, Y. "The Tafsīr of 'Abdallāh b. 'Abbās." *Der Islam* 58 (1981): 125-35.
Goldziher, Ignaz. *Die Richtungen der islamischen Koranauslegung.* Leiden, 1920. Reprint, Leiden: E. J. Brill, 1970.

Gräf, Erwin. *Jagdbeute und Schlachttier im islamischen Recht.* Bonn: Selbstverlag des Orientalischen Seminars der Universität Bonn, 1959.

Gramlich, Richard. *Abu l-'Abbās b. 'Aṭā': Sufi und Koranausleger.* Stuttgart: Franz Steiner, 1995.

——. *Die Gaben der Erkenntnisse des 'Umar as-Suhrawardī.* Wiesbaden: Franz Steiner, 1978.

——. *Muḥammad al-Ghazzālīs Lehre von den Stufen zur Gottesliebe.* Wiesbaden: Franz Steiner, 1984.

——. *Die Nahrung der Herzen.* 4 vols. Stuttgart: Franz Steiner, 1992–95.

——. *Schlaglichter über das Sufitum.* Stuttgart: Franz Steiner, 1990.

——. *Das Sendschreiben al-Qušayrīs über das Sufitum.* Wiesbaden: Franz Steiner, 1989.

Haeuptner, Eleanor. "Koranische Hinweise auf die materielle Kultur der alten Araber." Phil. F. diss., University of Tübingen, 1966.

Halm, H. "*Bāṭenīya.*" *EIr,* 3:861–63.

——. *Shiism.* Edinburgh: Edinburgh University Press, 1991.

Heide, A. van der. "PARDES: Methodological Reflections on the Theory of the Four Senses." *Journal of Jewish Studies* 34 (1983): 147–59.

Hodgson, M. G. S. "Ja'far al-Ṣādiq." *EI,* new ed., 2:374–75.

Horovitz, Josef. *Jewish Proper Names and Derivatives in the Koran.* Reprint, Hildesheim: Georg Olms, 1964 (originally published in *HUCA* 2 [1925]:145–227).

al-Hujwīrī, Abū 'l-Ḥasan. *Kashf al-maḥjūb.* Ed. V. Zhukowsky. Leningrad, 1926. Reprint, Tehran: Kitabkhānah-i Ṭahūrī, 1399/1979.

——. *The Kashf al-Mahjúb,* Trans. Reynold A. Nicholson. Leiden: Brill, 1911. Reprint, London: Luzac, 1970.

Ibn Sa'd, Muḥammad. *al-Ṭabaqāt al-kubrā.* 9 vols. Beirut: Dār al-Ṣādir, n.d.

Ibn Taymiyya, Taqī al-Dīn Aḥmad. *Risāla fī 'ilm al-bāṭin wa l-ẓāhir.* In *Majmū'at al-rasā'il all-munīriyya.* Vol. 1, 229–52. Beirut: Dār Ihyā' al-Turāth al-'Arabī, 1970.

Jeffery, Arthur. *The Foreign Vocabulary of the Qur'an.* Baroda: Oriental Institute, 1938.

al-Kalābādhī, Abū Bakr. *The Doctrine of the Ṣūfīs.* Trans. A. J. Arberry, Cambridge, 1935; reprint, London: Cambridge University Press, 1977.

——. *Kitāb al-ta'arruf li-madhhab ahl al-taṣawwuf.* Ed. A. J. Arberry. Cairo: Librairie El-Khandgi, 1934.

Lazarus-Yafeh, Hava. *Intertwined Worlds.* Princeton, N.J.: Princeton University Press, 1992.

Lory, Pierre. *Les commentaires ésotériques du Coran d'après 'Abd ar-Razzāq al-Qāshānī.* Paris: Les Deux Océans, 1980.

Lubac, Henri de. *Exégèse médiévale: les quatre sens de l'Écriture.* 4 vols. Paris: Aubier, 1959–64.

al-Makkī, Abū Ṭālib. *Qūt al-qulūb fī mu'āmalāt al-maḥbūb.* 2 vols. Cairo: Muṣṭafā al-Bābī al-Ḥalabī, 1381/1961.

Massignon, Louis. *Essai sur les origines du lexique technique de la mystique musulmane.* 2d ed. Paris: J. Vrin, 1968.

al-Mawṣilī, Majd al-Dīn al-Ḥusayn b. Naṣr al-Ka'bī Ibn Khamīs. *Manāqib al-abrār wa-maḥāsin al-aḥyār.* Istanbul, Topkapi Sarai, MS Ahmet III, 2904, fols. 166v–168r.

al-Maybudī, Rashīd al-Dīn. *Kashf al-asrār wa-'uddat al-abrār.* 10 vols. Ed. 'Alī Aṣghar Ḥikmat. Tehran: Mu'assasah-intishārāt Amīr-i kabīr, 1341.

Meier, Fritz. *Abū Sa'īd-i Abū l-Ḥayr.* Leiden: E. J. Brill, 1976.

——. "Stambuler Handschriften dreier persischer Mystiker." *Der Islam* 24 (1937): 1–42.

al-Muḥāsibī, Abū 'Abdallāh al-Ḥārith b. Asad. *al-'Aql wa fahm al-Qur'ān.* Ed. Ḥusayn al-Quwatlī. Beirut: Dār al-Fikr, 1391/1971.

al-Nasafi, Abū Mutī Makḥūl. *Al-Radd 'alā l-bid'a.* Ed. Marie Bernard. *Annales islamologiques* 16 (1980). Leiden: Brill, 39–126.

Nwyia, Paul. *Exégèse coranique et langage mystique.* Beirut: Dar el-Machreq, 1970.

——. "Sentences de Nūrī cités par Sulamī dans *Ḥaqā'iq al-tafsīr.*" *Mélanges de l'Université Saint-Joseph* 44 (1968): 145–47.

——. "Le Tafsīr mystique attribué à Ǧa'far al-Ṣādiq." *Mélanges de l'Université Saint-Joseph* 43 (1968): 179–230.

——. *Trois oeuvres inédites de mystiques musulmans.* Beirut: Dar el-Machreq, 1973.

Paret, Rudi. "Furqān." *EI*, new ed., 2: 949–50.

——. *Der Koran: Kommentar und Konkordanz.* Stuttgart: Kohlhammer, 1971.

——. "Sure 57,12f. und das Gleichnis von den klugen und den törichten Jungfrauen." In *Der Koran.* Ed. R. Paret, 192–96. Darmstadt: Wissenschaftliche Buchgesellschaft, 1975.

al-Qāshānī, 'Abd al-Razzāq. *Tafsīr al-Qur'ān al-karīm lil-shaykh al-akbar.* Ed. Muṣṭafā Ghālib. 2 vols. Beirut: Dār al-Andalus, 1978.

al-Qushayrī, Abū l-Qāsim. *Laṭā'if al-ishārāt.* 3 vols. Cairo: al-Hay'a al-Miṣriyya al-'Āmma lil-kitāb, 1981–83.

——. *al-Risāla.* Ed. 'Abd al-Ḥalīm Maḥmūd and Maḥmūd al-Sharīf. 2 vols. Cairo: Dār al-Kutub al-Ḥadītha, 1972–74.

——. *al-Risāla al-qushayriyya.* Ed. 'Abd al-Ḥalīm Maḥmūd and Maḥmūd b. al-Sharīf. 2 vols. Cairo: Maṭba'at al-Bābī al-Ḥalabī, 1385/1966.

Radtke, B. ed. *Adab al-mulūk.* Beirut: Franz Steiner, 1991.

Radtke, Bernd. "*Bāṭen.*" *EIr*, 3:859–61.

——. *Drei Schriften des Theosophen von Tirmiḏ.* 2 vols. Beirut; Stuttgart: in Kommission bei Franz Steiner Verlag, 1992–96.

Rippin, Andrew. "Ibn 'Abbās's al-Lughāt fi'l-Qur'ān." *BSOAS* 44 (1981): 15–25.

——. "Ibn 'Abbās's Gharīb al-Qur'ān." *BSOAS* 46 (1983): 332–33.

Ritter, H. "Ḥasan al-Baṣrī." *EI*, new ed. 1: 247–48.

Rivlin, Josef J. *Gesetz im Koran: Kultus und Ritus.* Jerusalem: Bamberger & Wahrman, 1934.

Salqīnī, 'Abdallāh Muḥammad. *Ḥabr al-umma 'Abdallāh b. 'Abbās.* Cairo: Dār al-salām, 1406/1986.

al-Sarrāj, Abū Naṣr. *The Kitāb al-luma' fī l-taṣawwuf.* Ed. R. A. Nicholson. Leiden: Brill, 1914. Reprint, London: Luzac, 1963.

——. *Pages from the Kitab al-luma.* Ed. A. J. Arberry. London: Luzac, 1947.

Schimmel, A. *Mystical Dimensions of Islam.* Chapel Hill: University of North Carolina Press, 1975.

Scholem, Gershom G. "The Meaning of the Torah in Jewish Mysticism." In Scholem, *On the Kabbalah and Its Symbolism.* Trans. Ralph Manheim, 32–86. New York: Schocken, 1965.

Sharī'at, Muḥammad Jawād. *Fihrist-i Tafsīr Kashf al-asrār wa-'uddat al-abrār.* Tehran: Mu'assasah-intishārāt Amīr-i Kabīr, 1343.

Shpall, W. "A Note on Najm al-dīn al-Rāzī and the *Baḥr al-ḥaqā'iq.*" *Folia orientalia* 22 (1981–84): 69–80.

Strack, Hermann L., and Paul Billerbeck. *Kommentar zum Neuen Testament aus Talmud und Midrasch.* 6 vols. Munich: Beck, 1956.

al-Suhrawardī, Abū Ḥafṣ 'Umar. *'Awārif al-ma'ārif.* Beirut: Dār al-Kitāb al-'Arabī, 1966.

——. *'Awārif al-ma'ārif.* Ed. 'Abd al-Ḥalīm Maḥmūd and Maḥmūd b. al-Sharīf. Cairo: Dār al-Kutub, n.d.

al-Sulamī, Abū 'Abd al-Raḥmān. *Ḥaqā'iq al-tafsīr.* In Massignon, *Essai sur les origines*, 359–412.

——. *Ḥaqā'iq al-tafsīr.* London, British Library, MS Or. 9433 (dated 564/1168–69), fol. 318r; Istanbul, Fatih, MS 261 (dated 600/1203–4), fol. 269r; Alexandria, Baladiyya, MS 1018v (dated 795/1392–93), fol. 248v.

——. *Ṭabaqāt al-ṣūfiya.* Ed. J. Pedersen. Leiden: E. J. Brill, 1960. Also ed. N. Shurayba. Cairo, 1969.

——. *Ziyādāt ḥaqā'iq al-tafsīr.* Ed. G. Böwering. 2d ed. Beirut: Dar el-Machreq, 1997.

al-Tustarī, Sahl. *Tafsīr al-Qur'ān al-'aẓīm*. Cairo: Muṣṭafā al-Bābī al-Ḥalabī, 1329/1911.

Vadet, J. C. "Ibn Mas'ūd." *EI*, new ed., 3: 873–75.

Vaglieri, L. Veccia. "'Abd Allāh b. al-'Abbās." *EI*, new ed., 1: 40–41.

Versteegh, C. H. M. *Arabic Grammar and Qur'anic Exegesis in Early Islam*. Leiden: E. J. Brill, 1993.

Völker, Walther. *Kontemplation und Ekstase bei pseudo-Dionysius Areopagita*. Wiesbaden: Franz Steiner, 1958.

Wagtendonk, K. *Fasting in the Koran*. Leiden: E. J. Brill, 1968.

Wansbrough, John. *Quranic Studies*. Oxford: Oxford University Press, 1977.

Weiss, J. "Die arabische Nationalgrammatik und die Lateiner." *Zeitschrift der Deutschen Morgenländischen Gesellschaft* 64 (1910): 349–90.

Wensinck, A. J. "Lawḥ." *EI*, new ed., 5: 698.

Zay'ūr, 'Alī . *al-Tafsīr al-ṣūfī lil-Qur'ān 'inda l-Ṣādiq*. Beirut: Dār al-Andalus, 1979.

24

Are There Allegories in Ṣūfī Qur'ān Interpretation?

HAVA LAZARUS-YAFEH†

Ṣūfī Qur'ān interpretation is well known for both its beautiful metaphors and its enigmatic mystical depths. From Sahl al-Tustarī to Pseudo-Ibn al-'Arabī—and even before and after these protagonists—this literature flourished among other genres of mystical literature, often using the Qur'ān as an external framework or even only as a pretext to give expression to mystical ideas, metaphors, similitudes, or stories. Thus, for example, the verses dealing with the Pilgrimage (*ḥajj*) in *Baqara* in the second sūra of the Qur'ān serve as a starting point for Pseudo-Ibn al-'Arabī (or fourteenth-century al-Qāshānī, who is apparently the author of the so-called *Tafsīr Ibn al-'Arabī*) to construct an excursus on mystical meditation and mystical ascent that has very little to do with the Ḥajj itself. His commentary speaks about the "*ṭawāf* (circumambulation) of the heart around the essence of God" or about "the sacrifice of one's earthly desires in the territory of the Ka'ba of the Heart"(*dhabḥ al-ahwā fī fanā ka'bat al-qalb*).[1] Mystical metaphors occur in several Ṣufī commentaries of the Qur'ān , for example with regard to the famous Verse of Light in Q 24:35 or the dog that accompanied the famous Sleepers in Q 18:18 and in many other instances.

Most Ṣūfī authors, however, do not go much further than using similes and metaphors in their qur'ānic interpretations. Metaphors, in this context, means short allegorical explanations for qur'ānic words, idioms, or verses which do not build up to a whole story and do not constitute what I will call a "full-fledged allegory." Full-fledged allegories are rather rare in this literature and one can discern a clear trend of avoidance of the use of such allegories in Ṣūfī Qur'ān interpretation, as in most medieval Muslim religious literature. This avoidance of full-fledged allegory is, I suppose, related to the well-known fact that allegorical interpretation of the Qur'ān very early became a vehicle for expressing dissident and even heretical views and later served as an identification mark of the philosophers, Mu'tazilites, and Shī'ites, especially the Ismā'īlīs. Allegory became connected with the latter's political dissent, and when the famous al-Ghazālī (d. 505/1111), for example, mocks Ismā'īlī allegorical interpretation in his writings against them—as he does for instance in his *Faḍā'iḥ al-Bāṭiniyya*[2]—he seems to take allegory for an Ismā'īlī political revolutionary instrument. In addition, allegory was taken to be a potential threat to religious thought and practice, especially with respect to the basic dogmas of Islam and the punctilious performance of the religious commandments. Here, as well, Ismā'īlī allegorical interpretation of the law serves as the worst example of this kind. Anti-Ismā'īlī literature, by authors like al-Ghazālī or the eleventh-century Yemenite author Muḥammad b. Mālik al-Ḥamādī al-Yamanī, who wrote a book against the famous Ismā'īlī *dā'ī* al-Kirmānī,[3] abounds with examples from Ismā'īlī literature to prove the potential danger for Islam inherent in allegorical interpretation of qur'ānic and other injunctions. Some Ṣūfī extremists were charged with the same accusations, often rightly so, and Ibn al-Jawzī (d. 597/1200) in his famous book *Talbīs Iblīs* gives several examples of how Ṣūfī mystical ideas and metaphors promote negligence in the performance of the prescribed religious commandments.[4] The commonly accepted term *Ibāḥiyya* for both Ismā'īlī Shī'ites and Ṣūfīs in this context (meaning those who advocate that everything is permitted and no laws or commandments must necessarily be observed) proves that allegorical interpretation per se was a primary concern for many Muslim authors, regardless of who was engaged in it.

The political and religious dangers of allegorical interpretation (*ta'wīl*) engendered one of the longest continuous religious debates in medieval Islam.[5] It was closely connected with the far- reaching dogmas about the unique character of the uncreated Qur'ān, especially the dogma about its miraculous inimitability, whereby the rhetorical uniqueness of the Qur'ān, its language, style, and contents became the main argument for its divine character. All this may have created a certain wariness on the part of many authors, including the moderate Ṣūfīs, with regard to the use of allegory in their Qur'ān commentaries. As was previously stated, Ṣūfī commentators used many metaphors and similes to give expression to their mystical ideas but usually refrained from developing full-fledged allegories in their Qur'ān commentaries. This may be true, though to a lesser extent, with regard to Ṣūfī literature in general, in which fully developed allegories do exist but are rather rare. One of the best examples is, of course, the famous Allegory of the Birds (*Manṭiq al-ṭayr*) rewritten by several Ṣūfī authors such as the two al-Ghazālīs (apparently Abū Ḥāmid in Arabic and his Ṣūfī brother, Aḥmad, in Persian) and especially the later Persian Ṣūfī author Farīd al-Dīn 'Aṭṭār (d. ca. 627/1229).[6] The story tells of a group of birds setting out to search for a king, only to find out, after a long and tortuous journey, that what they had been looking for is either unattainable or had existed all along in their own hearts.

In more orthodox mainstream Muslim literature and commentaries, full-fledged allegories are even scarcer. They seem to really flourish only in modern Arabic literature, apparently under Western influence. In addition to the political and religious dangers, however, there may exist a deeper reason for the Ṣūfī—and general Muslim—reluctance to indulge in allegory and symbolic parables. According to the Qur'ān itself, creating parables is for God alone and only He is the true coiner of similitudes: "Seest thou not how Allāh coineth a similitude (*a-lam tara kayfa ḍaraba Allāh mathalan*)? A goodly saying as a goodly tree, its roots set firm, its branches reaching into heaven; giving its fruit in every season by permission of its Lord; Allāh coineth the similitudes for mankind (*yaḍribu Allāh al-amthāl lil-nās*) in order that they may reflect" (Q 14:23–24).

According to the Qur'ān, however, most people find it difficult to understand these "Mathals" of God and only the wise and learned among the believers can comprehend them (Q 29:43). How much more would this be so with regard to parables coined by men and with their allegorical interpretation of qur'ānic verses, both those clearly understood (*muḥkamāt*) and those whose meaning is ambiguous (*mutashābihāt*)? The human creation of similitudes (*amthāl*) is recognized as a "suspect enterprise" by the Qur'ān[7] and is contrasted therein with God's truth: "[for] every similitude they bring thee, We bring thee the truth as against it and it is better as an explanation" (Q 25:33). The coining of parables is even linked by some commentaries directly to God's power of creation.[8]

This means, I believe, that the creation of full-fledged allegories, which resemble linguistic paintings or sculptures, was considered to be unlawful, since God alone is the creator of all things.[9] This far-reaching understanding of God as the one and only creator and this prohibition against interference with his modes of creation permeate very deeply the whole of Muslim medieval religious thought and can be found in connection with very different issues.[10] It may, perhaps, be likened to adoption, which seems to be taken as the creation of a family against God's decree (although this prohibition may have stemmed in the first place from the Prophet's personal desire for his adopted son's wife).[11] It may also be akin to the forbidden intercalation of a month to the lunar year,[12] which God created to be shorter than the solar year and which should therefore remain shorter. It certainly is very close to the well-known Muslim prohibition of drawing pictures or making sculptures of humans and animals,[13] which should not be explained only in terms of the biblical fear of idolatry. In several *ḥadīth* sayings, painters and sculptors are explicitly accused of having attempted to imitate God as creator in their work (*yuḍāhūna bi-khalq Allāh*). Therefore, on Judgment Day they will be called upon to instill life into their works of art but will not be able to do so and will be punished severely.[14] We may have here another expression of Islam's constant longing for the abstract or of its strict, almost Spartan, puritanical monotheism. Muslim authors tried to understand and express the unity and transcendence of God (*tawḥīd*) in the most abstract way possible.They shunned not only the painting and sculpture of living creatures, but also visual symbolism of every kind, perhaps following in this attitude an ancient pre-Islamic Christian trend for abstract art.[15] Islam has no visual symbol parallel to the cross, for example, and most Muslim medieval authors (except for some Ṣūfī authors!) found it very difficult to understand the symbolic meaning of the cross.[16] They also did not develop any symbolic rituals and refrained from instilling any symbolic signification into the two festivals of Islam, which are curiously devoid of any deeper meaning.[17]

One later Muslim author, al-Samhūdī (d. 911/1505), who collected all the sayings in praise of Medina, even quoted an extraordinary statement by a Damascene Shāfi'ite jurisprudent to the effect that Islam does not acknowledge any holy time (Friday is no Sabbath!) or space (even Mecca, which is, according to Muslim law, considered to be sacred territory!) and ascribes holiness to God alone.[18] Islam also shuns music, liturgy, drama, and myth, all in stark contrast to Christianity and even to Judaism, especially to Jewish mystical kabbalah.[19] If we accept the simple definition of a symbol as being "something presented to the senses or the imagination . . . which stands for something else,"[20] we can easily associate imaginary allegory with it. This thinking would allow us to understand better the curious fact that, in the unusually rich religious literature of medieval Islam, very few authors stand out as giving free reign to their imagination and engaging in allegorical creativity.[21] Notable among them are the great philosopher Ibn Sīnā (d. 428/1037) and the tenth-century authors of the Epistles (*Rasā'il*) of the Pure

Brethren (Ikhwān al-Ṣafā),[22] as well as Shihāb al-Dīn al-Suhrawardī (d. 587/1191)[23] and Ibn al-ʿArabī (d. 638/1240),[24] all deeply influenced by Neoplatonic philosophy. Most Muslim authors, however, following Aristotelian philosophers, considered imagination to be a very low level of perception and this assessment may have added to their reluctance to create imaginary stories and allegories.

To return to the rare use of full-fledged allegory in Muslim Qur'ān commentaries in general (the use of metaphors, partial allegories, and similes was, of course, widespread), we can say that the Muʿtazilites (with some Ashʿarites, such as the great Qur'ān commentator Fakhr al-Dīn al-Rāzī [d. 606/1210] following them) and the philosophers (especially Ibn Rushd in his *Faṣl al-maqāl*) accepted allegory as a permissible tool in Qur'ān interpretation, but they used it mainly to explain away the anthropomorphic expressions in the Qur'ān, and rarely if ever otherwise. The Ḥanbalites went, of course, much further and tried to forbid the use of allegorical interpretation altogether. Ibn Ḥanbal is said to have used *ta'wīl* in only three instances, with regard to three *ḥadīth* sayings which cannot be taken literally in any way: one stating that the Black Stone in the Kaʿba is God's right hand on earth (*al-ḥajar al-aswad yamīn Allāh fī l-arḍ*) another saying that the believer's heart is held by two fingers of God's hand (*qalb al-mu'min bayna iṣbaʿayn min aṣābiʿ Allāh*), and the third being the Prophet's saying that he feels God's breath from the south (*innī la ajidu nafas al-Raḥmān min qibali l-Yaman*).[25] The famous tenth-century Jewish Muʿtazilite author Saadia Gaon makes use of the same approach but states more clearly that allegorical interpretation may be used only if the literal sense of a biblical verse contradicts the senses, reason, another verse, or tradition.[26]

Of course, the tendency to read allegory into the Qur'ān could not be stopped completely. It became, however, mainly a hallmark of sectarian interpretation. The Shīʿītes, and especially the Ismaʿīlīs, engaged in it unrestrainedly, since they could find no better way to link their respective political and religious claims to the Qur'ān. Unfortunately, scholarship has often connected Ṣūfī Qur'ān interpretation with these sectarian enterprises, because both came to be known by the term *ta'wīl*. Yet any comparison between Shīʿīte and Ṣūfī interpretation will easily reveal the latter's restraint with regard to allegory, unlike the Shīʿīte and Ismāʿīlī ways of interpretation. It is not easy to find full-blown mystical allegorical explanations for qur'ānic verses in the commentaries of authors such as Sufyān al-Thawrī (d. 162/778), Sahl al-Tustarī (d. 283/896), Abū ʿAbd al-Raḥmān al-Sulamī (d. 412/1021), ʿAbd al-Karīm al-Qushayrī (d. 467/1074), and others.[27] To be sure, their writings abound in mystical statements and mystical metaphors, but seldom if ever are these developed into true allegories. The exceptions are the previously mentioned Ibn al-ʿArabī and ʿAbd al-Rāziq al-Qāshānī (d. 730/1329), the author of the *Tafsīr* attributed to Ibn al-ʿArabī. Al-Qāshānī, for example, following Ibn al-ʿArabī's *Futūḥāt*, turned the whole qur'ānic story of Joseph in the twelfth sūra into a full-fledged Philo-like allegory about the struggle between man's inner faculties such as his heart (*al-qalb al-mustaʿidd*—Joseph) and his intellect (*al-ʿaql*—Jacob), his outer and inner senses (*al-ḥawāss al-ẓāhira wa-l-bāṭina*—the brothers), and his carnal soul which incites to evil (*al-nafs al-ammāra bi-l-sū'*—his master's wife, *imra'at al-ʿazīz*).[28]

For further elucidation let us look at some early Ṣūfī commentaries on the famous Verse of Light in Q 24:35. In Shīʿite commentaries the whole verse is explained as a full allegory pertaining to the house of ʿAlī: Fāṭima is the "niche wherein is a lamp" (*ka-mishkāt fīhā miṣbāḥ*) as well as the "shining star" (*kawkab durrī*), while the two Ḥasans

(Ḥasan and Ḥusayn) are represented by the "lamp" which is mentioned twice in the verse. Continuing the interpretation, the Shīʿite pure Abrahamic belief, which has nothing to do with either Judaism or Christianity, is the "blessed olive tree neither of the East nor of the West," and the "light upon light" represents the generational chain of the *Imāms*, and so on.[29] Ṣūfī authors, however, are very careful even with regard to this most mystical of all qur'ānic verses. Not only do they refrain from developing an overall allegorical explanation to fit all its beautiful details, they even try to explain away the explicit beginning of the verse: "Allāh is the light of the heavens and the earth; the similitude of his light is as a niche wherein is a lamp." The famous ninth-century exegete Sahl al-Tustarī, whose mystical doctrine of light was so well described by G. Böwering,[30] explains that "God is the light of the heavens and the earth, meaning that he is adorning the heavens and the earth with lights" (*muzayyin al-samawāt wa-l-arḍ bi-l-anwār*) and that "the similitude of his light" is the light of Muḥammad.[31]

Al-Tustarī's whole theory of light centers on the light of Muḥammad in which the divine articulates itself. Although al-Tustarī conceives of God as light, he is very careful to speak only about the manifestation of this divine light in the primordial light of Muḥammad. In any case, it seems that his theory is closer to a Neoplatonic theory of emanation than to a symbolic allegory. Al-Tustarī also quotes al-Ḥasan al-Baṣrī (d. 110/728) in his interpretation of the verse. According to al-Ḥasan, the verse does not refer to the heart of a prophet but to the heart of an ordinary believer which is lit up by the pure monotheistic belief. The light mentioned in the verse is the light of the Qur'ān which evokes in the heart of the believer gnostic insight and sincerity in performing the religious commandments. There can be little doubt that al-Tustarī consciously avoided the great mystical challenge of the beginning of this verse, which states clearly that God is the light of the heavens and the earth. In this he is followed by other Ṣūfī Qur'ān commentators such as al-Qushayrī, who takes up al-Ḥasan al-Baṣrī's explanation and completely avoids dealing with the beginning of the verse. Both seem to be in perfect harmony with the Muʿtazilite explanation of the verse; for example, the famous Qāḍī of Hamadhān ʿAbd al-Jabbār (d. 416/1025) in his *Tanzīh al-Qur'ān ʿan al-maṭāʿin* (which could be translated as "The Defense of the Qur'ān against Criticism") says: "This verse ("Allāh is the light of the heavens and the earth") may [wrongly] seem to imply that God is a composite thing (*jism*) perhaps the most beautiful of all *jisms*, as some say. Therefore we explain that the meaning of the verse is that God lights up the heavens and the earth" (*munawwir al-samawāt wa-l-arḍ*).[32] Both Muʿtazilites and Ṣūfīs, usually so different from each other, combine here to explain away the plain meaning of the verse so as not to liken God even to light, a most commonly used metaphor and religious symbol. This seems to be the overriding concern even for the Ṣūfīs, who avoided this opportunity to use the whole verse for the creation of an allegory of divine light.

If we now examine the great al-Ghazālī's attitude toward allegorical interpretation of the Qur'ān, we shall find him to be very cautious as well. In his book about how to read and understand the Qur'ān, he demands strict adherence to the literal meaning of the text and to its traditional explanation and leaves little room for other modes of interpretation. These *ta'wīl* modes, if used at all, have to be based on a thorough knowledge of the Arabic language and the plain meaning of the text and kept far removed from any political or other self-interested interpretation.[33] Al-Ghazālī seems to permit allegorical and symbolic explanations only insofar as they serve to deepen the religious understanding of a verse or a commandment[34] and always as an addition to the plain literal meaning of the text. Thus, for example, the Pilgrimage (*ḥajj*) may be understood as a rehearsal and preparation for the pilgrim's last journey after his death, and its various rituals may therefore be explained allegorically in this context: the pilgrim's departure from home and the dangers awaiting him on his journey to Mecca are likened to his departure after his death to his grave, while his riding mount symbolizes his bier. His standing (*wuqūf*) at 'Arafāt on the ninth of *Dhū al-Ḥijja* symbolizes his future standing before God on the Day of Judgment, and his running between the Ṣafā and Marwa hills near the Ka'ba symbolizes either his scales of good and bad deeds going up and down on that day before God or his running forward and back in front of the great Judge's palace expecting his final judgment in great anxiety, and so on.[35] All these explanations, however, are permitted only as an *addition* to the literal understanding of the text and the punctilious performance of every detail of the ritual commandments.[36] Al-Ghazālī's insistence upon every allegorical explanation's being only *additional* to the plain literal meaning of the text is no doubt directed at the Ismā'īlīs who substituted allegory for the literal meaning of both texts and commandments and ended up with no commandments at all to fulfill. For example, fasting means to withhold true esoteric knowledge from the uninitiated; ritual purification means the renewal of the covenant of Ismā'īlī loyalty; the seven circumambulations of the Ka'ba mean "the circumambulation of the seven true *Imāms* in your heart"; prayer (*ṣalāt*) and alms-giving (*zakāt*), which together consist of seven consonants in Arabic, mean loyalty to Muḥammad and to 'Alī, also a total of seven consonants, and so on.[37] Al-Ghazālī's words are also directed at some earlier Ṣūfī authors, like those quoted by the eleventh-century Persian al-Hujwīrī in his *Kashf al-maḥjūb*, who spoke about "the temple of the heart" in contrast to "the temple of the stone" in Mecca, and preferred "the journey away from sin" and "contemplation and annihilation in the abode of friendship [of God]" to the pilgrimage itself.[38]

In his *Fayṣal al-tafriqa*, al-Ghazālī goes a step further and dismisses as unfounded speculation (*dalālāt ẓanniyya wa-laysat bi-barāhīn*) even Ṣūfī allegorical interpretations of the qur'ānic stories, the narratives that involve no commandments, because these confuse the hearts of the simple people.[39] Although al-Ghazālī is very careful not to label those who use *ta'wīl* as heretics, he does so explicitly with regard to anyone—such as the philosophers and the *zandaqa* (a general term for heretics)—who explains allegorically the basic dogmas of the faith, such as the belief in the (physical) resurrection of the dead, reward and punishment, or God's knowledge of the particulars.[40] This attitude must have inhibited his own natural inclination toward mystical Qur'ān interpretation. Even his most mystical book, the *Mishkāt al-anwār*, which deals with the qur'ānic Verse of Light, is not truly allegorical. In it he formulates a kind of mystical epistemology of the qur'ānic verse and derives man's different sources of knowledge and understanding from it (the senses, imagination, reason, prophecy, etc.). In one passage that deals with Moses being told by God to take off his shoes in the sacred valley of *Ṭuwā* (Q 20:12), al-Ghazālī states again that this verse—like any other—must first be understood literally. Only later may one add the deeper religious meaning that both shoes mean both worlds and that Moses was also commanded to detach himself from this world and the next, not to hope for anything in either world. In the same way, the *ḥadīth* saying that angels will never enter a house in which there is a painting or a live dog must first be understood and followed literally—namely, that one should not keep any paintings or dogs in one's house. After that one could and should add other meanings such as that: the dog represents the "dog of anger" in your heart, all your low passions, while the angels represent true knowledge (*ma'rifa*), which comes from above as they do, and therefore no heart consumed by passion will ever obtain true knowledge. According to al-Ghazālī, only he who combines both modes of interpretation may be considered to be perfect (*kāmil*).[41] This attitude of al-Ghazālī became the dominant one in Islam and it may well be that the strict demand never to abandon the plain literal meaning of a verse and always to give to that meaning first priority served also to subdue any imaginative inclinations to create full-fledged allegorical explanations.

What I have tried very cautiously to suggest here is that just as Islam shunned icons, painting, sculpture, drama, myth, and visual symbols in a deep search for the most abstract understanding of God's transcendence (*tawḥīd*), the mainstream of this civilization, including the mystics, may also have developed a reserved attitude toward linguistic paintings, as it were—that is, full-fledged allegories. This does not mean, of course, that allegorical language is absent from the great and huge religious literature of Islam, certainly not from Ṣūfī literature. As was mentioned at the beginning of this chapter, Ṣūfīs, like all mystics, make plentiful use of metaphors and partial allegorical interpretations. This is a hallmark of every mystical literature. But the use of what I termed full-fledged allegories, which is rather common in Christian mystical and other literature, is sparse in Ṣūfī literature and almost absent from classical Ṣūfī Qur'ān interpretation (with the exception of rare figures like Ibn al-'Arabī). This phenomenon may be similar to what happened with regard to prohibiting the depiction of live creatures in paintings and sculpture. We do find beautiful paintings in Islam despite this prohibition, such as in Umayyad palaces and public baths or in the well-known Persian miniatures, but we never find any painting or sculpture in a mosque. Similarly, we may find some full-fledged allegories in Ṣūfī and other religious literature of Islam, but they are extremely rare in Qur'ān commentaries. This in clear contrast to sectarian Shī'ite Qur'ān interpretation, which makes much use of full-fledged allegory.

This impressionistic suggestion must, of course, still be checked very thoroughly, and perhaps quantitatively, in many more Qur'ān commentaries. In a wider context it could also mean that any study of medieval Islamic imagination parallel to that done by Jacques Le Goff for the Western medieval imagination[42] has to proceed very differently and may come to very different conclusions.

Notes

1. Ibn al-'Arabī, *Tafsīr al-Qur'ān al-karīm*, 1:120 (Q2:195). See also his *al-Futūḥāt al-Makkiyya*, 1: 226–27.
2. See al-Ghazālī, *Faḍā'iḥ al-Bāṭiniyya*, 58–68.
3. See his *Kashf al-asrār al-bāṭiniyya wa-akhbār al-Qarāmiṭa*.
4. Ibn al-Jawzī, *Naqd al-'ilm wa-l-'ulamā aw Talbīs Iblīs*, for example 278–89.
5. See, for example, Bello, *The Medieval Islamic Controversy Between Philosophy and Orthodoxy*.
6. See Ritter, *Das Meer der Seele*, 8–18.
7. See Ivry, "Ibn Rushd's Use of Allegory."
8. See, for example, Ibn Kathīr's (d.774/1373) commentary to Q 2:26, *Tafsīr*, 1:64.
9. See al-Ghazālī, *al-Maqṣad al-asnā fī sharḥ ma'ānī asmā' Allāh al-ḥusnā*, 79–84: the attributes

of God as creator (*khāliq, bārī'*, and to a lesser extent also *muṣawwir*) cannot be used by man even figuratively.

10. See Q 5:110, which stresses the fact that even Jesus' miracles, including the creation of a bird of clay, were performed only with the permission (and help) of God.

11. Q 33: 4–5, 37.

12. Q 9:37.

13. There exist a large number of studies on this topic. I have mentioned several in the bibliography (e. g., Arnold, Crone, Creswell, Grabar).

14. *Ṣaḥīḥ al-Bukhārī*, 4: 103–4 (*Kitāb al-libās* [77], *Bāb al-taswīr* [88]); *Ṣaḥīḥ Muslim, Kitāb al-libās wa-l-zīna* [37], *Bāb* 26, no. 81–102, 1664–73. Even tattooing (*washm*) is forbidden because it changes the creation of God (*Bukhārī*, ibid., 87; *Muslim*, ibid.).

15. See Dodd, "The Image of the Word."

16. Lazarus-Yafeh, "Some Neglected Aspects of Medieval Muslim Polemics against Christianity."

17. Lazarus-Yafeh, *Some Religious Aspects of Islam*, 38–47.

18. Nūr al-Dīn 'Alī b. 'Abdallāh al-Samhūdī, *Wafā' al-wafā' bi-akhbār dār al-muṣṭafā*,1: 21. He apparently quotes 'Abd al-'Azīz b.'Abd Al-Salām (d. 661/1262), who wrote a book entitled *al-Qawā'id al-kubrā* (I am grateful to my student Lee Baron for this information). The context of the quotation is that of the rivalry between Mecca and Medina. See Lazarus-Yafeh, "Jerusalem and Mecca," 205.

19. Most scholars agree that both Judaism and Islam, in contrast to Greek thought, prefer aniconic and aural representations of God and are in general auditory and nonvisual in their religious orientation. In spite of this basic common attitude, many deviations are to be found in Jewish writings—much more so than in Islam—especially in Jewish mysticism. See the detailed discussion of these topics in Wolfson, *Through a Speculum that Shines*.

20. This is one of many definitions, taken from Bevan, *Symbolism and Belief*, 11.

21. Of course allegory is only one product of the human imagination, which includes much more. For the study of Western imagination, including allegory, and its importance for the study of history in general, see the work of Jacques Le Goff, especially his *L'imaginaire médiéval*. There is as yet no parallel to this kind of work in the study of Islam.

22. Even in these *Epistles* it is difficult to find full-fledged allegories, although imagination reigns high in them. See, for example, the famous debate between the animals and man in the twenty-second *Risāla*, which is certainly a fable but not an allegory. This fable was newly translated, with introduction and commentary by Lenn Evan Goodman as *The Case of the Animals versus Man Before the King of Jinn*.

23. He is al-Suhrawardī al-Maqtūl, who developed the theory of illuminative wisdom, a special symbolism of light (*ishrāq*), and was executed as a heretic in 1191. See R. Arnaldez, "*Ishrāq*," *EI*, new ed., 4:119-20.

24. See Corbin, *L'imagination créatrice dans le soufisme de 'Ibn 'Arabī*.

25. See al-Ghazālī, *Fayṣal al-tafriqa bayn al-Islām wa-l-zandaqa*, 184–86.

26. See his *al-Mukhtār fī l-amānāt wa-l-i'tiqādāt*, 219–20 (beginning of chap. 7).

27. I have not checked the later Ṣūfī commentaries, after Ibn al-'Arabī.

28. See Pseudo-Ibn al-'Arabī, *Tafsīr*, 590, and Goldziher, *Richtungen der islamischen Koranauslegung*, 233, who sums up the *Futūḥāt*.

29. See, for example, al-Ḥasan b. 'Alī al-Qummī, *Tafsīr* , 103.

30. Böwering, *The Mystical Vision of Existence in Classical Islam*, 147-53, 216–20.

31. Sahl b. 'Abdallāh al-Tustarī, *Tafsīr*, 68.

32. 'Abd al-Jabbār b. Aḥmad, 'Imād al-Dīn, *Tanzīh al-Qur'ān 'an al-maṭā'in*, 286. See also Fakhr al-Dīn al-Rāzī's commentary on the Verse of Light.

33. *Iḥyā' 'ulūm al-dīn*, 1.8: *Kitāb asrār tilāwat al-Qur'ān*, 527–28 (*al-Bāb al-rābi'*).

34. See Lazarus-Yafeh, *Studies in al-Ghazzali*, 264–348, on his symbolism of light.

35. *Iḥyā 'ulūm al-dīn*, 1:7: *Kitāb asrār al-ḥajj*, 483–91 (*al-Bāb al-thālith, Bayān al-a'māl al-bāṭina*).

36. The same attitude can be found among medieval Jewish authors. See, for example, Saperstein, "The Social and Cultural Context."

37. These examples are taken from the books mentioned in notes 2 and 3.

38. See al-Hujwīrī, *The Kashf al-maḥjūb*, trans. Nicholson, 326–29.

39. al-Ghazālī, *Fayṣal al-tafriqa*, 190–91.

40. Ibid., 191–93. He explains this in detail in his *Tahāfut al-falāsifa* and repeats it in other books.

41. al-Ghazālī, *Mishkāt al-anwār*, in *al-Quṣūr al-'awālī*, 32–33.

42. Le Goff, *L'imaginaire médiéval*; idem, *The Medieval Imagination*.

Bibliography

'Abd al-Jabbār, Imād al-Dīn. *Tanzīh al-Qur'ān*. Beirut: Dār al-Nahḍa al-Ḥadītha, 1967.

Arnaldez, R. "*Ishrāḳ*," *EI*, new ed., 4: 119–20.

Arnold, Thomas Walker. *Painting in Islam: A Study of the Place of Pictorial Art in Muslim Culture*. New York: Dover Publications, 1965.

Bello, Iysa A. *The Medieval Islamic Controversy between Philosophy and Orthodoxy: Ijma' and Ta'wil in the Conflict between al-Ghazali and Ibn Rushd*. Leiden: E. J. Brill, 1989.

Bevan, Edwyn. *Symbolism and Belief*. Boston: Beacon Paperback, 1957.

Böwering, Gerhard. *The Mystical Vision of Existence in Classical Islam: The Qur'anic Hermeneutics of the Ṣūfī Sahl al-Tustari (d. 283/896)*. Berlin: Walter de Gruyter, 1980.

Corbin, Henry. *Creative Imagination in the Sufism of Ibn 'Arabi*. Trans. Ralph Manheim. Bollingen Series, 91. Princeton, N.J.: Princeton University Press 1969.

——. *L'imagination créatrice dans le Soufisme d'Ibn 'Arabī*. Paris: Flammarion, 1958.

Creswell, Keppel Archibald. "The Lawfulness of Painting in Early Islam." *Ars islamica* 11/12 (1946): 159–66.

Crone, Patricia. "Islam, Judeo-Christianity and Byzantine Iconoclasm." *JSAI* 2 (1980): 59–95.

Dodd, Erica Cruikshank. "The Image of the Word: Notes on the Religious Iconography of Islam." *Berytus: Archeological Studies* 18 (1969): 35–62.

al-Ghazālī, Abū Ḥāmid. *Faḍā'iḥ al-Bāṭiniyya*. Ed. 'Abd al-Raḥmān Badawī. Cairo: al-Dār al-Qawmiyya lil-Ṭibā'a wa l-Nashr, 1383/1973.

——. *Fayṣal al-tafriqa bayna l-Islam wa l-zandaqa*. Ed. Sulaymān Dunyā. Cairo: Dār Iḥyā al-Kutub al-'Arabiyya, 1381/1961.

——. *Iḥyā' 'ulūm al-dīn*. 4 vols. Cairo: Muṣṭafā al-Ḥalabī, 1939.

——. *al-Maqṣad al-asnā fī sharḥ ma'ānī asmā' Allāh al-ḥusnā*. Ed. Fadlou A. Shehadi. Beirut: Dār al-Machreq, 1982.

——. *Mishkāt al-anwār*. In *al-Quṣūr al-'awālī*. Ed. Maḥmūd Muṣṭafā Abū l-'Alā. Cairo: Maktabat al-Jundī, 1970.

——. *al-Quṣūr al-'awālī*. 4 vols. Cairo: Maktabat al-Hindī, 1970–73.

——. *Tahāfut al-falāsifa*. Ed. Sulaymān Dunyā. Cairo: Dār al-Ma'ārif, 1980.

Goldziher, Ignaz. *Die Richtungen der islamischen Koranauslegung*. 2d ed. Leiden: E. J. Brill, 1952.

Goodman, Lenn Evan. *The Case of the Animals versus Man before the King of Jinn: A Tenth-Century Ecological Fable of the Pure Brethren of Basra*. Boston: Twayne, 1978.

Grabar, Oleg. *The Formation of Islamic Art*. New Haven, Conn.: Yale University Press, 1973.

al-Ḥammadī, Muḥammad b. Mālik. *Kashf asrār al-Bāṭiniyya wa-akhbār al-Qarāmiṭa*. Ed. Muḥammad 'Uthmān al-Khisht. Cairo: Maktabat Ibn Sina, 1988.

Ibn al-'Arabi, Muḥyī l-Dīn. *al-Futūḥāt al-makkiyya*. Ed. 'Uthmān Yaḥyā. 12 vols. Cairo: al-Majlis al-A'lā lil-Thaqāfa, al-Maṭba'a al-'Arabiyya, 1392/1972.

Ibn al-Jawzī, Abū l-Faraj 'Abd al-Raḥmān. *Talbīs Iblīs*. Amman: Dār al-Fikr, 1986.

——. *Zād al-masīr fī 'ilm al-tafsīr*. 9 vols. Beirut: Dār al-Yaqẓā al-'Arabiyya, 1968/1378.

Ibn Kathīr, Ismā'īl b. 'Umar. *Tafsīr al-Qur'ān al-'aẓīm*. 7 vols. Beirut: Dār al-Fikr lil-Ṭibā'a wa l-Nashr, 1970.

Ibn Rushd, Abū l-Walīd Muḥammad b. Aḥmad. *Faṣl al-maqāl*. Cairo: Dār al-Ma'ārif, 1983.

Ivry, Alfred. "Ibn Rushd's Use of Allegory." In *Averroës and the Enlightenment*. Ed. Mourad Wahba and Mona Abousenna, 113–25. Amherst, N.Y.: Prometheus Books, 1996.

Lazarus-Yafeh, Hava. "Jerusalem and Mecca." *Judaism* 46 (1997): 97–105.

——. "Some Neglected Aspects of Medieval Muslim Polemics Against Christianity." *Harvard Theological Review* 89 (1996): 61–84.

——. *Some Religious Aspects of Islam*. Leiden: E. J. Brill, 1981.

——. *Studies in al-Ghazzali*. Jerusalem: Magnes Press, 1975.

Le Goff, Jacques. *L'imaginaire médiéval*. Paris: Gallimard, 1985.

——. *The Medieval Imagination*. Trans. Arthur Goldhammer. Chicago: University of Chicago Press, 1988.

al-Ḥujwīrī, 'Alī b. 'Uthmān. *Kashf al-maḥjūb*. Ed. Reynold A. Nicholson. Leiden: Brill, 1911.

——. *The Kashf al-maḥjūb, The Oldest Persian Treatise on Sufism*. Trans. Reynold A. Nicholson. Gibb Memorial Series, vol. 17. London: Luzac, 1959.

Pseudo Ibn al'-Arabi, Muhyī l-Dīn. *Tafsīr al-Qur'ān al-karīm*. 2 vols. Beirut: Dār al-Yaqẓā al-'Arabiyya, 1968.

al-Qummī, Abū l-Ḥasan b. 'Alī b. Ibrāhīm. *Tafsīr*. Ed. Ṭayyib al-Jazā'irī. 2 vols. Najaf: Maṭba'at al-Najaf, 1387/1967.

Ritter, Helmut. *Das Meer der Seele*. Leiden: E. J. Brill, 1955.

Saadia ben Joseph. *Kitāb al-amānāt wa-l-i 'tiqādāt*. Ed. S. Landauer. Leiden: E. J. Brill, 1880.

——. *al-Mukhtār fī l-amānāt wa-l-i'tiqādāt* (Book of Beliefs and Opinions). Ed. and trans. Joseph Kafih. New York-Jerusalem: Sura Institute and Yeshiva University, 1970.

al-Samhūdī, 'Alī b. 'Abdallāh. *Wafā' al-wafā' bi-akhbār dār al-Muṣṭafā*. 2 vols. Cairo: Maṭba'at al-Ādāb, 1908.

——. *Wafā' al-wafā'*. Ed. Muḥammad Muḥyī l-Dīn 'Abd al-Ḥamīd. 4 v. in 2. Beirut: Dār Iḥyā' al-Turāth al-'Arabī, 1981.

Saperstein, Marc. "The Social and Cultural Context: Thirteenth to Fifteenth Centuries." In *History of Jewish Philosophy*. Ed. Daniel H. Frank and Oliver Leaman, 294–324. London: Routledge, 1997.

al-Tustarī, Sahl b. 'Abdallāh. *Tafsīr al-Qur'ān al-'aẓīm*. Cairo: Muṣṭafā al-Bābī al-Ḥalabī, 1911.

Wolfson, Elliot R. *Through a Speculum that Shines: Vision and Imagination in Medieval Jewish Mysticism*. Princeton, N.J.: Princeton University Press, 1994.

al-Yamanī, Muḥammad b. Mālik al-Ḥamādī. *Kashf al-asrār al-bāṭiniyya wa-akhbār al-Qarāmiṭa*. Najaf: Maktabat al-Khanānjī, 1374/1955.

25

From the Sacred Mosque to the Remote Temple

Sūrat al-Isrā' between Text and Commentary

ANGELIKA NEUWIRTH

The Problem and Its Context

Three honorary titles are assigned to Jerusalem in Islam: It is "the first of the two directions of prayer" (*ūlā l-qiblatayn*), the "second of the two sanctuaries (for temples; *thānī l-masjidayn*)," and the "third [important sacred site] after the two places of pilgrimage" (*thālith al-ḥaramayn*).[1]

These three honorifics serve to express the significance of the city for the educated Muslim and his religious community to the present.[2] They do not, however, constitute a purely panegyrical expression of the momentous "merits of Jerusalem";[3] rather they summarize the *ambivalent* position of Jerusalem in Islam, an ambivalence that emerged as the result of extended theological controversies. The rhetorically suggestive augmentation of the numerical value in the beginnings of the three honorifics should not obscure the fact that the seemingly ascending sequence of these individual honorary titles actually is inversely related to the acutal development of Jerusalem's official recognition as a religious center. While the sequence of the titles certainly reflects a development of *increasing plurality* and *complexity* in the perception of the holy places, it simultaneously marks a process of successive *demotions* of Jerusalem from its inherited primacy as a central place of monotheistic worship.

Let us briefly review the implications of the three epithets found in this succinct, tripartite formula. The opening honorific, "first [i.e., historically earlier] of the two directions of prayer," refers to the physical ritual of turning oneself toward an imagined, distant sanctuary, a custom introduced during the time of the Prophet's activity in Mecca. This practice not only served to open the central ceremony of the newly developed verbal worship of the early community, but also, as I will argue, it was understood to be closely connected with an important spiritual experience of the Prophet reflected in the Qur'ān itself, that of his nocturnal translation to the "remote temple" (*al-masjid al-aqṣā*), that is, to Jerusalem. Although Muslims later faced Mecca (instead of Jerusalem) while praying, they remembered Jerusalem as the initial *qibla* of the community.

The middle honorific, "second [i.e., historically later] of the two sanctuaries," recalls the *rivalry*, conceived during the Prophet's activity in Medina, between the founding places of the two basic forms of monotheistic worship—the ritual and the verbal—regarded as subsequent stages of development. Mecca, which houses the Kaʿba, was recognized as the origin of the Abrahamic cult, which manifests itself above all in the physical rites of pilgrimage; by contrast, *al-masjid al-aqṣā*, the sanctuary of the *Banū Isrāʾīl*, appeared as the center of the "Blessed Land" (*al-arḍ allatī bāraknā fīhā*), the land of the activity of Moses and Jesus, qurʾānic prophets whose message survived primarily in verbal forms. Among these two places, as Q 3:96 declares for the first time, the Kaʿba is to be regarded as the earlier sanctuary and Jerusalem the later one.

The last honorific name, "third after the two sanctuaries," reflects a later compromise, which emerged a few generations after the death of the Prophet. As doubts about the orthodox character of revering Jerusalem as a holy place began to coalesce, theologians and legal scholars responded with a restriction:[4] "Jerusalem retained a place in the restricted canon of sanctuaries, the prominent places of pilgrimage, while other sites seeking that privilege remained excluded, but its rank was relegated to third after Mecca and Medina."[5] This limited canonization was meant to control the still powerful tendency to credit Jerusalem with its traditional rank as the center of the world, the starting point of creation and, ultimately, of the dissolution of the created world,[6] a trend enhanced by the Umayyad building policy—the Dome of the Rock was completed by ʿAbd al-Malik in 692—but widely regarded as dogmatically dubious.[7]

While the developments summarized in the last two epithets are based on unambiguous passages in the Qurʾān or on *ḥadīths* and historical texts that are approximately datable, the role of Jerusalem for the early Islamic cult, as reflected in the first honorary name, is by no means uncontroversial in modern research. On the contrary, the problem of the relevance of Jerusalem as the nucleus of significant religious institutions developed in the two older "book religions," and reclaimed to play a part in the genesis of the Qurʾān and the Islamic cult—a problem that crystalizes in the question of the direction of prayer, the *qibla*—is in no way solved. It has remained among the most controversial points in the current discussion about the historicity of the traditional Islamic presentation of the early period.[8]

This essay is an attempt to deal with the question of the *qibla* from a new angle, bringing it down from the lofty heights of exegetical discussion based on a wide spectrum of heterogeneous religious ideas to the more limited forum of plain though sometimes fragmentary qurʾānic debates. By critically reconsidering some *ḥadīth* evidence accepted as early in recent research, I shall further try to elucidate the significance of the initial orientation toward Jerusalem and provide the background of its later abrogation in favor of a *qibla* toward Mecca (part 1). A necessary precondition for such a deeper understanding of the cultic significance of the *qibla* is an inquiry into the form and structure of the key verse Q 17:1 as well as a reconstruction of its qurʾānic context, which it has been sadly denied in modern research (part 2). But the investigation into Q 17:1 cannot dispense with a consideration of some representative texts from the amply developed narrative commentary on this verse which, in spite of substantial differences, can be shown to converge on certain focal points (part 3). Since this study is meant last but not least to highlight the relations feasible between text and commentary, it will focus on sūra 17 as a specimen of internal qurʾānic exegesis. The references to the *qibla* in sūra 17 will be placed in the context of the particular process of scriptural growth—the qurʾānic "canonical process"—and thus will be shown to mark relevant stages in the development of the rite of prayer and the debate about the signs of prophethood (part 4). After attempting to demonstrate that a reading of the qur'ānic text as the scenario of a canonical process may yield insights into the emergence of a cultic community, I will return to narrative exegesis and argue that its mythologizing tendency constitutes a fundamentally different hermeneutical paradigm of reading the Qur'ān from that which has been termed internal qur'ānic commentary. Inasmuch as it permits the dissolution of the qur'ānic context, narrative mythologizing exegesis claims a rank above the restrictively parenetic and eschatological discourse of the Qur'ān allowing us to recontextualize qur'ānic wordings. (part 5).

Focusing on the Qur'an, this investigation is constructed on a textual basis that more recently has been marginalized in favor of a focus on the much richer exegetic *ḥadīth* literature. A number of recent studies in *ḥadīth* texts have contributed substantially to a more complex image of the earliest Islamic developments, often strongly revising older positions. Results of such research are, however, seldom related to the qur'ānic vision question.[9] In spite of the often repeated observation that the Qur'ān, with its peculiar structure, which follows neither chronological nor systematic criteria, yields little as an immediate source of history, I will for my purpose of clarifying the problem of the qibla, look for exegetical evidence in the Qur'an itself.[10] The undeniable obstacles presented by the qur'ānic structure should not preclude the Qur'ān from historical investigations. This essay is meant to vindicate the perusal of qur'ānic references as exegetical evidence.

Any evaluation of qur'ānic evidence has, of course, in one way or another to respond to the radical reevaluation of the generally accepted authenticity of the Qur'ān as a text corpus going back to the prophet Muḥammad, which was introduced into the scholarly discussion by John Wansbrough's revolutionary *Quranic Studies*.[11] Depending on the particular premise a researcher chooses to follow—crediting the Qur'ān as an authentic testimony from the years 610 to 632 or considering it as merely a further "collection of traditions" that were canonized later—varying conclusions may be reached. As long as one clings to the heuristic basis of the historicity of the Prophet as a mediator of the texts collected in the Qur'ān,[12] it seems advisable to confront the results of *ḥadīth* research with those of an analysis of the qur'ānic evidence itself. The qur'ānic texts in such an analysis should, of course, be viewed not as already fixed and binding statements but rather as attestations to a process of growth, the "canonical process" turning the Qur'ān into scripture (see part 4 of this chapter). This approach will be pursued in the following discussion of the question of the community's first orientation of prayer (*qibla*)—a case where qur'ānic and *ḥadīth* evidence contradict each other and recent research has argued in favor of the accounts presented in *ḥadīth* literature.

Part 1: Ūlā al-qiblatayn

1. The *Qibla* as a Case. Was the Ka'ba the first orientation of prayer? "In any case it is clear that the façade of the Ka'ba was his [Muḥammad's] first *qibla*."[13] This assumption, which contradicts the initial honorific, has been deduced by Uri Rubin through partly explicit and partly implicit information yielded by numerous *ḥadīth* traditions. It is true that exegetical *ḥadīth* literature offers a different picture from the finally reached Islamic consensus, which holds, in keeping with the honorary title *ūlā al-qiblatayn*, that

the Jerusalem *qibla* goes back to the Prophet's Meccan activities, even though it is no longer possible to date the practice exactly.[14] In many instances in *ḥadīth* literature, the Jerusalem *qibla* is viewed as a gesture of compromise toward the Jews, and thus its introduction is transferred to the time immediately after the Prophet's emigration to Medina (the *Hijra*).[15] This attempt at dating—particularly frequent in the *ḥadīths* related by al-Ṭabarī (d. 923)—echoes the polemical stance maintained in the qur'ānic context of the abrogation of the first *qibla* (Q 2:142–45) and relativizes the unpopular but undeniable fact that a *qibla* toward Jerusalem was shared with the Jews for a longer period until its replacement some eighteen months after the *Hijra*.

Ḥadīths also record divergent datings of the introduction of the Jerusalem *qibla*, such as "eighteen months before the Hijra,"[16] implying that the *qibla* was taken over from neo-Muslims resident in Medina, or "at the same time as the revelation of *Sūrat al-Isrā'* (Q 17)."[17] Rubin has rightly rejected the overstated assumption, held by some traditionalists, that Muḥammad prayed toward Jerusalem "since his first revelation." He interprets the tradition, however, as being a tendentious repression of an earlier *qibla* toward the Ka'ba, "its aim being to suppress the fact that Muḥammad, at a certain stage, abandoned his original *qibla* (the Ka'ba) in favor of Jerusalem. In fact, most of the traditions that describe his praying toward Jerusalem while in Mecca maintain that he used to stand opposite the southeastern wall of the Ka'ba in order to have the Ka'ba between himself and Jerusalem."[18] However, the consideration of both the Ka'ba and Jerusalem as the *qiblatāyn*, as Wensinck stressed,[19] looks far more like a compromise, one that can be easily explained as an effort of the respective transmitters to honor the final *qibla* of Islam with an early supererogatory exercise of the Prophet or to ascribe to the Prophet a supernatural talent of knowing in advance religious practices that were to be divinely sanctioned later on, a pattern of thinking which can frequently be traced in the biographies of Muḥammed (*sīra*).[20]

The question of the *qibla* thus cannot be solved by investigating the Islamic tradition alone. Rubin, who in his study relies exclusively on *ḥadīth* material, justly noted the uncertain premises involved in accepting the theory of an early adoption of Jerusalem as the first *qibla*. He has demonstrated that the Ka'ba, which at the time of Muḥammad already had attracted varied cultic practices, functioned as a place of ritual prayer for the *Jāhilī* Meccans and, hence, for Muḥammad's community in the earliest period of his activities prior to the development of his own cultic practices. The question arises, however, as to whether the *ḥadīth* material can be regarded as sufficiently free from tendentiousness simply because of its broad base of evidence to disqualify the view of the "official version"—and to establish the Ka'ba as the "first *qibla*" in lieu of Jerusalem—or whether individual *ḥadīths* should not rather be read as expressing certain apologetic motives of a later period. Such tendentiousness, as Wensinck rightly stressed, could be excluded on the assumption that the "Jewish" *qibla* was adopted during the Prophet's time of activity in Mecca. Since this assumption—that is, Jerusalem being the final *qibla*—though not supported by an explicit qur'ānic text, did become the dominant view, let us examine the evidence supporting it.

2. Imagining the "Remote Temple" (*al-masjid al-aqṣā*). Perhaps the complex notion of a *qibla* itself provides the most convincing argument in favor of the primacy of Jerusalem. For, even if one accepts as probable that Muḥammad and his community did initially pray facing the Ka'ba, or at the Ka'ba, the question arises of whether this practice alone fulfills the notion of "taking up a direction of prayer." Does not a ritual *qibla*, like that mentioned

in the Medinan verses Q 2:143–45, point instead to an orientation toward a sanctuary not directly accessible to the person praying but rather sought after in the imagination? Let us take a look at the qur'ānic statements themselves: It is well known that the Qur'ān speaks only about the abolishment of the "earlier direction of prayer," evidently presupposing the listener's knowledge of that earlier direction toward Jerusalem. Q 2:142–44 reads:

> The fools among the people will say,
> "What has turned them from the direction
> they were facing in their prayers aforetime?" . . .
> We did not appoint the direction thou wast facing,
> except that We might know
> who followed the messenger from him who turns on his heels. . . .
> We have seen thee turning thy face to heaven;
> now We will surely turn thee to a direction that shall satisfy thee.
> Turn thy face towards the holy mosque (*al-masjid al-ḥarām*);
> and wherever you are, turn your faces towards it.

The verses seem to reflect a crisis as well as its final solution. On the one hand the abolishment of the initial *qibla* (toward Jerusalem), about whose duration the text says nothing, meets with criticism by outsiders ("they") against whom it has to be asserted. The initial *qibla* is thus demoted in importance and viewed as a merely provisional orientation, a test of the community. The newly introduced *qibla* (of the Ka'ba), presented as a substitute apt to give satisfaction to those addressed, is, however, not marked as the resumption of an older practice, as would be expected had the Meccan worship already entailed turning to such a *qibla*. The new *qibla* is certainly novel, yet not in need of justification, since it fits into the cult reform initiated at Medina where the newly developed concept of Islam encompasses a revival of an "Abrahamic monotheism."[21] At the same time, the passage clearly shows the peculiar intention underlying a divinely institutionalized *qibla*: the worshipper who is *outside* the holy place ("wherever you are") must turn his face towards it in prayer. These verses presume the possibility of the worshipper's being remote from the Ka'ba, perhaps even in exile.

It is precisely this remoteness of the worshippers from the sanctuary intended as their point of orientation that underlies the earlier Jerusalem *qibla*. Indeed, the very fact of its material inaccessibility enhances its significance. The typological difference between an accessible sanctuary in which, or in whose surroundings, rites are performed and a holy place that serves as the orientation and direction of prayer from which the worshippers are remote and for which they must search in their imagination is obvious. The latter understanding of a *qibla* echoes throughout the qur'ānic verse and reminds us of the biblical text 1 Kings 8, especially vv. 33–34, with its reference to the tradition of facing Jerusalem while praying:

> When thy people Israel be smitten down before the enemy,
> because they have sinned against thee,
> and shall turn again to thee, and confess thy name, and pray,
> and make supplication unto thee in this house:
> then hear thou in heaven, and forgive the sin of thy people Israel
> and bring them again unto the land
> which thou gavest unto their fathers.

The worshipper's assumption of such an orientation is based upon more complex preconditions than his simply being present at the holy place: it presupposes the intention to maintain one's own indigenous cult even against obstacles. In the case of believers living in a situation of exile it further presupposes the hope of a resumption of their cult *in situ*.

A corresponding awareness with regard to the rites at the Kaʿba can hardly be asserted for Muḥammad and his community before their Medinan exile. In the Meccan community, complex forms of verbal worship clearly based on elements of the two older monotheistic religions had emerged, complementing the inherited rites.[22] Prayers[23] and other rites of the early community may have been performed in front of the Kaʿba and the worshippers may be imagined to have "faced" (*istaqbala*)[24] the Kaʿba. It would be a gross anachronism, however, to understand the lexeme in its later sense of "ritually facing an imaginary point for the convergence of prayers" for the early Meccan community. As against that, the Medinan community, or at least the Meccan emigrants among them, should have viewed the Kaʿba from a different perspective. To them, the Kaʿba should have appeared as a meaningful replacement of Jerusalem, since by then their own situation had come close to that of exile. In any event, with the newly evolving cultic concept, Mecca and the Kaʿba gradually came to mark a starting point within salvation history, as is clearly documented in Q 3:96: "The first House established for the people was that at Bakka, a place holy, and a guidance to all beings." What was founded here are the rites of Islam, a heritage mentioned in diverse Medinan verses and integrated into biblical salvation history in Q 14:35–37: "And when Abraham said, My Lord, make this land secure, and turn me and my sons away from serving idols . . . , our lord let them perform the prayer . . . " and Q 2:128f.: "Our lord show us our holy rites." It is noteworthy, however, that Mecca was to inherit still another merit of Jerusalem, to be the cradle not of ritual worship alone but of monotheist verbal worship as well—Q 2:127: "And, our Lord, do Thou send among them a Messenger, one of them, who shall recite to them Thy signs, and teach them the Book and the Wisdom, and purify them; Thou art the Almighty, the All-wise." Thus the most important prerogative of Jerusalem (suggestively pronounced by Isaiah 2:3: "The Law will go out from Zion and the word of the Lord from Jerusalem") had been transferred to Mecca, the locale of the most ancient temple.[25]

Part 2: The Enigmatic Verse, Q 17:1 and Its Exegesis

Let us now try to situate Jerusalem on the mental map of the early community by investigating the qur'ānic texts related to the sanctuary so as to construct a context fot the event of Jerusalem's elevation to the rank of a qibla.

1. Salvation History Localized in Jerusalem. It is true that Jerusalem, whose official (Roman) name in qur'ānic times was Aelia Capitolina,[26] is never explicitly mentioned in the Qur'ān. Likewise, Mecca figures explicitly not more than twice,[27] being mentioned only in Medinan sūras. The only place mentioned directly in Meccan texts is Mount Sinai, which appears nine times always in early sūras.[28] Otherwise toponyms are generally replaced by paraphrastic characterizations[29] or evoked through the particular sanctuaries by which they are distinguished.[30] It is a topographia sacra, not profane geogra-

phy, that the Qur'ān designs, where places are represented by emblems. Jerusalem, though not mentioned explicitly, is, of course, not absent from the Qur'ān.

A clear reference to Jerusalem, and specifically its temple, is found in sūra 19 ("Mary"), which is ordinarily dated to the middle Meccan period. Zachary is presented as receiving a divine message in the *miḥrāb* unanimously understood as the Temple (Q 19:11). That the continuation of the episode, Mary's seclusion at "an eastern place" (Q 19:16), should also be located in the Temple is suggested by the later Medinan account (Q 3:37, 39).[31] Earlier in salvation history, David acts as a judge (Q 38:21) in the *miḥrāb*. In these cases the temple is understood primarily in the physical sense as monumental architecture. Likewise, *miḥrāb* in the plural (*maḥārīb*) in the sense of "palaces," "monumental buildings" figures in an account of Solomon (Q 34:13). Yet, in sūra 17, which is also considered middle Meccan, the Temple, understood as the spiritual center, or emblem of the *Banū Isrā'īl*, is not presented as a *miḥrāb* but is designated by "*masjid*" (Q 17:7), a title otherwise reserved[32] for the Meccan sanctuary. This term is used with reference to two different epochs of the Jerusalem Temple history: the Temple of Solomon and the Temple of Herod. It is noteworthy that here reference to the Jerusalem Temple can be made with the single word *masjid*, qualified only by its relation to the *Banū Isrā'īl*, without further geographic determination. The isolated expression "temple," (*masjid*) thus either presupposes the listeners' familiarity with the notion of the "Jerusalem Temple" or has to be taken as a reference to a less ambiguous mention of the Temple in a preceding passage, that is, Q 17:1.

All these references to the Temple evoke the sanctuary as the scenario of major events in salvation history. Yet they imply little about the significance of Jerusalem in the Prophet's and the community's consciousness. To explore this relation we have to look for a reference to the Temple that has a direct bearing on the personal experience of the Prophet himself.

2. Q 17:1: Evidence of the Prophet's Personal Relation to Jerusalem. There is indeed a single qur'ānic text that conveys a direct relationship between Jerusalem and the Prophet: in Q 17:1, Jerusalem functions as the destination of the nocturnal departure of the Prophet. Here too the location is mentioned only indirectly, but it is made unambiguous through geographical localization in the "Holy Land" and confirmed in its high rank through a parallelization with the Meccan "temple" (*al-masjid al-ḥarām*) as its antipode, with respect to which it is the "remote temple" (*al-masjid al-aqṣā*). Yet this reference to Jerusalem has raised problems. Unlike all the indirect references to Jerusalem, it lacks a direct connection with events of the earlier salvation history familiar to the listeners. Rather, it figures as the scene of a mysterious, though obviously important, biographical experience of the Prophet himself, one that is related in the Qur'ān only on this occasion in a fairly unambiguous form.

Sūra 17:1 reads:

a Glory be to him, who carried his servant by night
b from the holy mosque to the further mosque
c the precincts of which we have blessed,
d that we might show him some of our signs.
e He is the all-hearing, the all-seeing.[33]

The verse entails individual praise of God uttered by the Prophet[34] and introduced through a hymnic exclamation. What is celebrated here is unique in the qur'ānic representation of the Prophet: a nightly experience of closeness to the divine Other during which the Prophet felt himself transferred from his Meccan sanctuary (*al-masjid al-ḥarām*)—or in a general sense, from Mecca—to the "remote sanctuary," situated in the Holy Land. It is true that describing the Jerusalem Temple or the Temple Mount with the expression "remote temple" (*al-masjid al-aqṣā*) is unique to the Qur'ān, but viewed in its relation to Mecca, site of the *masjid al-ḥarām* as the starting point of the departure, it functions not as a toponym but simply as an appellative.

Though Q 17:1 may lack an explicit salvation history context familiar to the listeners, there is at least the allusion to such a context in the phrase, "whose surroundings we have blessed."[35] The ensuing indication of a divine-human interaction "to show him our signs" attests for the prophet a salvation history rank that recalls, in an abridged form, an earlier experience of a similar kind, namely of visions reflected in Q 53:18: "he truly saw the greatest of the signs of his Lord" (*laqad ra'ā min āyāti rabbihi l-kubrā*).[36] In both instances, the perception of signs is the essence of the experience. The question arises as to how this 'biographical' verse relates to the rest of the sūra.

3. Formal Problems: Is Q 17:1 in Its Original Place? Western research proceeds unanimously from the hypothesis that the first verse was not originally part of the corpus of the sūra,[37] a problem not raised in the traditional Islamic chronology.[38] Still, the relationship of the first verse to the rest of the sūra is of great relevance for the interpretation of this seemingly isolated verse, which cannot be fully clarified without an attempt at contextualization. Indeed, the verse displays some striking traits that distinguish it from the corpus of the sūra, the first being its peculiar closing. The verse ends in an otherwise uncommon end rhyme *-īr*, forming an isolated unit vis-à-vis the following text rhyme in *-ūrā/īrā, -ūlā/ īlā*, an irregularity that calls for an explanation, especially since it could easily have been avoided: a penultimate rhyme on *-īrā* conforming with the rest of the sūra could have been attained through a simple repositioning of the syntagmas.[39]

Indeed, the "corpus of the sūra," Q 17:2–111, appears self-sufficient. The first verse aside, the sūra is well proportioned consisting of three sections made up of (1+)20/60/30 verses. Still, the second verse is obviously unfit to form the beginning of a sūra, both stylistically and rhetorically. Starting with a *wa*-syndesis, it seems to continue a preceding text. With its reference to the familiar *topos* of the revelation of a scripture serving as a divine "sign," it also seems to provide an additional argument to a discourse already initiated. Now, the first verse without the clausula that isolates it structurally would be perfectly plausible as an initial verse, since a hymn that forms the beginning of a narrative section is by no means uncommon in the Qur'ān. Already within the Meccan texts, numerous sūras begin with a hymn followed by discursive sections. What is irregular about the first verse is not so much its complex structure and unique contents, but its special rhyme closure, even more so its clausula, which appears somewhat alien to the whole sūra: *innahu huwa l-samī'u l-baṣīr*. Closures of this kind[40] become predominant in late Meccan and Medinan sūras, where the loose flow of speech is regularly interwoven with hymnic or parenetic insertions, or "*clausulas*," that function as an intrinsic commentary. In sūra 17, however, all verses except Q 17:1 end with a rhymed phrase that is not a parenetic comment, but which forms part of the main strand of speech—a stylistic economy that places the sūra close to the group of middle Meccan texts.

Now, one might consider the possibility that Q 17:1 was once recited as a verse group made up of four short verses, inasmuch as its first three cola still resonate with a rhyme pattern (aCCā/ah-*aṣrā/aqṣā/ḥawlah*) that has been blurred by their integration into the structure of a long verse. A comparison with the similar text in sūra 53 may clarify this hypothesis. The recollection of the two visions of the Prophet recorded there culminates in the appraisal (Q 53:18), "truly he saw the greatest signs of his Lord" (*laqad ra'ā min āyāti rabbihi l-kubrā*). Similarly, the fourth colon of Q 17:1, (d), *li-nuriyahu min āyātinā*, which also entails the culmination of an experience, might have originally been the closing element of a short verse group of its own. It is true that the antepenultimately stressed *āyātinā* is not very suggestive as a rhyme ending and would as such be without parallel in the Qur'ān.[41] Also, as the keyword of its colon, it hardly appears fit simultaneously to fill the place of an ornamental element. If, however, the qualification *kubrā* given to the *āyāt* of a divine vision in sūra 53 could be conferred on the *āyāt* of the encounter with the divine recorded in sūra 17, the verse would gain a suitable rhyme ending, and the entire ensemble 17:1, a–d, would end with a convincing closure. The rhymes of the three preceding cola, *asrā*, *aqṣā*, and *ḥawlah*, would regain their functionality as markers of verse endings in a group consisting of four verses. Their transmitted final shape as one long verse, unambiguously closed through a stereotypical clausula, may be due to their initially isolated transmission at a time when the main body of the sūra had not yet been composed. As I will argue, the corpus of this sūra (Q 17:2–111) could have grown around the nucleus of the first verse in the course of the canonical process. The initial verse, according to this hypothesis, should be viewed not as a secondary addition to the corpus of the sūra, but rather as a temporarily independent pronouncement which was later elaborated through a "commentary" setting it in its proper theological and cultic context, as found in Q 17:2–111.

Part 3: Interpretations of Q 17:1 Offered by the Islamic Tradition

Before turning to the key for understanding verse 1—namely, the corpus of sūra 17—let us take a look at the exegesis of the verse as offered by the Islamic tradition. Two different narratives have emerged, establishing substantially different ways of remembering the biographical episode. They may be labeled "plain" and "mythologizing," respectively. A brief analysis of the structural elements of both types will reveal some essential traits of the narrative commentary whose rereading of the Qur'ān atomizes the scriptural discourse into a host of isolated elements that invite employment at random to form new meaningful combinations. The resulting picture will serve as a backdrop for the clearer discernment of the tenets and techniques of that inner-qur'ānic exegesis which manifests itself in the particular process of the growth of the text itself.

1. The "Nocturnal Departure"—*Isrā'*—as a Translation to Jerusalem in a Dream. Among the most popular of the "plain" and "sober" reports is a narrative, transmitted by al-Ṭabarī from Ibn Isḥāq that dispenses entirely with legendary trends of interpretation, in which the destination of the Prophet's nocturnal movement was Jerusalem. Umm Hāni', a cousin of the Prophet, reports:

> The nocturnal departure [*isrā'*, a term derived from the qur'ānic *asrā*, "he made him depart by night," A.N.] of the Messenger of God took place as follows: He was staying at my house [indication of an ordinary place in Mecca instead of the precise location of the Ka'ba, a strikingly free exegesis of the qur'ānic *al-masjid al-ḥarām*, A.N.[42]], where he spent

> the night [interpretation of the qur'ānic *laylān*—"by night," A.N.]. When he had performed the final evening prayer he went to sleep and so did we. In the early morning God's Messenger woke us for the morning prayer and when we had concluded it together he said to me: "Umm Hāni', I have been praying here together with you the evening prayer, as you remember. But then I was in *Bayt al-Maqdis* [Jerusalem; an explication of the qur'ānic "remote temple"—*al-masjid al-aqṣā* A.N.] and prayed there ["prayer"being an explication of the qur'ānic allusion to the vision of divine "signs," *āyātinā*, A.N.]. And now I have been praying with you the morning prayer in this place.[43]

Although we are not entitled to take this report as a firsthand testimony about the experience of the Prophet—the term *Bayt al-Maqdis* (the Arabic rendition of the Hebrew *beit ha-miqdash*, "Temple") would perhaps not yet have figured in such a context[44]—it is remarkable for the paucity of its semantic preconceptions. It does not display any particular ideological tendency, nor does it refer to any supernatural power or experiences irreconcilable with the qur'ānic self-image of the Prophet. Also in favor of its genuineness is the observation that the qur'ānic text is not interpreted verbatim but is dealt with like a specimen of ordinary discourse so that *al-masjid al-ḥarām*, taken *pars pro toto* for Mecca, can be represented by a private house. The miraculous traits, though, are given proper attention. The transmitters relate that the event occurred within a specific time frame, the limited hours between two periods of prayer. This would, however, not necessitate a supernatural agency, had it happened in a dream as the report suggests. A claim to a supernatural experience is, however, resounding in the qur'ānic verse with its triumphant tenor (*subḥāna*), its expressive mention of a locomotion between the two most momentous sanctuaries of the ecumene—an event felt to have taken place "out of time." Looking for a *sitz im leben* for sūra 17, one might hypothesize that it originated out of a public provocation. The initial verse with the striking news of the Prophet's translation to Jerusalem—once recited to the Meccans in public—is reported to have aroused protests and derision. These reactions, which are also mirrored in the harsh polemics adduced in the corpus of sūra 17 itself, could not be ignored but had to be confronted. The response was presented in a sophisticated reflection on the entire context of prophetical self-representation, verses 17:2–111, a text that should have been composed a short time after the promulgation of the event itself. Be that as it may, the *ru'yā*, the vision of the Prophet as well as the (rejected) notion of an ascension (*ruqiyy*) occupy important places in the corpus of the sūra. Central, however, is the performance of prayer,—not surprisingly so since prayer in the exegesis of 17:1 is not only the starting point of the experience but also its culmination and, finally, the end mark of the venture.

2. The "Nocturnal Departure" (*Isrā'*) as a Miraculous Ride to Jerusalem Followed by an Ascent to Heaven (*Mi'rāj*).[45] As against that plain and sober report, there stands a narrative richly adorned with images and fantastic traits in which the nocturnal departure culminates in an ascent to heaven. The story first appears separately from the translation report, but already the classical biography of the Prophet by Ibn Isḥāq (d. 768), the *sīra* par excellence,[46] which transmits different versions of the "nocturnal departure," contains a miraculous ride to Jerusalem culminating in a detailed description of an ascent to heaven. Both movements, the longitudinal leading to the earthly sanctuary and the vertical to the heavenly spheres though ascribed to different transmittors (al-Ḥasan al-Baṣrī and 'Abdallāh b. Mas'ūd, respectively), are dealt with as successive phases of the same event (the reports going back to only a few generations after the death of the

Prophet). The perspectives of these presentations differs radically from that of the "plain" report.

In the transmission of al-Ḥasan al-Baṣrī, which is adduced here as representative of the accounts of the miraculous journey to Jerusalem, the event is clearly framed as an initiation rite. The novice sleeping in the sanctuary is awakened with three strokes by the initiator, is led out by him and subjected to a test. Inserted between these steps is a scene staged in Jerusalem—completely in harmony with qur'ānic imagery—a gathering of the prophets familiar from Jewish and Christian salvation history. Among them Muḥammad has to assert his rank. At the end, the story returns to the "real" scenario at Mecca, where the report of the nocturnal journey with its supernatural traits has provoked criticism and even derision among the Qurayshites:

> I was told that al-Ḥasan said that the Prophet said: While I was sleeping [interpretation of the qur'ānic *laylān*, A.N.) in the Ḥijr [narrow understanding of the *masjid al-ḥarām*, A.N.] Gabriel came and stirred me with his foot. I sat up but saw nothing and lay down again. He came a second time and stirred me with his foot. I sat up, but saw nothing and lay down again. He came to me a third time and stirred me with his foot. I sat up and he took hold of my arm and I stood beside him and he brought me out to the door of the mosque and there was a white animal, half mule, half donkey [indication of an interpretation of the qur'ānic *asrā* as a movement on horseback, A.N.], with wings on its sides with which it propelled its feet, putting down each forefoot at the limit of its sight and he mounted me on it. Then he went out with me keeping close to me.[47]

In this story al-Hasan said:

> The apostle and Gabriel went their way until they arrived at the Temple [narrow understanding of the qur'ānic *al-masjid al-aqṣā*, A.N.] at Jerusalem. There he found Abraham, Moses, and Jesus among a company of the prophets [as bearers of the divine blessings, a representation of the Blessed Land, the qur'ānic *al-arḍ allatī bāraknā fīhā*, A.N.]. The apostle acted as their imām in prayer [identification of the qur'ānic *āyāt* with the performance of a prayer in the community of the prophets, A.N.]. Then he was brought two vessels, one containing wine and the other milk. The apostle took the milk and drank it, leaving the wine. Gabriel said: "You have been rightly guided to the way of nature and so will your people be, Muḥammad. Wine is forbidden you." Then the apostle returned to Mecca and in the morning he told Quraysh what had happened. Most of them said, "By God, this is a plain absurdity! A caravan takes a month to go to Syria, and a month to return and can Muḥammad do the return journey in one night?" Many Muslims gave up their faith.[48]

Ibn Isḥāq, then reporting on the authority of Abū Sa'īd al-Khuḍrī, has the ascension story directly follow that of the miraculous journey to Jerusalem: "I heard the apostle say: 'After the completion of my task in Jerusalem a ladder [*mi'rāj*] was brought to me finer than any I have ever seen. . . . My companion mounted it with me until we came to one of the gates of heaven.'" This report is followed by visions of hell, then further climbings across the spheres, which are each occupied by one prophet until the seventh sphere is reached, from which a vision of paradise is opened up. The further description of the ascension attributed by Ibn Isḥāq to 'Abdallāh b. Mas'ūd, a secretary of the Prophet, concludes with the following scene:

> (Finally) they reached the seventh heaven and his Lord. There the duty of the fifty prayers a day was laid upon him. The apostle said: "On my return I passed by Moses and what

a fine friend of yours he was! He asked me how many prayers had been laid upon me and when I told him fifty he said, 'Prayer is a weighty matter and your people are weak, so go back to your Lord and ask him to reduce the number for you and your community.' I did so and He took off ten. Again I passed by Moses and he said the same again; and so it went on until only five prayers for the whole day and night were left. Moses again gave me the same advice. I replied that I had been back to my Lord and asked him to reduce the number until I was ashamed and I would not do it again. Anyone of you who performs them in faith and trust will have the reward of fifty prayers."[49]

3. Attempt at an Evaluation of the Accounts of the Nocturnal Ride (*Isrā'*) and Ensuing Ascent (*Mi'rāj*). The peculiar fact that the two "phases" of the movement, the longitudinal nocturnal departure to Jerusalem and the vertical ascension through the spheres, do not belong together typologically has already been pointed out by Horovitz (1919). For their proper religio-historical context we need only refer to the detailed studies by Widengren (1955) and, more recently, by Busse (1991) and van Ess (1999).[50] For our purposes, it suffices to note the structural elements comprised in each of the reports. For the miraculous ride to Jerusalem, these are as follows: (1) the awakening of the novice by the initiator; (2) his mounting a miraculous animal (donkey/mule) with the ability of time-lapse movement; (3) after arrival at the destination, Muḥammad's performance of a prayer rite by assuming the function of imām among the older prophets; (4) the testing of the novice.

It is noteworthy that elements (1) and (4) as parts of a rite of initiation and (2) as an obscure evocation of a messianic entrance into Jerusalem are alien to the horizon of qur'ānic imagery.[51] As against that, element (3), the core of the report, can be read as a narrative application of the qur'ānic prophetology that culminates in the "seal word" (Q 33:40: "Muhammad is . . . the seal of the Prophets") and the elevation of the Prophet to a close relationship with the heavenly hierarchy (Q 33:56, "God and His angels bless the Prophet"). In this narrative account, the Prophet's elevation to his superior rank vis-à-vis the other prophets is established through his acting as an imām in the collective prayer offered in the Jerusalem sanctuary with the previous prophets.

The components of the ascension story are similarly heterogeneous: (1) the prophet's climbing up a heavenly ladder; (2) his visiting of the prophets situated in the diverse spheres; (3) after arriving at the destination, his receiving the obligation of fifty daily prayers; (4) his following of Moses' advice to ask for a reduction in number; (5) divine confirmation of the value of the five daily prayers.

Here again, elements (1) and (2) are alien to the qur'ānic imagery. They presuppose the psychological type of an ecstatic hardly reconcilable with Muḥammad's qur'ānic profession as a messenger.[52] The situation of the prophets in the spheres, moreover, reflects the image of planetary deities governing the movement of the spheres that is familiar from antiquity. Elements (3) and (4) appearing at the center of the narrative are more in line with the qur'ānic imagination. Here the central role of Muḥammad is complemented by the important, yet marginal role played by Moses. It is noteworthy that Moses, rather than Muḥammad, initially appears to be the superior in authority; it is he who gives advice based on his experience as the leader of a community, a tribute of honor, inspired, as we will see, by sūra 17 itself. The account of the ascension culminates, as did the stories of the nocturnal translation and the miraculous ride, in the idea of prayer. The *āyāt*—that according to Q 17:1 are bestowed on the Prophet and that are elaborated in the narrative exegesis into miraculous adventures of a cultural hero—even in the most daringly mythologizing version culminate in none other than the divine communication of the institution of prayer.

Part 4: The Corpus of Sūra 17 (Q 17:2–111) as a Commentary on Q 17:1

1. Sūra 17 and Its Position in the Canonical Process. Having thus digressed into the narrative commentary on Q 17:1, let us turn to the internal qur'ānic elaboration of the verse. For discussion of the relation of Q 17:1 to the "corpus" of the sūra Q 17:2–111, as well as to other qur'ānic texts, it is useful to rely on the new approach developed by the American biblical scholar Brevard Childs, who has proposed an understanding of the genesis of a canon as a process of growth. "Canon" in this context is no longer limited to the officially codified final form of a text, but rather means "the consciousness of a binding covenantal character deeply rooted in the texts" that is affirmed by the continuous references of later emerging text units to a text nucleus, and by recurrent instances of intertextuality mirrored in the text units developing around that nucleus. It attests to a "canonization from below," the driving force behind this process of growth being the continual publication of texts and their acceptance by the community. This process aptly accounts for the shape of the Qur'ān, which reflects the dialogic mode of its genesis. It is mirrored in a striking shape in the relationship between the initial verse and the corpus of sūra 17. The corpus unfolds and discusses the implications, both textual and "political," of the initial verse. Interpretation of previously communicated texts is thus one of the primary functions underlying textual growth. The final shape of the corpus simply relocates interpretation, which until then took place in productive additions or changes within the text, and which henceforth takes place through exegesis and interpretation that are separate from the text.[53] The situation of these exegetes is obviously different from that of the early community's. As van Ess has recently stressed again, "the scholars contined to be aware of the fact that revelations had been reactions to specific situations; this is why they talked about asbāb al-nuzūl."[54] But the Qur'ān, which had become a scripture, a collection of equally venerated revelations to the Prophet, was not to be fit into diverse—locally and socially conditioned—theological frameworks and thus was stripped of its referentiality and leveled in terms of its peculiar historical expression.

2. Q 17:2–111 as a Document of a Controversy about the Significance of Prophetic "Signs" (*āyāt*). The sūra, despite the diversity of its *topoi* and the allusive nature of their discussion, displays a well-balanced composition. The text as a whole provides an elaboration of the frequently treated theme of divine communication with men through prophets, with particular focus on the significance and diversity of "signs" (*āyāt*) as ascribed to the prophets. Uniquely in the Qur'ān, the sūra presents in parallel two prophetic figures, Moses[55] and Muḥammad, who alternately play the main roles in its narrative, other prophetic agents being only marginally recalled. Though they are chronologically separated, their roles are closely related, the gap being bridged by a number of shared experiences and notions, not the least of which is sacred topography, as introduced through Q 17:1, wherein the Meccan Prophet is understood to have entered the imagi-

nary territory associated with Moses, the Holy Land. The sūra is built around the nuclear elements of (1) two prophets in synopsis: Muḥmmad and Moses, characterized by their prophetic signs as developed in previous sūras; (2) significant movements: the liberating experience of a movement out of familiar space, the fear from an enforced movement out of familiar space (exodus, *isrā'*, vs. expulsion, *istifzāz*, as experienced by both) as well as spiritual movements, *mukhrāj*, *mudkhāl*, and demanded, but not performed ecstatic movements, *ruqiyy*; (3) "movements in spirit": that is, enactments of divine-human communication through the related experience of a vision, (*ru'yā*), the transcendence of familiar horizons of perception; and finally (4) other signs, such as the communal prayer as a novel liturgical achievement of the emerging Meccan community.

The sūra can be read as a matrix of what will later be fantastically elaborated to form the narratives of *isrā'* and *mi'rāj* in *ḥadīth* literature. The central difference between the qur'ānic and the *ḥadīth* discourse, however, is less the diverse amount of imaginary elements than the distinct cast of the experience. In the Qur'ān we witness a communication process in which divine prerogatives (guardianship, providence, etc.) and human attitudes and perceptions (gratitude, reason, etc.) as links between the speaker and the audience never fade, while leaving the modalities of the transcendent experience undisclosed, whereas the *ḥadīth* version has taken the form of a narration that unfolds particular elements in a fantastic way to satisfy an audience requesting a narrative closure for some of their most cherished qur'ānic images and an etiological explanation for the core elements of their rituals.

3. First Section of the sūra Q17:2–21: Nocturnal Departure/History of the Temple and the Teaching of Moses/the Rank of the New Revelation. The first section starts with a hymnic appraisal of the divine sign granted to Muḥammad, that is, his nocturnal departure (*isrā'*),[56] recalled through a hymnic exclamation (*subḥāna*, Q 17:1), and it continues with the sign granted to Moses, a figure whose memory, through the association of the exodus with "*isrā'*," has already been evoked.[57] Moses' sign is the "book" (*kitāb*, Q 17:2), whose essence is the commandment of the exclusive worship of one God: "Do not take unto yourselves any guardian apart from me" (*lā tattakhidhū min dūnī wakīlān*, Q 17:2). The servant of God complying with this command proves grateful (*kāna 'abdān shakūrān*, Q 17:3). The book (or the heavenly archetype of the revealed scriptures)[58] subsequently (Q 17:4) reveals itself as the book of providence, which has destined for the people of Moses, the *Banū Isrā'īl*, that they will twice commit grave sins through arrogance: "you shall do corruption in the earth twice, and you shall ascend exceedingly high" (*la-tufsidunna fī l-arḍi marratayni wa-la-ta'lunna 'uluwwan kabīran*, Q 17:4). They will both times be punished through the desecration of their sanctuary (*al-masjid*, Q 17:7) which, in Q 17:1, qualified by the attribute "whose precincts we have blessed" (*alladhī bāraknā ḥawlāh*), is understood to be situated in the Holy Land.

After this report, marked by "predictions of calamities" (sg. *wa'd*, Q 17:2–8) visited upon the *Banū Isrā'īl* who sin despite the scriptural law communicated to them by Moses, a return to the time of the speaker, Muḥammad, relates the scripture of Moses to the new scripture, "*hādhā l-qur'ān*." This comes first to "spread good tidings" (*yubashshir*), but also comes to blame humankind in general, who despite having been given divine directives, behaves unreasonably and rashly (*'ajūl*, Q 17:11) in its relationship with God. Everyone will be given his "book" (*kitāb*, now taken in the meaning of an account of deeds, Q 17:13–14). In addition, a worldly punishment is pending, one that is always brought about—due to divine predestination—through the mighty of a community who cause the "destruction of a city" (*ihlāk qarya*, Q 17:16). Eschatological retribution will affect everyone according to his own deeds, even if some may have been more privileged than others in this life (*faḍḍalnāhu tafḍīlan*, Q 17:21).

4. Second Section (Q 17:22–81): Decalogue, Miraculous and Spiritual Signs, Ritualia of Prayer. The second section, again, starts with an enunciation relating to Moses, namely an Islamic paraphrase of the decalogue (Q 17:22–39), introduced by and ending with an appeal to worship God alone (cf. Q 17:2).[59] This rendition of the decalogue, as well as that of the Temple history in sūra 17, figure uniquely in the Qur'ān. The former, put explicitly into relation with Moses, may, however, be as well intended to serve an immediate need of the community. For somewhat abruptly thereafter follows a polemic address to the contemporaries of the Prophet, which takes up a central discourse of the closely related sūra, 53 (Q 53:19–27): the Prophet's insistent refusal to ascribe an angelic rank (*malā'ika*) to the goddesses revered by the pagan Meccans, in keeping with his defiance of any infringement on the worship of God alone (Q 17:39). In Q 17:42 the idea is further expanded: a plurality of gods would threaten the predominance of one God reigning solely, they "would have sought a way unto the Lord of the Throne" (*ibtighā' sabīl*, Q 17:42). Such an assumption is proof of "arrogance" (*'uluww kabīr*, Q 17:43; cf. reference in Q 17:4 to the *Banū Isrā'īl*), and it is rejected with a hymnic-apotropaic exclamation (*subḥāna*, Q 17:43; cf. Q 17:1). The polemical debate about the problem of revelation proceeds from the qur'ānic idea that God imposed the inability to understand upon the unbelievers, who deride the Prophet, denouncing him as "bewitched" (*masḥūr*, Q 17:47) , a stereotypical polemic against his prophethood (cf. Q 25:8), and who provocatively demand a fixed time for the awakening of the dead (Q 17:51). As a consolation, the Prophet is cleared of the responsibility for being a guardian to them (*wakīl*, Q 17:54; cf. Q 17:2). God alone knows about all creatures in heaven and on earth and it is for Him alone to grant "privileges" to individual prophets over others ("*tafḍīl*", Q 17:55, cf. Q 17:21). Even the powers invoked along with Him are in need of Him, "they are seeking the means to come to their Lord" (*ibtighā' al-wasīla*, Q 17:57, cf. Q 17:42). A worldly punishment, the "destruction of a city" (*ihlāk qarya*, Q 17:58, cf. Q 17:16), will surely strike all of them before the Last Day, thus it has been fixed in the book of predestination (*kitāb*, cf. Q 17:4).

Thereupon the question of divine signs (*āyāt*) is explicitly addressed: the response to these has always been unbelief, be they conspicuous signs like the camel stud (she-camel Q 17:59, the sign of Ṣāliḥ, the messenger dispatched to Thamūd; a reference to the older texts Q 91:13f. and 54:28); or allusive ones like the "vision that we showed Thee" (*al-ru'yā llatī araynāka*, Q 17:60; cf. Q 17:1: "that We might show him some of Our signs"); or simply qur'ānic images like that of the "cursed tree" of hell (bearing satans' heads as fruit, a reference to Q 56:51–55). All this should serve as a "test" (*fitna*), to inspire respect or even fear, but it only increases obstinacy (Q 17:60). The rebellious stance taken by the adversaries is the effect of the assignment given to Satan by God Himself, namely to inspire man forcefully to revolt (*istifzāz*, Q 17:64, a reference to the account of the "deal in heaven," first related in Q 15:30). He has, however, no power over the faithful servants of God, since for them God is a reliable "guardian" (*wakīl*, Q 17:65, cf. Q 17:2). With reference to Q 17:67, the believer should consider that, in analogy to the accepted truth, it is solely God, not the other powers invoked, who can rescue humans from trouble at sea. Insomuch as people respond to their rescue "without gratitude" (*kafūr*, cf. Q17:2), God should also be credited with the power to bring about a catastrophe, which no "guardian" (*wakīl*, Q 17:68, cf. Q 17:2, 54, 65) can prevent. Human beings are from the beginning "favored" (*tafḍīl*) over other creatures by divine providence (Q 17:70; cf. Q 17:21, 55). They will therefore render account on the Day of Judgment and "receive their book in their hands" (*kitāb*, Q 17:71; cf. Q 17:13–14).

Once more, with a clear reference to the self-deception temporally suffered by Muḥammad regarding the authenticity of a particular revelation, an experience that is traditionally connected with sūra 53, the Meccans are accused of a grave transgression. They are charged (as they had been before—e.g., Q 68:9) with having urged the Prophet (*iftān*, Q 17:73; cf. Q 17:60: *fitna*) to invent a revelation.[60] This charge would have been of lethal consequence for him had he not, thanks to divine support, remained steadfast. Furthermore they are reprimanded for ongoing attempts to "force" him out of the country (*istifzāz*, Q 17:76, cf. Q 17:64), attempts that would have fateful consequences for themselves. Section II ends with an appeal to hold daily liturgical services: two ritual prayers and a vigil, so as to attain a "superior rank" (*maqāman karīman*). A particular formula of prayer is recommended that pleads for divine benevolence, for the "exit" (*mukhraj*) and "entrance" (*mudkhal*) related to the enigmatic "dispatch" to that rank (Q 17:80).[61] A movement away from the accustomed space thus has positive connotations, in contrast with the three references to attempts at expulsion (Q 17:64, 76, 103), movements that have a negative association. This positive departure experience is strikingly in line with the liberating "departure," *isrā'*, recalled in Q 17:1.

Since this enigmatic verse (Q 17:80) about the exit–entrance movement is without a parallel in the Qur'ān, it can hardly be interpreted in eschatological terms. It appears, however, in this given context of prayer, to be a reference to the worshipper's exit from and reentry into the profane realm. This psychic movement into a sacred realm, the "state of sacredness," (*iḥrām*) is ritually enacted by a preparatory gesture of taking up a direction of prayer toward a remote sanctuary. The verse might therefore be intended as a plea for a similarly profound experience of an exit from the profane and entry into the sacred world, as occurred in the *isrā'*, which is assumed to be still fresh in his memory.

5. Third Section (Q 17:82–111): Confirmation of the Revelation—Controversies about Prophetic Signs. The third section begins with an observation of the effect that the Qur'ān has on the believers on the one hand, and on transgressors on the other, lamenting the ingratitude (*kafūr*, Q 17:89; cf. Q 17:11–12: *'ajūl*; cf. Q 17:67: *kafūr*) of humans. This is followed by the provoking queries of the unbelievers about the "spirit" (*rūḥ*) as a mediator of revelation (Q 17:85; cf. Q 19:17 and 26:193, where *rūḥ* figures as mediator instead of an angel). These questions can be answered by Muḥammad in coded form only: revelation depends on God alone, who can deprive him of the messages mediated through the spirit, leaving him without a "guardian" to ward off a divine punishment (*wakīl*, Q 17:86; cf. Q 17:2; 54, 65, 68). But, irrespective of the mysterious way of mediation, the imparted word speaks for itself as a clear "sign": even if spirits and men united, they would not be able to bring about a "*qur'ān*" like this (Q 17:86). Still, the positively recognizable "sign" of the uniqueness of the qur'ānic recitation does not satisfy the unbelievers. They voice further challenges, calling for miraculous signs ranging from the production of a source of water (Q 17:90, perhaps an allusion to a miracle worked by Moses; cf. Exod 17:6 and Q 2:60) to the act of an "ascension to heaven"

(*ruqiyy*, Q 17:93), from where Muḥammad should bring down a "book" (*kitāb*), that is a complete scripture rather than single revelations arriving gradually. The claim is rejected vehemently, again with a hymnic apotropaic exclamation (*subḥāna*, Q 17:93; cf. Q 17:1, 43), pointing to the Prophet's merely human nature. It would be meaningful to dispatch "angels" (*malā'ika*, Q 17:95) as messengers only if the community itself were a host of angels. "Signs" (*āyāt*, Q 17:98; cf. Q 17:1, 2 [book to Moses], 59, 60) are plentiful; he who remains an infidel will suffer punishment in the world beyond.

Again a section focusing on Muḥammad is followed by a passage on Moses. Nine "signs" (*āyāt*, Q 17:101) had been given to Moses but had been answered by Pharoah, the leader of the infidels, with mockery and derision. Moses, not unlike Muḥammad, was accused of being "bewitched" (*masḥūr*, Q 17:101; cf. Q 17:47). The unbelievers defied Moses as Muḥammad was defied, by an insistence upon retaining their idolatry and, not unlike Muhammad's adversaries, tried to "expel" him from the country (*istifzāz*, Q 17:103; cf. Q 17:64, 76, a reverse image of the "exodus," which is always presented as *asrā/isrā'*). These earlier transgressors, however, received punishment while yet living, whereas the *Banū Isrā'īl* were given land to inhabit until the second "prediction of a calamity" (*wa'd*, Q 17:104; cf. Q 17:5, 7) came to pass. The story of Moses and the *Banū Isrā'īl*, as recorded in the third section of sūra 17, ends where it began: at the Temple in Jerusalem (Q 17:104), the same place to which Muḥammad's enigmatic translocation, recorded in Q 17:1, had led him.

The topic of confirmation of the revelation to Muḥammad, familiar as a closure of sūras since the middle Meccan period, forms the end of the third section. Once again Muḥammad's role as simply "a transmitter of good tidings" (*mubashshir*, Q 17:105; cf. Q 17:9) and "a warner" (*nadhīr*) is stressed. The "sign" that is divinely communicated to him is the *qur'ān* itself, a message that he should recite distinctly and slowly to the community, and which is sent down to him in the right, "adequate" way (*ḥaqqan*), that is, as a series of successive communications, not as a complete volume of scripture handed to him during a miraculous ascension to heaven; cf. Q 17:93. Whether it meets with belief or disbelief on the part of the pagan Meccans is secondary to the importance of adherents to the earlier revelations accepting it with due respect, praising God with the hymnic exclamation *subḥāna* (Q 17:108; cf. Q 17:1, 43, 93) for his fulfillment of a "promise" (*wa'd*). The final passage is dedicated to issues related to prayer. These include a discourse on the equality of the divine names Allāh and al-Raḥmān as addressees in prayer, and an exhortation to perform the liturgy of prayer, which should not be uttered too loudly or softly, and in which God's uniqueness (cf. Q 17:2, 22, 39), his exaltedness above humankind with respect to procreation (cf. Q 17:40), and his sole regency should figure as themes of praise. The liturgy should also contain a repeated evocation of God's greatness, a multiple *takbīr*. In these rulings, we can easily identify significant elements of the ritual prayer as it was later set forth for the community: Thus, the divine names Allāh and al-Raḥmān alternate in the communal prayer *al-Fātiḥa*,[62] which is the opening of the liturgy. The *takbīr* serves as the formula for the worshipper's entrance into the state of sacredness maintained throughout the prayer; it is also repeated several times during the prayer itself. Finally, the question of the performance of liturgy in a loud or soft voice becomes relevant if a communal prayer service involving multiple worshippers is intended. It is such a communal service to which the end of the sūra obviously refers.

6. Progress of the Canonical Process: Sūra 17 and Its Nucleus, Sūra 53.[63] Sūra 17 begins, in perfect accordance with sūra 53, with a spiritual experience by Muḥammad that is *sui generis*. After the two visions reported there, which may be located in Muḥammad's own surroundings—though certainly experienced as "extraterritorial"—(Q 53:1–18 and 81:19–21), the "nightly departure" of sūra 17 unfolds a new geography that reaches beyond the local horizons to include the religious centre of the *Banū Isrā'īl* and the locations of the experiences of Moses, their leader. The understanding that the *āyāt* revealed to Muḥammad relate to the rite of prayer (an interpretation enhanced by the three types of narrative commentary on the verse, irrespective of serious differences among particular exegetical positions) accounts for the spiritual aura that surrounds the destination of Muḥammad's nocturnal translation, the Solomonic Temple, which was the orientation for prayer for Muḥammad's monotheistic contemporaries. This sūra ends, like sūra 53, with a reference to the rite of prayer. Much like the final canonical version of sūra 53,[64] sūra 17 must be viewed as having emerged under the still powerful impression of a narrow escape from peril: the danger of blending the divine message with human desires.

However, sūra 17 takes a very different position on the *āyāt* than does sūra 53: like Moses, who had also been induced through powerful signs to take up this mission (Q 20:9–22), Muḥammad received miraculous *āyāt*. The two visions from sūra 53 that may have been Muḥammad's initiation are evoked anew, if only indirectly, through an almost verbatim repetition of the closing phrase of the second report (compare Q 53:18 and 17:1; and see also Q 20:22 where Moses is addressed with the same phrase). They are complemented by the new experience, related to the exodus prototype that directly involves Moses, of the movement towards the *masjid* of the *Banū Isrā'īl*. Like Moses before him, Muḥammad earns only derision, being ridiculed as "bewitched" and threatened with expulsion from the land. Like Moses, no more than a human warner, he too has received a scripture to be recited, the *qur'ān*. The experience recalled to at the beginning of the sūra, the vision (*ru'yā*) of divine *āyāt*, which is referred to again in Q 17:60 unlike that of sūra 53, does not refer to a vision of the Prophet in the sense of an intimate encounter with God; rather, it refers to his translation into a miraculously perceived "different world," a topographia sacra located in the Holy Land where God's prophets have worked. The experience focuses on the Prophet's adherence to the realm of the biblical prophets. It is—unlike the situation in sūra 53—less an initiation into a new relation with the divine Lord than an entrance into the territory and community of the biblical prophets.

The Prophet is aware that he cannot meet the challenge of the Meccans to perform the miraculous acts they demand, such as his ascent to heaven. His communication with God takes place, as is expressed in sūra 73, either in vigils, where revelations come down to him in portions, "in the right way" (*ḥaqqan*), or in the rite of prayer. It is in the context of such a prayer period during a performance that is in itself a temporary exit out of the world, that he appears to have been granted the divine reward of the nightly translation, the imagined exodus, to that central point where the prayers of monotheistic worshippers converge to ascend to God.

7. Sūra 17 and Other Early Polemical Texts about Prophethood. Sūra 17 continues a debate which already dominated the later sūras of the early Meccan period and especially those of the middle Meccan period: the discussion of the origin and transmission

of the revelation.[65] After the evidence about the two visions produced in sūras 53 and 81 apparently aroused doubts among pagan listeners (Q 53:12), a new point of contention emerges: the question of the reality of the angel (Q 81:19–21) responsible for the transmission. The Prophet is thus urged to produce not only that angel (Q 15:7, 17:92) but even God himself (Q 17:92), perhaps with reference to the visions mentioned in sūra 53. What remaining evidence can meet the unbelievers' demand now that even the supernatural signs granted to the Prophet have failed to convince them of the seriousness of his message? Already in Q 52:34, in an attempt to reject the charge of having invented revelations, the idea is voiced that the revelations speak for themselves and betray their supernatural origin: "Then let them bring a discourse like it, if they speak truly!" (*fal-ya'tū bi-ḥadīthin mithlihi in kānū ṣādiqīn*), an argument that in Q 17:88 is sharpened into a statement on the inimitable character of the qur'ānic recitation: "Say: If man and jinn banded together to produce the like of this Qur'ān, they would never produce its like" (*Qul: la-ini jtamaʿati l-insu wa-l-jinnu ʿalā an ya'tū bi-mithli hādhā l-qur'āni lā ya'tūna bi-mithlihi*). The recitation itself becomes an *āya*, a sign confirming its superhuman origin.[66] Sūra 17 reflects the perception that signs, more precisely those accessible to rational control, are sufficiently available. Accordingly, the qur'ānic reflection of the *isrā'* experience—whose earlier public promulgation had, according to Islamic tradition, met with so little acknowledgment by the Meccans—is no longer used as an apology, as were the reports of the visions in sūras 81 and 53; rather it is publicized in the triumphant form of a hymn. The sūra as a whole reclaims the proportions existing between miraculous and simple *āyāt*, proportions that had been blurred by the provocative demands of the unbelievers. The vision or dream experience, *ru'yā*, is not what counts; rather the divine word speaks for itself.

There is, however, one other important argument adduced to enhance the reality of one divine communication enjoyed by the Prophet: the rite of prayer (*ṣalāt*) as it takes shape in the middle Meccan period. Here a glance at sūra 15 proves useful. This text, which opens with antagonistic challenges to produce those angelic mediators to whom the vision account in sūra 81 has alluded, refers in its final part to a distinctly different kind of *āya*. It reassures the Prophet that he has at his disposal not only the Qur'ān, the growing corpus of texts for recitation, but also the "seven verses of litany" (*sabʿan mina l-mathānī*, Q 15:87), that is, the *Fātiḥa*, the core of the communal prayer. This should be understood as a decisive advantage that the harrassed community possesses over those who, by their worldly possessions and power, are inspired to act arrogantly.[67] The argument that there is a confirmation of prophethood implied in the achievement of a distinct prayer formula recurs twice in sūra 17. At the end of section II, the exhortation to pray at three different times combines with the plea for a particularly blessed sequence of movements, an exit and an entrance that are otherwise unknown in the Qur'ān. In my view this can most plausibly be explained in the sense of an exit from and a subsequent reentrance into the profane realm. To accept this interpretation, one would have to presuppose that the later canonized elements of the *takbīr al-taḥrīm*, that is, the formula *Allāhu akbar* marking the worshipper's entrance into the state of sacredness and thus the beginning of the rite of prayer, already belonged to the service in Meccan times. The experience of a new achievement, then, would be clearly reflected in the triumphal tone of the final statement of the sūra, which asserts that the idle has given way to the essentially true (Q 17:84).

The powerful evidence, implicit in the rite of prayer, for the authenticity of the divine origin of Muḥammad's message is taken up again at the end of the sūra, where a unique scene from a prayer service is evoked: adherents of the earlier scriptures bow down weeping from the impact of the recitation of the Qur'ān (Q 17:107–109). This reminiscence leads to a discourse on the technicalities of conduct while praying. It is to be uttered at a medium level of volume and should encompass particular contents, maybe even particular texts. The hymnic introduction of the adjuration with "Praise belongs to God" (*al-ḥamdu li-llāh*) reminds one of the *Fātiḥa*, while the ensuing enumeration of elements sounds like a paraphrase of Q 112, "The Unity" (*Sūrat al-ikhlāṣ*). At the end, there is the call to utter the *takbīr*, the formula demanded for the "exit" (cf. Q 17:80) from the profane state into that of the sacred and vice versa.

This allusion in Q 17:80 to the imaginary departure from the profane space for an entrance into the sacred realm returns us to the notion of the *qibla*. The state of sacredness can be viewed as the mental realization of the inner movement toward God, which began with facing the *qibla* leading to "his house," the converging point of all prayer. The symbolic direction (*qibla*) is thus pursued spiritually by the praying person. A "vision" (*ru'yā*) of the sacred sphere, an "exodus" (*isrā'*) to the focal point of prophetic tradition itself, does, of course, go beyond that experience. It remains a unique event whose frame can perhaps best be explained psychologically as a unique dream experience of the Prophet that continues his conscious act of directing himself toward Jerusalem at the beginning of a prayer, but whose modalities remain concealed.

What seems to be triumphantly resounding in Q 17:1 is the Prophet's and the community's overwhelming perception that they are not only in the possession of a scripture to recite, the *qur'ān*, but also of the constitutive elements of a communal prayer service. These consist of the introital prayer of the *Fātiḥa*, already celebrated as a novel accomplishment in sūra 15, and of a sequence of ritual formulas of verbal and body language that begins with the gesture of facing the *qibla* to initiate the "exit" into a state of sacredness. Thus at this stage of the community's formation, the Prophet has been able to enhance substantially his already achieved function as a "a warner" (*nadhīr*, *mudhakkir*) and "herald of good tidings" (*mubashshir*), that is, a human mouthpiece of a divine message. He has become the founder and leader of a cultic ceremony that fosters the coherence of the covenantal community. He can thus rightly claim the rank of apostle (*rasūl*) (Q 17:15, 93), equal to the earlier prophets.[68]

Part 5: Plain and Mythologizing Exegesis: *Isrā'* versus *Mi'rāj*

1. Q 17:1 in Western Research. After these reflections, it may appear surprising that not only the branch of Islamic tradition that later became dominant, but also most Western research, which is based chiefly on the fundamental study by J. Horovitz (1919), has interpreted Q 17:1 not as the experience of a nocturnal translation of the Prophet to the Jerusalem sanctuary in a dream, but rather as an ascension of the Prophet to heaven. The arguments presented to support this view will be briefly reexamined in light of the results reached by the preceding textual analysis of sūra 17.

According to Horovitz, "nobody would have thought to connect *al-masjid al-aqṣā* with Jerusalem had this interpretation not been suggested by the Islamic tradition. The fact that European research, too, has accepted it without prior reexamination proves that it has not yet freed itself from the spell of Islamic tradition." The credit goes to Schrieke, Horovitz insists, "for having broken the spell for these particular texts and having realized that the 'remotest *masjid*' (*das 'fernste Masgid'*) is not to be sought in Jerusalem nor anywhere else on earth, but in heaven."[69]

Upon this basis, Horovitz attempted to prove that a heavenly sanctuary was the final point of Muḥammad's nocturnal translation. His argument is based on linguistic and typological similarities that exist among the three passages in the Qur'ān (sūras 81, 53, and 17) that deal with extraordinary spiritual experiences of Muḥammad, and on the parallels found in biblical and apocryphal literature. Since he proceeds from the hypothesis (without attending to the aforementioned redactional problematic reflected in the beginning of the sūra) that Q 17:1 "has no connection to the following whatsoever,"[70] he cannot use the corpus of the sūra as an elucidating context for the first verse, and thus he remains dependent upon external evidence. He has at his disposal both the *ḥadīth* tradition that views the ascension to heaven (*mi'rāj*) as the climax of the *isrā'* experience, and older texts that ascribe ecstatic experiences to salvation history figures in the other Abrahamic religions. This latter material, with its copious evidence for ascension experiences, supports the *mi'rāj* version rather than the interpretation that it was a translation to Jerusalem in a dream, for which there would be no more than a single parallel.[71]

Horovitz's assertion that the "idea of an ascension toward heaven kept Muḥammad's mind busy"[72] appears rather questionable, however, since no more than four qur'ānic passages, two Meccan and two Medinan, touch upon the subject. They are certainly overinterpreted by Horovitz. The oldest evidence should be Q 15:14–15:

> though We opened to them a gate in heaven
> and still they mounted through it,
> yet would they say, "Our eyes have been dazzled;
> nay, we are a people bewitched!"[73]

Irrespective of the hyperbole marked by the use of the *irrealis* as a rhetorical *ultima ratio* that expresses the utmost degree of divine inclination to communicate with man, Horovitz tries to connect this passage directly to Muḥammad: "The Prophet wants to say that his compatriots would believe in the ascension to heaven of former men of God, but thought the ascension of the Prophet in their midst to be a mere deception of his senses."[74] But this illustration of disbelief refers not to an experience of Muḥammad but to demands of the infidels, as is shown unambiguously by Q 17:93:

> They say, 'We will not believe thee till
> thou makest a spring to gush forth from the earth for us [Q 17:90];
> or till thou goest up into heaven;
> and we will not believe thy going up
> till thou bringest down on us a book that we may read.[75]

Horovitz's reading of Q 17:93 as an indirect confirmation of an ascension—"They want to see with their own eyes the heavenly book which Muḥammad should bring to them as proof of his stay in heaven"[76]—is possible only because he ignores its direct context, which ends in a clear rejection (of such an ascent) by the Prophet: "Say: 'Glory be to my Lord! Am I aught but a mortal, a messenger?" (*qul: subḥāna rabbī, hal kuntu illā basharan rasūlan?*)

Given this explicit rejection of an ascension as inappropriate for a human messenger, it is not surprising that the further verses adduced by Horovitz as evidence for the hypothesis of Muḥammad's ascension only confirm this negative result. Q 6:35 reads:

> And if their turning away is distressful for thee,
> why, if thou canst seek out a hole in the earth,
> or a ladder in heaven, to bring them some sign—
> but had God willed, He would have gathered them to the guidance
> so be not thou one of the ignorant.[77]

If this verse were to be taken as evidence for a factual ascent to heaven, it would also have to be read as evidence for Muḥammad's search for a hole in the earth to impress the Meccan unbelievers with a supernatural sign. Finally, Q 6:125 reads:

> Whomsoever God desires to guide,
> He expands his breast to Islam;
> whomsoever He desires to lead astray,
> He makes his breast narrow, tight,
> as if he were climbing to heaven.
> So God lays abomination upon those who believe not.[78]

The verse has no connection whatsoever to the Prophet. Rather, the metaphor of the ascension as an image for a situation of extreme pressure has negative connotations and is related to obstinate unbelievers. Therefore it is all the more remarkable that it is precisely the ensemble of these two elements—the "widening the breast" and "ascension to heaven"—that in the mythologizing *ḥadīth* comes to constitute the twin tradition of the Prophet's initiation and his ascension, encountered earlier *in nuce* (see "Nocturrnal Departure" as a Miraculous Ride to Jerusalem in part 3). Horovitz's conclusion from his consideration of the qur'ānic texts is therefore difficult to accept: "Muḥammad's ecstatic ascension to heaven as an experience of his prophetical career can be taken for granted on the basis of his self-testimony" [i.e., the Qur'ān, A.N.].[79] Horovitz's work remains valuable as a basic study of the traditional Islamic descriptions of the ascension, although it does, contrary to the reservations expressed in the initial quotation from his essay, eventually concede that the interpretation of qur'ānic evidence can gain something from a consultation of the exegetical tradition: "The fact that Islamic tradition directly connects the ascension of Muḥammad to the night journey to Jerusalem that is deduced from Q 17:1 can be viewed as a proof that it has preserved the memory of the correct interpretation of this qur'ānic passage."[80] Horovitz's study has certainly contributed substantially to the task of putting the ascension accounts of *ḥadīth* literature into their appropriate religio-historical context, while elucidating them by adducing potential prototypes. It has, however, contributed less to the elucidation of the qur'ānic stance toward miraculous deeds as a means of prophetic persuasion. Horovitz's surrender to the overwhelmingly powerful *ḥadīth* literature, contradicting explicit and unambiguous qur'ānic evidence, calls for some basic remarks on the techniques applied in narrative exegetical *ḥadīth*. Meanwhile the problem "ascension or translation" seems to be solved: J. van Ess, in his essay "Vision and Ascension," has lately argued convincingly that the image of an ascension of the Prophet is an exegetical construct. Adducing ample testimonies, not only qur'ānic and ḥadīth texts but doctrinal and heresiographic material as well, he has suggested that the interpretation of *isrā'* in the sense of an ascension resulted from an extended theological debate involving popular beliefs, on the one hand, and a strong opposition against anthropomorphism, on the other. For the "orthodox," the idea of an ascension of the Prophet, a movement of a human toward God, in the end proved easier to accept than that of a prophetical vision, presupposing a divine movement toward man. The *isrā'* thus attracted those images that had previously grown around the complex of the Prophet's visions whose qur'ānic attestations, contrary to that of the *isra'*, do bare an affinity to cosmic and other imaginary speculations.

2. The Preconditions of Mythologizing Exegesis: The Dissolution of the Qur'ānic Discourse into Isolated Elements. Since our vantage point is not exegesis, however, but the Qur'ān itself, for us, the hermeneutical question still lingers how the qur'ānic text—made up of veritative as well as metaphorical speech—can be transformed so profoundly as to fit the diverse needs of the broad spectrum of later disputant groups. Let us therefore briefly return to the different types of exegetical unfolding of the qur'ānic *isrā'*. The two examples of interpretation of Q 17:1, cited above—the one plain and sober, the other "mythologizing" (see part 3)—demonstrate two basically different approaches to the text. Of these the second, by its very intention, does not aim to elucidate the historical or the discursive context at all. While the "plain" exegesis tries to provide a plausible social and historical framework for the particular text thus coming close to the genre of *asbāb al-nuzūl*, the mythologizing exegesis dissolves the qur'ānic statement into its individual elements in order to construct out of these elements side-plots and background images. Recall that the mention of the time of night (*laylan*) evoked the deep sleep of the Prophet. Given the local point of the departure (*al-masjid al-ḥarām*), this had to be taken as sleeping *in* the sanctuary itself, as demanded for the rite of initiation intended in the story. Further, in this expanded exegesis, the epithet of the destination "whose precincts we have blessed" evoked the personal presence of the bearers of that blessing, the prophets. The provocative demand for an ascension presented to the Prophet later in the sūra evoked the unfolding of his ascension, despite the denial he expressed in his immediate answer to the challenge.

The consistent role of Moses as a prototype of Muḥammad in sūra 17 was also integrated into the story by narrative exegetical *ḥadīth*, but with less extreme deviations from the qur'ānic model. Moses, in the ascension account, became Muḥammad's side-figure, whose experience as an adviser was appreciated, though renounced in the end.

Finally, we found that a complete sequence of *ḥadīth* episodes was based on the mere coincidence of the use of two opposing metaphors that, in their qur'ānic context, are particularly expressive: the widening of the breast, which is a qur'ānic reference to belief; and its tightening to a degree that makes the person feel that he was climbing to heaven, which serves as an image for stubborn unbelief (see earlier). Consequently, what is simply a set of metaphors in the Qur'ān becomes, in the *ḥadīth*, the nucleus of a complex account of the Prophet's initiation and ascension.[81] Therefore two complete subplots emerge: the first comprising a "widening of the breast" and a cleansing of the Prophet's heart[82] to prepare for the implantation of the gift of prophecy;[83] the second, a miraculous ascension to heaven.

This kind of exegesis is not meant to elucidate the overall discourse of the underlying text; rather it focuses on individual images, which, isolated from their contextual function, invite an elaboration into new narrative units. These, in turn, open the way for further expansions through new imaginary traits. "Mythologized" exegesis has as its *raison d'être* a new religiously complex, mythologized image of the Prophet[84] that emerged soon after Muḥammad's death, when his awareness of his merely human dimension had become obscured.[85] It is thus easy to identify this image as a later construct. Though such a verdict would be rash in the case of the "plain" narrative commentary (see part 3), which respects the contextuality of qur'ānic texts and therefore can temptingly be read as historically plausible, one should still be aware of its fundamental divergence and thus distance from the qur'ānic text itself.

The Qur'ān, as against the biography (*sīra*), does not relate the narrative of a messenger and his fate among his community; rather it reflects a complex communication process, involving a number of *dramatis personae*, themes, developments, and tenets. Its many voices, bridging vast spatial and chronological distances, clearly resound with the urgency of accepting a novel notion of time as the framework for human interactions. It is this discursive character of an ongoing debate, the striking phenomenon of qur'ānic self-referentiality—so widely lost in narrative commentary—that characterizes *inner qur'ānic commentary*. The subsequent unfolding of the discourse through the successive growth of the scripture clearly reflects the parallel process of the emergence of a community relying on the development and refinement of a coherence-generating cult. Tracing these double processes of emergence—the scriptural and cultic—demands a close contextual reading of qur'ānic texts, a reading that exhibits respect for the Qur'ān as a literary corpus claiming integrity and consistency. Taking this heuristic premise seriously, I have tried here to promote a microstructural approach to the Qur'ān rather than following the macrostructural project that dominates present qur'ānic research.

From the elaborate textual edifice of the Qur'ān, an edifice that becomes fully recognizable when viewed through the microstructural perspective, it appears that individual elements were expounded upon by exegetes soon after the closure of the corpus. These exegetes, inspired by more complex religious anticipations than those held by the qur'ānic *dramatis personae* (i.e., the early community), reused these elements as *spolia* in the occasionally fantastic structure of a mythologized history of the Prophet. *Ḥadīth* literature still promises important new insights into early Islamic history; it should not, however, block us from seeing the sober qur'ānic discourse, which, given our present state of knowledge, should be assigned priority over other texts as evidence of the twofold canonical process, the emergence of an Islamic scripture and the development of an Islamic cult.

Notes

This essay is based on a lecture given at the Görres Institute, Jerusalem, in November 1991. Its basic ideas have been published in German as "Erste Qibla—Fernstes Masğid? Jerusalem im Horizont des historischen Muḥammad," in *Zion: Ort der Begegnung*, 227–70. An important aspect of the early community's imagination of Jerusalem, its association with scripture and hence with a written preservation of scriptural memory, is discussed by Neuwirth, "Face of Man—Face of God." The important essay by J. van Ess on a related topic, "Vision and Ascension," appeared only after this chapter had been delivered to the publisher. Thus only a few references to it could be inserted during the proofreading.

1. For the emergence of particular epitheta ornantia for Islamic cities and regions, see E. Gruber, *Verdienst und Rang*. The triple epithet can be traced back as far as to the Ayyubid era. It is cited by the preacher Zakīyaddīn in his sermon in praise of the reconquest of Jerusalem by Saladin. Cf. Ibn Khallikān, *Wafayāt al-a'yān*, ed. Ihsan Abbas, iv (Beirut no date), 232. An English translation is given by De Slane in *Ibn Khallikan*, ii (Paris 1842), 636–37.

2. Cf. Ibrāhīm Zayd Kīlānī, *Makānat al-Quds fī l-Islām*. Unpublished lecture given at *Al-Mu'tamar al-dawlī al-thālith li-ta'rīkh bilād al-Shām*, Amman, 1980.

3. On the traditions that have emerged since the end of the first Islamic century and have been collected since the third century, on the "merits of Jerusalem" (*faḍā'il al-Quds*), cf. Hasson, "'Les Titres de Gloire de Jérusalem' par Abū Bakr Muḥammad b. Aḥmad al-Wāsiṭī" (Fr. intro.), in *Faḍa'il al-bayt al-muqaddas*; Kister, "A Comment on the Antiquity of Traditions Praising Jerusalem," 185–86; Goitein, "Jerusalem in the Arab Period (638–1099)," 168–96; and more recently, Elad, "The History and Topography of Jerusalem during the Early Islamic Period."

4. Cf. Kister, "'You Shall Only Set Out for Three Mosques"; Goitein, "al-Ḳuds," in *EI*, new ed.

5. See Watt, "al-Madīna," in *EI*, new ed.

6. Cf. Hasson, "Titres"; Sivan, "Le Caractère sacré de Jérusalem."

7. For a detailed dicussion of the possible motives of the erection on the Dome of the Rock see J. van Ess, "'Abd al-Malik."

8. A basic revision of the immediate pre-Islamic and early Islamic history was initiated by Crone and Cook in their work *Hagarism*.

9. A significant exception is J. van Ess's "Vision and Ascension," a study that highlights the complex scene of heterogeneous theological trends emerging during the first Islamic centuries and sheds new light on the tensions between the qur'ānic and the ḥādith discourse.

10. See Paret, "Der Koran als Geschichtsquelle," reprinted in idem, ed., *Der Koran* (Darmstadt, 1975), 137–58; Peters, "The Quest of the Historical Muhammad." More recently, see Schoeler, *Charakter und Authentie der muslimischen Überlieferung über das Leben Muhammeds*.

11. Wansbrough, *Quranic Studies*. Wansbrough's work is to be recognized as revolutionary not only for its basic thesis, but also for its richness of thought and the precision of its revision of traditional qur'ānic research. Even if his basic thesis, inasmuch as it does not give due attention to the literary form of the Qur'ān, fails to refute the traditional perception of the genesis of the Qur'ān, any analysis of qur'ānic materials will profit from a comparison with Wansbrough's reasoning. For Wansbrough, the process of the canonization of the Qur'ān has little to do with the measures undertaken by the third caliph, 'Uthmān b. 'Affān, to standardize and refine the partial collections of the qur'ānic text circulating in his lifetime. He reconstructs the process as follows: Initially there was the "attribution of several partially overlapping collections of logia (exhibiting a distinctly Mosaic imprint) to the image of a biblical prophet (modified by the material of the Muhammadan evangelium [i.e. the *sīra*; A.N.] into an Arabian man of God) with a traditional message of salvation (modified by the influence of rabbinic Judaism into the unmediated and finally immutable word of God)" (p. 83). Cf. his basic outline, p. 51. More recently, see Donner, *Narratives of Islamic Origins*.

12. This essay maintains the view that all qur'ānic texts eventually may be traced to Muḥammad and that most of them, especially the Meccan parts, also received their final redaction from him. Much of the material dating from the Medinan period, however, is considered to owe its transmitted form to the initiative of collecting and editing undertaken by 'Uthmān. See Neuwirth, "Koran."

13. Rubin, "The Ka'ba," 97–131, esp. 108.

14. Wensinck, art. "Ṣalāt," in *Handbuch des Islams*. For background, see Watt, *Muhammad at Medina*, 198–204.

15. Rubin, "Ka'ba," 103, n. 29.

16. Ibid.

17. The date of the introduction of the Jerusalem *qibla* indicated by Rubin in note 29 of his article "Ka'ba" is traceable only in al-Ḥalabī, *al-Sīra al-ḥalabiyya*, 1:264. This date would fit well with the thesis presented here that the assumption of the direction of prayer triggered the nightly journey of the Prophet to the imaginary Jerusalem. However, al-Ḥalabī's ascription of the *qibla* to the time of Q 17 cannot be used as evidence of the simultaneity of the *qibla* and the *isrā'* experience, since it can just as easily have been inspired by their common relation to Jerusalem. Duri, "Jerusalem in the Early Islamic Period," 105–25, has dated Q 17:1 "about a year before the Hijra."

18. Rubin, "Ka'ba," 105, n. 29.

19. Wensinck, art. "Ṣalāt."

20. See Sellheim, "Prophet, Caliph und Geschichte." For an example of Muḥammad's abstention from sacrificial meat prior to the canonical prohibition, see Kister, "A Bag of Meat."

21. On a similar concept developed by the pre-Islamic "Ḥanīfs", see U. Rubin, "Ḥanīfiyya and Ka'ba: An Inquiry into the Arabian Pre-Islamic Background of Din Ibrahim" (transcript of a lecture given at the Third International Colloquium on "*From Jahiliyya to Islam: Aspects of Social, Cultural and Religious History in the Period of Transition*," Jerusalem June 30–July 7, 1985). The notion of Ḥaniyya notion which focuses on Abraham as the prototype of the messenger of God appears only at the end of the Meccan period. Up until then, Moses held that rank in the communal imagination.

22. Cf. Baumstark, "Jüdischer und christlicher Gebetsstypus im Koran"; Goitein, "Prayer in Islam"; Neuwirth, "Images and Metaphors."

23. Cf. Birkeland, *The Lord Guideth*. For a critical evaluation see Paret, *Koran: Kommentar*.

24. For *ḥadīths* presenting this interpretation, see the commentary on Q 2:143 in al-Ṭabarī, *Jāmi' al-bayān fī tafsīr al-qur'ān*.

25. For the process of the expansion of the community's "mental map" at Medina cf. the article "Geography" in *Encyclopaedia of the Qur'ān vol. II*.

26. Goitein, "Shemot Yerushalayim," 32–35 and Khalil Athaimina, "Le jovenier Siecle de l'Islam."

27. Bakka: Q 3:96; Makka: Q 48:24.

28. *al-Ṭūr*: Q 19:52; 20:80; 28:29; 28:46; 52:1; *Ṭūr sīnīn*: Q 95:2 (Mecc.); *al-wād al-muqaddas Ṭuwā*: Q 20:12; 79:16 (Mecc.).

29. *Al-balad al-amīn* for Mecca: Q 95:3 (Mecc.); *hādhā l-balad*: Q 14:35, 90:1, 2 (Mecc.); *al-mu'tafika* for Sodom and Gomorrha: Q 53:53 (Mecc.); *al-mu'tafikāt*: Q 69:9 (Mecc.); 9:70 (Med.), see Horovitz, *Koranische Untersuchungen*, 13f.; *al-arḍ allatī bāraknā fīhā* for Palestine: Q 17:1; 21:71, 81; 34:18 (Mecc.); 7:137 (Med.); *al-arḍ al-muqaddasa*: Q 5:21 (Med.).

30. *Al-masjid al-ḥarām* for Mecca: Q 17:1; 22:25; 48:25 (Mecc.); Q 2:144, 150, 191, 217; 5:2; 8:34; 9:7, 19, 28 (Med.); *ḥaram āmin* for Mecca: Q 28:57; 29:67 (Mecc.); *al-Ka'ba* for Mecca: Q 5:97; *al-bayt al-ma'mūr* for Mecca: Q 52:4 (Mecc.); *al-miḥrāb* for Jerusalem: Q 19:11; 38:21 (Mecc.); Q 3:37, 39 (Med.).

31. Cf. Busse, *Theologische Beziehungen*, 117ff.

32. The term *masjid* occurs only once in the Meccan period (Q 18) and there refers to the monument above the cave of the Seven Sleepers. Elsewhere in the Qur'ān, when used in the singular, the word denotes the Ka'ba.

33. Translations from the Qur'ān in this article are taken from Arberry, *The Koran Interpreted*. Its verbal rendering of *asrā*, however, is insufficiently precise, as is the traditional association of *isrā'* with a "nocturnal journey." The translation of *isrā'* as "nocturnal departure" in the following is based on Wansbrough's observation that the verb of motion *asrā* in the Qur'ān refers to an exodus. When used with *'ibād*, it refers to that of Moses: (cf. Q 20:77; 26:52; 44:23), otherwise, to the flight of Lot (cf. Q 15:65; 11:81 [Mecc.]). An association with these cases of

urgent departure resounds in Q 17:1. The corpus of the sūra refers more than once to a forced departure (Q 17:64; 76:103) but also contains a positive reference to a departure (Q 17:80).

34. *'Abd* in the singular most often refers to the Prophet, see Q 53:10, 18:1 and often.

35. See n. 29.

36. It is not astonishing that the vision—more precisely the second vision recorded in sūra 53—in Islamic exegesis has been related to an ascension of the Prophet's and thus been closely linked to Q 17:1, cf. Van Ess, "Vision and Ascension."

37. Cf. Horovitz, "Muhammeds Himmelfahrt"; Paret, *Koran: Kommentar.*

38. See Schwally, in *GdQ*, on the sūra.

39. A rhyme clause ending in *samī'an baṣīran*, which would harmonize with the rhyme of the corpus of the sūra, appears twice in the Qur'ān: 4:58, 134.

40. On the notion and the development of the *clausula* in the Qur'ān, see Neuwirth, *Studien. Clausulae* as verse closures became the rule in the Medinan sūras. They are found only sporadically in middle Meccan sūras but appear more often in late Meccan sūras.

41. See the list of all qur'ānic rhymes in Neuwirth, *Studien.* For the notion of a canonical process, see part 4.

42. For the gradual evolution of topographical attributions such as individual place names in connection with a sanctuary, see Hawting, "The Origins of Islamic Sanctuary at Mecca."

43. al-Ṭabarī, *Jāmi'*, 15:3.

44. Cf. Goitein, "Shemot Yerushalayim."

45. Cf. Van Ess, "Vision and Ascension," where the notion of an ascension is discussed in the context of both the Qur'ān and various exegetical trends of the first and second Islamic centuries.

46. Ibn Sa'd, *al-Ṭabaqāt al-kubrā*, II/1:142–45, could be quoted; see Busse, "Jerusalem."

47. Ibn Hisām, *al-Sīra al-nabawiyya* Ibn Isḥāq, *The Life of Muhammad*, trans. Guillaume, 181.

48. Ibn Hishām, *al-Sīra al-nabawiyya*, I, 398, Ibn Isḥāq, *The Life of Muḥammad*, 181f.

49. Ibn Hishām, *al-Sīra al-nabawiyya*, I, 407, Ibn Isḥāq, *The Life of Muḥammad*,187.

50. Horovitz, "Himmelfahrt"; Widengren, *The Apostle of God and his Ascension*; Busse, "Jerusalem"; van Ess, "Vision and Ascension."

51. Horovitz, "Himmelfahrt," 179–83.

52. Horovitz raises doubts about the direct transferability to the person of Muḥammad of the ecstatic practices which Schrieke, "Die Himmelsreise Muhammeds," assumes to have been common among the pre-Islamic *kāhins* (cf. Horovitz, "Himmelfahrt," 165). Still, Horovitz retains the possibility that, through ascetic practices, Muḥammad might have reached an ecstatic disposition sufficient for the experience of a spiritual ascension. However, in view of Muḥammad's outright rejection of such supernatural faculties, this is quite problematic.

53. Cf. Childs, *Biblical Theology of the Old and New Testaments*, and Dohmen and Oeming, *Biblischer Kanon warum und wozu?* The quotations are taken from Dohmen and Oeming, 25. For a more elaborate presentation and application of the approach, see Neuwirth, "Vom Rezitationstext über die Liturgie zum Kanon" and Neuwirth, "Referentiality and Textuality in the Qur'ān."

54. Cf. Van Ess, "Vision and Assension," 58.

55. On the dominant role of Moses as the qur'ānic prophetic prototype, see Goitein, "Ramadan, the Muslim Month of Fasting," in *Studies*, 90–111, and the more recent study by Zwettler, "The Mantic Manifest," 75–119, 205–31. In accordance with his revisionist theory of the genesis of the Qur'ān, Wansbrough, *Quranic Studies*, regards Moses as the model for the creation of an image of Muḥammad by the later community. See also the critical reevaluation of related qur'ānic research by Radscheit, *Die koranische Herausforderung*, 71–74.

56. See Wansbrough, *Quranic Studies*, 67–69, where he tends to identify the unspecified *'abd* from Q 17:1 with Moses instead of Muḥammad (*isrā'* then must be taken as an allusion to

the exodus of the Israelites); the argument requires, however, discounting the two topographic indications as later glosses.

57. See n. 33.

58. On the various aspects of the qur'ānic *kitāb*, see Jeffery, "The Qur'an as Scripture"; for *kitāb* as the emblem of a prophet, cf. Radscheit, *Koranische Herausforderung*.

59. The decalogue is analyzed by Neuwirth, "Der Koran."

60. These references clearly point to Meccan adversaries rather than to Jews or Jewish Christians as held by Wansbrough, *Quranic Studies*, 78–80.

61. In view of the verb *ba'atha* used in Q 17:79, Paret, *Der Koran; Übersetzung*, argues for an eschatological interpretation of Q 17:80, which is hardly convincing in the context of the performance of a prayer.

62. Neuwirth and Neuwirth, "*Sūrat al-Fātiḥa*."

63. For the following paragraph cf. van Ess, "Vision and Ascension," which through a thorough investigation of the exegetical discussion unfolds hidden dimensions of sūra 53.

64. On the so-called "Satanic verses" see GdQ, 100–103.

65. An essentially new evaluation of the topoi of polemics about prophethood has been presented by Radscheit, *Koranische Herausforderung*.

66. Wansbrough considers the argument presented here, pertaining to the challenges to the unbelievers to produce a text for recitation comparable to the Qur'ān (the so-called *taḥaddī* verses), to be a clear proof of the emergence of the Qur'ān in a Jewish surrounding (*Quranic Studies*, 78–80). The observation, however, that these verses respond polemically to the charge of the Prophet's invention of a revelation, a charge obviously familiar in Mecca ever since the episode of the "Satanic verses" (Q 17:73; 11:13, 52:33–34), contradicts such an assumption of a non-Meccan origin of the text. On the problem of the "inimitability of the Qur'ān," see Radscheit, *Koranische Herausforderung*.

67. See Neuwirth and Neuwirth, "*Sūrat al-Fātiḥa*."

68. On the development of the notions of *rasūl* and *nabī* in the Qur'ān, see H. Bobzin, "'Das Siegel der Propheten,' Zum Verständnis von Mohammeds Prophetentum" (unpublished transcript of a lecture delivered in the summer of 1992), and Radscheit, *Koranische Herausforderung*.

69. Horovitz, "Himmelfahrt," 162.

70. Ibid., 160.

71. In addition to the references by Horovitz already noted, further material has been produced by Wansbrough, *Quranic Studies*, and Busse, "Jerusalem."

72. Horovitz, "Himmelfahrt," 164.

73. *wa-law fataḥnā 'alayhim bāban mina l-samā'*
fa-ẓallū fīhi ya'rujūn (*ruqiyy*)
la-qālū: innamā sukkirat abṣārunā bal naḥnu qawmun masḥūrūn.

74. Ibid.

75. *wa-qālū: lan nu'mina laka ḥattā tafjura lanā mina l-arḍi yanbu'an*, 'Q 17:90)
aw tarqā fī l-samā'i (*ruqiyy*)
wa-lan nu'mina li-ruqiyyika ḥattā tunazzila 'alaynā kitāban naqra'uhu

76. Ibid.

77. *wa-in kāna kabura 'alayka i'rāḍuhum*
fa-ini staṭa'ta an tabtaghiya nafaqan fī l-arḍi
aw sullaman fī l-samā'i fa-ta'tiyahum bi-āyatin
wa-law shā'a llāhu la-jama'ahum 'alā l-hudā
fa-lā takūnanna mina l-jāhilīn

78. *Fa-man yuridi llāhu an yahdiyahu*
yashraḥ ṣadrahu li l-islāmi
wa-man yurid an yuḍillahu

yaj'al ṣadrahu ḍayyiqan ḥarajan
ka-annamā yaṣṣa"adu fī l-samā'i
ka-dhālika yaj'alu llāhu l-rijsa 'alā lladhīna lā yu'minūn

79. Ibid., 169.

80. Ibid., 165.

81. The ensemble of narratives given, for example, in book V, *ḥadīth* 9 of al-Bukhārī, *Kitāb al-Jāmi' al-Ṣaḥīḥ*, ed. Krehl and Juynboll, has already been criticized as incompatible by Bevan, "Muhammad's Ascension to Heaven," 49–62, esp. 58–60; cf. also Widengren, "Apostle."

82. For a qur'ānic application of the first image to the Prophet, but again in only a metaphorical sense, see sūra 94.

83. On the *topos* of the cleansing of the heart and the implanting of the gift of prophethood, cf. Widengren, "Apostle"; Birkeland, *The Legend of the Opening of Muhammad's Breast*; Paret, review of Birkeland, *Legend*; Wansbrough, *Quranic Studies*.

84. Cf. Andrae, *Person Muhammads* and Sellheim, "Prophet."

85. In more recent research, after Paret in 1957 had once again supported a "plain" interpretation, Busse, "Jerusalem," readdressed the subject. His study, based on rich source material from *ḥadīth* traditions as well as non-Islamic religious texts, focuses on the genesis and development of both narrative complexes. However, he completely overlooks the function of the *isrā'* account for the processes of growth, both of the Qur'ān as scripture and of the Islamic cult. It is thus not surprising that the Qur'ān does not figure as the focal point of the *isrā'* discussion, but remains in the background as a mere collection of traditions, albeit a particularly prominent one, an approach very much in line with the concepts developed by Busse: "[S]everal versions of the journey to heaven exist in the ḥadīth literature, the story told in Surah 17, 1 being only one of them. It differs from the account transmitted in the ḥadīth only in the circumstance that it was ascribed a higher degree of authority than the others on account of its inclusion in the Koran" ("Jerusalem," 3).

Bibliography

Andrae, T. *Die Person Muhammads in Lehre und Glauben seiner Gemeinde*. Stockholm: Norstedt, 1918.

Arberry, A. J. *The Koran Interpreted*. Oxford: Oxford University Press, 1964.

Athaminaghh. "Le premier siècle de l'Islam. Jérusalem capitale de la Palestine." In *Jérusalem le Sacré et le Politique*. Ed. F. Mardam-Beyet Elias Sanbar. Paris: Actes du Sud 2000. 115–148.

Baumstark, A. "Jüdischer und christlicher Gebetsstypus im Koran." *Der Islam* 16 (1927): 229–48.

Bevan, A. A. "Muhammad's Ascension to Heaven." In *Studien zur semitischen Philologie und Religionsgeschichte (Festschrift Julius Wellhausen)*. Ed. K. Marti, 49–62. Giessen: Töpelmann, 1914.

Birkeland, H. *The Legend of the Opening of Muhammad's Breast*. Oslo: J. Dybwad, 1955.

——. *The Lord Guideth: Studies on Primitive Islam*. Oslo: H. Aschehong, 1956.

al-Bukhārī, Muḥammad. *Kitāb al-Jāmi' al-ṣaḥīḥ*. Ed. L. Krehl, T. W. Juynboll. 4 vols. Leiden: E. J. Brill, 1862–.

Busse, Heribert. "Jerusalem in the Story of Muḥammad's Night Journey and Ascension." *JSAI* 14 (1991): 1–40.

——. *Die theologischen Beziehungen des Islams zu Judentum und Christentum: Grundlangen des Dialogs im Koran und die gegenwärtige Situation*. Darmstadt: Wissenschaftliche Buchgesellschaft, 1988.

Childs, Brevard S. *Biblical Theology of the Old and New Testaments: Theological Reflection on the Christian Bible*. London: SCM, 1972.

Crone, P., and M. Cook. *Hagarism: The Making of the Islamic World*. Cambridge: Cambridge University Press, 1977.

DeSlane, G. *Vie des hommes illustres de l'islamisme en Araba par Ibn Khallihan*. 2 vols. Paris 1838/42.

Dohmen, Christoph, and Manfred Oeming. *Biblischer Kanon warum und wozu?* Freiburg: Herder, 1992.

Donner, F. M. *Narratives of Islamic Origins: The Beginnings of Historical Writing*. Princeton, N.J.: Princeton University Press, 1998.

Duri, A. A. "Jerusalem in the Early Islamic Period: 7th–11th Centuries A.D." In *Jerusalem in History*. Ed. K. J. Asali, 105–25. Essex, England: Scorpion Publishing, 1989.

Elad, Amikam. "The History and Topography of Jerusalem during the Early Islamic Period: The Historical Value of *Faḍā'il al-Quds* Literature; A Reconsideration." *JSAI* 14 (1991): 41–70.

Goitein, S. D. "Jerusalem in the Arab Period (638–1099)." In *The Jerusalem Cathedra* 2 (1982): 168–96.

——. "Al-Ḳuds." *EI*, new ed. 5: 322–39.

——. "Prayer in Islam." In *Studies in Islamic History and Institutions*, 73–84. Leiden: E. J. Brill, 1966.

——. "Ramaḍān, the Muslim Month of Fasting." In *Studies in Islamic History and Institutions*, 90–111. Leiden: E. J. Brill, 1966.

——. "Shemot Yerushalayim (The Names of Jerusalem)." In *ha-Yishuv be-Erets Yisra'el be-reshit ha-Islam uvi-tequfat ha-ṣalbanim: le-'or kitvei ha-Genizah*, 32–35. Jerusalem: Yad Yitshak Ben-Tsevi, 1979.

Gruber, E. *verdienst und Rang: Die Faḍā'il ak literarishches und gesellschaft-liches Problem im Islam*. Freiburg, 1975.

Ḥalabī, 'Alī b. Ibrāhīm. *al-Sīra al-Ḥalabiyya*. Cairo: al-Maktaba al-Ẓāhiriyya; reprint, Beirut: Dār al-Ma'rifa lil Ṭibā'a wa-l-Nashr, 1980.

Hasson, I. "'Les Titres de Gloire de Jérusalem' par Abū Bakr Muḥammad b. Ahmad al-Wāṣitī (= introduction française)." In *Faḍā'il al-Bayt al-Muqaddas li-Abū Bakr Muḥammad b. Aḥmad al-Wāṣitī*. Ed. I. Hasson, 7–29. Jerusalem: Dār Maghnis lil Nashr, 1979.

Hawting, G. R. "The Origins of the Islamic Sanctuary at Mecca." In *Studies on the First Century of Islamic Society*. Ed. G. H. A. Joynboll, 25–47. Carbondale: Southern Illinois University Press, 1982.

Horovitz, J. *Koranische Untersuchungen*. Berlin: Walter de Gruyter, 1926.

——. "Muhammeds Himmelfahrt." *Der Islam* 9 (1919): 159–83.

Ibn Ḥishām, 'Abd al-Malik. *al-Sīra al-nabawiyya*. Ed. Aḥmad Muḥammad Shākir. Cairo: n.p., 1373/1954.

Ibn Sa'd, Muḥammad. *al-Ṭabaqāt al-kubrā*. Ed. E. Sachau. Reprint, Beirut: n.p., 1960.

Ibn Isḥāq, Muḥammad. *The Life of Muhammad: A Translation of Ibn Isḥāq's Sīrat Rasūl Allāh*. Trans. Alfred Guillaume. Lahore, Pakistan: Oxford University Press, 1974

Ibn Khallikān. *Shamsuddin, Wafayātal-a'yān*. Ed. Ihsan Abbas. Beirut: n.d. n.p.

Jeffery, Arthur. "The Qur'an as Scripture." *Muslim World* 60 (1950): 41–55, 106–34, 185–206, 257–75.

Kister, M. J. "A Comment on the Antiquity of Traditions Praising Jerusalem." In *The Jerusalem Cathedra* 1 (1981): 185–86.

——. "'You shall only set out for three mosques': a study of an early tradition." *Le Muséon* 82 (1969): 173–96.

——. "A Bag of Meat: A Study of an Early Hadith." *BSOAS* 33 (1970): 267–75.

McAuliffe, J. D., ed. *Encyclopaedia of the Qur'ān*. Vol. 2, E-I. Leiden: Brill 2002.

Neuwirth, Angelika. "Erste Qibla—Fernstes Masǧid? Jerusalem in Horizont des historischen Muḥammad." In *Zion: Ort der Begegnung; Festschrift für Laurentius Klein zur Vollendung des 65. Lebensjahres*. Ed. F. Hahn et al., 227–70. Bodenheim: Athenäum Hain Hanstein, 1993.

——. "Face of Man–Face of God: The Significance of the Direction of Prayer in Islam." In *Self, Soul and Body in Religious Experience*. Ed. A. Baumgarten, J. Assmann, and G. Stroumsa, 298–312. Leiden: E. J. Brill, 1998.

——. "Images and Metaphors in the Introductory Sections of the Makkan Suras." In *Approaches to the Qur'an*. Ed. G. R. Hawting and Abdul-Kader A. Shareef, 3-36. London; New York: Routledge, 1993.

——. "Koran." In *Grundriß der arabischen Philologie*. Vol. 1. Ed. H. Gätje, 96–147. Wiesbaden: Reichert, 1987.

——. "Der Koran–Mittelpunkt des Lebens der islamischen Gemeinde." In *Weltmacht Islam*. Ed. R. Hilf, 69-91. Munich: Bayerische Landeszentrale für politische Bildungsarbeit, 1988.

——. "Referentiality and Textuality in the Sūrat al-Ḥijr. Some Observations on the Qur'ānic 'Canonical Process' and the Emergence of a Community." In *Literary Structures of Religious Meaning in of the Qur'an*. Ed. Issa Boullata. London: Curzon Press, 2000. 143-172.

——. "Vom Rezitationstext über die Liturgie zum Kanon: Zu Entstehung und Wiederauflösung der Surenkomposition im Verlauf der Entwicklung eines islamischen Kultus." In *The Qur'an as Text*. Ed. S. Wild, 69-105. Leiden: E. J. Brill, 1996.

——. *Studien zur Komposition der mekkanischen Suren*. Berlin: Walter de Gruyter, 1981.

Neuwirth, A., and Neuwirth K. "*Sūrat al-Fātiḥa*–'Eröffnung' des Text-Corpus Koran oder 'Introitus' der Gebetsliturgie?" In *Text, Methode und Grammatik (Festschrift W. Richter)*. Ed. W. Gross, H. Irsigler, and T. Seidl, 332–57. St. Ottilen: EOS Verlag, 1991.

Paret, Rudi. "Der Koran als Geschichtsquelle." *Zeitschrift für Geschichte und Kultur des islamischen Orients* 37 (1961): 24–42. Reprint in *Der Koran*. Ed. R. Paret, 137–58. Darmstadt: Wissenschaftliche Buchgesellschaft, 1975.

——. *Der Koran: Kommentar und Konkordanz*. Stuttgart: W. Kohlhammer, 1971.

——. *Der Koran: Übersetzung von Rudi Paret*. Stuttgart: W. Kohlhammer, 1962.

——. Review of *The Legend of the Opening of Muhammad's Breast*, by H. Birkeland. *Orientalische Zeitschrift* 52 (1957), 248–50. Reprint in *Der Koran*, 278–80.

Peters, F. E. "The Quest of the Historical Muhammad." *International Journal of Middle Eastern Studies* 23 (1991): 291–315.

Radscheit, M. *Die koranische Herausforderung: die tahaddi-Verse im Rahmen der Polemikpassagen des Korans*. Berlin: Klaus Schwarz, 1996.

Rubin, Uri. "The Ka'ba: Aspects of Its Ritual Functions and Position in Pre-Islamic and Early Islamic Times." *JSAI* 8 (1986): 97–131.

Schoeler, G. *Charakter und Authentie der muslimischen Überlieferung über das Leben Muhammeds*. Berlin: Walter de Gruyter, 1996.

Schrieke, B. "Die Himmelsreise Muhammeds." *Der Islam* 6 (1916): 1–30.

Sellheim, R. "Prophet, Caliph und Geschichte: Die Muhammad-Biographie des Ibn Ishaq." *Oriens* 18/19 (1967): 33-91.

Sivan, Emmanuel. "Le caractère sacré de Jérusalem dans l'Islam aux XIIe–XIIIe siècles." *Studia Islamica* 27 (1967): 149–82.

al-Ṭabarī, Abū Ja'far Muḥammad b. Jarir. *Jāmi' al-bayān fī tafsīr al-qur'ān*. 30 vols. in 15. Bulaq: al-Maṭba'a al-Maymūniyya, 1314/1896; reprint, Beirut: Dār al-Ma'rifa, 1972.

Van Ess, J. "'Abd al-Malik and the Dome of the Tock: An Analysis of some texts." In *Raby and J. Johns. Bayt al-Magdis: 'Abd-al-Malik's Jerusalem*. Ed. Oxford Studies in Islamic Artg. Oxford: Oxford University Press 1992, 89–103.

——. "Vision and Ascension: *Sūrat al-Najm* and its Relationship with Muḥammad's *mi'rāj*." *Journal of Qur'ānic Studies* 1 (1999): 47–62.

Wansbrough, John. *Quranic Studies: Sources and Methods of Scriptural Interpretation*. Oxford: Oxford University Press, 1977.

Watt, W. M. "Al-Madīna." *EI*, new ed. 5: 994–98.

——. *Muhammad at Medina*. Oxford, 1956; reprint, Oxford: Clarendon Press, 1981.

Wensinck, A. J. "*Ṣalāt*." In *Handbuch des Islams*. Leiden, 1941; reprint, Leiden: E. J. Brill, 1979.

Widengren, Geo. *Muhammad, the Apostle of God and his Ascension*. Uppsala: Uppsala Universitet Årsskrift, 1955.

Zwettler, M. "The Mantic Manifest: the Sura of the 'Poets' and the Qur'anic Foundations of Prophetic Authority." In *Poetry and Prophecy: The Beginnings of a Literary Tradition*. Ed. J. L. Kugel, 75–119, 205–31. Ithaca, N.Y.: Cornell University Press, 1990.

26

Qur'ānic Exegesis and History

GERALD HAWTING

The interpretation of any text involves at least two parties—the text itself and the interpreter. The interpreter will approach the text with aims, preconceptions, tools, and methods of interpretation, many of which derive not from the text but from the mind of the interpreter and the society to which he or she belongs. In some cases, the interpreter's agenda can dominate to such an extent that "exegesis" could legitimately be described as the imposition of meanings upon the text, meanings that may have been foreign to its "authors." The imposition of meanings on a text can be so successful that it may obscure what, for an outsider, would count as earlier and perhaps more authentic levels of meaning. In some cases the whole character of a text may be transformed by the way in which a particular community understands and uses it. Comprehending the way in which a community understands and makes use of a text is of great importance, but it is difficult for the academic observer to grasp the nature of that understanding and usage so long as he or she depends on the community's tradition alone and is cut off from other meanings. In the case of the Qur'ān, academics have had limited success in developing understandings independent of those provided by the traditional Muslim scholars.

One of the fundamental ingredients of qur'ānic commentaries is elucidation of who is addressed or referred to in the various passages of the scripture. The style of the Qur'ān is characteristically allusive and referential, containing very few proper names (of people, places, social groups, etc.) associated with the time or places in which it is usually understood to have originated, and it is therefore natural that establishing addressees and referents has been one of the basic concerns of the commentators. For example, Q 2:6–7 refers to a group that disbelieves (*alladhīna kafarū*) and that will continue to refuse to believe, whether "you" warn them or not. It is the commentators who identify for us the "you" and the group of unbelievers. There is unanimity that the "you" addressed is the prophet Muḥammad, but disagreement about the unbelievers: some commentators understood it as a reference to the Jews of Yathrib (Medina), some to the pagans of Mecca.[1]

Often these identifications are made in a summary fashion, the commentator interrupting his citations of the scripture with words that may be translated as "i.e." or "meaning" and then providing the identification, or simply by glossing the passage and introducing phrases such as "O Muḥammad." Frequently the identification is achieved in a more complex way through a story about the circumstances in which a particular or passage of the Qur'ān was revealed. In the course of the story, the identifications are provided and so is an interpretation of the passage. These "occasions of revelation" (*asbāb al-nuzūl*) stories are to be found in several genres of Muslim literature, not merely in works that proclaim themselves as commentaries on the scripture. They occur in large numbers, for example, in works of *sīra* (traditional accounts of the life of the Prophet).

Some of the features and functions of these "occasions of revelation" stories, in the course of which are identified anonymous or ambiguous individuals or groups (*ta'yīn al-mubham*), have been discussed recently by John Wansbrough and by Andrew Rippin.[2] The stories could sometimes have a legal significance in that the chronology of revelation, the order in which the verses of the Qur'ān were revealed, could affect their authority in disputed questions of law. More generally, however, they were important in providing context, and therefore meaning, for portions of the text. A characteristic of such stories is that the identifications of the anonymous and ambiguous references of the scripture are often inconsistent or even contradictory. Different stories pertaining to the same verse or passage will provide variant names and other details, and often the same verse will be the subject of variant and contradictory stories about the occasion of its revelation. The result is that different understandings of particular qur'ānic verses and passages developed, and works of commentary often assemble several different interpretations of a given part of the qur'ānic text. There was room for disagreement about the precise meaning of a passage, about the circumstances in which it had been revealed, or about the identification of individuals or groups mentioned in it.[3]

Those variants and inconsistencies, however, are confined within certain limits. There might be disagreement about the meanings of particular words, about whether a particular verse was revealed in Mecca or Medina, about the circumstances leading to the revelation of a particular passage and hence about its significance, but there was no disagreement that the Qur'ān was God's revelation to Muḥammad nor, in broad terms, about the time, place, and circumstances in which the text as a whole was revealed. It may be argued, therefore, that differences and contradictions regarding the circumstances and meaning of individual parts of the Qur'ān were less important than the common ground concerning the circumstances—and hence to some extent the significance—of the work as a whole. It was less important to have unanimity about individual parts of the text than it was to have agreement that the Qur'ān was a record of a revelation made to Muḥammad in Mecca and Medina. Traditional exegesis thus establishes not only the possibilities for the interpretation of the various parts of the Qur'ān but also the limits within which those possibilities are confined.

In thus establishing the image of the setting in which the Qur'ān originated, an image that has been generally accepted both within and outside Islam down to modern times, how far is a balance maintained between exegesis in the literal sense of that word and the imposition on the text of ideas that originated independently of it? Of special concern here is the traditional idea that the text emerged in a society in which the majority were Arab polytheists and idolaters of a crude and literal sort and that the fundamental message of the Qur'ān was directed against those people. How far might that idea be said to be substantiated by the Qur'ān itself, and how far might it be judged as something imposed on the text for reasons not arising from the book itself?

Much of the Qur'ān attacks a group (or perhaps groups) which it accuses of the sin of *shirk* (literally, "associationism") and whose members are referred to by terms such as *mushrikūn* and *alladhīna ashrakū* (literally, "those who commit *shirk*," "those who make or recognize associates"). This group is the major target of qur'ānic polemic. They are sometimes explicitly (and generally implicitly) distinguished in the text from Jews or Christians,[4] and that sin is ascribing associates or partners to God (as objects of prayer and worship, or as having a share in the power of God). In the history of Islam, *shirk* has continued to be regarded as the major sin, incompatible with Islam, and groups of Muslims have often designated their opponents, some of them non-Muslims and others claiming to be Muslims, as *mushrikūn*. Perhaps the best-known example is the application of the term in traditional polemic to Christians, in spite of the fact that the Qur'ān itself does not specify Christians or Christianity as the object of its attacks on *shirk*. In Muslim polemic, on the other hand, the Christian doctrines of the divine sonship of Jesus and of the Trinity have been frequently attacked as incompatible with true monotheism, as in fact *shirk*.[5] In Muslim polemic, *shirk* often functions as the equivalent of "idolatry" and other related words and concepts in Jewish and Christian polemic.

The Muslim exegetical tradition, and the traditional literature in general (lives of Muḥammad and other works), identify the qur'ānic "associators" (*mushrikūn*) as the Arabs of the time of Muḥammad who believed in many different gods and worshipped them in the form of idols. These idolatrous and polytheistic Arabs were the inhabitants of Mecca and the neighboring town of Ṭā'if, the bedouins of the surrounding regions, and a majority of the population of Yathrib (Medina), where, however, there also lived a significant community of Jews.

The following three examples illustrate how the tradition portrays these *mushrikūn* of the Qur'ān as polytheists and idolaters. Many more examples could be provided, but these should establish the point. The image transmitted of these polytheists and idolaters is rather complicated, a point that will be discussed later. At this stage, however, I simply wish to stress how the tradition is more explicit than the Qur'ān in its portrayal of the *mushrikūn* as polytheists and idolaters.

1. *Q 6:136*: "They have assigned to God, from the crops and cattle which he has created, a portion saying, 'This is for God'—so they assert—'and this is for our associates (*li-shurakā'inā*).' What is for the associates does not reach God but what is for God does reach the associates. Evil is their judgment!"[6]

In his *Sīra* (life of Muḥammad), Ibn Isḥāq (d. 151/768) reports the following story, also found in other traditional texts. The tribe of Khawlān (a tribe of pre-Islamic Arabia) had an idol (*ṣanam*) whose name is given as 'Ammanās or some variant. It was asserted that they used to divide their crops and cattle between God (Allāh) and the idol. If any designated for God came into the portion designated for the idol, they would let it lie there; but if any designated for the idol came into the portion allotted to God, they would retrieve it for the idol. The name of this clan is given by Ibn Isḥāq. Some say, he tells us, that it was in connection with this practice that Q 6:136 was revealed.[7]

This is an example of the "occasions of revelation" (*asbāb al-nuzūl*) stories. In works of a more explicitly exegetical type we find several similar reports in explication of this verse, often without any names of specific tribes or idols. In this way it is established generally that the verse alludes to the practice of pre-Islamic Arab idolaters and that the word "associates" (*shurakā'*) alludes to their idols, to which they gave priority over God.

2. Q *6:148*: "Those who have committed *shirk* will say, 'If God had not willed it, we would not have committed *shirk* and neither would our fathers, and we would not have declared anything [scil. lawful] as prohibited.' . . . "[8]

The commentator al-Ṭabarī (d. 310/923), reflecting the tradition well established by his time, here identifies "those who have committed *shirk*" as "those *mushrikūn* of Quraysh (i.e., the Meccan fellow townsmen of Muḥammad) who put idols and representations on the same level as God (*al-ʿādilūna bi-llāh al-awthān wa-l-aṣnām*)." Ṭabarī tells us that in the verse these opponents are reported as arguing, "If God had desired that we believe in him and worship him alone apart from the idols (*awthān*) and (other) gods (*āliha*), . . . we would not have appointed a partner (*sharīk*) to God and neither would our forefathers. . . . because he has the power to prevent us from doing it. . . . But he has accepted that we persist in worshipping the idols and the representations, assigning him a partner and equals (*andād*) in worship. . . . "[9]

Again *shirk* is established here as a form of idolatry in which worship of idols is included in a (limited) recognition of God: the *mushrikūn* worship idols and gods although they also accept the existence of God and even accord him supreme power. (In the previous example they were accused of giving their idol preference over God.)

3. Q *29:61–65*: "If you ask them [i.e., the opponents], 'Who created the heavens and the earth, and subjected the sun and the moon?' they will say, 'God' (Allāh); how then are they deflected [from this truth]? . . . If you ask them, 'Who sends down rain from the heavens and thus gives life to the dead earth?' they will say, 'God.' Say, 'Praise be to God,' but most of them have no understanding. . . . When they embark on a ship they call upon God, offering worship to him alone, but when he delivers them safely to land, they commit 'association.'[10]

Again al-Ṭabarī's commentary may be cited.

> God is here saying: "If you ask, O Muḥammad, these who give associates to God (*hā'ulā'i l-mushrikīn bi-llāh*), 'Who created the heavens and the earth?'" . . . And he says to his prophet Muḥammad: "If you ask, O Muḥammad, these of your people who give associates to God (*hā'ulā'i l-mushrikīna bi-llāh min qawmika*), 'Who sends down rain from the heavens?' . . . [They would, of course, answer: 'God']," but most of these who give associates to God have no understanding of what is beneficial or harmful in the matter of their religion (*lā yaʿqilūna mā lahum fīhi al-nafʿu min amri dīnihim wa-mā fīhi al-ḍarr*). In their ignorance they reckon that by worshipping the gods other than God they obtain a closeness and nearness to God (*fa-hum li-jahlihim yaḥsabūna annahum li-ʿibādatihim al-āliha dūna llāh yanālūna ʿinda llāh zulfatan wa-qurbatan*). . . . And when these associaters travel on the sea in ships and fear drowning and death, they call upon God alone . . . and do not ask for aid from their gods and those whom they recognize as equals of God (*ālihatahum wa-andādahum*) but from God who created them. . . . But when he brings them safely to land they appoint to God a partner (*sharīk*) in their acts of worship, praying to gods and idols (*awthān*) together with him as lords.[11]

Such examples, therefore, identify for us the opponents called *mushrikūn* in the Qur'ān as Arab idolaters and polytheists of the society in which Muḥammad lived; their sin of *shirk* involved the recognition and worship of idols (*aṣnām* or *awthān*) and of gods (*āliha*) other than God (Allāh). In addition to these and many other examples which are professedly exegetical in the sense that they refer to and present themselves as explanations of particular verses of the Qur'ān, Muslim tradition reinforces the message by providing us with a relatively large amount of information about the idols, gods, and sanctuaries of the Arabs of central Arabia before Islam. That information is provided sometimes in qur'ānic commentary, but also in works such as biographies of the Prophet, genealogical literature, geographical accounts, collections of *ḥadīths*, and others. Much of this material does not refer directly to the Qur'ān. Some works were produced that were devoted entirely to the compilation of information about pre-Islamic Arab idolatry, the best known being the *Kitāb al-aṣnām* (Book of Idols), attributed to Hishām b. Muḥammad al-Kalbī (d. 206/820). Taken as a whole, the interpretations provided by the exegetes and the material gathered in other traditional texts have been effective in establishing that the first and fundamental targets of the qur'ānic attack on *shirk* were Arabs who were quite literally polytheistic and idolatrous. In other words, the material has been accepted as evidence that the Qur'ān—and to some extent Islam—was revealed in (or, according to non-Muslim understanding, emerged from) a predominantly pagan Arab milieu.

It is not possible to explain fully here why I think we need to reconsider this common view of the Qur'ān's polemic against the *mushrikūn*. That a major development in the monotheist tradition should result from a confrontation with people who were "real" polytheists and idolaters is an idea strange enough to warrant at least some hesitation before it is accepted,[12] and a full discussion would require consideration of the nature of polemical language in the monotheistic tradition as well as of the nature and value of the traditional Muslim accounts of pre-Islamic Arab idolatry. Here I wish to focus on the question of how far there is continuity or disjunction between the qur'ānic material against those opponents whom it accuses of *shirk* on the one hand, and the "exegetical" material which identifies them for us as Arab idolaters on the other.

First, it is clear that the Qur'ān itself does to some extent equate the *shirk* of the opponents with polytheism and idolatry. It accuses them in various passages of worshipping or recognizing gods other than (or "before," *min dūni*) God,[13] and it refers to them as partisans of the *ṭāghūt* and the *jibt*.[14] The origins and precise meaning of those two words are rather obscure, but the tradition associates them with idols and idolatry (among other things) and it is possible to relate them to terms used in pre-Islamic monotheist allusions to "idolatry" in Aramaic/Syriac or possibly Ethiopic.[15]

On the other hand, we are told in the Qur'ān that these *mushrikūn* thought that those whom they regarded as "associates" (*shurakā'*) would intercede with God for them at the Last Day;[16] that (as we have seen in the example just cited) they would recognize God as the creator of all things and would call on him alone when in peril on the sea, but when they reached land they would again commit *shirk*; that they believed in angels and jinn and regarded them as offspring of God;[17] that they defended their recognition of "associates" by saying they were a means of drawing closer to God;[18] and that they said God could have prevented their *shirk* had he so wished.[19] These are not arguments which one would expect of polytheists and idolaters in any literal sense of those words.

The Qur'ān is notably reticent regarding the details of the opponents' idolatry. It refers to eight names, five in one passage and three in another, which the extra-qur'ānic tradition explains as names of idols worshipped by the Arabs, although the scripture itself does not make that claim. One of those passages refers by name to the five gods worshipped by the idolatrous contemporaries of Noah.[20] The extra-qur'ānic tradition tells us that these five were worshipped too by the pre-Islamic Arabs and it provides considerable detail about them, their sites, the tribes that worshipped them, and how they were destroyed in early Islam.[21] The other qur'ānic passage mentions by name Allāt, al-ʿUzzā, and Manāt, whom it implies the opponents regarded as female offspring of God, and it seems to suggest that they identified these as angels who could intercede with God.[22] The extra-qur'ānic tradition tells us that these three were in fact idols worshipped by the Meccans and others, it supplies the same sort of information as it does about the five gods of the people of Noah, and, notoriously, it has them figure large in the story of the satanic verses. According to that story, not widely transmitted but nevertheless a feature of Muslim tradition, the Prophet, misled by Satan, temporarily recognized these three "goddesses" of the Meccans as possible intercessors with God—a compromise with Arab paganism which won the adherence of the Meccans to Islam. Once Gabriel had pointed out his error to the Prophet, and once the true words of the scripture were established—and these three dismissed as mere names—the Meccans reverted to their former polytheism and idolatry.[23]

Even if one is prepared to follow the tradition in its development of the two qur'ānic passages where these eight names occur, that would seem to be the sum total of specific information in Muslim scripture about the "idolatry" of the *mushrikūn*. Elsewhere, it is a general accusation only and not always a consistent one. While some passages accuse them of worshipping gods before God, others refer to their "friends" or "patrons" (*awliyā'*) or to their "associates" (*shurakā'*) rather than to their "gods."[24] Although they are charged with following the *ṭāghūt* and the *jibt* in some verses, the most common Arabic words for idols, *aṣnām* and *awthān*, are rarely if ever used in the accusations against them. When those two words occur in the Qur'ān it is nearly always in connection with earlier peoples—usually the contemporaries of Abraham or of Moses—and not with the opponents attacked as *mushrikūn*.[25]

The Qur'ān thus presents a rather two-sided general image of the opponents: on the one hand vocabulary with connotations of idolatry and polytheism is applied to them; on the other, they appear to know about the one God and to share some of the concepts of the monotheist religion, especially the eschatological ones. It is just that normally they "associate" others with God. We will return to the question of how this image might be understood.

When we look at the extra-qur'ānic material, we find, not surprisingly, that to some extent this double-sided image is reflected especially when the traditional material is a more or less direct commentary on the qur'ānic texts. Thus in the three examples given, both the "occasion of revelation" story about Khawlān and its idol and the more direct glosses and expansions of the qur'ānic text by al-Ṭabarī present the *mushrikūn* as sharing monotheistic ideas to some extent, especially a knowledge of the one God (Allāh), but as worshipping idols and other gods at the same time. However, it is apparent that those exegetical materials, while reflecting what the Qur'ān says about the opponents' awareness and occasional worship of the one God, are much more explicit than the scripture is about the nature of their idolatrous and polytheistic characteristics. Where the Qur'ān has innuendoes of idolatry and more frequent charges of *shirk* ("associationism"), the three passages of commentary cited here have more specific references to the "idols" (*aṣnām*, *awthān*) and "gods" (*āliha*) of the opponents, sometimes identifing the opponents, and, in the case of the report about Khawlān, supplying some detail about the idolatrous practices of those who make sure that their offerings reach their *shurakā'* but are not concerned that their offerings to God do in fact reach him.

When we move away from the material that is closely associated with qur'ānic texts, we find ourselves in an even more explicitly idolatrous and polytheistic world. Texts like the *Kitāb al-aṣnām* are full of stories about the idols of the Arabs, how they originated and were destroyed, where in Arabia they were situated, which tribes worshipped them, and so on. In these the possibly monotheistic tendencies of the qur'ānic *mushrikūn* tend to be lost and we are dealing more with the typically one-dimensional, hostile, and mocking view of polytheism as crude idolatry which is characteristic of much monotheistic writing about perceived polytheists.[26] The ambiguous and two-edged qur'ānic material becomes clear and more uniform in the traditional literature about pre-Islamic Arab idolatry.

This clearly observable shift in emphasis is, however, to some extent cut across and obscured by material in the traditional accounts of Arab idolatry that *does* associate the pre-Islamic Arabs with elements of monotheism. For example, we are told that among the idolatrous and polytheistic Arabs of the time of Muḥammad and before, there were certain individuals who did believe in the one God and had abjured the idolatry of their fellows. Generally they are referred to as *ḥanīfs*.[27] We are told that Arab idolatry had developed by a process of corruption of a pure monotheism which had been brought to Arabia by Abraham, who had traveled to Mecca at God's command and rebuilt the Ka'ba (the house of God) in Mecca. The gradual corruption of Abraham's monotheism over time by the Arabs had not been complete: remnants of that monotheism still survived among the *ḥanīfs*. Even among the pagan Arabs there was a residual memory: they regarded the Ka'ba as the chief sanctuary of the Arabs, associated it with a god whom they referred to as Allāh, and gave the Ka'ba and Allāh a status above that of the other local and tribal sanctuaries, gods, and idols. It is the combination of this sort of material with a description of crude and simple idolatry which characterizes texts like the *Kitāb al-aṣnām*. The description of the idols and sanctuaries of the pagan Arabs is given within a framework account of Arab idolatry as a corruption of Abrahamic monotheism.[28]

How are we to understand this material: the qur'ānic passages attacking the *mushrikūn*; the commentaries identifying them as idolaters and polytheists who to some extent and on certain occasions were monotheists; and the other traditional material which portrays them as much more stereotypical idolaters and polytheists but explains their paganism as a corruption of an earlier monotheism whose elements still lingered on (and which the prophet Muḥammad was commissioned to restore)? It would be possible to accept the material as coherent and to explain it the way the tradition does, as reflecting the religion of the people of central and western Arabia at the time the Prophet was sent to them by God, a society fundamentally idolatrous and polytheistic but still containing elements of the ancestral monotheism. Much modern non-Muslim scholarship has in fact been content to follow that approach although, as one would expect, it has reformulated the traditional material to emasculate or totally remove its religious and theological elements.

The most widely accepted understanding of the material results from reading it in the light of evolutionary theories of religion. This was the approach adopted by Julius Wellhausen, whose work on the paganism of pre-Islamic Arabia has had a lasting influence on academic accounts of Arab religion and the rise of Islam.[29] In essence, this approach proposes that the Arabs around the time of Muḥammad were emerging from the polytheistic stage of religious development into the monotheistic stage. The old paganism was in a state of decline or even collapse; monotheistic ideas—whether as a result of foreign influences or through a process of natural evolution—were beginning to emerge, and the work of Muḥammad was simply to further this process by providing the impetus that finally toppled the decrepit edifice of the old Arab paganism and drew out and developed the emerging monotheism in ways especially congenial to the Arabs of the time. This approach does not question the traditional picture of the setting within which the Qur'ān (here equated with Islam) emerged; it simply explains it according to a theory that was more persuasive to the scholars concerned than was the traditional Muslim explanation.

An interesting variant on the evolutionary interpretation attempts to apply the idea of protomonotheism or *Urmonotheismus* to the traditional material. The notion, developed by Andrew Lang, Nathan Söderblom, and Wilhelm Schmidt among others, was that a type of monotheism was the earliest form of religion in the world and that other types of religious ideas—including animism, fetishism, polydemonism, and polytheism—have to be understood as subsequent developments (read corruptions). This idea seems to have been first applied to the traditional Muslim material by Carl Brockelmann,[30] who argued that the strange combination, portrayed in the Muslim evidence, of monotheistic elements, idolatry, and polytheism among the Arabs of the Prophet's time in fact reflected the survival of elements of a hypothetical monotheism native to Arabia amid the general polytheism and idolatry which had developed there. Muḥammad was able to build upon, not so much elements of monotheism emerging out of an earlier stage of polytheism, but rather survivals of an earlier stage of monotheism which still remained among the later layers of polytheism. The Muslim idea of the religion of Abraham and its fate in Arabia could be understood in part as an earlier and more specific form of the modern *Urmonotheismus* idea of comparative religion.

These two approaches, not always clearly distinguished and their theoretical bases not always understood, have dominated academic accounts of pre-Islamic Arabia and the emergence of Islam over the past century or so. Fundamentally they accept the evidence of the Qur'ān and of the non-qur'ānic tradition as all of a piece, and they accept the "facts" reported in the tradition while divesting them of the significance which they have there. For example, the dominant status accorded by the tradition to the Ka'ba among the sanctuaries of pre-Islamic Arabia is accepted as a historical fact, but the tradition's explanation of the fact by reference to the role of Abraham in building the Ka'ba and to the survival of elements of Abrahamic religion among the Arabs of Muḥammad's time is replaced by notions of evolutionary development or of the persistence of native Arabian monotheism. Unfortunately, the quarrying of the traditional material for historical fact, without too much concern for questions about why particular stories or themes exist in the tradition or what they mean there, has been a feature of much modern scholarship.

I am concerned here with, if not the absolute disjunction, at least the marked difference in emphasis between the image of the *mushrikūn* derivable from the rather ambiguous qur'ānic materials attacking them, on the one hand, and, on the other, the more one-sided portrayal of them as crude and literal idolaters in the professedly exegetical literature and in the traditional texts purporting to describe the idols, gods, and sanctuaries of the pre-Islamic Arabs. I suggest that the traditional descriptions of pre-Islamic Arab paganism—although their explicit references to the Qur'ān are limited—

can be understood as a form of exegesis in that their primary purpose is to give substance to the idea that the Qur'ān (and therefore, in the traditional understanding, Islam) was revealed in a pagan Arab society. The question of the value of those descriptions as a source of real information about religious conditions in Arabia before Islam is a separate issue, although it is relevant to the general theory being outlined here. Essentially, even if it could be shown that the traditional accounts of Arab pagan religion before Islam contain a substantial amount of accurate information, the question of their truth content should be secondary to that of their purpose and the reasons for their existence.

It is not only that the extra-qur'ānic material is more explicit about the idolatry and polytheism of the opponents than is the scripture itself: there is also a difference in the way the tradition and the Qur'ān explain the combination of monotheist and "idolatrous" elements which they ascribe, respectively, to the pagan Arabs and to the opponents attacked for their *shirk*. In the traditional texts identifying the qur'ānic *mushrikūn* as idolatrous Arabs, the elements of monotheism among them are explained mainly as the persistence in Arabia of ideas or institutions of the Abrahamic monotheism (*dīn Ibrāhīm*) which had become corrupted but never entirely obliterated. In the Qur'ān, on the other hand, the traditional monotheist concept of Abraham as the father of monotheism and as the spiritual ancestor of those who adhere to the true faith is attested, but there is little to suggest that Abraham had introduced monotheism into Arabia. He is, indeed, connected with the sanctuary in a number of verses (Q 2:127, 3:97, 22:26), but the sanctuary (*bayt*) and its site are not identified, and the theme of the corruption of Abraham's religion among the Arabs is nowhere visible. Instead, in the Qur'ān, the *shirk* of the opponents seems to be explained as the result of religious and psychological weakness and error—the need to have an intercessor and the desire to draw closer to God through the *shurakā'*. A certain level of monotheism among them is assumed (they recognize that God is creator of everything) and it becomes heightened in certain circumstances (e.g., when in peril on the sea). In the tradition, crude idolatry (*'ibādat al-aṣnām*) appears to be contrasted with simple monotheism (*tawḥīd*); in the Qur'ān, the contrast is between debased monotheism (*shirk*) and pure monotheism (*ikhlāṣ*).

My suggestion is, therefore, that we need to distinguish between the Qur'ān and the traditional Muslim literature and not run them together as historical evidence for one and the same phenomenon. The qur'ānic material attacking *shirk* makes sense if it is read as polemic against a group or groups who would have considered themselves—and may be regarded by uncommitted outside observers—as monotheists. The polemic of the Qur'ān, however, regards their religion as at best an inconsistent and weak form of monotheism, one that is really the equivalent of idolatry and polytheism and that it sometimes attacks as in fact such. It is the nature of polemic to distort the position of the opponents, often by exaggerating or misinterpreting aspects of their practices and ideas. It may be difficult for those not involved in the polemic, or with no other information to put it into a context, to recognize the nature of the language involved, and it must always be a problem to decide how much those involved in a polemic are themselves aware of the special nature of the language they are using.

The extra-qur'ānic material, on the other hand, is concerned to identify those qur'ānic opponents as the Arabs of inner Arabia who believed in a plurality of gods and worshipped them in the form of idols. Not only is the polemic of the Qur'ān transformed into a portrayal of gross polytheism and idolatry, it is also given a relatively precise setting in time and place. The description of pre-Islamic idol worship, however, had to take account of the related ideas of Abraham as the founder of the Muslim sanctuary at Mecca and of his son Ishmael as the progenitor of the Arabs, and as a result the religious condition of the Arabs before Islam came to be portrayed as the result of the corruption over time of a previously pure monotheism brought to Arabia by the two patriarchs. In describing how this corruption had occurred, Muslim tradition developed accounts used in Jewish and Christian tradition which described idolatry as something that had come into the world by the debasement of an earlier state of monotheism. This had occurred as the result of a combination of usually well-intentioned human stupidity and satanic guile.[31]

The difference in quality between the extra-qur'ānic material and the scripture itself, and the monotheistic character of the opponents attacked in the Qur'ān for their *shirk*, have sometimes been sensed by modern scholars, but the consequences have been obscured by a failure to understand the way in which the extra-qur'ānic tradition has imposed its own version of the historical setting within which the scripture was revealed (in other words, by treating the different types of evidence as all of a piece). Duncan Black Macdonald, notably, after surveying the qur'ānic material relating to the *mushrikūn*, wrote in his entry "Allāh" in the first edition of the *Encyclopaedia of Islam*: "The religion of Mecca in Muḥammad's time was far from simple idolatry. It resembled much more a form of the Christian faith, in which saints and angels have come to stand between the worshippers and God." No doubt Macdonald's own Protestantism made him especially alert to the import of the qur'ānic polemic against *shirk*, but such was the authority of the tradition that his remarks seem to require no more than an adjustment to our evaluation of the religion of the *mushrikūn*: accepting the identification of them provided by the tradition, we need do no more than than give them rather more credit than does the tradition. Macdonald's allusion to Christianity was strongly rejected by Brockelmann, who was committed to interpreting the qur'ānic *mushrikūn* as adherents of an indigenous Arabian monotheism.[32]

But if the tradition's presentation of the opponents attacked in the Qur'ān for their *shirk* as literal idolaters and polytheists is, as argued here, misleading, why should its identification of them as Arabs (whether of Mecca, Medina, or the tribes) of the society of Muḥammad be thought any more secure? That latter identification is also entirely dependent on the tradition and not on the text of the scripture itself, and it is achieved in precisely the same way as is the view of them as polytheists and idolaters. Furthermore, where there is at least some link between the text of scripture and the extra-scriptural tradition realizing the *mushrikūn* as idolaters and polytheists, there is little in the scripture to generate the idea that Arabia was the place in which the *mushrikūn* lived, or to suggest a time frame. Those elements of identification too depend upon the tradition rather than on the words of scripture.

The identification of the *mushrikūn* in Muslim works of qur'ānic commentary and other texts, therefore, may be said to reflect ideas about the society and place in which Islam originated which are largely independent of the text itself. Rather than arising out of the relevant verses and passages, those verses and passages have been read in the light of ideas which, I suggest, developed independently and are not exegetical in the usual meaning of that term.

It might be possible to explain the traditional portrayal of the *mushrikūn* as idolaters and polytheists in a literal sense as a result of a simple misunderstanding of the qur'ānic polemic and to that extent as not completely divorced from the text. In other words, it might be thought that the attacks in the scripture on the *mushrikūn*, which sometimes associated them with polytheism and idolatry, were interpreted literally because their character as polemic was not understood by the early Muslim scholars. Once the historical setting that had generated it was left behind, the polemic, it might be argued, was so opaque to those who established qur'ānic commentary, the traditional life of the Prophet, and other forms of tradition that they unconsciously transformed the polemic into literal fact—*shirk* became *'ibādat al-aṣnām* merely as a result of a failure to understand.

That explanation would require a level of insensitivity to the polemical tenor of the scripture which might be thought unlikely given Islam's own tradition of polemic, a tradition in which the notion of *shirk* has played a central role. Muslim historical tradition tells us that already during the first civil war (the *fitna* of 36/656–40/661) the Khārijites accused 'Alī b. Abī Ṭālib of *shirk*, citing a qur'ānic verse against him, because they considered that he had derogated from the authority of God when he appointed human arbitrators to settle his dispute with Mu'āwiya.[33] Whether or not that incident in fact took place, it is clear that Muslims used the notion of *shirk* from an early date in their arguments with one another and with outsiders, and it is therefore hard to imagine that they were oblivious of the meaning and polemical function of the term in passages of the Qur'ān. Naturally, once the tradition of identifying the qur'ānic *mushrikūn* as pagan Arabs had become established, later generations would have followed it, and there is no reason to suspect a conscious process of reinterpretation among the later Muslim scholars upon whose works we depend for our knowledge of the early tradition.

Even if the hypothesis of a mistaken literalist interpretation of the qur'ānic polemic is preferred, it is still legitimate to ask what predisposed the understanding of the attack upon *shirk* as an attack on Arab idolatry and polytheism. I have suggested that that understanding arose not from the text of the Qur'ān itself but from other considerations which led to the reading of the Qur'ān in a certain way. The most obvious of those considerations would be a need—conscious or unconscious—to emphasize the association of the Qur'ān with the activity of the prophet Muḥammad in western central Arabia.

Notes

This essay contains some material and arguments that were subsequently elaborated in Hawting, *Idea of Idolatry*.

1. See, e.g., al-Suyūṭī, *Lubāb al-nuqūl fī asbāb al-nuzūl*, 11 ad loc.
2. Wansbrough, *Quranic Studies*, 141–42, 177–85; Rippin, "The Function of the *asbāb al-nuzūl*."
3. On diversity of interpretation as a characteristic of *tafsīr* literature and on its narrowing down in certain texts, see Calder, "*Tafsīr* from Ṭabarī to Ibn Kathīr."
4. See, e.g., Q 2:96; 2:105; 98:1; 98:6; 5:82.
5. Presumably the Muslim accusation of *shirk* against Christians is reflected in those Greek Christian texts that say the Ishmaelites called the Christians *hetairiastas*, a likely Greek rendition of *mushrikūn*. See the *De haeresibus* attributed to John of Damascus (d. ca. 754), text and translation in Sahas, *John of Damascus on Islam*, 134, 136 (text) = 135, 137 (trans.). There is a new edition of the text in *Die Schriften des Johannes von Damaskos*, iv, *Liber De haeresibus*, ed.

B. Kotter. For the problem of the authenticity of the attribution, see Abel, "Le chapitre CI du Livre des hérésies de Jean Damascène." The same information about the use of *hetairiastas* is contained in the ritual of abjuration for those converting to Christianity from the religion of the Saracens, which, although it can be no earlier than the late ninth century in the form in which we have it, may contain materials originating earlier than that; see Montet, "Un rituel d'abjuration des musulmans," 145–63, esp. 154; on the date of the text, see Cumont, "L'origine de la formule grècque d'abjuration."

6. "wa-ja'alū li-llāhi mimmā dhara'a mina l-ḥarthi wa-l-an'āmi naṣīban fa-qālū hādhā li-llāhi bi-ja'mihim wa-hādhā li-shurakā'inā fa-mā kāna li-shurakā'ihim fa-lā yaṣilu ilā llāhi wa-mā kāna li-llāhi fa-huwa yaṣilu ilā shurakā'ihim sā'a mā yaḥkumūna."

7. Ibn Hishām, *Sīrat rasūl Allāh*, ed. Muṣṭafā al-Saqā, et al., 1: 80–81; = *The Life of Muhammad*, trans. A. Guillaume, 36–37; Ibn al-Kalbī, *Das Götzenbuch*, trans. Rosa Klinke-Rosenberger, 27 (text) = 53 (trans.).

8. "sa-yaqūlu lladhīna ashrakū law shā'a llāhu mā ashraknā wa-lā abā'unā wa-lā ḥarramnā min shay'in. . . . "

9. al-Ṭabarī, *Jāmi' al-bayān fī tafsīr āy al-Qur'ān*, ed. M. Shākir, 12:208 ad loc.

10. "wa-la-in sa'altahum man khalaqa l-samawāti wa-l-arḍa wa-sakhkhara l-shamsa wa-l-qamara la-yaqūlunna llāhu fa-annā yu'fakūna . . . wa-la'in sa'altahum man nazzala mina l-samā'i mā'an fa-aḥyā bihi l-arḍa min ba'di mawtihā la-yaqūlunna llāhu qul al-ḥamdu li llāhi bal aktharuhum lā ya'qilūna . . . a-idhā rakibū, fi l-fulki da'aw llāha mukhliṣīna lahu l-dīna fa-lammā najjāhum ila l-barri idhā hum yushrikūna."

11. al-Ṭabarī, *Jāmi' al-bayān* (Bulaq ed.), 21:9, ad loc.

12. Cf. Waardenburg, "Un débat coranique contre les polythéistes," 2:143: "Le surgissement d'un monothéisme qui se dresse contre une religion polythéiste est un phénomène poignant dans l'histoire des religions." I do not mean to suggest, of course, that terms such as "polytheism" or (especially) "idolatry" have a meaning independent of that implied by those who use them. Both words usually occur in "monotheist" evaluations of other systems of religion, and they imply a hostile value judgment.

13. E.g., Q 17:42; 19:81; 25:43; 37:36; 43:58.

14. See Q 2:256, 257; 4:51, 60, 76; 5:65; 16:36; 39:17.

15. Nöldeke, *Neue Beiträge*, 47–48; Jeffery, *Foreign Vocabulary*, 99–100, 202–3; Levy, *Wörterbuch*, 2:170b-71a, s.v. *ṭ-'-w-t*; Köbert, "Das koranische 'ṭaġ ūt.'"

16. E.g., Q 2:225; 6:94; 10:3, 18; 32:4; 30:13; 40:18.

17. E.g., Q 6:100–101; 17:40; 21:26–28; 37:158; 43:15, 19.

18. Q 39:3.

19. Q 6:148 (example "b" earlier); 16:35.

20. Q 71:23: Wadd, Suwā', Yaghūth, Ya'ūq, and Nasr.

21. In addition to the commentaries ad loc., see, e.g., Ibn al-Kalbī, *Götzenbuch* = *Aṣnām*, 6–7, 17, 32–36 (text) = 34–35, 43, 57–61 (trans.), and the editor's notes thereto.

22. Q 53:19–28.

23. See the articles s.v. each of the three "goddesses" in the *EI*. The story of the satanic verses, when it occurs in *tafsīr*, is usually adduced not in connection with Q 53:19, but with 22:52. Probably the best-known version of the story is that transmitted by al-Ṭabarī in his *History* from Ibn Isḥāq: al-Ṭabarī, *Ta'rīkh al-rusul wa'-l-mulūk*, 1:1192–95 (trans. Guillaume, in Ibn Hishām, *The Life of Muhammad*, 165–67). For further references and discussion, see Rubin, *Eye of the Beholder*, 156–66.

24. Patrons/friends (*awliyā'*): e.g., Q 29:41; 36:3; 42:6; equals/peers (*andād*): e.g., Q 2:165; 14:30; 39:8; 41:9; associates (*shurakā'*): e.g., Q 30:13; 6:94; 10:18.

25. But note Q 22:30, where the opponents are exhorted to avoid "the filth of idols" (*al-rijs min al-awthān*), apparently designating food considered unclean.

26. In the words of the Wisdom of Solomon 14:27: "The worship of idols with no name is the beginning, cause, and end of every evil." For a conspectus of stories about the origins of idols and idolatry in the Jewish tradition, see Ginzberg, *Legends of the Jews*, index, s.vv. "idols" and "idolatry." For the influence on early Christianity of Hellenistic critiques of popular superstition portrayed as crude polytheism and idolatry, see Bevan, *Holy Images*.

27. The locus classicus is probably Ibn Hishām, *Sīrat rasūl Allāh*, 1:222–32 (= *Life of Muḥammad*, 98–103). Cf. Rubin, "Ḥanīfiyya and Ka'ba," and Rippin, "RḤMNN and the Ḥanīfs."

28. See esp. Ibn al-Kalbī, *Götzenbuch* = *Aṣnām*, 1–6 (text) = 32–34 (trans.); Ibn Hishām, *Sīrat rasūl Allāh*, 1:76–78 (= *Life of Muḥammad*, 35–36).

29. Wellhausen, *Reste arabischen Heidentums*.

30. Brockelmann, "Allah und die Götzen."

31. Muslim tradition itself shared the common monotheistic stories about how idolatry had entered the world among the descendants of Adam; see, e.g, Ibn al-Kalbī, *Götzenbuch* = *Aṣnām*, 31–33 (text) = 56–58 (trans.). The desire to commemorate in a material form the honored dead, which is a theme in those stories and others (perhaps best known is the passage in Wisdom of Solomon 14:12–31), is transformed in the Muslim tradition about the origins of stone and idol worship in Arabia into the desire to commemorate the Ka'ba and its rituals.

32. See n. 30.

33. al-Ṭabarī, *Ta'rīkh*, 1:3362, 3363, 3377.

Bibliography

Abel, Armand. "Le chapitre CI du *Livre des hérésies* de Jean Damascène: son inauthenticité." *Studia islamica* 19 (1963): 5-25.

Bevan, Edwyn. *Holy Images: An Inquiry into Idolatry and Image-Worship in Ancient Paganism and in Christianity*. London: G. Allen, 1940.

Brockelmann, Carl. "Allah und die Götzen: Der Ursprung des islamischen Monotheismus." *Archiv für Religionswissenschaft* 21 (1922): 99–121.

Calder, Norman. "*Tafsīr* from Ṭabarī to Ibn Kathīr: Problems in the Description of a Genre, Illustrated with Reference to the Story of Abraham." In *Approaches to the Qur'ān*. Ed. G. R. Hawting and Abdul-Kader A. Shareef, 101–40. London: Routledge, 1993.

Cumont, Franz. "L'origine de la formule grècque d'abjuration imposée aux musulmans." *Revue de l'histoire des religions* 64 (1911): 143–50.

Ginzberg, Louis. *Legends of the Jews*. 7 vols. Philadelphia: The Jewish Publication Society of America, 1909–38.

Ibn Hishām, 'Abd al-Malik. *The Life of Muhammad: A Translation of Isḥāq's Sīrat rasūl Allāh*. Trans. Alfred Guillaume. Oxford: Oxford University Press, 1955.

——. *Sīrat rasūl Allāh*. Ed. Muṣṭafā al-Saqā, et al. 2 vols. [Cairo?], 1955.

Ibn al-Kalbī. *Das Götzenbuch: Kitāb al-Aṣnām des Ibn al-Kalbī*. Trans. Rosa Klinke-Rosenberger. Leipzig: Otto Harrassowitz, 1941.

Jeffery, Arthur. *The Foreign Vocabulary of the Qur'ān*. Baroda: Oriental Institute, 1938.

John, of Damascus. *Die Schriften des Johannes von Damaskos*. iv, *Liber De haeresibus*. Ed. B. Kotter. Berlin: Walter de Gruyter, 1981.

Köbert, R. "Das koranische 'ṭaġūt.'" *Orientalia* n.s. 30 (1961): 415–16.

Levy, Jacob. *Wörterbuch über die Talmuden und Midraschim*. 2d ed. Berlin and Vienna: B. Harz, 1924.

Montet, Édouard. "Un rituel d'abjuration des musulmans dans l'église grecque." *Revue de l'histoire des religions* 53 (1906): 145-63.

Nöldeke, Theodor. *Neue Beiträge zur semitischen Sprachwissenschaft*. Strassburg: Karl J. Trübner, 1910.

Rippin, Andrew. "The Function of the *Asbāb al-nuzūl* in Qur'ānic Exegesis." *BSOAS* 51 (1988): 1-20.

——. "RḤMNN and the Ḥanīfs." In *Islamic Studies Presented to Charles J. Adams*. Ed. Wael B. Hallaq and Donald P. Little, 153-68. Leiden: E. J. Brill, 1991.

Rubin, Uri. *The Eye of the Beholder*. Princeton, N.J.: Darwin Press, 1995.

——. "Ḥanīfiyya and Ka'ba." *Jerusalem Studies in Arabic and Islam* 13 (1990): 85-112.

Sahas, Daniel J. *John of Damascus on Islam: The "Heresy of the Ishmaelites"*. Leiden: E. J. Brill, 1972.

al-Suyūṭī, Jalāl al-Dīn. *Lubāb al-nuqūl fī asbāb al-nuzūl*. Tunis, 1981.

al-Ṭabarī, Muḥammad b. Jarīr. *Jāmi' al-bayān fī tafsīr āy al-Qur'ān*. 30 vols. Bulaq: al-Maṭba'a al-Maymaniyya, 1905-12.

——. *Jāmi' al-bayān fī tafsīr āy al-Qur'ān*. Ed. M. Shākir. 16 vols. to date. Cairo, 1954-.

——. *Ta'rikh al-rusul wa-l-mulūk*. Ed. M. J. de Goeje, et al. 15 vols. Leiden: E. J. Brill, 1879-1901.

Waardenburg, Jacques. "Un débat coranique contre les polythéistes." In *Ex orbe religionum: studia Geo Widengren oblata*. Vol. 2, 143-54. Leiden: E. J. Brill 1972.

Wansbrough, John. *Quranic Studies: Sources and Methods of Scriptural Interpretation*. Oxford: Oxford Universty Press, 1977.

Wellhausen, Julius. *Reste arabischen Heidentums*. Berlin: Reimer, 1887; 2d rev. ed., Berlin: Reimer, 1897.

27

The Self-Referentiality of the Qur'ān

Sura 3:7 as an Exegetical Challenge

STEFAN WILD

The self-referentiality of the Qur'ān is increasingly viewed as one of its central features. Given the fact that the Qur'ān is primarily a text to be recited to an audience, this self-referentiality reflects a constant challenge in which the audience questions the qur'ānic recitation and that qur'ānic recitation, in turn, reacts. The audience is addressed directly as well as indirectly. The Qur'ān answers questions which were asked about it, about its origin, about its meaning, about its true aims. It describes itself by various generic terms, comments, explains, distinguishes, puts itself into perspective vis-à-vis other revelations, denies hostile interpretations, and so on. It almost never mentions by name those who ask, challenge, seek guidance, doubt, or abuse, which is one of the reasons the Qur'ān has been named a "text without a context."[1]

Some of the terms with which the qur'ānic revelation referred to itself seemed to later generations to be contradictory or at least in need of clarification. It was "in clear Arabic" (*bi-lisānin 'arabiyyin mubīnin*, Q 26:195) on the one hand, yet certain parts of it needed an interpretive authority. Some parts were declared to be opaque, ambiguous, clear only to God himself and thus incomprehensible to humanity. "The Qur'ān" was "sent down" in a single night of one month, yet it was revealed to the prophet Muḥammad during a long period of time.[2] It was absolutely clear and binding, yet God's pronouncements could be vague at first only to be set right later. The Prophet who received the divine revelation could not be in doubt about the factuality and infallibility of his prophethood, yet Satan was sometimes allowed to intervene in the text, so that the Prophet hastily ascribed or came very close to ascribing words to God which were, in fact, not God's words.

The *locus classicus* in which the qur'ānic revelation sets the tone for the history of qur'ānic exegesis is Q 3:7. Ignaz Goldziher has already commented upon it in his *Die Richtungen der islamischen Koranauslegung.*[3] The transcribed standard version of this passage reads:

> huwa lladhī anzala 'alayka l-kitāba minhu āyātun muḥkamātun hunna ummu l-kitābi wa-ukharu mutashābihātun fa-ammā lladhīna fī qulūbihim zayghun fa-yattabi'ūna mā tashābaha minhu btighā'a l-fitnati wa-btighā'a ta'wīlihī wa-mā ya'lamu ta'wīlahū illā llāhu wa-l-rāsikhūna fī l-'ilmi yaqūlūna āmannā bihī kullun min 'indi rabbinā wa-mā yadhdhakkaru illā ulū l-albābi.[4]

The two possible translations reflect two different readings and two different interpretations of this verse. The translation of the standard reading with the relevant passage in italics, is:

> It is he who sent down upon thee the Book, wherein are verses clear that are the Essence of the Book, and others ambiguous. As for those in whose heart is swerving, they follow the ambiguous part, desiring dissension, and desiring its interpretation; *and none knows its interpretation, save only God. And those firmly rooted in knowledge say,* "We believe in it; all is from our Lord"; yet none remembers, but men possessed of minds.

The translation of the minority reading is:

> It is he who sent down upon thee the Book, wherein are verses clear that are the Essence of the Book, and others ambiguous. As for those in whose heart is swerving, they follow the ambiguous part, desiring dissension, and desiring its interpretation; *and none knows its interpretation, save only God and those firmly rooted in knowledge. They say,* "We believe in it; all is from our Lord"; yet none remembers, but men possessed of minds.

John Wansbrough once, perhaps not without slight exaggeration, called this verse, with its distinction between "clear" (*muḥkam*) and "ambiguous" (*mutashābih*) verses, "a passage, unanimously agreed to represent the point of departure for all scriptural exegesis."[5] This chapter aims at clarifying the scriptural prehistory of this verse, at putting the terms used in their context, at examining some of the various interpretations of the verse as they have been put forward in Islamic exegesis, and finally at placing the verse within the broader perspective of the self-referential character of many qur'ānic passages.

Precanonical Tradition

According to the Arabo-Islamic tradition of the canonization of the qur'ānic text, there are two pre-'Uthmānic variants of this verse. "Pre-'Uthmānic" is defined here as belonging to a recitational or scriptural tradition which Islamic scholarship has identified as precanonical. These variants were transmitted not as postcanonical admissible "readings" (*qirā'āt*) but as rejected noncanonical variants. Despite this rejection, however, their existence as *variae lectiones* has been kept in memory. 'Abdallāh b. Mas'ūd read in this verse, in place of the italicized words in the translations: "*and there is no interpretation of it except with God. And those firmly rooted in knowledge say.*"[6] With its added preposition ("with"), Otto Pretzl considers this reading "a change in the text in order to preclude a misunderstanding."[7] For the same verse Ubayy b. Ka'b offers another reading which can only be rendered as "*and only God knows its interpretation. And those who are firmly rooted in knowledge say.*"[8]

We have, of course, no way to determine an "Urtext," quite apart from the problem that we should have to take into account primarily a "Urrezitation" as well. If the principle of the *lectio difficilior*—or perhaps rather the *recitatio difficilior*—is to be invoked, then the standard version should seem preferable. It shows an ambiguity which the other two readings do not, one that they most likely deliberately eliminated. These differences in the earliest versions of the Qur'ān available to us mean that the controversy which the qur'ānic text reports about itself during the time of revelation, and which linked interpretation (*ta'wīl*) and dissension (*fitna*), survived even though the text tried to settle it. We cannot be sure about the extent to which this controversy in the early Muslim community may have spilled over into the different exegetical traditions known to us from later times. Because in this instance, pre-'Uthmānic versions of this verse have been preserved, we are allowed a glimpse into the textual history of the Qur'ān as it was shaped by the early community. The text that the Islamic community finally accepted as canonical—the so-called 'Uthmānic text, on which all existing qur'ānic texts are based—is a version in which the Arabic script cannot distinguish between two contradictory interpretations, here given as "Standard Reading" and "Minority Reading." According to the Standard Reading, part of the qur'ānic revelation is interpretable only by God; according to the Minority Reading, also some humans, namely those rooted in knowledge, know the interpretation of this part of the holy text. The problem of ambiguity did not arise in the oral tradition, because the human voice, the mode of recitation, easily expressed the difference. Breaking off the sentence after *illā llāhu* or, in the terminology of the Qur'ān-reciters, "inserting a pause (*waqf*)" signified that only God knew the interpretation of these verses. If, however, the text was read without a pause, "continuing the sentence (*waṣl*)," it meant that also some men could know it. This difference could be transmitted only orally until the graphemes for pause and nonpause reading had been invented. These signs, however, were never considered to belong to the holy text but were deemed nothing more than human inventions. Numerous Muslim scholars of the Qur'ān seem to have resisted the temptation to equate themselves with God as masters of the meaning of the text.

The official qur'ānic text in its written form, therefore, "carries" the two contradictory interpretations. Perhaps we may even go so far as to say that its whole point is this lack of decision for one of the two versions. The community could agree only on the opaque version of the qur'ānic verse, because its ambiguity made it acceptable to the rival factions who had the power to decide on the canonical text. Roughly 1,400 years later, the official qur'ānic text approved by the Azhar University in Cairo, dating from the year 1344/1925–26[9] and reprinted millions of times, places above the final letter of *Allāhu* the pausal abbreviation *mīm* (meaning *al-waqf al-lāzim*), which makes pause obligatory, thus enforcing what I have called the Standard Reading. The question, however, remains unsettled: a Qur'ān recently printed in Medina[10] follows a different tradition by putting the abbreviation *qly* (meaning *al-waqf al-awlā*) above the word *Allāh*. According to this text, to pause at this word is preferable but not obligatory. This reading, therefore, recommends the interpretation of the Standard Reading while not completely ruling out the Minority Reading.

There is no way to answer the question of what was the original form and meaning of this verse. It seems obvious to me that the canonized text took pains to uphold the possibility that the Prophet himself did not know the true interpretation of the ambiguous (*mutashābih*). Yet for some later theologians this idea seemed to border on blasphemy. Ibn Qutayba (d. 276/889) asked rhetorically in his *Mushkil al-Qur'ān* ("The difficult passages in the Qur'ān"): "Is anyone allowed to say that the Prophet did not know the ambiguous?" And he proceeded to deduce from the inadmissibility of such a proposition that also those "who are firmly rooted in knowledge must know the interpretation of the ambiguous."[11] Similarly, but for different reasons, Shī'ite exegesis[12] has always insisted that the Imāms knew the interpretation of the ambiguous verses, and most but not all of the Mu'tazilite exegetical tradition insisted that the meaning of these verses could be grasped by sound scholarship.[13] Important early Sunnī exegetes were also sure that "those firmly rooted in knowledge" did, in fact, know the meaning of the ambiguous in the holy text, and they usually counted themselves among them.[14] Whatever the later generations made of this verse, few of its "operative terms"—to borrow John Wansbrough's expression[15]—are clear in their precise pre-exegetic meaning. These operative terms are as follows: (1) "clear verses" (*āyāt muḥkamāt*), and the corresponding (2) "ambiguous" (verses) (*mutashābihāt* along with *mā tashābah*), (3) "the Essence of the Book" (*umm al-kitāb*), (4) "swerving" (*zaygh*), (5) "trial, dissension" (*fitna*), (6) "interpretation" (*ta'wīl*), and (7) "those firmly rooted in knowledge" (*al-rāsikhūna fī l-'ilm*).

The Operative Terms: The Qur'ānic Vocabulary

There is something tantalizing in this verse, as in many other self-referential passages of the Qur'ān. Such passages imprint on the hearer and reader, with great vigor and often with much detail, the unique importance of the character of the text. But frequently, and certainly in this instance, the text tells neither the believer nor the skeptic precisely what these characteristic traits consist of. In reflecting itself, the text hides, at least for Islamic exegesis, what precisely is meant. For us, as well as for the exegetes from the earliest times onward, most of the "operative terms" of this passage are opaque. Neither a close reading of the rest of the qur'ānic text nor an investigation of the biographical literature on Muḥammad (*sīra*) nor a recourse to Arabic lexicography will help to clarify this sentence completely.

1. "Clear" (*muḥkam*). The term "verse" (*āya*) connected with a derivation of *ḥkm* IV is to be found at three other places in the Qur'ān (Q 11:1; 22:52–53; 47:20–21). In Q 11:1 it occurs in something that resembles the heading of a sūra: "Alif Lām Rā'. A book whose verses are *set clear*, and then distinguished, from One all-wise, all-aware." This verse seems to indicate a sequence of divine care for the revealed word, first the "clear setting" (*uḥkimat*), then the act of "distinguishing" (*fuṣṣilat*). Both expressions gave rise to many exegetical theories.

The second verse cited has been connected to the Verses of the Cranes, the so-called Satanic Verses (Q 22:52–53): "We sent not ever any messenger or prophet before thee, but that Satan cast into his fancy, when he was fancying; but God annuls what Satan casts, then God *confirms* his signs—surely God is all-knowing, all-wise (53) that he may make what Satan casts a trial for those in whose hearts is sickness, and those whose hearts are hard. . . . " In this verse, the divine "confirmation" (*iḥkām*) abrogates and corrects a satanic intervention into the prophetic text, and "trial" (*fitna*, usually in the sense of "dissension") is a divine punishment affecting those with sick and hard hearts.

Finally Q 47:20–21: "Those who believe say, 'Why has a sūra not been sent down?' (20) Then, when a *clear* sūra is sent down, and therein fighting is mentioned, thou seest those in whose hearts is sickness looking at thee as one who swoons of death; but better (21) for them would be obedience, and words honourable." In this case "a clear sūra" (*sūratun muḥkamatun*) seems to mean a clear, unambiguous, decisive passage—not necessarily a sūra, in its later sense of a complete chapter of the qur'ānic text.

2. "Ambiguous" (*mutashābih*). This complement of "clear" (*muḥkam*) poses even more of a problem. Apart from its occurrence in Q 3:7 it is attested in the Qur'ān in other

places: Q 2:25: "This is that wherewithal we were provided with before; that they shall be given in *perfect semblance*" (*hādhā lladhī ruziqnā min qablu wa-utū bihī mutashābihan*).

In the following examples the *shbh* VI means nothing more than "to resemble, to be alike": Q 2:70, "Cows are much alike to us" (*inna l-baqara tashābaha 'alaynā*); Q 2:118, "Their hearts resembled each other" (*tashābahat qulūbuhum*); Q 6:99, "and olives, pomegranates, like each to each and each unlike to each" (*wa-l-zaytūna wa-l-rummāna mushtabihan wa-ghayra mutashābihin*); and minimally different form the preceding Q 6:141, "and olives, pomegranates, like each to each, and each unlike to each" (*wa-l-zaytūna wa-l-rummāna mutashābihan wa-ghayra mutashābihin*); Q 13:16, "Are the blind and the seeing man equal? Or are the shadows and the light equal? Or have they ascribed to God associates who created as he created, so that creation is all alike to them?" (*hal yastawī l-a'mā wa-l-baṣīru am hal yastawī l-ẓulumātu wa-l-nūru am ja'alū li-llāhi shurakā'a khalaqū ka-khalqhihī fa-tashābaha l-khalqu 'alayhim*). Paret translates here: "so daß ihnen die Schöpfung mehrdeutig vorkommt (und sie nicht wissen, wieweit sie das Werk Gottes und wieweit sie das seiner Teilhaber ist)?"

In Q 39:23 the word refers to the holy book: "God has sent down the fairest discourse as a Book, *consimilar in its oft-repeated* whereat shiver the skins of those who fear their Lord" (*Allāhu nazzala aḥsana l-ḥadīthi kitāban mutashābihan mathāniya taqsha'irru minhu julūdu lladhīna yakhshawna rabbahum*). Paret translates: "Gott hat die beste Verkündigung . . . herabgesandt, eine sich gleichartig wiederholende Schrift (mit) Erzählungen (*mathāniya*)" (God has sent down the best announcement, a scripture repeating itself with narrations); Horovitz suggests that *mutashābih* could refer to the well-balanced structure of the different parts of the Qur'ān ("könnte auf die ebenmäßige Anordnung der Teile gehen").[16] Angelika Neuwirth, basing herself on Uri Rubin's study of the concept *mathānin*, translates *kitāban mutashābihan mathāniya* with "eine Schrift voller Ähnlichkeiten, voller Wiederholungen" (a scripture full of similarities, full of repetitions).[17]

The term *mutashābih* and its synonym *mushtabih* are used in Q 2:70, 2:118, 6:99, and 6:141 for objects resembling each other wholly or partly. The participles of *shbh* VI and VIII, *mutashābih* and *mushtabih*, in Q 6:99 and 6:141 are used synonymously. Outside the Qur'ān, the latter term usually means "doubtful." In Q 39:23 the question remains: What exactly does the *kitāb* resemble? Does *kitāb mutashābih* mean a book containing interior similarities and repetitions or does the expression mean a *kitāb* resembling something else? In Q 3:7 *mutashābih* must mean more than mere similarity; it must mean a similarity which induces ambiguity and may therefore lead to doubt. Unfortunately, in Q 39:23 both words, *mutashābih* and *mathānin*, are terms whose precise meanings are unclear. The recitation as a written text is called both *mutashābihun* and *mathānin*. And it is doubtful whether the juxtaposition of *mutashābihun* and *mathānin* in this verse helps to explain the distinction between a verse that is *mutashābih* and a verse that is *muḥkam* according to Q 3:7. What seems clear, however, is that next to the simple and direct meaning "similar," the term denotes in Q 3:7 and Q 39:23 a feature which refers to scriptural or recitational features of the Qur'ān. It was evidently used as an interpretive, text-centered term, but apparently not with exactly the same function in both verses. Q 13:16, in which *mutashābih* appears as an attribute to *khalq*, can mean only that those who practise polytheism consider God's creation as something *mutashābih*. The existence of the created world leads them wrongly to assign partners to God, that is, it leads to polytheism. So, in this verse *mutashābih* means "leading to erroneous, doubtful conclusions." Therefore, *mutashābih* in Q 3:7 could also refer to parts of the *kitāb*. And since the word *kitāb* in Q 3:3 in its context must mean the revelation revealed to the prophet Muḥammad, *mutashābih* could be taken to designate those parts of the qur'ānic text that resemble pre-Islamic scriptures and deal with the same persons or events but are not identical to these earlier revelations. Furthermore, this lack of identity may lead the wavering believer to the conclusion that one of the scriptural versions must be wrong and that this wrong version could be the Qur'ān.

3. The Essence of the Book (*umm al-kitāb*). The "Essence of the Book" (literally, "Mother of the Book") is identified in Q 3:7 with the "clear verses" of the qur'ānic revelation. The much discussed term appears also in Q 13:39 and 43:4. Q 13:39 states, "God blots out, and he establishes whatsoever he will; and with him is the *Mother of the Book*"; while Q 43:3–4 says, "Behold, we have made it an Arabic Qur'ān; haply you will understand; and behold, it is in *the Mother of the Book*, with us; sublime indeed, wise."

The graphic term "the mother of the book" is a riddle. Horovitz, and following him Paret[18] and Wansbrough,[19] distinguish between the *umm al-kitāb* as a heavenly archetype of all scripture ("himmlische Urschrift") which contains at the same time all revelation and the records of all human acts (Q 13:39 and 43:3), and *umm al-kitāb* in a more limited sense as part of the qur'ānic revelation which is somehow a nucleus containing the essential qur'ānic message as in the verse, Q 3:7.[20] Wansbrough explains, "Only in Q 3:7, where it could be an interpolation, may *umm al-kitāb* refer not to a scriptural archetype, but rather to an exegetical *point d'appui*."[21] In that case, *umm al-kitāb* in Q 3:7 is another purely exegetical term. But does the identification of *umm al-kitāb* with the *muḥkam*-verses really exclude its identification with the heavenly prescripture? Apparently, the qur'ānic recitation and text were attacked for inconsistencies by people striving for dissent, and the Qur'ān concedes that it contains verses that were not clear. The text insists, however, that its main points consist of revealed material which is identical with the divine archetype and which the Jews and the Christians ought to find in their scriptures as well. Muqātil b. Sulaymān (d. 150/767) taught that the verses known as the "Essence of the Book" "were not only preserved with God . . . but also in the scriptures of all peoples."[22] That notion could suggest that "clear" (*muḥkam*) means what was primarily and most distinctly revealed in the Qur'ān, whereas "ambiguous" (*mutashābih*) means what was similarly, but with differences, to be found also in other scriptures. In other words, I suggest that "ambiguous" in Q 3:7 meant qur'ānic revelations that resembled but were not identical with passages in Jewish and Christian scriptures. Q 3:7 thus tried to settle the problem of competing and sometimes conflicting scriptural authorities that included Christian and Jewish scripture.

As usual, early Islamic traditions tell us different stories about the occasion(s) and reason(s) of revelation with regard to this part of Q 3. For example, we are told that the first large segment of the third sūra, a section that runs from the first verse to somewhere in the eighties of this sūra and thus includes Q 3:7, was revealed in connection with a controversy between the Prophet on the one hand and a Christian delegation from Najrān on the other hand. We find other traditions that Q 3:12 referred to a discussion between the Prophet and the Medinan Jews.[23] In the third sūra itself, the verses preceding verse 7 explain the fact that the book (*kitāb*) sent down to the prophet

Muḥammad confirms what was earlier sent down in the Torah and the Gospel. Verse 8 then continues with a prayer of the Muslim community to protect it from "swerving." These and other stories, therefore, seem to relate Q 3:7 to a scriptural discussion between Muslims and either Christians or Jews.

4. "Swerving" (*zaygh*). Unlike the previous terms, this one is clear. The infinitive "swerving" occurs only in Q 3:7. In Q 3:8, "Our Lord, make not our hearts *to swerve* after that thou hast guided us," the concept of "guidance" (*hudā*) is set against *zaygh*. In Q 33:10 another form of this verb is used to describe eyes that "swerve" with alarm. In Q 38:63 together with *'an* it means, "to fail to perceive." In Q 53:17 the finite forms of *zāgha* and *azāgha* are used with "hearts" (*qulūb*), and Q 5:63, 9:117, 61:5 read, "When they *swerved* God *caused* their hearts *to swerve*." Q 9:117 has "God has turned toward the Prophet and the Emigrants and the Helpers who followed him in the hour of difficulty, after the hearts of a part of them wellnigh *swerved* aside." In Q 34:12 the word is used metaphorically and means "to turn aside from a command." "Swerving" means the human heart's turning in the religiously wrong direction, causing it to disregard the teachings of the prophets. In the same sense, the hearts of the disbelievers show "sickness" (*maraḍ*, Q 22:53).

5. "Trial, dissension" (*fitna*). This word occurs frequently in the Qur'ān. It usually denotes the grave danger of religious and political dissension and strife which plagued the early Muslim community just as it did pre-Muslim communities.[24] In Q 3:7 as in Q 22:53 Satan sows intercommunal dissension with what he throws into diseased hearts.

6. "Interpretation" (*ta'wīl*). The word *ta'wīl*, here always translated as "interpretation," has apparently two different qur'ānic meanings. Whereas "interpretation of tales" (Q 12:6; 12:21, etc.) and "interpretation of dreams" (Q 12:44–45, etc.) seem straightforward enough, in at least some instances (Q 4:59, 17:35, and perhaps 7:53) the word *ta'wīl* is generally considered not to mean "interpretation" but rather "consequence, end of a story" (*'awāqib*), a meaning which if applied to Q 3:7 would alter the sense of the whole passage. But in Q 3:7 this connotation seems rather farfetched. The danger of interior or internal strife, which is named as a corollary of *ta'wīl*, makes the meaning "interpretation" in Q 3:7 safe.

In Q 10:38–39 the implicit object of *ta'wīl* is scripture: "Or do they say, 'Why, he has forged it'? Say: 'Then produce a sūra like it, and call on whom you can apart from God, if you speak truly.' No, but they have cried lies to that whereof they comprehended not the knowledge, and whose *interpretation* has not yet come to them." In Q 18:78, "Now I will tell thee the *interpretation* of that thou couldst not bear patiently," God's mysterious servant, who is usually identified with al-Khiḍr, reveals to Mūsā the real significance of his strange deeds, as he does in Q 18:82.

7. "Those firmly rooted in knowledge" (*al-rāsikhūna fī l-'ilm*). This expression occurs only once except for Q 3:7. Q 4:162: "But those of them that are *firmly rooted in knowledge* and the believers believing in what has been sent down to thee and what was sent down before thee, that perform the prayer and pay the alms and those who believe in God and the last day—them we shall surely give a mighty wage." The third person plural refers here to Medinan Jews who are accused in verses 160 and 161 of having taken usury; it is further stated that God as a punishment made certain foods, which were originally good and wholesome, unlawful for them. Verse 162 follows. Here the expression "those firmly rooted in knowledge" refers beyond doubt to those Medinan

Jews who, because of their intimate knowledge of the Jewish scriptures, acknowledged the prophethood of Muḥammad and therefore converted to Islam. It seems to me that the same meaning is the proper one in Q 3:7. Those Jews who find in their scriptures the confirmation of Muḥammad's prophethood are called "well-grounded in knowledge." These righteous Jews are not confused by passages that seem to be different in the Qur'ān and in the Torah, but they say, "we believe in it, all of it [i.e., the Qur'ān *and* Jewish scripture] is from God." This reading again seems to make it very likely that the "ambiguous" verses were originally those passages of the Qur'ān and Jewish scripture which treated the same subject and were in this sense similar to each other (*mutashābih*) but showed differences in wording and sense. Muslim exegetical tradition connects this type of "learned" Jewish convert and Q 4:161 with famous Medinan Jews like ʿAbdallāh b. Salām.[25] The "knowledge" in these passages is, of course, knowledge of scripture: Solomon had in his court "a man who possessed knowledge of the Book" (Q 27:40). And "those who have knowledge of the Book" in Q 13:43 refers to Jews or Christians.[26]

The Qur'ān also insists in Q 75:18–19 on the necessity of a divine exegesis: "So when we recite it, follow thou its recitation. Then Ours is it to explain it." This explanation is called *bayān*.[27] If one scrutinizes the textual environment of Q 3:7 one sees—disregarding the *Alif Lām Mīm* of verse 1—that verses 2–9 are metatextual. Verses 3–4 preshadow verse 7 by addressing the Prophet saying, "He has sent down upon thee the Book with the truth, confirming what was before it, and he sent down the Torah and the Gospel aforetime, as guidance to the people, and he sent down the Furqān." Here, the order in which scripture is revealed to mankind is Torah, Gospel, Book with the truth (in the sense of the revelation sent to the prophet Muḥammad) and then Furqān, which in this verse can scarcely be the same as those three but seems to be a fourth genre of revelation or a different aspect of revelation.[28]

Exegetical Currents

At this point a brief summary of what Muslim exegesis did with the terms "clear" (*muḥkam*) and "ambiguous" (*mutashābih*) seems in order. I follow in this the studies of Leah Kinberg, Michel Lagarde, and Jane Dammen McAuliffe,[29] who discuss in detail, drawing from the earliest sources down to those of our time, the question of what these two terms were believed to mean. A fairly good idea of the general issues in premodern time can be acquired from the various traditions preserved in the qur'ānic handbook *al-Itqān fī ʿulūm al-Qur'ān* ("The Perfection in the Sciences of the Qur'ān"), written by al-Suyūṭī (d. 911/1505).[30] Helmut Gätje translated and interpreted the relevant passage of the last major Muʿtazilite commentary in the Sunnī world, al-Zamakhsharī's (d. 538/1144) *Kashshāf*, on this question.[31] Daniel Gimaret in a recent publication has partially reconstructed the Muʿtazilite commentary of Abū ʿAlī al-Jubbāʾī (d. 303/915), who also dealt with this verse.[32]

The primary exegetical question was this: Must each qur'ānic verse be either clear or ambiguous, or were these terms not mutually exclusive? Ibn Ḥabīb al-Nīsābūrī (d. 553/1158) summarizes three possible opinions on this point: (1) the whole Qur'ān is clear (*muḥkam*), (2) the whole Qur'ān is ambiguous (*mutashābih*), (3) part of the Qur'ān is *muḥkam*, part *mutashābih*.[33] Al-Suyūṭī adds a fourth possible opinion: that there are verses which are neither or both. Muslim exegesis in premodern times showed three different ways to deal with the dichotomy of clear/ambiguous: legal interpretation, rhetorical interpretation, and anti-exegetical interpretation.

Legal interpretations defined the clear verses as those pertaining to legal matters, that is, human behavior; these had to be clear and unambiguous because of their legislative function. Ambiguous verses, on the other hand, concerned matters of belief. Because these qur'ānic statements could be expressed in different wordings, they were, in this sense, ambiguous. In another variant, the dichotomy between a clear and an ambiguous verse was identified with the distinction between an "abrogating verse" (*nāsikh*) and an "abrogated verse" (*mansūkh*). Islamic jurisprudence insisted that those verses which served as basis for the religious law (*sharīʿa*) could not be open to debate and could therefore not be ambiguous. Sometimes the "clear" verses were identified with a selection presenting some of the most basic religious duties of every Muslim and usually including Q 6:151–153 and 17:23–25. All other verses of the Qur'ān could, according to this view, be ambiguous. Fakhr al-Dīn al-Rāzī (d. 606/1210), on the other hand, argued that both "clear" and "ambiguous" referred to verses containing commandments of God: "But whereas the clear ones are absolute and never change, the ambiguous ones are relative and open to change."[34] Furthermore, according to al-Rāzī, the ambiguous verses deal with details that differentiate Islam from other religions, while the clear verses contain principles valid for other religions as well."[35]

Rhetorical interpretation saw in the ambiguous verses those in which the same words were used to denote different matters or in which identical meanings were expressed in different wordings. "Ambiguous" could then be those verses in which words and expressions were repeated in different contexts. According to another distinction, the clear verse could bear only one interpretation while the ambiguous verse is open to more than one interpretation, especially a metaphorical or allegorical one and a nonmetaphorical one. A similar view sees in the clear verses "those whose nature and basic meaning cannot be distorted," whereas the ambiguous ones are verses "whose true meaning can be easily distorted."[36] This distinction was mainly used to argue for the inimitability of the Qur'ān (*iʿjāz al-Qur'ān*).

Anti-exegetical interpretation creates an entirely different response: The group that favored this type of exegesis of Q 3:7 had in common that they opposed all (human) interpretation of the ambiguous parts of the Qur'ān and allowed human interpretation for the clear verses only. The verses that should not be submitted to exegesis dealt with matters like the day of resurrection, the conditions of hell and paradise, the eschatological appearance of the apocalyptic Dajjāl, the appearance of Gog and Magog, the coming of Christ, and others.[37] Usually counted among the verses not to be subjected to exegesis were the opening letters of some sūras and those verses used by the philosophers to discuss the question of God's attributes.

One of the most important, yet widely ignored exegetical attempts to deal with the question of who was qualified to interpret the *mutashābih* and under which conditions was that of Ibn Rushd (d. 595/1198), known in medieval Europe as Averroës. In his book "The Authoritative Treatise and Exposition of the Convergence between Religious Law and Philosophy" (*Faṣl al-maqāl wa-l-taqrīb mā bayna sharīʿa wa-l-ḥikma mina l-ittiṣāl*) he used the two possible ʿUthmānic readings of Q 3:7 mentioned earlier to justify two different approaches to truth. Friedrich Niewöhner[38] has convincingly analyzed Ibn

Rushd's attack on al-Ghazālī (d. 505/1111), in which Ibn Rushd discussed the questions of whether the world is eternal, of whether God knows the *particularia*, and whether, with regard to the resurrection of the body, qur'ānic verses were open to different interpretations. Ibn Rushd's exegetical argument is as follows:

> Moreover, it is evident from what we have said that a unanimous agreement cannot be established in questions of this kind, because of the reports that many of the early believers have said that there are allegorical interpretations [of the qur'ānic text] which ought not to be expressed except to those who are qualified to receive allegories.[39]

And Ibn Rushd bases his argument on Q 3:7. Those qualified to "receive allegories" are "those firmly rooted in knowledge." Ibn Rushd clearly subcribes to the position that "ambiguous" refers to verses that can and should be interpreted metaphorically; those firmly rooted in knowledge are no longer the traditionalists, but the philosophers. To support this point of view, he understands the verse to mean that these philosophers, together with God, do know the interpretation of the "ambiguous" verses. Ibn Rushd, in rejecting the pause after the word Allāh in Q 3:7 and in reading the sentence as continuous, opts thereby for the interpretation that I have called the "Minority Reading." But, he says, this reading is a restricted reading, reserved for the philosopher alone. Ibn Rushd goes on to say:

> Allegorical interpretations then, ought not to be expressed to the masses, nor set down in rhetorical or dialectical books. . . . And with regard to a text with an apparent meaning, when there is a [self-evident] doubt, whether it is apparent to everyone and whether knowledge of its interpretation is impossible for them, they [the masses] should be told that it is ambiguous (*mutashābih*) and [its meaning] known by no one except God; and that the pausal stop should be put here after the sentence "And no one knows the interpretation thereof except God."[40]

This interpretation serves to introduce the doctrine of a dual way to truth in the name of a single truth. There is one truth for the philosophers and another truth for those who are not philosophers, but they ultimately mean the same. As Niewöhner notes, "truth is double because Averroës insists that the non-philosophers must consider their interpretation true—otherwise they would start to doubt. The philosopher, on the other hand, must not divulge his truth, which contradicts the supposed truth of the others."[41] Averroism, which in European thought was largely synonymous with the bitterly contested teaching of a double truth, can be said to have originated in an interpretation of Q 3:7.

As may have become clear, Islamic exegesis never adopted a decisive stand on how to distinguish between "clear" and "ambiguous." And modern exegesis has continued to develop further the specter of multiple meanings. One of the most contemporary and contested approaches is that of Muḥammad Shaḥrūr in his monumental study "The Book and the Qur'ān" (*al-Kitāb wa-l-Qur'ān*).[42] According to Shaḥrūr, the "clear verses" are those which guide human conduct, which indicate the forbidden and the commanded. This division corresponds to an older exegetical tradition, as was mentioned earlier. The ambiguous verses, on the other hand, deal with creation, the day of judgment, the earlier prophets, and the like. An important angle of Shaḥrūr's interpretation is his statement that, in addition to clear and ambiguous verses, the Qur'ān contains a third category of verses which are neither clear nor ambiguous. While such a theoretical possibility was at least mentioned by earlier exegetical traditions, Shaḥrūr introduces a revolutionary element by asserting that "those firmly grounded in knowledge" are not, in the first place, the religious scholars in the traditionally accepted sense, but rather modern natural scientists, philosophers, sociologists, and anthropologists. Shaḥrūr takes "knowledge" (*'ilm*) here in the sense of (natural) science(s),[43] not scriptural knowledge. In Shaḥrūr's exegetical work, the prime example of a qur'ānic verse that is neither "clear" nor "ambiguous" is Q 3:7, the subject of this study. There are not a few verses, says Shaḥrūr, which "explain" the contents of the holy book. Shaḥrūr calls these verses, which have here been called "self-referential," "the exposition of the Book" (*tafṣīl al-kitāb*).[44] According to him, Q 3:7, which establishes the difference between a clear verse and an ambigous verse, is itself neither the one nor the other but rather a third category of verse, a self-referential verse.

Q 3:7 also became a key verse to many a modern convert. Muhammad Asad (1900–92, born Leopold Weiss), a Jewish convert to Islam, called this verse a key to any understanding of the Qur'ān. The difference between "clear" and "ambiguous" (or "allegorical") verses, and the fact that according to this verse God alone knows the true meaning of the latter, led him to this conclusion: "It is this concept which is the basis for understanding the Qur'an and for the principle of religion in general. All religious knowledge is based on the fact that only a small segment of reality is accessible to human thought and human imagination. Its greater part is closed to our attempts to understand."[45] It is clear that Muhammad Asad's understanding of this verse is based on what I have called the "Standard Reading."

The Self-Referentiality of the Qur'ān

The self-referentiality of the Qur'ān has, I think, little to do with what Wansbrough called the "Deutungsbedürftigkeit"[46] of the text. All scripture is in need of exegesis. It has even been argued convincingly that textual canonicity is unthinkable without a certain degree of exegesis.[47] In this, the Qur'ān does not stand alone. But the Qur'ān is unique in that much of the canonical text itself is already exegesis, much more so than other comparable holy texts.[48] In the case of the Qur'ān, self-referentiality means more than the concentration of much of the text on its own textuality. Its self-referentiality predates the canonization of the text. In the Qur'ān, exegesis itself becomes scripture.

Whatever the "original" meaning of the words and verses in Q 3:7 was—and I insist on putting the word "original" in quotation marks—we will never know it. What we do know are the different, often contradictory attempts of the Islamic exegetical tradition to establish one correct interpretation, or in many cases to accept a multitude of equally acceptable correct interpretations. We cannot know "the" correct interpretation today; we are even sure that while the text was in the process of canonization, there were rival meanings ascribed to rival wordings of one and the same verse. Therefore, the quest for a single "correct" interpretation is pointless. Still, one aspect comes out clearly: Q 3:7 is only one of many qur'ānic passages that reflect the essential self-referentiality of Islamic revelation. Whatever the terms discussed here meant, whatever in other verses sūra, *kitāb*, and *qur'ān* and many other basic qur'ānic terms describing Islamic revelation at the time of the Prophet meant, and whatever they came to mean in the process of the canonization of what is today the holy book of Islam—an important aspect of the qur'ānic revelation from its beginning to the death of the prophet Muḥammad was the interest the Qur'ān expressed in itself, its interest in the form as well as in the content of the divine message. Stated in religious terms, the divine text underlined its own divinity by constant reference to different aspects and stages of this very divine origin. Stated in human terms, the qur'ānic text emerges as a contested and embattled text, embattled because it was under constant pressure of a contextuality with other holy texts. This contextuality was problematic because it was in some aspects acknowledged by the Prophet and by the text revealed to him and in other aspects denied.

Notes

1. Radscheit, *Die koranische Herausforderung*, 14–23.

2. See Wild, "We Have Sent Down to Thee the Book with the Truth," in *The Qur'ān as Text*, ed. S. Wild, 137–53.

3. Goldziher, *Richtungen*, 127–29; 262. Denny, "Exegesis and Recitation," 94, mentions this verse without discussing the recitational differences caused by different traditions of *waqf* and *waṣl*.

4. The English translation usually follows Arthur A. Arberry's version, *The Koran Interpreted* (Oxford: Macmillan, 1964).

5. Wansbrough, *Quranic Studies*, 149.

6. *wa-in ta'wīluhū illā 'inda llāhi*. The syntax of this sentence precludes combining the following phrase, *wa-l-rāsikhūna fī l-'ilmi*, with the pronoun governing a genitive *'inda llāhi*.

7. "Abwehr eines Mißverständnisses durch Textänderung," GdQ, 3:78, n. 3.

8. *wa-yaqūlu l-rāsikhūna fī l-'ilmi* . . . , which is another way to make the grammatical link between *allāhu* and *al-rāsikhūna fī l-'ilmi* impossible. Cf. GdQ, 3:84, n. 7, referring to al-Suyūṭī's *Itqān* and to al-Ṭabarī's *Tafsīr*.

9. Bergsträsser, "Koranlesung in Kairo," 5.

10. *Muṣḥaf al-Madīna al-Munawwara. Al-Qur'ān al-karīm wa-tarjamat ma'ānīhi wa-tafsīruhū ilā l-lughati l-anklīziyya. Tanqīḥ wa-i'dād al-ri'āsa al-'āmma li-idārat al-buḥūth al-'ilmiyya wa-l-iftā' wa-l-da'wa wa-l-irshād. Majma' al-malik Fahd li-ṭibā'at al-muṣḥaf al-sharīf, al-Madīna*, 1410/1989–90.

11. Ibn Qutayba, *Mushkil al-Qur'ān wa-gharībuhā*, 1:95.

12. Lawson, "Akhbārī Shī'ī Approaches to *Tafsīr*."

13. See Gimaret, *Une lecture mu'tazilite du Coran*, and al-Zamakhsharī, *Kashshāf* apud sūra 3:7.

14. See al-Mujāhid's paraphrasis: *al-rāsikhūna fī l-'ilmi ya'lamūna ta'wīlahū wa-yaqūlūna: āmannā bihī*, "Those firmly rooted in knowledge know its interpretation and they say: We believe in it"—as quoted in Abū 'Ubayd's (d. 224/838) *Faḍā'il al-Qur'ān* ("The Excellent Qualities of the Qur'ān," ed. Aḥmad al-Khayyāṭī) I:279. Abū 'Ubayd adds, according to a tradition not to be traced to al-Mujāhid: *intahā 'ilmuhum ilā an qālū: āmannā bihī kullun min rabbinā*, "their knowledge was at its end, until they said, 'We believe in it, everything is from our Lord'" (ibid.).

15. Wansbrough, *Quranic Studies*, 149.

16. Horovitz, *Untersuchungen*, 27.

17. Neuwirth, "Sūrat al-Fātiḥa," 343, and Rubin, "Exegesis and *Hadith*," passim.

18. Paret, *Kommentar*, 264–65.

19. Wansbrough, *Quranic Studies*, 149, 153, 170.

20. Horovitz, *Untersuchungen*, 65–66.

21. Wansbrough, *Quranic Studies*, 153.

22. Ibid., 149.

23. al-Wāḥidī al-Nīsābūrī, *Asbāb al-nuzūl*, 61–62.
24. Cf. as-Sirri, *Religiös-politische Argumentation*.
25. See Horovitz, "'Abdallāh Ibn Salām."
26. See also Wansbrough, *Quranic Studies*, 152.
27. Ibid., 153.
28. See the article by Paret, "Furḳān," in *EI*, new ed.
29. McAuliffe, "Qur'ānic Hermeneutics"; Kinberg, "*Muḥkamāt* and *Mutashābihāt*"; Lagarde, "De l'ambiguité (*mutashābih*) dans le Coran."
30. al-Suyūṭī, *al-Itqān fī 'ulūm al-Qur'ān*, 3:7–32: *Fī l-muḥkam wa-l-mutashābih.*
31. See Gätje, *Koran und Koranexegese*, 80–83, for a translation of the Zamakhsharī passage.
32. See n. 10.
33. al-Suyūṭī, *Itqān*, 3:7.
34. Kinberg, "*Muḥkamāt and Mutashābihāt*," 152–53.
35. Ibid.
36. Ibid., 157.
37. Ibid., 156.
38. Niewöhner, "Zum Ursprung."
39. Hourani, *Averroes on the Harmony of Religion and Philosophy*, 53; Ibn Rushd, *Faṣl al-Maqāl*, 38–39.
40. Niewöhner, "Zum Ursprung," 31; Hourani, *Averroes*, 66; Ibn Rushd, *Faṣl*, 53.
41. Niewöhner, "Zum Ursprung," 32.
42. Shaḥrūr, *al-Kitāb*.
43. Ibid., 104.
44. Ibid., 121.
45. *The Message of the Qur'ān*, 1980, here quoted according to Karl Günter Simon, "Nachwort," in Asad, *Der Weg nach Mekka*, 446.
46. Wansbrough, *Quranic Studies*, 148–55.
47. Assmann and Gladigow, eds., *Text und Kommentar*, passim.
48. Instances of self-referential verses in Jewish scripture are mentioned by Wansbrough, *Quranic Studies*, 152: Ezra 7:10; Nehemiah 8:7. His references are L. Zunz, *Die gottesdienstlichen Vorträge der Juden* (Frankfurt, 1892), and I. Elbogen, *Der jüdische Gottesdienst in seiner geschichtlichen Entwicklung* (Frankfurt, 1931). An impressive self-referential statement in the Gospels is John 20:30–31: "There were indeed many other signs that Jesus performed in the presence of his disciples, which are not recorded in this book. Those here written have been recorded in order that you may hold the faith that Jesus is the Christ, the Son of God, and that through this faith you may possess life by his name." See Helms, *Gospel Fictions*, 10–11 and passim on the "self-reflexive" aspect of the "two Testaments." A comparable remark in the qur'ānic text is Q 4:164 :"And to David we gave the Psalms. And messengers we have already told thee of before, and messengers we have not told thee of before" (*wa-rusulan qad qaṣaṣnāhum 'alayka min qablu wa-rusulan lam naqṣuṣhum*). Another self-referential verse in the Gospels is John 21:24–25: "This is the disciple which testifieth of these things, and wrote these things: and we know that his testimony is true. And there are also many other things which Jesus did which if they should be written every one, I suppose that even the world itself could not contain the books that should be written. Amen." In a way, the Gospel of John could be said to be related to the three other "synoptic" gospels in the same way the Qur'ān claims to be related to the Jewish and Christian scriptures.

Bibliography

Abū 'Ubayd al-Qāsim b. Salām. *Faḍā'il al-Qur'ān wa-ma'ālimuhā wa-ādābuhā*. Ed. Aḥmad b. 'Abdalwāḥid al-Khayyāṭī. 2 vols. Rabat: n.p., 1415/1995.

Asad, Muhammad. *Der Weg nach Mekka: Reporter, Diplomat, islamischer Gelehrter; Das Abenteuer eines Lebens.* Hamburg: Luchterhand, 1992.

Assman, Jan, and Gladigow, Burkhard, eds. *Text und Kommentar: Archäologie der literarischen Kommunikation IV.* Munich: W. Fink, 1995.

Bergsträsser, Gotthelf. "Koranlesung in Kairo." *Der Islam* 20 (1932): 1–42; 21(1933):110–40.

Birkeland, Harris. *Old Muslim Opposition against Interpretation of the Koran.* Oslo: J. Dybwad, 1955.

Denny, Frederick M. "Exegesis and Recitation. Their Development as Classical Forms of Qur'ānic Piety." *In Transitions and Transformations in the History of Religions. Essays in Honor of Joseph M. Kitagawa.* Ed. Frank E. Reynolds and Theodore M. Ludwig, 91–123. Leiden: E. J. Brill, 1980.

Gätje, Helmut. *Koran und Koranexegese.* Zurich: Artemis, 1971.

Gimaret, Daniel. *Une lecture mu'tazilite du Coran: Le Tafsīr d'Abū 'Alī al-Djubbā'ī (m. 303/915) partiellement reconstitué à partir de ses citateurs.* Louvain: Peeters, 1994.

Goldziher, Ignaz. *Die Richtungen der islamischen Koranauslegung.* 2d ed. Leiden: E. J. Brill, 1952.

Hawting, G. R., and Abdul-Kader A. Shareef, eds. *Approaches to the Qur'ān.* London: Routledge, 1993.

Holms, Randal. *Gospel Fictions.* Buffalo, N.Y.: Prometheus Books, 1988.

Horovitz, Josef. "'Abdallāh Ibn Salām." *EI*, new ed. 1: 52.

——. *Koranische Untersuchungen.* Berlin: Walter de Gruyter, 1926.

Hourani, George F. *Averroes on the Harmony of Religion and Philosophy.* A translation, with introduction and notes, of Ibn Rushd's *Kitāb faṣl al-maqāl* with its appendix (*Ḍamīma*) and an extract from the *Kitāb al-kashf 'an manāhij al-adilla.* London: Luzac, 1961.

Ibn Qutayba. *Mushkil al-Qur'ān wa-gharībuhu.* 2 vols. Beirut: Dār al-Ma'rifa, n.d.

Ibn Rushd. *Kitāb faṣl al-maqāl wa-taqrīr mā bayna sharī'a wa-l-ḥikma mina l-ittiṣāl.* Ed. Albert N. Nader. Beirut: n.p., 1961.

Kinberg, Leah. "*Muḥkamāt and Mutashābihāt* (Koran 3/7): Implication of a Koranic Pair of Terms in Medieval Exegesis." *Arabica* 35 (1988): 143–72.

Lagarde, Michel. "De l'ambiguité (*mutashābih*) dans le Coran: Tentatives d'explication des exégètes musulmans". *Quaderni di studi Arabi* 3 (1985): 45–62.

Lawson, B. Todd. "Akhbārī Shī'ī Approaches to *Tafsīr*." In *Approaches to the History of the Interpretation of the Qur'ān.* Ed. Andrew Rippin, 173–210. Oxford: Clarendon Press, 1988.

McAuliffe, Jane Dammen. "Qur'ānic Hermeneutics: The Views of al-Ṭabarī and Ibn Kathīr." In *Approaches to the History of the Interpretation of the Qur'ān.* Ed. Andrew Rippin, 46–62. Oxford: Clarendon Press, 1988.

——. "Text and Textuality: Q 3:7 as a Point of Intersection." In *Literary Structures of Religious Meaning in the Qur'ān.* Ed. Issa J. Boullata, 56–76. London: Curzon Press, 2000.

Neuwirth, Angelika. "*Sūrat al-Fātiḥa*—'Eröffnung' des Text-Corpus Koran oder 'Introitus' der Gebetsliturgie?" In *Text, Methode und Grammatik: Wolfgang Richter zum 65. Geburtstag.* Ed. Walter Gross, Hubert Irsigler, and Theodor Seidl, 321–57. Saint Ottilien, Germany: Eos Verlag, 1991.

Niewöhner, Friedrich. "Averroismus vor Averroes? Zu einer Theorie der doppelten Wahrheit im 10. Jahrhundert." *Mediaevalia philosophica Polonorum* 32 (1994): 33–39.

——. "Zum Ursprung von der Lehre von der doppelten Wahrheit: Eine Koran-Interpretation des Averroes." In *Averroismus im Mittelalter und in der Renaissance.* Ed. F. Niewöhner and Loris Sturlese, 23–41. Zürich: Spur, 1994.

Paret, Rudi. "*Furkān.*" *EI*, new ed. 2: 949–50.

——. *Der Koran: Übersetzung.* Stuttgart: W. Kohlhammer, 1962.

——. *Der Koran: Kommentar und Konkordanz.* Stuttgart: W. Kohlhammer, 1971.

Radscheit, Matthias. *Die koranische Herausforderung: Die taḥaddī-Verse im Rahmen der Polemikpassagen des Korans.* Berlin: Klaus Schwarz, 1996.

Rubin, Uri. "Exegesis and Hadith: The Case of the Seven Mathānī." In *Approaches to the Qur'ān*. Ed. G. R. Hawting and Abdul-Kader A. Shareef, 141–56. London: Routledge, 1993.

Shaḥrūr, Muḥammad. *Al-Kitāb wa-l-Qur'ān. Qirā'a mu'āṣira. Wa-bi-ākhirihī kitāb asrār al-lisān al-'arabī li-D. Ja'far Dakkal-bāb*. Cairo/Damascus: Sharikat al-Maṭbū'āt lil-Tawzī' wa l-Nashr, 1992.

as-Sirri, Ahmed. *Religiös-politische Argumentation im frühen Islam (610–685): Der Begriff Fitna; Bedeutung und Funktion*. Frankfurt: P. Lang, 1990.

al-Suyūṭī. *Al-Itqān fī 'ulūm al-Qur'ān*. Ed. Muḥammad Abū l-Faḍl Ibrāhīm. 3d ed., 4 vols. in 2. Cairo: Dār al-Turāth, 1985.

al-Ṭabarī, Abū Ja'far Muḥammad b. Jarīr. *Jāmi' al-bayān 'an ta'wīl āy al-Qur'ān*. Ed. Maḥmūd Muḥammad Shākir and Aḥmad Muḥammad Shākir. 16 vols. Cairo: n.p., 1954–68.

al-Wāḥidī, 'Alī b. Aḥmad. *Asbāb al-nuzūl*. Ed. al-Sayyid Jumaylī. Beirut: Dār al-Kitāb al-'Arabī, 1985.

Wansbrough, J. *Quranic Studies: Sources and Methods of Scriptural Interpretation*. Oxford: Oxford University Press, 1977.

Wild, Stefan, "We Have Sent Down to Thee the Book with the Truth . . ." In *The Qur'an as Text*. Ed. S. Wild, 137–53. Leiden: E. J. Brill, 1996.

28

The Designation of "Foreign" Languages in the Exegesis of the Qur'ān

ANDREW RIPPIN

Jalāl al-Dīn al-Suyūṭī, who died in 911/1505, wrote at least two separate works on "foreign" words in the Qur'ān. One is called *al-Mutawakkilī fīmā warada fī l-Qur'ān bi-l-lughāt, mukhtaṣar fī mu'arrab Qur'ān*, a treatise named after the caliph who died in 943/1536, who commanded that the learned author compile a list of qur'ānic words that are "to be found in the speech of the Ethiopians, the Persians, or any people other than the Arabs."[1] This list, al-Suyūṭī says, was extracted from his longer book *Masālik al-ḥunafā' fī wāliday al-Muṣṭafā*.[2] The list, 108 words attributed to eleven languages, is organized according to language and, within that organization, according to the textual order of the Qur'ān.[3]

Al-Suyūṭī's second work, *al-Muhadhdhab fīmā waqa'a fī l-Qur'ān min al-mu'arrab*, is very similar but is arranged in the alphabetical order of the words themselves.[4] The book contains a greater measure of variant opinion than the *al-Mutawakkilī* (that is, a given word is likely to be attributed to more than one language), while at the same time it notes some words as simply "foreign" without specifying the language from which they are thought to derive.

Al-Suyūṭī's compendium of the qur'ānic "sciences," *al-Itqān fī 'ulūm al-Qur'ān*, also contains a chapter on "foreign vocabulary."[5] Al-Suyūṭī makes reference to his *al-Muhadhdhab* in the introduction to this chapter of *al-Itqān*, but not to *al-Mutawakkilī*, so it is likely that *al-Muhadhdhab* was written first. The lists in *al-Itqān* and *al-Muhadhdhab* are not identical but are extremely close; they are also arranged in the same manner, alphabetically. There are 118 words listed in *al-Itqān* and 124 in *al-Muhadhdhab*, but the content of the entries is clearly related and the overlap between the two works is almost complete.

Al-Suyūṭī is often viewed as a compiler of material par excellence, and with good reason. His reuse of material is certainly one of the notable tendencies which may be observed within his large corpus of works, as demonstrated by these three books, bringing together similar material in slightly different organizational patternings. But al-Suyūṭī's works also exhibit an attribute of the mature Muslim exegetical tradition which Norman Calder has termed its "fundamentally acquisitive" nature.[6] The material al-Suyūṭī presents on foreign words has been culled from many sources and contains several substantial differences of opinion on any given item. Many of these words are cited as "foreign" within a variety of earlier exegetical works, and al-Suyūṭī's collation of all of these suggestions, has produced a stock of vocabulary deemed "foreign" which remains relatively constant. Exegetes such as al-Suyūṭī frequently cite the foreignness of a given word with very little elaboration about why or how it should be considered so: the nature of the "acquisitive" tradition is such that the foreign status of a word is an element of exegesis which is accepted without necessarily any questioning. A major factor here is the power of tradition: the acquisitive nature of the exegetical tradition has meant that nothing can be thrown away (at least, up to the time of Ibn Kathīr in the eighth/fourteenth century).[7]

In analyzing the lists of foreign words compiled by al-Suyūṭī, it is easy to see the reasons behind the inclusion of some of the words:[8] difficult morphological structures, barren roots, and irregular phonetic features.[9] The isolation of these features, of course, depended upon the establishment of a set of criteria to define Arabic as such, criteria developed by early grammarians such as Sībawayhi (d. ca 180/796) and al-Khalīl (d. ca 160/776). Examples of such criteria would include the permissible morphological forms of Arabic words and the combinations of letters that do not occur in Arabic. *Hapax legomena* and other infrequently used words were also among the likely candidates for the lists of foreign words.

In some of the other words in these lists, however, especially those that appear to be common Arabic words, the reasoning is less clear. In these cases the immediate suspicion is that an exegetical problem has led to the suggestion of the "foreignness" of the word, as Arthur Jeffery has already proposed in his work *The Foreign Vocabulary of the Quran*.[10]

In addition to the judgment that a word is foreign, whether because of its irregularities or an exegetical problem, another interesting aspect of the exegetical treatment of these words is the determination of the language to which a word belongs. In their procedures for specifying non-Arabic language, Muslim exegetes appear to have incorporated two elements: first, some knowledge of foreign languages and, second, typical Muslim exegetical tools. On occasion, it would appear that these two procedures intertwined, but at other times they seemed to work independently, resulting in what must have appeared even to the exegetes as intuitively "wrong" designations.

Muslim knowledge of Semitic languages other than Arabic has been studied admirably by Ramzi Baalbaki.[11] Syriac—known as *suryānī* or *nabaṭī* (with the latter perhaps referring to a specific Eastern Aramaic dialect)—was well known as a spoken language, according to anecdotes found in the works of Ibn Qutayba (d. 276/889) and Ibn Durayd (d. 321/933). The association of Syriac with Christianity is clear in the work of al-Bīrūnī (d. 456/1048). Such is also the situation with Hebrew (*'ibrī* or *'ibrānī*), for which al-Bīrūnī is able to provide a reasonably accurate system of transliteration into Arabic, and Judaism. Baalbaki also suggests that there appears to have been an awareness of the relationship between these languages and Arabic. He claims, for example, that Ibn Ḥazm (d. 456/1064) makes his understanding of the relationship explicit,[12] although whether we would really wish to equate Ibn Ḥazm's observations with genuine linguistic reflection is, in my opinion, still open to doubt. Ibn Ḥazm talks of the language of Abraham being Syriac; that of Isaac, Hebrew; and that of Ishmael, Arabic. It seems doubtful that in noting the genealogical relationship, Ibn Ḥazm is seriously saying anything about the relationship of the languages.

It is frequently pointed out that, among the classical Arab grammarians, lexicographers, and exegetes, there were a substantial number for whom a language other than Arabic was their mother tongue or a part of their religious upbringing. It has always been suspected, therefore, that knowledge of some kind was brought to the study of "loan words" in Arabic, a topic of interest both within the exegesis of the Qur'ān and in general lexicography. The book by al-Jawālīqī (d. 539/1144) is the most reknowned of its kind in the realm of general lexicography.[13] He traced much of his material back to early exegetes and grammarians such as Abū 'Ubayd (d. 224/838), Abū Ḥātim al-Sijistānī (d. 256/869), and Ibn Durayd, and in a large number of cases (although primarily non-qur'ānic ones), their opinions about the source of words agree with that of modern philologists, a fact that suggests a good measure of knowledge of the non-Arabic languages.

Even so, it is clear that the classical sources are often at a loss as to which language to suggest. This characteristic may be seen in two ways: first, a suggestion is made for the attribution of a word to a language for which there are absolutely no historical or linguistic grounds on which to establish a relationship; and, second, evident relationships are ignored even though the exegetes apparently had a knowledge of the language in question, as Baalbaki's discussions make clear they did.

The explanation for these two situations, at least as they relate to qur'ānic vocabulary, lies in exegetical procedures and in the development of *tafsīr* as an enterprise. Those odd suggestions that do arise may be rooted in the fact that the original assertion that a word was foreign was made by those who did not know the language in question. When those who might know better came along, it was not possible to override the weight of tradition. It is worth pointing out, however, that the sense of the acquisitive tradition cannot easily be equated with the inherited stock of works of *tafsīr*; in a significant number of cases, I have not been able to find evidence of the traditions in earlier works of *tafsīr* even though such traditions are included in the lists of al-Suyūṭī, for example. This may mean we are dealing with traditions not recorded in works that still exist (or, at least, works to which I have ready access) or that these traditions were more a part of living, popular Islam than of the intellectual tradition and that they become incorporated into "official" Islam at a late date.

A more detailed examination of the some of the words al-Suyūṭī has included in his lists will illustrate all of the foregoing points. It is relatively easy to observe the way exegetical problems are solved by the use of a narrative context which is seen to suggest the presence of a certain non-Arabic language. To use a famous example,[14] exegetes were unclear about the statement of Zulaykha, the governor's wife, to Joseph, *hayta laka* in Q 12:23. The supposition arose that she must have been speaking a foreign language which was then recorded in the Qur'ān. "Now the woman in whose house he was, solicited him and closed the doors on them. 'Come,' she said, 'take me! [*hayta laka*]' 'God be my refuge,' he said." There was, however, clearly some doubt as to just which language she would have spoken. Al-Suyūṭī reports in his *al-Mutawakkilī* that Ibn Abī Shaybah and Ibn Abī Ḥātim report on the authority of Ibn 'Abbās that the expression *hayta laka* means "Come here!" in Aramaic, while al-Ṭabarī is reported to have cited al-Ḥasan as saying this expression is Syriac. In his *Muhadhdhab*, however, al-Suyūṭī reports that Ibn Abī Shayba considers it to be Nabatean; Ibn Abī Ḥātim, Aramaic (*al-ḥawrāniyya* equals *al-ārāmiyya*); and al-Ṭabarī, Syriac. For the exegetes, there seems to be little doubt as to what the text means, since that can be deduced easily from the context: the words are always taken to mean "Come here!" How to explain the words, however, remained the problem. *Hayta laka* is an odd Arabic expression (although it does have a resemblance to some other verbal conjugations in Arabic) and could well be considered to have stimulated thought of its foreignness not on the basis of exegetical problems but on the basis of it being a "barren root" and apparently non-Arabic in formation. Some lexicographers did consider the word Hebrew, and that conclusion, on the surface, might be thought to make sense, given the biblical context. The lexicographers suggested that *hayta laka* was an Arabized version of a Hebrew phrase *hayetah lakh* (sometimes written as *kakh*), which E. W. Lane has suggested is an attempt by the Arab lexicographers to represent the Hebrew *'attah lekhah* of Genesis 31:44.[15] Many exegetes however, did not entertain this solution and saw issues of the supposed narrative context (as opposed to the textual source, i.e., the Hebrew Bible) as more important. It is this approach that became embedded in the exegetical tradition and codified in works such as those of al-Suyūṭī, regardless of the philological "merit" of the proposed solutions.

Overall, while there appears to be an awareness that the Jewish Bible was written in Hebrew, the language of the people mentioned in the Qur'ān is not often connected to Hebrew, nor an ancient Egyptian language in the case of Zulaykha. In *al-Mutawakkilī*, only nineteen words are cited as possibly being Hebrew, and seven of those are cited in a manner which clearly indicates that al-Suyūṭī did not consider these claims to have much support. Other languages, such as Syriac and Coptic, seem to be more significant. This tendency suggests that the ideas surrounding the languages from which "foreign" words were thought to originate were dictated, to some extent, by the languages then known to the Arabs, suggesting a nonhistorical view of the world: that is, the belief that the language a person spoke now was the languge they had always spoken.

Looking at the words al-Suyūṭī ascribes to Coptic (*al-qibṭiyya*) provides some interesting examples to illustrate this observation.

Muttakā' is a classic exegetical puzzle from the story of Joseph, Q 12:31: "When she heard their sly whispers, she sent to them, and made ready for them *muttakā'*; then she gave each one of them a knife." Whether the word means "banquet," "orange," or "cushion" was a subject of great debate. The idea that the word was Coptic clearly places it in a perceived Egyptian context; in that language, the word was said by some to mean "orange." But this opinion was rivaled by the suggestion that the term was Ethiopian (*al-Ḥabash*), a suggestion that conveys a conception of the language that we might suppose becomes associated with a narrative context of Africa in general, and a solution that al-Suyūṭī appears to prefer, according to his *Muhadhdhab*.

Manāṣ is a *hapax legomenon* found only in Q 38:3 and is said to be Coptic for "time of escape." This is a meaning provided by the overall context with an emphasis on the preceding *ḥīna*, "when": "How many generations before them did We destroy, and they called, but there was not a moment when there was a time of escape." Perhaps this is to be taken as a reference to Moses and Egypt among the "generations before them," but the passage is not at all specific.

Min taḥtihā, meaning "from within her" as found in Q 19:24, is ascribed to Coptic.[16] The context is one of Mary giving birth to Jesus. While the expression is common in Arabic, simply meaning "under her," commentators apparently found this signification nonsensical, and the idea of the infant Jesus speaking from within the womb appeared more adequate. The presumed narrative context of the birth of Jesus in Egypt is, of course, not textually obvious but neither is it an uncommon elaboration within the Muslim tradition, probably as a result of some exegetical confusion with the later flight of Joseph and Mary.

There may be another explanation for this instance of *min taḥtihā*, however, given the existence of three other expressions which, in certain passages, are attributed to Coptic with a meaning that is the reverse of their Arabic meaning. Perhaps Coptic played a cultural role as a language of deception for Arabic speakers; there may well be a larger social imagination behind this that pictures Copts as deceptive in their dealings with Muslims and twisting the Arabic language to their own advantage.[17]

Baṭā'inuhā, Q 55:54, is said to be Coptic for "their outward parts" (*ẓawāhir*). The righteous recline on carpets whose "outward parts" are of rich brocade (*istabraq*). The term's common meaning of "inner" or "hidden," a root sense which occurs twenty-five times in the Qur'ān, could not be understood to convey the correct image of luxury: what was the point of luxurious carpets if one could not see their rich brocade? This expression occurs in a depiction of the afterlife in paradise in which the blessed recline on carpets. It is possible, therefore, that a reflex here of the "reclining" in the Joseph story could provide the Egyptian context and the Coptic language suggestion, but that is certainly a weak narrative connection.

Al-ūlā is said to be Coptic for "the last, previous" in Q 33:33 rather than its normal meaning of "first." The phrase here of the "previous *jāhiliyya*" occurs in a context of the wives of the Prophet, which would make the thought of its having an Egyptian setting remote: "Remain in your houses and display not your finery as in *al-jāhiliyya al-ūlā*." The exegetical problem seems to have been stimulated by the problematic implication that there was more than one period of *jāhiliyya* and by the desire to make it clear that this was a reference to the period immediately preceding the coming of Muḥammad.

Al-ākhira is given a Coptic meaning as "the former" when used in Q 38:7, rather than its more normal Arabic signification as "the latter." The reference here is to the "former community" (*al-milla al-ākhira*), often taken to be the Christians when glossed in this manner, thus providing the possibility of an Egyptian context: "And the council of them depart saying, 'Go! Be steadfast to your gods; this is a thing to be desired. We have not heard of this in *al-milla al-ākhira*; this is surely an invention. What, has the remembrance been sent down on him out of all of us?'" Once again, confusion over which community was meant led to speculation over how to understand *al-ākhira* here.

Clearly what brings these three (or perhaps four) examples together is a sense of the Coptic language as being opposed to, or even opposite to, Arabic in meaning. Such an understanding does not seem to stem from early exegetical works, however, as far as I have been able to determine. Al-Suyūṭī takes some of these examples from an earlier compiler of information, al-Zarkashī (d. 794/1392),[18] who in turn does not provide a source. As I suggested earlier these ideas may well be popular elements, which have become incorporated into the intellectual tradition. I can only speculate as to the cultural situation between Arabs and Copts that might have led to this distrust of Coptic speakers; further investigation of this point is necessary.

These Coptic words, as cited by al-Suyūṭī, may be profitably compared to the words he ascribes to Greek (*al-Rūmiyya*). Once again, it is apparent that it is not always possible to see what has prompted an association with a certain language.

Fa-ṣurhunna is said to be Greek for "cut them into pieces" or "twist them," as used in Q 2:260, a sense not otherwise associated with this root. It occurs in the context of the story about Abraham and the four birds which, after having been "cut up" and placed on "every hill," will come flying back. Could the context of the elaboration of this story be Christian? Regardless, al-Suyūṭī seems to prefer the idea that this word is Nabatean.

Ṭafiqā is said to mean "they two undertook" in Greek when used in Q 7:22 and 20:121 (but not Q 38:33 in which it is translated as "to begin to"). Both instances occur in the story of Adam and Eve and the temptation of Satan, and Greek is the only language suggested as the source of this meaning.

Al-firdaws is said to be Greek for "garden" when used in Q 18:107 and 23:11,[19] but the word was also said to be Nabatean, or Syriac (secondarily in al-Jawāliqī). Al-Farrā' (d. 207/822)[20] cites *firdaws* as Greek on the authority of al-Kalbī, but he himself considers it to be Arabic because it was used by the Arabs. Al-Suyūṭī speaks of this word as either Greek or Aramaic. While the origin of this word is undoubtedly Iranian, it spread widely through the ancient world. Jeffery's opinion is that it came from Syriac into Arabic through Christian sources.[21] There is nothing in the context of the passage in Q 23:11 (which speaks of the reward of the faithful Muslim) that would suggest the association with Christianity. The word is clearly non-Arabic by formation, and there was never any doubt as to what it meant, since that was easily established by the context and in parallel passages where *janna* is used. (The word *firdaws* is usually glossed as *bustān*.)

More interesting, perhaps (or at least more profitable for speculating on these issues), is a series of words associated with the marketplace that are ascribed to Greek: *al-qisṭ*, meaning "justice" in Q 3:18, 21—fifteen times in total—a sense that has no verbal root in Arabic (Greek is the only language al-Suyūṭī ascribes this to); *al-qisṭās* meaning "scales" in Q 17:35 and 26:182, a word that appears to have a nonstandard Arabic formation (once again, Greek is the only language mentioned as a source); *al-ṣirāṭ* meaning "a road" in Q 1: 6, 7 and elsewhere (used forty-five times and ascribed to Greek uniquely), a barren root in Arabic; and *al-qinṭār* meaning "12,000 ounces" or "a hundredweight" in Q 3:14, 3:75, and 4:20, a word that could also be Syriac or "African" according to al-Suyūṭī.

It is worthy of note that while in a number of instances, perhaps all instances, modern philology might agree with the early Muslim thoughts that these particular words have some connection to Greek, this idea does not account historically for the appearance of these words in an Arabic text. In no instance is it likely that the word passed directly into Arabic from Greek. It is far more likely that Aramaic or Syriac would have been the vehicle. In a number of cases, Greek is not the ultimate source anyway; rather, the words are Latin and have moved into the Middle Eastern languages through their Hellenized forms during times of Greek administrative rule. The idea that the words are Greek, therefore, is unlikely to have been the result of observations of linguistic parallels or of linguistic knowledge. Rather, such speculation was likely based upon observations of the non-Arabic nature of the words combined with conjectures involving certain cultural assumptions about the nature of other societies in the past (and perhaps the present)—that is, the association of the Greek world with the marketplace.

In the context of discussing the exegetical procedures of Muqātil b. Sulaymān (d. 150/767), Kees Versteegh has opined in his recent book that "it is much more difficult to understand how the assumption of a foreign origin for obscure qur'ānic words can contribute to their understanding."[22] It seems to me, however, that Versteegh has misunderstood the nature and purpose of Muslim exegesis.[23] What is characteristic of *tafsīr* is that there was rarely a problem deciding whether a word meant one thing or another, even though there could be some disagreement and a good measure of tolerance for different solutions. Rather, the writing of commentaries may be viewed as a process of finding solutions—and solutions were always found. Muslim exegetes were forever in search of an explanation for how something could mean what it had to mean. And there the concept of the "foreign word" played an important role. The presence of foreign words in the text of the Qur'ān provided the explanation for why words meant things that were not otherwise known among Arabic speakers or scholars of the language.

Tafsīr, then, might best be conceived, at least in part, as an explanatory device: it is not so much a search for understanding as it is an attempt to explain the text of the Qur'ān within the cultural, theological, social, political, and legal context existing at the time of the exegetes. It is also characterized by its acquisitive nature, which means that some elements that were relevant to the time and place of a particular exegete remain within the transmitted exegetical material even though their precise exegetical motivation may have been lost.

Notes

1. *The Mutawakkili of as-Suyuti*, ed. and trans. Bell, 14. See also GAL, 2:145, no. 13.
2. See GAL, 2:147, no. 44; I have not had access to this book.
3. Note that no words generally considered to be proper names are found within this list or any of the other lists discussed in this essay. However, some names such as Mūsā and Nūḥ are discussed as being foreign words by some early exegetes; on this point, see the intelligent discussion of al-Rāzī, *Mafātīḥ al-ghayb*, 7:159–60, on *tawrāt* and *injīl* as "foreign."
4. Ed. 'Abdallāh al-Jubūrī. Also see GAL, 2:145, nos. 5 and 12.
5. Ed. Muḥammad Abū Faḍl Ibrāhīm, 2:108–19.
6. "Tafsir from Ṭabarī to Ibn Kathīr," 133.
7. Overall, the very idea that there were foreign words in the Qur'ān was a contentious one in Islam (in both early and contemporary times), but for our purposes let it simply be observed that, for many people within the Muslim exegetical tradition, the assertion of the presence of foreign words was readily accepted and was not seen as overly significant. See Gilliot, *Exégèse, langue et théologie en Islam*, 95–110, which contains references to much of the scholarly discussion of this topic.
8. Earlier studies of Lothar Kopf have discussed this issue; see his "Religious Influences" and "The Treatment of Foreign Words." Both articles are reprinted in his *Studies in Arabic and Hebrew Lexicography*.
9. Kopf, "The Treatment of Foreign Words," 198.
10. 32–41.
11. "Early Arab Lexicographers and the Use of Semitic Languages."
12. Ibn Ḥazm, *al-Iḥkām fī uṣūl al-aḥkām*, 1:37.
13. *al-Mu'arrab min al-kalām al-'ajamī 'alā ḥurūf al-mu'jam.*
14. See Jeffery, *Foreign Vocabulary*, 33.
15. See Lane, *An Arabic-English Lexicon*, 2910; also see al-Suyūṭī, *al-Itqān*, 2:118, although in the edition the word is written with a *jīm* at the end.
16. Among other languages, see Jeffery, *Foreign Vocabulary*, 32.

17. See Dvorák, *Über die Fremdwörter im Koran*, 22–23, cited in Jefferey, *Foreign Vocabulary*, 29.
18. *al-Burhān fī 'ulūm al-Qur'ān*, 1:287–90.
19. Also see al-Jawāliqī, *Mu'arrab*, 109–10.
20. *Ma'ānī Qur'ān*, 2:231.
21. Jeffery, *Foreign Vocabulary*, 223–24.
22. Versteegh, *Arabic Grammar and Qur'ānic Exegesis*, 89.
23. For a full analysis of Versteegh's book, see Rippin, "Studying Early *tafsīr* Texts."

Bibliography

Baalbaki, Ramzi. "Early Arab Lexicographers and the Use of Semitic Languages." *Berytus* 31 (1983): 117–27

Brockelmann, Carl. *Geschichte der arabischen Litteratur*. 2 vols. Weimar: Felber, 1898–1902.

Calder, Norman. "Tafsir from Ṭabarī to Ibn Kathīr: Problems in the Description of a Genre, Illustrated with Reference to the Story of Abraham." In *Approaches to the Qur'ān*. Ed. G. R. Hawting and Abdul-Kader A. Shareef, 101–40. London: Routledge, 1993.

Dvořák, R. *Über die Fremdwörter im Koran*. Wien, 1885.

al-Farrā', Yaḥyā b. Ziyād. *Ma'ānī al-Qur'ān*. 3 vols. Cairo: Dār al-kutub al-Mistiyya, 1966–72.

Gilliot, Claude. *Exégèse, langue et théologie en Islam: l'exégèse coranique de Tabari (m. 311/923)*. Paris: J. Vrin, 1990.

Ibn Ḥazm, 'Alī b. Aḥmad. *al-Iḥkām fī uṣūl al-aḥkām*. Cairo, 1978.

al-Jawāliqī, Mawhūb b. Aḥmad. *al-Mu'arrab min al-kalām al-'ajamī 'alā ḥurūf al-mu'jam*. Ed. A. M. Shākir. Cairo, 1361.

Jeffery, Arthur. *The Foreign Vocabulary of the Quran*. Baro'da India: Oriental Institute, 1938.

Kopf, Lothar. "Religious Influences on Medieval Arabic Philology." *Studia islamica* 5 (1956): 33–59. Reprint in Kopf, *Studies*.

——. *Studies in Arabic and Hebrew Lexicography*. Jerusalem: Magnes Press, 1976.

——. "The Treatment of Foreign Words in Mediaeval Arabic Lexicography." *Scripta hierosolymitana* 9 (1961): 191-205. Reprint in Kopf, *Studies*.

Lane, E. W. *An Arabic-English Lexicon*. London: Williams and Norgate, 1863–93.

al-Rāzī, Fakhr al-Dīn. *Mafātīḥ al-ghayb*. 6 vols. Tehran, n.d.

Rippin, Andrew. "Studying Early *tafsīr* Texts." *Der Islam* 72 (1995): 310–23.

al-Suyūṭī, Jalāl al-Dīn. *al-Itqān fī 'ulūm al-Qur'ān*. Ed. Muḥammad Abū l-Faḍl Ibrāhīm. Cairo: Dār al-Turāth, 1967.

——. *The Mutawakkili of as-Suyuti*. Ed. and trans. William Y. Bell. Cairo: [Nile Mission Press, 1924].

——. *al-Muhadhdhab fīmā waqa'a fī l-Qur'ān min al-mu'arrab*. Ed. 'Abdallāh al-Jubūrī. *al-Mawrid* 1 (1971): 97-126.

Versteegh, C. H. M. *Arabic Grammar and Qur'ānic Exegesis*. Leiden: E. J. Brill, 1993.

al-Zarkashī, Muḥammad b. Bahādur. *al-Burhān fī 'ulūm al-Qur'ān*. Ed. Muḥammad Abū l-Faḍl Ibrāhīm. Cairo: al-Ḥalabī 1957.

29

The Genre Boundaries of Qur'ānic Commentary

JANE DAMMEN MCAULIFFE

Most twentieth-century surveys of qur'ānic exegesis, whether produced in Muslim or non-Muslim academic environments, remain remarkably uniform. Several widely available texts demonstrate this symmetry, circumscribing the subject field of *tafsīr* within well-defined parameters. A few volumes can serve as representative examples. Ignaz Goldziher's *Die Richtungen der islamischen Koranauslegung*, first published in 1920, has held its place as the standard Western survey of Islamic scriptural exegesis.[1] The most frequently cited sources are precisely what one would expect: 'Abdallāh b. 'Abbās (d. 68/686–7), the *tafsīrs* of al-Ṭabarī (d. 310/923) and al-Zamakhsharī (d. 538/1144), the *Itqān* of al-Suyūṭī (d. 911/1505), among others.[2] A quick glance at the index of a more recent volume, one that was planned as an attempt to update Goldziher, confirms this frequency count.[3]

In 1381/1961 Muḥammad Ḥusayn al-Dhahabī, a professor of the qur'ānic sciences in the Faculty of Islamic Studies (Kulliyyat al-Sharī'a) of the University of al-Azhar, published his *al-Tafsīr wa-l-mufassirūn* ("Commentary and Commentators"), a work that has since gone through several editions and reprintings.[4] Al-Dhahabī's survey quickly became the standard secondary source for contemporary *tafsīr* studies throughout the Muslim world. Numerous volumes have been issued which are essentially summarizations of it.[5] Much of the text is devoted to a description of the major works of commentary, and the list of names echoes and expands that of Goldziher: al-Ṭabarī, al-Zamakhsharī, al-Ṭabarsī (d. 638/1240), Fakhr al-Dīn al-Rāzī (d. 606/1210), al-Bayḍāwī (d. probably 716/1316–7), Ibn Kathīr (d. 774/1373), al-Suyūṭī, Muḥammad 'Abduh (d. 1905), Rashīd Riḍā (d. 1935), and others.

It is worth noting that the Arabic translation of Goldziher's text is the only Western, non-Muslim work listed among the sources in al-Dhahabī's bibliography, where it is included as a sciences of the Qur'ān (*'ulūm al-Qur'ān*) work.[6] Both Goldziher and al-Dhahabī subdivide their respective surveys in quite similar fashion. Goldziher starts by describing the earliest period and then chronicles five "directions" or orientations: traditional (based on tradition/*ḥadīth*) dogmatic, mystical, sectarian (non-Sunnī), and modern. Al-Dhahabī does much the same. He begins with the first two centuries and then moves on to the commentary era itself with a segmentation that is virtually identical to that of Goldziher. In fact, Goldziher's chapter titles could easily be substituted[7] with but two additions: al-Dhahabī includes sections on (1) legally oriented commentary, which draws religio-legal injunctions (*aḥkām*) from particular qur'ānic verses, and (2) "scientific" commentary, which associates qur'ānic allusions with contemporary levels of scientific knowledge and achievement.

These two works, in turn, follow a pattern that was well established by the late classical period, as evidenced by various exegetical "introductions" (*muqaddimāt*) and "sciences of the Qur'ān" works, and was fixed definitively in the summatory, encyclopedic efforts of Badr al-Dīn al-Zarkhashī (d. 793/1391)[8] and Jalāl al-Dīn al-Suyūṭī (d. 911/1505).[9] These genres of Islamic religious literature manifest stable and perduring forms of classification encompassing both the contents of the Qur'ān and the approaches or perspectives of those who undertook its interpretation. For example, Ibn Taymiyya (d. 728/1328) in his *Muqaddima fī uṣūl al-tafsīr* divides the extant exegetical output into "traditional" and "dogmatic," to use Goldziher's terms, while inveighing against the inaccuracies or excesses of Mu'tazilī, Shī'ī, and Ṣūfī commentators like al-Zamakhsharī, al-Ṭūsī, and al-Sulamī.[10] Consequently, studies of qur'ānic *tafsīr*, both classical and contemporary, tend to concentrate on the same cast of characters. Al-Ṭabarī, of course, takes pride of place, but close behind him follow other members of the pantheon—or pantheons, for each of the subcategories has generated its "short list." One need have no quarrel with this pattern, as far as it goes. *Tafsīr* in its "linked" (*musalsal*) commentary form is a distinct genre of Islamic literature and deserves to be treated and studied as such. But is *tafsīr* as an exercise of the Muslim religious mind and imagination confined to this well-charted territory? Those of us who work in this field would immediately answer, "of course not," because we are ever conscious of Islamic literature, in all of its variety, as being thoroughly Qur'ān-saturated. But what is the relation between *tafsīr* as it occurs *within* that genre-bounded territory and *tafsīr* beyond its borders? Does the exegetical activity to be found in other forms of Islamic literature simply echo that of the *musalsal* commentary tradition? A brief exemplative analysis would suggest that such is not necessarily the case.

The Transformation of a Qur'ānic Condemnation

Recently I made a study of "debate" or "disputation" in the Qur'ān, or, more precisely, how the activity of debate is assessed and evaluated in the Qur'ān.[11] This involved an analysis of the relevant qur'ānic vocabulary, particularly the key qur'ānic term *jadal* (debate or disputation) in its various forms. There are many qur'ānic occurrences of this term and its cognates, and taken in their entirety they present a clear semantic pattern. Most often debate and disputation receive negative judgment and are associated with human ignorance or willful rejection of the probative value of God's "signs." In some passages, debate is prompted by Satan and prevalent among his followers. In other instances, disputation is directed at prophets and constitutes a form of derision and repudiation. Yet the Qur'ān does not place all uses of *jadal* and its cognates in a negative context. Examples of a more positive connotation would include the soul's capacity to dispute on its own behalf when faced with the day of resurrection and judgment or the divine permission accorded Abraham to engage in debate about the compatriots of Lot and the destruction of their city. In two significant qur'ānic pericopes there is even an etiquette[12] expressed and an encouragement to "summon to the way of your Lord with wisdom and fine exhortation and debate with them in the better way" (*ud'u ilā sabīli rabbika bi-l-ḥikmati wa-l-maw'iẓati l-ḥasanati wa-jādilhum bi-llatī hiya aḥsanu*).[13] Despite these ameliorating exceptions, however, the predominant qur'ānic usage of *jadal* and its cognates is negative. Q 18:54 seals this view with a descriptive, disapproving characterization: "More than anything, man is disputatious" (*wa-kāna l-insānu akthara shay'in jadalan*).

Perhaps the inescapability of this aspect of qur'ānic anthropology accounts in part for the post-qur'ānic transformation of debate and disputation, for the negative associations of *jadal* and its cognates, as well as other relevant vocabulary, did not inhibit the emergence of dialectical argument as a primary discourse mode in fields such as *fiqh* and *kalām*. The extent to which this process was prompted by the the emergence of Greek dialectic as a major method of intellectual engagement itself remains a subject of scholarly debate.[14] But for present purposes what is more intriguing is the post-qur'ānic transformation of *jadal* from negative to necessary. In charting the stages of this transformation, one finds that the Qur'ān itself was soon used to prove both the efficacy and the exigency of disputation. As the literature of *fiqh* and *kalām* develops, passages that censure this activity give way to pericopes of another sort. The exegetical spotlight shifts to highlight textual distillations of debate. In fact, the qur'ānic text frames and focuses upon striking scenes of disputation: Iblīs argues with God about his superiority over humans;[15] Abraham and Noah dispute with their disbelieving peoples, as do other prophets such as Hūd, Ṣāliḥ, and Shu'ayb. Lengthy pericopes report the exchanges between Moses and Pharaoh. Even the parable of the two gardens in the eighteenth sūra (*sūrat al-Kahf*) is cast in the form of a debate. Classical scholars of *fiqh* and *kalām* closely examined these exchanges, subjecting them to detailed technical analysis so that the lessons of qur'ānic argumentation could be assimilated and conveyed.

The exhortation of Q 16:125 (*sūrat al-Naḥl*) to "debate with them in the better way" provided the most prominent prooftext to justify this classical ratification of disputation as an indispensable intellectual instrument. This instruction becomes the central warrant for disputation as a mandatory religious obligation. The achievement of this centrality can be charted through several centuries of Islamic theological, philosophical, rhetorical, and legal works. The justification of debate or *jadal* is basic to the theoretical structuring of each of these forms of religious thought, and Q 16:125 provides the foundation upon which this justification is constructed.[16]

The Testimony of Tafsīr

In *tafsīr* literature, however, one finds quite a different view of this verse. The earliest exegetical stratum either passes over Q 16:125 in silence or provides but the simplest glossing. Zayd b. 'Alī (d. 122/740), Sufyān b. 'Uyayna (d. 196/811), Abū 'Ubayda (d. 207/822), and 'Abd al-Razzāq b. Hammām al-Ṣan'ānī (d. 211/827) make no comment on the verse.[17] Mujāhid b. Jabr (d. 104/722) suggests that the phrase "debate with them in the better way" means avoiding situations in which people can harm or offend you.[18] For another early exegete, Muqātil b. Sulaymān (d. 150/767), the better way is the Qur'ān, as is the "wisdom" (*ḥikma*) by which one is commanded, at the beginning of this verse, to "summon to the way of your Lord." Muqātil clearly defines those who are to be the object of this summons and debate as the "people of the book" (*ahl al-kitāb*).[19]

Two lines of interpretation emerge in this earliest layer of commentary and, not unexpectedly, they are both represented in the exegetical compendium of al-Ṭabarī: (1) the Qur'ān is the generative source of both "wisdom" and "fine exhortation"; (2) situations of disputation can expose one to offensive behavior for which an aggressive counterattack is not "the better way."[20] The tenth-century Shīʿī exegete al-Qummī combines these by simply glossing "debate with them in the better way" as disputation based on the Qur'ān.[21]

Both al-Samarqandī (d. 375/985) and al-Ṭūsī (d. 460/1067) introduce a new element: the importance in debate of the deployment of proof (*ḥujja*) and clarification (*bayān*). They both, however, continue to correlate this with the prior emphasis on eschewing a situation of escalating verbal retaliation. Al-Samarqandī speaks of the need for gentleness (*līn*),[22] while al-Ṭūsī counsels courteousness (*rifq*), dignified deportment (*waqār*), and tranquility (*sakīna*).[23] Al-Zamakhsharī (d. 538/1144) adds a few additional synonyms to this list but provides no further interpretive development.

At the close of the twelfth century, Ibn al-Jawzī (d. 597/1200) supplies another moment of summation, like that produced by al-Ṭabarī at the end of the ninth. He is, however, much more concise, offering but three points: (1) The "them" encountered in disputation either are the *ahl al-kitāb*, as Muqātil b. Sulaymān had said much earlier, or are, more generally, the people with whom Muḥammad interacted in Mecca. (2) The "better way" of debate could be basing oneself on the Qur'ān, or responding with a proclamation of faith, or presenting a posture of civility and forbearance. (3) The verse, according to some of the *tafsīr* scholars, is abrogated by the famous "sword verse" (*āyat al-sayf*, Q 9:5):[24] "When the sacred months have passed, kill the *mushrikūn* where you find them and take them and besiege them and prepare every ambush for them. But if they repent and establish the *ṣalāt* and pay the *zakāt*, then make free their way. Truly God is forgiving, merciful."

Ibn al-Jawzī's third option opens up a new stage of exegetical discussion. The possibility of abrogation, the displacement of the legislative force of a particular verse by another revelation, is entirely absent from the earlier exegetical works, at least those of the *musalsal* tradition.[25] It does appear in dedicated *nāsikh/mansūkh* texts, those texts that deal specifically with abrogation, but not until the mid-tenth century. The verse is not mentioned, for example, in the text of Abū ʿUbayd al-Qāsim b. Sallām (d. 224/838) nor in the text attributed to Qatāda b. Diʿāma (d. 117/735).[26] *Al-Nāsikh wa-l-mansūkh* of Abū Jaʿfar al-Naḥḥās (d. 338/949) cites both possible positions: i.e., either the verse is abrogated (by the command to fight in Q 9:29) or it is not.[27] With Ibn Salāma (d. 410/1019) only abrogation is mentioned,[28] with the abrogating verse being either the "sword verse" (*āyat al-sayf*, Q 9:5) or the "battle verse" (*āyat al-qitāl*, Q 9:29).[29] Makkī b. Abī Ṭālib al-Qaysī (d. 437/1045), while citing both possibilities, argues that the verse should be deemed *muḥkam*, that is, not abrogated, because of its connection with both command and prohibition.[30]

Abū Bakr b. al-ʿArabī (d. 543/1148), who is most noted for his legal (*aḥkām*) *tafsīr*, provides the fullest treatment of this abrogation issue. The earlier works of *aḥkām* commentary, such as al-Jaṣṣāṣ (d. 370/980) or Ilkiyā al-Harrāsī (d. 504/1110), do not treat this verse, nor does Ibn al-ʻArabī in his own *aḥkām* work.[31] But in his text on abrogation he includes lexical information about the qur'ānic term for "debate" and its cognates and then states, "In the beginning of Islam, disputation (*mujādala*) was the entire work of the Prophet, but when God commanded fighting, this original disputation was abrogated and what remained was arguing (*muḥajja*) with those who call for that."[32] In other words, debate retains a place in the repertoire of interreligious contact but it no longer constitutes the only mode of engagement.

Exegesis in Other Genres

If we take a closer look at the line of interpretation with which this study of Q 16:125 began, it quickly becomes apparent that the discussion has moved in quite a different direction. The justification for disputation as a basic mode of intellectual operation in both jurisprudence and theology could be constructed only on the conception of debate as obligatory, as a responsibility grounded in the imperative to command the good and proscribe the bad (*al-amr bi-l-maʻrūf wa-l-nahy ʻan al-munkar*). The argument, whether explicit or implicit, affirms that expressed error cannot stand unchallenged. For example, the author of a treatise entitled *al-Kāfiya fī l-jadal* insists that the religiously learned are divinely mandated to engage in persuasive disputation in order to eradicate mistaken beliefs and obstinate rejection of the truth.[33] Aspects of this theme are developed in a variety of works on rhetoric, dialectic, and legal reasoning, such as those of Isḥāq b. Ibrāhīm [b. Sulaymān b. Wahb al-Kātib] (d. mid-third century), the author of an early treatise on the theory of aesthetic effectiveness,[34] and Abū Bakr b. Fūrak (d. 406/1015), a disciple of Abū l-Ḥasan al-Ashʻarī (d. 324/935).[35]

The Mālikī jurisprudent (*faqīh*), Abū l-Walīd Sulaymān b. Khalaf al-Bājī (d. 474/1081),[36] who studied in Baghdād with another disciple of al-Ashʻarī, Abū Isḥāq al-Shīrāzī (d. 476/1083),[37] but who is probably best remembered for his Majorcan debates with Ibn Ḥazm (d. 456/1063),[38] also wrote on this topic,[39] as did Nāṣiḥ al-Dīn Abū l-Faraj al-Anṣārī, known as Ibn al-Ḥanbalī (d. 634/1236–37). The latter, one of a famous family of Damascene *ʻulamā'*,[40] was a preacher and *faqīh* during the period of that city's Ayyūbid ascendancy.[41] While the contributions of those just mentioned, as well as several others, are recorded and recognized within their respective genres, authors whose names have much wider currency also participated in creating this parallel exegetical trajectory for Q 16:125. Several of these, Ibn Ḥazm, al-Ghazālī, Ibn Rushd, Ibn Ṭufayl, and Ibn Taymiyya, deserve particular consideration.

The first of these, ʻAlī b. Aḥmad b. Ḥazm, stands out as one of the most distinctive voices to emerge in medieval Muslim Spain. An Andalusian poet, philosopher, and theologian as well as Ẓāhirī jurist, Ibn Ḥazm produced a foundational work on the sources of Islamic jurisprudence, *al-Iḥkām fī uṣūl al-aḥkām*, that provided the fullest exposition of the obligatory nature of *jadal* to have yet appeared. Drawing upon an extended range of qur'ānic citations, he develops several lines of argumentation. The essential imperative for his endeavor is Q 4:59: "O, you who believe, obey God and obey the Messenger and those among you who are in authority (*ūli l-amr*). Should you dispute about anything (*fa-in tanāzaʻtum fī shay'in*), refer it back to God and the Messenger, if you are believers in God and the Last Day."[42] Clearly, this injunction to refer all to the Qur'ān and *ḥadīth*, the two touchstones of Ẓāhirī literalism, anticipates the inevitability of disputation, and this very anticipation constitutes an additional form of legitimation.

In this treatise Ibn Ḥazm shows himself to be an assiduous scripture scholar, one who has culled an important collection of qur'ānic passages to support his argument.[43] As a first step he must respond to those qur'ānic verses that have been used to argue the position that all forms of debate (*jadal* or *jidāl*) are proscribed.[44] In each passage that he cites, Ibn Ḥazm carefully qualifies the proscriptive force by explaining what has rendered debate illicit or illegitimate. These clarifications constitute a necessary prelude to the extended justification he provides for debate as a praiseworthy religious activity.

Important for his appreciation of the qur'ānic approbation of *jadal* is Q 4:82, "If it were from other than God, they would have found much disagreement (*ikhtilāf*) in it," which removes the Qur'ān as a source of *jadal* while still affirming its support of the procedure itself. For that procedure, that is, debate based on truthful premises (*jidāl bi-l-ḥaqq*), Ibn Ḥazm culls citations of praise as well as pertinent examples that demonstrate the success of such conduct.[45] Consonant with this exegetical trajectory he uses Q 16:125 as the primary prooftext with which to insist that debate is not merely a possible mode of discourse but an obligatory exercise in defense of the truth: "In this verse God has made debate mandatory and has taught the entire etiquette and procedure (*ādāb*) of debate (*jidāl*), including courtesy, clarity, adherence to the truth, and having recourse to whatever decisive argument requires."[46]

Proof is the defining quality of disputation for Ibn Ḥazm, and the preeminence of proof stands centrally in his subsequent elaboration of disputation as obligatory. Both *ḥujja* (proof) and its qur'ānic synonym *sulṭān* are the lexical targets as he searches for verses to underscore this point, a search that yields such passages as Q 10:68–69.[47] These verses, which recount and deny the assertion that "God has taken for himself a son," afford Ibn Ḥazm a clear example in which *sulṭān*, which can also mean such things as "authority" and "power," is synonymous with *ḥujja*. There is complete scholarly agreement on this point, he insists, as well as on the unequivocal responsibility to provide adequate proof for all such pronouncements.[48]

In citing Q 6:83, Ibn Ḥazm highlights as a qur'ānic model for proper disputation (*mujādala*) the prophet Abraham: "This is our convincing proof (*ḥujjatunā*); we gave it to Abraham [to use] against his people." The earlier exhortation in Q 3:95 to "follow the religious community (*milla*) of Abraham" provides further confirmation of this prophet as a role model in the conduct of praiseworthy disputation (*munāẓara*). Ibn Ḥazm cites Abraham's use of argumentation with both his people and Nimrod as exemplary instances of this. The proclamation in Q 3:68 that "those people who have the most compelling claim to Abraham are those who followed him" impels Ibn Ḥazm to declare that "We are the followers of Abraham in [our use of] reasoned argument and disputation, so we are the people who have the most compelling claim to him." With such assurances, Ibn Ḥazm seeks to counter the declarations of those who disallow debate and disputation on the basis of particular qur'ānic prooftexts. All that is being disallowed in such instances, Ibn Ḥazm insists, is either disputing in a state of utter ignorance or falsely pretending to knowledge and truthfulness in order to deceitfully persuade one's opponent.[49]

Half a century later this alternate avenue of exegesis on Q 16:125 finds another prominent voice, that of the famous theologian and religious reformer Abū Ḥāmid al-Ghazālī (d. 505/1111). And once again the prophet Abraham is held up as the qur'ānic model of skillful and successful disputation. In his work *al-Qisṭās al-mustaqīm* ("The True Balance"), which draws its title from a phrase in Q 17:35 and Q 26:182, al-Ghazālī weaves Abraham's debate with Nimrod through his dialogue with the imagined Bāṭinī[50] interlocutor, eliciting from Abraham's encounter an extended example of praiseworthy disputation.[51] The question of how true knowledge is achieved precipitates this philosophical dialogue, a question for which the interlocutor first offers the combined possibilities of considered opinion (*ra'y*) and analogical reasoning (*qiyās*) or that of authoritative instruction (*ta'līm*).

Abruptly rejecting these two options, at least in their initial presentation, and dismissing those who would argue for *ra'y* and *qiyās* as ignorant friends of religion, more to be feared than its intelligent enemies, al-Ghazālī introduces his extended justification for syllogistic logic with an educational psychology grounded in Q 16:125. Cleverly he switches the exegetical emphasis that had previously been given to this verse. Where earlier attention had fallen almost entirely on the imperative to "debate with them in the better way" (*wa-jādilhum bi-llātī hiya aḥsanu*), al-Ghazālī features its prefatory injunction, "summon to the way of your Lord with wisdom and fine exhortation" (*ud'u ilā sabīli rabbika bi-l-ḥikmati wa-l-maw'iẓati l-ḥasanati*) as well.

The three foci of this charge correlate, for al-Ghazālī, with three groups of people: "God taught that some people are summoned to him by wisdom (*ḥikma*),[52] others by exhortation (*maw'iẓa*), and yet others by disputation (*mujādala*)."[53] To secure his argument, he creates a succession of feeding metaphors that are as memorable as they are engaging. For example, al-Ghazālī contends that people suited only to vigorous exhortation cannot be reached by wisdom any more than a nursing infant can be fed the flesh of fowl. Similarly, one who can be approached with wisdom would recoil from disputation the way a powerful man would recoil from being nursed with human milk.[54]

The ninth chapter of *al-Qisṭās al-mustaqīm* further elaborates the three methods, detailing the appropriate approach to the insightful elite, the common people, and the contentious.[55] Al-Ghazālī links these last-named, the "people of disputation" (*ahl al-jadal*), to Q 3:7's rebuke of "those who follow what is ambiguous [in the Qur'ān], seeking dissension." Again, he enjoins "debate with them in the better way" (Q 16:125), urging an etiquette of civility and courtesy, devoid of both fanaticism and vehemence.[56]

The negative effects of unbridled debate and the harsh emotions aroused by it occupy al-Ghazālī's attention in the fourth book of the third quarter (that dealing with *al-muhlikāt*) of his *Iḥyā' 'ulūm al-dīn*. This fourth book deals with the "evils of the tongue" (*āfāt al-lisān*), among which he includes the "evils of quarreling and disputation."[57] Earlier in this same work he details the eight conditions and characteristics that the legitimate use of disputation demands. Exchanges conducted within these parameters, al-Ghazālī contends, conform to the consultations of the Companions and are easily distinguished from the forms of self-aggrandizement that mark contemporary debating practice.[58] Those that fail to meet these standards inevitably degenerate into mere intellectual aggression and self-promotion and become "the fountainhead of all the traits deemed blameworthy by God but praiseworthy by God's enemy, Iblīs."[59]

Scanning forward within the corpus of medieval Islamic literature reveals additional instances of this alternate avenue of exegesis for Q 16:125. Less than a century after al-Ghazālī, the great philosopher and scientist Ibn Rushd/Averroës (d. 595/1198) constructed a similar elaboration of Q 16:125 in his *The Decisive Treatise* (*Faṣl al-maqāl*). Following the same tripartite educational psychology as his philosophical predecessor, Ibn Rushd postulates that the natural capacities of human beings are characterized as being susceptible to demonstrative (*burhān*), dialectical (*al-aqāwīl al-jadaliyya*), and rhetorical (*al-aqāwīl al-khiṭābiyya*) arguments, respectively.[60] The consequences of such classification are then closely linked to Ibn Rushd's qur'ānic hermeneutics. A particular passage's exegetical accessibility becomes for Ibn Rushd a function of both the text itself and the mode of intellectual receptivity appropriate to each of the three categories of people.[61]

As with al-Ghazālī, Q 3:7 offers Ibn Rushd the liberating exegetical entrée necessary to match scriptural meaning with human intellectual capacity.[62] When his version of the tripartite classification is presented in his *Kitāb al-kashf 'an manāhij al-adilla fī 'aqā'id al-milla*, Ibn Rushd readily connects it to the condemnation cast by Q 3:7. Those who engage in disputation (*ahl al-jadal*) are linked with "those in whose hearts is doubt (*zaygh*)," the ones "who follow what is ambiguous in it (*mā tashābaha minhu*), seeking dissension."[63] They deem ambiguous what is not and arrogate to themselves an exegetical capacity that is beyond their ken.

It is worth noting that a similar, but more elliptical, connection of Q 16:125 with the categorization of human cognitive capability had been made somewhat earlier by Ibn Rushd's Andalusian contemporary and mentor, the philosopher-physician Abū Bakr b. Ṭufayl (d. 581/1185–86). The latter facilitated Ibn Rushd's introduction to the caliph Abū Ya'qūb Yūsuf and preceded him as court physician. In his philosophical romance *Ḥayy b. Yaqẓān*, Ibn Ṭufayl's protagonist has cause to lament the limits of human receptivity. Surveying humankind, Ḥayy notes that for most people "exhortation (*al-maw'iẓa*) has no beneficial effect on them, nor do fine words; debate (*al-jadal*) but compounds their intractability. As for wisdom (*al-ḥikma*), they have no way to attain it nor any allocation of it."[64] While in this instance the apposite qur'ānic text is not directly cited, there can be no doubt that the passage quoted partakes of the same exegetical tradition.[65]

Several generations later, the Ḥanbalī theologian and jurisconsult Ibn Taymiyya (d. 728/1328) followed this new established exegetical itinerary, debating his own amplification of the threefold imperative posed by Q 16:125. In some of his remarks on this issue he especially rebuked those "would-be philosophers" who refuse to acknowledge the genuinely experiential character of "wisdom" (*ḥikma*) as knowledge that is both understood and acted upon (*ma'ārifat al-ḥaqq wa-l-'amal bihi*).[66] Those who are capable of both can be reached by a summons to the fully developed spiritual intuitions of *ḥikma*. Others, however, who can recognize the truth but whose passions and preoccupations prevent their following it can be reached only by strong exhortation (*maw'iẓa*). Such forceful rhetoric must play upon both positive and negative emotions. It should stimulate a craving for the truth and instill a fear of falsehood. To underscore this point, Ibn Taymiyya cites but small segments of two relevant verses, letting their remainders echo his argument: "If they had done what they were exhorted to do [then it would have been better for them and more affirming]" and "God exhorts you never to repeat the like of it [if you are believers]."[67]

Only for those who neither accept nor act upon the truth should debate be the appropriate approach. To establish both that the qur'ānic text contains many scenes and situations of disputation and that it demonstrates the proper modes of such discourse, Ibn Taymiyya cites a number of passages. In presenting such textual exemplification, however, and in his accompanying discussion of instances and strategies of qur'ānic debate, he clearly distinguishes it from the forms of dialectic that are practiced by the heirs of Greek logical methodology (*al-ṭarīqa al-jadaliyya 'inda ahl al-manṭiq*).[68] In fact, Ibn Taymiyya's lengthy refutation of Greek logic and its practitioners, *al-Radd 'alā l-manṭiqiyyīn*, also expands his interpretation of Q 16:125. This topic is addressed in the eleventh section of the last quarter of the work.[69] Not unexpectedly, the arguments and the particular qur'ānic citations overlap with those of *Ma'ārij al-wuṣūl*, but in *al-Radd* the focus is more tightly fixed on what Ibn Taymiyya takes to be the fallacious interpretations of the philosophical logicians. Contending that these latter equate the three terms of the qur'ānic injunction conveyed by Q 16:125 (*ḥikma*, *maw'iẓa*, and *jadal*)[70] with the demonstrative (*burhān*), the rhetorical (*khiṭāba*), and the dialectical (*jadal*), Ibn Taymiyya proceeds to challenge this reading.

Their philosophical misinterpretations of these qur'ānic categories, he maintains, constitute a much greater contradiction than do the views held by the Jews and Christians. Ibn Taymiyya is willing to admit the terminological equivalences, if they are correctly conceived, but of course the argument hinges precisely on how the two sides differ in defining these crucial terms. In *al-Radd*, moreover, his exegesis of Q 16:125 builds quite strongly on a grammatical distinction in the verse. Reopening those perspectives of pedagogical psychology that had surfaced earlier in this corresponding interpretive track, Ibn Taymiyya sketches the three kinds of people and their respective receptivities.[71] But arguing from the two imperatives in this verse,[72] he draws a sharp distinction between those who can be summoned to the truth and those who can only be confuted. The point he is trying to make here is that, as he reads Q 16:125, it is not a command to summon people via three modes or methods of approach, each well suited to a particular type of person. Rather it is a command to summon by one of two methods, wisdom or exhortation, and to contest with those who resist or reject the truth by quite another means—disputation. By this reading, *jadal* functions not as a means by which to evoke wholehearted acceptance of the truth but only as a mechanism of repudiation.[73]

Expanding the Search

The names of Isḥāq b. Ibrāhīm, Ibn Fūrak, al-Bājī, and Ibn al-Ḥanbalī, or even those of Ibn Ḥazm, al-Ghazālī, Ibn Rushd, Ibn Ṭufayl, and Ibn Taymiyya, do not ordinarily appear on standard lists of qur'ānic commentators. Yet each has contributed significantly to the exegetical development of this verse. In concert with several others, they have created a parallel exegetical pathway, one that evolves in quite a different fashion from that found in the *musalsal tafāsīr*. I do not want to claim that these trajectories never intersect. Both the philosophical commentary of Fakhr al-Dīn al-Rāzī and the later encyclopedic "sciences of the Qur'ān" works (e.g., al-Zarkashī and al-Suyūṭī) exhibit some points of interconnection. But these works are the exception. As this case study indicates, *tafsīr* as a genre and *tafsīr* as an intellectual exercise of the Muslim religious imagination are not necessarily coterminous categories. Despite the countless shelves of published commentaries and the many collections of *tafsīr* manuscripts that await editing, medieval exegesis of the Qur'ān cannot be caught and contained within these boundaries. But ordinarily, studies of particular qur'ānic pericopes limit themselves to those sources that fall within the genre borders of *tafsīr*, as the term is technically construed. Such limitation, in turn, is quite understandable, because that genre itself is so vast that no individual study can exhaust its riches. Nevertheless, such limitation can blind us to the interpretive insights waiting to be found in sources that do not usually appear in the standard exegetical who's who.

Notes

1. This work was originally conceived as a series of invited lectures that were to be given in 1913 at the University of Uppsala.

2. A fuller list would be: 'Abdallāh b. 'Abbās, al-Bukhārī (d. 256/870), al-Ṭabarī, and al-Suyūṭī's *Itqān* for Sunnī sources; 'Alī b. Ibrāhīm al-Qummī (lived in mid-4th/10th cent.) for Shī'ī; Muḥyī l-Dīn b. al-'Arabī's (d. 638/1240) *Fuṣūṣ al-ḥikam* and *Futūḥāt makkiyya*, for Ṣūfī; al-Zamakhsharī for Mu'tazilī, etc.

3. Rippin, ed., *Approaches to the History of the Interpretation of the Qur'ān*.

4. This was issued as a three-volume work by the Egyptian publishers Dār al-Kutub al-Ḥadīthah, with subsequent editions by that house (3 vols., 1976), and Maktaba Wahba (2 vols., 1405/1984).

5. For example, Manī' 'Abd al-Ḥalīm Maḥmūd, *Manāhij al-mufassirīn*; Fahd b. 'Abd al-Raḥmān b. Sulaymān al-Rūmī, *Uṣūl al-tafsīr wa-manāhijuhu*; Muḥammad b. Luṭfī al-Ṣabbāgh, *Lamaḥāt fī 'ulūm al-Qur'ān wa-ttijāhāt al-tafsīr*.

6. *al-Madhāhib al-islāmiyya fī tafsīr al-Qur'ān al-karīm*, trans. 'Alī Ḥasan 'Abd al-Qādir.

7. *al-tafsīr bi-l-ma'thūr* = traditional; *al-tafsīr bi-l-ra'y* (both acceptable and unacceptable) = dogmatic; Shī'ī and Khārijī = sectarian; Ṣūfī and philosophical = mystical; modern = modern.

8. al-Zarkashī, *al-Burhān fī 'ulūm al-Qur'ān*.

9. al-Suyūṭī, *al-Itqān fī 'ulūm al-Qur'ān*.

10. Ibn Taymiyya, *Muqaddima fī uṣūl al-tafsīr*. He makes a nice distinction, however, between operating with false doctrine along with inaccurate exegesis and holding true doctrine but mistaken exegesis. Al-Sulamī (d. 412/1021) is his example of the latter. *Muqaddima*, 92.

11. "'Debate with Them in the Better Way': The Construction of a Qur'ānic Commonplace," 163–88.

12. Q 22:67–68: "To every *umma* we have appointed a *mansak* which they should observe. Do not let them contend with you on the matter (*fa-lā yunāzi'unnaka fī l-amr*) but invite them to your Lord, for you are surely on the right course (67). If they dispute with you (*wa-in jādalūka*) then say 'God knows best what you are doing'"(68).

13. Q 16:125; also Q 29:46: "Do not dispute (*la tujādilū*) with the People of the Book except in the better way (*illā bi-llatī hiya aḥsanu*) unless [with] those of them who have done wrong." As the following pages will demonstrate, Q 16:125 became a key verse in the classical apologetic for *jadal bi-l-ḥaqq*.

14. The influence of Greek logic has generated a large literature, much of it cited in the Ph.D. thesis of Larry Miller, "*Islamic Disputation Theory*." An increasing willingness to credit Stoic as well as Aristotelian models can also be traced. See, for example, Rosenthal, *Knowledge Triumphant*, 207; van Ess, "The Logical Structure of Islamic Theology," 27–35; Shehaby, "The Influence of Stoic Logic on al-Jaṣṣāṣ's Legal Theory."

15. Q 15:30–33; 17:61; 7:11–12; 38:73–76.

16. Further to this, see McAuliffe, "'Debate with Them in the Better Way.'"

17. Zayd b. 'Alī, *Tafsīr gharīb al-Qur'ān*; Sufyān b. 'Uyaynah, *Tafsīr*; Abū 'Ubaydah Ma'mar b. al-Muthannā l-Taymī, *Majāz al-Qur'ān*; 'Abd al-Razzāq b. Hammām al-Ṣan'ānī, *al-Tafsīr*.

18. Mujāhid b. Jabr, *al-Tafsīr*, 2:355.

19. Muqātil b. Sulaymān al-Balkhī, *al-Tafsīr*, 2:494.

20. al-Ṭabarī, *Jāmi' al-bayān 'an ta'wīl āy al-Qur'ān*, 14:194–95.

21. al-Qummī, *al-Tafsīr*, 1:392.

22. al-Samarqandī, *Baḥr al-'ulūm*, 2:255. He also draws attention to such cognate verses as "Do not dispute (*lā tujādilū*) with the People of the Book except with that which is better" (Q 29:46) and "Do not quarrel with them except in an open manner" (Q 18:22).

23. al-Ṭūsī, *al-Tibyān fī tafsīr al-Qur'ān*, 6:439.

24. Ibn al-Jawzī, *Zād al-masīr fī 'ilm al-tafsīr*, 4:506. In his *naskh* text, *Nāsikh al-Qur'ān wa mansūkhuhu*, 453, Ibn al-Jawzī simply repeats this with the addition of *ḥadīth* from Mujāhid.

25. See Powers, "The Exegetical Genre *nāsikh al-Qur'ān wa-mansūkhuhu*."

26. Abū 'Ubayd al-Qāsim b. Sallām, *Kitāb al-nāsikh wa-l-mansūkh*, and Qātada b. Di'āma, *Kitāb al-nāsikh wa-l-mansūkh*. For the latter, see GAS, 1:31. Reference to this verse is absent from some later *nāsikh/mansūkh* works as well, e.g., 'Abd al-Qāhir b. Ṭāhir b. Muḥammad al-Baghdādī (d. 428/1037), *al-Nāsikh wa-l-mansūkh*.

27. al-Naḥḥās, *al-Nāsikh wa-l-mansūkh*, 543–44.

28. Ibn Salāma, *al-Nāsikh wa-l-mansūkh*, 114. Ibn al-Bārizī (d. 738/1337), *Nāsikh al-Qur'ān wa-mansūkhuhu*, 38, lists only *āyat al-sayf*, while Ibn al-'Atā'iqī (d. c. 790/1308), *al-Nāsikh wa-l-mansūkh*, 58, lists both.

29. "Among those who were given the Book, fight those who do not believe in God or the Last Day and do not forbid what God and his Messenger forbid and who do not follow the religion of truth until they pay the *jizya* from/to hand when they are humbled." The closing phrases of this verse have been the subject of much scholarly discussion. For a contribution to this, which also cites the relevant bibliography, see McAuliffe, "Fakhr al-Dīn al-Rāzī on *āyat al-jizya* and *āyat al-sayf*."

30. "It both leads to what God commanded and abstains from what he prohibited and thus cannot be abrogated." Makkī b. Abī Ṭālib al-Qaysī, *al-Īḍāḥ li-nāsikh al-Qur'ān wa-mansūkhihi*, 336.

31. Abū Bakr Aḥmad b. 'Abdallāh al-Jaṣṣāṣ al-Rāzī, *Aḥkām al-Qur'ān*; Ilkiyā al-Harrāsī ('Imād al-Dīn b. Muḥammad al-Ṭabarī), *Aḥkām al-Qur'ān*; Ibn al-'Arabī, *Aḥkām al-Qur'ān*.

32. Ibn al-'Arabī, *al-Nāsikh wa-l-mansūkh fī l-Qur'ān al-karīm*, 2:279. See also al-Mashnī, *Ibn al-'Arabī*. Ibn al-'Arabī even provides examples of the Prophet's arguments with Christians, Jews, and *mushrikūn*.

33. Pseudo-Juwaynī, *Kāfiya*, 24. For this author, the obligation to know the *sharī'a* as a whole (*farḍ 'alā l-kāffa*) or in its detail (*farḍ 'alā l-kifāyah*) is the more comprehensive imperative. This treatise has been published as that of 'Abd al-Malik al-Juwaynī (d. 478/1085), by Fawqiyya Ḥusayn Maḥmūd, but this attribution has been sharply questioned on both bibliographic and stylistic grounds. See Gimaret, *La doctrine d'al-Ash'arī*, 183, n. 2. Cf. his earlier acceptance of this edition in "Un document majeur pour l'histoire du kalām," 216, n. 147bis. A magisterial study of *al-amr bi-l-ma'rūf wa-l-nahy 'an al-munkar* has recently been published. See Cook, *Commanding Right and Forbidding Wrong in Islamic Thought*.

34. Isḥāq b. Ibrāhīm b. Sulaymān b. Wahb al-Kātib, *al-Burhān fī wujūh al-bayān*.

35. Ibn Fūrak, *Muğarrad maqālāt al-Aš'arī*. Gimaret argues for his attribution of the Medinese manuscript upon which this edition is based in "Un document majeur," and, with additional justification, in his introduction to this edition.

36. GAL, 1:419, and GAL *Supplementa* 1:743–44.

37. This noted *faqīh* wrote an early juristic *jadal* work, a very succinct introduction that he conceived as "an aid for the beginner and a reminder for the adept (*ma'ūnah lil-mubtadi' wa-tadhkira lil-muntahī*)." Given its intended brevity, the commonplace of commendable/reprehensible *jadal* is not included. He composed it after his longer *al-Mulakhkhaṣ fī l-jadal fī uṣūl al-fiqh* and meant it to be a summary of the latter. al-Shīrāzī, *al-Ma'ūna fī l-jadal*, 123. A Kuwait edition published a year earlier makes frequent cross-reference to the Ṣan'ā' manuscript of the *Mulakhkhaṣ*.

38. Turki, *Polémiques entre Ibn Hazm et Bagi*.

39. Abū l-Walīd al-Bājī, *al-Minhāj fī tartīb al-ḥijāj*, 8.

40. His great-grandfather was Abū l-Faraj al-Shīrāzī (d. 486/1093); his grandfather, also known as Ibn al-Ḥanbalī, was Sharaf al-Islām 'Abd al-Wahhāb b. 'Abd al-Wāḥid (d. 536/1141); and his father was Abū l-'Alā' Najm al-Dīn (d. 586/1190), *shaykh* of the Ḥanābila during his own lifetime.

41. al-Dhahabī, *Siyar a'lām al-nubalā'*, 19:54; Ibn Ṭūlūn, *al-Qalā'id al-jawhariyya fī ta'rīkh al-ṣāliḥiyya*, 1:158–59; Ibn Taghrībirdī, *al-Nujūm al-zāhira*, 6:297; Ibn al-'Imād, *Shadharāt al-dhahab fī akhbār man dhahab*, 5:164–66; al-Ḥiṣnī, *Muntakhabāt al-tawārīkh li-Dimashq*, 2:502–3; Pāshā, *Hadiyyat al-'ārifīn*, 1:524.

42. Ibn Ḥazm, *al-Iḥkām fī uṣūl al-aḥkām*, 1:13. Another Andalusian scholar and a contemporary of Ibn Ḥazm, the Mālikī *faqīh* Abū 'Umar Yūsuf b. 'Abdallāh b. 'Abd al-Barr (d. 463/1070) assembled the Prophetic *ḥadīth* that proscribed debating or quarreling about the Qur'ān, e.g., "al-mirā' fī l-Qur'ān kufrun," but carefully circumscribed their range of applicability. Recognizing that the Companions frequently argued about the meaning of particular qur'ānic passages and about the legal implications of various verses, Ibn 'Abd al-Barr maintains that the proscription applies to the sort of contention that culminates in doubt or denial. See his *Jāmi' bayān al-'ilm*, 2:92–99.

43. For Ibn Ḥazm's work on another scriptural text—the Bible—see esp. Lazarus-Yafeh, *Intertwined Worlds*, and Adang, *Muslim Writers on Judaism and the Hebrew Bible*.

44. Q 30:15-16, 43:58, 42:35, 3:20.

45. Q 41:33, 16:125, 28:49–50, 10:68–69, 29:46. Ibn Ḥazm, *Iḥkām*, 1:22.

46. Ibn Ḥazm, *Iḥkām*, 1:22.

47. Also Q 55:33; 2:258, and 6:83.

48. Ibn Ḥazm, *Iḥkām*, 1:23.

49. Ibn Ḥazm, *Iḥkām*, 1:26. His principal citations here are Q 40:69, 22:3, 22:8–9, and 40:4-5.

50. al-Ghazālī's principal work against the Bāṭiniyya, his *Kitāb Faḍā'iḥ al-Bāṭiniyya* = *al-Mustaẓhirī*, was first edited and translated by Goldziher, *Streitschrift des Ġazālī gegen die Bāṭinijja-Sekte*, and more recently by 'Abd al-Raḥmān Badawī. Bouyges, *Essai de chronologie des oeuvres de al-Ghazali*, 57, lists *al-Qisṭās al-mustaqīm* as Ghazālī's fifth anti-Bāṭinī work. Further to this see van Ess, *Die Erkenntnislehre des 'Aḍuddīn al-Īcī*, 285–86 and, more briefly, his "Logical structure," 47–49.

51. al-Ghazālī, *al-Qisṭās al-mustaqīm*. English translation by McCarthy, *Freedom and Fulfillment*, 287–332; a discussion and French translation by Chelhot, "'al-Qiṣtās al-mustaqīm' et la connaissance rationnelle chez Ġazālī," 7–98.

52. In this context, and others to be discussed, *ḥikma* is usually translated as "philosophy," but I have preferred the more inclusive term "wisdom" to signal the difference between medieval and modern understandings of the scope of philosophy.

53. al-Ghazālī, *Qisṭās*, 42. On Ghazālī's use of the first and third of these terms see Jabre, *Essai sur le lexique de Ghazali*, 74–76 and 47–48, respectively. He also provides an extended discussion of *jadal* and *mujādala* in his *La notion de certitude selon Ghazali*, 117–19.

54. al-Ghazālī, *Qisṭās*, 42.

55. al-Ghazālī, *Qisṭās*, 84–93. According to Lazarus-Yafeh, the lack of technical terminology

in the *Qisṭās* may itself be a conscious pedagogical effort to suit the presentation to the intended audience. *Studies in al-Ghazzali*, 251. For a contemporary discussion of the three classes of Q 16:125 see Muḥammad Abū Zahra, *al-Qur'ān, al-mu'jiza al-kubrā*, 335 ff.

56. al-Ghazālī, *Qisṭās*, 89–90. Should civil disputation prove useless, however, powerful means (*sulṭān*), or what al-Ghāzalī, following Q 57:25, calls "iron (*ḥadīd*)," must be used: "These must be kept from disputation by the sword and the spear." *Qisṭās*, 90.

57. al-Ghazālī, *Iḥyā' 'ulūm al-dīn*, 3:113–15.

58. al-Ghazālī, *Iḥyā'*, 1:42–48.

59. al-Ghazālī, *Iḥyā'*, 1:45.

60. Ibn Rushd, *Faṣl al-maqāl*, 12–13. See also the notes to his translation of this treatise in Hourani, *Averroes on the Harmony of Religion and Philosophy*, 92. Leaman, *Averroes and His Philosophy*, 149, notes, with some surprise, Ibn Rushd's corroborative use of Q 16:125 and does not mention its prior exegetical connection with the categorization of human intellectual capacity.

61. Ibn Rushd, *Faṣl al-maqāl*, 22–23.

62. Ibn Rushd, *Faṣl al-maqāl*, 8–9. Further to this see, Bello, *The Medieval Islamic Controversy between Philosophy and Orthodoxy*, 66–74, and Fakhry, "Philosophy and Scripture in the Theology of Averroes."

63. Ibn Rushd, *Kitāb al-kashf*, 67–69.

64. Ibn Ṭufayl, *Ḥayy b. Yaqẓān*, 96.

65. For some comments on Ibn Ṭufayl's use of qur'ānic citation, see Conrad, "Introduction: The World of Ibn Ṭufayl," 24–25, and idem, "Through the Thin Veil," 250.

66. Ibn Taymiyya, "Ma'ārij al-wuṣūl," in *Min majmū'at al-rasā'il al-kubrā*, 1:186–87.

67. Portions of Q 4:66 and 24:17, respectively.

68. E.g., Q 50:14, 36:81, 75:36, 56:58, 9:10, 6:91. Ibn Taymiyya, "Ma'ārij al-wuṣūl," 1:186–90. Further to this, see Brunschvig, "Pour ou contre la logique grecque," 1:303–27.

69. Ibn Taymiyya, *Kitāb al-radd 'alā l-manṭiqiyyīn*, 438–69. This section was dropped from the abridgement of *al-Radd* created two centuries later by al-Suyūṭī (d. 911/1505) and entitled *Jahd al-Qarīḥa fī tajrīd al-Naṣīḥa*. See the translation of the former work by Hallaq as *Ibn Taymiyya Against the Greek Logicians*.

70. It is interesting to see how condensed this exegetical course has become at this point. Ibn Taymiyya, *al-Radd*, 467, does not even cite all or part of Q 16:125 but simply makes an elliptical reference to "the three things mentioned in *al-Naḥl*."

71. Ibn Taymiyya, *al-Radd*, 467–68.

72. (1) *ud'u ilā sabīli rabbika* and (2) *wa-jādilhum*.

73. Ibn Taymiyya, *al-Radd*, 468: *wa-ammā l-jadalu fa-lā yud'ā bihi bal huwa bābu daf'i l-ṣā'il*.

Bibliography

'Abd al-Razzāq b. Hammām al-Ṣan'ānī. *al-Tafsīr*. Ed. Muṣṭafā Muslim Muḥammad. 3 vols. in 4. Riyadh: Maktaba al-Rushd, 1410/1989.

Abū 'Ubayd al-Qāsim b. Sallām. *Kitāb al-nāsikh wa-l-mansūkh*. Ed. John Burton. Cambridge: E. J. W. Gibb Memorial Trust, 1987.

Abū 'Ubayda Ma'mar b. al-Muthannā l-Taymī. *Majāz al- Qur'ān*. Ed. F. Sezgin. 2 vols. Cairo: al-Khanjī, 1954–62.

Abū Zahra, Muḥammad. *al-Qur'ān, al-mu'jiza al-kubrā*. Cairo: Dār al-Fikr al-'Arabī, n.d.

Adang, Camilla. *Muslim Writers on Judaism and the Hebrew Bible: From Ibn Rabban to Ibn Hazm*. Leiden: E. J. Brill, 1996.

al-Bājī, Abū l-Walīd. *al-Minhāj fī tartīb al-ḥijāj*. Ed. 'Abd al-Majīd Turkī. Paris: Maisonneuve et Larose, 1978.

Averroës. *Averroes on the Harmony of Religion and Philosophy.* Trans. George Hourani. London: Luzac, 1961.

Bello, Iysa. *The Medieval Islamic Controversy between Philosophy and Orthodoxy: Ijmā and Ta'wīl in the Conflict between al-Ghazālī and Ibn Rushd.* Leiden: E. J. Brill, 1989.

Bouyges, Maurice. *Essai de chronologie des oeuvres de al-Ghazali.* Ed. Michel Allard. Beirut: Imprimerie catholique, 1959.

Brunschvig, Robert. "Pour ou contre la logique grecque chez les théologiens-juristes de l'Islam: Ibn Ḥazm, al-Ghazālī, Ibn Taimiyya." In *Études d'islamologie.* 1: 303–27. Paris: G.-P. Maisonneuve et Larose, 1976.

Chelot, Victor, S. J. "'al-Qiṣtās al-mustaqīm' et la connaissance rationelle chez Ġazālī." *Bulletin d'études orientales* 15 (1955–57): 7–98.

Conrad, Lawrence. "Introduction: The World of Ibn Ṭufayl." In *The World of Ibn Ṭufayl: Interdisciplinary Perspectives on Ḥayy ibn Yaqẓān.* Ed. Lawrence Conrad, 1–37. Leiden: E. J. Brill, 1996.

——. "Through the Thin Veil: On the Question of Communication and the Socialization of Knowledge in *Ḥayy ibn Yaqẓān.*" In *The World of Ibn Ṭufayl: Interdisciplinary Perspectives on Ḥayy ibn Yaqẓān.* Ed. Lawrence Conrad, 238–66. Leiden: E. J. Brill, 1996.

Cook, Michael. *Commanding Right and Forbidding Wrong in Islamic Thought.* Cambridge: Cambridge University Press, 2000.

al-Dhahabī, Muḥammad b. Aḥmad. *Siyar a'lām al-nubalā'.* 25 vols. Beirut: Mu'assasat al-Risāla, 1413/1993.

Fakhry, Majid. "Philosophy and Scripture in the Theology of Averroes." *Mediaeval Studies* 30 (1968): 78–89.

al-Ghazālī, Abū Ḥamīd. *Faḍā'iḥ al-Bāṭiniyya.* Ed. 'Abd al-Raḥmān Badawī. Cairo: al-Maktaba al-'Arabiyya, 1383/1964.

——. *Iḥyā' 'ulūm al-dīn.* Ed. Badawī Ṭabāna. 4 vols. Cairo: Dār Iḥyā' al-kutub al-'Arabiyya, 1957.

——. *al-Qisṭās al-mustaqīm.* Beirut: al-Maṭba'a al-Kāthūlīkiyya, 1959.

Gimaret, Daniel. *La doctrine d'al Ash'arī.* Paris: Cerf, 1990.

——. "Un document majeur pour l'histoire du kalām: le *Muġ arrad maqālāt al-Aš'arī* d'Ibn Fūrak." *Arabica* 32 (1985): 185–218.

Goldziher, Ignaz. *Die Richtungen der islamischen Koranauslegung.* Leiden, 1920; reprint, Leiden: E. J. Brill, 1970. *al-Madhāhib al-Islāmiyya fī tafsīr al-Qur'ān al-karīm.* Trans. 'Alī Ḥasan 'Abd al-Qādir. Cairo: Maṭba'at al-'Ulūm, 1944.

——. *Streitschrift des Ġazālī gegen die Bāṭinijja-Sekte.* Leiden: E. J. Brill, 1916.

Hallaq, Wael. *Ibn Taymiyya against the Greek Logicians.* Oxford: Oxford University Press, 1993.

——. "A Tenth-Century Treatise on Juridical Dialectic." *The Muslim World* 77 (1987): 197–228, with glossary printed as an editorial errata in the 1988 volume.

al-Ḥiṣni, Muḥammad Adīb. *Muntakhabāt al-tawārīkh li-Dimashq.* 3 vols. Damascus: al-Maṭba'a al-Ḥāditha, 1346/1927.

Ibn 'Abd al-Barr, Abū 'Umar Yūsuf b. 'Abdallāh. *Jāmi' bayān al-'ilm wa-faḍlihi wa-mā yanbaghī fī riwāyatihi wa-ḥamlihi.* Medina: al-Maktaba al-Salafiyya, n.d.

Ibn al-'Arabī, Muḥammad b. 'Abdallah Abū Bakr. *Aḥkām al-Qur'ān.* 2d ed. 4 vols. Cairo: 'Isā al-Bābī al-Ḥalabī, 1392/1972.

——. *al-Nāsikh wa l-mansūkh fī l-Qur'ān al-karīm.* Ed. 'Abd al-Kabīr al-'Alawī al-Mudaghrī. Rabat: Wizārat al-Awqāf, 1988.

Ibn al-'Atā'iqī, 'Abd al-Raḥmān b. Muḥammad. *al-Nāsikh wa-l-masūkh.* Ed. 'Abd al-Hādī l-Faḍlī. Najaf, Iraq: Maṭba'at al-Adab, 1970.

Ibn al-Bārizī, Hibat Allāh. *Nāsikh al-Qur'ān wa-mansūkhuhu.* Ed. Ḥātim Ṣāliḥ al-Ḍāmin. Beirut: Maktabat al-Nahḍa al-'Arabiyya, 1403/1983.

Ibn Fūrak, Abū Bakr. *Muǧarrad maqālāt al-Aš'arī. Exposé de la doctrine d'al-Aš 'arī.* Ed. Daniel Gimaret. Beirut: Dar el-Machreq, 1987.

Ibn Ḥazm, Abū Muḥammad 'Alī. *al-Iḥkām fī uṣūl al-aḥkām.* 2 vols. Cairo: Dār al-Ḥadīth, 1984.

Ibn al-'Imād, 'Abd al-Ḥayy. *Shadharāt al-dhahab fī akhbār man dhahab.* 8 vols. Cairo: Maktaba al-Qudsī, 1351/1932.

Ibn al-Jawzī, Abū l-Faraj 'Abd al-Raḥmān b. 'Alī. *Nāsikh al-Qur'ān wa mansūkhuhu.* Beirut: Maktabat al-Nahḍa al-'Arabiyya, 1411/1990.

——. *Zād al-masīr fī 'ilm al-tafsīr.* Introduction by Muḥammad Zuhayr al-Shāwīsh. 9 vols. Damascus: al-Maktab al-Islāmī lil-Ṭibā'a wa-l-Nashr, 1384–85/1964–65.

Ibn Rushd, Abū Walīd. *Faṣl al-maqāl.* Ed. Muḥammad 'Imāra. Cairo: Dār al-Ma'ārif, 1972.

——. "Kitāb al-kashf 'an manāhij al-adilla fī 'aqā'id al-milla wa-ta'rīf mā waqa'a fīhā bi-ḥasb al-ta'wīl min al-shiba al-muzīga wa-l-bida' al-muḍilla." In *Philosophie und Theologie von Averroes.* Ed. Marcus J. Miller, 67–69. Munich: G. Franz, 1859.

Ibn Sālama, Hibat Allāh. *al-Nāsikh wa-l-mansūkh.* Ed. Zuhayr al-Shāwīsh and Muḥammad Kan'ān. Beirut: al-Maktab al-Islāmi, 1404/1984.

Ibn Taghrībirdī, Abū l-Maḥāsin Yūsuf. *al-Nujūm al-ẓāhira.* 16 vols. Cairo: al-Mu'assasa al-Miṣriyya, 1963.

Ibn Taymiyya, Taqī l-Dīn Aḥmad. *Kitāb al-radd 'alā l-manṭiqiyyīn.* Ed. 'Abd al-Ṣamad al-Kutūbī. Bombay: 'Abd al-Ṣamad Sharaf al-Dīn al-Kutubī, 1368/1949.

——. "Ma'ārif al-wuṣūl." In *Min majmū'at al-rasā'il al-kubrā.* 2 vols. in 1. Cairo, 1323.

——. *Muqaddima fī uṣūl al-tafsīr.* Ed. 'Adnān Zurzūr. Kuwait: Dār al-Qur'ān al-Karīm, 1391/1971.

Ibn Ṭufayl, Abū Bakr. *Ḥayy ibn Yaqẓān.* Ed. Albayr Naṣrī Nādir. Beirut: al-Maṭba'a al-Kāthūlīkiyya, 1963.

Ibn Ṭūlūn, Muḥammad. *al-Qalā'id al-jawhariyya fī ta'rīkh al-ṣāliḥiyya.* 2 vols. Damascus, n. p., 1368/1949.

Ilkiyā al-Harrāsī ('Imād al-Dīn b. Muḥammad al-Ṭabarī). *Aḥkām al-Qur'ān.* 4 vols. Cairo: Dār al-Kutub al-Ḥāditha, n.d.

Isḥāq b. Ibrāhīm b. Sulaymān b. Wahb al-Kātib, Abū al-Ḥusayn. *al-Burhān fī wujūh al-bayān.* Ed. Aḥmad Maṭlūb and Khadīja al-Ḥadīthī. Baghdad: n. p., 1387/1967. Also ed. Ḥifnī Muḥammad Sharaf. Cairo: Maktabat al-Shabab, n.d. Also ed. Ṭāhā Ḥusayn and 'Abd al-Ḥamīd al-'Abbādī as *Kitāb Naqd al-nathr* of Qudāma b. Ja'far. Cairo: Maṭba'at Dār al-Kutub al-Miṣriyya, 1933.

Jabre, Farid. *Essai sur le lexique de Ghazali.* Beirut: Publications de l'Université Libanaise, 1970.

——. *La notion de certitude selon Ghazali.* Paris: J. Vrin, 1958.

al-Jaṣṣāṣ al-Rāzī, Abū Bakr Aḥmad b. 'Abdallāh. *Aḥkām al-Qur'ān.* 4 vols. Istanbul: Maṭba'at al-Awqāf al-Islāmiyya, 1335–38/1916–19.

al-Juwaynī, 'Abdal-Malik, see Pseudo-Juwaynī.

Lazarus-Yafeh, Hava. *Intertwined Worlds: Medieval Islam and Bible Criticism.* Princeton, N.J.: Princeton University Press, 1992.

——. *Studies in al-Ghazzali.* Jerusalem: Magnes Press, 1975.

Leaman, Oliver. *Averroes and His Philosophy.* Oxford: Oxford University Press, 1988.

Maḥmūd, Manī' 'Abd al-Ḥalīm. *Manāhij al-mufassirīn.* Cairo: Dār al-Kitāb al-Miṣrī, 1978.

Al-Mashnī, Muṣṭafā Ibrāhīm. *Ibn al-'Arabī al-Mālikī al-Ishbīlī wa-tafsīruhu Aḥkām al-Qur'ān.* Amman: Dār al-'Ammār, 1991.

McAuliffe, Jane Dammen. "'Debate with Them in the Better Way': The Construction of a Qur'ānic Commonplace." In *Aspects of Literary Hermeneutics in Arabic Culture: Myths, Historical Archetypes and Symbolic Figures in Arabic Literature.* Ed. A. Neuwirth, S. Günther, and M. Jarrar, 163–88. Beiruter Texte une Studien. Wiesbaden: Harrassowitz, 1999.

——. "Fakhr al-Dīn al-Rāzī on *āyat al-jizyah* and *āyat al-sayf*." In *Conversion and Continuity: Indigenous Christian Communities in Islamic Lands, Eighth to Eighteenth Centuries*. Ed. M. Gervers and R. Bikhazi, 103–19. Toronto: Pontifical Institute for Mediaeval Studies, 1990.

McCarthy, Richard Joseph. *Freedom and Fulfillment*. Boston: Twayne, 1980.

Miller, Larry. "Islamic Disputation Theory: A Study of the Development of Dialectic in Islam from the Tenth through Fourteenth Centuries." Ph.D. diss., Princeton University, 1984.

Mujāhid b. Jabr, Abū l-Ḥajjāj. *al-Tafsīr*. Ed. 'Abd al-Raḥmān b. Ṭāhir b. Muḥammad al-Suwartī. 2 vols. Beirut: al-Manshūrāt al-'Ilmiyya, n.d.

Muqātil b. Sulaymān al-Balkhī, Abū l-Ḥasan. *al-Tafsīr*. Ed. 'Abdallāh Maḥmūd Shiḥāta. 4 vols. Cairo: al-Hay'a al-Miṣriyya al-'Āmma lil-Kitāb, 1980–87.

al-Naḥḥās, Abū Ja'far. *al-Nāsikh wa-l-mansūkh*. Ed. Muḥammad 'Abd al-Salām Muḥammad. Kuwait: Maṭba'at al-Falāḥ, 1408/1988.

Niewöhner, Friedrich. "Zum Ursprung der Lehre von der doppelten Wahrheit: eine Koran-Interpretation des Averroës." In *Averroismus im Mittelalter und in der Renaissance*. Ed. F. Niewöhner and L. Sturlese, 23–41. Zurich: Spur, 1994.

Pāshā, Ismā'īl. *Hadiyyat al-'ārifīn*. Istanbul: Milli eğitim bas_ mevi, 1951.

Powers, David S. "The Exegetical Genre *nāsikh al-Qur'ān wa-mansūkhuhu*." In *Approaches to the History of the Interpretation of the Qur'ān*. Ed. Andrew Rippin, 117–38. Oxford: Oxford University Press, 1988.

Pseudo-Juwaynī. *al-Kāfiya fī l-jadal*. Ed. Fawqiyya Ḥusayn Maḥmūd. Cairo: Dār Iḥyā' al-Kutub al-'Arabiyya, 1399/1979.

Qatāda b. Di'āma. *Kitāb al-nāsikh wa-l-mansūkh*. Ed. Ḥātim Ṣāliḥ al-Ḍāmin. Beirut: Mu'assasat al-Risāla, 1404/1984.

al-Qummī, Abū l-Ḥasan 'Alī b. Ibrāhīm. *al-Tafsīr*. Ed. Ṭayyib al-Mūsāwī l-Jazā'irī. 2 vols. Najaf, Iraq: Maktabat al-Hudā, 1387/1967.

Rippin, Andrew, ed. *Approaches to the History of the Interpretation of the Qur'ān*. Oxford: Oxford University Press, 1988.

Rosenthal, Franz. *Knowledge Triumphant: The Concept of Knowledge in Medieval Islam*. Leiden: E. J. Brill, 1970.

al-Rūmī, Fahd b. 'Abd al-Raḥmān b. Sulaymān. *Uṣūl al-tafsīr wa-manāhijuhu*. Riyadh, Saudi Arabia: Maktabat al-Tawba, 1413.

al-Ṣabbāgh, Muḥammad b. Luṭfī. *Lamaḥāt fī 'ulūm al-Qur'ān wa-ttijāhāt al-tafsīr*. Beirut: al-Maktab al-Islāmī, 1406/1986.

Shehaby, Nabil. "The Influence of Stoic Logic on al-Jaṣṣāṣ's Legal Theory." In *The Cultural Context of Medieval Learning*. Ed. J. H. Murdoch and E. D. Sylla, 61–85. Dordrecht, Holland/Boston: D. Reidel, 1975.

al-Shīrāzī. Abū Isḥāq Ibrāhim b. 'Alī b. Yūsuf. *al-Ma'ūna fī l-jadal*. Ed. 'Abd al-Majīd Turkī. Beirut: Dār al-Gharb al-Islāmī, 1408/1988. Also ed. 'Alī b. 'Abd al-'Azīz al- 'Umayrīnī. Kuwait: Iḥyā' al-Turāth al-Islāmī, 1407/1987.

Sufyān b. 'Uyayna. *Tafsīr*. Ed. Aḥmad Ṣāliḥ Muḥāyirī. Riyadh, Saudi Arabia, 1403/1983.

al-Suyūṭī, Jalāl al-Dīn 'Abd al-Raḥmān. *al-Itqān fī 'ulūm al-Qur'ān*. Ed. Muḥammad Abū l-Faḍl Ibrāhīm. 4 vols. in 2. Cairo: Dār al-Turāth, 1387/1967.

al-Ṭabarī, Abū Ja'far Muḥammad b. Jaīir. *Jāmi' al-bayān 'an ta'wīl āy al-Qur'ān*. Ed. Aḥmad Sa'īd 'Alī et al. 30 vols. Cairo: Muṣṭafā al-Bābī al-Ḥalabī, 1373–77/1954–57; reprint, Beirut: Dār al-Fikr, 1984.

Turki, Abdel Magid. "Argument d'autorité, preuve rationnelle et absence de preuves dans la méthodologie juridique musulmane." *Studia islamica* 42 (1976): 59–91.

al-Ṭūsī, Muḥammad b. al-Ḥasan. *al-Tibyān fī tafsīr al-Qur'ān*. Introd. Aghā Buzurk al-Ṭihrānī. 10 vols. Beirut: Dār Iḥyā' al-Turāth al-'Arabī, n. d.

van Ess, Josef. *Die Erkenntnislehre des 'Aḍuddīn al-Īcī*. Wiesbaden: Steiner, 1966.
——. "The Logical Structure of Islamic Theology." In *Logic in Classical Islamic Culture*. Ed. G. E. von Grunebaum, 21–50. Wiesbaden: Harrassowitz, 1970.
al-Zarkashī, Badr al-Dīn Muḥammad b. 'Abdallāh. *al-Burhān fī 'ulūm al-Qur'ān*. Ed. Muḥammad Abū l-Faḍl Ibrāhīm. 4 vols. Cairo: Dār al-Turāth, 1404/1984.
Zayd b. 'Alī. *Tafsīr gharīb al-Qur'ān*. Beirut: al-Dār al-'Ālamiyya, 1412/1992.

Subject Index

S of S = Song of Songs

Index to Citations from the Bible, Rabbinic Literature, and the Qur'ān

CPSIA information can be obtained at www.ICGtesting.com
Printed in the USA
BVOW06s0545280516

449885BV00003B/4/P